CINEMA
OF SWORDS

CINEMA OF SWORDS

OF SWORDS

A HISTORY AND GUIDE TO MOVIES ABOUT
KNIGHTS, PIRATES, BARBARIANS, AND VIKINGS
[AND SAMURAI AND MUSKETEERS AND GLADIATORS AND OUTLAW HEROES]

LAWRENCE ELLSWORTH

APPLAUSE
THEATRE & CINEMA BOOKS
Essex, Connecticut

An imprint of Globe Pequot, the trade division of
The Rowman & Littlefield Publishing Group, Inc.
4501 Forbes Blvd., Ste. 200
Lanham, MD 20706
www.rowman.com

Distributed by NATIONAL BOOK NETWORK

Library of Congress Cataloging-in-Publication Data

ISBN 978-1-4930-6562-2 (cloth: alk. paper)
ISBN 978-1-4930-6563-9 (electronic)

CONTENTS

INTRODUCTION

On a Caribbean beach, two scruffy pirate crews eye each other as their leaders, Captain Peter Blood (Errol Flynn) and Capitaine Levasseur (Basil Rathbone), stand and parley. The men are partners, having signed Articles together, but they are also rivals; their talk is tense, and behind their false smiles, it's clear they hate one another. At issue is the fate of a prisoner, Arabella Bishop (Olivia de Havilland), whom both want and who watches anxiously from the sidelines. Blood makes the highest bid, 12 perfect pearls, and is the winner according to the Articles, but as he claims his prize, Levasseur, wild-eyed, cries out, "Wait! You'll not take her while I live."

"Then I'll take her when you're dead!" Blood replies, and both men draw their swords.

This was always what they wanted, and they leap eagerly to the fray, clashing their slender cup-hilted rapiers, beating hard and thrusting fast, both smiling confidently, Blood with a grim smirk and Levasseur with a feral leer. They are evenly matched, and the bout ranges fiercely down the beach, across the sand, into the low surf, and then up onto wet rocks, both swordsmen panting. The footing is treacherous, and Levasseur falls onto his back; Blood pauses, shows his teeth, and says, "Up!" Levasseur rises into a lunge, and the furious duel resumes. When Blood stumbles, Levasseur gives him no time to recover, pressing him down, and Blood fights his way to his feet by sheer force. Then Levasseur overreaches his attack; Blood steps inside his guard and runs him through. The Frenchman staggers and falls back into the surf, already dead as a wave breaks over his face.

And that's what it's all about. This is not a serious book; it's an informed appreciation of a popular genre, a guide for a general audience. Your editor is not a media historian, has not been to film school, and is not an expert fencer: I'm a veteran designer of narrative video games, and a writer and translator of historical fiction, specializing in swashbucklers. My most recent project in that field has been compiling and translating new versions of Alexandre Dumas's Musketeers novels, including *The Three Musketeers*. I used to fence with rapier and dagger as a hobby, before arthritis robbed me of my knees and wrists; and though I haven't written screenplays like some of my fellow narrative game designers have, I've worked for many years as a visual storyteller. Add that all up, and I think I have some claim to expertise about movies where the subjects are pirates, knights, Vikings, and sword-slinging cavaliers.

Mainly, though, I just love this stuff—as you probably do, or you wouldn't have picked the book up in the first place. It's a popular genre, and there sure is a lot of it, so I set out to compile a handy guide to movies and shows of swordplay that would hopefully answer the question, *Do I want to watch this?* My method is to briefly describe what each entry is about, so you know whether the subject matter is up your street, calling out highlights that make a flick enjoyable and memorable or weak points that make it lean toward suck, all summarized with a rating system of one to five stars. Because I'm recommending films for a general audience, which tends to prefer more modern presentations, I'll often knock off a star because a movie is black-and-white, is subtitled, or is really long (so when I tell you that *Seven Samurai*, which is all those things, is nonetheless a five-star essential, you can damn well believe that's just what it is).

Above all, I'm a storyteller, not an academic, and I write to entertain. My goal is for every mini-retro-review in this book to be a fun and interesting read, even if it's clear that the film being reviewed isn't your jam. If *The Cinema of Swords* succeeds as what you might call a bathroom book, then I'm happy. If you enjoy it so well that it merits a place on your regular bookshelf, that's even better. As a former fencer, I'll always take a point scored, even if it's a low blow.

WHAT'S IN THIS BOOK

Here you will find 400+ short but informative reviews of live-action movies and TV shows about swashbucklers: knights, pirates, samurai, Vikings, barbarians, musketeers, gladiators, and outlaw heroes. *The Cinema of Swords* covers releases from the silent era up through the 1980s, where I stopped because that's all I could fit into one volume. (What about more recent movies? If this book is a success perhaps there will be a second volume, *The Nineties to Now*.) I've tried to include only films and shows that an interested person can find on streaming services or disc without paying a fortune; thus long-out-of-print or otherwise unavailable titles didn't make the cut.

WHAT ISN'T IN THIS BOOK

- Movies and shows without English-language versions or subtitles.
- Historical dramas that have little or no action.
- Animated films and cartoons.
- Stories set before recorded history (i.e., no cave people) or after the early nineteenth century, when people started settling their differences with guns rather than swords (with a few exceptions, such as *Red Sun*, because it's my rule, and I can break it if I want to).
- Religious epics of any faith, because reverence and swashbuckling make uncomfortable bedfellows. This leaves out some fine films, such as *Ben-Hur* (1959), but I felt I had to draw a line on this somewhere, so accept my apologies.

SOME TERMINOLOGY

Chambara (sometimes rendered *chanbara*): A Japanese historical swordplay adventure, usually featuring samurai, ninja, and/or armed yakuza crooks.

Jidaigeki: A Japanese historical that's more drama than adventure, though it may include some swordplay.

MacGuffin: Cinematic, and now general storytelling, term for an object of desire that drives character motivation; the classic example is the statuette of the black bird in *The Maltese Falcon*.

Maciste: A hero of Italian cinema, a sort of mighty-muscled everyman who appears most often in tales set in ancient times, though he may show up in almost any time period.

Peplum: Named after the brief tunics worn by the ancients, an Italian sword-and-sandal adventure, many of which feature strongman heroes such as Hercules or Maciste.

Ronin: A samurai warrior who doesn't belong to a clan, a "masterless" samurai.

Spaghetti Western: 1960s Westerns, mostly grim and violent, made by Italian filmmakers and often shot on the dry plateaus of Spain.

Wuxia: Chinese historical adventures featuring martial arts with weapons, though the term translates more accurately as "martial chivalry."

Yakuza: Japanese organized crime gangs or "families" that oversee prostitution rings and gambling dens, occupying a semiofficial but very low tier in the social structure.

A NOTE ABOUT TITLES

Many films were released in different countries under varying titles. When a movie has multiple titles, I've listed its American release first, for the simple reason that due to market size, this book will have more American readers than British or Irish. If a movie had no American theatrical release, I've listed its title in its country of origin first. If you don't spot what you're looking for, all titles, first or alternative, are listed in the index.

ALPHABETICAL REVIEWS

THE ADVENTURER OF TORTUGA (OR COLD STEEL FOR TORTUGA)

Rating: ★★★☆☆ • *Origin:* Italy, 1965 • *Director:* Luigi Capuano • *Source:* 4001 DVD

Piracy, Italian style! Rakish Captain Pedro Valverde (Rik Battaglia) and his crew are buccaneers in the Caribbean in the late eighteenth century, past the peak of the great age of piracy. (Their costumes all say it's 100 years earlier than that, but never mind, they're good costumes.) The crew is trying to raise enough gold to take Tortuga back from the Spanish, and Valverde's dubious method of moneymaking is to pose as a Spanish grandee smitten by a nobleman's daughter, propose marriage, and then escape with the dowry before the nuptials are concluded. This is supposed to be roguishly amusing but, sorry, nope. The scheme goes badly wrong when Valverde's latest target, Soledad Quintero (Ingeborg Schöner), also happens to be the intended romantic prey of a rival, Governor Montélimar (Guy Madison). The wicked governor is after the young lady's hidden treasure—because the half-nonwhite Soledad is a princess of the fabled Darien Indian tribe.

This is a light comedy swashbuckler that aspires to the tone and quality of a Disney live-action adventure, and it comes close to the mark. The pirates are all good-hearted rogues, certainly better than that ruthless scoundrel of a governor, and though there's lots of fighting, it's all family-friendly and bloodless. One of the pirates uses a bola, another a bullwhip, which becomes sort of a theme, as the governor promises that one day the whip will be in *his* hand. Battaglia as Valverde is handsome, charming, and active, but my favorite sea dog here is his dour and stone-faced quartermaster, Pen (Giulio Battiferri), who lurks grimly in the back of every melee, cracking the heads of Spaniards who get too close without ever changing his expression. A total hero.

This film's story was "suggested" by one of the lesser-known tales of Emilio Salgari, an Italian author who wrote as many as 200 adventure novels from the 1890s through the 1920s; as beloved on the European continent as Rafael Sabatini or the earlier Alexandre Dumas, Salgari wrote mostly about pirates or about colonial adventurers who might as well have been called that. The screenplay was written by the director, Luigi Capuano, who'd made several other Salgari films based on the author's Sandokan series. Taken on its own mild terms, the film is a success: the story checks all the piracy boxes, the acting is adequate, the costumes and sets are better than average, the buccaneers have a catchy song, and the final showdown between Valverde and the governor is, I think, the only double-bullwhip duel in the entire *Cinema of Swords*. Crackin'!

THE ADVENTURES OF DON JUAN (OR *THE NEW ADVENTURES OF DON JUAN*)

Rating: ★★★☆☆ • *Origin:* USA, 1948 • *Director:* Vincent Sherman •
Source: Warner Bros. DVD

Errol Flynn had given up doing swashbucklers after *The Sea Hawk* (1940), but with the revival of the historical adventure genre in the late 1940s, Warner Bros. gave him a sword and put him back in trunk hose for *The Adventures of Don Juan*. It must be said, Flynn doesn't seem entirely comfortable in the role of Don Juan de Maraña, a scandal-plagued womanizing rogue who is forced to give up his naughty ways and turn over a new leaf. After disgracing himself by picking forbidden fruit at the English court, Don Juan is summoned back to Madrid by the Queen of Spain (Viveca Lindfors) and commanded to reform. And, however improbably, he does, because his soul is purified for the first time by true love . . . for the queen herself. (No, really.) Unfortunately, purged of the rakish qualities that made the character distinctive, Don Juan becomes a conventional noble who gets entangled in conventional court intrigues, saving the queen from a conventional treasonous minister by foiling his conventional plot at the last minute—as usual.

Flynn seems vaguely embarrassed by all this, while Swedish beauty Lindfors looks majestic but seems to have just two emotional states, detached or petulant. Only Robert Douglas as the villainous Duke de Lorca gets his teeth into his part, oozing arrogance and cruelty and going out in fine style in an epic rapier duel with Don Juan on the palace's grand staircase.

Don Juan, of course, is the notorious antihero of a long tradition of fables, operas, and epic poems, but strangely, this movie draws on almost none of that rich background, with one curious exception: that final duel takes place at the foot of a colossal, armored statue of the Commander, the figure of ultimate justice that appears at the end of so many Don Juan stories. Why that and nothing else? Who knows? At least there's a fine Spanish-tinged score by Max Steiner, the Oscar-winning costumes are excellent, production values are high, and the fencing is better than usual. But compare this merely adequate film with John Barrymore's stunning *Don Juan* (1926) and you'll shake your head ruefully at what might have been.

THE ADVENTURES OF HAJJI BABA

Rating: ★★☆☆☆ • *Origin:* USA, 1954 • *Director:* Don Weis • *Source:* Turner Classic Movies

Maybe the beautiful princess was the real treasure all along!

This film was "suggested" by James Justinian Morier's popular 1824 novel *Hajji Baba of Ispahan*, but about all it takes from the book is the name recognition of its title and its stilted dialogue style (e.g., "By Allah, I shall slay you!").

But let's give the movie credit for its good qualities: it's a colorful spectacle shot in lush wide-screen photography; it has a surging score by Dimitri Tiomkin, who also wrote a goofily endearing theme song sung by Nat King Cole; it's fast paced and doesn't lag; and it features a gang of fierce female bandits called the Turcoman Women, escaped slaves who fight with scimitars and sash bolas, which is pretty great.

However, those Turcoman Women wear a lot of lipstick, because this film is an example of what our queen of the swashbucklers, Maureen O'Hara, called a "tits and sand" movie, a throwback to the Sheik of Araby films of the silent era, but updated to the '50s with snappy patter—or patter that would be snappy if it wasn't dreck-like, as in "I seek adventure as some seek wine." This awful dialogue is delivered in performances every bit as stiff as the script, from the leads on down, starting with pretty lad John Derek as Hajji Baba and pretty lass Elaine Stewart as Princess Fawzia, who should have been thrown out of the Screen Actors Guild for this travesty. The rest of the cast is no better, not even the villains, whom you can usually count on to chew the scenery in an entertaining fashion when the leads are wooden mannequins. Not this time.

Okay, some plot: Despite the warnings of her father, the Caliph of Ispahan, the selfish and petulant Princess Fawzia is determined to wed an obvious villain, the power-hungry Prince Nur-El-Din, and sets off in disguise to meet the agent of the prince, who will take her to him. Hajji Baba is a humble barber with ambitions to make his fortune; he stumbles on this plot, takes the place of the agent, and engages to take the princess to Nur-El-Din in exchange for her emerald ring and 100 dinars. The princess is insulted that he's more taken with the ring than with her beauty, but he fobs her off, which is how you know they're fated to fall in love. They head out into the desert (Southern California doing a good job of standing in for Persia) and into a series of caravans and captures and escapes and betrayals, all ornamented by bevies of half-clad starlets. Hajji is supposed to be a resourceful and charming rogue with amusingly flexible morals, but Derek is unconvincing in the role and doesn't look like he believes the drivel he's saying even as he says it. The horses are handsome and the costumes are sumptuous, but the jokes aren't funny and the scimitar fencing is crap. So, naturally, it was a solid hit at the box office. John Derek went on to lend his last name to his fourth wife, Bo Derek, whom maybe you may have heard of.

THE ADVENTURES OF LONG JOHN SILVER

Rating: ★☆☆☆☆ • *Origin:* USA/Australia, 1955 • *Directors:* Lee Sholem, Byron Haskin • *Source:* Echo Bridge DVD

After the completion of 1954's *Long John Silver* feature, though that film had had a lukewarm reception at the box office, director Byron Haskin formed Treasure Island Productions and the cast and crew stayed in Australia to film 26 half-hour episodes of this TV show. It was filmed in color, which was unusual because color broadcasting was still a rare thing in the mid-1950s. And then, shortly after the series debuted in the United States, its star, Robert Newton, died at the age of 50 from alcoholism after returning to Hollywood for his final role in *Around the World in 80 Days*.

Newton's undeniable charisma notwithstanding, this show should've been scuttled at the wharf. It's unable to settle on a tone, veering from serious pirate drama one week to broad situation comedy the next, as Purity Pinker (Connie Gilchrist), the proprietress of the Cask and Anchor, tries to dry-dock Long John into matrimony. Half the time Silver is the rapacious scoundrel he is in the films, and half the time he's semireformed and just a sort of con man, no worse or more ill-intentioned than Sergeant Bilko. Color film notwithstanding, the production values are low, the acting is weak, the dialogue is worse, and even having a pint-size pirate with a hook in Silver's crew isn't enough to save it. Avast! These be shoal waters, mates—steer clear.

THE ADVENTURES OF QUENTIN DURWARD (OR *QUENTIN DURWARD*)

Rating: ★★★☆☆ • *Origin:* USA/UK, 1955 • *Director:* Richard Thorpe •
Source: Warner Archive DVD

After Robert Taylor's smash hit as a knight in *Ivanhoe* and a follow-up in *Knights of the Round Table*, MGM dug up another Walter Scott potboiler in *Quentin Durward*, to try for three. The result is mixed at best: the novel doesn't adapt well to the Hollywood treatment, being slow to start and spending too much time on the politics of fifteenth-century France; the romance is obvious and perfunctory, with the talented comedian Kay Kendall miscast as an overserious countess who never gets a funny line; plus the villain is a cartoon caricature; the depiction of the funny Roma sidekick is an ethnic abomination; the costumes, gear, and settings are rife with anachronism; and the dialogue is one sad cliché after another. But there are two important reasons to watch it anyway, especially the scene where . . . but wait. We'll get to it.

Scottish knight Quentin Durward (Taylor) is summoned by his elderly uncle, who's contemplating matrimony, and after a few unfunny Scots-are-stingy jokes, Durward is sent to France to inspect the prospective bride, Countess Isabelle (Kendall)—and evaluate her dowry. She's a ward of Charles the Bold, the Duke of Burgundy, who for a Scottish alliance is marrying her off against her will to Durward's uncle. There follows an hour of court politics with brief interludes of action in which Durward displays his knightly courage. The Scottish knight is represented as a romantic but obsolete relic of chivalry, and in fact, throughout the film, all his plans rely solely on reckless bravery. How can Isabelle fail to fall for him?

Durward follows Isabelle from the court of Duke Charles to that of his rival, the nominal monarch of France, King Louis XI. And finally we get to a place where the movie is worth the time invested, because the wily and shameless King Louis is played to perfection by Robert Morley, at the height of his wry, eyebrow-waggling powers. He's just so good. Never one to miss an opportunity, the king co-opts the honest and simple Durward and employs him as a tool in a rather unlikely intrigue, assigning him as Isabelle's bodyguard to protect Louis's reputation, for Isabelle is to be abducted and forcibly married to La Marck, "the Beast of the Ardennes" (Duncan Lamont), that cartoon villain mentioned earlier. Durward, sadly, is to be slain for defending Isabelle's honor.

It doesn't work out that way, of course. Away from courts and kings, in its last third, the movie kicks into gear at last, as La Marck's black-clad goons erupt from ambush to pursue our knight and his countess. Taylor gets to do some very credible swashbuckling in a running fight at a country inn and then successfully escorts the countess to the forest-girt castle of her archbishop uncle, where she will presumably be safe. But La Marck uses Louis's gold to buy cannon, the walls are breached, and the foxes are in the henhouse. Which brings us to the other compelling reason to watch this flick: the absolutely insane final duel between Durward and La Marck, whacking at each other with swords as they both desperately swing back and forth on bell ropes at the top of a burning cathedral belfry, the great bells tolling out above them. No, I'm serious! It's glorious madness that's not to be missed.

THE ADVENTURES OF ROBIN HOOD

Rating: ★★★★★ (Essential) • *Origin:* USA, 1938 • *Directors:* Michael Curtiz
and William Keighley • *Source:* Warner Bros. DVD

This is a nigh-perfect film—as you know, because you've seen it (and if you haven't, then I'm very sorry, but we can no longer be friends). Let's just mention in passing some of the many reasons why you'll want to watch it again sometime soon:

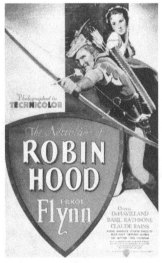

The Adventures of Robin Hood (1938) WIKIMEDIA COMMONS

- The matchless and heart-uplifting romantic chemistry between Errol Flynn and Olivia de Havilland.
- The rich and vivid look of this many-hued Technicolor fairy tale of the Middle Ages.
- The edgy interplay between the unforgettable villains, Basil Rathbone, Claude Rains, and Melville Cooper.
- The best Merrie Men ever assembled onscreen, most memorably Eugene Pallette as Friar Tuck.
- The brilliant script: witty, terse, thoughtful, romantic, and inspiring.
- The rousing, Oscar-winning score by Erich Wolfgang Korngold.
- That final, climactic battle and duel in Nottingham Castle.

Many 55-gallon drums of ink have been spilled in praising, analyzing, dissecting, and interpreting this film, for which the word "classic" almost seems to have been invented. I'll just cite a few things you may not have heard or considered. First, for a film that was perfectly cast, it's curious that the initial choice of director was not as on-target (archery reference intentional). William Keighley, who had directed Flynn in *The Prince and the Pauper*, occupied the director's chair for the first half of the movie's extensive shoot, but he turned out to have no knack for lensing large-scale action scenes, essential in a film intended to evoke the spirit of Flynn's predecessor, Douglas Fairbanks Sr. So halfway through production, Keighley was replaced by the more versatile Michael Curtiz, who had also directed Flynn before (in *Captain Blood*). It was Curtiz who helmed the fights and chase scenes, the arboreal antics in Sherwood Forest, and the battle in the castle.

Then there's Erich Wolfgang Korngold's personal tale of involvement with the film. An Austrian Jew, the famous composer and his family were natives of Vienna, where in early 1938 he was engrossed with completing a new opera for performance later in the year. But the opera was postponed, so when the call came from Warner Brothers asking him to do the music for *Robin Hood*, Korngold was unexpectedly available. Shortly after he arrived in Hollywood, the news came from Vienna that the Anschluss, Hitler's merger of Austria into Germany, was imminent. Korngold instantly sent for his family to join him, and they got out of Austria on the very last train before travel for Jews was interdicted. It was a daring escape for his family and poetically appropriate for the composer to a film about resistance to tyranny. From then on, Korngold always said that his and his family's lives had been saved by Robin Hood.

Back to the movie: You know those sheriff's goons who look like they get shot in the chest with arrows? They got shot in the chest with arrows. Each goon wore a chest plate of metal to stop the arrow, covered with a slab of balsa wood so the arrowhead would stick. A $150 bonus compensated for the risk, pain, and shock.

Our final fun fact involves Golden Cloud, the horse ridden in the film by Lady Marian. Another Hollywood character, Roy Rogers, was so taken with Golden Cloud's looks and obvious intelligence that he made inquiries and eventually bought the horse from Warner Brothers. Rogers took Golden Cloud over to the Republic Pictures lot, renamed him Trigger, and made him the most famous horse in Hollywood.

Now, go watch *The Adventures of Robin Hood* again. You know you want to.

THE FIRST BRITISH INVASION

Television and TV broadcasting had many forebears, but the first regular national service was Great Britain's BBC TV in 1936. It was suspended in 1939 during World War II so enemy aircraft couldn't home in on its signals, but broadcasting resumed in 1946 and expanded rapidly thereafter. In 1955 the BBC was joined on the British airwaves by the Independent Television network, or ITV. Unlike the BBC, ITV was a commercial network, its programming supported by advertising and, it was hoped, by selling its content for rebroadcasting in the burgeoning American markets.

ITV programmed a broad range of content, but what's important to us is that there were entertaining swashbuckler series in the mix, starting from the very beginning in September 1955 with *The Adventures of Robin Hood* and *The Adventures of the Scarlet Pimpernel*. In *Robin Hood*, at least, ITV had a smash success, and its production company added two additional series in 1956: *The Adventures of Sir Lancelot* and *The Buccaneers*, joined by a *Count of Monte Cristo* series from a different producer. All of these shows were syndicated regionally across the United States, and *Robin Hood* in particular is fondly remembered.

THE ADVENTURES OF ROBIN HOOD, SEASON 1

Rating: ★★★★☆ • *Origin:* UK, 1955 • *Directors:* Ralph Smart et al. • *Source:* Network DVDs

This series, which premiered in 1955 in both the United States and the UK, heralded a brief vogue for swashbuckling TV shows, most of them produced in Britain—but this is the one that really mattered, because it was smart and dependably entertaining, found a devoted audience, and ran for four seasons in the 1950s and then for decades in syndication. Its success inspired its only significant rival in Disney's *Zorro*. Though shot in the UK with a British cast and crew, its producers were Americans whose politics leaned left, and most of its scripters were American screenwriters such as Howard Koch and Waldo Salt, who'd both been blacklisted in Hollywood. They gave the stories an antiauthoritarian edge that accorded well with Robin Hood's outlaw legend.

Much of the series' success rested on the matinee-idol charisma of star Richard Greene, who invested the role of Robin with a charm and wry wit unmatched since Errol Flynn's portrayal. With a foil in the equally charming Bernadette O'Farrell as Lady Marian Fitzwalter, and a determined and intelligent adversary in Alan Wheatley as the Sheriff of Nottingham, each episode's brief (25-minute) morality play delivered solid entertainment week after week for 143 episodes over the life of the series.

The first season (39 episodes) establishes the situation: Saxon noble Robin of Locksley, loyal to King Richard, returns to England during the corrupt reign of Prince John and is outlawed. Robin then leads a band of Merrie Men from Sherwood Forest, fighting oppression with the aid of romantic interest Lady Marian and advisor Friar Tuck, both of whom are somewhat protected by their positions in the social hierarchy. This was the standard pop culture version of Robin Hood for a good 20 years until the first of the revisionist Robin Hoods, *Robin and Marian*, in 1976.

The opening episodes that set the stage are among the best. In "The Coming of Robin Hood," written by Ring Lardner Jr., Locksley, "back from the Holy Wars," finds that a Norman (played by a young Leo McKern) has usurped his domain; when Robin tries to reclaim it, an attempt to assassinate him kills the Norman instead, but Robin gets the blame and is outlawed. In "The Moneylender," Robin joins a band of outlaws in Sherwood, converts them to robbing from the rich to give to the poor, and inherits their leadership when their chief, Will Scathlock, dies in an ambush that Robin had warned them against. "Dead or Alive" introduces Little John (Archie Duncan), with the traditional quarterstaff fight on the log bridge, while "Friar Tuck," of course, brings that mettlesome priest (the amusing Alexander Gauge) into the band—and thereafter the outlaws have *two* schemers in their number. Finally, episode 5, "Maid Marian," introduces Robin's ladylove in her first full appearance, already adopting male garb and outshooting most of the outlaws.

Atypically for British shows of the period, *Robin Hood* wasn't shot all on soundstages, having exteriors set in the English greenwood in nearly every episode. The scripts are generally sharp, with an edge lacking in most conformist 1950s teleplays, though the overtly comic episodes haven't aged very well. The swordplay choreography is largely quite good, and archery is often central to the plot, which is gratifying—and the outlaws actually pause to string their bows before going into action! Even better, for a '50s TV show, Lady Marian is quite assertive, plus she's capable with a bow and shown to keep a French maître d'armes who trains her in handling a sword. Later episodes worth your time include 18, "The Jongleur"; 22, "The Sheriff's Boots"; 36, "The Thorkil Ghost"; and what is essentially the season closer, episode 38, "Richard the Lion-Heart." Note that some DVD collections jumble the episode order, which actually matters with this show, considering the way characters are introduced and developed; look online for a detailed reference so you're sure to watch them in proper succession.

THE ADVENTURES OF ROBIN HOOD, SEASON 2

Rating: ★★★★☆ • *Origin:* UK, 1956 • *Directors:* Ralph Smart et al. • *Source:* Network DVDs

The first season had been a big success, and the second season continued the formula, with the same cast, writers, and directors. And while it didn't quite have the freshness of the first time around, in the second season the actors were looser and more comfortable with each other, and the writers began to expand their themes. There had been a couple of experiments with continued stories, or rather sequel episodes, in the first season, and in the second there were quite a few more, and these were some of the best installments in the series. A particular standout was the sequence involving Prince John and his pursuit of young Prince Arthur,

King Richard's heir, in the episodes "The Dream," "Shell Game," "Ambush," "The Bandit of Brittany," and "Flight from France."

Prince John is played with relish by Donald Pleasance as a cowardly sociopath, and an episode in which he appears is always a standout, including some of those mentioned above as well as "Isabella," in which both John and Robin (Richard Greene) are outwitted by an amoral French princess. Other top-notch episodes showcase individual cast members, including "The Black Patch," in which Marian (Bernadette O'Farrell) takes the lead; "The Friar's Pilgrimage," in which Tuck (Alexander Gauge) exercises his formidable wits; and "The Blackbird," wherein Little John (Archie Duncan) gets his turn. But the two best episodes are ensemble efforts: "A Year and a Day," in which Robin and company perform a nip-and-tuck dance to keep a wanted serf out of the hands of the Sheriff (Alan Wheatley) until the bells at the end of the day declare his freedom; and "The York Treasure," in which Robin and his band help Jewish refugees find a safe haven following anti-Semitic riots in York and persecution on the continent. Robin and Little John even adopt Jewish disguises when necessary and apparently without a qualm, which puts them one up on Ivanhoe.

It must be said that some episodes, particularly in the second half of the season, feature particularly cringeworthy caricatures of Scots, Irish—pretty much anyone, in fact, who isn't English. Moreover, Robin's and Tuck's attitudes toward women are frequently condescending, but just as often Marian isn't having it. O'Farrell's strong portrayal of a smart, competent, and independent Marian outweighs any number of snide remarks and must have been quite encouraging to the girls in the audience. *Robin Hood*'s writers' room included far more women than was usual for the period, and it showed on the screen. Recommended.

THE ADVENTURES OF ROBIN HOOD, SEASON 3

Rating: ★★★☆☆ • *Origin:* UK, 1957 • *Directors:* Don Chaffey et al. • *Source:* Network DVDs

Robin Hood goes soft! Okay, that's an overstatement, but the third season of the successful series does feature a change in tone toward stories that are somewhat more gentle and, alas, considerably more didactic. The show has attracted a large audience of children, and a recognition of that is responsible for the shift. In season 3, combat is less frequent and, when it does occur, less deadly, and the civics lessons taught in most episodes have become less subtle.

Otherwise, the series largely maintains the high quality of the first two seasons, with one sad exception: the replacement of the excellent Bernadette O'Farrell as Maid Marian by the less-excellent Patricia Driscoll, who lacks O'Farrell's sharp intelligence and impish sense of mischief. O'Farrell is missed, though Driscoll does grow into the part over the course of the season.

There are thirty-nine 25-minute episodes in season 3, but if you don't have time for all of them, we have some standouts to recommend. Two of them feature the always entertaining Alexander Gauge as Friar Tuck: episode 2, "A Tuck in Time," in which we meet Tuck's brother Edgar in a classic evil-twin tale featuring the threat of black powder from Cathay, and the final episode, "Farewell to Tuck," in which the Sheriff of Nottingham (still played by Alan Wheatley, thankfully) suspects the friar is in league with the outlaws (took him long enough) and tries to engineer his transfer to a different parish. Episode 8, "An Apple for the Archer," concerns an orchardman whose fiancée is an excellent archer and refuses to marry anyone who isn't, so Robin takes the apple-grower under his wing and teaches him everything there is to

The Adventures of Robin Hood TV series   WIKIMEDIA COMMONS

know about medieval archery, including time spent with bowyers and fletchers; it's fascinating. Episode 14, "The Challenge of the Black Knight," harks back to the more hard-edged swashbuckling of the previous seasons, with John Arnatt very good as a knight returned from the Crusades looking for an opponent who can match his fighting skill, whom the Sheriff persuades him is Robin Hood. And Donald Pleasence returns as the creepiest Prince John in episode 38, "Marian's Prize": the prince co-opts a minor noble's archery tournament, putting up a large prize as a trap to catch Robin Hood, but the outlaw is away. The Merrie Men decide someone must take his place to try to claim the prize, and when Marian outshoots the outlaws, she determines to compete dressed in male guise. Fun stuff.

THE ADVENTURES OF ROBIN HOOD, SEASON 4

Rating: ★★★★☆ • *Origin:* UK, 1958 • *Directors:* Terry Bishop et al. • *Source:* Network DVDs

In the fourth and final season of *Robin Hood,* just when you would expect it to be at its weakest, the show regains its swashbuckling mojo and how! The civics lessons are mostly gone, replaced by banditry, suspense, and a sense of peril that's been missing since season 1. There are no major changes to the preexisting cast, but new characters join, both among the Merrie Men and on the side of the villains—most notably Sir Ralph, the Deputy Sheriff of Nottingham, who replaces the regular Sheriff as Robin's main antagonist for most of the season. Memorably played by John Arnatt, the Deputy Sheriff is more cunning and less scrupulous than the Sheriff, exactly the foe Robin (Richard Greene) needs to shake up the status quo in Sherwood Forest.

Season 4 is relatively short, 27 episodes instead of the usual 39, but there's less filler, and nearly every episode is worth your time. The return to deadly, high-stakes danger is set immediately with episode 1, "Sybella," which starts with a cold-blooded murder as one knight kills another for his credentials—signed by Robin—that will enable him to get close enough to King Richard overseas to assassinate him. The plot is discovered in Nottingham by a traveling entertainer whose Middle Eastern assistant, Sybella (Soraya Rafat—an actual Asian, for a wonder), is a memory prodigy who doesn't understand English but remembers everything she hears. However, traumatized by the death of the entertainer, she doesn't remember his entire last message until Marian (Patricia Driscoll) has fallen into the hands of the murderers.

Among the other top episodes in this outstanding season is 2, "The Lady-Killer," which reintroduces the sarcastic Will Scarlet (Paul Eddington) into the band. He's captured by Alan Wheatley as the Sheriff, who proves, in one of his last appearances, that he can be just as sharp and biting as Scarlet. Episode 7, "Six Strings to His Bow," adds the aristocratic minstrel Alan-a-Dale (Richard Coleman) to the outlaws in a tense tale of pursuit and capture in which the Sheriff plays detective and Marian, Will, and Alan all end up wounded.

The next episode, 8, "The Devil You Don't Know," brings in the aforementioned Deputy Sheriff, appointed by King John to take the Sheriff's place while he attends the royal court in London. Wily and ruthless, Sir Ralph is determined to capture or kill Robin Hood and thereby become the high sheriff of Nottingham for good. A master of deceit, he initially persuades Robin that he's a fugitive who's stolen the Deputy's identity, and Robin is tricked and very nearly taken. In episode 11, "Hue and Cry," which revolves around the medieval English practice of raising the yeomanry to hunt down a criminal but to suffer the punishment of a prisoner who isn't captured, the Deputy condemns nine innocent men to hang and is only foiled by the combined wits of Marian and Robin.

The rest of the season is of similar quality, but we can't leave Richard Greene's Robin Hood without noting episode 24, "The Edge and the Point," because it's all about swordplay rather than archery. Guest star Michael Gough brings the star power as Sir Boland, a master swordsman returned from the Crusades who enters Sherwood looking for trouble. He beats both Little John (Archie Duncan) and Will Scarlet, challenges Robin—and after an hour-long duel, defeats him! Robin is only saved from capture by Marian's dead-eye archery, but Boland escapes to Nottingham, where he teaches the Deputy Sheriff all his best fencing tricks for a final duel with Robin Hood. The bout between Gough and Greene is impressive, the finest swordplay in the show's four seasons, and a fitting farewell to what is arguably the best and most influential swashbuckling TV show of the twentieth century.

THE ADVENTURES OF SIR LANCELOT

Rating: ★★☆☆☆ (first half) / ★★★☆☆ (second half) • *Origin:* UK, 1956 •
Directors: Ralph Smart et al. • *Source:* Amazon streaming video

With the first season of *The Adventures of Robin Hood* a runaway success on both sides of the pond, the British ITV network called for companion series, and Sapphire Films was happy to comply. *Lancelot* was made at the same studios as *Robin Hood*, employing the same writers and directors, and sharing actors, costumes, and sets. But despite this, the new series seemed to lack the spark of its predecessor and got off to a slow start. Star William Russell as Lancelot wasn't as sharp or versatile as Richard Greene, and the initial episodes are flat, clichéd, and seemingly aimed at a juvenile *Hopalong Cassidy* level.

The stories are reasonably well grounded in the Arthurian legends, though without using the actual tales and with 100 percent less adultery. Oh, Lancelot and Guinevere make eyes at each other for the first few episodes, but then they dial it down, and the bold knight takes up flirting with whoever is the lady guest star of the week. Merlin is a fraud and a charlatan, as in Twain's *Connecticut Yankee*, but here is seen as a wise advisor who uses chemistry and optics to appear to cast spells. Lancelot, however, sees through his tricks, though he doesn't reveal them, and takes advantage of his cleverness. Unfortunately, the show's limited budget meant a smallish cast, and battles and sieges seem faintly ridiculous when conducted with five combatants per side. And though there are at least two sword fights in every episode, the swordplay is rubbish.

However, halfway through the first season, somebody seemed to have noticed that the series was flagging and decided to do something about it, because after episode 13 the scripts show a marked improvement. Russell doesn't get any better, but the stories suddenly come alive, the situations are more complex, and the characters show some depth. Furthermore, starting with episode 16, the series is shot in full color, a first for a British TV show. Alas, it must have been too little, too late to save the series, because it wasn't renewed for a second season.

But that does leave a good eight or ten episodes that are worth seeking out. Start with episode 10, "Roman Wall," an early outlier in which Lancelot finds a lost and forgotten Roman outpost. The first of the improved later episodes is 14, "Shepherds' War," which is clearly inspired by Kurosawa's *Seven Samurai*. Episodes 23 and 27, "Lady Lilith" and "The Missing Princess," address the situation of women in medieval (and, by extension, 1950s) Britain, going about as far toward advocating equality of the sexes as could be done on '50s TV. But the best episode is 29, "The Thieves," in which Arthur and Lancelot, for a wager, are disguised as branded thieves and learn for themselves how the lowest of the realm's underclass are treated by their betters. (Did I mention that this series was written by the same progressive American scripters as *Robin Hood*?)

THE ADVENTURES OF THE SCARLET PIMPERNEL

Rating: ★★★★☆ • *Origin:* UK, 1955 • *Directors:* David MacDonald et al. • *Source:* Network DVDs

This British TV series dates from the very beginning of ITV, but good as it was, it lasted only half a season. Echoing the stories by Baroness Orczy and the film adaptations of the 1930s, during the French Revolution Sir Percy Blakeney is a wealthy and foppish English lord who has a secret identity as the Scarlet Pimpernel, leading a league of adventurers dedicated to saving fugitive and condemned French aristocrats from the guillotine. The main differences from the source material are that, to suit egalitarian postwar attitudes, this Pimpernel doesn't really sympathize with the aristos, but he saves them out of common decency. And he's unmarried, leaving him free to romance the lady of this week's episode—or just to wish he dared risk it.

Though the series' budget was low, the writing and acting were good, with a solid ensemble cast led by coproducer Marius Goring playing Sir Percy and the Pimpernel. Goring was charming, handsome, and a talented character actor, essential in a role heavy on disguise and impersonation. In most episodes the Pimpernel is supported by his able lieutenants, Lord Richard Hastings (Anthony Newlands) and Sir Andrew Ffoulkes (Patrick Troughton, a decade before his turn as the Second Doctor Who). The droll Alexander Gauge (Friar Tuck in the *Adventures of Robin Hood* TV show) brings the avoirdupois as the Prince of Wales, and Stanley Van Beers more than carries his own weight in the thankless role of the irascible and ever-outsmarted Citizen Chauvelin, the Scarlet Pimpernel's French nemesis.

The 25-minute episodes fall, with some overlap, into three categories: *Mission: Impossible*-style schemes of deceit and impersonation, thrillers rife with gun- and swordplay (Goring is a two-fisted Pimpernel), and lighter-toned comedy installments that are less successful, though the Christmas episode is a standout. Episodes move fast, scenes change quickly, and much of the fun comes in trying to discern which just-introduced character is actually Sir Percy in disguise. It's a series that's worth tracking down if you're a Scarlet Pimpernel fan.

AGAINST ALL FLAGS

Rating: ★★★★☆ • *Origin:* USA, 1952 • *Director:* George Sherman •
Source: Universal Studios DVD

I know it isn't true, but I like to think that in the late 1990s, when the wonks at Disney were considering what tone to take for the movie on which they planned to base their *Pirates of the Caribbean* theme-park ride, they watched a lot of old pirate movies, saw *Against All Flags*, and said, "That's it!" Though a few historical names appear in it, this is a story set in an age of piracy beyond history, or at least no closer than next door to it. The bustling Madagascar port of Libertatia is run by the Captains of the Coast, a diverse gang that includes the Latino Roc Brasiliano (Anthony Quinn), Englishman William Kidd, a Black Jamaican called Captain Death, and a woman, the fiercely independent Spitfire Stevens (Maureen O'Hara), daughter of the master gunsmith who built the impregnable defenses that protect the pirate port "against all flags"—that is, the navies of the world.

Enter Lt. Brian Hawke (Errol Flynn), who's been drummed out of the Royal Navy and arrives in Libertatia to join the pirates. Flynn looks a trifle puffy and worn down here, to be honest, but acting-wise he's got much of his old, prewar swashbuckler mojo back. That mischievous glint is in his eye once more, and he seems to be enjoying himself, especially in his scenes with O'Hara. (I mean, who wouldn't be?) She is great here, on top of her game, striding around in thigh-high leather boots and swinging a sword with the best of them, alternately trying to kiss Flynn or kill him. Anthony Quinn just wants to kill him—and he may be the

Against All Flags Author's Collection

villain, but as Captain Roc he looks damned dashing swaggering about in his black mustachio and gaudy pirate garb. He's the one who engineers Flynn's most dangerous challenge, a one-on-one fight in which Hawke must prove his pirate's bona fides by dueling a giant buccaneer wielding hooked boarding pikes. Ouch!

Flynn, of course, is actually a navy spy, come to Libertatia to steal the plans of its fortifications, spike the guns, and call down condign punishment upon the pirates. He has a busy agenda: he must romance Spitfire Stevens, go a-pirating with Captain Roc, rescue an East Indian princess, and survive being lashed to the deadly Tide Stakes as the claw-clacking surf crabs crawl closer . . . ever closer. But the action's all served up with a light hand and tongue not quite in-cheek. Eventually everything comes to a head in a mass sword fight on the deck of Roc's brigantine, with Flynn, O'Hara, and Quinn all fencing away like fury, but finally virtue, or at least cunning, is triumphant, and we've all had a thoroughly satisfying piratical romp. Bonus: watch for Flynn, alone at night at the ship's wheel, singing "Haul on the Bowline" to himself.

ALEXANDER NEVSKY

Rating: ★★★★☆ • *Origin:* Russia, 1938 • *Director:* Sergei Eisenstein • *Source:* Criterion DVD

Alexander Nevsky is a towering achievement, an enduring classic of world cinema, except for the parts where it's goofy and awful. Director Sergei Eisenstein, who'd made his name in the silent era with *Battleship Potemkin* (1925), had been trying ever since the advent of sound in film to get another movie made, but under the strictures of Stalin's Russia, it was nigh impossible. Finally, by selecting as subject a historical tale of Russian resistance to German aggression (Hitler was then saber-rattling at Stalin) and by collaborating on the script with a Communist Party bigwig, Eisenstein was able to bring *Nevsky* to the screen.

It's set in the thirteenth century, when the lands of the Kievan Rus, already plundered by the Mongols from the east, are beset by a new threat from the Teutonic Knights to the west. To counter the German assault, the boyars of Novgorod turn to the war hero who'd also staved off the Swedes from the north, Prince Alexander Nevsky (Nikolai Cherkasov). From a story standpoint, this isn't a complicated film: there's the main, heroic plot, in which Alexander rallies the Russians to resist the heinous Germans, plus a goofy romantic subplot in which two cartoonish would-be heroes vie for the affections of a glorious Russian war maiden. But ignore all that and just look at this movie, because the matchless visuals are what we're here for.

After a run-in with some Mongols from the Golden Horde—who look *perfect*—Alexander is off to Novgorod to start building a coalition to fight the Germans. The reconstruction of medieval Novgorod is painstaking and beautiful: this is Old Russia, built of wood and earth and complete in every lovely detail. And the Germans are coming to destroy it.

Cut to the city of Pskov, newly conquered, and the Teutonic Knights, its conquerors. Here history has been augmented by art to depict a truly evil enemy. The knights are armored automatons, faceless and inhuman in their full helms, dealing death with cold, fanatical zeal. Even their foot soldiers' heads are enveloped in coal-scuttle helms that deliberately evoke the helmets of the German Wehrmacht. Imperial Stormtroopers? Here's where they come from, *Star Wars* fans. Only the Knights' robed and hooded priests have faces—but their visages are the cadaverous faces of vultures—Emperor Palpatine in the medieval flesh.

These Germans are bad. How bad are these Germans? They burn babies and throw live children right into bonfires. That's how bad.

On to the arousing-the-Russian-people-to-fight montage, and high time to mention the stirring orchestral and choral soundtrack by Sergei Prokofiev. Eisenstein worked closely with Prokofiev to fully integrate the music with the moving images. The director had distinct ideas about how to do this, because he'd been studying the recent revolution of the synchronization of music and film by its undisputed master: Walt Disney.

The last half of the movie is pretty much all medieval war and its aftermath, as Alexander maneuvers the Teutonic Knights into a final confrontation on the ice of frozen Lake Chudskoye. The climactic battle is justly famous for its setup and onset. The advance and charge of the Teutonic Knights established the look and feel for medieval warfare on film for everything to follow, from Laurence Olivier's *Henry V* all the way to Peter Jackson's *Lord of the Rings*. It must be said, this is one long-ass battle, but it's organized into several clear and distinct phases, so the viewer never loses track of what's going on. The goofy romantic rivals get too much screen time, and Prokofiev's pursuit theme is shrill, frenetic, and overwrought, but the climax on the icy lake, as the surface cracks and disintegrates under the heavily armored Germans, pays for all.

Victory, however, leads to deep melancholy and extended brooding over the carnage, because Russians. "I kiss your sightless eyes and caress your cold forehead," the chorus sings. But at least the romantic subplot ends happily, and there's even a parade! Hats are waved, babies are kissed, and all is well again in Mother Russia.

ALEXANDER THE GREAT

Rating: ★★★☆☆ • *Origin:* USA, 1968 • *Director:* Phil Karlson •
Source: YouTube streaming video

An action TV movie with William Shatner (Captain Kirk) as Alexander and Adam West (Batman) as his loyal general Cleander? Can this be true?

It is. Shot in 1963 as a one-hour pilot for an unproduced series, this wasn't broadcast until 1968, after the breakout TV success of stars Shatner and West. West is the second banana here and doesn't get much screen time, but Shatner as the conquering king of Macedonia is in full-on Kirk mode, and no fan of original *Star Trek* should miss this. There are many other familiar faces in the cast, including John Cassavetes (*The Dirty Dozen*) and Joseph Cotten (frickin' *Citizen Kane*) both listed as guest stars, which means, of course, that they won't survive the episode.

Alexander has conquered the east coast of the Aegean Sea and is pushing his army east into Persia, seeking a confrontation with King Darius. Not just the King of Macedonia, Alex here is also an action hero who's personally riding ahead with his scouts when he comes upon a squad of his troops tortured and hung upside down on a dead tree. "There's no soul . . . to these barbarians!" Alex emotes. "I'll . . . *teach* them!" One of the soldiers, not yet dead, reveals that Alex's buddy Cleander was captured by the Persians—and *there he is*, tied to a horse among a squad of Persian cavalry on the hilltop just ahead! Who cares if it's a trap? Charge!

Cut to the Greek camp five days later, where the generals are arguing about what to do, since the missing Alex must certainly be dead. One of them has to be the traitor who set up the ambush that apparently killed the king, but who? Well, there's no time to waste in a TV pilot, so the traitor is obvious: it's Karonos (Cassavetes), who is reluctantly supported by Antigonus (Cotten) to be the new Greek leader. Karonos orders a retreat west to the coast, but then—surprise! Alex shows up with Cleander, rescued, 'cause he's an action hero, no explanation needed. He confirms Karonos's order to break camp but instead commands a forced march *east*, to catch the Persian army by surprise.

First, though, Alex and his generals have a party, so the conqueror's buxom lover, Persian princess Ada (Ziva Rodann), can do a gratuitous exotic dance while Shatner smirks and leers. (So good.) Then it's on to the confrontation with the Persians, the treachery of the traitors, and the deaths of the Guest Stars. The big battle scene reuses footage from the Steve Reeves sword-and-sandal epic *Giant of Marathon* (1959), and that's fine, because it gives us plenty of shots of Persian soldiers in their doofy, bulbous helmets. The episode's swordplay is directed by Albert Cavens, son of the great fight master Fred Cavens, but though Shatner is enthusiastic, Albert still isn't able to get him to wield a bronze short sword convincingly. The excellent music is instantly recognizable as by composer Leonard Rosenman, who scored 151 episodes of *Combat!*, and his overwrought soundtrack is a good match for the hyperbolic Shatner as he looks moodily into the setting sun, emoting over the deaths of so many good Greek and Persian soldiers. What a shame this wasn't picked up as a series.

ALFRED THE GREAT

Rating: ★★★☆☆ • *Origin:* UK, 1969 • *Director:* Clive Donner • *Source:*
Cinema & Cultura DVD

This film flopped upon release in 1969, and it's easy to see why: out of step with the times, it's too slow, too long, and too self-important, while the lead, David Hemmings as King Alfred, overacts and is no fun. The historical Alfred should be a fine subject for a film, so what the hell?

To be fair, it starts out well: it's the ninth century in England, and the scholarly Prince Alfred, about to be confirmed as a priest, is called away by his brother, King Aethelred of Wessex (Alan Dobie), because the Danes under King Guthrum (Michael York, quite good) are invading. Aethelred is wounded, so Alfred reluctantly takes command of the troops, comes up with a brilliant tactical plan, and defeats the Danes in a battle that's as period-authentic as anyone could wish. Prince Alfred marries Princess Aelswith of Mercia (Prunella Ransome, quite dull), Aethelred promptly dies, Alfred is proclaimed king—and then proceeds to spend the next 90 minutes making mistake after mistake. Come on, royal dude! He mistreats his queen, alienates his nobles, gives Aelswith as a hostage to Guthrum, loses a battle to the Danes, and is driven into hiding in the marshes. As a captive, Aelswith even bears Alfred's son and follows up by getting involved with Guthrum. D'oh! Alfred is angsty about it.

But then, while spying on the Danes, Alfred is captured by the bandits of the marshes, whose leader Roger is played by none other than Ian McKellen, and the movie is saved. In a daring raid with Roger's help, Alfred abducts his wife and son from Guthrum and then builds a coalition of nobles and commoners to resist the Danes. He learns about Greek phalanxes from a book in a monastery, musters his forces, and defeats Guthrum and company in a climactic battle. Whew!

Director Clive Donner got the job because he'd never done a historical epic and the producer wanted to avoid clichés, which sort of worked: the clichés of historical epics were avoided but not those of Donner's previous specialty, stories of overwrought and tormented youth. To their credit, every effort was made to get the ninth-century details right, and the movie was shot far from modern civilization in County Galway in western Ireland, so it mostly looks good, barring a few murky interior scenes lit only by torches. For most of the picture, Hemmings chews the scenery to shreds, but when he doesn't, McKellen and York declaim effectively like proper British-trained stage actors, with strong support from Colin Blakely as Alfred's monkish chum. Their efforts make this film worth seeing—once.

ALI BABA AND THE FORTY THIEVES

Rating: ★★★☆☆ • *Origin:* USA, 1944 • *Director:* Arthur Lubin • *Source:* Universal DVD

After the success of the dumb *Arabian Nights*, Universal decided to give the genre another go with substantially the same cast—and we're glad they did, because this second movie is 100 percent less dumb than the first. It starts out with an actual historical event, the 1258 siege and sacking of Bagdad by the Mongols of Hulagu Khan, and scenes of the massacre of the Bagdadis immediately set this film's more serious tone. The Caliph is betrayed by his Grand Vizier and killed in a Mongol ambush (note to self: if you're a Sultan or Caliph, never have a Grand Vizier), but the Caliph's only son, Ali, escapes. Though historically the boy was captured by the Khan, here he gets away into the desert, where he stumbles upon the secret hideout of a band of 40 thieves. And yes, the magic words "Open, sesame" do open the lair's stone doors, the only fantasy element in this film. To the bandits, Ali reveals his identity as the Caliph's son, and their leader, Old Baba, adopts him as his own, hiding him under the new name Ali Baba. Old Baba appoints his aide, Abdullah—squeaky-voiced Andy Devine, best known for playing comic sidekicks in Westerns, here in regrettable brownface—to be Ali's guardian and also, inevitably, his comic sidekick.

Ten years pass, and Ali, now grown (and henceforth played by Jon Hall), emerges as the leader of the gang, which he's reforged into a band of freedom fighters conducting a guerrilla war against the occupying Mongols—the theme that marks this as a true wartime movie. The 40 thieves now wear uniform red and blue robes, and they even have a catchy theme song they sing while galloping across the desert! "We riiiiide . . . plundering sons, thundering sons, forty and one for all, and all for one." Hmm, that part sounds familiar. Wait, so does the next part: "Robbing the rich, feeding the poor. . . ." Okay, got it: the Forty Thieves are the Merrie Men.

The film has an actual plot: Robin Hood—I mean, Ali—is scouting a Mongol camp when he meets Lady Amara (Maria Montez) swimming fetchingly in the water of the oasis. Amara, the daughter of the treacherous vizier, is on her way to Bagdad to be married to Hulagu Khan—but as a little girl she had been the boy Ali's childhood sweetheart, so this marriage must be stopped! Swashbuckling follows, with raids, abductions, and captures, throughout which Amara is aided by her loyal knife-throwing servant, young Jamiel (Turhan Bey, making an impression; the role had been written for teen star Sabu, but having become a naturalized citizen, he had joined the Army Air Force to serve as a tail gunner in B-24s). Ali decides the time has come for full-scale revolt against the Mongols, but he gets captured himself. To save him, the thieves have to get smuggled into the palace inside 40 man-sized oil jars—the only other nod, besides the cave doors, to the original Ali Baba story in *The Arabian Nights' Entertainment*. In the end the uprising occurs in the nick of time, and—spoiler!—Lady Amara doesn't have to marry Hulagu Khan. Somehow, it all works.

AMAZONS (1986)

Rating: ★★☆☆☆ • *Origin:* Argentina/USA, 1986 • *Director:* Alejandro Sessa • *Source:* ENDLESSCLASSICS DVD

This heroic fantasy has a screenplay by Charles R. Saunders based on his fine story "Agbewe's Sword" from the *Amazons!* anthology edited by Jessica Amanda Salmonson, and therefore one could hope it might be good. But in the end, it's one more example of how anything good fed into the Roger Corman wood chipper comes out the other end as mulch.

Still, this barbarian boob-fest may be the best of Corman's cheapo Argentine action fantasies, though that's admittedly a low bar. The bad news: what passes for acting isn't any better than usual; the costumes, sets, and fight direction are bottom of the barrel; and the special effects for the wizard magic are acutely embarrassing. Saunders's story, though, is just interesting and complex enough to pull you through, even while you're shaking your head at the terrible performances. In outline, the plot is nothing special: a sorcerer-king named Kalungo (Joseph "Cool" Whipp—okay, I made up the "Cool" part) uses his lightning powers and black-clad mercenaries to conquer a generic fantasy town and threatens to conquer the rest of the Emerald Land unless a warrior can bring back a magic sword from a distant, mystic cave. But because this is called *Amazons*, Kalungo is opposed by a corps of warrior women in leather bikinis, and the warrior with the quest, Dyala (Mindi Miller), is the bikiniest and blondest of them all.

This may sound dumb, and it mostly is, but the interest comes from the character interplay between Dyala, her treacherous bottle-blond aide Tashi (Penelope Reed), and Tashi's even more treacherous but equally blond mother Tashinge (Danitza Kingsley), who is the commander of the Amazons but is selling them out to Kalungo for wizard nookie and future queen rights. As played by Mr. Whipp, Kalungo in this setting is jarringly incongruous, less the usual gloating mad tyrant than an oily self-satisfied California producer who has somehow ended up in a fantasy world with lightning powers. It's so wrong that after a while you kind of get to like it.

There's a lot of gratuitous female nudity on display here, so be prepared for that, and the battles between Kalungo's troops and the Amazons are unusually feeble, even by low-budget fantasy flick standards. However, there's this one action sequence, where Dyala has to save Tashi from being sacrificed by a tribe of masked goons to their creepy sacred tree, that's not half bad—like, somebody spent time and effort on setting it up, and it works. It totally makes up for the scene where Dyala has to wrap a tame snake around herself to make it look threatening and then roll around in the dirt. (Yep.) Just . . . don't let your expectations get out of hand.

AMBUSH AT BLOOD PASS (OR INCIDENT AT BLOOD PASS OR MACHIBUSE)

Rating: ★★★★★ • *Origin:* Japan, 1970 • *Director:* Hiroshi Inagaki • *Source:* Warrior DVD

Who doesn't love a movie in which seven strangers, each with their own secret agenda, come together in a lonely inn in a snowy mountain pass with murder in the icy air?

Toshiro Mifune dons the gray kimono and gruff mannerisms of the nameless ronin from *Yojimbo* and *Sanjuro* again for the second time in a year (see *Zatoichi Meets Yojimbo*), once more costarring with Shintaro Katsu. This time the itinerant samurai is offered a mysterious job from a hooded man in the shadows known only as "Crow," who tells him to go to Shansu Pass and "Wait until something happens—you'll know what to do." Intrigued, the laconic yojimbo (bodyguard) does just that. On the way up the mountain, he liberates a woman named Okuni (Ruriko Asaoka) from an abusive husband, and she follows him to the Minoya Inn. This remote teahouse, run by an elderly man and his granddaughter, is already housing Gentetsu (Katsu), a man on the run who claims to be an ex-doctor from Edo. They're soon joined by a handsome but shady gambler named Yatarou (Yujiro Ishihara) and Ibuki (Kinnosuke Nakamura), a wounded police officer with a captive crook, Tatsu the Wild Monkey (Ryonosuke Yamazaki). As the others begin quarreling, the wandering yojimbo . . . waits for something to happen.

And things do begin to happen, slowly at first and then all in a rush. Gentetsu makes a pass at Okuni, but she rebuffs him. Then two riders arrive, claiming to be police, enticing officer Ibuki to bring Tatsu along and leave with them, but the gambler and the yojimbo smell a rat and butt in. In a quick scuffle, the yojimbo kills one rider, but the other gets away. The dead man's tattoos prove him a gangster, but no one can explain why two gangsters would try to rescue a cheap crook like the Wild Monkey. The yojimbo goes out to scout the pass, and in the meantime Okuni's brutal husband arrives. He tries to get Okuni to leave with him, and when she refuses, he gets aggressive—but suddenly the inn is invaded by an entire criminal gang, and everything changes. The gang takes over the inn, and Gentetsu comes forward and reveals himself as their leader. When the gruff yojimbo returns, he assesses the situation, and when he's challenged, he just tells Gentetsu that they work for the same employer and he was sent to help him—and he shows Crow's letter to prove it.

As usual, the yojimbo is just going along with the goons until he sees his opportunity. Gentetsu lets him in on their caper: they're planning to rob a shogunate gold shipment that will be coming through the pass. But it's more than just a heist, there's a political angle to the job as well. And that's all the yojimbo needs to hear to realize that he's caught in the middle of a classic double cross. Time to loosen his sword in its sheath.

This is the final feature film of the veteran director Hiroshi Inagaki, and he handles the story's taut suspense and sudden violence with complete mastery. Mifune is wryly self-possessed, Katsu is menacing, Asaoka is brave under pressure, and the evil mastermind Crow gets what he deserves. In its own small way, this movie is kind of perfect.

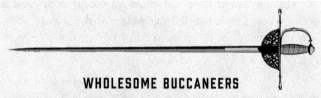

WHOLESOME BUCCANEERS

After the grim years of World War II, much of the moviegoing public was looking for lighter fare in their entertainment, and Hollywood returned to making swashbucklers, many of them in the happy hues of Technicolor. Pirates were back on the menu, but as America headed into the conformist 1950s, the pirates on its movie screens were more rascals than cutthroats, good-hearted rogues who would plunder some buried treasure and maybe hold a lady for ransom but for whom keel-hauling and suchlike barbarisms were out of the question. Wholesome buccaneers as family entertainment! Absurd, of course, but fun if it was done with a wink at the viewer.

ANNE OF THE INDIES

Rating: ★★★★☆ • *Origin:* USA, 1951 • *Director:* Jacques Tourneur • *Source:* Amazon streaming video

We usually award the title Queen of the Swashbucklers to Maureen O'Hara, but Jean Peters makes a grab for O'Hara's crown in this fine pirate melodrama. As a feisty orphan girl, Anne (Peters) was raised aboard ship by Edward Teach—Blackbeard himself!—and now commands her own fighting ship, the *Sheba Queen*, under the name Captain Providence. She's a real hellion, and since her brother was hanged as a pirate by the English, she preys on English shipping and kills English sailors without mercy, making the captives walk the plank. But one captive sailor is the strikingly handsome Louis Jourdan playing a Frenchman named (what else?) François, who claims to be a privateer's navigator who'd been captured by the Royal Navy. Captain Providence frees him, adds him to her crew, and takes him to Nassau to meet Blackbeard—which is where the real trouble starts.

This story as originally developed was supposed to be about historical female pirate Anne Bonny, but then Hollywood happened, and history was shown the door. However, the story we got instead, a nautical love triangle punctuated by sword fights and naval actions, is perfectly fine, with the seeds of tragedy planted in the first act bearing woeful but believable fruit in the last. And history didn't entirely get the boot, because somebody did some research into the pre-steam Age of Sail and for once they got all the details right. The sailing orders the officers bark out are accurate and appropriate, the gun crews serving the cannons follow authentic routines instead of just miming, and we get the rarely seen spectacle of a pirate ship careened on her side on the beach of a hidden cove, as her crew use their boarding axes to clear the barnacles from her foul bottom. Nice!

We also get brief but spot-on looks at three Caribbean ports: the brawling pirate hell of Nassau, the private club of the perfidious officers of the Royal Navy in Port Royal, and the exotic mix of traders and sailors from every sea at the slave market in the Spanish colonial town of Maracaibo. During all this sailing around in pursuit of the plot, Jean Peters stays in fine form as the ever-smoldering Captain Providence—and she can fence too! Louis Jourdan sells it as the suave but two-faced François, and the ursine Thomas Gomez makes a memorable Blackbeard. There's even a solid early appearance by Debra Paget in a supporting role as Anne's rival. Add stylish direction by Jacques Tourneur and a rollicking soundtrack by Franz Waxman, and it makes for a tidy package o' piracy that's well worth digging for.

ARABIAN ADVENTURE

Rating: ★★★☆☆ • *Origin:* UK, 1979 • *Director:* Kevin Connor • *Source:* StudioCanal DVD

This is a movie that isn't afraid to ask the question, "If one magic carpet is good, wouldn't *nine* be *better?*"

Arabian Adventure is an utter throwback to the 1950s, a love letter to *The Thief of Bagdad* and its ilk. You've seen just about every bit in it in earlier *Arabian Nights*-inspired films, and that's the whole point, really—it's Bagdad fairy tale comfort food. There's a hero, Prince Hasan, played by Oliver Tobias (Arthur in *Arthur of the Britons*), and a plucky princess, Zuleira (Emma Samms), and a villain, Caliph Alquazar (top-billed Christopher Lee), but the real protagonist is an 11-year-old beggar boy named Majeed, played with charm and brio by the charismatic young Puneet Sira—who has, of course, a mischievous pet monkey.

Arabian Adventure Author's Collection

It's the kind of movie in which the hero invades the caliph's palace and fights a running scimitar battle with black-clad guards, engaging in athletic swashbuckling until he stumbles into the boudoir of the beautiful princess. It's the kind of movie where the hero gets thrown into the dungeon and finds that his scruffy fellow prisoner is a former wazir, played by Peter Cushing. The kind of movie where a street urchin's kindness to a ragged old beggar woman is repaid with a magic sapphire containing a lovely female jinni. The kind of movie where the sets are right out of Technicolor-era Hollywood, and all the magic and monsters are old-school practical effects. That kind of movie.

Despotic Caliph Alquazar has only one desire: a magical MacGuffin called the Rose of Al-Il that will make him all-powerful—but he needs a hero to get it for him. Heroic Prince Hasan of Bagdad comes to town, and he and the caliph's daughter fall in love at first sight, so Alquazar offers him his daughter's hand if he'll go into dire peril and bring back the rose. Quest time! Young Majeed joins Hasan's expedition, and with the help of his sapphire jinni, the adventure is on.

The heroes encounter an evil jinni, a laughing giant clearly inspired by Rex Ingram's genie in the 1940 *Thief of Bagdad,* but the princess tells them the secret of how to beat it: by speaking through her father's haunted magic mirror. More challenges follow, and then, an hour into the movie, just as it's all becoming a bit overfamiliar and you think it's never going to show you anything you haven't seen before, there it is: a trio of fire-breathing, mechanical, way pre-steampunk "brasspunk" demons controlled by a deranged engineer-wizard, played in an absolutely unhinged performance by none other than Mickey Rooney (no lie). The evil caliph commences a long-range betrayal of the heroes, with Christopher Lee relishing such commands to his minions as, "Do not fail me!" (just before, inevitably, they fail him). Despite his efforts, Hasan and Majeed return to the city with the magical rose and hook up with the desperate citizen freedom-fighters who've only been waiting for a leader, and we get a climax with a flying carpet dogfight with multiple carpets on each side. Created with all practical effects, it's actually kind of awkward, but you have to give them credit for the idea.

Arabian Adventure was not a box-office success—it was a film past its time, and its uninspired title didn't help matters. But, man alive, *brasspunk fire demons.*

ARABIAN NIGHTS

Rating: ★★☆☆☆ • *Origin:* USA, 1942 • *Director:* John Rawlins •
Source: Universal Cinema Classics DVD

In the 1940s, Universal was a modest-sized studio whose business was cranking out low-budget adventure pictures in every genre. After he starred in the 1940 British *Thief of Bagdad*, Indian teen star Sabu moved to Hollywood and signed a contract with Universal. They cast him in some jungle adventures but also decided to try him in their own Arabian Nights fantasy, titled, er, *Arabian Nights*. The studio splurged on fancy costumes and big sets, and they shot it all in Technicolor but relied on their usual stable of B- and C-list actors to round out the cast.

The movie's title notwithstanding, it doesn't seem like anyone involved with this story read *The Arabian Nights' Entertainment* beyond the list of characters, cherry-picking the ones that sounded familiar. Haroun-al-Raschid (Jon Hall), Caliph of Bagdad, is betrayed by his grand vizier in favor of his evil half-brother, Kamar, who is determined to steal the throne because he figures it's the only way he can win the love of the ambitious dancing girl Sherazade (Maria Montez). Yeah, that's how dumb this is. Sherazade is part of a troupe of "humorous" traveling entertainers that includes an acrobat, Ali (Sabu), a doofus named Aladdin whose shtick is that he's always searching for his lost lamp, and another doofus who tells boring sea stories and goes by the name Sinbad, played by Shemp Howard of the Three Stooges, no less.

So the plot: Haroun, wounded in the vizier's coup but saved by Ali and then disguised, falls in with his troupe of entertainers; Haroun and Sherazade make eyes at each other, guards with scimitars appear, and gags and pursuits ensue. Evil Kamar openly wants the throne and the love of Sherazade; his evil vizier secretly wants the throne and the love of Sherazade; disguised caliph Haroun wants his throne back and . . . well, you get it. Despite the references to magic lamps, this is a conventional dynastic struggle with no fantasy elements to it, unless you count the male fantasy in which Ali hides among the caliph's scantily clad harem women while two of them distract the eunuch guards with a hair-pulling catfight. (Yup.) We do get ornery camels and shiny turbans and scenic sand dunes, but the story doesn't make a lick of sense, the acting is uniformly terrible, and all the scimitar-clashing fights are at the level of community-theater stage combat. So naturally it was a big hit, and thenceforth Hollywood had a new ongoing adventure genre, the Arabian fantasy! Allah preserve us.

ARTHUR OF THE BRITONS, SEASON 1

Rating: ★★★☆☆ • *Origin:* UK, 1972 • *Directors:* Sidney Hayers et al.
Source: Network DVDs

Britain's ITV network had several fine historical adventure shows early on, including *The Adventures of Sir Lancelot* (1956) and *Sir Francis Drake* (1961), but it was a long decade until their next one, *Arthur of the Britons*, in 1972, and in that time a lot of things changed, including tastes in historical sagas. Hollywood's Technicolor past was out, replaced by gritty realistic history, at least as it was seen 50 years before now. This series is set during the time of the historical Arthur—if he existed—a time shortly after the Romans left British shores and the Saxons came across the narrow sea to fill the power vacuum. Here, "King" Arthur is one of many Celtic warlords resisting the Saxon advances but the only one with the vision to see that the Celts must unite under a single leader if they are to hold the parts of Britain still under their control.

There isn't much of the classic Arthurian tales and legends here: Arthur (Oliver Tobias) still has a foster brother named Kai (Michael Gothard), but here it's Kai who is adopted, the son of the Celtic warrior Llud (Jack Watson), a craggy old veteran who trained both boys in arms. The arms are those of the sixth century: axes, spears, and swords both short and long, with nary a jousting lance or suit of plate armor to be seen. Instead, it's all furs, studded leather, and the occasional shirt of mail; think of it as an early take on the period depicted in Bernard Cornwell's *Last Kingdom* series. But in these tales, there's no Merlin, no Lancelot, and no Guinevere, though there are a couple of quarreling cousins named Gawain and Gareth.

The twelve 25-minute episodes are discontinuous, each telling its own story, so the situation doesn't really change as the season unfolds. The stories are quite good, most of the first season penned by veteran screenwriter Terence Feely, with a solid mix of characterization, medieval Celtic politics, and action. The combat, and there's plenty of it, is well staged and credible, and the battle tactics the Celts use against the Saxons match what little we know of the period. Once past the first episode, in which everyone shouts all the time, the acting is quite decent, though top-billed Tobias as Arthur is outdone by Gothard's Kai, with his rugged charisma and crooked smile. The only person more rugged than Kai is walking oak tree Jack Watson as Llud—except for the four episodes in which force-of-nature Brian Blessed appears as the loud and robust Mark of Cornwall. The best of these is the last episode, "The Prize," but other standout episodes include the third, "The Challenge," and the sixth, "The Duel," which pits Llud against Mark.

This series was rerun frequently in the UK in the 1970s and was also shown in France, Germany, and Brazil. Several episodes were edited into a feature titled *King Arthur, The Young Warlord* (1975), but you may find that it's out of print. Worth a look, though.

ARTHUR OF THE BRITONS, SEASON 2

Rating: ★★★☆☆ • *Origin:* UK, 1973 • *Directors:* Sidney Hayers et al. • *Source:* Network DVDs

This series picks back up where season 1 left off but with a couple of differences. First, several recurring characters are added to the cast, and stories and themes are carried on from one episode to the next, so watching order makes a difference. Second, where the first season seemed almost to be more about Kai (Michael Gothard) than Arthur (Oliver Tobias), this time most of the stories center squarely on Arthur as the leader of the Celtic alliance. Of the recurring characters, two in particular stand out: Princess Rowena (Gila—that's her whole name), the spirited daughter of Yorath, a Jute warlord, and the rousing return of King Mark of Cornwall (Brian Blessed), who steals every scene he appears in. There's real chemistry between Arthur and Rowena, and when Mark is added into the mix as well, things get spicy.

The high quality of the writing established in the first season is retained in the second and maybe even improved upon. The production budget is still low, but the attention to historical detail is impressive for a 25-minute afternoon adventure show, and the vigorous combat is often intense and suspenseful. Ninety percent of the scenes are exteriors, shot in the lovely, muddy British countryside, and it does wonders for the ol' verisimilitude.

Several episodes in particular stand out. The third regular member of the cast, craggy Jack Watson as Llud of the Silver Hand, gets an episode to himself, "Go Warily," in which he's dogged by a premonitory dream. The nightmare gets repeated a few too many times, but we don't mind, because the Celtic warlord Brandreth and his evil twin brother are both played with gusto by Tom Baker (*Doctor Who*).

Then there's the Rowena sequence, starting, naturally enough, with "Rowena," which introduces the feisty princess and her on-again, off-again romance with Arthur. In "Some Saxon Women," Rowena single-handedly maneuvers Arthur into opposing the traffic of captive slaves, which is right for Arthur's character though ahistorical as hell, as every tribe in the period engaged in the dreadful practice of slavery and would for centuries more. Third and best of all is "The Marriage Feast," in which King Mark persuades Rowena that he loves her, when what he really loves is the land she would bring as his bride. Arthur tries to put the kibosh on the wedding by tricking Mark into losing his temper, but the smug king of Cornwall just smiles at every outrage and remains "as sweet as hazelnuts," as he puts it. It's hilarious. Both Rowena and Mark are featured in two other episodes apiece, and they're all worth watching.

It's also worth mentioning that the series has a catchy fanfare-blaring title theme by Elmer Bernstein (*The Magnificent Seven*) that he probably knocked out in about 90 minutes, but which I guarantee you'll be humming for a week. Duh-dun-da-DAH, dun-duh-dun-da-dah. . . .

ATLAS IN THE LAND OF THE CYCLOPS

Rating: ★★☆☆☆ • *Origin:* Italy, 1961 • *Director:* Antonio Leonviola • *Source:* Mill Creek DVD

Disregard the American title of this Italian peplum romp: the hero of this feature isn't Atlas; it's Maciste.

Atlas in the Land of the Cyclops was the second 1960s Maciste film and the only one that starred Gordon Mitchell in the title role, which is a shame because Mitchell was quite charming in the part, playing the big lug as a good-hearted simpleton who just happened to probably be a demigod. He smiles a lot, flexes often, performs an even dozen Mighty Feats of Strength, and speaks in simple, declarative sentences like, "I have heard of your bad queen," and "I am a prisoner of your beauty." You have to love him.

The movie is a solid 90 minutes of near-nonstop action, most of which makes approximate sense on its own terms, reminiscent of a Republic serial from the 1940s. It's set in the

MIGHTY MACISTE

The character of Maciste originated in Italian cinema in 1914 and appeared in over two dozen films in the silent era. A heroic strongman of ancient times, Maciste was revived in 1960 during the post-*Hercules* peplum craze, appearing in another two dozen films before the sword-and-sandal fad faded. Maciste was never given a specific origin; he was just a shirtless, roving hero with godlike strength whose movies were set in any period from prehistoric times to the sixteenth century. At least 10 different actors starred as Maciste in 1960s films, most of them American bodybuilders cast for their looks rather than their acting ability. Most of the Maciste movies were dubbed into English for American release, but some were shot in both Italian and English versions.

times of Greek myth, when, as the introductory narration informs us, the descendants of Circe the sorceress and Polyphemus the cyclops were driven by fate to take revenge on the descendants of Ulysses. Thus the "bad queen" Capys (Chelo Alonso) sends out her troops to wipe out her enemies' village with the concise command, "Destroy everything!" They do, capturing Good Queen Penope (Vira Silenti) in the process, but her infant son is carried off into the mountains by a loyal but dying bodyguard, to be protected by Maciste.

The strongman is found sleeping on a lakeshore, slowly arising and stretching his mighty limbs to a prolonged physique fanfare. He accepts responsibility for the babe in arms without hesitation, but isn't simpleton enough to try to care for the child himself, immediately fobbing him off on a convenient shepherd before setting off downhill to sort things out in the city of Queen Capys. Inside the palace, Maciste's chest enters the room long before the rest of him, a quality easily matched by the impressive bosom of Queen Capys. Maciste is determined to find a way to free the captives, but Capys tells him she isn't all bad, she's just a pawn of fate, so Maciste hangs around for some feasting and vintage '60s "exotic dancing." But you can't argue with fate, and Mighty Feats of Strength ain't gonna perform themselves, so soon enough there's lion wrestling, boulder rolling, bodyguard wrestling, ceilings held up and ceilings pulled down, cyclops wrestling, and lots of drugged wine—Capys really has a thing for drugging the wine. Fate made her do it.

ATOR, THE FIGHTING EAGLE

Rating: ★☆☆☆☆ • *Origin:* Italy, 1982 • *Director:* Joe D'Amato • *Source:* Cine DVD

Wow, this is really bad. Even the fact that the hero has an adorable bear cub sidekick can't save it.

The story follows standard sword-and-sorcery plot B: a fantasy realm is oppressed by an evil high priest, but a prophecy foretells that a son shall be born who will slay him. When the signs indicate the birth of the child, the priest sends forth his wicked minions to kill him, but the child is borne off to a remote village to be raised by foster parents. When the child, a mighty warrior, comes of age, the high priest's wicked minions find the village and slaughter his foster parents, so the young warrior vows revenge.

Aside from the aforementioned bear cub, this lazy *Conan* knockoff has nothing whatsoever to recommend it. Its star, Miles O'Keeffe, had first afflicted movie screens the year before in the Bo Derek *Tarzan* travesty, and he does no better here; he's handsome and muscular, and he has a winning smile but acts like someone who's never in his life had to work hard and can't think why he should start now. His costar, Italian horror actress Sabrina Siani, who plays the Amazon thief Roon, does her best to imitate Sandahl Bergman but can't seem to stay interested from one scene to the next, and who can blame her? Ator's quest to slay the priest of the Spider Cult takes the pair on a series of disconnected adventures that lead to one damn mystic cave after another, fighting zombies, a witch, Spider Cult goons, blind shrine guards, and a giant spider called the Ancient One. These would-be adventures are tired and tiresome. For example, Roon tells Ator, "Now we must pass through the Lands of the Walking Dead," to which Ator replies, "Well, if we gotta go . . ." In this flick, that counts as snappy patter. They then wander through a series of mystic caves while zombies stagger after them until suddenly they don't, and Ator remarks with unconcern, "They disappeared. C'mon, let's get outta here."

Characters come and go without motive or explanation, the main example being Griba (Edmund Purdom, nearly unrecognizable in a terrible blue-black wig), who initially saves the infant Ator and then shows up at random points thereafter to advance the plot with cryptic utterances about destiny, before flipping without warning from mentor to villain. Why? The costumes are cheesy and ridiculous, the sluggish combat looks like nobody cares, and the giant spider is a farcical puppet that wouldn't scare a toddler. If you shoot a film like this in Italy, at least you get to use ancient, ruined amphitheaters and aqueducts as backgrounds, which is cool, but in that case, why bother with all the shabby mystic caves? Pfah.

Cute bear cub, though.

ATOR 2: THE BLADE MASTER (OR CAVE DWELLERS)

Rating: ★☆☆☆☆ • *Origin:* Italy, 1984 • *Director:* Joe D'Amato • *Source:* Quadrifoglio DVD

This is a legendarily bad fantasy adventure. Now, plenty of low-budget fantasy adventures are bad, but they're usually bad in predictable ways. *The Blade Master*'s badness is largely unpredictable and unexpected, a whole film of WTF moments.

That's not to say it isn't also bad in the ways one would expect: a script that's dead on arrival, terrible lip-synching, third-rate acting, and somnambulistic combat—I mean, the blade choreography isn't bad, but it looks like they didn't practice very much, so they go through the moves slowly to make sure nobody gets hurt. Safety first, I guess.

"Knowledge is nothing against fate. My discovery is everything . . . and nothing."

The movie starts with a long scene in a cave full of brutal Neolithic folk, cave people who have virtually nothing to do with anything except that *Quest for Fire* (1981) had been popular recently. Grunt! Switcheroo, and suddenly we're in a Renaissance castle where, in a cavern laboratory (every interior in this film is staged in a cave) the wise sage Akronos (Charles Borromel) is showing his nubile and weirdly fur-clad daughter Mila (Lisa Foster) his latest discovery, a glowing box he calls the Geometric Nucleus, literally the worst MacGuffin name ever. It mustn't fall into the hands of the evil Zor (David Brandon), who is approaching with his mounted and weirdly fur-clad warriors. Akronos sends Mila to find their only possible savior, the mighty Ator (Miles O'Keeffe). This enrages Zor, who wears a helmet that looks like a big black bird is nesting on his head, and he sends three goons after her.

"The dividing line between goodness and stupidity is very, very fine."

So Mila sets out to find Ator . . . on foot. Apparently, her dad the wise sage has been too busy to teach her about horses. The goons, out of a sense of fair play, I guess, also forgo their horses and run after her. In a scuffle, they shoot her with a crossbow, but though wounded she staggers gamely on. Meanwhile Ator, in a cave, of course, is practicing his swordplay with his Asian sidekick, whose name is, er, *Thong* (Chen Wong). Mila stumbles in, bleeding from the bolt in her shoulder, and Ator and Thong put her on a surgical table,

Ator 2 AUTHOR'S COLLECTION

because Ator is not just a muscle-bound, shirtless swordsman in a fur Speedo but also a learned scholar! Thong puts big green leaves on Mila's face while Ator pulls out the bolt. Soon she's all better—but Ator decides Mila must "prove herself" before he'll believe her story, so he locks her in a convenient iron-barred cell. Mila shows her stuff by grinding some rocks together and combining their dust to make black powder, and then blowing the door off her cell. Didn't see that coming, did you?

The three of them head back to rescue Akronos . . . on foot. The journey that formerly took Mila about 20 minutes now takes several days, as Ator gets ambushed a whole bunch and goes on frequent side quests. The ambushes include costume-party samurai, a mystic cave full of invisible assailants (always the easiest enemies to costume), and cannibal cavemen, while the side quests include returning to Ator's birth village, where he fails to prevent a clumsy massacre, and then gets captured by serpent cultists. In yet another cave, Mila gets thrown into a snake pit, and to save her Ator must fight a giant rubber snake puppet so flaccid he has to wrap it around himself to make it look dangerous.

"It would be less repugnant to be strangled by a thousand serpents than to have to endure your smile."

They finally get back to Akronos's castle, where Ator splits the party again (he does that a lot), telling Mila and Thong to sneak in the back way while he attacks from the front. He vanishes into the underbrush and then reappears over the hilltop—on a *hang glider* that he apparently built from sticks, his shoelaces, and a bolt of fabric he had in his quiver. (Didn't see that coming, did you?) He spends about five minutes on a scenic glide over an *entirely different* castle, dropping black powder bombs on Zor's goons, and then drops down for the climactic battle.

"My life is too dangerous to share."

Victorious, mighty Ator rides off to oppose evil wherever he finds it. And, hey, he found a horse after all!

ATOR 3: THE IRON WARRIOR

Rating: ★★☆☆☆ • *Origin:* UK/Italy, 1987 • *Director:* Alfonso Brescia (Al Bradley) •
Source: YouTube streaming video

Other than starring Miles O'Keeffe, this action fantasy has almost nothing to do with its two predecessors: Ator is given an entirely new origin, and stylistically this film is completely different from the previous barbarian adventures. In fact, it's more like an artsy Italian horror film than a heroic fantasy, a hallucinogenic series of weird nightmare scenes loosely connected by dream logic, in which many strange events occur with little or no explanation.

In other words, this thang don't make a lick o' sense. In the opening scene, twin boys play ball amid crumbling ruins until one of them is abducted by a cackling hag. The hag, Phoedra (Elisabeth Kaza, in an unhinged performance), is then judged by her fellow witches in a tediously talky trial and sentenced by Good Witch Deeva (Iris Peynado) to 18 years on a desert island. When her time is served, Phoedra is collected by metal-skull-masked Trogar (Franco Daddi), "part man, part machine," and then goes to attend the 18th name day celebration of the kingdom's Princess Janna (Savina Gersak), who for some reason has one scarlet eyebrow. After cackling out assorted curses and threats, Phoedra summons Trogar, who kills the king and abducts the princess. But meanwhile Good Witch Deeva has summoned Ator, who mounts a white steed and rides to the princess's aid.

A bunch of stuff happens, much of it illusory, inexplicable, and filmed with cheap yet pretentious camera tricks. Ator repeatedly fights Trogar, who apparently can't be killed and is, of course, Ator's abducted twin brother from the first scene, a fact that's eventually just put out there rather than revealed for effect. Phoedra has an apparently unlimited number of burly goons armed with broadswords and wearing Evil Armor™, and they chase Ator and Janna around every scenic site on the Mediterranean islands of Malta and Gozo. Ator fights lots of sluggish and unexciting duels with the goons, sometimes moving in slo-mo, so you know he must actually be moving really, really fast. Janna leads Ator to a town where she expects to be able to raise some loyal troops to take back her throne, and—*omigod, my head's spinning*—because it's the set of the town of Sweethaven, from Robert Altman's *Popeye* (1980) with Robin Williams! Except instead of a population of E. C. Segar's cartoon characters, Sweethaven's only inhabitants are corpses, because Phoedra's goons got there first. But what the hell?

Though this film is tonally at utter variance with the first two Ator films, there's one thing you can depend on being the same: O'Keeffe can't act worth a damn and doesn't even try. Fortunately, he doesn't have much to say here. "What if they kill you?" Janna asks. "Then I'll be dead," Ator replies. (A real philosopher, that Ator.) The longer this film goes on, the closer it comes to achieving its apparent goal of resembling a never-ending nightmare. But hey, at least, when it finally does finish, the ending is pointlessly ambiguous. Thanks for that!

AT SWORD'S POINT (OR *THE SONS OF THE THREE MUSKETEERS*)

Rating: ★★★★☆ • *Origin:* USA, 1952 • *Director:* Lewis Allen • *Source:* Warner Bros. DVD

This sequel to *The Three Musketeers* was made by RKO a couple of years earlier than but not released until 1952, possibly to get it out of the long shadow of the 1948 MGM version. There have been dozens of screen versions of *The Three Musketeers*, but Hollywood has never quite figured out how to adapt Dumas's sequel, *Twenty Years After*, into a successful film. This story uses some of the elements of that novel, in particular, France on the verge of civil war after the deaths of Louis XIII and Richelieu, as the aging Queen Anne tries to preserve order until Louis XIV can come of age. Meanwhile the fractious nobles, personified here by the scheming Duke de Lavalle (Robert Douglas) vie to seize power. The novel calls on the older versions of the four musketeers to step in and sort things out, but this tale calls on their grown-up children to rise to the occasion. Could this be Hollywood ageism at work? Well, it certainly isn't sexism, because one member of the younger generation is Athos's daughter Claire (Maureen O'Hara), and she's as good with a blade of any of the men—with the possible exception of the younger d'Artagnan, who's played by an Olympic fencer (Cornel Wilde).

Let's get right to the point: this is the first serious movie representation of a female swashbuckler who is the equal of the men—and accepted by them as such! There's still plenty of flirtation with Claire by the younger Aramis and d'Artagnan—I mean, these *are* musketeers—but it's not condescending, and she gives as good as she gets. The people who underestimate Claire are the villains, and they learn to be sorry they did. The best moment in the picture is when Lavalle, who has strong-armed the queen into letting him marry Princess Henriette, leads her to the altar, lifts her veil, and finds that Claire has taken his bride's place and that the princess is safely in the hands of the other musketeers. And Claire, faced with the wrath of the most powerful man in France, just laughs in his face!

The plot here is nothing to write home about, being the usual series of sword fights, kidnappings, escapes, pursuits, betrayals, traps, and rescues, but the writers were clearly admirers of Dumas, and there are a number of fun callouts to the novels—for example, minor characters named Planchet and Rochefort and, at one point, Claire, hoodwinking some guards, assumes the name Countess de La Fère—the family name of her father, Athos. Plus, the costumes are better than average, Wilde does some nicely acrobatic swashbuckling, and the familiar blue tabards of the king's musketeers come out of the wardrobe for the grand finale. All good stuff, but it's still Maureen O'Hara who walks away with the prize.

THE AVENGER

Rating: ★★★☆☆ • *Origin:* Italy/France/Yugoslavia, 1962 • *Director:* Giorgio Venturini • *Source:* YouTube streaming video

This sequel to *The Trojan Horse* (1961) is thoroughly adequate, though it's not as good as its predecessor; it's smaller in both budget and ambition. Steve Reeves stars once again as the hero Aeneas, and in fact this is adapted from Virgil's *Aeneid* (20 BCE); in Italy its title is *The Legend of Aeneas,* changed for American release because presumably nobody in the United States ever heard of that guy.

Aeneas and his tribe of refugee Trojans have fled west across the Mediterranean, and after many tribulations, they've fetched up in Italy at the forks of the Tiber. This is in the realm of King Latino (Mario Ferrari), who to stave off the encroaching Etruscans has allied with several petty monarchs: arrogant bully-boy King Turno (Gianni Garko), noble but naive King Pallante (Robert Bettoni), and fiercely independent Queen Camilla (Liana Orfei). In contrast with the *Aeneid*, the gods play no active role, so what we get is straight politics. King Turno, who hopes to grab Latino's throne by landing either Queen Camilla or Latino's daughter Lavinia (Carla Marlier), immediately sees the famous hero Aeneas as a threat and tries to run him and his Trojans out of town. However, wise old Latino grants Aeneas the Tiber marshland, at which Turno flips out and puts his usurpation plans into action, framing the Trojans for murder and moving to attack their stockade. Pallante sides with Aeneas, Camilla is on the fence, and then the Etruscans march in. And Aeneas finds himself once again reluctantly at war.

With no Troy in the background and considerably smaller armies maneuvering on the plains of Yugoslavia (standing in for central Italy), this film is less epic than *The Trojan Horse,* but Reeves is as stoically charismatic as ever and fights a couple of well-staged single combats. Pallante is pallid, but the fiery Turno and Camilla stand out from the otherwise wooden cast, and the stage direction of the talking-heads scenes is more dynamic than usual for an Italian sword-and-sandal flick. The plight of the Trojan refugees in their stockade, once again defending their walls against attackers, is affecting, plus there's a bonus European longhorn cattle stampede. The costumes are good, and the four-sided final battle is well handled. Summary: solid fare, though nothing special.

Caveat (that's Latin, see?): this film also exists in a slightly shortened English dub rendered into black-and-white for American television. Pass on that and find the color version if you can.

THE AVENGING EAGLE

Rating: ★★★★☆ • *Origin:* Hong Kong, 1978 • *Director:* Sun Chung • *Source:* Dragon Dynasty DVD

A wounded man on a lame horse rides blearily across dry, rocky terrain, losing blood until he tumbles from the horse in a faint. Eventually a second man comes riding along, spots the wounded man, dismounts, wakes him, and offers him a drink. The first man comes to in a wild terror, gulps down all the second man's water, refuses to give his name, and then steals his benefactor's horse and gallops off.

The first man has . . . issues. He is a bandit, Chik Sing (Ti Lung), a member of the notorious Iron Boat Clan—or, rather, an ex-member now pursued by the Twelve Eagles, the clan's enforcers. We learn this when the second man (Alexander Fu Sheng) catches up to Chik and starts asking questions, ironical but persistent. Like his former brothers, the other Eagles, Chik is an orphan who was raised in villainy by Yoh Xi Hung (Feng Ku), the wicked leader of the Iron Boat Clan, an older man but still mighty in his kung fu. When he sends his Eagles on a raid and Chik is wounded and left behind, the young man is helped to recovery by an altruistic family, and for the first time he learns about love and compassion. It changes him, and he begins to question the cruel methods of the master of the Eagles.

However, Chik has long lived the life of a thief and a killer and still has a lot to answer for. And he's going to have to answer for some of it to his mysterious and inquisitive benefactor.

This film is structured as an extended flashback in which Chik tells the story of his life and gradual change of heart, punctuated by colorful *wuxia* duels with exotic Chinese weapons whenever another squad of Eagles catch up to him. It's a simple story but it's effective, primarily because of the sympathetic star power of Ti Lung and the sardonic charisma of Alexander Fu Sheng as his nameless new friend. Suspicious and wary though they are, the two share a genuine, comradely chemistry that makes the film work.

A large percentage of the film's running time is spent in fast-paced wuxia beatdowns, and it's a tribute to director Sun Chung that these fights are sufficiently varied that they stay fresh all the way to the end. That end, of course, pits Chik and his finally named (but we won't spill it here) mysterious friend against Yoh Xi Hung himself, whose brass-clawed kung fu is matched only by his cunning and deceit. The shock ending, though it was foreshadowed well in advance, still comes as a punch to the gut. Recommended.

THE BANDIT OF SHERWOOD FOREST

Rating: ★★☆☆☆ • *Origin:* USA, 1946 • *Directors:* George Sherman and Henry Levin • *Source:* Columbia Pictures DVD

The aging Robin Hood, for 20 years now the Earl of Huntingdon, rides into Sherwood and blows a horn to summon his old comrades. Mounted bandits, scores of them, with bows come riding out of the woods, waving their weapons, all galloping and gathering—geez, there are more horse archers in Sherwood Forest than the Mongols had in the Golden Horde. Once assembled before Huntingdon, the earl reveals that he's called them all together . . . for exposition! The King of England is a child; a royal regent governs in his name and is convening a meeting of nobles, where the earl suspects the regent wants to *revoke the Magna Carta*! But don't worry, Merrie Men, Huntingdon has sent for his son Robert, so thanks for galloping, now go chill for a day or two.

POSTWAR IN THE GREENWOOD

In the middle of the last century, you couldn't say "Robin Hood" without evoking the image of Errol Flynn in 1938's classic *The Adventures of Robin Hood*—every movie and TV show in the next 30 years about the bandit of Sherwood Forest was made in its long, green shadow. The Robin Hood story depicted in the Flynn film became the de facto standard version of the legend, cinematic comfort food, with subsequent screen incarnations not straying far from its characters and situation. Still, there were good times to be had in that long, green shadow, and tales of Robin and his Merrie Men owned Saturday afternoons for the sleepy '50s and well afterward.

Huntingdon arrives at the meeting of nobles, and as soon as he sees that the regent is played by the sneering Henry Daniell, he knows the deal is going down. In short order, the Magna Carta is rescinded, tyranny is ascendant, the regent plots to usurp the throne, and the uncooperative Earl of Huntingdon is banished. And the next day Robin Hood is back in Sherwood, organizing the resistance.

This movie is pretty standard Robin Hood fare, of the kind quite common between V-E Day and 1960 or so. The twist this time is that the older and now silver-haired Robin (Russell Hicks) is relegated to the background, while his son Robert (Cornel Wilde) takes point handling the derring-do. Young Robert is virile and active but kind of an arrogant jerk at first, trouncing the older Merrie Men while sparring, snatching kisses from unwilling ladies, and being a general show-off. Really, Robert just needs a serious challenge, like saving the young king from his unscrupulous regent, and he'll straighten right out—especially if he listens to that smart lady he stole the kiss from (Anita Louise), because she's going to save his neck when he gets captured and thrown into the Nottingham Castle dungeon. Fortunately, Nottingham Castle has the worst postern gate security protocols *ever*.

This picture's not bad, but it has this weird and unexpected flaw: it keeps forgetting it isn't a Western. The extras all sound like cowboys; everybody has horses and gallops everywhere, riding Western style (there's *so much riding*), and it's clear that the cast and crew, who were making a Western just last week, are really looking forward to getting out of their green tights and making another Western next week. At least there's a final duel between Wilde and Daniell, with their giant shadows fencing across the castle wall behind them—because traditions, after all, must be upheld.

THE BANDITS OF CORSICA (OR THE RETURN OF THE CORSICAN BROTHERS)

Rating: ★★★☆☆ • *Origin:* USA, 1953 • *Director:* Ray Nazarro •
Source: Amazon streaming video

This overlooked film is often described as a remake of the 1941 *Corsican Brothers* or as based on Alexandre Dumas's short novel of that name, but it's actually a full-fledged sequel that stands on its own. Producer Richard Small had done well with low-budget sequels to his *Count of*

Monte Cristo, so he tried the same trick with his *Corsican Brothers*, and with some success. It's strictly to Small's by-then-familiar formula, drawing heavily on elements of its predecessor and from Small's similar *Son of Monte Cristo*. So it doesn't cover any new ground, but it's pretty enjoyable nonetheless, thanks mainly to the charm and intelligence of its star, Richard Greene—the same actor who would make such an indelible impression later in the decade starring in the title role of the *Adventures of Robin Hood* TV show. In some ways, this film can be regarded as an extended screen test for that part, as its engaging and clever hero, the fugitive noble Mario Franchi, leads a band of outlaws in a desperate fight against tyranny.

But this is another of those double-lead-role swashbucklers in which Greene plays not just Mario Franchi but also his separated-at-birth twin brother Lucien who, through his psychic connection to Mario, lives a tormented double life. Greene bases his tragic Lucien on Douglas Fairbanks Jr.'s haunted performance in the 1941 *Corsican Brothers* and carries it off admirably. Set five years after the earlier film, once again the Franchi brothers pit their doppelgänger hijinks against a ruthless aristocrat who wants to rule all of Corsica, in this case Raymond Burr in the role of evil Baron Jonatto. Burr may not have the wicked gusto of Akim Tamiroff, the villain of the first film, or the urbane arrogance of George Sanders in *Son of Monte Cristo*, whom he's clearly emulating, but he seems to be making an effort and is more lively than usual. Better is his brutal lieutenant, Nerva, played by a young but steely Lee van Cleef, who sneeringly steals the scenes from his stolid boss.

Count Mario has a comely but helpless countess (Paula Raymond), whose function is to be loved hopelessly by Lucien when she's not being held captive by Jonatto. The plot is the standard mix of midnight raids, impersonations, abductions and escapes, villainous ultimatums, vows of vengeance, and a guards-oppressing-the-people montage spiced with amnesia, Roma, a secret passage, and a dungeon torture chamber, all climaxing in a perfectly fine four-way sword fight. A well-worn tale, but solidly executed, and worth it for Greene and van Cleef.

BARBARIAN QUEEN

Rating: ★★☆☆☆ • *Origin:* Argentina/USA, 1985 • *Director:* Héctor Olivera •
Source: Shout! Factory DVD

This movie is a fraud: ostensibly it's about women warriors taking revenge on their abductors and rapists, but actually the women's rape and abuse are the true point of the picture. All these fierce women in buckskin bikinis and big 1980s hair are put into harm's way solely to be harmed for the titillation of the viewer. This sort of heavy-breathing misogyny has a long history in cheap exploitation horror movies, but it took a while in coming to fantasy films.

It would be tempting with a movie this reprehensible to simply dismiss it as utter crap, but though born of evil intentions, *Barbarian Queen* is nonetheless made with a certain craft and care—which only makes it all the more clear that the filmmakers knew exactly what they were doing. The sets and costumes make the best of the movie's low budget, and star Lana Clarkson is at least enthusiastic about her leading role, adding a level of energy lacking in the rest of the cast.

The setting is a generic barbarian fantasy world, and for that it's hard to find better scenery than rural Argentina, where this was shot. A village of blond and tanned farmers is preparing for a wedding between Amethea (Clarkson) and Argan (Frank Zagarino, zero charisma) when they are attacked by dark-haired raiders who burn, rape, and enslave. Amethea and two of her friends escape the raid and set out in pursuit of the raiders, determined to somehow liberate their abducted people. The trail leads to a generic fantasy city ruled by, as usual, an evil tyrant, in this case named Arrakur (Arman Chapman). (Yes, there are too many characters in this film whose names start with *A*.) There's a resistance group in town that's preparing to fight back but isn't yet ready to move, which frustrates the impatient Amethea, because her stolen tribesmen are being pitted against each other as gladiators while the women are added to Arrakur's harem or forced to service the gladiators.

One of Amethea's friends is arrested by Arrakur's guards, and when Amethea tries to rescue her she, too, is captured. Amethea is taken to a torture dungeon where she is stripped down to a skimpy thong, tied spread-eagled to a board, and tormented. This is not a mere aside in the plot: this is the centerpiece of the film, an extended scene in which Amethea is cruelly abused and then outright raped. The means by which she escapes from her rapist we won't describe here, but it's a sweaty-palmed lad's masturbation fantasy.

However, escape she does, and the film then proceeds to its final phase, in which Amethea leads the gladiators and resistance fighters in an uprising to overthrow Arrakur. It's the same scene that ends every sword-and-sandal movie, but here the combat is sadly inept, with the entire cast clearly looking forward to finishing up and collecting their paychecks. One can only hope that what they got made it worth what they had to go through.

THE BARBARIANS (OR BARBARIANS & CO.)

Rating: ★★★☆☆ • *Origin:* Italy/USA, 1987 • *Director:* Ruggero Deodato • *Source:* Quadrifoglio DVD

This Italian heroic fantasy appears on the face of it to be a terrible 1980s barbarian flick. Actually, it's a lively parody of terrible barbarian flicks while at the same time still being a terrible '80s barbarian flick. Got it? Good!

The eponymous barbarians are Kutchek and Gore, "the Barbarian Brothers," twins who are played by Peter Paul and David Paul, a pair of bellowing, musclebound lunkheads who don't even begin to try to act, which is just as well, as their entire repertoire consist of hooting and flexing and performing Mighty Feats of Strength. The film appears to have been inspired by the first three *Mad Max* movies, both visually and in its feverish, headlong exuberance, an energy entirely missing from the Roger Corman barbarian films. In fact, it opens with an extended action sequence in which the wagons of a band of traveling entertainers are pursued by mounted, leather-clad raiders, a scene that answers the burning question, "What if *Mad Max* was set in the world of *Conan the Barbarian*?" Now we know.

The entertainers are being chased by the goons of a mad warlord named Kadar (Richard Lynch) who is after the magic ruby held by the troupe's queen, Canary (Virginia Bryant). She manages to send the ruby off to be hidden before the troupe is captured by Kadar, who demands the gem, only to have his demanding fingers bitten off by a pair of fierce twin 12-year-old boys. Canary agrees to become Kadar's slave if he swears never to harm the boys, and he accepts—and then raises them as brutal pit fighters so they'll kill each other. That plan fails: the now-adult bros tear up the combat arena and escape, and then they find the remnants of the entertainer troupe, who tell them what they need to do to find the ruby and free Canary. Quest time!

The bros go with a thief named Ismene (Eva La Rue) to a tavern to buy weapons. But there are no weapons; it's really just an excuse to get the bros into a barbarian dive bar and the inevitable ensuing brawl. And you know what? The ridiculous brawl is both tightly directed and pretty darn funny. It's followed by a series of lampoons of barbarian flick clichés that are mostly spot on: sacking the Tomb of the Ancient King for magic weapons and armor, fighting random fang-toothed monsters that leap out of nowhere ("Who the hell were they?" "Hur hur, forgot to ask!"), eventually leading to a swamp haunted by blue klieg lights and fog machines where the bros must face a giant phallic dragon puppet. How they kill it, and what they find inside, is too good a joke to spoil.

After that climax, the film keeps going, mostly so it can parody the requisite Final Duel with the big, bad Kadar, but it's a mistake: we've already had our fun and don't really need one more high-five and "Hur!" But I guess you can't expect barbarian bros to know that the essence of comedy is brevity.

BARDELYS THE MAGNIFICENT

Rating: ★★★☆☆ • *Origin:* USA, 1926 • *Director:* King Vidor • *Source:* Flicker Alley DVD

This is an adaptation of an early novel by Rafael Sabatini, a book revived, like *The Sea Hawk*, in the wake of the worldwide success of Sabatini's *Scaramouche* (1921). Its star, matinee idol John Gilbert, was riding high at the time and was paired here with the hit-making director King Vidor, best known for *The Big Parade* and (much later) *Duel in the Sun*. The setting is France in 1632, midway through the reign of King Louis XIII, who is putting down the last major revolt of the rebellious Prince Gaston. Gilbert plays the Marquis de Bardelys, an elegant Paris playboy who excels at romantic conquest, his seductions fueling the gossip and petty scandals of the French Court. Bardelys is one of King Louis's spoiled favorites, and he rivals another favorite, the supercilious Comte de Chatellerault (in a delicious mustache-twirling performance by Roy D'Arcy). When Chatellerault tries and fails to win the hand of a provincial heiress, Bardelys mocks him and is then maneuvered into accepting a challenge to win her himself—much to the displeasure of the king, played with epicene preciosity by Arthur Lubin. Against the royal wishes, Bardelys sets off into rebellion-torn Languedoc to win the hand of Roxalanne de Lavedan, whom he's never even met.

Complications ensue, and after a couple of far-fetched coincidences, Bardelys ends up recovering from wounds in the Château de Lavedan, but under an assumed name, that of a slain rebel and traitor. Once he meets Roxalanne, Bardelys finds himself in true love for the first time, but he has to romance Mademoiselle de Lavedan under a false name while being hunted by royal troops. What follows is a tangle of honor and dishonor, spies, jealous rivals, secret vows, betrayals, and athletic escapes, and a fine climactic duel.

John Gilbert is genuinely charming and charismatic as Bardelys, and fortunately the smart and spirited Eleanor Boardman is cast opposite him as Roxalanne. They play well off each other, and their scenes together are the best in the film, especially the famous episode in which Gilbert woos her in a sun-dappled boat drifting through a long screen of trailing willow branches. Sadly, everyone else in the picture hams it up outrageously, which I guess we have to blame on King Vidor's direction. One caveat: this silent film was thought lost for decades, until a single copy was discovered in Paris in 2006. It's been magnificently restored except for several scenes in the middle of the film that had to be reconstructed from stills and the shooting script. That and the fact that almost everything in this movie is strictly to formula are all that keep it from being a four-star film. Lurid visual bonus: skull-faced priests with sinister, pointy-cowled monkshood minions!

THE BEASTMASTER

Rating: ★★★☆☆ • *Origin:* USA/West Germany, 1982 • *Director:* Don Coscarelli •
Source: Magic Sign DVD

This is a sword-and-sorcery film about a hero who has a telepathic connection with a squad of loyal animal allies. Maax (Rip Torn), evil high priest of the god Ar of the desert city of Aruk, hears a prophecy that he will die at the hands of the unborn son of the city's King Zed (Rod Loomis). Maax tells Zed that Ar demands his unborn son as a sacrifice, so Zed banishes Maax—but the priest's witchy ally magically steals the fetus from its mother's womb by transferring it to that of a cow! The infant is cut from the cow by the witch and its hand is branded, but before it can be slain, a passing warrior kills the witch and takes the babe.

The warrior names the child Dar and raises it in his remote village as his own son, concealing the boy's origins but teaching him combat skills. When Dar (Marc Singer) reaches maturity, so does his telepathic connection with animals. Then the villagers are massacred by barbaric Jun warriors commanded by the exiled Maax, so Dar vows revenge and sets out to follow them, collecting along the way a gang of beasts that includes an eagle, a pair of clever ferrets, and a gigantic black panther. When he nears Aruk, Dar also collects a love interest in Kiri (Tanya Roberts), a condemned slave of the priests of Ar.

Reaching Aruk and its pyramid of sacrifice, Dar soon finds that even with his beasts, he's no match for the power of Maax, and though he saves a sacrificial child, the rightful King Zed is held prisoner. Dar is forced to retreat back into the desert where, fortunately, he finds more allies in Zed's loyal war leader Seth (John Amos) and Zed's young son Tal (Josh Milrad). He's going to need them, for in addition to Maax's sorcery, Dar must face undead Death Guards, fanatical priests, uncanny witches, and barbaric Jun warriors.

This film is based on a 1959 young-adult science fiction novel by Andre Norton, but she disagreed with adapter and director Don Coscarelli's changes to the story and asked to have her name removed from the credits. One can see her point, as despite the strong plot, the film's story has serious problems with structure and pacing. The movie shines during its action

The Beastmaster AUTHOR'S COLLECTION

scenes, but otherwise the storytelling is muddled and wanders all over the place. The beasts are more charismatic than the actors and frequently steal the show, though star Marc Singer is personable enough and Rip Torn makes a fine villain. The sorcery, mostly practical effects, is restrained and effective, and for a low-budget barbarian flick, the fight direction is solid. The film looks good, the American Southwest providing a vast and scenic setting that is matched by Lee Holdridge's grandly epic soundtrack.

The Beastmaster didn't do very well in its initial theatrical release, but it found new life in repeat on TV's cable channels (the joke was that HBO stood for "Hey! *Beastmaster*'s on!"), where it developed enough of a following to spawn two sequels and a TV show in the 1990s. Plus it makes everyone who watches it yearn for a pet ferret. See if you don't.

THE BELOVED ROGUE

Rating: ★★★☆☆ • *Origin:* USA, 1927 • *Director:* Alan Crosland • *Source:* Warner Bros. DVD

The Beloved Rogue is a strange one: it's ostensibly based on events from the life of the first great poet of the French language, François Villon (1431–1463), a man whose life we know next to nothing about, and what little we do know doesn't exactly support this movie's story. About the only thing they got right is that the great poet was also a petty criminal, a thief and ruffian who frequently ran afoul of the law. But this silent film is no biopic; it's more a romantic fable of the Middle Ages, so maybe the facts don't matter.

We know we're in fable territory from the very first scenes set in a medieval Paris deep in the grip of winter, the city's crazy gambrel roofs covered in snow and dripping with icicles. (The exaggerated sets are by William Cameron Menzies, who also did *The Thief of Bagdad*.) Villon, who enters the film in mid-robbery, stealing a jug of frozen wine, is played by John Barrymore, who gives his daring rogue a devil-may-care attitude lacking in Douglas Fairbanks's earnest heroes. Barrymore switches back and forth from heartthrob to buffoon without hesitation, always three sheets to the wind, and as King of Revels on All Fools' Day, he clowns like he just don't care. Villon, already famous for his poetry, darling of both the beggars and the nobility, gets caught up in a political struggle between King Louis XI and the Duke of Burgundy, who wants Louis's throne. The poet writes scathing satirical doggerel skewering both king and duke, romances the king's adorable ward, dodges death and exile, and engages in assorted drunken shenanigans involving a catapult, a performing bear, a capering dwarf, Burgundian crossbow-

men, and an army of beggars from the Court of Miracles. Barrymore's Villon is a blond Byron who does all his fighting with his words and his wits, winning the day through sheer cleverness.

But the impish Villon doesn't own this picture; he has to share it with King Louis XI, the master conniver of his day, played here by the great German actor Conrad Veidt (in his first Hollywood role) as a saturnine vulture, alternating between cruel gloating and cowardly cringing. It's a bravura performance that even overshadows Barrymore's in

The Beloved Rogue WIKIMEDIA COMMONS

the scenes they share. There's also some fairly daring direction for the day from Alan Cros-land, who shoots at unusual angles, splits an image tenfold through a mullioned window, and employs long takes dwelling on Barrymore's features as he has an inspiring idea or comes to a horrified realization, his every thought written clearly on his face. Fine stuff.

THE BLACK ARROW

Rating: ★★★★☆ • *Origin:* USA, 1948 • *Director:* Gordon Douglas •
Source: Columbia Pictures DVD

Say, this is good. Based, somewhat loosely, on Robert Louis Stevenson's 1888 novel, it compresses and abridges but gets the essence right. This is another of independent producer Edward Small's swashbucklers starring Louis Hayward, a story of the War of the Roses in which Hayward plays one of the victorious Yorkists, Sir Richard Shelton, returning home after the defeat of the Lancastrians. He pauses to drink at a stream, and a black arrow thuds into a tree next to him—an arrow wrapped with a note in rhyme from a mysterious "John Amend-All," warning him of treachery ahead. And in fact, Shelton arrives at his home estate to find that his father has been murdered, a crime blamed on a neighboring Lancastrian noble who has already been executed but is survived by a spirited daughter, Joanna Sedley (Janet Blair). More black arrows arrive with rhymed warnings, and gradually Sir Richard realizes that there was something fishy about his father's murder. Interestingly, we know whodunit from the start: Richard's grasping Uncle Daniel (George Macready), whom we see meeting with his three accomplices plotting to pull the wool over Richard's eyes. Following the clues of the black arrows leads Richard to a gang of outlaws in nearby Tunstall Forest, a band deliberately evocative in Stevenson's novel of Robin Hood's men, and the similarities are emphasized even more in the film. The rest of the story is about how Richard, with the help of Joanna and John Amend-All, learns the truth—and what he does about it.

If the sets look familiar, it's because we've seen them before in *Bandit of Sherwood Forest* and *Prince of Thieves* and will see more of them in *The Swordsman* and others to come. Hayward's Sir Richard is one of his best performances, and Macready does good work as the villainous uncle, but Janet Blair as the heroine deserves special notice. Blair, a big-band vocalist who had a second career acting in the movies, is sharp and spicy, and her byplay with Hayward is delightful. Kudos also to Lowell Gilmore, suave and malicious, as the slightly hunchbacked Duke of Gloucester—yes, the eventual Richard III. And though the film's budget is modest, veteran director George Douglas keeps the action spare and tight. Douglas made several swashbucklers, and we're always glad to see his name in the credits; you may know him best as the director of the sci-fi classic *Them!* (1954).

BLACKBEARD, THE PIRATE

Rating: ★★☆☆☆ • *Origin:* USA, 1952 • *Director:* Raoul Walsh •
Source: Amazon streaming video

On November 22, 1718, Edward Teach, the notorious pirate known as Blackbeard, was killed on his ship the *Adventure* during a fierce boarding action led by Royal Navy Lt. Robert Maynard. By the time he was brought down, Blackbeard had been shot five times and suffered 20 wounds from edged weapons. For the most famous image depicting this event, look no further than the painting by Jean Leon Gerome Ferris on the cover of my *Big Book of Swashbuckling Adventure* anthology.

Blackbeard, The Pirate WIKIMEDIA COMMONS

Blackbeard's career and death are also depicted in this film, in which Lieutenant Maynard, ordered to Port Royale in pursuit of Henry Morgan and the loot from the sack of Panama . . . wait, what? Whoa, this film's story is set in the 1670s, before Ned Teach and Rob Maynard were even born. God blind me, this entire moving picture is naught but a tissue of lies! Avast! Bloody pirates—they'll steal half a century right out from under you if you so much as look the wrong way.

History failure notwithstanding, this was one of the most popular pirate movies of the 1950s, thanks mainly to Robert Newton's unhinged and completely over-the-top performance as Blackbeard. Newton took all the mannerisms and speech patterns he'd developed for the role of Long John Silver in *Treasure Island* and cranked them up to 11, frequently veering into farce and self-parody, but was no less entertaining because of that. (So many *Ahr*s!) Unfortunately, the rest of the film doesn't hold up so well. The plot is sadly muddled, starting out with Maynard undercover chasing Morgan (Torin Thatcher) but then captured by Blackbeard, along with Edwina, a pirate-captain's daughter who's secretly stolen Morgan's treasure, all four of them blundering about loudly at cross-purposes, and it never really gets sorted out. Characters' motives change suddenly from scene to scene, people stranded on islands show up back in port without explanation, and even the big ship-to-ship showdown between Blackbeard and Morgan ends in an unsatisfying draw. It's a mess.

One could overlook the ham-handed story if the performances supporting Newton were entertaining, but the rest of the cast is just bland and forgettable. Worst is Keith Andes, who plays Maynard, the English naval lieutenant and ostensible protagonist, exactly as if he were a tough-talking New York district attorney going up against the mob—imagine a slim Peter Graves but with no sense of humor. We're supposed to root for this guy against Blackbeard and the other pirates, but it's flat-out impossible. His intermittent romance with Edwina (Linda Darnell) is likewise arid and unconvincing, no matter how hard Darnell tries to look adoringly at him. Yeah, no.

At least there's a lot of action, solidly directed by Raoul Walsh; the cutlass duels in particular are quite good. The shipboard scenes are also decent, with the quarters below decks properly close and cramped, including visits to the lazaret and the orlop (or, as Newton calls it, the *ahr*-lop). And Blackbeard's crew are as filthy and repulsive a set of brutes as you're likely to see in the otherwise over-tidy '50s, so bonus points for that. But you won't be able to swallow the story unless you swallow a stiff rum or three first.

THE BLACK KNIGHT

Rating: ★☆☆☆☆ • *Origin:* UK/USA, 1954 • *Director:* Tay Garnett •
Source: Amazon streaming video

Where to start with this one? *The Black Knight* is a very silly movie. Its hugely popular star, Alan Ladd, has in only three years since his career-defining Western *Shane* become a self-caricature, playing the same part in every picture: a bluff, laconic good guy whose solution to every problem is a sock on the jaw. For tax purposes he stayed out of the United States for 19 months in the period between 1952 and 1954 and made four films overseas, including this medieval Arthurian travesty. A bluff, laconic smith known only as John (Ladd) forges arms and armor in the Earl of Yeonil's smithy. John and the earl's daughter Linet (Patricia Medina) are in love, but John, a commoner, knows it's hopeless. A bluff, laconic visiting knight from nearby Camelot tells John not to despair and reveals that he, too, was once a commoner. "You made your own sword," he tells John. "Now let your sword make you." This is the only good line in the picture.

Cue the Viking raid! Obviously phony Norsemen in crazy, horned helms burst into the castle, pillaging and killing. One of them strikes down the earl; then he and his leader set fire to the place and ride away. John pursues and sees the raiders doff their Viking gear, revealing themselves to be secret Saracens! They ride to Camelot, and John chases their leader right into King Arthur's throne room, where he socks him in the jaw. Arthur doesn't like this, because the Saracen is Sir Palamides (Peter Cushing!), one of his Knights of the Round Table. (No round table appears in this film.) Bound by immutable law, Arthur sentences John to death but is then reminded that it's a holiday, so by immutable law, Arthur must grant John a boon. John asks for time to prove Palamides is a traitor, and Arthur grants him three months.

John does what anyone would do in this situation: he adopts a secret identity! He becomes the Black Knight, wearing a suit of armor he made himself, and this ploy enables him to . . . well, it's not really clear how it helps, but stuff happens, the bad guys do more bad things, and John fights a lot, except when he's galloping off to another fight. There are at least 25 minutes of fighting in this 85-minute movie, and not a second of it bears any resemblance to actual medieval combat. The knights' armor is all hilariously awkward and wrong, as if the costumers had never seen a real suit of armor and just copied images from bad comic books—couldn't someone from Pinewood have popped down to the British Museum for an hour? The knights' helms all have tall, lurid totems on top and weird protruding visors, but in the Black Knight's case, this has the advantage of covering his face, which means all that fighting can be done by Ladd's stunt double. Now and then the Black Knight pauses in mid-combat, steps back, and they cut to Ladd in rear-screen projection, flipping up his visor for a moment so you can see it's really him. Smile, Alan!

Meanwhile, there's treachery in Camelot: Palamides is in league with Arthur's putative ally, King Mark of Cornwell (Patrick Troughton—yes, the Second Doctor Who), but Mark is a crypto-pagan who secretly wants to wipe out Arthur and his new Christians, because pagans are just like that. The pagans capture Lady Linet and plan to sacrifice her at Stonehenge, which is complete and unruined, albeit cardboard, but John spoils their fun and then Arthur orders his knights to throw lassos around the great stones and pull them down. And That's How Stonehenge Got Ruined. But the naughty pagans and Saracens just won't give up, even after their Viking imposture is exposed, so John has to sneak into Mark's castle to steal their secret plans to attack Camelot. He has to do this twice, because the first time he leaves without taking the plans—I am not even making this up. Stay to the end to see the newly dubbed Sir John marry Lady Linet in a dress made of iridescent cellophane feathers. I think Thomas Malory would dig it.

THE BLACK PIRATE

Rating: ★★★★★ • *Origin:* USA, 1926 • *Director:* Albert Parker • *Source:* Kino Video DVD

The Black Pirate was a risky experiment with a new technology that went by the name of "Technicolor"—a risk that, in the main, paid off. It was also the first big-budget Caribbean pirate movie, and Douglas Fairbanks went all-in on an original story that drew heavily on Howard Pyle's tales, drawings, and paintings, and on Stevenson's *Treasure Island*—the best possible sources, really.

The silent film opens with a pirate crew plundering a captured merchantman and immediately establishes that these sea rovers are bad, bad people, as atrocities are committed in the name of plunder and sheer bloody cruelty. The pillaged ship is sunk by having its powder magazine exploded, after which Fairbanks, the sole survivor, makes it ashore to a desert island, where he vows to live for revenge.

This is the film that established the visual look of all Hollywood pirate films to follow—right up to the current day, really. Waistcoats and sashes, peg legs and parrots, eye patches and cutlasses, tattoos, piercings, and questionable facial hair—it's all here. And then there are the familiar tropes: treasure buried in hidden caves, the crew dividing the spoils on the quarterdeck, drunken roistering, walking the plank—look no further for their cinematic origins.

The Black Pirate Albert Parker / Wikimedia Commons

DOUGLAS FAIRBANKS SR.

In the silent era, after Charlie Chaplin, Douglas Fairbanks (1883–1939) was the biggest male star in Hollywood. And the actress who became his wife, Mary Pickford—"America's Sweetheart"—was the biggest female star. From 1915 to 1920 Fairbanks made 28 films, nearly all romantic comedies, mainly for groundbreaking director D. W. Griffith. Handsome, charming, and expressive, Fairbanks was an ideal lead for light romances, but he was also a dynamic physical actor, strong and athletic, a side that wasn't getting any play in the rom-coms. He decided to reinvent himself as a popular action hero, a risky move, but with *The Mark of Zorro* (1920) he pulled it off, simultaneously inventing the modern cinematic swashbuckler. For the next 10 years he could do no wrong, making one historical adventure after another; after Zorro he played d'Artagnan, Robin Hood, the Black Pirate, the Thief of Bagdad, his own son in *Don Q, Son of Zorro* (1925), and finally d'Artagnan again in *The Iron Mask* (1929). Along the way, to avoid being controlled by the big studios, Fairbanks, Griffith, Chaplin, and Pickford founded United Artists, the first creator-owned media powerhouse. Fairbanks's career cratered in the 1930s, when the talkies came in and suddenly his style of acting was out of style. But he'd made an indelible contribution to the look and feel of Hollywood action films, and his acrobatic approach to swashbuckling still sets the standard for sword-swinging heroes 100 years later.

As the buccaneers are conveniently burying their treasure on the island where he was marooned, Fairbanks, posing as a cutthroat, boldly makes a bid to join the band. He beats their best fighter in a fencing match—nice sword fighting, with some fine rapier-and-dagger work—and joins the crew. Challenged by a Basil Rathbone–cognate to show he understands that there's more to piracy than swordplay, Fairbanks takes a merchant ship by stratagem to prove he has brains as well as brawn.

The stunts in this film are amazing, as Fairbanks personally swings through the rigging like Spider-Man. This is the movie where the riding-your-dagger-as-it-slices-its-way-down-the-sail gag was invented. It's such a great stunt, he does it three times.

Clad all in black silks and leather, Fairbanks takes the name "Black Pirate" and sets out to become the pirates' leader—and then immediately betray them. There's a captive princess to rescue in the bargain, a woman with whom he's fallen in love at first sight. But his plans are foiled by a clever rival, and a series of sudden reversals, clever ruses, daring escapes, and unexpected twists follow. Most unexpected of all, for me at least, is when Fairbanks, having escaped from the pirates, returns to rescue the princess in command of a long, slim galley rowed by three dozen bodybuilders clad in little more than shiny leather straps. And then, frankly, things get really weird. But the weird ending notwithstanding, this is a fabulous picture, grand and exciting, and not to be missed.

THE BLACK ROSE

Rating: ★★☆☆☆ • *Origin:* USA, 1950 • *Director:* Henry Hathaway •
Source: Fox Cinema Classics DVD

This movie works well as a showy spectacle depicting thirteenth-century England and parts of Mongolia and China. However, as an adventure or a character-driven story, it's not so good. This is one of those films in which the angry and stubborn protagonist is told at the beginning what he needs to do to find peace and purpose, spends the next two hours determinedly rejecting that advice, and then finally embraces it in the last 10 minutes of the picture. Weak! Walter of Gurnie (Tyrone Power), an illegitimate son of a Saxon lord, is our angry protagonist, who's suffered injustice at the hands of his Norman relatives. Edward II (Michael Rennie)—the King of England, no less—tells Walter he needs to put aside his hatred of Normans for his own good and that of the realm and its people, but Walter angrily insists on leaving England to seek his fortune in distant lands—even in far Cathay, if he must, which he's heard about from his Oxford mentor, Roger Bacon.

Cut to central Asia, to which Walter has fast-traveled with his loyal sidekick, English longbowman Tristram Griffin (Jack Hawkins in an early role, his cragginess softened by youth). They join a Mongol caravan headed further east to the court of Kublai Khan, bearing tribute of gifts and women to the great conqueror. One of these women is Maryam, a half-English daughter of a captured Crusader, known as the "Black Rose" for her rare beauty. Maryam escapes the harem, joins the Englishmen disguised as a serving boy, and immediately falls in love with Walter, but he thinks having a girl along is a dangerous nuisance and irritably refuses her affections. (Do you see the pattern?) Maryam is played with conviction by the French actress Cécile Aubry, who though she was 21 at the time of filming really looks like she's about 14 (ew!), which makes Walter delaying his inevitable fall for her something of a relief.

The commander of the caravan as it grows into an army is a genuine historical figure, a Mongol general called Bayam of the Hundred Eyes, played by Orson Welles as an engaging rogue. Since Welles was himself an engaging rogue, this isn't much of a stretch, and though he's a pleasure to watch here, one can see that he isn't really working very hard. Bayam acts as a counterweight to good King Edward, giving Walter diametrically opposed advice, which actually starts him at last on the road to realizing what a sap he's been. Along the way there's a deadly archery contest, several offstage battles, a torture gauntlet, and Walter's discovery of the Eastern secrets of gunpowder and the magnetic compass. When the gang finally reaches Cathay, there's a long half hour of clichéd orientalism before a muddled ending that returns Walter, with Maryam, to England. Alas, we already know how it's going to end, because every single event in the plot has been thoroughly telegraphed. Ah, well, at least it looks good: the movie was shot at scenic locations in England and Morocco (standing in for Asia), and the desert scenes include camel jokes that are almost funny.

THE BLACK SHIELD OF FALWORTH

Rating: ★★★☆☆ • *Origin:* USA, 1954 • *Director:* Rudolph Maté •
Source: Amazon streaming video

The Victorian children's novel *Men of Iron* (1891) by the American author and artist Howard Pyle had a big influence on the "knights in shining armor" medieval adventure tales that were popular right up through the 1950s. Pyle's story was a simple morality play in which Myles, a young Englishman whose father was betrayed by an ambitious noble, trains as a squire and then as a knight and finally avenges his father's betrayal. Pyle's vivid depiction of would-be knights training with sword, shield, armor, and lance was recycled countless times in tales of medieval chivalry over the following three-quarters of a century. *Men of Iron* also established in popular fiction the convention of trial by combat ("And may God defend the right!"), the favorite climactic plot device of the lazy knight-pulp writer.

All of these tropes are on display in classic fashion in *Falworth*, Universal's adaptation of *Men of Iron*. Concocted as a starring vehicle for Tony Curtis, here in his first big-budget epic, Pyle's simple tale is simplified even further for the screen, while its romance aspect is fleshed out to provide additional screen time for the radiant Janet Leigh, Curtis's then-wife, in the role of the female romantic lead, Lady Anne. Curtis's nimble athleticism serves him well in the part of the hot-headed and energetic Myles, though when reading his lines, his delivery is still rather awkward. It doesn't help that a lot of the dialogue is in the hifalutin elevated diction that had been considered appropriate for tales of medieval chivalry ever since Sir Walter Scott—stuff like "Have you not had your fill of buffoonery?"—but thankfully it's toned down considerably from the stilted language in Pyle's novel.

The guy who gets the best lines is Torin Thatcher—you know him as the sorcerer in *The 7th Voyage of Sinbad*—appearing here as Sir James, the surly one-eyed master-of-arms-cum-drill sergeant who trains Myles in the knightly martial arts. Thatcher's is easily the film's most enjoyable performance, clichéd though it may be, and when he threatens to hurl Myles from the battlements if he gets into just one more brawl, you believe him.

Falworth was Universal's first Cinemascope extravaganza, and no expense was spared on the colorful costumes and expansive sets, with absurdly spacious castle interiors and grand courtyards where platoons of men-at-arms ply their medieval weaponry. The romance story is familiar, and the villains' plots are all too predictable, but the fight scenes are tight and well choreographed. The film is a pleasure to look at and doesn't pretend to be anything but a simple tale of pluck and virtue triumphant over mean-spirited wickedness. (Oh, and persistent movie myth notwithstanding, Curtis never says, "Yonda stands the castle of my fadda"—for that, see *Son of Ali Baba*.)

THE BLACK SWAN

Rating: ★★★★★ (Essential) • *Origin:* USA, 1942 • *Director:* Henry King •
Source: Fox Studio Classics DVD

Trust me, mates, this is one of the finest pirate movies ever made. It's not as iconic or influential as *Captain Blood* or *Treasure Island*, but it's every bit as good and deserves to be better known. Like *Blood*, it's a reasonably close adaptation of a Rafael Sabatini novel, with crackling dialogue by Seton Miller (*Adventures of Robin Hood, The Sea Hawk*) and the great Ben Hecht (*The Front Page, Gunga Din*). It's one of director Henry King's many collaborations with star Tyrone Power and the first of their series of swashbucklers. King understood that the audience wanted a vivid, fast-moving tale, and that Power was looking for roles with both strength and nuance to them. And in this Technicolor epic, the team delivered all of that.

This movie pulls no punches: even before the main titles, a pirate ship takes down an English merchantman, and immediately after the opening, two buccaneer crews raid and sack a Spanish colonial port. And these are real pirates, not Robin Hood's Merrie Men: murder and pillage are rife, and rape is implied. Less than five minutes into the film, Captain Jamie Waring (Power) and Captain Leech (George Sanders, that magnificent bastard) are lolling on the beach, splitting the spoils, as Waring laments the capture of their leader, Captain Henry Morgan. Then Spanish reinforcements counterattack, and Waring is captured and put on the rack by an oily Spanish don who demands to know where Morgan really is. Boom! Pirates swarm the castle, Waring is freed, and in walks their commander, Captain Morgan himself.

So far, the movie's been good, even better than good, but when Laird Cregar enters in the role of Henry Morgan, it's elevated to remarkable. Because Cregar simply *is* Sir Henry Morgan, brought back from the dead after three centuries, larger and more alive in every way than every other person in Port Royal, Jamaica, and the entire Caribbean. His screen presence even outpowers Tyrone Power. Indeed, there's only one other star in the film with the megawattage to match him. . . .

Maureen O'Hara, of course, in the first of her many memorable swashbuckling roles, playing the fiery Lady Margaret Denby, daughter of the governor of Jamaica—that is, the former governor, since Morgan has replaced him. Pirate Jamie Waring and Lady Margaret fall into smoldering love/hate at first sight, and off we go!

The plot works well, with plenty of moving parts that satisfy: new governor Morgan trying to compel peace, renegade pirates plundering the Main, treacherous nobles selling out to the sea rovers—events keep moving without ever getting too complicated. The real fun in the middle part of the film comes from the interactions between the respectable citizens of Jamaica and Morgan's buccaneers—theoretically the swabs have been rehabilitated, but they just can't get the hang of polite society, because pirates gonna pirate.

Then treachery rears its head and we're roaring into act three, bedad! Rather than tip the final twists and turns of the brilliant finale, I'll just point out a few things about this movie that shouldn't be overlooked. First, there's a fine and flavorful score by Alfred Newman that sets the mood perfectly. Second, we get the reliably rascally Anthony Quinn leering and wearing an eye patch as George Sanders's second in command. And last but by no means least, it's a thrill to report that the tavern where the pirates meet is called Ye Porker's Sterne, with an appropriately lurid pictorial sign hanging above its front door. Bedad, indeed!

THE BLACK TULIP

Rating: ★★★☆☆ • *Origin:* France/Italy/Spain, 1964 • *Director:* Christian-Jaque •
Source: Video Dimensions DVD

When French matinee idol Alain Delon saw how much fun Jean-Paul Belmondo had making *Cartouche* (1962), he decided he wanted to star in a swashbuckler, too, and the result is *The Black Tulip*. It takes its title, but nothing else, from a novel by Alexandre Dumas—though it has another Dumas connection, as we'll see.

In 1789, at the very beginning of the French Revolution, the aristocrats of a remote province are robbed and terrorized by a masked outlaw who calls himself the Black Tulip, a man of mystery who fences like a master and rides an intelligent wonder horse named Voltaire. Secretly the Tulip is a nobleman himself, the smug and supercilious Guillaume de Saint-Preux (Delon); unfortunately, when he barely escapes being caught by his nemesis Baron de La Mouche (Adolfo Marsillach), he gets scarred on one cheek. If Guillaume shows his face in public before the wound heals, he'll be revealed as the Tulip, so he summons his lookalike brother Julien (also Delon) to temporarily take his place. Twin heroes are a staple of the genre, of course, realized here through the miracle of split-screen photography. Julien, though diffident, prim, and priggish, is an ardent revolutionary, so he's thrilled to help his brother by making social appearances as Guillaume. In that guise, Julien learns of the approach of a regiment bent on putting down the rebels, so he warns Guillaume about it, assuming the Black Tulip will want to lead a counterattack—but is disillusioned to find that Guillaume cares nothing for his revolutionary ideals.

So Julien puts his diffidence aside and assumes the identity of the Black Tulip as well as that of Guillaume, allying with the revolutionary Plantin (Francis Blanche), who turns out to be a grandson of "the musketeer Porthos." Plantin has raised his daughter Caro (Virna Lisi) as a boy and taught her the family's "secret thrust," so she's able to train Julien to be as good a fencer as Guillaume—and naturally they fall in love in the process. Swashbuckling ensues.

This film maintains its tone of light adventure more successfully than *Cartouche*, never veering too far into the silly or the grim, and if it's maybe five minutes too long, we'll forgive it. We'll also forgive its so-so swordplay because, for a change, most of the fencing is with cavalry sabers instead of small swords or rapiers, which is refreshing. Plus, you know, it has a wonder horse named Voltaire. *Vive la Tulipe Noire!*

THE BLOOD BROTHERS

Rating: ★★★★☆ • *Origin:* Hong Kong, 1973 • *Director:* Chang Cheh •
Source: Dragon Dynasty DVD

With this film, director Chang Cheh's storytelling achieves a new maturity centered on solid character development and the evolving relationships between his four leads. *The Blood Brothers* trades some of the colorful theatrical sets of Cheh's earlier movies for the grand expansiveness of southern China.

The entire story is told in flashback: frantic shouts inform us that Officer Ma Hsin has been assassinated, but his killer has been captured and is quickly hauled in chains before an imperial judge. The assassin, Chang (David Chiang, the man with the world's most charming smirk), asks for paper and a brush so he can write out the story of why he did it.

Four years earlier: Chang and his partner Huang (Chen Kuan Ti) are martial artists who have been forced to stoop to highway robbery, though they're cheerful about it. A lone man on a horse approaches, and the pair decide to relieve him of both horse and whatever money he's carrying. But the horseman is Ma Hsin (Ti Lung), another martial artist who fights Chang and Huang to a standstill—until Huang's wife, Mi Lan (Li Ching), rides by and mockingly grabs up Ma Hsin's purse. Ma Hsin tracks the robbers to their lair, not because he wants his money back but because he thinks they're wasting themselves on a life of petty crime. Join me, Ma Hsin says, and together we'll take over a powerful nearby bandit gang and establish ourselves as a serious local force!

After considerable leaping, hacking, and whacking, the deed is done, and Chang and Huang congratulate themselves on finally arriving at the good life they'd dreamed of. But Ma Hsin has bigger dreams: he not only trains the bandits into a fierce fighting troop, at night he studies for the imperial exam, takes it and gets top marks, and then goes off to become a government officer. Ma Hsin prospers in his new role, becomes a minor general, and sends for his blood brothers and their trained troops to add to his forces.

Together, they succeed in defeating the powerful Long Hair Bandits, and Ma Hsin is made the governor of two provinces. Brother Huang starts spending time in gambling houses,

The Blood Brothers Author's Collection

while his wife, Mi Lan, starts spending time with Ma Hsin, though Brother Chang sees what's going on and doesn't like it. The dissolute Huang has become an embarrassment to the increasingly ambitious Ma Hsin; Chang tries to warn Huang about what's going on, but Huang refuses to believe it, and unfortunately it's too late—Ma Hsin has set Huang up to be murdered during a phony bandit raid. This, Chang cannot forgive, and he sets out to take Ma Hsin's own life in revenge for Huang's.

This story of loyalty, ambition, and betrayal is engaging and well paced from beginning to end with scarcely a lag. There's a lot of combat here, and it's about evenly split between armed and unarmed bouts. And it must be said, the unarmed fighting is quicker and more exciting than the clashes with weapons—you can almost see director Cheh deciding that he's done with *wuxia* and moving on to kung fu. Most of the rest of Hong Kong filmmaking went with him.

THE BOLD CABALLERO

Rating: ★☆☆☆☆ • *Origin:* USA, 1936 • *Director:* Wells Root • *Source:* Alpha Video DVD

This is the first Zorro film of the sound era, made by Republic Pictures, a minor studio best known for cranking out 12-part serials. In an astounding splurge, this film was shot in full color, a rare thing in the mid-1930s. The story was "from an idea by Johnston McCulley," Zorro's creator, and was written and directed by Wells Root, who the following year would script the Ronald Colman version of *The Prisoner of Zenda*.

As we're told before the movie begins, Zorro had been leading a Native American revolt against Spanish oppression but was captured; thus he starts the movie as a convict on his way to the scaffold for execution. (It's like the beginning of an *Elder Scrolls* videogame!) Spoiler: he escapes!

Alas, this film is a typical low-budget Republic production, color notwithstanding: it looks cheap, the direction is shoddy, and the acting is uniformly terrible. Much of it is played for laughs, but the jokes are weak. Zorro/Don Diego de Vega is played by a handsome non-entity with no discernible talent named Robert Livingston. No, I never heard of him either. There's an impostor Zorro, a weak murder mystery, a bullfight, a pallid romance, a lot of dusty galloping, and some truly feeble stunts in imitation of Doug Fairbanks. To be fair, B-list actress Heather Angel does a passable job as the love interest, and there are a couple of laughs from an Austrian "Commandante" character played by German comic actor Sig Rumann, better known for chasing the Marx Brothers around opera houses and racetracks. Everything else is just embarrassing.

THE BUCCANEER (1938)

Rating: ★★★☆☆ • *Origin:* USA, 1938 • *Director:* Cecil B. DeMille • *Source:* Olive DVD

This may be the only patriotic American pirate movie with a president in it, except for the remake from 20 years later. It's based on the 1930 novel *Lafitte the Pirate* by Lyle Saxon, which I haven't read, but if its plot has as little to do with history as this movie, Mr. Saxon has a lot to answer for. High concept: "Jean Lafitte helps ol' Andy Jackson beat the British at the Battle of New Orleans." This is not only a surefire, can't-miss basis for a Hollywood movie but it even actually happened—just nothing like the way it's depicted in *The Buccaneer.*

All right, so this is claptrap—but is it entertaining claptrap? In the main, it is, mostly because it knows it's claptrap and therefore doesn't take itself very seriously. This is a relief, frankly, after DeMille's pompous and overblown *Cleopatra* and *The Crusades;* it shows he still knows how to tell a story with a light hand. But this is also flag-waving, chest-thumping American history as told in the mid-twentieth century, and therefore more about America's idea of itself than what really occurred.

Jean Lafitte, the titular buccaneer, is played by Fredric March, one of the most respected leading men of the 1930s, acclaimed in roles both dramatic and romantic. His Captain Lafitte is a dark and curly-haired dandy who mocks the respectable in a suave French accent while secretly aspiring to gentility, more an unorthodox, free-trading entrepreneur than an unscrupulous cutthroat. The real Lafitte was the last of the Caribbean pirates, a double-dealing scoundrel with no principles to speak of—but that won't do for DeMille, who must have a heroic privateer who respects the American flag and will raid only foreign shipping. Claptrap, but it provides the film some early conflict between Lafitte and a captain who disobeys his orders and sinks an American vessel. This gives March a chance to conduct a boarding action, show off his piratical grit, and then turn around and display his decency by saving the life of a captive, a Dutch woman named Gretchen, played for laughs by Franciska Gaal. She's not the only funny-foreigner character in the film: for DeMille, the melting pot of New Orleans is an opportunity for a parade of cartoon ethnics and racial stereotypes. This is irksome, hard to forgive, and unfunny, with one exception: the ursine Akim Tamiroff and his mighty mustache in the role of Dominique Youx, a former Napoleonic cannoneer in the service of Lafitte (true story). Tamiroff becomes Gretchen's protector, and his blustering ebullience is one of the chief pleasures of this film.

Other pleasures include the re-creation of Lafitte's legendary pirate haven of Barataria, his battalion of buccaneers gliding through the bayous on their long, narrow flatboats, and the swaggering and smirking Anthony Quinn as Lafitte's shady lieutenant. (Quinn's presence seems to be statutorily required in every pirate movie of the time.) But best of all is the dawning realization that the so-serious Fredric March has a genuine talent for sly comedy.

Over an hour into the movie, the other major historical figure finally appears: Hugh Sothern as General Andrew Jackson, in a fun over-the-top portrayal of Old Hickory, outdone only by his aide, the even-more-cartoonish frontiersman Ezra Peavey (Walter Brennan, in an early triumph). Brennan even out-hams Akim Tamiroff. Anyway, the British are coming!

After a tense negotiation held at mutual gunpoint, Jackson and the outlawed Lafitte join forces—but not until Lafitte slays a British-paid traitor in a fine cutlass duel and frees his captive men from prison in the nick of time.

And then the Battle of New Orleans is on! In the big finale, DeMille reminds us that, if nothing else, that son of a bitch sure knew how to set up a shot. Lafitte and his men are given the critical center of the line of defense, whereas historically they held the extreme left flank, but what the hell, it's Hollywood. Flags wave, redcoats marching to skirling bagpipes are no match for Jackson's squirrel hunters and Napoleon's cannoneer, and America is saved from perfidious Albion. So it's a happy ending for everyone, right? Well, not so much, because pirates. No spoilers here: see it for yourself.

THE BUCCANEER (1958)

Rating: ★★☆☆☆ • *Origin:* USA, 1958 • *Director:* Anthony Quinn • *Source:* Olive Films DVD

This is Cecil B. DeMille's 1958 wide-screen, Technicolor remake of his 1938 film about pirate Jean Lafitte and the Battle of New Orleans. It stars Yul Brynner (as Lafitte) and Charlton Heston (as Andrew Jackson), both of them breakout stars for DeMille in *The Ten Commandments* two years before, and for that reason you might expect to like it even more than the earlier version. And for a fact, Brynner and Heston do not disappoint. Brynner's brooding screen presence is even more imposing than that of predecessor Fredric March, though he lacks the glimpses of touching vulnerability that March gave the character: Brynner is bulletproof. And Heston's towering charisma eclipses even Brynner's formidable magnetism. To take advantage of it, Jackson here gets triple the screen time he got in the '38 version, and it was a wise move.

It comes at a cost, however: the expansion of Jackson's role is at the expense of Lafitte's, meaning we get a lot less piratical scoundrelry and Gallic swagger and a lot more self-congratulatory American mythmaking. And unfortunately, the story's told with an old-school staginess that's even hokier than it was 20 years earlier. DeMille was ailing—this was his final picture—so his son-in-law, Anthony Quinn, is the nominal director, but this film has ol' Cecil's showy fingerprints on every frame. The entire production is bloated with self-importance, and the Technicolor is so damn bright it often looks cartoonish.

The script is substantially rewritten from the original, and the dialogue somehow got even more clichéd and wooden in the process, so stiff that it's more than most of the supporting cast can comfortably handle. Inger Stevens as Lafitte's love interest, the governor's daughter (historical interruption: Lafitte actually romanced the governor's *wife*), is a blond mannequin, and the aging Charles Boyer as Napoleonic cannoneer Dominique You can't compete with the energetic performance of his predecessor, Akim Tamiroff. E. G. Marshall and Lorne Greene are similarly wasted. The only actors who can mouth these awful lines with conviction are Brynner, Heston, and Claire Bloom in an early standout role as a hard-bitten pirate wench.

The piratical antics of the original are sadly diminished, because this time around the emphasis is on building up to the set piece of the Battle of New Orleans, expanded from 10 minutes in the '38 version to a full half hour here. This does not improve it: all the extra fussing about supply shortages and scouting the British lines just drains the urgency out of the fray, and by the time of the battle's inevitable end in windrows of fallen redcoats, we're glad it's over. At least this version retains Lafitte's post-battle humiliation, repudiation, and escape to the freedom of the high seas, an ending that comes across as a strange refutation of all the nationalistic breast-beating that precedes it. All in all, *The Buccaneer* is an interesting failure almost redeemed by the sheer star power of its two leads.

THE BUCCANEERS

Rating: ★★★★☆ • *Origin:* UK, 1956 • *Directors:* Ralph Smart et al. • *Source:* Network DVDs

The Buccaneers AUTHOR'S COLLECTION

After Hannah Weinstein's Sapphire Films had a hit in 1955 with *The Adventures of Robin Hood,* it added two more swashbuckling series the following year, and *The Buccaneers* was arguably the best of them. Its writers and directors came from the same talent pool Sapphire used for *Robin Hood,* and the stories had a similar progressive slant, as Captain Tempest and the reformed buccaneers of his ship the *Sultana* drew on their piratical pasts to fight tyranny and oppression through unorthodox means. The stories were set in the Caribbean in the early 1700s, based mainly around New Providence in the Bahamas, though for the last quarter of the 39 episodes, the *Sultana* weighed anchor to the coasts of the southern American colonies.

Main man Captain Dan Tempest is played by Robert Shaw in his first major starring role (though for the first two episodes Shaw was unavailable, so Alec Clunes fills in as former pirate Woodes Rogers). Tempest initially arrives in New Providence too late to accept the new king's pardon and is slapped in prison for piracy by acting governor Beamish (Peter Hammond), but when Blackbeard attacks the port, Beamish needs Tempest to lead the defense and lets him out, so long as Tempest agrees to reform. He does, and thereafter Captain Dan is New Providence's main protector against sea rovers and the Spanish, along with his regular Merrie Sailormen on the *Sultana.*

Most of the 25-minute episodes have engaging scripts and taut direction, though a few outright comedy entries fall flat compared to the thrillers. There's an interesting tension between the reformed pirates' duty to enforce the law on the sea lanes while resisting the urge to revert to pillage and slaughter, and Shaw's Captain Tempest, with his crooked smile, never quite loses his feral edge. Over the length of the season, all the piracy boxes are checked: buried treasure, sea shanties, decent cutlass fencing, threats of keelhauling, sailors shanghaied off the docks, a devious Spanish *marquesa,* even ghost pirates! The best episodes are those in which Tempest turns the tables on the authorities to rescue marginalized folk, like slaves, prisoners of debt, and women trying to make it on their own, serious matters that are faced honestly, not just dismissed with a wink. It's a shame this fine series wasn't renewed for a second season.

BUCCANEER'S GIRL

Rating: ★★☆☆☆ • *Origin:* USA, 1950 • *Director:* Frederick de Cordova •
Source: Universal DVD

It looks like the idea here was to make a film like the classic Greta Garbo–Jimmy Stewart Western *Destry Rides Again*—but with pirates! Not a bad idea, but if that's where Universal Pictures was aiming, it missed the mark by a wide margin. Around 1800, a singer and dancer from Boston named, er, Debbie (Yvonne De Carlo) stows away on a southbound ship that gets captured by pirates, but she's spunky and takes no guff from mere filibusters, so she winds up in New Orleans instead of marooned on a desert isle, as the suave Captain Baptiste (Philip Friend) originally threatened. Once everyone arrives in the Crescent City, it becomes clear that this is not just a pirate adventure but also a comedy, a musical, and a romance. Unfortunately, the jokes aren't funny, the songs are mediocre, and there's no chemistry between the romantic leads. Production values are good, the Technicolor is lovely, and there are a couple of naval actions portrayed by decent Hollywood ship models, but otherwise this is a write-off.

THE CAPTAIN (OR LE CAPITAN)

Rating: ★★★★☆ • *Origin:* France/Italy, 1960 • *Director:* André Hunebelle •
Source: Pathé DVD

This French film may be the best swashbuckler you've never seen. It's set in France a dozen years before the events of *The Three Musketeers*, when King Louis XIII is only 15 years old and still ruled by his mother, Marie de Médicis, and her lover, the Italian adventurer Concino Concini, whom Marie has elevated to the rank of prime minister. Concini's hired thugs are killing nobles who oppose him and looting their estates, and the movie opens with a melee in which Concini's assassins, led by their boss Rinaldo, are raiding a count's château. The count's friend, the Chevalier de Capestang (Jean Marais), gallops up and leaps into the fray, turning the tide, but not before Rinaldo knifes the count in the back. As the thugs retreat, Capestang is wounded by another thrown knife and is about to be slain by the last assassin when the killer is shot down by a mysterious lady (Elsa Martinelli) in a male cavalier outfit.

The mystery woman nurses Capestang back to health but then disappears. Was she just a vision of delirium? Once healed, Capestang agrees to represent the grievances of the local nobles and travel to Paris to appeal to Concini—and maybe even to the young king. Concini (Arnoldo Foà) tries to co-opt the capable Capestang, but he haughtily refuses, and Concini, in Italian, dubs him *il capitano* after the stock commedia dell'arte character of the strutting braggart. Capestang accepts the moniker as a badge of honor.

Fortunately, le Capitan is no buffoon—that part goes to the comic actor Bourvil in the role of Cogolin, Capestang's loyal jester-slash-valet. Cogolin has a comic horse and a comic dog and does all the funny bits, leaving the derring-do to Capestang. And unlike director Hunebelle's 1953 version of *The Three Musketeers*, this time the do is daring indeed. Marais is an athletic swashbuckler who compares well with Errol Flynn and Doug Fairbanks Sr., and moreover, he knows how to handle a blade; the swordplay in this film is impressive. Marais is said to have done all his own stunts, and while there are some long shots when Capestang is scaling a castle wall—where I'd wager they used an expert climber—there are plenty of close-ups where it's clearly Marais leaping from a window or dangling on the end of a rope.

And as in Hunebelle's *Three Musketeers*, the locations are nearly all authentic period sites, with scarcely a studio stage set to be seen.

Based on a now-forgotten 1907 novel by Michel Zevaco, the story gets the history mostly right but best of all nails the genre conventions. Capestang eventually finds his mysterious pistol-packing cavalier lady, and along the way we get carriage chases, a dwarf alchemist, a masked impostor, a dynamited drawbridge, and a torture dungeon under the Louvre. It's grand good fun. Spoiler: the young king is saved from his evil councilors. *Vive le roi!*

CAPTAIN BLOOD

Rating: ★★★★★ (Essential) • *Origin:* USA, 1935 • *Director:* Michael Curtiz •
Source: Warner Bros. DVD

Captain Blood AUTHOR'S COLLECTION

After the success of swashbucklers *Treasure Island* and *The Count of Monte Cristo*, Warners decided to go all-in on a remake of Rafael Sabatini's *Captain Blood*. (There'd been a silent version in 1924, now lost.) The stars they initially had in mind for the leads bowed out, and in the end the studio took a huge risk and cast two complete unknowns: Errol Flynn and Olivia de Havilland. Luckily, they were both excellent, ideal for the roles—and even better, they had great onscreen chemistry together, so good they were paired seven more times in the next 10 years. The director's chair went to studio veteran Michael Curtiz, who in 1938 would codirect another swashbuckling essential, *The Adventures of Robin Hood*, before his career pinnacle helming *Casablanca*. Add in Basil Rathbone as the villain, supported by a slate of the best character actors in Hollywood, plus a stirring soundtrack by Erich Wolfgang Korngold, and you have the makings of a true classic.

The story starts in 1685 during Monmouth's Rebellion against England's King James II. Dr. Peter Blood, treating one of the wounded, is swept up with the captured rebels and sentenced to death in the Bloody Assizes, where we first get a sense of his indomitable character. Throughout the film Blood is aflame with a mocking defiance of oppression and tyranny, but Flynn's characterization also sparkles with wry intelligence, and he delivers razor-sharp remarks with such conviction it seems he'd thought them up himself. Blood's death sentence, and that of his fellow rebels, is commuted to slavery on the plantations of Jamaica, and the crew is shipped off to Port Royal. At a degrading slave sale, Blood catches the eye of Arabella Bishop (Olivia de Havilland), daughter of one of the plantation owners, who buys the sullen Irishman herself to save him from being bought by the most brutal rancher on the island. Now, there's a "meet cute" for you!

The film's next half hour is this amazing back-and-forth as the story contrasts the luxury and brutality of colonial Jamaica with Blood's step-by-step engineering of an escape attempt by himself and his fellow slaves, meanwhile currying favor with the governor (only Blood can cure his gout) and engaging in a half-serious courtship dance with Arabella. (Neither of them really means it—or do they?) Then the escape plans go awry, and all seems lost until the "timely interruption" (as Blood himself puts it) of a raid by Spanish pirates. The slaves take advantage of the chaos to turn the tables on both the Spanish and the English, and after some derring-do, Blood and his crew are free and in command of a fighting ship. And then, with all the world their enemy, what option do they have but to sail to Tortuga and join the Brotherhood of the Coast?

However, when you ally with pirates, you must consort with such scoundrels as Captain Levasseur (Basil Rathbone)—and that might not end well. But oh, those scenes of Caribbean piracy: the buccaneers swearing to the Articles, drunken pirates pillaging a seaport, freebooters roistering in the taverns of Tortuga, the boarding actions—"Grappling hooks to larboard!" They've all been done many times since, but never better, to my mind. The rapier duel in the surf between Flynn and Rathbone fighting over the captured de Havilland is worth the price of admission alone. Guilty pleasure: Basil Rathbone's outrrrrrageous French accent.

CAPTAIN FROM CASTILE

Rating: ★★★☆☆ • *Origin:* USA, 1947 • *Director:* Henry King •
Source: 20th Century Fox Classics DVD

This is a magnificent failure, a classic case of Hollywood buying a novel for its strengths and then lacking the guts to put those strengths on the screen. And it's a damn shame, because it could have been great. Samuel Shellabarger's best-selling 1945 novel tells the story of a naive young Spanish nobleman who runs afoul of the Inquisition; to escape persecution and certain death, he joins Hernán Cortez's expedition to Mexico, becoming one of the conquistador's trusted officers. Shellabarger's novel pulls no punches in its depiction of the excesses of the Inquisition and the horrific events of the Conquest of Mexico, but the screenplay for the film chokes on both those points, soft-pedaling the Inquisition (and changing its name) and waffling on whether the slaughter and suppression of the Aztecs is deplorable or glorious.

And that's not even the worst of it. When a historical fiction author involves a protagonist in great historical events, it's essential to make that protagonist a mover and driver of the action rather than a mere spectator. This is where the script for *Captain from Castile* fails in a big way, as Captain Pedro de Vargas is nearly always swept along by other forces rather than directing or influencing them himself. Poor Tyrone Power, who plays Vargas: much of the time, he simply seems clueless or bewildered. The exceptions are when the story calls for some swashbuckling, briefly giving him a clear purpose, or when he's romancing the fabulous Jean Peters as Catana, dazzling here in her début role. There's genuine chemistry between Powers and Peters, especially in a white-hot scene at a Mexican campfire where they dance a blazing *zarabanda.* Vaya!

This movie does have other things going for it as well. For one thing, it's bloody gorgeous, shot in full color largely on location in Mexico at or near the actual sites of the Conquest. Historically, part of Cortez's march on the Aztec capital took place against the backdrop of an active volcano, and while shooting this film, the peak of Paricutín obligingly erupted, enabling jaw-dropping scenes of the conquistadores marching across country with a great volcanic-ash cloud smeared across the sky behind them. Another visual home run: meticulous research went into re-creating the arms and clothing of the Aztecs, and they're worn in the film by descendants of the Aztec people instead of Hollywood extras. Plus, Cesar Romero gives an energetic performance as Cortez, alternating between inspiring leader and rapacious plunderer. And it's all backed up by one of composer Alfred Newman's greatest scores. Alas, ultimately the tonal inconsistency and the flaws in the story take the wind out of the sails of what should have been a masterpiece.

CAPTAIN HORATIO HORNBLOWER

Rating: ★★★★★ • *Origin:* USA, 1951 • *Director:* Raoul Walsh • *Source:* Warner Bros. DVD

Drawing from three of the *Hornblower* novels by C. S. Forester, this movie is easily the best depiction of Napoleonic-era naval warfare until, well, the British TV *Hornblower* adaptations in the late 1990s. It also works as a character study, a romance, and an unflinching reminder of the high human cost of war. Forester himself plotted the adaptation, though the script was handled by three Hollywood screenwriters. The film was originally developed as a vehicle for Errol Flynn, but after the disappointing reception of *The Adventures of Don Juan*, Flynn was passed over; instead, the movie stars Gregory Peck as Royal Navy Captain Hornblower. It's a great choice: Peck, though not English, has the sort of awkward grandeur the role requires, formal and severe on the surface but gnawed by doubt underneath. Hornblower wins his battles against the odds by outthinking his opponents, and Peck deftly conveys the character's native intelligence. Plus he just plain looks great in a Royal Navy captain's rig, like a statue from the Admiralty come to life.

The story is wide-ranging, from the tropical Pacific to the cold North Atlantic, and if it has a flaw, it's overambition, cramming in a midnight boarding expedition, a gun duel between ships of the line, a mad warlord, a jealous commodore, imprisonment and escape, a ship hijacked from port, and a surprise attack on an anchored French squadron under the guns of a cliff-top fortress—all in just under two hours. Somehow there's still time for character development, camaraderie among the English officers, and the mourning of losses after the battles. Credit must be given to veteran director Raoul Walsh for keeping all these elements moving swiftly and coherently without ever feeling rushed.

And we haven't even gotten to the romance yet! The changing politics of war mean that Lady Barbara Wellesley (Virginia Mayo) needs a sudden ride out of Panama, and Hornblower's is the only English ship for thousands of miles, so he's stuck with carrying her around the Horn and back to England. Lady Barbara shows courage and heart by caring for the wounded during battle, Hornblower returns the favor by personally nursing her through a bout of debilitating tropical fever, and love blooms. But they're adults with commitments, neither one is free, and obstacles must be surmounted. Mayo, who in a lightweight part could sometimes rely on her smile and phone it in, excels here as Lady Barbara, showing how well she can act when she's engaged with the role. That and her genuine chemistry with Peck really make the love story work. But of course, Forester had a feel for stories of strong women romancing eccentric captains: he also wrote *The African Queen*. By the way, watch for Christopher Lee as a Spanish captain fighting a fierce cutlass duel with Hornblower—he's the only guy in the movie who's taller than Gregory Peck.

CAPTAIN KIDD

Rating: ★★★☆☆ • *Origin:* USA, 1945 • *Director:* Rowland V. Lee •
Source: American Home Treasures DVD

Charles Laughton had a strange career for a movie star. Enormously talented, with an outsize screen presence despite his modest stature, he made an early name for himself in the 1930s playing big roles like King Henry VIII, the Emperor Nero, and Captain Bligh. But no matter how talented he was, Laughton was far from conventionally handsome and only grew more homely with time; his looks limited his options, and by the '40s, about the only lead parts he could get were in low-budget melodramas like *Captain Kidd*. Though theoretically based on the life of the historical pirate, other than a few names and some disconnected incidents, this movie has less to do with history than with including as many pirate-movie tropes as possible: rascally crew members signing the Articles, buccaneers burying their ill-gotten treasure in a hidden cave, a sword duel over possession of a captive lady, a candle burning down to set off a ship's powder magazine, and even a medallion that reveals the wearer's true parentage. All good fun, but this film's principal pleasure comes from watching Laughton's portrayal of the supremely duplicitous William Kidd, who indulges in treachery, corruption, cruelty, and murder because he genuinely enjoys it and openly revels in his utter lack of scruples. When he's lying to someone he plans to betray (i.e., everyone), he can scarcely conceal his evil glee. At one point John Carradine calls him a cold-blooded shark, to which Laughton replies, "Ah, you flatterer!"

Speaking of the gaunt and ever-sinister John Carradine, he may be the best of the fine character actors supporting Laughton in this film, but he's not the only one: there's Gilbert Roland as another of Kidd's lieutenants, the suave but avaricious Spaniard Lorenzo; the haughty Henry Daniell as King William III; and Reginald Owen as the snooty Shadwell, the butler Kidd hires to teach him how to act like a "person of quality." The only wrong note comes from the casting of Randolph Scott as Adam Mercy, the ex-pirate who joins Kidd's crew as master gunner but whose manners and attitude betray an aristocratic background. The problem is that Scott, a tall, square-jawed American best known as a two-fisted cowboy in Western movies, is about as aristocratic as beer and about as piratical as an Eagle Scout. As the king's infiltrator in Kidd's crew, it's just unbelievable that the wily Kidd and his cutthroats would be taken in by him for a moment. But this is Hollywood, so in the end, cowboy virtue wins out over ruthless duplicity. At least Laughton gets in a mocking final speech.

Fun fact: according to Nikita Khrushchev's memoirs, this was one of Josef Stalin's favorite films. He's said to have been delighted by Laughton's portrayal of the unrepentant and utterly unprincipled pirate captain. Is good!

CAPTAIN KRONOS—VAMPIRE HUNTER

Rating: ★★★★☆ • *Origin:* UK, 1974 • *Director:* Brian Clemens • *Source:* Feel Films Blu-ray

By the early 1970s, the UK's Hammer Films was on the rocks; their brand of gothic horror had become passé, and other genres, including swashbucklers, were no longer working for them either. This was an attempt to establish a new series with a fresh take on both swashbucklers and horror.

It should have worked. In late eighteenth-century England, among tricornes and tail-coats, Captain Kronos (Horst Janson) is a former member of the Imperial Guard who finds a new career after his family is slain by vampires and he nearly succumbs to the monsters himself. A master fencer armed with a cavalry saber and a Japanese *katana*, and backed by the hunchbacked scholar Professor Grost (John Cater), who drives a rattling wagon full of anti-undead paraphernalia, Kronos becomes a professional vampire hunter. But he needs one more sidekick: on his way to a summons from his old friend Doctor Marcus (John Carson), Kronos frees the young beauty Carla (Caroline Munro) from the stocks where she's been imprisoned for dancing on a Sunday, and she joins his band.

A vampire is indeed preying on Doctor Marcus's remote village, but of what kind? This undead threat drains the life force from its victims rather than blood, and the usual counter-measures are of no use. However, as Professor Grost points out, "There are many species of vampires," and he has ways of figuring out how to respond to this one. The puckish Grost is delightful, and so are his methods, including the Toad-in-the-Hole vampire detector: a dead toad in a box is buried where you think a vampire will pass, because as the old saying goes, "Then the vampire life shall give, and suddenly the toad shall live." Sure, professor.

Besides the vampire attacks, there are some run-ins with sword-armed malefactors hired by someone to take Kronos out. But the only real suspects in the neighborhood are the creepy aristocrats of the old Durward family, so at first it looks like there isn't much of a mystery here. However, the story takes some unexpected twists and turns in its final act—and because it's a swashbuckler, it has to end in a climactic sword duel. This is an exciting clash reminiscent of the brawls in Richard Lester's *Musketeers* films, which makes sense because Kronos's undead swordsman opponent is played by fight director William Hobbs, who also choreographed the swordplay in the *Musketeers* movies. Clang!

This film was written and directed by Brian Clemens, who along with coproducer Albert Fennell had been the showrunner for the Steed and Mrs. Peel *Avengers* TV series. *Kronos* exhibits the same kind of dark whimsy as *The Avengers*, and it should have worked here as well. It was made in 1972 and not released until '74, after the success of *The Three Musketeers*, but by that time Hammer Films was failing and couldn't support it properly. Too bad—based on this first film, a few more entries in the series would have been welcome.

CAPTAIN PIRATE

Rating: ★★★★☆ • *Origin:* USA, 1952 • *Director:* Ralph Murphy •
Source: Columbia Pictures DVD

The black-and-white *Fortunes of Captain Blood* (1950) must have done well, because Columbia upped the production ante for this Technicolor sequel, which is quite good despite its reeee-ally stupid title. Like *Fortunes*, it stars Louis Hayward and Patricia Medina in a story loosely based on a book by Rafael Sabatini, in this case *Captain Blood Returns* (1932). The writers bor-rowed a few incidents, characters, and names from *Returns*, but mostly this is an original story and a good one; it hews closely to the historical feel and character of Sabatini's tales, which hinge on the balance between Peter Blood's ruthless cunning and innate decency.

The plot here belongs to the "the only way to prove I'm not the murderer is to catch the real killer" club, piracy chapter. Blood, now a retired and respectable Jamaica planter, is on the verge of marrying Doña Isabella, whom he rescued in *Fortunes*, when he's arrested and accused of returning to piracy by leading an attack on the port of Cartagena, based on the lying evidence of Isabella's Spanish cousin and that of Hilary Evans (John Sutton), Blood's rival for Isabella's hand. Blood winds up in prison, but happily, Isabella takes charge; at her behest Blood's first mate reforms his old crew (there's a fine rallying-the-crew montage delightfully scored to the tune of "Drunken Sailor"), Evans's ship is boarded and captured in Port Royal harbor, and Blood is broken free to sail off and try to discover who really raided Cartagena in his guise.

What follows is a high-seas detective story on the Spanish Main that takes Blood and his crew from Port Royal to Tortuga, Martinique, Santo Domingo, and Puerto Bello, bargaining with, bamboozling, and bullying a series of gratifyingly unsavory characters of every stripe, always just ahead of the pursuing English and Spanish navies. There are some tense action scenes, in which Hayward shows that he's not only improved his already-capable fencing skills but has added judo into the bargain, throwing scurvy dogs and Royal Marines around with equal abandon. The final duel with Sutton in a burning fortress is thrilling. Does Blood finally track down the true culprit, clear his name, and marry Doña Isabella? What do *you* think? It's a fitting end to Hayward's career in swashbucklers, as after this film he hung up his rapier for good.

CAPTAIN SCARLETT

Rating: ★★☆☆☆ • *Origin:* USA, 1953 • *Director:* Thomas Carr •
Source: Amazon streaming video

This bit of fluff is low-budget, Saturday-matinee fare of interest solely because it stars Richard Greene, appearing here a couple of years before his run as Robin Hood in the fine 1955–1959 *Adventures of . . .* TV series—in fact, he plays a hero similar enough to the bandit of Sherwood Forest that the film is almost a 72-minute audition for the role. This movie's story is nominally set in "France, after the Napoleonic wars," but the only thing French about it is some of the character names, and it bears no relation to actual history. Bad, oppressive nobles are bad, good, oppressed commoners are good, and Captain Scarlett, unjustly robbed of his estate, is back from the wars to put things right.

The film was shot in Mexico with a largely Latin American cast, and though the landscape looks even less like France than the usual Southern California locations, at least the architecture is more-or-less European. The protagonists are Greene as Captain Scarlett, whose first name seems to be "Captain," his sidekick Pierre DuCloux (Nedrick Young), another dispossessed gentleman, and Princess Maria (Leonora Amar), who has no more last name than Scarlett has a first. The princess is being forced into a loveless marriage with a bad noble because he's bad, and though Scarlett rescues her, she isn't very gracious about it. In fact, she spends most of the film being sullen and/or jealous, and the few scenes where she smiles and tries to be pleasant are unpersuasive. She's supposed to be the hero's reluctant love interest, but there's zero chemistry between Maria and Scarlett, despite Greene's considerable charm. *Captain Scarlett* was Amar's last role in motion pictures, and it's no wonder, really.

Greene, however, has what fun he can with the part of Scarlett, bounding around in a flowing red cape, tossing off clichéd heroic quips, and wielding a smallsword with dash in a half dozen duels. The frequently embarrassing script was written by producer Howard Dimsdale, so presumably director Thomas Carr didn't have much leeway to tinker with it, and he and the cast just do the best they can. Virtuous peasants are saved from brutal and lecherous tax collectors, an execution by guillotine is duly foiled, and about every 10 minutes, there's another thunderous chase on horseback through the Mexican hills. There's a brief departure from formula when Princess Maria, on the feeblest of pretexts, joins Scarlett and DuCloux to become a third freedom fighter, but it lasts only as long as the middle act before she falls off her horse and is captured by the chief bad noble's soldiers. Then, alas, she has to be rescued by Scarlett and DuCloux before the final confrontation. For a few minutes there, it looked like *Captain Scarlett* was going to break the mold, but nope, no such luck.

CAPTAIN SINDBAD

Rating: ★★★☆☆ • *Origin:* West Germany/USA, 1963 • *Director:* Byron Haskin •
Source: Warner Bros. DVD

What do you do if you want to make a Sinbad movie capitalizing on the success of *7th Voyage*, but you're not Columbia Pictures and you can't get Ray Harryhausen to do the effects? First, you hire Byron Haskin as your director, because he's experienced with swashbucklers like *Treasure Island* (1950) and SF films chock-full of practical effects, like *From the Earth the Moon* (1958). Second, for your Sinbad you hire Guy Williams, arguably the leading American swashbuckler star of the time coming off his run as Disney's Zorro. Third, you add a letter to Sinbad's name to cover your legal ass. And then, fourth: profit!

It's worth pointing out that this film and *Jason and the Argonauts*, Harryhausen's own follow-up to *7th Voyage*, were released on the same day in June 1963. *Jason* is maybe the finest fantasy film of the 1960s; but *Captain Sindbad* is not without its charms, and though nearly forgotten today, at the time it made just as much money as Harryhausen's epic.

Unlike *Jason*, which is as serious as seven skeletons, *Sindbad* is a comic fantasy, an exuberant fable with a light touch for most of its running length. A lot of the gags seem flat and dated nowadays, but hang on, it'll be worth it. The mythical *Arabian Nights*–style country of Baristan has been taken over by the wicked El Kerim (Pedro Armendáriz)—you can tell he's

Captain Sindbad Author's Collection

bad because he has evil mustachios. El Kerim seeks to marry the dotty king's daughter, Princess Jana (Heidi Brühl), to legitimize his usurpation of the throne, but Jana loves Sindbad, who is returning from a voyage of several years' duration all unknowing of Jana's plight. The princess appeals to her "uncle," the comic wizard Galgo (Abraham Sofaer), who transforms her into a firebird and sends her to warn Sindbad—but El Kerim gets wise and has Galgo change some of his guards into rocs, giant birds carrying boulders that sink Sindbad's ship. Despite this, Sindbad and most of his crew wash up safely in Baristan, where they plot to free the princess. Sindbad's bold plan is to get himself captured and then confront El Kerim directly, which he does, running the villain through with a scimitar—to no effect, because his heart has been magically removed, making him invulnerable! Uh-oh.

It's a rule that in every Sinbad movie, the evil wizard gets the best part, and that's certainly true here, as the mocking El Kerim has all the best lines and also all the best outfits—is he a Persian, a Cossack, a Prussian, or a Mongol? The only person who's better dressed is his leading henchman, Colonel Kabar (Henry Brandon), who has one of the finest black goth villain suits ever. Anyway, Sindbad is captured and sentenced to the Arena to fight an invisible monster that's right out of *Forbidden Planet*. But he swashbuckles an escape, pokes the goofy Galgo with a scimitar to make him talk, and learns that El Kerim's heart is sequestered in an ancient tower on the other side of a haunted swamp. Main quest time!

Up to this point the film has been a light but uninspired romp with plentiful though unimpressive special effects, but now it gets good. Like, really good. The haunted swamp sequence is genuinely tense as Sindbad leads his crew through the mire and loses them, one by one, to strangler vines, sinkholes, crocodile puppets, boiling pools, and lava vents. And the ancient tower is even better. I won't spoil the ending, but I will point out that the next-to-final boss monster is the clear inspiration for the Bigby's Hand spells in *Dungeons & Dragons*. Plus there's a 12-headed hydra, and that's five more heads than on the hydra in *Jason and the Argonauts*. Take that, Harryhausen!

CARDINAL RICHELIEU

Rating: ★★☆☆☆ • *Origin:* USA, 1935 • *Director:* Rowland V. Lee •
Source: Fox Cinema Archives DVD

This film's story comes from an 1839 play by Edward Bulwer-Lytton, he of "It was a dark and stormy night" fame, the man renowned as a writer so bad that there's an annual bad-writing award named after him. And this is nothing if not a creaky old potboiler, a romance shoehorned into a pastiche of various events from the reign of King Louis XIII, combining four different conspiracies against king and cardinal into one. The movie retains the play's theatrical staginess, with just enough carriage chases and swordplay thrown in to allow it to qualify for inclusion in this book.

Still, if you're interested in the period, as I am, there are several things *Cardinal Richelieu* gets right, starting with its depiction of His Red Eminence, who is wily, bold, articulate, and as generous one minute as he is ruthless the next. Richelieu is played by George Arliss, an English actor of stage and screen who was very popular in his day though now he's largely forgotten. His characterization of the cardinal is easily the mildest and least menacing of any film portrayal of Richelieu, and it's jarring at first to have such a milquetoast in the role, until gradually Arliss reveals the steel fist beneath the red velvet glove.

Francis Lister, playing Prince Gaston, also deserves a mention, as his portrayal of King Louis's ambitious but weasely and craven younger brother is spot on. The costumes are all period-perfect, and Maureen O'Sullivan and Cesar Romero, as the star-crossed lovers caught up in the conspiracy, look good in them. But the script doesn't give them anything interesting to say, and you won't see any turns of plot that you haven't seen many times before. Nonetheless, it wouldn't be fair not to acknowledge the capable direction of Rowland V. Lee, without whom this old pot wouldn't boil at all.

CARTOUCHE (OR *SWORDS OF BLOOD*)

Rating: ★★★☆☆ • *Origin:* France, 1962 • *Director:* Philippe de Broca • *Source:* Anchor Bay DVD

This swashbuckler fictionalizing the life of a historical outlaw in eighteenth-century France starts out as a light farce and gradually gets serious. Dominique (Jean-Paul Belmondo) is a charming and brazen thief who runs afoul of the head of the Paris thieves' guild and gets a price put on his head. He escapes Paris by joining the army, and since this is a French farce and everyone in authority is a buffoon, a satire-tinged massacre ensues. Dominique and two jovial accomplices, the knife-throwing Mole (Jean Rochefort) and simple strongman Gentle (Jess Hahn) escape the slaughter, stealing a carriage load of army payroll gold in the process. Making their getaway, they hook up with the dancing pickpocket Venus (Claudia Cardinale), add in a rogue monk, and a new outlaw gang is formed.

Gang leader Dominique takes the *nom de voleur* Cartouche and sets out to rob only oppressive aristocrats, distributing the excess spoils to the poor out of sheer ebullience and converting the downtrodden into willing accomplices. Cartouche is so successful that he returns to Paris and takes over the thieves' guild, turning their hideout into an opulent, treasure-draped lair for his lover, Venus. But all too soon, Cartouche's roving eye lands on a haughty countess, the wife of the lieutenant general of police, and that won't end well.

This film was a lavish production released just as Gallic heartthrob Belmondo's star was ascending to its height, and even in the silly first act, his confidence and élan carry him through. There's real chemistry between Belmondo and the youthful Cardinale, who glows with joy and exuberance. The supporting cast is also strong, especially the always enjoyable Rochefort as the Mole, who has a wry remark to make at every turn. However, beyond Rochefort's quips, the script isn't that great, consisting mostly of clichés recycled with a wink, and the humor is mainly broad slapstick, but as the story grows more serious, the action gets tighter and the early goofiness is forgiven. Cartouche is a hero who harks back to the Romantic era, so in the end his career turns from comic to tragic. *Mais bien sûr*, it's French.

A CHALLENGE FOR ROBIN HOOD

Rating: ★★★☆☆ • *Origin:* UK, 1967 • *Director:* C. M. Pennington-Richards • *Source:* StudioCanal DVD

Stump your film-fan friends! Ask them, "Did Hammer Films make one Robin Hood film or two?" Then, no matter how they answer, push up your glasses and say, "Actually, depending on how you count them, they made at least three."

This is the third, and it's pretty good, an effective recombination of the legend's familiar elements built around a new origin story. Robin de Courtenay (Barrie Ingham) is a nephew of the aging Norman lord John de Courtenay, a good man whose wicked sons Roger (Peter Blythe) and Henry (Eric Woofe) can hardly wait to see shuffle off this mortal coil. While out hunting, Roger de Courtenay (the wickeder son) spies a poacher and kills him without knowing or caring that he's the former Lord Fitzwarren, a Saxon who's been forced into poverty. Robin steps in and prevents Roger from killing Fitzwarren's son, which earns him the grudging admiration of the Sherwood outlaws. When Lord de Courtenay, on his deathbed, splits his inheritance between Roger, Henry, and Robin, wicked Roger, to get the whole shebang, murders Henry with Robin's dagger, and Robin, proscribed, must flee to the greenwood and join the outlaws. You know how it goes from there.

Considering it was made by Hammer, this is a surprisingly family-friendly movie, high-spirited and good-hearted without being sappy or silly—well, except for the pie fight at the country fair, but that's over quickly. Though lacking any real standouts, the main cast is all well up to the job, the best being Ingham as Robin, James Hayter as Friar Tuck, Leon Greene as Little John, and the villains: Blythe as Roger de Courtenay and John Arnatt as the Sheriff of Nottingham. The only real disappointment is Gay Hamilton as Lady Marian Fitzwarren, who's too young for the part and out of her depth. (She's much better a few years later, in *Barry Lyndon* and *The Duellists*.)

A Challenge for Robin Hood really marks the end of the era of the standard screen versions of the outlaw archer that began with Errol Flynn in *The Adventures of Robin Hood* in 1938. After this movie the Robin Hood genre disappears until the making of the first of the "revisionist" Robin Hoods, starting with Richard Lester's *Robin and Marian* in 1976. After that, Robin Hood onscreen becomes one new reinvention after another, and that's no bad thing. But you can still enjoy what was this last hurrah with the traditional Merrie Men in Sherwood before times inevitably changed.

CHIMES AT MIDNIGHT (OR FALSTAFF)

Rating: ★★★★★ • *Origin:* Spain/Switzerland, 1965 • *Director:* Orson Welles •
Source: Mr Bongo DVD

"Thou owest God a death."

This is Orson Welles's retelling of the life and death of Sir John Falstaff, one of Shakespeare's greatest characters, with a script Welles drew from five of the Bard's plays but reframed and reordered to suit his purpose, which is to find the heart beneath the surface of the rogue. This is a great film—Welles himself considered it his best, and I'd not dispute it—as visually rich as it is audibly challenging: unlike many cinematic adaptations of Shakespeare, where the language rings out with clarity and force, here it's often spoken in haste or muttered low and indistinctly. Welles forces you to listen closely and pay attention to what's being said, and it gives Shakespeare's words a new sort of power, an unfamiliar weight, as they emerge from obscurity, as spoken, to clarity, as heard.

But this is the *Cinema of Swords*, so enough about words: this film's great contribution to our genre is almost entirely wordless, the 20-minute Battle of Shrewsbury at the crux of the movie between the forces of King Henry IV (John Gielgud) and his son, the Prince of Wales (Keith Baxter) against the rebellious Northumberland (José Nieto) and his son Harry "Hotspur" Percy (Norman Rodway). The battle, when the two sides come to grips, is a storm

Chimes at Midnight AUTHOR'S COLLECTION

of chaos, muddy, bloody, and inglorious, shocking and lethal, horrific and absurd. Welles wanted the viewer to recoil from warfare rather than revel in it. And yet the single combat between the Prince of Wales and Hotspur, though sharp and brutal, is nonetheless exciting, forcing viewers to consider their own attraction to its violence. Influenced by Eisenstein before him, Welles's depiction of the fury of men in battle was a powerful influence on later films, including Spielberg's *Saving Private Ryan* and Branagh's *Henry V*, itself a sort of sequel to this film.

Welles shot this movie on a shoestring at medieval locations in Spain, and in many ways it's raw and unpolished, but that just makes its remarkable visuals all the more striking. Don't go into *Chimes at Midnight* expecting a slick, easy-to-swallow commercial production, because that's not what this is. This is art, unvarnished, unsettling, unexpected, art that laughs at humanity and loves it for all its flaws, and Welles's portrayal of Falstaff is indelible. Orson, for all those wretched wine commercials, you are forgiven.

CHUSHINGURA: THE LOYAL 47 RETAINERS (OR 47 SAMURAI)

Rating: ★★★★☆ • *Origin:* Japan, 1962 • *Director:* Hiroshi Inagaki • *Source:* Image DVD

The tale of the 47 ronin is sometimes called Japan's national epic, as it epitomizes the samurai virtues of courage and loyalty unto death. In Japan it's been filmed at least six times, with countless other dramatic adaptations, but Inagaki's sumptuous 1962 movie is probably the best-known retelling to Westerners. The film's subtitle for its English-language release was "The Loyal 47 Retainers," but in the original Japanese version it's "Story of Blossoms, Story of Snow." Not blossoms as in budding flowers, but the fluttering petals whose day is over and that fall as a harbinger of the death symbolized by the coming of snow.

The story is familiar: at the height of the shogunate, a high-ranking samurai lord is preparing to receive a delegation from the emperor, and his ritual reception must be precise and perfect. It's the job of Lord Kira (Chûsha Ishikawa) to instruct Lord Asano (Yuzo Kayama) in the proper ceremonies, but the corrupt Kira is angry because the stiff-necked Asano refuses to grease the wheels with rich bribes. Certain that he's untouchable, Kira repeatedly insults

Asano, slapping his face with a fan, until Asano loses control and attacks Kira with a dagger right in the shogun's palace. Kira is only scratched, but Asano is disgraced, ordered to commit ritual suicide, and his entire clan is disbanded.

That's just the setup, the "Blossoms" part of the film. Next comes "Snow," the plot of Asano's now-masterless samurai to regain their warrior's honor by taking the life of Lord Kira.

The first part of the film marches with a stately inevitability, as if every event is fated, the camera moving deliberately, almost majestically, except during the sudden chaos of Asano's attack on Kira. In part 2, the pace picks up: plans are laid and executed, spies lurk and are caught, and it's all deceit and intrigue until the final paroxysm of violence, the raid of the 47 ronin on Lord Kira's well-defended city estate.

This is a long movie, over three hours, and though it's capped by a superbly orchestrated 20-minute orgy of vengeance, it takes its time getting there. The pleasures along the way include a gorgeous wide-screen re-creation of Japan at the turn of the eighteenth century, plus a number of fine performances by a first-rate cast. Of particular note are Matsumoto Koshiro as Chamberlain Oishi, who masterminds the Asano clan's revenge while concealing his plans by pretending to become a degenerate wastrel, and Chûsha Ichikawa, the weaselly face of despicable cowardice as Lord Kira. For those who insist that every samurai film should have Toshiro Mifune in it, he's also here in a memorable supporting role as a powerful samurai-for-hire who holds off reinforcements while the Asano ronin hunt for Kira.

In short, which this movie isn't, *Chushingura* is a visual feast for those who can be as patient for the climax as the Asano samurai. But it's no dishonor if that's not for you.

CLASH OF THE TITANS

Rating: ★★★★☆ • *Origin:* UK/USA, 1981 • *Director:* Desmond Davis • *Source:* Warner Bros. Blu-ray

There are worse ways to learn about Greek myths than from a Ray Harryhausen adventure film. In this one the great stop-motion animator takes on the story of Perseus and Andromeda, while his fantastic creatures, such as Pegasus, Medusa, a mechanical owl, and some angry giant scorpions, as usual outact the human players, though this time not by much.

There are some changes to the tale of the myth to make the story hang together better as a movie script, but the basics are intact: Queen Cassiopeia (Siân Phillips, Livia from *I, Claudius*), makes the mistake of praising her daughter Andromeda (Judi Bowker) as more beautiful than the sea goddess Thetis (Maggie Smith), and the divine lady vows revenge, threatening to send the monstrous kraken to destroy their city within 30 days. But the hero Perseus (Harry Hamlin) falls in love with Andromeda and vows to save her. As a son of Zeus (Laurence Olivier), Perseus is granted the finest god-forged gear, a sword and magic helmet (plus shield) that are just what you want for monster fighting. But he's going to need more than that to defeat the Kong-sized kraken, so he goes on a quest to ask the creepy three Stygian witches what to do. After stealing their single eye to get the witches to talk, Perseus is advised that his only chance is to travel to the Isle of the Dead on the edge of the Underworld and there to take the head of the gorgon Medusa. On it!

The plot is thickened with the addition of some extra characters not in the original myth, including the devilish Calibos (well played by Neil McCarthy), who also desires Andromeda, the aforementioned Pegasus the flying horse, and some giant scorpions, who provide the best swordplay foils in the film. There's also a cutesy mechanical owl made by Hephaestus in

1981: THE OLD ORDER CHANGETH

1981 was a watershed year in fantasy films. The success of *Star Wars* had made it possible to fund and produce large-scale SF and fantasy movies, but it also heralded a change in the way such movies were made, placing high-quality (and thus expensive) special effects front and center. Prior to *Star Wars*, special effects in fantasy films were almost invariably low-budget and cheesy, reflecting movie producers' almost invariable belief that such films appealed only to a niche and rather undiscerning market.

The conspicuous exception to this rule was the films of master animator Ray Harryhausen, but even in his movies, beyond the creature animation, the production values, script, and human performances were often afterthoughts. However, the creatures were magnificent, and that was considered enough.

Not anymore. Harryhausen's painstaking stop-motion animation were superseded by new approaches that integrated stop-motion with puppetry, classical animation, and most importantly computer graphics. And indeed, 1981's *Clash of the Titans* was Harryhausen's final film. If *Clash* wasn't completely outdone by *Dragonslayer,* the effects in that film, largely produced by George Lucas's Industrial Light and Magic, nonetheless pointed the way toward a new era in fantasy.

However, it wasn't all about the special effects. John Boorman's *Excalibur* showed that a film of heroic fantasy could also be cinematic art, aspiring to the best the medium was capable of. After *Excalibur,* plenty of critics would continue to sneer at fantasy films, but the proof was in: they were wrong.

---

imitation of Athena's favorite familiar and sent to help Perseus after he loses his magic helmet in a haunted swamp. Best of all is Medusa, and the scene in which Perseus and his hoplite redshirts invade her eerie, flame-lit temple is tense and suspenseful.

For a Harryhausen epic, the human actors come off pretty well. Romantic leads Hamlin and Bowker are more than just pretty faces, dealing well with the lean script by Beverley Cross, and Burgess Meredith does a pleasant turn as Perseus's poetic sidekick Ammon. The role of the gods of Olympus is even more prominent than in *Jason and the Argonauts* (1963); the divinities push the mortals around like pieces on a game board, and it's clear that even the villains, such as Calibos and Medusa, were made into monsters by the whims of the gods.

But times are changing, and this is the last of Harryhausen's stop-motion animated fantasy films. At this point *Star Wars* is the new leading fantasy franchise, and its influence is felt in the John Williams–inspired soundtrack by Laurence Rosenthal and by the vocalizations of the mechanical owl, which are all too similar to the whistles, clicks, and beeps of R2-D2. But *Clash* was nonetheless a success, beaten out that summer only by *Raiders of the Lost Ark*, which was released on the same day—not a bad swan song for the venerable Harryhausen. And, of course, this film is the source of the "Release the kraken!" meme. But did you remember that the original line was spoken by Sir Laurence Olivier?

COLOSSUS AND THE AMAZON QUEEN

Rating: ★☆☆☆☆ • *Origin:* Italy, 1960 • *Director:* Vittoria Sala • *Source:* Mill Creek DVD

Terrible sword-and-sandal comedy starring Rod Taylor as clever guy Pirro and Ed Fury as Glauco, his doofus, musclebound pal, with a weirdly incongruous jazz soundtrack that one never quite gets used to. Pirro, Glauco, and a bunch of other ancient Greeks land on the island of the Amazons, where the women dominate the men but secretly just want to be put in their place. Ninety minutes of leering at half-clad Amazons, slapstick humor, and gags that fall flat. Big nope.

THE COLOSSUS OF RHODES

Rating: ★★★★☆ • *Origin:* Italy/Spain/France, 1961 • *Director:* Sergio Leone •
Source: Warner Bros. DVD

This is Sergio Leone's first film as a director, and it's mostly excellent. After working as assistant director on sword-and-sandal epics such as *Quo Vadis* (1951) and *Ben-Hur* (1959), Leone finally got to show what he could do as lead on this picture, which is probably the best-looking Italian historical epic of the peplum era. It has its drawbacks, though, particularly its questionable choice of lead in American cowboy star Rory Calhoun, who combines the glowering good looks of a Robert Mitchum with the leering insouciance of Dean Martin. An ancient Greek hero he ain't. And, frankly, seven screenwriters are too many, even if one of them is Leone himself.

It's 280 BCE, the Hellenistic period before the rise of Rome, and the Athenian war hero Dario (Calhoun) has arrived on the island of Rhodes on what he hopes will be a pleasure trip. Rhodes and its epicene King Serse (Roberto Camardiel) are celebrating the dedication of their spectacular new harbor defense, a 300-foot-tall bronze statue of Apollo that can dump flaming molten lead on attacking ships. Genius inventor Carete (Félix Fernández), who built the colossus, is the hero of the day, but Dario is more interested in pursuing the man's devious daughter Diala (Lea Massari). Politics get in the way, though: the defenses of Rhodes were built by slave labor, and the slaves are brewing a revolt, while the rival Phoenicians have promised to help Serse's evil defense minister Thar (Conrado San Martín) usurp the throne in return for letting Phoenicia use Rhodes as a naval base against Greece. Everyone assumes Dario is a Greek agent, and he gets caught up in the intrigues. And though Dario doesn't want any part of local politics, when he's thrown into a lurid torture dungeon with the leaders of the slave revolt, he learns the basic peplum equation of rebels good, tyrants bad. (Also, Phoenicians bad.)

The problem is that Dario just isn't very clever, and for two-thirds of the film, he makes one poor choice after another, acting more like the hapless patsy in a Hitchcock thriller than a war hero who can tip the balance between the three factions. But Leone keeps things moving, interleaving scenes of his trademark tension and suspense with exciting action sequences in eye-popping settings, including a gruesome Temple of Baal (with a ballet of sacrifice!) and the interior of the colossus itself. Indeed, the colossus alone is worth the price of admission, a towering statue crammed with bronze-forged mechanisms, infernal devices, and royal guards in gorgeous Greco-Rhodian armor. When Dario, pursued by the gleaming guards, escapes out Apollo's ear for a thrilling sword duel high atop the colossus's biceps, you'll think you've seen it all. And yet, you're wrong, there's more to come!

So, Rory Calhoun notwithstanding, this movie wins on the basis of sheer spectacle, which thanks to Leone's unerring eye is classy rather than cheesy. It is, dare I say it, colossal!

COME DRINK WITH ME

Rating: ★★★★★ • *Origin:* Hong Kong, 1966 • *Director:* King Hu • *Source:* 88 Films Blu-ray

Sometime during the Ming dynasty, a government official leads a file of troops who are escorting wheeled cages bearing captive bandits to prison. Suddenly they're stopped by a white-robed man with a petition, demanding the release of the leader of the Five Tigers criminal gang. The petition is refused, and the response of the Five Tigers is instant: the troops are slain in a bloody massacre and their commander, the son of the local governor, is captured as a hostage. What can the governor do but send the Golden Swallow to rescue him?

Come Drink with Me, written and directed by King Hu, is the beginning of the modern *wuxia* film. King Hu's brilliant cinematic innovation was to ignore the actual practices of historical martial arts and replace them with the theatricality of Chinese opera, depicting combat through the choreography of dance. This triggered a visual revolution that changed how fighting was depicted in cinema, a watershed that created, over time, a new paradigm that has become a standard in both East and West.

Not only that, but while he was at it, Hu smashed the gender barrier by casting a 19-year-old ballet dancer, Cheng Pei-pei, as one of his two protagonists, placing female fighters on the same footing as men without even bothering to explain it. And he did it in a film that was both strikingly beautiful and broke new ground in quick cuts and editing.

So this is hot stuff. Golden Swallow (Cheng Pei-pei) sets out to confront the Five Tigers and rescue the governor's son, who is also her brother, venturing into the bandits' territory in male guise. (It's a wuxia genre convention that a woman dressed as a man is seen as male by everyone until her gender is conclusively revealed—and indeed, that's an old swashbuckling standard in Western cultures as well.) The Swallow's first confrontation with the bandits is in a large restaurant perfect for a big brawl, but just as it gets going, a drunken beggar butts in on the fracas, cracking jokes and getting in the way like countless clown characters before him since the beginning of theater. However, there's a difference: this clown, Drunken Cat (the charming Yueh Hua), has superior kung fu abilities that he slyly and furtively deploys on the behalf of the badly outnumbered Golden Swallow.

The Swallow, stylish as hell, wins her initial combat with the Five Tigers' goons thanks to the hidden help of Drunken Cat, exhibiting as she does remarkable skills that are still nonetheless believably within the possibilities of human athletics. However, when she tracks the Five Tigers to their lair and faces their Number Two, Jade Faced Tiger (Chan Hung-lit), the jams are kicked out, and the combat begins to verge on the superhuman. Drunken Cat intervenes, changing the balance of power by revealing his true skills—but can even his powers match those of the supreme mastermind behind the Five Tigers, the wicked Abbot Liao Kung (Yeung Chi-hing)?

This movie was made for the Hong Kong studio of the Shaw Brothers, a film factory that had no patience for art, so after he finished it, King Hu bid the Shaws farewell and went to Taiwan to make *Dragon Inn*. But *Come Drink with Me*, art and all, was such a success that even the Shaw Brothers recognized they had a new genre on their hands, following it up with *Golden Swallow* and dozens more movies well into the 1980s. And thus, a new style of swashbuckler was born to the benefit of us all.

THE BARBARIAN BOOM [PART 1]

The '80s Barbarian Boom didn't start with *Conan the Barbarian* (1982), though its long prerelease hype train certainly primed the pump. In truth, the market was ripe for such films, and by mid-1981, a number of other sword-and-sorcery movies were in production or preproduction. The genre had been bubbling its way up in other mass media throughout the '70s, *Dungeons & Dragons* codesigner Gary Gygax had come to Hollywood talking up swords and sorcery, and the *Choose Your Own Adventure* paperbacks, which were largely heroic fantasy, were selling millions of copies. It was time, and the parade of Clonans was on. The barbarians were here, and they would rule the next decade.

CONAN THE BARBARIAN

Rating: ★★★☆☆ • *Origin:* USA, 1982 • *Director:* John Milius • *Source:* Universal DVD

Conan the barbarian was created by Texan pulp author Robert E. Howard in the 1930s for heroic fantasy stories published in *Weird Tales*. They were republished in the 1960s in paperbacks with fantastic and evocative covers by Frank Frazetta, and the character was picked up by Marvel Comics in the 1970s, with adventures running to hundreds of issues. Conan took a while to get to the screen due to rights tangles, but the 1982 film was the biggest swordand-sorcery movie up to its time, establishing that fantasy subgenre as a viable film form and launching star Arnold Schwarzenegger on his acting career.

The film, directed and cowritten by John Milius, is a mini-epic of the forging of a young man through hardship and suffering into a mighty warrior, a sword-swinging muscleman determined to avenge his parents' death by slaying Thulsa Doom (James Earl Jones), the charismatic but evil cult leader who murdered them. Along the way he finds a lover in the nimble thief Valeria (Sandahl Bergman) and two wisecracking sidekicks in Subotai (Gerry Lopez) and the Wizard of the Mounds (Mako [Iwamatsu]). They get into fights with cult warriors, wolves, giant snakes, and sky demons in between a lot of philosophizing about life and the purpose and place of humans in existence.

Conan fights his way through ancient cities and across barren wilderness to find the home of the cult, which has awesome serpent towers in the cities, and a snaky, peak-top subterranean lair called the Mountain of Power. The impressive combats are inspired by Japanese sword work and set against a driving *Carmina Burana*–ish score by Basil Poledouris. The film set the standard for all the warrior-versus-wizard movies to follow.

But for all that, *Conan the Barbarian* is also frequently cringey and embarrassingly dumb. The three main heroes, Schwarzenegger, Bergman, and Lopez, all inexperienced actors, were chosen by Milius for their unspoiled outlook, but their line readings are often awkward and amateurish. James Earl Jones as the archvillain is a solid and professional presence, but his longhaired hatchet men look and act like roadies for a heavy metal band. The story is rife with coincidental or unexplained plot events, and its philosophical meanderings are pompous and juvenile. "For us, there is no spring—just the wind that smells fresh before the storm." Really?

Conan the Barbarian Author's Collection

The role of women is problematic; there's Bergman's Valeria, who is strong and competent and who takes the lead during the trio's thieving—but every other woman is a victim, a whore, or a witch. It's pretty much an adolescent male's fantasy and nothing but. Milius's direction is uneven, but he does have one trick so good he uses it twice: the heroes' murderous infiltrations of a serpent tower and the Mountain of Power are wordless and deliberate dream dramas in which events unfold as if fated in time to Poledouris's hallucinatory music. It works, and if it misses achieving the operatic, it at least reaches the level of a heavy metal concept album. Rock on.

CONAN THE DESTROYER

Rating: ★★★★☆ • *Origin:* USA, 1984 • *Director:* Richard Fleischer • *Source:* Universal DVD

Conan the Barbarian (1982) established a new genre of film and introduced Arnold Schwarzenegger to most of the world, but this sequel is in many ways superior to it. In fact, it's one of the best movies of the 1980s barbarian boom.

Conan (Schwarzenegger again) is mourning his lost love Valeria when he and his thieving sidekick, Malak (Tracey Walter), are accosted by Taramis (Sarah Douglas), the witch-queen of Shadizar, who wants him to undertake a quest for her. Conan refuses until Taramis promises that if he succeeds, she'll bring Valeria back from beyond the gates of death. The task: escort a prophesied princess, Jehnna (Olivia d'Abo), to retrieve a crystal key from an evil wizard, use that key to unlock a second MacGuffin, a magic horn, and then bring horn and princess safely back to Shadizar. Conan agrees, and Taramis sends with them her guard captain, Bombaata (Wilt Chamberlain), a towering, seven feet tall warrior.

On the way, Conan recruits additional help by saving the wizard Akiro (Mako, reprising his role from the first film) from a band of cannibals and then liberating the fierce raider Zula (Grace Jones) from her merchant captors. Conan uses both brains and brawn to defeat the wizard Thoth-Amon in his island ice castle; he gains the key and then uses it, after a tense dungeon crawl through the trap-filled Temple of the Dreaming God, to obtain the horn. When Bombaata takes horn and princess and leaves Conan and the others behind to face a swarm of furious cultists, Conan realizes he's been duped and sets out to Shadizar to save the princess before she can be sacrificed to the abyssal god Dagoth.

With a solid story by Roy Thomas and Gerry Conway, the *Conan* comic book writers, and direction by veteran Richard Fleischer (*The Vikings*), this is a very satisfying sword-and-sorcery romp. Fleischer is a better action director than *Barbarian*'s John Milius, and he forgoes the first film's ponderous self-importance in favor of a brisker pace. Schwarzenegger's English is more fluent this time around, and he's backed by a solid cast, the standout being Grace Jones as Zula, who brings a thrilling feral edge and visual flair. The swordplay is as good as in the first film and there's more of it, plus Conan punches a camel *and* a horse. The set designs by concept artist William Stout are outstanding, and if you liked Basil Poledouris's distinctive soundtrack in *Barbarian*, you'll enjoy more of it here.

Controversially, the sex and violence of the first film were toned down in the second to secure a PG rating, under the assumption the move would increase *Destroyer*'s audience. Many fans of the first movie considered this a sellout, and in fact it seems to have hurt ticket sales more than it helped. But that doesn't keep *Conan the Destroyer* from being first-rate entertainment—and if you want more nudity and gore, the *Deathstalker* films are always there.

THE CONQUEROR

Rating: ★☆☆☆☆ • *Origin:* USA, 1956 • *Director:* Dick Powell • *Source:* Universal DVD

This is the legendarily awful Howard Hughes–produced turkey in which Big John Wayne is incredibly miscast as Big Genghis Khan. Miscast he may have been, but Wayne got the part because he wanted it, and you can see why: the role fulfills the male barbarian fantasy in which manly men kneel to you because you're the toughest, the loudest, and the most brutal, and desirable women love you because they just can't help themselves although you beat and sexually assault them. Also . . . Mongol mustaches.

Nothing in this noisy shambles of a movie makes a lick of sense; it's just nonstop riding and raiding and abductions and surprise attacks, surprises that always work because everyone on every side is a dope who will fall for anything. Genghis's "blood brother" Jemuga (Pedro Armendáriz), supposedly a brilliant tactician, gets captured no less than three times by his enemies, which are everybody. The Mongols hate the Merkits, the Merkits hate the Tartars, the Tartars hate the Mongols, and everyone hates the Han Chinese. (Accurate.) Plots and counterplots send everybody blundering about the desert at a full gallop while waving their swords.

But what you'll want to know is, Is this travesty just bad-bad, or is it hilariously funny-bad? Given Wayne's bombastic delivery of his totally cringeworthy dialogue, it definitely skews toward the latter. Hearing Wayne say stuff like "Dance, Tartar woman—dance for Temujin!" or (to Agnes Moorehead) "You didn't suckle me to be slain by Tartars, my mother!" is just

The Conqueror
Reynold Brown / Wikimedia Commons

wonderful, and there's so, so much of it because he never shuts up. "She's a woman, very much a woman. Could her perfidy be less than that of other women?" Come on, you can't ask for better entertainment than that.

Except for one lone Asian actor, cast as a treacherous Chinese shaman, every speaking role is filled by a Hollywood Caucasian, and few of them share Wayne's enthusiasm for their lines, most of the time just looking embarrassed (except for Robert Conrad and Lee van Cleef, who are shameless, as you would expect). Poor Susan Hayward as "the Tartar woman," one of the foremost leading ladies of her day, just pouts angrily in every scene, except when she has to pretend helpless passion for Wayne. You can only pity her.

Tragically, the film was shot downwind of a 1950s atomic testing range, and by the 1970s, the director and nearly all the leads had died of cancer, which also afflicted the rest of the cast and crew at three times the normal statistical rate. A sad coda for what is otherwise a sort of trash masterpiece, but to quote Big Genghis himself, "What venture is without hazard?"

THE CONQUEROR OF THE ORIENT

Rating: ★☆☆☆☆ • *Origin:* Italy, 1960 • *Director:* Tanio Boccia • *Source:* Mill Creek DVD

Standard *Arabian Nights* adventure fantasy that follows the usual formula of a tyrannical sultan and a true heir, Nadir (Rik Battaglia), who must prove himself against a series of challenges to win the throne. Production values are low, the acting is third-rate, and there are no surprises; you can find a better way to spend the evening.

THE CORSICAN BROTHERS

Rating: ★★★☆☆ • *Origin:* USA, 1941 • *Director:* Gregory Ratoff •
Source: Hen's Tooth Video DVD

Ever since his success with *The Count of Monte Cristo* in 1934, independent producer Edward Small made about one swashbuckler movie per year until World War II broke his streak. For his 1941 entry, Small turned once more to a story by Alexandre Dumas. Louis Hayward, Small's usual star, was slated for the lead, but he took a part in a prestige drama instead, so the dual role of the Corsican twins instead went to Douglas Fairbanks Jr., who delivered one of his best performances.

The plot is vintage Dumas: In old Corsica, two aristocratic families, the noble Franchis and the cruel and coarse Colonnas, have been feuding for generations. The Franchi family gather at their estate to await the birth of an heir to the count, an event the Colonnas take advantage of to attack and massacre the Franchis. Countess Franchi gives birth to conjoined, or Siamese, twins, but in the chaos of the Colonna attack they are spirited away by the family physician, Doctor Paoli, who successfully separates the twins and names them Lucien and Mario. Baron Colonna is aware that Countess Franchi gave birth to twins, so to put him off the trail, Mario is sent with wealthy family friends to be raised in Paris, while Lucien remains in Corsica, where he is raised by a Franchi retainer among a gang of bandits. But the twins share a psychic connection, and what one feels, the other feels as well. When the brothers come of age, Dr. Paoli summons Mario back to Corsica to meet Lucien and to inform them

CHARMING AND DANGEROUS: DOUGLAS FAIRBANKS JR.

Douglas Fairbanks Jr. was a fine actor with a considerable range, but he never got out of the shadow of his more famous father. Douglas Fairbanks Sr., after all, was more than a fine actor; he was a force of nature who single-handedly established the conventions of the cinematic swashbuckler in a series of grand, albeit silent epics. Doug Jr.'s parents divorced when he was young, and against his father's wishes he was raised in the movies, starting in the silent era as a child star with his own studio contract. He played mostly romantic and dramatic roles as he matured, but inevitably he made some swashbucklers of his own, showing that he had, unsurprisingly perhaps, a natural talent for them.

of their true parentage. The twins embrace and swear vengeance upon Count Colonna. "No one knows there are two of us," says Lucien. "It'll be our sharpest weapon!"

All this, which sets up the story, is just the first half hour. Now comes the fun: the conflict with the Colonnas, led by Akim Tamiroff as the baron, and the conflict between the brothers, who fall in love with the same woman, Lady Isabelle Gravini (Ruth Warrick)—who is also, of course, pursued by Baron Colonna. Besides genre-convention bingo (Secret passage! Villain's jealous mistress! Fop impersonation! Death-feigning potion!), the main pleasures here are in the performances of the two male leads. Fairbanks really nails his double role as the noble Mario and the tormented and jealous Lucien, and in both parts he gets in some fine athletic swashbuckling reminiscent of his father. And Tamiroff's Baron Colonna is a delightful mix of wily cunning, brutal bullying, and vain preening. Menacing one moment, laughing the next, he's a complete hoot. When the Franchi brothers repeatedly raid his holdings, he's outraged: "First my cousins, then my nephews," he cries, "and then my sheep!"

But in the end, it all works out with Doctor Paoli's help—because science! The final duel between Franchi and Colonna was Doug Fairbanks Jr.'s favorite sword fight of his entire career.

THE COUNT OF MONTE CRISTO (1913)

Rating: ★★☆☆☆ • *Origin:* USA, 1913 • *Directors:* Golden/Porter •
Source: Grapevine Video DVD

Alexandre Dumas's *The Count of Monte Cristo* (1844) is a long and complicated novel, one of our greatest revenge fantasies, and adapting it from a truncated theatrical play version (as this was), trying to tell its story in just over an hour, necessitates stripping it down to its barest skeleton. James O'Neill, who plays Edmond Dantès/Monte Cristo, had been famous for his stage production of the novel, and that's what he brought to the screen in this early silent version. The story zips right along (it has to), a lot of the interior scenes were moved to appropriate external locations, and it ends with some brief but satisfying swordplay. Still, as *Monte Cristo* adaptations go, this one's pretty perfunctory.

CHARGED WITH FIVE COUNTS OF MONTE CRISTO

Alexandre Dumas's most popular and enduring novels are *The Three Musketeers* and *The Count of Monte Cristo*, and one of the most remarkable things about them is that he wrote them at the same time. They were published in simultaneous serial form in two different Parisian periodicals, with *T3M* finishing first because *Monte Cristo* was the longer novel. Though written together, the two are very different: *T3M* is an action-packed tale of youthful heroism, practically the definition of a swashbuckler, while *Monte Cristo* is a slow-burn revenge fantasy, a swashbuckler more in its themes than its action. It still holds up today; if you haven't read it, or haven't read it lately, I recommend the Penguin Books translation by the late Robin Buss. (I know a little bit about translating Dumas, so take my word for it.)

THE COUNT OF MONTE CRISTO (1934)

Rating: ★★★★☆ • *Origin:* USA, 1934 • *Director:* Rowland V. Lee •
Source: Hen's Tooth Video DVD

After English stage actor Robert Donat had garnered acclaim playing opposite Charles Laughton in Alexander Korda's *The Private Life of Henry VIII*, he was brought over to Hollywood to star in the first talkie version of *Monte Cristo*. This is the first of director Rowland Lee's spate of swashbucklers, and he does an able job, supported by a stirring soundtrack from Alfred Newman. The story is necessarily streamlined from that of the lengthy novel, its European politics simplified for an American audience and the plot pared down to its essence of triple revenge. It's pretty tight, and there's a desperate urgency to Edmond Dantès's escape from the Château d'If that's missing from the earlier silent versions.

In due course Dantès finds the buried Spada treasure and utters Dumas's immortal line, "The world is mine!" The film's final hour is the clockwork accomplishment of his vengeance. Transformed by the Spada wealth and the imprisoned Abbé Faria's wisdom, Donat looks tremendous as the Count of Monte Cristo, silver-haired and rigid with purpose. Elissa Landi plays Dantès's old love, Mercédès, and when she first meets the count after 20 years of believing Dantès dead, the scene is genuinely affecting. After that the count's shocking revelations follow one upon the other, and it all ends as it should, with flashing swords and pistols at dawn. This was the definitive *Count of Monte Cristo* for a generation.

After this film's success, Donat was offered the lead in *Captain Blood*, but he didn't care for Hollywood and went back to Britain to work with Alfred Hitchcock. (And the part of Peter Blood, of course, went to Errol Flynn.) *Monte Cristo*'s producer, Edward Small, went on to make eight more swashbucklers over the next 15 years, mostly starring Louis Hayward, including two *Monte Cristo* sequels.

THE COUNT OF MONTE CRISTO (1956, SERIES)

Rating: ★★☆☆☆ (mostly) • *Origin:* UK, 1956 • *Directors:* Sidney Salkow et al. •
Source: Network DVDs

Though the novel was wildly successful, despite many requests Alexandre Dumas never wrote a sequel to *The Count of Monte Cristo*. That didn't stop other hands from writing Monte Cristo sequels after Dumas's death, signing his name to pastiches with titles such as *The Son of Monte Cristo* and *The Countess of Monte Cristo*. Dumas never wrote a sequel because he'd already written a superb fantasy of injustice fantastically avenged, and there was nothing more to say about the count once his vengeance was achieved. The sequel pastiches ignored that point, and this early British TV series missed it entirely. This successful and fabulously wealthy Count of Monte Cristo supports the very French establishment whose corruption he exposed in the novel and now has nothing better to do for 39 episodes than to help folk in trouble as a sort of do-gooder-without-portfolio. This is mostly just disappointing, stories of mundane intrigue with clichéd plots and obvious villains who always succumb to the count in quick smallsword duels just before the credits roll.

Monte Cristo is played by George Dolenz (and if that last name sounds familiar, it might be because George was the father of Mickey Dolenz of the Monkees). Dolenz is handsome and competent enough, but mostly humorless and lacking the savage edge of the character in the novel. Fortunately, the funny stuff is ably handled by his aide Jacopo, played by Nick Cravat—you remember Burt Lancaster's mute acrobatic sidekick in *The Crimson Pirate* and *The Flame and the Arrow*, right? That was Cravat, who here plays Monte Cristo's mute and acrobatic sidekick. Even without speaking, the charismatic Cravat outacts everyone else in the cast, including the guest stars, and is a bright spot in even the weak episodes, which is most of them. He's supported by another sidekick, a nonentity named Rico who's only there to speak with the count because Jacopo can't—though Jacopo makes up for it with amazing gymnastic fisticuffs.

For some reason, the first few episodes were shot in Hollywood before production moved to England for the bulk of the season, returning to Hollywood for episodes 29 through 39. Those jumps didn't help the series' quality, which was wildly inconsistent. So was the cast: after production returned to California Rico disappeared, only to be replaced on a rotating basis by two clones named Carlo and Mario, while the rest of the cast switched to third-rate Hollywood actors with flat American accents. Pretty shoddy.

However, one result of this inconsistency is that here and there you can find excellent episodes that stand head and shoulders above the rest. Three of the best installments are deliberate callbacks to the novel that feature characters from Dumas and plots that center on Monte Cristo–style revenge: episode 8, "Bordeaux," in which Mercédès returns to torment the count's heart; episode 19, "Sicily," which delves into Edmond Dantès's time as a fugitive and features the always excellent Alexander Gauge as the villain; and episode 27, "Point, Counterpoint," in which Monte Cristo is targeted by the daughter of the late Baron Danglars. Three other episodes from the late Hollywood run are worth tracking down: 31, "The Pen and the Sword," 33, "The Affair of the Three Napoleons," and 37, "The Duel," helmed by American feature director Sidney Salkow. If you're a Monte Cristo fan, look for these 6 episodes streaming on the web and let the other 33 go. I watched them so you don't have to; don't let my sacrifice be in vain.

THE COUNT OF MONTE CRISTO (1964, MINISERIES)

Rating: ★★★★☆ • *Origin:* UK, 1964 • *Director:* Peter Hammond •
Source: Simply Media DVDs

Alexandre Dumas's great novel *The Count of Monte Cristo* is many things: a thrilling adventure story, a romantic melodrama, a study in criminal psychology before that discipline existed, and an extended revenge fantasy, possibly the finest ever written. Screen adaptations, for obvious reasons, tend to focus on the romance and the thrilling adventure, boiling Dumas's long novel down to its most memorable high points. In contrast, this adaptation focuses almost exclusively on the psychological drama, and as a 12-part miniseries almost six hours in length, it's the only version of *Monte Cristo* long enough to get most of the novel onto the screen. And though what it leaves out of that classic swashbuckler novel is all of its swashbuckling, it's so riveting that not a single one of its 300 minutes is wasted.

This was a prestige drama for the BBC, and it has all the hallmarks of one of their classic adaptations: a top-notch script, brilliant stage-trained actors, and a tragically low budget that means grainy black-and-white video shot in close-up so you won't notice that the sets are made of plywood and burlap. But the script is so tight, the dialogue so taut, the acting so sharp, that you'll be sucked in despite the bargain basement settings. Alan Badel as Edmond Dantès, the eponymous count, is fantastic in the role, mostly underplaying his part so that when he suddenly shows his passion for revenge with a tigerish laugh, it's genuinely thrilling. There are no weak links in the cast; standouts include Michael Gough as the villainous de Villefort, Natasha Perry as Edmond's estranged love Mercédès, John Wentworth as the Abbé Faria, and Anthony Newlands as the shipowner Monsieur Morel. And despite what I said about the crappy sets, they found a genuinely horrific old stone prison for the scenes in the Château d'If, a shooting location it would be hard to top. Brrr.

The middle episodes are the best; as the series approaches its end, it gets a trifle self-important, as if to remind you that this is the BBC and you're watching a classic of world literature and not a mere melodrama. Really, by the rules of the *Cinema of Swords*, I shouldn't include this adaptation of *Monte Cristo* because it's all acting and no action, but I deem it relevant as a comparison to other versions—and besides, they're my rules, so I can break them if I want to, nyah. Solely from the standpoint of story, this is the best screen adaptation of *The Count of Monte Cristo* available. Just remember: no swashbuckling.

THE COUNT OF MONTE-CRISTO (1975)

Rating: ★★★☆☆ • *Origin:* UK, 1975 • *Director:* David Greene • *Source:* Network DVD

In 1956, British television network ITV had a one-season *Count of Monte Cristo* series, and it returned to the source almost 20 years later for this TV movie, which fortunately hews much more closely to Alexandre Dumas's novel. It's also fortunate in its cast: Richard Chamberlain as Edmond Dantès/Monte-Cristo (inexplicably hyphenated), with Tony Curtis, Donald Pleasence, and Louis Jourdan as the villains Mondego, Danglars, and de Villefort. Rounding out the cast is the excellent Trevor Howard as the abbé Faria, the wise old holy man Dantès meets during his long incarceration in the Château d'If, and the film benefits from the amount of time devoted to the relationship between the two prisoners. unfortunately, as a result the second half of the movie, Monte-Cristo's Parisian revenge on his four enemies, is rushed and

The Count of Monte-Cristo (1975) Author's Collection

in parts almost incoherent, as characters are quickly introduced and then suddenly disposed of two scenes later.

Due to its limited budget, in common with most TV movies of its era, the production values are rather low: the sound recording is atrocious, and though the costumes have some striking designs, particularly Monte-Cristo's outfits, the rest look cheap and off-the-rack new, as if they just came out of the prop shop. However, the exterior locations are excellent, and the interiors, shot at Rome's Cinecittà Studios, are fine. And though Dumas forgot to include a spirited final duel between Dantès and Mondego, screenwriter Sidney Carroll makes up for the lapse, with Chamberlain and Curtis going at each other with gusto. Sa-ha!

THE COURT JESTER

Rating: ★★★★★ (Essential) • *Origin:* USA, 1955 • *Directors:* Norman Panama and Melvin Frank • *Source:* Paramount DVD

There were swashbuckler parodies before this film, and others followed later, but *The Court Jester* is the one and only crown jewel, the chalice from the palace, the brew that is true.

The film was produced, written, and directed by the team of Melvin Frank and Norman Panama, Hollywood journeymen who'd first made their mark with Hope and Crosby comedies in the 1940s. By the mid-1950s they'd been working together for years and knew exactly what they were doing. Star Danny Kaye had made an impression with 1947's *The Secret Life of Walter Mitty* but followed that with a series of mediocre comedies that he felt didn't show off his real strengths. Panama and Frank agreed and formed a production company with Kaye to create for him a vehicle worthy of his array of talents.

The big studios had been churning out loud and hokey knights-in-shining-armor movies since about 1950, most of them bloated groaners ripe for parody. Panama, Frank, and Kaye decided some medieval mockery was in order, especially of the many knight-in-training

The Court Jester Wikimedia Commons

films, but then had the inspired idea of borrowing most of their tropes from an actual good movie, the beloved 1938 *Adventures of Robin Hood* with Errol Flynn. As icing on the cake, they even hired Flynn's antagonist, Basil Rathbone, to play their leading villain.

And then they wrote a script that is a work of goddamned genius, an action musical that never lets up except to pause for the next comic song, with stock characters spouting perfect parodies of Hollywood medieval bombast, interspersed with tongue-twisting, fast-talk vaudeville routines and punctuated by hilarious physical comedy, driving an intricate plot that has 17 moving parts that somehow all interweave and mesh perfectly.

And at the center of this controlled chaos, the focus and fulcrum of almost every scene, is Danny Kaye's Giacomo the Jester, mugging, swaggering, cowering, singing, japing, pratfalling, and blustering in the performance of a lifetime, somehow simultaneously evoking Laurel and Hardy, Abbott and Costello, Charlie Chaplin, and Douglas Fairbanks Sr. (Whew!)

Moreover, as if Kaye and Rathbone aren't enough, we also get the spirited and gorgeous (and slyly funny) Glynis Johns as Kaye's romantic and comedic foil, a glowing Angela Lansbury as a spoiled and self-centered princess, and the underrated Mildred Natwick nailing the whammy as the princess's sorcerous servant. Plus there's a Robin Hood–style masked outlaw, a secret passage, a baby in a basket, a troupe of midget acrobats, and a vessel with a pestle. If you haven't seen it, you must. Get it? (Got it!) Good.

CRIMSON BAT 1: THE BLIND SWORDSWOMAN

Rating: ★★★☆☆ • *Origin:* Japan, 1969 • *Director:* Sadatsugu Matsuda •
Source: YouTube streaming video

The popular Zatoichi *chambara* series about a blind swordsman ran for 19 entries from Daiei Studios from 1962 to 1968—and when that run came to its end, smaller Shochiku Studios quickly jumped in to fill the gap with a four-film series about a blind swords*woman*. The parallels between the two series are many and obvious: like Zatoichi, female counterpart Oichi wanders from place to place helping the helpless and combating the cruel and criminal, fighting with a straight blade hidden inside a cane and held in a reverse grip for close-quarters action, and though Oichi finds some solutions for the problems of others, she never finds satisfaction or a home for herself. Though imitative, the Crimson Bat series stands on its own, mainly due to the compelling performances of its lead, Yoko Matsuyama as Oichi.

Oichi's origin story is told in *Crimson Bat: The Blind Swordswoman*, a tale of pathos and greed among the criminal classes and their hired ronin enforcers. The repeated theme here is abandonment: in a terrible thunderstorm, seven-year-old Oichi is ditched by her mother as the woman elopes with a lover who doesn't want a child around. Oichi is seeking desperately for her mother in the storm when lightning strikes a nearby tree and she is blinded.

Flash forward: Oichi, now an adult and blind as a . . . well, you know, draws her cane sword to defend an old man who's fleeing from a gang of angry peasants. The old man, Nihei, turns out to be a fugitive yakuza with a price on his head, a thief who broke out of jail to try to find his daughter Oyone, whom he'd abandoned during his life of crime. But Oichi helps Nihei because he resembles. . . .

Yasuke, another former thief. Flash back to Oichi's childhood when Yasuke, whom Oichi calls "Grandpa," takes in the blind girl and raises her. They live in seclusion, because Yasuke is hiding from the vengeance of a third thief, Denzo, the worst of the lot and a master swordsman into the bargain. Eventually Denzo and his three goons catch up with Yasuke, murder him, and are preparing to slay Oichi when a wandering ronin, Ukita (Isamu Nagato of *Three Outlaw Samurai*), comes to her rescue, killing the attacking goons as Denzo escapes.

Impressed by Oichi's wild but untrained attempts to defend herself, Ukita takes Yasuke's place, not as father figure but as teacher, instructing her in fencing and training her to "see with her mind's eye." When Oichi has learned all that Ukita can teach her, he gives her a crimson cane with Yasuke's old blade mounted inside it—and then abandons her, sneaking off when Oichi says she wants to stay with him forever.

Oichi, bitter and alone, vows to track down Denzo and avenge Yasuke's death, but instead she is drawn into the tragedy of Nihei and his daughter Oyone, who's been sold to the yakuza as a prostitute to pay a family debt. And running the brothel is none other than Oichi's long-lost . . . well, that's enough spoilers. Suffice it to say that all the threads of the story tie back together long enough for Oichi to sever the knot with her flashing red cane sword.

CRIMSON BAT 2: TRAPPED, THE CRIMSON BAT

Rating: ★★☆☆☆ • *Origin:* Japan, 1969 • *Director:* Sadatsugu Matsuda •
Source: YouTube streaming video

Sadly, this isn't as good as the first *Crimson Bat* film. This entry basically tells us that due to her inherent female weakness, Blind Oichi is unable to find a way out of the emotional trap she's been caught in by a gang of predatory yakuza. That won't do.

Trapped starts out as a crime story that morphs into a romantic melodrama. Oichi (Yoko Matsuyama) is working as a bounty hunter and traveling with a young woman named Okyo, who idolizes her and says she's an orphan. However, she's actually the runaway daughter of a businessman who's hired a yakuza boss, Bunzo, to retrieve her. Bunzo's agent in the matter is Oen, a female gambler who wields a bullwhip made from the hair of disappointed women, which is admittedly awesome. When Oichi learns she's been lied to by Okyo, she's persuaded to give the girl up, but she's ashamed about it—and so are we, because there should have been another solution.

However, before the Okyo matter is sorted out, Oichi has killed several of Oen's goons, and Oen vows revenge. Oichi defeats her in a straight fight, but then Oen pulls some venomous snakes out of her kimono(!) and flings them at Oichi. The blind swordswoman is bitten and staggers away, poisoned and hallucinating.

Oichi is saved and nursed back to health by a lonely fisher named Mosaku, who falls in love with her. Oichi thinks she might be happy with Mosaku, but their love just makes her vulnerable to further manipulation by the yakuza. The story up to this point has been muddled and overcomplicated, but here it goes quite off the rails: Oichi couldn't save Okyo and now she can't save herself, because while the writers made her a badass sword fighter, they forgot to make her *smart*. In the end she gives up her hopes for happiness with Mosaku, picks her sword cane back up, and sets out to slaughter Boss Bunzo and his entire gang, Oen included. Director Matsuda makes a bold attempt to save the picture by turning the final mass combat into an artsy dance theater of death, but the fight direction isn't strong enough to pull it off, and a descent into bloody nihilism just isn't what we want from the Crimson Bat. Too bad.

CRIMSON BAT 3: WATCH OUT, CRIMSON BAT!

Rating: ★★★★☆ • *Origin:* Japan, 1969 • *Director:* Hirokazu Ichimura • *Source:* YouTube streaming video

A fine entry, this is the best of the series, thanks mainly to a script that restores Blind Oichi's agency and control so she's not a mere pawn to "feminine emotions," as in the previous film. The story is engaging but complex, featuring a pair of spunky teenaged orphans, a brutal yakuza boss, a corrupt and tyrannical clan overlord, forbidden love, and a ronin seeking redemption—in other words, this is a movie in prime Zatoichi territory, and all the better because of it.

A mounted man is shot in an ambush and then dragged down a mountainside by his runaway horse. Blind Oichi (Yoko Matsuyama), wandering as usual, frees the wounded man from the tangled reins with a slash of her cane sword, and he gasps out a dying request: that she take a scroll he gives her to Instructor Murobuse, in Naguno-Ga-Hara!

Oichi is immediately pursued by the dead man's assassins, clan warriors disguised as priests, but after she kills four of them in as many moves, the others back off and become more circumspect. They are soon joined by other pursuers: a masterless samurai named Gennosuke (Goro Ibuki) who wants the scroll for reasons of his own, a yakuza gang working for the mysterious clan, and Oichi's new friends, the plucky teenage orphans Hanji and Omiyo, who decide to help her retrieve the scroll when it goes missing after a fight. Gradually secrets are revealed: the Otawara clan is experimenting with Dutch gunpowder, trying to make powerful explosives and killing and injuring innocent villagers in the process, including the orphans' parents; the scroll has the formula the clan needs; and instructor Murobuse, a ballistics expert, is the one who knows how to use it. Gennosuke, who is Murobuse's former student, helps Oichi recover after she injures her sword arm in a fight with the yakuza, and the two become friends—and maybe, Oichi seems to hope, even more than that. But Gennosuke loves Murobuse's daughter Kotoe (Kyoko Inoue), so Oichi resigns herself to disappointment, until Sakon (Asahi Kurizuka), another attractive samurai sellsword, crosses her path. But wait: isn't he working for the Otawara clan?

This story succeeds because all these characters are given enough screen time to develop and reveal themselves, so we care what happens to them when the crunch comes in the final act. Given decent material to work with, Matsuyama as Oichi delivers a nuanced and even charming performance. The combat sequences are stylish and well directed, and the climactic fight is taut and credible, as Oichi is joined in taking down the Otawara by two other impressive sword masters. If you have time to watch only one *Crimson Bat* movie, this is the one to see.

CRIMSON BAT 4: OICHI, WANTED DEAD OR ALIVE

Rating: ★★★☆☆ • *Origin:* Japan, 1970 • *Director:* Hirokazu Ichimura •
Source: YouTube streaming video

This is the last film in the series before it went to a single season on Japanese television. It features yet another shift in tone for the character of Blind Oichi (Yoko Matsuyama), as the former bounty hunter gives up that shady career and goes full Robin Hood, dedicating herself to helping oppressed and bullied commoners against yakuza thugs and corrupt officials. This does the character no favors; it simplifies her means and motives and makes her, on the whole, less interesting.

The story opens on the wedding of a despotic magistrate and a reluctant bride, whose former fiancé has been arrested on false charges so the magistrate can steal his beloved. The ceremony is interrupted by Oichi, determined that this injustice shall be thwarted; she takes the magistrate hostage, and the groom and bride are reunited as Oichi covers their escape in a wild melee with the magistrate's constables. Oichi gets away, but a price of 100 ryo is placed on her head, and a trio of dangerous bounty hunters set out to collect it.

Oichi hides out in the fishing village of Fukuda, which has its own drama going on: the shogunate plans to build a new port facility in place of the fishers' homes, but the villagers have been offered only a paltry compensation and are resisting being moved, unaware that the corrupt magistrate and his yakuza boss accomplice are pocketing 90 percent of the government's compensation fee. When the yakuza thugs start abusing the villagers, trying to drive them out of their homes, Oichi can't stop herself from fighting back and defending them.

Meanwhile, those bounty hunters are hot on her trail—but one of them, the handsome Sankuro (Yuki Meguro), is a Fukuda native who hasn't gone completely bad and who is touched by Oichi's defense of the villagers . . . and maybe by more than that. Will Oichi be able to expose the machinations of the corrupt magistrate, save the villagers, and incidentally redeem Sankuro from his life in the criminal half-world? I bet you know the answer.

Though not quite up to the standards of the third film, this is a decent enough entry in the series. The villains are stock, but there are interesting characters among both the village fisher-folk and the bounty hunters, as well as variations on the usual duels, as Oichi must face a karate expert and a chain-and-sickle fighter. However, the combats are not as stylishly staged as in *Watch Out!*, and the final massacre of the yakuza is too long and too unbelievable. Moreover, the flattening of Oichi's character into a simple do-gooder robs her of any development, and in the end she goes off into the sunset the same person she was at the beginning. A missed opportunity.

THE CRIMSON BLADE (OR THE SCARLET BLADE)

Rating: ★★★☆☆ • *Origin:* UK, 1963 • *Director:* John Gilling • *Source:* StudioCanal DVD

This Hammer Films swashbuckler is set in 1648 during the English Civil War. Oliver Cromwell's Roundheads pursue the fugitive King Charles I to the home of Lord Beverly; Colonel Judd (Lionel Jeffries) and his aide Captain Sylvester (Oliver Reed) capture the king and execute Lord Beverly, but his son Edward Beverly (Jack Hedley) vows revenge. Disguised under the name of the Scarlet Blade, he organizes resistance and vows to liberate the king. Colonel Judd's daughter Claire (June Thorburn) is still fiercely loyal to the Royalist cause, but

Captain Sylvester desires her and is willing to betray Colonel Judd to get her—until he finds that Claire has fallen for the Scarlet Blade.

Though Jeffries as Colonel Judd gets top billing and Edward as the Scarlet Blade is the titular hero, this movie belongs to Oliver Reed as Captain Sylvester. Proud, brutal, passionate but utterly amoral, his portrayal is this film's centerpiece; he gets more screen time than anyone else and deserves it. June Thorburn as Claire Judd, fierce and idealistic, is almost his match but doesn't quite have the star power of the lambent and glowering Reed.

The story, written by director John Gilling, is the usual series of captures, escapes, betrayals, and rescues, with plenty of tense and well-directed fights and flights. There are desperate pursuits, impersonations, a secret passage, a torture dungeon, and two near hangings, all with that lurid Hammer touch, before the love triangle between Sylvester, Claire, and the Scarlet Blade sorts itself out and everyone gets what they deserve. Not bad at all.

THE CRIMSON PIRATE

Rating: ★★★★★ (Essential) • *Origin:* USA, 1952 • *Director:* Richard Siodmak •
Source: Amazon streaming video

This isn't the first swashbuckler farce, but it's the first great one, a hoot and a half from beginning to end. Burt Lancaster immediately sets the tone by breaking the fourth wall: high atop a ship's mast, he does an athletic aerial stunt, grins at the audience, and says, "Believe only what you see!" Then he does the stunt backward by reversing the film and says, "Well, believe *half* of what you see!" Then it's "Sail ho!" and we're off to the first ship battle.

This film is set in the revolutionary 1790s, so we're in Scarlet Pimpernel territory, and the original script by the blacklisted Waldo Salt is said to have been a serious anti-aristocratic call to arms. According to the memoirs of Christopher Lee, who has a small part here as a king's officer, director Richard Siodmak quickly rewrote it into a cartoony self-parody, full of action but high spirited and frequently hilarious. The chase scenes often bring to mind another Warner Bros. franchise, the Looney Tunes of Chuck Jones and Friz Freleng—and that's meant as a compliment. It even has a fine antic soundtrack by William Alwyn with a catchy main theme that evokes both sailing and circuses.

The setting is a bit fantastical: the pirate protagonists are opposed by the troops and navy of "the king," an unnamed imperial monarch who combines elements of England and Spain. However, the exterior scenes, which are most of them, were shot on the Italian island of Ischia, with its medieval town, harbor, and port, and that grounds the production in reality. And it needs that grounding, because Lancaster and sidekick Nick Cravat, his old circus partner, are in full-on bounding-acrobat mode, knocking down rows of soldiers with barrels, driving Da Vinci-inspired steampunk tank-wagons, and dive-bombing the king's troops from a hot-air balloon. There's a solid liberate-the-people revolution 'n' romance plot to support all these shenanigans, with good performances from Eva Bartok as the spunky liberation leader's daughter, Leslie Bradley as the ruthless aristo villain, and, best of all, Torin Thatcher as Humble Bellows, the pirate crew's scurvy but philosophical first mate. But really this is the Flying Burt and Nick Show—Lancaster even gets to act a bit as his Captain Vallo gradually falls in love with the liberator's daughter and grows some newly uncomfortable scruples. The best scene may be when Nick and Burt, the latter impersonating the villain, crash the island governor's fancy ball wearing outrageously foppish finery, Burt grinning like the Cheshire cat, and Nick eyeing all the ladies' jewelry through a gilded quizzing glass. Or the best scene might be another—it's just so hard to choose!

CROSSED SWORDS (OR *THE PRINCE AND THE PAUPER* [1977])

Rating: ★★★☆☆ • *Origin:* UK, 1977 • *Director:* Richard Fleischer • *Source:* StudioCanal DVD

Producers Alexander and Ilya Salkind had had a substantial success with *The Three Musketeers* (1973) and *The Four Musketeers* (1974) and decided to try another premium adaptation of a classic swashbuckler with an all-star cast, this time drawing upon Mark Twain's 1881 novel *The Prince and the Pauper*. It was a good plan, but a couple of things went wrong.

First, the resulting film has a problem with tone. Inspired by both Charles Dickens and Alexandre Dumas, Twain's novel is a light boys' adventure that nonetheless addresses issues of social inequality in Olde England. The movie retains, or even emphasizes, the novel's critique of society but drops nearly all of its humor and whimsy, and the result is pretty cheerless. Scripter George MacDonald Fraser was going for a corrective to the romantic view of the Tudor era as seen in films like *The Sword and the Rose* (1953), but he went too far into the grim and gritty for the material. It doesn't help that the prince and his pauper double have three father figures in John Canty (Ernest Borgnine), King Henry VIII (Charlton Heston), and soldier of fortune Miles Hendon (Oliver Reed), all of whom are perpetually shouty and angry.

However, this is a lavish production, well directed by Richard Fleischer, with a cracking cast, so the tone issue isn't fatal. The nearly lethal blow is the casting of former child actor Mark Lester (*Oliver!,* 1968) as the near-twins Prince Edward and Tom Canty. Lester is terrible, just embarrassingly bad, and his performance got such awful reviews that he retired from acting at age 18 and never made another picture. He's in nearly every scene in the movie, and he stinks.

But, but, but . . . Oliver Reed and Charlton Heston and Ernest Borgnine! Not to mention Rex Harrison, Raquel Welch, and George C. frickin' Scott. Yes, they do make a difference—Rex Harrison's cheerful snarkiness nearly saves the movie by itself. There are some fine rough-house melees, mainly because Oliver Reed still hadn't learned how to fence, and Scott's scene as the Ruffler, a sardonic beggar king, is a total hoot. Welch gets short shrift, alas, showing up late in the movie and given only a handful of lines, though she does fine with what she's granted. And despite the tonal issues, Fraser's script has plenty of sharp dialogue for these top-notch actors to snap at each other with. Plus the costumes are excellent, and the shooting locations, Penshurst Palace in England and city sites in Budapest, are lovely.

But Mark Lester . . . no. Just no.

Crossed Swords Author's Collection

THE CRUSADES

Rating: ★★☆☆☆ • *Origin:* USA, 1935 • *Director:* Cecil B. DeMille • *Source:* Universal DVD

If you know only two names associated with the Crusades, they'll likely be King Richard of England, known as the Lionheart, and Saladin of the Saracens, who in 1187 completed an Islamic conquest of the Holy Land. So when Cecil B. DeMille, who made big, crowd-pleasing movies, set out to make his film about the Crusades, he knew it had to be about those two characters. To his credit, he hired the great historical fiction author Harold Lamb as writer and researcher—but DeMille, who always played fast and loose with historical fact, used only the parts of Lamb's research that suited his melodramatic story.

After Jerusalem falls to the Muslims, the Holy Hermit (played by C. Aubrey Smith and his whiskers) rouses the kings of Christendom to join in a Third Crusade to liberate the city. All the monarchs of Christian Europe, including Philip of France, sign up for the picnic. Philip's sister, Princess Alice, is promised by treaty to marry King Richard, who is played by DeMille's go-to leading man, Henry Wilcoxon, as a brave but empty-headed, manly lout who cares little for politics, women, or religion but loves a good fight. To avoid wedding the surly Alice, Richard joins in with the Crusade and marches his army across France. However, by the time he reaches the Mediterranean coast, his men are starving, and he ends up marrying someone anyhow to get his troops enough food and fodder to get them to Palestine. His new wife is Princess Berengaria (Loretta Young), daughter of the King of Navarre, a gentle and well-meaning soul ill-matched to King Dude-bro. Richard humiliates her, but she puts up with everything he does—"for the Crusade."

This was a tremendously expensive film to make, and you can see every dollar on the screen: it looks great. Lamb did his research well, and this is the finest depiction of the pageantry and slaughter of the Crusades that the first half of the twentieth century has to offer. The battle scenes are spectacular and convincingly horrific. Unfortunately, the story in between the battles is sheer tripe, a lot of tiresome religious chest-beating, along with a ridiculous romantic soap opera that contrives a love triangle between Richard, Berengaria, and . . . Saladin. (Yes!) Surprisingly, Ian Keith's portrayal of Saladin is the picture's best performance, restrained yet powerful. But can it outweigh the wretched Alan Hale Sr. as Richard's "funny" minstrel Blondel? Perhaps not.

CYRANO DE BERGERAC (1925)

Rating: ★★★☆☆ • *Origin:* France, 1925 • *Director:* Augusto Genina •
Source: Image Entertainment DVD

Augusto Genina's *Cyrano de Bergerac*, based on Edmond Rostand's 1897 play, was actually shot in 1922, but wasn't released until '25 because it took three years to hand color every frame of the movie using a painstaking process called "stencil color." Dubbing prints of the result proved to be very expensive, so few copies were made, and it's a wonder the film has survived. For all that effort to give the film color, the results are strange—unconvincing, garish, and unevenly applied.

But is the movie any good? Adapting a beloved play known for its language to a silent medium was a major challenge, and you have to give Genina credit for trying. For one thing, he uses a lot of close-ups, relying on his actors' very expressive features to convey the story. For another, he just plain slaps more words up on the screen than is typical of most silents, sometimes three cue cards' worth in immediate succession. And during Cyrano's big duel in the theater, in place of cue cards, the words are printed right over the images as surtitles so the action isn't interrupted—which unfortunately is more jarring than effective. And all these expedients don't quite add up to success: the play is still a talkfest, and watching a silent talkfest is a strain.

That said, shooting the film in the actual older streets of Paris gives it a richness of setting no Hollywood backlot could match, and the costumes are uniformly excellent. Pierre Magnier, who plays Cyrano, is inspired, and the film overflows with character actors who mug up a storm. The swordplay, alas, is mediocre stage combat, but the classic story is as good as ever, the soldiers' camp at the Siege of Arras is convincingly depicted, and Linda Moglie is one of the best Roxanes you'll ever see, radiating intelligence, spirit, and wit, as that character should. Alas, the lugubrious last act is way too long, and the ending is sentimental sludge. A thoroughly mixed bag, all in all.

CYRANO DE BERGERAC (1950)

Rating: ★★★★★ (Essential) • *Origin:* USA, 1950 • *Director:* Michael Gordon •
Source: Alpha Video DVD

You've seen this, of course, probably more than once. If you haven't, just smile, nod, and pretend you have, and then tonight make the time to find it and watch it. It's based on the 1897 play by French poet and playwright Edmond Rostand, who wrote the original entirely in verse, in rhymed couplets. The play was a gigantic hit that ran for years and toured the world. In 1923 prominent American stage actor Walter Hampden commissioned the New York poet and playwright Brian Hooker to create an English translation in blank verse; it became the standard English translation for

José Ferrer as *Cyrano de Bergerac* (1950)
WIKIMEDIA COMMONS

the next half century, and Hampden, playing Cyrano, used it in touring productions throughout the '20s and '30s. (Fun fact: as good as the Hooker version of *Cyrano* is—and it's very, very good—there's another fine English version that appeared in 1970 from none other than Anthony Burgess, the author of *A Clockwork Orange.*)

The brilliant Puerto Rican actor José Ferrer revived the play on Broadway in 1946, winning a Tony Award. He reprised the role for a live TV production in 1949 and then again for this movie version in 1950, for which he took home the Oscar for Best Actor. The movie, an independent Stanley Kramer production made on the cheap, has been criticized for its low production values in an era of grand Hollywood epics, but really it looks fine, and frankly its approach suits the material, opening out just enough from the staginess of the play to avoid theatrical claustrophobia.

By the time he made the movie version, Ferrer had been playing the role of Cyrano for years and really came to inhabit the part. He loved it, and his enthusiasm is infectious to this day. The play was shortened somewhat to fit a feature's running time, with some new interstitial material written by Orson Welles (uncredited) to mask the transitions between acts; this included a brief scene between the Comte de Guiche (Ralph Clanton) and his uncle the "Cardinal," who though unnamed is clearly intended to be Richelieu. Also added to the film were the sword fight with the "100" thugs and the combat with the Spanish at the Siege of Arras. For a low-budget production, these battles were well done, but this should come as no surprise considering the film's fight director was the veteran sword master Fred Cavens, who coached the fencing in just about every Hollywood swashbuckler from the silent era on. (Get this: Cavens coached Douglas Fairbanks Sr. as Zorro in 1921, Tyrone Power as Zorro in 1940, and Guy Williams as Zorro in 1957!) Ferrer holds his own in these fights, and looks good doing it—and you can tell it's he and not a double, because who else would have such a big nose?

DAIMAJIN (OR MAJIN THE MONSTER OF TERROR)

Rating: ★★★★☆ • *Origin:* Japan, 1966 • *Director:* Kimiyoshi Yasuda •
Source: Mill Creek Blu-ray

By the mid-1960s, the Daiei studio was having success in two genres, giant monster movies and samurai adventure films. Why not cross the streams?

The earth is shaking, so the villagers overseen by the Hanabusa clan gather to conduct a midnight ritual to placate the Majin, the angry mountain demon. But a more prosaic danger is on the march: Samanosuke (Ryutaro Gomi), a ronin who'd been adopted by the Hanabusa, has masterminded a revolt, and his loyal cutthroats slay the clan chief and install Samanosuke as the new daimyo. However, the young son and daughter of the old daimyo escape with the help of the loyal samurai Kogenta (Jun Fujimaki). They are led by priestess Shinobu (Otome Tsukimiya) high onto the haunted mountain to take refuge in a cave guarded by a giant statue, the Daimajin god who keeps the mountain demon contained.

Ten years pass. Samanosuke has turned the village into a brutal slave labor camp, a stone quarry to build a fortress as a base for conquest. Meanwhile, the Hanabusa prince, Tadafumi (Yoshihiko Aoyama) and his sister, Kozasa (Miwa Takada), have grown to adulthood on the mountain under the guidance of Kogenta and Shinobu. Learning of the plight of the villagers, Kogenta sneaks down from the mountain to see what can be done, but he is captured; Tadafumi attempts to free him and is captured as well. Shinobu warns Samanosuke that his sins will anger the mountain god, but he kills her and orders the Daimajin statue destroyed. When his men pound a great metal spike into the Daimajin's forehead, the statue bleeds, there's lightning and landslides, and chasms open in the earth, swallowing the attackers. And then things get bad.

The 25-foot-tall Daimajin, possessed by the furious mountain demon, marches on Samanosuke's fortress. He's a modest monster as *kaiju* go, owing more to the original King Kong than to Godzilla, but he's more than a match for Samanosuke's samurai, despite their swords, muskets, catapults, chains, and flaming carts. The samurai are toast; the only question is, Can the good guys persuade the monster to stand down before he destroys the village as well?

This mash-up of the monster and samurai genres feels entirely natural: the direction easily changes gears from the spooky and supernatural to sharp samurai action, the acting is fine, and the cinematography is lush and colorful. Plus there's a clear moral: do not pound a metal spike into the forehead of a divine guardian statue. What more could you want?

SAMURAI VERSUS *KAIJU!*

In the menagerie of Japanese postwar film studios, the Toho Company was the 900-pound King Kong, known best for its crime and samurai films, including those of director Akira Kurosawa. Toho hit the international big time in 1954 with *Godzilla, King of the Monsters*, which, though inspired by *King Kong* and *The Beast from 20,000 Fathoms*, really counts as the first of the *kaiju*, or Japanese-style giant monster movies. Toho followed up in 1956 with *Godzilla Raids Again* and expanded the franchise late in that year with *Rodan*. By the early 1960s, other Japanese studios started getting in on the act. This included Daiei Films with their kaiju Gamera, who "starred" in seven features from 1965 through 1971. We know Daiei primarily for the Zatoichi series, which capitalized on its skill at churning out fair-to-exceptional historical samurai adventures mainly for the Japanese market. With Gamera, Daiei had a series that sold internationally as well, and they had the bright idea of mashing up their two most popular genres, kaiju and *chambara*, into a single series: samurai vs. a giant monster! Thus was born the *Daimajin* trilogy.

DAIMAJIN 2: RETURN OF DAIMAJIN (OR WRATH OF DAIMAJIN)

Rating: ★★★★☆ • *Origin:* Japan, 1966 • *Director:* Kenji Misumi • *Source:* Mill Creek Blu-ray

Immediate sequel! Lord Danjo of Mikoshiba (Takashi Kanda) is so cruel that his peasants are fleeing to the neighboring domain of Chigusa, a peaceful realm that shares Yagumo Lake with the benign domain of Nagoshi. In the middle of the lake is the island of the god that protects them both, embodied in a stone Daimajin statue. Right after a festival of peace between the two lake domains, Mikoshiba attacks Chigusa and slays its lord, but Chigusa's son, Juro (Kojiro Hongo), who is betrothed to Princess Saiyuri of Nagoshi (Shiho Fujimura), escapes the assault. Assuming Juro has escaped across the lake, Danjo uses that as a pretext to conquer Nagoshi as well. Then, as a morale crusher, Danjo sends a team with explosive gunpowder charges to blow up the Daimajin statue, and all is gloom around Yagumo Lake.

But Juro and Saiyuri have both escaped to the island, and Juro is determined to lead a rebellion against Danjo. There follows nearly an hour of excellent samurai action, with midnight raids, secret passages, captures, escapes, and desperate sacrifices. But Danjo's troops are just too numerous and ruthless, and eventually all the good guys are captured and tied to stakes for mass execution. Because it's the wickedest thing he could do, Danjo has Lady Saiyuri prepared to be burned alive, but she prays to their guardian god for aid, and her maiden tears bring him to life.

This, of course, is what we've been waiting for. Daimajin, though blown to bits, rises whole from the lake and is possessed by a demon of vengeance. The lake waters separate to allow Daimajin to plod thunderously to shore! He walks through stockade walls! He sneers at volleys of musket balls! He defies massed grappling hooks and exploding crates of gunpowder! He hurls boulders, summons lightning, and shoots fire bolts! It's super gratifying.

Kenji Misumi, who directed six *Zatoichi* and four *Lone Wolf and Cub* features, is in total charge here, and he directs this mini-epic with a sure hand. You might fault it for being predictable but you'd be wrong, because it delivers exactly what the audience is looking for.

DAIMAJIN 3: DAIMAJIN STRIKES AGAIN (OR THE RETURN OF MAJIN)

Rating: ★★★★☆ • *Origin:* Japan, 1966 • *Director:* Kazuo Mori • *Source:* Mill Creek Blu-ray

This is a boys' adventure flick in which four plucky lads face wicked samurai and a giant monster. You say you don't like child actors? Get over it!

In northern Japan, a whole team of loggers from the mountain village of Koyama has gone missing. One of them, wounded and dying, staggers back into town to report that the missing men were all captured by samurai of the Arakawa clan and taken to a forced labor camp in Hell's Valley. The wounded logger escaped and only made it home because he dared to cross the forbidden peak of the Majin, the mountain god. That's the only way to free the others, but the villagers dare not try it—except for four young boys who are determined to save their fathers and brothers.

With just a few supplies, the four set off to climb the mountain of the Majin and make their way to Hell's Valley to free the captives. There's a good half hour kids versus nature adventure in spectacular scenery, struggling until they reach the peak and find the statue of Daimajin; awed, they honor it and pay their respects, and in return the mountain god sends an avatar, a great hawk, to watch over them. And they're going to need help, because Lord Arakawa (Toru Abe) has sent a squad of his nastiest samurai to close off the mountain approach.

Meanwhile, in Hell's Valley, the Koyama loggers are being worked to death in an atrocious environment of boiling springs and noxious gases, mining sulfur so the Arakawa can make industrial quantities of gunpowder with which to conquer their neighbors. The Majin is angered and wreaths his mountain in a snowstorm, but that just enables the nasty samurai to follow the tracks of the plucky lads. Trapped, one of them sacrifices himself to the mountain god while calling for aid, and the Daimajin statue becomes animate, possessed by the spirit of a demon of vengeance. The statue marches on Hell's Valley, bringing a blizzard with it, and not even artillery can save Lord Arakawa when, after three movies, Daimajin finally draws his catastrophic *kaiju katana*.

The Daiei Film studio shot all three *Daimajin* films back-to-back and then released them a few months apart throughout 1966. Kazuo Mori, one of the regular Zatoichi directors, found a way to keep the formula fresh by turning the third film into a kids' adventure, and very successfully too. Gunpowder goes boom!

DANGEROUS LIAISONS

Rating: ★★★★★ • *Origin:* USA, 1988 • *Director:* Stephen Frears •
Source: Warner Bros. Blu-ray

Typically, a swashbuckler story is about a hero who fights injustice but does so while following a personal code of behavior, in defiance of the strictures of society.

Dangerous Liaisons is a sort of reverse swashbuckler in which, though the protagonists are villains, they, too, live by personal codes to which they are no less devoted than heroes are to their own. Adapted by the playwright Christopher Hampton from the scandalous 1782 novel by Pierre Choderlos de Laclos, the story's villain protagonists are the Vicomte de Valmont (John Malkovich) and Madame de Merteuil (Glenn Close), a pair of romantic predators in *ancien régime* Paris who are rivals in a game of debauching the naive and innocent. To gain revenge on an ex-lover, Merteuil wants Valmont to seduce the ex-lover's young fiancée Cécile (Uma Thurman) so that he will marry not a naïf right out of the convent but a woman trained for sex like a prostitute. However, Valmont declines because he has his sights set on bigger game, the chaste and devout Madame de Tourvel (Michelle Pfeiffer). So Merteuil sweetens the deal: if Valmont can seduce both Cécile and Tourvel, she'll reward him with a night in her own arms. Valmont accepts, but meanwhile Merteuil spins up a backup plan, introducing Cécile to young Danceny (Keanu Reeves), a penniless but dreamy music teacher whom she shapes to her own ends.

At first, the villains have it all their own way, so they keep raising the stakes ever higher until they're playing for prizes they can't afford to lose. Then events spin out of control. Tautly directed by the acclaimed Stephen Frears, this brilliant film was nominated for seven Academy Awards and won three of them. The performances, especially by leads Close, Malkovich, and Pfeiffer, are intense and memorable, the cinematography by Philippe Rousselot is dazzling, the settings in majestic period French châteaux are stunning, and the costumes won one of those Oscars.

This is a movie you can watch again and again and still find new, telling details in it that you never noticed before. And, as if just to make sure it would qualify for the *Cinema of Swords*, it has a gritty smallsword duel in the snow between Keanu Reeves and John Malkovich choreographed by the great fight master William Hobbs. Dangerous, indeed.

(See also *Valmont.*)

D'ARTAGNAN AND THREE MUSKETEERS

Rating: ★★★★☆ • *Origin:* Russia, 1978 • *Director:* Georgy Yungvald-Khilkevich •
Source: Twister DVD

There are several musical versions of Dumas's *The Three Musketeers*; this Russian TV miniseries is the best of them. (Admit it: that's a sentence you didn't expect to read today.)

Dumas's novels have been wildly popular in Russian translation since the nineteenth century, maintaining their popularity right through the Soviet era, especially *The Three Musketeers*, which can be read as a critique of European social inequality. But it was really the musketeers' manly comradeship that Russian readers found most appealing.

D'Artagnan and Three Musketeers Author's Collection

This is a three-part miniseries first broadcast in 1978. Though a lavish production for Russian TV of its time, it looks ludicrously low-budget to Western capitalist eyes, particularly the fanciful costumes with their polyester satin, fake fur, and multicolored wool knits. On the other hand, the period sets, mostly shot in the old Ukrainian city of Lvov, are just wonderful, far better than those of most historical swashbucklers shot in Western Europe.

The main roles are all well cast with the type of strong character actors suited to musical comedy. D'Artagnan (Mikhail Boyarsky) is played as a lovable goofball whose chief qualities are overconfidence and boundless enthusiasm. The musketeers, Athos, Porthos, and Aramis, are close to Dumas's depictions, as are the villains, Cardinal Richelieu, Rochefort, and Milady. The royals, King Louis, Queen Anne, and Buckingham, also come off well.

And everybody sings. This version is absolutely chock-full of catchy songs, some of which have become popular Russian oldies. You haven't lived until you've heard Cardinal Richelieu sing a trio with Milady de Winter and the Comte de Rochefort, suavely harmonizing in purple polyester. The music, mainly electric organ with drums and occasional guitar and bass, sounds like it's played by a hotel lounge band, which adds to its charm, and the bouncy songs are right for the show's light tone of cheesy melodrama. (And by the way, if you think *cheesy melodrama* is inappropriate for a classic of world literature, you're just wrong—where would Charles Dickens be without it?)

In fact, this adaptation of the novel is closer than most. With three 80-minute episodes, it runs to four hours, the length of most of the best screen versions of *T3M*. The book has a two-part structure, and by necessity many of its later events are reordered here to match this production's three-act configuration, but it's cleverly done. Some key scenes were clearly inspired by their rendition in Richard Lester's adaptation, which doesn't hurt them at all. The romantic plots drive the story forward, there's plenty of action, though the fencing is more histrionic than convincing, and even the jokes are pretty good. Bonacieux the mercer is portrayed as an ugly Jewish caricature, but we'll overlook that lapse to gaze in wonder at the dreaded Cardinal singing a melancholy song of his hopeless love for Queen Anne, a balalaika tune that dissolves into a dream sequence in which he leads the queen through a mock-formal court ballet. It's even better than the Catholics-versus-Huguenots song the soldiers belt out at the Siege of La Rochelle. Ochen horosho, da!

DEATHSTALKER

Rating: ★★☆☆☆ • *Origin:* Argentina/USA, 1983 • *Director:* James Sbardellati • *Source:* Shout! Factory DVD

In the early 1980s, filmmakers on the lower end of the budgetary spectrum seemed to assume that sword-and-sorcery movies appealed primarily to horny adolescent males, an audience who would be fascinated by a muscular hero who pursues gory sword fights and a ready supply of bare-breasted women, all presented without unnecessary clutter like character development or social commentary. *Deathstalker*, produced by schlockmeister Roger Corman, follows that formula with slavish devotion, wasting no effort on being original, clever, or even fun.

The story is bare-bones cliché: a barbarian warrior whose only name is Deathstalker (Rick Hill) is informed by a witch that the evil ruler Munkar (Bernard Erhard) has two of the three Powers of Creation, an amulet and a chalice, and if Munkar gets the third, the Sword of Justice, he will become all-powerful. But if Deathstalker obtains the sword, he can defeat Munkar, take the other two magical objects, and wield all the power himself. The warrior initially refuses the quest but then changes his mind, defeats an ogre in a mystic cave to get the sword, and then sets off for Munkar's generic fantasy city, where the ruler is holding a tournament to choose an heir to his throne. However, the tournament is really a trick to eliminate any rivals who might be strong enough to threaten Munkar's power—and to lure Deathstalker to bring the Sword of Justice to the hands of the evil wizard.

Along the way Deathstalker picks up the usual barbarian-hero sidekicks: a rogue named Salmaron (Augusto Larreta) whose main job is to do double takes, and a barbarian swordswoman named Kaira (Lana Clarkson) who mostly goes shirtless and sleeps with Deathstalker on the first date. This film is the start of Clarkson's brief career as the queen of barbarian movies, making an impression here because no one else in the cast has an ounce of charisma, including *Playboy* starlet Barbi Benton as a captive princess whose main function is to almost get raped a lot. Indeed, there's a great deal of almost-sex going on, but except for the tryst between Kaira and Deathstalker, it's all forced, which is distasteful at best and despicable at worst. Even Deathstalker, the putative hero, isn't above coercing an unwilling woman if the opportunity arises—not that this makes us think any less of him, because he's already thoroughly unlikeable: mean, humorless, and dull.

So much for the sex, now what about the violence? There's plenty of it, all terrible, just cheesy professional wrestling but with pointy weapons added to the drops and slams. Ugh.

And yet, this film was popular enough to spawn three sequels, so mustn't it have some good qualities? A few, the chief of which is its headlong pace, which piles on one incident after another so rapidly that you're rarely tempted to make the mistake of thinking about what's going on. Then, too, nobody has anything interesting to say, which keeps the dialogue taut. And there's a beast-man warrior in a pig mask—a *porc*, we used to call 'em back in the day—who is almost amusing. And apparently, that was enough.

DEATHSTALKER II: DUEL OF THE TITANS

Rating: ★★★☆☆ • *Origin:* Argentina/USA, 1987 • *Director:* Jim Wynorski • *Source:* Shout! Factory DVD

This is the last of the low-budget barbarian flicks producer Roger Corman made in Argentina. The genre was nearing the end of its popularity, and there was no money for magic or monsters, so director Jim Wynorski threw out the script he'd been given and rewrote it as a comedy. Of his two stars, one, John Terlesky as Deathstalker, is replacing Rick Hill in that role, while the other, model Monique Gabrielle, has never done comedy before, but they manage to hit it off and even display some onscreen chemistry together, a thing nearly unheard-of in a cheap sword-and-sorcery film. It's chemistry at the middle school chem-lab level, but still, that's not nothing.

Unfortunately, the story doesn't even try to make sense, and the comedy isn't very funny, most of the jokes being older than the stars' grandparents. Since it's a farce, you might think that the story doesn't *need* to make sense, but only the wildest farces can get away with that, and this ain't one of those. It's a fantasy quest movie, of course: A princess in disguise, Reena (Gabrielle), cons Deathstalker into helping her regain her throne from evil Evie (also Gabrielle), a clone created by the sneering swordsman-and-sorcerer Jarek (John LaZar). On the way Stalker and Reena face hapless pirate thugs, shambling zombies, the usual black-clad villains' goons, and their most dangerous opponents, a tribe of Amazon warriors. The Amazons capture them and sentence Stalker to fight a duel to the death with their champion, a very large woman named Gorgo (wrestler Queen Kong). Manly hero Stalker getting thrown around the ring by a very large woman—funny stuff, eh? Eh?

The exterior sets are the same ones seen in previous Corman fantasies, but by this time they're looking pretty ragged and ratty. The interiors are worse: new, but clearly made of painted plywood with textures barely sketched in. The costumes are of sub–Ren Faire leatherette, and don't ask about the props and weapons. (A glass doorknob fills in for a crystal ball.) Fights between the faceless guards and Amazons are as dull and terrible as ever, but Terlesky, who is active and enthusiastic, shows an unexpected talent for stage fencing that's almost matched by LaZar, who tries to keep up.

In fact, it's Terlesky, Gabrielle, and LaZar who sell this thing, especially the romantic leads, who seem to be having a genuinely good time. Nobody is under any illusions that they're involved in serious filmmaking, and that may have freed them up to be engagingly goofy. It's still a flimsy exploitation flick with gratuitous nudity and gore, but at least it knows it's no more than that.

DEATHSTALKER III: THE WARRIORS FROM HELL

Rating: ★☆☆☆☆ • *Origin:* USA/Mexico, 1988 • *Director:* Alfonso Corona • *Source:* YouTube streaming video

A barbarian flick, *Deathstalker III*
Was suitable only for mockery.
With swordplay amusing
But story confusing,
It impressed everyone with its suckery.

DESTINY'S SON (OR *KIRU*)

Rating: ★★★☆☆ • *Origin:* Japan, 1962 • *Director:* Kenji Misumi • *Source:* YouTube streaming video

This is a curiosity, an artsy, almost experimental *chambara* film from Kenji Misumi, a director best known for his contributions to the *Zatoichi* and *Lone Wolf and Cub* series. The story firmly identifies itself as a tragedy from the beginning, when a young samurai woman of the Iida murders her lord's wicked concubine "for the good of the clan." She's arrested and condemned, but her infant son is sent away to be raised in the Komoro clan. Twenty years later, handsome Shingo (Raizô Ichikawa), unaware that he's adopted, asks permission to leave Komoro and travel about "a little bit everywhere" for three years. He returns with an air of romantic melancholy and a new fencing style he's invented, a "shamisen stance" so threatening that even experienced swordsmen, when faced with it, begin to tremble and then admit defeat. In a tournament, this stance enables Shingo to defeat a powerful challenger and protect the Komoro clan's honor, but it also earns him the enmity of jealous rivals, who kill his foster family. In a dying revelation, Shingo's adoptive father tells him of his real origins in the Iida clan. The young man sets out to find the truth of his background, learning in the process that life is both wonderful and cruel.

Only slightly longer than 70 minutes, with a story told almost in shorthand and with abrupt changes of scene, *Destiny's Son* often sacrifices coherence for poetic impressionism, every sequence ending in some dark outbreak of violence. (Using his shamisen stance, Shingo kills an ambusher *with a flowering branch*.) Many of these scenes are striking and memorable, but the characters are mostly archetypes with little space for development. Even Shingo only gets more romantically melancholy with time, drifting into reveries of three women whose lives he couldn't save: his mother, his sister, and an unnamed, fierce fugitive who died fighting (in the nude, for extra art points) so her brother could escape their pursuers. The story slides into the Bakumatsu, the period of civil strife at the end of the shogunate, and Shingo is inevitably caught up in politics. But dreaming of his three lost ladies, he pays little attention until the lord he is sworn to protect is assassinated on his watch. "There is no excuse," he tells himself, as he prepares for his inevitable end.

Right, fair enough: we've known all along that Shingo's tale is about finding beauty in the face of implacable fate and suchlike, so you have no one to blame but yourself if you're looking for an incongruously happy ending. Enjoy it for what it is anyway.

THE DEVIL-SHIP PIRATES

Rating: ★★★☆☆ • *Origin:* UK, 1964 • *Director:* Don Sharp • *Source:* Sony Pictures DVD

In 1588, after the defeat of the Spanish Armada in the English Channel, the surviving Spanish ships sailed north and then west around the coasts of Scotland and Ireland, making for the open Atlantic and a route back to Spain. As many as two dozen Spanish ships wrecked on the Irish coast; some crews fought their way to rescue by their compatriots, but others were hunted down and killed or captured.

This is a Hammer Films swashbuckler, low-budget and lurid but not to be sneered at. Christopher Lee is top billed as Captain Robeles, skipper of the *Diablo*, a Spanish privateer that joined the Armada, was badly damaged, and had to put in to a remote marsh on the English coast to make repairs. The Spanish crew, pirates all except for the young officer Don Manuel (Barry Warren), take over a small coastal town and coerce the inhabitants into forced labor to repair the ship before the English militia can arrive. Local lord Sir Basil and the weaselly Vicar Brown counsel patient compliance with the pirates, but fiery young Harry (John Cairney), a wounded sea dog who'd sailed with Drake, organizes a resistance that seems hopeless—until Don Manuel, outraged by Captain Robeles's brutality, comes over to their side.

The Pirates of Blood River, its Hammer predecessor, was good, but this is better, with a superior story tightly and tautly told. The acting is solid, the costumes and sets are convincing, and in the end most everybody gets what they deserve. Along the way we're entertained by buccaneers roistering in the town tavern and playing Stupid Pirate Games, some admirable fencing with cutlass and rapier, a spiffy, double-barreled flintlock pistol, and everyone's favorite, death by quicksand. But the weaselly vicar lives to weasel another day, cursed be all the fates!

THE DEVIL'S SWORD

Rating: ★★☆☆☆ • *Origin:* Indonesia, 1984 • *Director:* Ratno Timoer • *Source:* Asia Line DVD

Trigger warning: softcore porn, gory horror effects, and a cheesy single-synth soundtrack. This is an Indonesian sword-and-sorcery exploitation flick, interesting mainly because where will you see another such film from this period with an English dub? It's an experience.

A sinister meteorite crashes near the remote hut of an old hermit guru, who forges the glowing meteoric metal into a magic blade that grants (unspecified-but-great) power to its wielder. Four evil martial artists are gathered to go after the sword by the wicked Crocodile Queen (Gudi Sintara), who wears silver mylar bikinis and also collects hypnotized boy toys for orgies in her big, fanged, crocodile-mouth bed. When the Croc Queen sends the best of her four warriors, Banyunjaga (Advent Bangun), on a flying boulder to a village to break up a wedding and collect the groom for her, the villagers resist and he gleefully slaughters them, all but the bride, Pitaloka (Enny Christina), who turns out to be the most badass fighter in town. But she's on the verge of defeat when a hero arrives on a golden palomino: it's Mandala the mighty (Barry Prima)! He saves Pitaloka, though Banyunjaga grabs the groom and summons a half dozen Croc Men out of the ground to cover his retreat. The groom is taken back to the Crocodile Cave, duly hypnotized, and then it's mylar bikini sexy time!

But even mylar bikini sexy time must come to an end, and then everybody must go after the devil's sword, which is hidden in a mystic cave that's so nasty, it has red lighting all through it. Scary! Mandala retrieves the sword, and then he and Pitaloka have to fight Banyunjaga and the other three wicked martial artists, one of whom has a decapi-hat that pulls your head off if it lands on your cranium. This movie has plenty of other ideas like that: it's wildly inventive but the budget is rock-bottom, so the sorcery effects and monsters all suffer from a whiff of the ridiculous. Swordplay and kung fu fill about half the running time, but the combat is marred by poor direction and cheap effects. Frankly, this movie isn't very well made, but the real fun here is seeing standard heroic fantasy quest tropes through the lens of Indonesian culture. And there are so many varieties of Croc Men! Who knew?

DON JUAN

Rating: ★★★★★ • *Origin:* USA, 1926 • *Director:* Alan Crosland • *Source:* Warner Bros. DVD

Don Juan features screen idol John Barrymore in the title role, playing a character quite a bit different from the standard swashbuckling hero. He's pretty much a bad apple, a vain, selfish, dishonest conniver obsessed with the seduction of women, and if he does the right thing, it's usually for the wrong reason. In short, he's nothing like the sanitized Don Juan of the later Errol Flynn movie, and for most of the picture we wonder how he and his ladylove are ever going to get together and win free of his appalling situation and reprehensible conduct. In this the story draws heavily on the 40-something Barrymore's own reputation as "the world's greatest lover," a rake and roué with a string of abandoned starlets behind him. In a bit of inspired casting, one of his real-world discarded lovers, the barely legal Mary Astor, plays the part of Don Juan's one true love, Adriana della Varnese, and their scenes together are smoking. In fact, generally speaking, the acting in this silent film is unusually good, especially from the villains, who are delicious—but more about them below.

After a short gothic-horror first act that establishes the reasons for Don Juan's eternal distrust and disloyalty to women—adultery, murder, and bad parenting, the usual excuses—the story moves to Rome circa 1499 during the bloody reign of the Borgia family. To further establish Don Juan's character, we then get a 20-minute bedroom farce in his Roman townhouse during which the great lover simultaneously juggles the affections, and locations, of three different young ladies. Eventually the women's menfolk intrude in high dudgeon, hilarity ensues, and everyone runs off, leaving Juan to consult with his valet on his romantic schedule for the evening ahead. But Lucrezia Borgia (the sneering and lascivious Estelle Taylor) has cast her acquisitive eye on Don Juan, and he is summoned to a ball that evening at the palace of the Borgias. Lucrezia is determined to have Juan to herself, and she's a lethally jealous lover, but Juan sees and is smitten by the innocent young Andrea della Varnese—who is herself desired by Count Donati, a Borgia crony. In no time we are hip deep in burning gazes, derisive taunts, poisoned chalices, and any number of balcony climbs.

Love and politics are intertwined, and when the Borgias finally break with the Varneses, blood runs in the streets of Rome, and Don Juan has to decide what's really worth fighting for. The bells announcing the impending forced marriage of Andrea to Donati drive him nearly mad, and during his climactic confrontation with the Borgias, he seems more dangerous than they do; he's genuinely unhinged, where the villains are merely wicked. There's a very satisfying and acrobatic sword duel, but though that's where most swashbucklers conclude, here it's just the prelude to the lurid final act, where both Andrea and Juan are clapped in durance vile. By the time Juan escapes the dungeon, it may be too late to redeem himself.

This film looks fantastic: "lush" and "opulent" don't even begin to describe it. It also marks a technical advance in the march to the talkies, a process called "Vitaphone," with a prerecorded musical soundtrack synced up to the action, augmented by sound effects like bells, thumping blows, and clashing swords. The Borgias' Roman orgies, with their dancing damsels clad only in swirling veils and a bibulous Bacchus surrounded by vine-draped maenads, are very convincing, plus this overstuffed film gives us leopard skin–clad African sedan chair porters, an evil dwarf castellan, a sinister alchemist who makes poisons, and a jilted lover sealed up alive in a castle's walls. Also watch for the striking Myrna Loy in an early role as Lucrezia's intriguing maidservant. And did I mention that Don Juan wears striped, asymmetrical trunk hose? Don't miss this one.

DON Q, SON OF ZORRO

Rating: ★★★★☆ • *Origin:* USA, 1925 • *Director:* Donald Crisp • *Source:* Kino Video DVD

Douglas Fairbanks returns to the well in *Don Q, Son of Zorro*, once more donning the mask and cape that made him a superstar in *The Mark of Zorro*. This time around Fairbanks plays both the aging Don Diego de Vega—Zorro—and his son, Cesar de Vega, in a story adapted from a non-Zorro novel, *Don Q's Love Story*. Returned from California to Spain, young Cesar astounds his high-society friends with his tricks with an American bullwhip. (Fairbanks trained with the whip for six weeks to get it right.) Shenanigans with the whip get him into trouble with the queen's guards, and in no time he's using it in signature Fairbanks style to hogtie sergeants, swing from balconies, and lasso a bull that broke out from the corrida. But then, escaping the guards through a noble's garden, he meets the luminous Dolores de Muro, played by Mary Astor. You know Astor as the femme fatale Brigid O'Shaughnessy in John Huston's

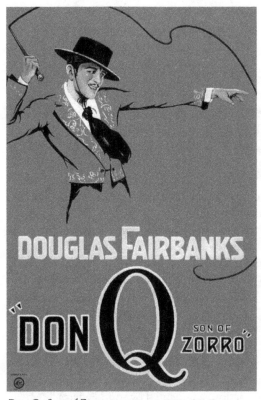

Don Q, Son of Zorro UNITED ARTISTS / WIKIMEDIA COMMONS

version of *The Maltese Falcon*, but 15 years earlier she was a silent movie star, a dewy ingenue with a languishing look. Cesar falls in love with Dolores at first sight—but so does the pursuing guard captain, Don Sebastian, and soon he and Cesar are rivals for Dolores's affection. Sebastian is a dastard, however, who stoops to foul play.

After colossal epics painted on broad canvasses in *Robin Hood* and *Thief of Bagdad*, it must have been a relief to return to the drawing rooms and cabarets of a romantic melodrama, and indeed, the ever-charismatic Fairbanks seems relaxed and comfortable in this film, happy to be doing what he does best. He dances flamenco, brawls with a gang of back-alley goons, and cuts out his rival at the archduke's ball. When Cesar is framed by Sebastian for the murder of the archduke, things get serious. He fakes his own death in a trick worthy of his father, and then it's masked-outlaw time until he can clear his name. It takes both clever chicanery and dashing sword- and whip play, but virtue wins out in the end, as the son of Zorro proves himself the equal of his father. The exciting finale, with its callbacks to the first film, is quite satisfying.

DOUBLE CROSSBONES

Rating: ★★☆☆☆ • *Origin:* USA, 1951 • *Director:* Charles Barton • *Source:* Universal DVD

This isn't the first pirate comedy, and it's far from the last, but it's even further from the best. Musical star Donald O'Connor, his career apparently on the downslide, appears as the Charleston shop boy David Crandall, who by a series of accidents becomes pirate captain Bloodthirsty Dave—and that name, I'm sorry to say, is the best joke in the picture. Production values are decent, and the Technicolor is lush, but the story is laughable without being funny, and the songs are weak: O'Connor sings, dances, and romances the ward of the corrupt Carolina governor, all the while looking vaguely embarrassed. It's notable that when Bloodthirsty Dave gets to Tortuga to join the Brotherhood of the Coast, his fellow captains include pirates from many eras: Blackbeard, Captain Kidd, Henry Morgan, Anne Bonney, and Long Ben Avery. Clearly time travel is involved; you might want to borrow some of that so you can get to the end of this quicker.

KING HU, THAT'S WHO

Even if you're not a big fan of *wuxia*, or Chinese historical martial arts films, you've likely seen *Crouching Tiger, Hidden Dragon*, so you're aware of their distinctive visual style. That style, of course, didn't come out of nowhere; it developed over time and can be traced back to the work of one man, Hong Kong writer-director King Hu, the creator of the modern wuxia movie. His breakout hit was *Dragon Inn* (1967), a film that continues to be influential even today.

DRAGON INN (OR DRAGON GATE INN)

Rating: ★★★★☆ • *Origin:* Taiwan, 1967 • *Director:* King Hu • *Source:* Eureka! Blu-ray

King Hu's follow-up to his standard-setting *Come Drink with Me*, this film builds on the successes of its predecessor but is also quite different from it. *Dragon Inn* was an even bigger hit in Asia than *Drink* and in some ways is even more influential.

At the beginning of the film, there's a major background story dump that you immediately forget because it really doesn't matter. Set in 1457 during the Ming dynasty and under the reign of the emperor's eunuch advisors, the great General Yu is framed for treason and executed because the eunuchs consider him a threat. His three children are exiled and sent on foot toward the distant western border with only a few guards, and the eunuchs, being thorough, send two companies of martial arts agents from the Eastern Group after them to slay the kids once they're sufficiently far from the capital. Summary: the government agents are bad.

A company of these agents, under three capable officers, ventures ahead to a desolate, rocky plain where the only food and hospitality available is at the lonely Dragon Inn. The agents barge in and take over the place, terrorizing the staff and showing how awful they are by murdering their hired porters instead of paying them. Now all they have to do is wait for General Yu's children to arrive and slaughter them and their escorts, and Bob's your uncle. But a smiling stranger with a folded parasol comes in through the door to the desert and, ignoring every hint that he should leave or else, calmly sits down and orders noodles and a bottle of wine. Needless to say, the stranger, Xiao (Shih Chun), is a total martial-arts badass, and the government agents have suddenly got trouble.

The central scene in *Drink* is when Golden Swallow intrudes on a city inn full of evil goons and, as the suspense rises, gradually reveals her considerable abilities. *Dragon Inn* perfects that scene and then turns it around and replays it in new variations, adding further wandering badasses to Xiao's side and gradually increasing the number and level of enemies they face inside and outside the inn. Eventually the children and their escort arrive, closely followed by the bulk of the agents and their commander, General Zhao, reputedly the finest sword fighter in China, and things get desperate. The action only pauses long enough to introduce new badasses on both sides, and the fights expertly ratchet up in intensity up to the final battle, which pits Xiao and all his new allies against the nigh-invincible General Zhao.

Where this film suffers in comparison to *Come Drink with Me* and Hu's third film, *A Touch of Zen*, is that *Dragon Inn* has almost no time for characterization. The only characters who really stand out are the urbane and sardonic Xiao and the fierce Miss Zhu (Lingfeng Shangguan), who dominates her every scene. Once again, without explanation or justification, Hu presents a female warrior who can more than hold her own with the men. Where does she come from? Who cares? She's tremendous. If you're interested in the origin and development of the *wuxia* film genre, you need to see *Dragon Inn*.

DRAGONSLAYER

Rating: ★★★★☆ • *Origin:* USA, 1981 • *Director:* Matthew Robbins • *Source:* Paramount DVD

Dragonslayer AUTHOR'S COLLECTION

Dragonslayer is one of the few early '80s fantasy films that has improved with age. At the time, its rather dark vision was a shock to mainstream audiences, especially in a film coproduced by Disney, but by the standards of our current day, it's damn near lighthearted.

In Urland, a fictional kingdom somewhere in Britain in the sixth century, one of the last of the race of dragons, Vermithrax Pejorative, terrorizes the countryside until the king institutes a lottery to select virgin sacrifices, a single young woman chosen every six months to sate the dragon's hunger. But the sacrifices are always borne by the peasant class, so a band of fed-up commoners led by a young man named Valerian (Caitlin Clarke) sets out to persuade Ulrich (Ralph Richardson), the last of the great wizards, to slay the dragon. However, the band has been followed by the king's hatchet man, the ruthless Tyrian (John Hallam), who is determined that no one will meddle with Urland's precarious détente with the dragon. Tyrian challenges Ulrich's magical credentials and the wizard defies him, offering his breast and daring Tyrian to try to kill him with a wicked dagger. Alas, the dagger goes home and the wizard falls, leaving the quest in the hands of Ulrich's young and inexperienced apprentice, Galen (Peter MacNicol).

Galen, armed with nothing but overconfidence and his late master's magical amulet, sets out to kill the dragon along with Valerian, whom he discovers is a young woman her father had passed off as a man to avoid the dragon lottery. Cue the seemingly doomed romance! The film is shot in the magnificently austere landscape of North Wales, which along with a grimly dramatic soundtrack by the great Alex North gives the film a tone of dark portent, a tone alleviated only by Galen and Valerian's emerging love for one another and the young apprentice's heroic determination to try to slay the dragon regardless of consequences. The script, by director Matthew Robbins and producer (and video game designer) Hal Barwood, is taut and literate, and the cast is solid, particularly Ralph Richardson, who was born to play a medieval wizard.

However, the most important member of the cast is arguably the dragon Vermithrax, though it speaks only by breathing fire on its opponents. Robbins and Barwood set out to create the finest dragon anyone had put on film to that date, and by most measures they succeeded: Vermithrax, a combination of large-scale puppetry with stop-motion and classical animation, is scary and convincing. The dragon's final visuals were realized by George Lucas's effects studio Industrial Light and Magic, one of its early efforts lending its talents to non-Lucas productions. The dragon's savage young, rendered by puppets, are less successful than the parent, and the overwrought wizardry of the finale is more pompous than persuasive, but those are nitpicks. It's remarkable that this film got made as well as it did when it did, and its practical effects hold up remarkably well against the computer-generated graphics of later decades. Give it a look.

THE DUELLISTS

Rating: ★★★★★ (Essential) • *Origin:* UK, 1977 • *Director:* Ridley Scott •
Source: Paramount DVD

The Duellists is the sine qua non of the *Cinema of Swords*, the essential of essentials. It's based pretty closely on Joseph Conrad's 1908 novella *The Duel*, expanded with added historical context by screenwriter Gerald Vaughan-Hughes. Acclaimed director Ridley Scott's first feature, its stunning visual look is directly influenced by Stanley Kubrick's *Barry Lyndon* (1975); like that film, *The Duellists* is

The Duellists Author's Collection

shot almost entirely with natural lighting, including the interiors, lending it a painterly look and Renaissance-style compositions but without Kubrick's fussiness.

The story is an account of six duels between two French cavalry officers over a period of 16 years during the Napoleonic wars, 1800 to 1816, told from the viewpoint of Armand d'Hubert (Keith Carradine), a cool-headed rationalist who is nonetheless trapped by the gentleman warrior's code of honor into a succession of fights with the fiercely irrational Gabriel Feraud (Harvey Keitel). Between the duels, d'Hubert's life evolves from that of a footloose lieutenant to a brigadier general who is a settled family man, raising the stakes so that he has more to lose at every encounter. The historical settings—situations, politics, costumes, equipment—are meticulously drawn, detailed and colorful yet clear, and the locations in the Dordogne of central France are stunning. It's a gorgeous picture.

The duels themselves, mounted or on foot, with smallswords, cavalry sabers, or pistols, are all different yet similar in how suspensefully they are staged and in their convincing realism. The fights were choreographed by the great William Hobbs, who was told by director Scott, "I don't want any of that old tosh, I want it *real*." Every duel conveys the profound sense that death is only a moment away, and both opponents know it. "We wanted to get across the awful feeling that you believe you'll be dead on the floor," said Hobbs. "In the end, the realism is the fear." In this, Hobbs is entirely successful, and the fencing in *The Duellists* is the breakthrough that established him as the best European-style fight director of his generation.

The performances by leads Carradine and Keitel are excellent, despite the occasional incongruity of their American accents, with Keitel's glowering and incendiary Feraud particularly memorable. They get strong support from Albert Finney, Tom Conti, and Edward Fox in minor roles, and especially from Diana Quick and Cristina Raines as d'Hubert's mistress and wife and Meg Wynn Owen as his sister. The haunting soundtrack is an early effort by Howard Blake, a classical-sounding score that betrays another Kubrick influence. If you haven't seen *The Duellists*, don't delay—there, that's your evening sorted.

DUEL OF CHAMPIONS

Rating: ★☆☆☆☆ • *Origin:* Italy/Yugoslavia, 1961 • *Directors:* Ferdinando Baldi and Terence Young • *Source:* Mill Creek DVD

Set early in Roman history, this is based on the legend of the Horatii–Curiatii duel, when triplet brothers from Rome (the Horatii) fought triplet brothers from Alba (the Curiatii) to settle a war between the two countries. That ought to be cool, but it isn't; instead, before that final triple duel, there's a whole lot of tiresome backstory involving treachery, hopeless romance, hasty assumptions, and mistaken disgrace, all weakly acted in crummy costumes in front of shoddy sets. The exteriors were mostly shot in Yugoslavia, which is a change, at least. Alan Ladd as Horatio, by this time a Hollywood has-been, is the token American star, and he barely makes an effort. This was one of a number of junk films made by director Terence Young before his breakthrough with the first James Bond movie, *Dr. No* (1962). Let's remember him for that and his later features—you don't want to blow an hour and a half on this one.

EL CID

Rating: ★★★☆☆ • *Origin:* USA/Italy, 1961 • *Director:* Anthony Mann • *Source:* Genius Products DVD

This grandiose three-hour retelling of the tale of Spain's national hero is worth your time, as it's lush and splendid to look at, has a memorable and soaring score by Miklós Rózsa, and some of the best scenes of medieval combat ever filmed up to its time. But it also has its downsides: you're going to have to put up with a choppy and inconsistent script, periods of barely coherent storytelling, and some hammy actors treating the scenery like Bazooka bubble gum.

Did I mention *El Cid* is three hours long? It even has an intermission, which is fine because it means 10 extra minutes of Rózsa's music—and believe me, after the second hour you'll be ready for an intermission. But let's go back to the beginning: the story is set during the *Reconquista*, those long centuries when the Christian kingdoms slowly drove the Moors out of Spain. Don Rodrigo Díaz (Charlton Heston), known as El Cid, is a knight who champions any ruler who behaves honorably, whether Christian or Muslim. This epic was made during the peak of Hollywood's era of grand historical sagas, and in the first hour, the film reveals its ambitions, which are considerable: the scenery, sets, and costumes all look spectacular; the main characters, all self-importance incarnate, posture and moralize without letup; and there's a lot of action in between the proud chatter. There are four fight scenes in that first hour alone, two of them simply tremendous: broadsword battles that by themselves are worth the price of admission. Those two sword fights were overseen by Yakima Canutt, the

THE FALL OF THE HOLLYWOOD EPIC

Big-studio Hollywood historical epics had a good run, arguably starting with the films of Cecil B. DeMille in the 1920s, flourishing throughout the 1950s and peaking around 1960 with grand features like *Ben-Hur* (1959) and *Lawrence of Arabia* (1962). But in the early '60s, the theatergoing public seems to have lost their taste for big epics. It happened right about the time those same epics began letting them down, either becoming unbearably ridiculous in their depictions of other cultures or bogged down in turgid self-importance. Actors—for example, Charlton Heston, who'd made a career out of swaggering through ancient and medi-eval studio sets with a sword on his hip—gave historical epics one last go and then shrugged and reinvented themselves as '70s action stars.

great stuntman turned action director, who also helmed the better battle sequences. Alas, the not-so-good fights were the work of lead director Anthony Mann, who did well composing character confrontations and grand scenic shots but was a duff hand when it came to combat.

El Cid is a prestigious star vehicle for its two leads, Heston and Sophia Loren as Ximena, Don Rodrigo's wife, but in the movie's first hour, they just don't seem to have much chem-istry. Then we get into the second hour, and the wheels come off entirely as the movie begins to display the kinds of problems that often result when movies are written piecemeal by five different scripters. There are abrupt changes of scene and motivation, and characters make rash and even ridiculous decisions while spouting self-righteous speeches at each other—really, it's like an opera without songs. If it were mounted on a big stage behind a full orchestra, its plot might seem more credible, or at least you wouldn't mind the flaws, because there'd be arias. By the end of that second hour, everyone hates everyone else and the Cid is exiled, just in time for the intermission.

There's a lovely entr'acte—and then surprisingly, in the third hour, everything improves. Heston and Loren finally seem comfortable with each other, the scenery-chewers mostly shut up or are dead, and a coherent plot emerges that builds properly to a stirring climax. It's quite good. What a relief!

In the twelfth century, there was a real Don Rodrigo Díaz, a.k.a. the Cid, who even did some of the things Heston does in this movie, but history is outclassed by the legend, which has been told and retold in books, plays, verse sagas, and yes, even operas (a lot of operas). With so many successful models to draw upon, if this version of the tale is something of a jumbled mess, blame it on the Hollywood machine that elevated the roles of the leads above all so that every piece of the production had to defer to aggrandizing the stars. Meanwhile, below the exalted plane of the stars, the good actors get short shrift, while the weaker actors resort to the aforementioned scenery-chewing in hopes of being noticed.

But I guarantee you'll be happy with the third hour of *El Cid*. Two immense medieval sieges are staged on a broad Mediterranean beach, which is genius, because you really couldn't pick a better location to throw a war. The action, mostly directed by Canutt, is solid to excel-lent, and the actors, stars included, deliver their lines with a gravitas that was missing before the intermission. Plus that buoyant Rózsa score just never quits. See, and hear, for yourself.

ERIK THE CONQUEROR

Rating: ★★★☆☆ • *Origin:* Italy/France, 1961 • *Director:* Mario Bava • *Source:* Arrow
Blu-ray

A devotee of 1960s cinema might wonder, "What if Italian director Mario Bava, the master of stylish horror films, had shot a remake of the 1958 epic *The Vikings?*" Fortunately, we don't have to wonder, because Bava did exactly that! *Erik the Conqueror* is a loose remake, but it does follow the major plot points of its predecessor: after sea rovers raid the coast of Britain, two sons of a Viking warlord grow to manhood, one Norse and one English, to oppose each other in a clash both personal and cultural, culminating in a Viking assault on a British castle. However, there are significant variations on the theme, as the English son Erik (George Ardisson) isn't enslaved by the Norse Eron (Cameron Mitchell), and instead of the brothers competing for the affections on one curvaceous blonde, Bava gives them two: Daya and Rama, a pair of Nordic "vestal virgins" played by the Kessler twins, Alice and Ellen.

That's really just the start of the variations, because Bava's approach to filmmaking couldn't be more different from that of *The Vikings*'s Richard Fleischer. Where the earlier film is grand, expansive, yet grounded in its sweeping scenery, *Erik* is lurid, sensationalistic, and fanciful, filmed in bold primary colors and daring camera angles, every scene limned in smoke, flame, and blood. Bava's film makes no pretense to historical accuracy, as you might guess from the vestal virgins mentioned above: mounted knights thunder to the attack bearing crimson lances thick as logs, cartoonish longships have their steering rudders on the wrong sides, and tarantulas infest Scottish dungeons. And the costumes! Holy hell! In fact, in all but its lack of overt supernatural elements, this is a fantasy film, a fever dream in which Nordic maidens swirl in a sword dance under a titanic purple Yggdrasil before blond barbarians fight a savage duel wielding glowing red-hot axes. Wow!

This movie has the best ridiculous medieval combat ever, and there's plenty of it. Bava's direction for the fight scenes appears to have amounted to "Just go wild!," as scores of seemingly untrained extras chop vigorously at each other with swords, axes, spears, and torches while screaming and howling. This is an approach that's failed in countless low-budget hacktaculars, but Bava makes it work. It may be overwrought but it's effective, and *Erik*'s final siege and sacking is just as exciting as the classic castle assault in *The Vikings*. The whole thing is a delirious and utterly unrestrained extravaganza. There's nothing else quite like it.

ERIK THE VIKING

Rating: ★★☆☆☆ • *Origin:* UK/Sweden, 1989 • *Director:* Terry Jones • *Source:* Vitrafilm DVD

File this one under Interesting Failure. Written and directed by Terry Jones, of the Monty Python troupe, this Viking comedy seems on the face of it to be just another historical farce like *Jabberwocky* or *Yellowbeard*, recycling jokes from *Holy Grail*—ha ha, weren't the Middle Ages filthy and casually brutal? But Jones, one of the more thoughtful Pythons, has something else in mind besides an action fantasy, couching the story as a study of belief and how it changes reality, at least for believers. So though the humor, familiar and derivative, is unfortunately not very funny, the philosophy—well, that doesn't really land either.

Which is a shame, because the story has plenty of interesting ideas, even if they don't pan out. Midgard has fallen into the eternal winter that precedes Ragnarok, the sun has disappeared from the sky, and life is nothing but pain and strife. Erik (Tim Robbins) finds he has no taste for rape and slaughter, and after he accidentally kills a woman he was trying to save, he decides that somehow, things must change. He consults with Freya the wise woman (Eartha Kitt, in a marvelous and spooky cameo), who tells him that he must sail west beyond the Viking world to the lost island of Hy-Brasil, where he will find the Horn Resounding: blowing it will bring him to Asgard, where a second sounding will awaken the sleeping gods who have abandoned Midgard to its fate.

Quest time! Erik assembles a crew of Norse misfits to sail off the edge of the world, but first he must evade the dragon ship of Halfdan the Black (John Cleese), who wants to prevent the return of peace, as it will put raiders and pillagers like him out of business. Next the crew must get past the Dragon of the North Sea, an imaginative and impressive giant puppet monster, and then persuade the goofy people of Hy-Brasil to give them the Horn before Halfdan catches up.

Robbins is good as the anachronistic hero, a well-meaning American stuck in a time where he doesn't belong, and Cleese is fine as his opposite number, an incongruously modern villain. Imogen Stubbs plays a spirited princess of Hy-Brasil and Tim McInnerny does a fine comic turn as a Funny Berserker, but best of all is Mickey Rooney as Erik's grandfather, in a bonkers performance recalling Ernest Borgnine in *The Vikings* but far more deranged. This is a good-looking film, even when it lapses into Pythonesque cartoonery, thanks in part to concept art from Alan Lee, famous for his Tolkien paintings. However, scenes are often too dark for clarity, and during the action the dialogue is mixed so low it's often unintelligible. Worth a gander if you're a Python fan or must see every movie about Vikings, but otherwise it's far from essential.

EXCALIBUR

Rating: ★★★★★ • *Origin:* USA, 1981 • *Director:* John Boorman • *Source:* Warner Bros. DVD

In the late 1470s, English knight Thomas Malory decided to collect all the major Arthurian stories in French, Welsh, and English, put them into a coherent order, and retell them as the book *Le Morte Darthur*. In the late 1970s, English director John Boorman decided to collect all the major incidents of Malory's book and retell them as a visionary feature film. Both efforts were ambitious to the point of madness, and yet both were resoundingly successful.

Filming Malory meant making changes to adapt to the medium of cinema, of course, and Boorman and cowriter Rospo Pallenberg decided to focus on King Arthur's legendary sword Excalibur, bringing it onstage before Malory did and investing it with mystical significance beyond what it had in *Le Morte*. The other major decision was

Excalibur Author's Collection

to expand the part of the wizard Merlin, making him more central to the story and keeping him around longer than in Malory. Both choices strengthened the movie's core narrative.

The resulting film is long and episodic, like the book, but it hangs together, and most important, considering it's a movie, it looks fabulous. Shot in the lush forests of Ireland's County Wicklow, it's drenched in saturated color, vivid and magical. The sumptuous costumes are exaggerated fantasies of medieval clothing, like opera costumes, an approach that works well against a sonic backdrop of soaring music by Richard Wagner and Carl Orff.

And the acting is a treat. King Arthur is played by classically trained Nigel Terry, who portrays him from his teens to his 50s, but the film really revolves around the rivalry between sorcerers Merlin and Morgana, memorably played by Nicol Williamson and Helen Mirren. Williamson in particular is not your father's comfortable old Merlin; he's *strange*, speaking his lines in a high, singsong pattern that gives his gnomic pronouncements uncanny significance. In addition, Nicholas Clay and Cherie Lunghi practically glow as Lancelot and Guenevere, and even the minor roles are filled by soon-to-be heavyweights like Patrick Stewart, Liam Neeson, and Gabriel Byrne.

The dialogue is mostly simple and direct, avoiding florid ye olde knightspeak, allowing the imagery to carry most of the storytelling weight. The story itself stretches from Arthur's conception, in an act of adultery enabled by Merlin's magic, through his youth drawing the sword from the stone, gathering Lancelot to his side, marrying Guenevere, and founding Camelot and the brotherhood of the Round Table. The knightly combats, orchestrated by fight director William Hobbs, are taut and exciting, particularly during the period of Arthur's early struggles. The story lags a bit during the Grail quest, as it does in the book, but Boorman ties the holy relic back into the tale of Arthur, reviving him in time to face the threat of Mordred (Robert Addie), his evil son conceived in sorcerous sin on his half-sister Morgana, echoing Arthur's own conception. The Christian mysticism never impedes the drive of the story much, and in the finale Boorman raises the tone to epic without going too far into ponderous.

In short, this is the best cinematic adaptation of *Le Morte Darthur* made up to its time, and as of 2022 it still hasn't been topped. If you haven't seen it, you have a memorable couple of hours ahead of you.

THE FALL OF THE ROMAN EMPIRE

Rating: ★★☆☆☆ • *Origin:* USA, 1964 • *Director:* Anthony Mann •
Source: Genius Products DVD

A grand historical epic from the producer and director who'd made *El Cid* (1961), starring Sophia Loren, Christopher Plummer, Alec Guinness, and James Mason, with cinematography by the great Robert Krasker and action scenes directed by Yakima Canutt, in the same late Roman setting as Ridley Scott's *Gladiator* (2000). What could go wrong?

The Fall of the Roman Empire is an object lesson in how little the above matters when your movie has a crap story. The script here is dead in the water, with characters continually talking past each other, declaiming in tone-deaf speech after speech, but all those grandiose speeches still aren't enough exposition to put the story across, so they're backed up by ill-placed internal monologues that drag it down further. The dialogue is pompous, self-important, and oh-so-significant, and the visual storytelling is little better. Oh, it's pretty enough, especially the first hour, set in the snowy forests of central Europe, with magnificent sets and fabulous costumes, but the costumes are worn by passionless mannequins sleepwalking through their parts. And the worst of these is Stephen Boyd as the nominal lead, General Gaius Livius: Boyd is a handsome nullity, an empty suit of Roman armor, and if he doesn't strike a single spark with Sophia Loren as his supposed great love Lucilla, it's no surprise.

Loren is wasted here, and so is James Mason as the saintly philosopher Timonides—saintly just isn't a good look for Mason. On the plus side, Alec Guinness does his best as the dying Caesar Marcus Aurelius, but he'd have done a lot better if his dialogue didn't sound like it came out of a textbook. In truth, only Christopher Plummer manages to find any juice in his role, but then he gets to be the odious villain, the increasingly mad Emperor Commodus. Plummer is the only one who's really jumped aboard this train wreck, and he gleefully seizes the engineer's levers and drives the train right off the bridge. When Plummer is onscreen, this movie is worth watching, but otherwise its three-plus hours of speeches and Roman processions—so many processions!—are barely tolerable.

True, occasionally there's some action between the speeches and processions. There are two fairly decent battles directed by Canutt, the best being a skirmish between the legionaries and the Germanic barbarians in the wintry forest. There's a ridiculous fight between two chariot drivers as their rigs careen down narrow mountain roads, jumping downed trees and teetering on precipices—come on, guys, just stop those things, step down and fight it out on terra firma. There are also a couple of unconvincing clashes with short swords, but it's all made up for by the finale, a two-man javelin duel in a square walled in by Roman soldiers with interlocking shields. It's spectacular and worth putting up with an hour of speeches and processions—but probably not two hours and certainly not three. This overwrought turkey tanked at the box office, and the verdict of the viewing public was spot on.

FANFAN LA TULIPE

Rating: ★★★★☆ • *Origin:* France/Italy, 1952 • *Director:* Christian-Jaque • *Source:* Criterion DVD

In this classic French comedy swashbuckler, Gérard Philipe plays the role of Fanfan, a name that's a term of endearment for a charming child, and this film is nothing if not charming and endearing. But though childlike in some ways, Fanfan is no child: we first see him in a haystack where he's just seduced a farmer's daughter. Active and confident, for a while he escapes the farmer and his pursuing friends, but eventually Fanfan is caught and sentenced to a shotgun wedding. While being frog-marched to the altar, Fanfan meets the voluptuous Adeline (Gina Lollobrigida): she pretends to read his fortune, telling him he will join the army, become a famous war hero, and marry the daughter of the king!

Faced with life married into a farming family, Fanfan decides he prefers to believe in this fortune and follow it to his destiny. As it's the middle of the 18th century and France is recruiting soldiers for the Seven Years' War, Fanfan flees his would-be in-laws and signs up with the Regiment of Aquitaine—only to find that Adeline is the daughter of the regiment's recruiter and told him that story just so her father would get a bonus for the new recruit. Destiny or no, Fanfan makes a terrible soldier and seems bound for a permanent home in the brig until his troop encounters a noble's coach being attacked by bandits. While the other soldiers cower, Fanfan single-handedly takes on the bandits, all the more eagerly when he finds the coach contains two beautiful ladies, and drives off the attackers. Fanfan is pleased with himself and then stunned to find that the ladies in the coach are the Marquise de Pompadour (Geneviève Page), the mistress of the king, and Princess Henriette (Sylvie Pelayo), the king's daughter!

The marquise gives Fanfan a brooch shaped like a tulip, earning him the moniker Fanfan la Tulipe—but Princess Henriette gives him a kiss. Destiny calls!

As Fanfan, Philipe is winning and irrepressible, even when being marched to the gallows or thrown in prison for yet another exploit. And, *sacre bleu*, the man can fence, bounding around saber in hand, grinning from ear to ear, in a performance that can't help but bring to mind Gene Kelly as d'Artagnan in the 1948 *Three Musketeers*. As soon as one bout is over, you want to watch it again, just to savor it.

The story is slight and knowingly improbable, all but winking at the viewer so you won't take it too seriously. Lollobrigida is just on the cusp of her international stardom, and her Adeline is feisty enough to slap the faces of both Fanfan and King Louis XV. The direction is clean and unencumbered by artsy flourishes, sharp and quick in the action scenes while giving the character actors plenty of space during the comedy bits. For a fun evening, pair director Christian-Jaque's *Fanfan la Tulipe* with his later swashbuckler *The Black Tulip* from 1964. *Délicieux!*

THE FATE OF LEE KHAN

Rating: ★★★★☆ • *Origin:* Hong Kong, 1973 • *Director:* King Hu • *Source:* Eureka! Blu-ray

After the commercial failure of *A Touch of Zen*, writer-director King Hu turned to a new variation on his blockbuster success *Dragon Inn*. Though less ambitious than *Zen*, *Lee Khan* still sees Hu pushing the envelope in several areas. For one thing, instead of a single strong female character, as in previous Hu *wuxia* films, this time around there is a half dozen—nearly half the combatants here are women. Moreover, the cast is full of top-notch character actors, and much of the story is conveyed by their expressions, sometimes subtly, sometimes as broadly as if this was a silent film.

The story is set toward the end of the Yuan dynasty, when China is ruled by the Mongols, and one of their leaders, Lee Khan (Tien Feng), is seeking to crush the rising revolt of the Han Chinese under General Zhu. Khan's sister and collaborator, Lee Wan-erh (Hsu Feng), corrupts one of Zhu's officers into selling them a map of Zhu's deployments, and the pair arrange to meet the traitor at the remote Spring Inn. But the rebels have their own spies among Lee Khan's forces, so agents from both sides—all martial artists, of course!—converge on Spring Inn to try to get hold of the map.

Almost the entire film is set inside the inn; it could almost be a stage play. The inn is run by Madame Wan (the great Li Li-Hua), and in preparations for the shenanigans to come, she hires four women, rebel outlaws all, as her new table servers. They are joined by Wang (Ying Bai), the leading rebel agent, and his sidekick Yun (fight director Sammo Hung), a comically obnoxious musician. In the lighthearted first half of the movie, the inn's rebel agents are tested by several waves of troublemakers—bandits, cheating gamblers, and crooked cops—which gives the outlaw waitresses a chance to show their chops as they settle the intruders' hash.

But some of the troublemakers are actually Lee Khan's advance agents, and when Khan and Wan-erh arrive suddenly, accompanied by a troop of murderous guards, the tone of the film darkens. The crooked cops are arrested by Khan's guards and taken away for summary execution, and then Khan's spymaster, Tsao (Roy Chiao), tipped off by the advance agents, begins a fierce interrogation of the employees of the inn. But Tsao stops short of denouncing any of the rebels because he is secretly a rebel, too, determined to help get the traitor's map and, if possible, put an end to Lee Khan.

The movie's second half is a suspenseful heist drama, with tense scenes savoring of Hitchcock, especially when Black Peony (Angela Mao), the lockpicking rogue waitress, steals the wrong document from Lee Khan and then has to find a way to return it. The tension ratchets tighter and tighter until the final explosion, when the masks come off and the blades come out—though in keeping with where Hong Kong action films were going in 1973, there's as much unarmed combat as armed. The final, extended melee bursts the bounds of the Spring Inn, and director Hu moves the mass combat outdoors for the slam-bang climax. Very satisfying.

THE 5TH MUSKETEER (OR *BEHIND THE IRON MASK*)

Rating: ★★★☆☆ • *Origin:* Germany/Austria, 1979 • *Director:* Ken Annakin • *Source:* Columbia DVD

This adaptation of Dumas's *The Man in the Iron Mask*, another attempt to replicate the success of *The Three* and *The Four Musketeers*, follows Richard Lester's formula of a large-scale production with an all-star cast. It was shot in 1976, but release was delayed when the Richard Chamberlain version of *Iron Mask* beat them out of the gate, and to distinguish this film from Chamberlain's, the name was changed to *The 5th Musketeer*, a rather obvious attempt to associate it with the Lester films.

This one's a loose remake of the 1939 *Iron Mask*, to the extent that George Bruce, the scripter of that film, even gets a writing credit, but screenwriter David Ambrose goes Bruce one better by making the characters of Prince Philippe and Maria Teresa active heroes rather than passive victims. In fact, this could have been one of the best screen versions of *Iron Mask* if only it had been made with enthusiasm instead of mere professionalism and if it didn't have for its lead the woefully miscast Beau Bridges in the double role of Prince Philippe and King Louis XIV. Bridges is simply out of his depth, bland and uncharismatic, his voice breaking when he raises it to give royal commands. Ugh.

Young King Louis is a weak bully who spends his time in bed with his mistress Ursula Andress, playing the meanest and sluttiest Louise de La Vallière ever. Meanwhile, in far Gascony, his unknown twin brother Philippe is being raised in seclusion by d'Artagnan (Cornel Wilde, playing the role for second time) and the Three Musketeers, secretly advised by Colbert the Good Minister (Rex Harrison, playing himself as usual). However, Fouquet the Bad Minister (a young Ian McShane) finds out about Philippe and has him abducted for a rather silly evil plot in which the prince, dressed up as King Louis to receive his bride, Spanish Infanta Maria Teresa (Sylvia Kristel), will be assassinated by "rebels." The real king will then miraculously reappear, thus confirming his divine right to absolute rule. However, assassinating a young man raised by the Four Musketeers isn't quite so easy: Philippe spots the black powder death trap and leaps at the last moment, grabs a convenient rapier, and then we're off into the usual dance of sword fights, kidnappings, impostures, rescues, love affairs, secret passages, and dreadful metallic headgear.

The direction by old hand Ken Annakin is merely passable except in scenes of suspense, which he still shows a talent for. The swordplay is perfunctory, and the costumes, though colorful, are a bit cheap and look rented—but the settings, in the palaces, castles, and cathedrals of Austria, are amazing. Lloyd Bridges as Aramis is as miscast as his son, but it's a pleasure to see the venerable José Ferrer and Olivia de Havilland in small roles as Athos and the Queen Mother. Awful old Alan Hale Jr. plays Porthos for the second time, as his father did before him in the 1939 *Iron Mask*, and this time he finally, finally gets it right. Alan Hale: redeemed after all his cinematic sins! Who could have guessed?

FIRE OVER ENGLAND

Rating: ★★★★☆ • *Origin:* UK, 1937 • *Director:* William K. Howard •
Source: Nobility Studios DVD

This film was adapted from the 1936 novel of the same name by A. E. W. Mason, the English historical fiction author best known for *The Four Feathers* (1902). Producer Alexander Korda was looking for a suitably inspiring and cautionary tale that would evoke the rising threat of Hitler's Germany, and he found it in this story of England's resistance to Spain's warmongering King Philip and his invading Armada. Korda was also looking for a vehicle with a romantic subplot to show off his drop-dead gorgeous new stars, Laurence Olivier and Vivien Leigh, who were already lovers offscreen. However, as undeniably attractive as Olivier and Leigh were, this picture really belongs to the actors in the roles of the opposing monarchs: Raymond Massey as King Philip II, and the unforgettable Flora Robson as Queen Elizabeth I.

It's 1588, and mighty Spain threatens tiny England; at the English Court, Spanish spies are everywhere, and their assassination plots threaten the life of the queen. In her audience hall, Elizabeth receives the Spanish ambassador, come to complain about the raid on Cadiz by Francis Drake, where he burned a Spanish fleet. Robson's Elizabeth immediately establishes herself as a commanding presence, adroitly alternating between defiance and conciliation; she refuses to reign in Drake and the sea rovers but gives Spain leave to punish them . . . "if they can."

The perilous situation established, cut to a boarding action at sea, where Michael Ingolby (Olivier), in a fine gleaming back-and-breast, leads a crew of English sea dogs onto the deck of a Spanish galleon. But the attack goes wrong, the Englishmen are overwhelmed, and Ingolby and his father, the English captain, are taken to Spain in irons. There, bad turns to worse, and by the time Ingolby escapes to return to England, he has terrible crimes to avenge.

Back in London, all is plots and intrigue. Ingolby is reunited with his beloved Cynthia (Vivien Leigh), one of Elizabeth's ladies-in-waiting, but their time together is short. After Ingolby saves the queen from an assassin, she gives him a new mission, to impersonate a Spanish agent and return to Spain as a spy.

Madrid: enter King Philip, calmly commanding, "*Employ rigorous means. Only by fear can people be made to do their duty—and not always then.*" Philip is a cold tyrant, all domineering intellect driven by frigid religious zeal. In the Palacio Real, a desperate duel of wits unfolds between the suspicious king and the impersonating young spy, a contest that's a symbol of the war between Spain and England and the fulcrum upon which the whole plot pivots. Philip's lip curls, masks are torn away, swashbuckling happens, and Ingolby hastens back to England just ahead of the sails of the Armada. All the plots and intrigues collide as Robson magnificently rouses her realm to resist the Spanish Armada for the exciting climax, in which Ingolby plays a key part. (Two words: fire ships!)

This is a handsome film, shot by the great Chinese American cinematographer James Wong Howe, but like most of the prewar Korda pictures, it's fallen into the public domain, and it's hard to find a good, clean digital transfer. Nobility Studios has done a painstaking restoration, and it's that version which I recommend. Watch for James Mason in a small, uncredited role as the traitorous Englishman Hilary Vane.

THE FLAME AND THE ARROW

Rating: ★★★★☆ • *Origin:* USA, 1950 • *Director:* Jacques Tourneur •
Source: Warner Bros. DVD

Burt Lancaster burst onto the Hollywood scene in 1946 playing a tender tough guy in *The Killers*, a dark film noir based on a Hemingway story, and he soon earned a reputation for excelling at edgy, dramatic roles. But before Hollywood, and before his service in World War II, Lancaster had been . . . a circus performer. In the 1930s he was one half of Lang & Cravat, a comical acrobatic act with his diminutive partner and lifelong friend Nick Cravat, who, as part of his shtick, never said a word, leaving all the snappy patter to Lancaster.

The Flame and the Arrow AUTHOR'S COLLECTION

By 1950 Lancaster was a big enough star that he was coproducing his own films, and he decided to expand his repertoire beyond gritty noir by doing a swashbuckler costarring his old partner Cravat. The screen chemistry of the laughing pals was palpable, their acrobatic antics hilarious, and the film was a big hit.

That film was *The Flame and the Arrow*. It's set in northern Italy in the twelfth century, when the mountains of Lombardy were occupied by the Germans of Holy Roman Emperor Frederick Barbarossa. In a mountain town ruled by the brutal Count Ulrich of Hesse, known as the Hawk (Frank Allenby), the villagers are thrilled by the return of their favorite son, the carefree hunter and crack archer Dardo (Burt Lancaster). The townspeople try to persuade Dardo to join their plans to resist the Hessians, but Dardo says he depends on no one but himself, and says he's "not out to right anybody's wrongs but my own." Well, we know he won't be singing that selfish tune for long once collective action is called for, especially since this film was written by Waldo Salt, who was about to be blacklisted in the imminent McCarthy era when he refused to testify before the House Un-American Activities Committee. Time to join the revolution, Comrade Dardo!

The personal wrong that Dardo's out to right is that he has a five-year-old son, Rudi, whom he's raising alone because his wife left him to become the Hawk's mistress. After Dardo, for the doubtful benefit of Rudi, publicly humiliates his mother in front of the Hawk, Count Ulrich decides to abduct Rudi into the castle to raise him as a Hessian. And thus begins the cycle of kidnappings, raids, and escapes that make up the exciting action of the rest of the picture, as Dardo reluctantly assumes the leadership of the anti-Hessian resistance.

The script is quite good, sharp without ever getting too dark, and with some clever byplay that almost justifies the romance between Dardo and the Hawk's niece Lady Anne (Virginia Mayo, as pale and bland as the condiment), whom Dardo kidnaps in a bid to trade her for Rudi. Lancaster rules the screen with his infectious grin and the twinkle in his eye, and he's an even more athletic swashbuckler than his obvious model, Douglas Fairbanks Sr., because he performs his lithe acrobatics with a virile muscularity Doug Sr. couldn't match. The director's chair is capably filled by Jacques Tourneur, who keeps things light, bright, and quick until the final confrontation in a darkened castle hall, which is staged with some of his signature moody lighting and artistic angles. Top it off with a score by Max Steiner, and you've got a very satisfying 90 minutes.

THE FLASHING BLADE

Rating: ★★★☆☆ • *Origin:* France, 1967 • *Director:* Yannick Andrei • *Source:* Network DVDs

It's 1630, and during one of the conflicts between Spain and France, the War of the Mantuan Succession, the fortress of Casal, held by the French, is besieged by a much larger Spanish force. But an adventurous Frenchman, the young Chevalier de Recci (Robert Etcheverry), accompanied only by his loyal lackey Guillot (Jacques Balutin), fights his way through the Spanish lines and into the besieged garrison. Does he bring an important message? No, he comes solely in search of glory!

The French commander, General de Thoiras (Gilles Pelletier), is in a desperate plight and has no place in his ranks for glory hounds, so he sends Recci on a secret mission to Marshal de La Force for reinforcements. To reach La Force, Recci sets out to cross the neutral Duchy of Savoy but runs afoul of the Spanish troops of Don Alonso (Mario Pilar). Alonso plots to wreck the truce negotiations between France and Spain at the Savoyard château of the Duke of Sospel. Unable to cut his way through the Spaniards, Recci is caught in Savoy in a web of international intrigue—but, entranced by the blue eyes of Isabelle de Sospel (Geneviève Casile), there's nowhere he'd rather be.

This action-packed swashbuckler was originally a full-color French miniseries of four 75-minute episodes called *Le Chevalier Tempête*. Bought by the BBC, it was cut up into twelve 25-minute episodes for British broadcast and dubbed, spectacularly well, into English. Originally shown in the UK in 1969, it was so popular it was rerun repeatedly during the 1970s. The story is a heady mixture of political intrigue, headlong chases, and sudden swordplay, and if the heroes don't have the depth of a d'Artagnan or a Cyrano, at least they're good-looking and active. The best characters are the intriguers: Claude Gensac as Mademoiselle Mireille, sly and convincing as a cunning secret agent of Cardinal Richelieu, and Giani Esposito, delightful in the role of Jules Mazarin, a wily papal envoy. Historically, Mazarin would go on to become a protégé of Richelieu, replacing him after his death as a cardinal and France's prime minister. Mazarin is the only character who appears both here and in Alexandre Dumas's novel about the War of the Mantuan Succession, *The Red Sphinx*, but *The Flashing Blade* owes its entire look and feel to Dumas's Musketeers novels.

This series isn't deep, but it's heartfelt. For a TV show, the period-perfect costumes are excellent, the forts and châteaux are all authentic locations, and the fencing with cup-hilt rapiers isn't bad. The French and Spanish musketeers—with muskets!—are spot on. And it has a dumb but ridiculously catchy galloping theme song that you can't get out of your head.

Bizarrely, during the initial British broadcast, there was a catastrophic technical fault a few minutes into the 12th and final episode, and the show went dark. In the attempt to save it, the dubbed version was somehow scrubbed and lost, so the last episode, a sort of epilogue, was never shown in British rerun. For the DVD release, Network went back to the original French show and subtitled it for episode 12, giving us a glimpse of *Le Chevalier Tempête* in its original form. *Très fascinant!*

FLESH + BLOOD (OR *FLESH AND BLOOD* OR *THE ROSE AND THE SWORD*)

Rating: ★★★★☆ • *Origin:* USA/Netherlands/Spain, 1985 • *Director:* Paul Verhoeven •
Source: MGM DVD

This historical drama is a stark and unflinching look at the damage war does to people. Good though it is, it won't be for everybody, as it's explicit and often brutal, even macabre, so fair warning.

The setting is northern Italy in 1501, a period of flowering Renaissance scholarship, bubonic plague, and bloody warfare between the Italian city-states. Lord Arnolfini (Fernando Hilbeck) has been thrown out of the city he ruled and has hired the mercenary Captain Hawkwood (Jack Thompson, playing a character based on the historical John Hawkwood), to retake it for him. Among Hawkwood's mercenary troops is a band of soldiers led by the hard-boiled but charismatic Martin (Rutger Hauer). They are promised that if they take the city, they can loot it to their heart's content. But after they succeed Arnolfini breaks his promise, disarms the mercenaries with Hawkwood's help, and turns them away empty-handed. Martin vows revenge.

Arnolfini's son Steven (Tom Burlinson), a would-be scholar, is engaged to the young Agnes (Jennifer Jason Leigh), a princess from a neighboring realm. They meet, and though Steven doesn't wish to marry, Agnes, who wants him and is both determined and resourceful, persuades Steven to change his mind. But then Agnes's dowry caravan, with Agnes hiding inside it, is hijacked by Martin and his mercenaries. When she's discovered, Agnes is raped by Martin in an ugly scene, but she quickly identifies him as the leader and decides her best chance of living through her captivity is to become his accomplice and lover. Together they invade a castle by stealth, opening the gates to let Martin's mercenaries in for massacre and looting. But Steven and Hawkwood are in close pursuit, and when they put the castle under siege, Steven tells Agnes that she's going to have to choose between him and Martin. "Winner takes all," she says.

This is the first English-language film for director Paul Verhoeven (*Robocop*, *Starship Troopers*), displaying his signature mix of violence, sex, and astringent social commentary. The visuals are, rich, evocative, and devoid of sentimentality—the camera never looks away, and neither can you. The leads all deliver sharp, even biting, performances, and even the secondary characters are sharply drawn and memorable. If the story rambles a bit, it's usually to give some side character some well-deserved screen time, but soon enough it returns to its central point: when war has destroyed ethics, morals, and honor, the only virtue left is survival. There are no good guys here, only those who die and those who do not.

Shot in superb locations in Spain, with nail-biting and savage combat offset by an exuberant score from Basil Poledouris, the action holds your attention all the way to the unexpected ending. Extra points for the scholastic Steven's Leonardo da Vinci–inspired wooden turtle tank siege engine with its ultra-phallic telescoping ramp. Unbelievable.

FORTUNES OF CAPTAIN BLOOD

Rating: ★★★☆☆ • *Origin:* USA, 1950 • *Director:* Gordon Douglas •
Source: Columbia/Sony DVD

This starts out as a conventional pirate adventure but takes an unusual turn after Captain Blood (Louis Hayward) learns that six of his crew have been captured and enslaved by the heartless Marquis de Riconete (George Macready). To find a way to free them, Blood leaves his ship and the rest of his crew and makes his way alone, disguised as a peasant, into the Spanish colonial port of La Hacha. There, acting much like an undercover detective, he moves through a shadowy world of devious slavers, murderous smugglers, greedy jailers, and desperate women, in a story that feels less like a pirate adventure than a filibuster noir. (See, that's *clever*, because "filibuster" is an old word that also used to mean "buccaneer.")

Though some sources call this a remake of the 1935 *Captain Blood*, it very much is not, being based on writer Rafael Sabatini's *The Fortunes of Captain Blood* (1936), a collection of six linked stories about Peter Blood. In fact, the plot here ably reflects the tales of shifting loyalties and betrayal that Sabatini did so well. And as always in a Sabatini story, victory goes to the man who is adroit and clever but who never betrays his code of honor.

Matching the dark tone of the story, when violence breaks out, it's rough and brutal, unusually so for the Hollywood of 1950. The escape from the prison feels genuinely dangerous. Likewise, the final confrontation at sea between Blood's ship, trapped in a bay, and the marquis's much larger galleon, takes some sharp and unexpected turns—thanks, once again, to ideas borrowed from Sabatini. Thus despite a slow start in La Hacha, this film pays off handsomely in the end.

THE FOUR MUSKETEERS (OR THE REVENGE OF MILADY)

Rating: ★★★★★ (Essential) • *Origin:* UK, 1974 • *Director:* Richard Lester •
Source: StudioCanal Blu-ray

This is the sequel to *The Three Musketeers* (1973), the second half of a two-part adaptation of Alexandre Dumas's greatest novel. The first half of the book, the tale of the queen's diamonds, is largely a self-contained story that ends on a triumph, so it's understandable that screen adaptations often confine themselves to just that part of the saga. The novel's second half is more complicated, darker in tone, and its ending is bittersweet, so it's rare for it to get the full cinematic treatment, as it does here. This is a reasonably close adaptation, and if screenwriter George MacDonald Fraser takes more liberties with the plot than he did with the first half, it's understandable. Some of his changes are actually improvements, clarifying and tightening, that rectify plot flaws in the original.

Though the story in *T4M* jumps around more and is less cohesive than in *T3M*, the second film contains scenes that are more intense and memorable than any in the first. Those involving Athos and Milady are the standouts here, as Oliver Reed and Faye Dunaway walk away with the movie. Dunaway didn't get much screen time in *T3M*, but her performance here more than makes up for that; she's subtle and layered, simultaneously sinister and affecting, and Reed is her mirror-image, wounded and vengeful: "I knew a man once . . ."

As mentioned above, the tone is darker this time 'round: France and England are going to war, the stakes in the game are higher, and the loss of a hand means somebody dies. The

The Four Musketeers Author's Collection

action sequences are just as inventive as in *T3M*, exciting but with touches of comedy. One of the best scenes in the novel, the siege of the St. Gervais bastion where the musketeers have breakfast on a battlefield while secretly discussing the threat of Milady, is marvelously rendered; that chapter rarely makes it into film adaptations, but it receives the full treatment here. Best of all is the final extended fight at the convent of Armentières between the musketeers and a full dozen of the Cardinal's Guards, a scene that isn't even in the book, added here to provide a final showdown with the Comte de Rochefort (Christopher Lee). First Rochefort duels Athos, and it's a delight to see the old Hammer Films compatriots Lee and Reed going at it hammer and tongs. The final battle between Rochefort and the enraged d'Artagnan (Michael York), who's just come from discovering the corpse of his beloved Constance (Raquel Welch), is just tremendous: staged in the nave of the chapel, in sunbeams tinted by the stained glass in the great rose window, the two men, nearly dead from fatigue, flail away at each other in desperate fury until finally d'Artagnan gets his revenge.

Of course, the great Cardinal Richelieu (Charlton Heston) gets the last word. In his final scene, where he ruefully acknowledges that he's lost the game to d'Artagnan and his comrades, the cardinal-duke lives up to the acid advice he'd given Milady earlier in the film: "If you should lose, do it with a becoming grace."

FREELANCE SAMURAI (OR *DEMON CRUSADER* OR *DEMON HUNTER SAMURAI*)

Rating: ★★★★☆ • *Origin:* Japan, 1957 • *Director:* Kenji Misumi •
Source: YouTube streaming video

This is a genial samurai adventure in the swashbuckling subgenre of princes separated at birth and then used as pawns in dynastic struggles. Its protagonist is the charming Shinjiro (Raizô Ichikawa), the "lost" coheir to the Wakagi clan who goes by the moniker Momotaro, the name of the legendary demon hunter "Peach Boy." An orphan now that his samurai mother has died, Momotaro has in fact come to Edo (Tokyo) to hunt demons and fight injustice because, as he says, he "can't let outlaws go unpunished." When we first see him, Momotaro is playing with some street kids but almost immediately comes to the aid of Kosuzu (Michiyo Kogure), a woman being harassed by two out-of-town samurai who accuse her of theft.

Kosuzu is taken with Momotaro and attaches herself to him, as does a street rogue named Inosuke the Monkey Man (Shungi Sakai), who becomes his comedy sidekick. (In the legends, Momotaro is always accompanied by animal chums, one of whom is a monkey.)

The story turns darker when Momotaro comes to the aid of Lady Yuri (Yoko Uraji) when she's assailed by masked abductors. There's a simmering conflict in the Wakagi clan in which an ambitious councilor is attempting to elevate an illegitimate son of the lord over the true son and heir, Shinnosuke (also Raizô Ichikawa). Yuri is on the side of the real "young lord," who must travel to the Wakagis' province to protect his claim—but on the eve of leaving, he's poisoned almost to death by the villain Hankuro (Seizaburo Kawazu). Momotaro, who's been brought in by Yuri, realizes Shinnosuke is his long-lost twin brother and reluctantly decides to act as his stand-in for the dangerous journey to the provinces. (You got all that, right?)

Momotaro, of course, is hot stuff with a *katana*, though the bad Wakagi are big cheaters who also use firearms, so the odds are frequently against him. The story has just enough twists and reversals in it to keep the plot hopping, plus for spice there's a romantic tug of war for Momotaro's heart between good beauty Yuri and bad beauty Kosuzu. This film is an early standout for director Kenji Misumi, who handles all these elements with confidence. Ichikawa, a former kabuki actor, is expressive and charismatic and to this day is the subject of a Japanese fan club. Kawazu as Hankuro is a solid villain, but this film is more comedy than tragedy, and you never doubt that Momotaro will win through in the end. Go go, Peach Boy!

THE FURTHER ADVENTURES OF THE MUSKETEERS

Rating: ★★★☆☆ • *Origin:* UK, 1967 • *Directors:* Christopher Barry and Hugh David •
Source: Simply Media DVDs

This, the BBC's follow-up to its 1966 *The Three Musketeers* miniseries, is based on Alexandre Dumas's first sequel to that novel, *Twenty Years After*, a book so large that my modern translation of it had to be published in two volumes: *Twenty Years After* and *Blood Royal*. And indeed, the BBC, which needed ten 25-minute episodes to adapt *The Three Musketeers*, needed 16 episodes for its sequel. Being the BBC, it adapted the novel straight, though with a sadly low budget, but the result, low budget or no, is the most authentic version of *Twenty Years After* ever filmed.

Which begs the question, Is a nearly seven-hour, low-budget, authentic film version of Dumas's long and complex novel worth the effort? The surprising answer is *yes*, if you have a sharp script and the four musketeers as strongly cast as in this version. Jeremy Young as Athos and Brian Blessed as Porthos return from the previous series, with the excellent John Woodvine stepping in as Aramis and, best of all, Joss Ackland as the mature d'Artagnan. In this story d'Artagnan comes into his own as a leader and master planner, a role in which Ackland excels—but if d'Artagnan is the brains of these musketeers, Brian Blessed is their heart and soul. To take advantage of Blessed's irrepressible joie de vivre, the role of Porthos is expanded here to be almost equal to d'Artagnan's, and the result is the finest screen depiction of the plus-size musketeer ever.

Frankly, the tale needs all the Porthos it can get. The complex story starts with a rebellion in France, moves across the Channel to the English Civil War and the trial of King Charles I, and then heads back to Paris to conclude the rebellion there. Politics and personal ambition mean the musketeers are split and on opposite sides in both conflicts, until the brilliant d'Artagnan finds a way to reunite them behind a single cause. The first five episodes move quickly, but the middle half dozen bog down in too much intrigue and too many characters; fortunately, however, the pace picks up again for the ending. Though the four musketeers are outstanding, the rest of the cast are basically just good enough, unusual for a prestige BBC production. The swashbuckling and swordplay are also adequate, and there's plenty of them, with a number of action scenes added that don't appear in the novel. Dumas felt that he had put enough of everything into *Twenty Years After* except romance, and this miniseries addresses that by elevating two of his female characters to greater prominence and then giving them something to do beyond just being objects of adoration. So extra points for that. Nonetheless, unless you're a big Dumas fan, you may find this a long slog, even with Blessed's glorious performance as Porthos.

FURY OF ACHILLES

Rating: ★★★☆☆ • *Origin:* Italy, 1962 • *Director:* Marino Girolami •
Source: YouTube streaming video

If you're interested in Greek warfare of the classical period, you might want to read Homer's *Iliad*, the story of the end of the Trojan War. (I recommend the recent translation by Caroline Alexander.) But if 500 pages of Hellenic proper names don't sound appealing, as an alternative you could do worse than to watch *Fury of Achilles*. This Italian sword-and-sandal mini-epic may have a modest budget and a few wooden actors, but it hews closer to the source material than most mid-century Trojan War movies, featuring divine magic and active meddling by the gods, which technically makes it a fantasy rather than a historical war story. Focusing on Achilles (Gordon Mitchell), this tells the tale of the 10th year of the war from the Greek perspective, with solid portrayals of movers and shakers such as King Agamemnon (Mario Petri), Ulysses (Piero Lulli), and Achilles's best bud Patroclus (Ennio Girolami). The Trojans get comparatively short shrift, with a spotlight only on the noble Hector (Jacques Bergerac).

However, this is an action film rather than a political thriller, with the mighty Gordon Mitchell front and center. The man looks like a marble statue of a Greek warrior come to life, radiating a compelling screen presence that makes up for his limited emotional range. With the Greeks short on provisions, Achilles with Agamemnon and Ulysses goes raiding in the Trojan back country, conquering a small city and claiming its aristocratic daughters as their personal slaves. Against all the omens, Agamemnon chooses as his prize Chryseis (Eleonora Bianchi), a priestess of Apollo, while Achilles takes the sullen-but-gorgeous Briseis (Gloria Milland) back to his tent. Achilles washes off the blood and comes around for lovemaking, but Briseis is defiant and tries to stick a dagger into him—and the blade melts because Achilles, of course, is a son of the goddess Thetis and 98 percent divinely invulnerable. However, he knows he is fated by prophecy to die before the walls of Troy, and rather than struggle against fate, he accepts that he is doomed. Briseis thinks that's hot, and they snog.

Agamemnon isn't so lucky with Chryseis, as Apollo, offended, smites the Greek army with a tempest and a nine-day plague. To end the smiting, the king gives up Chryseis, but he demands Briseis from Achilles as compensation, and that's where things start to go wrong. Achilles pulls himself and his Myrmidons out of the siege, Hector and his Trojans counterattack the weakened Greek forces, and Patroclus makes the fatal decision to don Achilles's armor and fight Hector in his place. This begins the last of the film's three big battle sequences, which is where *Fury of Achilles* really shines. With a limited number of troops onscreen, director

Girolami nonetheless manages, by clever staging, to give the impression of titanic battles, and unlike most Italian historicals, the combat is top-notch, with the extras fired up and working at it. The single combats are all tense and suspenseful, and the final duel between Achilles and Hector is one of the best short-sword bouts on film. Kudos to stunt coordinator Remo De Angelis for the dynamic action.

Bonus: with a slight overlap, this film ends where Steve Reeves's *The Trojan Horse* (1961) starts. Watch 'em both.

THE FURY OF HERCULES

Rating: ★★☆☆☆ • *Origin:* Italy, 1962 • *Director:* Gianfranco Parolini •
Source: Mill Creek DVD

This is a standard peplum that follows the usual formula: there's an ancient Greek city ruled by a tyrannical Bad Queen who is opposed by a faction of virtuous rebels. Our hero—in this case Hercules (Brad Harris)—is romanced by Queen Cnidia (Mara Berni) but ultimately throws in his lot with the rebels and overthrows the tyrants. The only twist in this iteration on the formula is that the bad queen might actually be a good queen who was given terrible advice by a bad minister (Serge Gainsbourg). The story is unusually muddled for a peak peplum, with some inexplicable plot turns and a few too many characters, but at least there are Mighty Feats of Strength involving lion wrestling, colossal lever turning, and stone block wrangling. There's also a guy in a gorilla suit, but the less said about him, the better.

The final battle, involving Herc, the rebels, and the good/bad queen's royal guard is actually pretty good, but Zeus! It was a long haul getting there. To quote the Bad Minister, "Without violence, power gives no satisfaction." I guess this time the joke's on you, Bad Minister!

GATE OF HELL

Rating: ★★★★★ • *Origin:* Japan, 1953 • *Director:* Teinosuke Kinugasa •
Source: Criterion DVD

Kôtarô Bandô in *Gate of Hell*
DAIEI / WIKIMEDIA COMMONS

This samurai tragedy is really more of a *jidaigeki*, a period costume drama, than a *chambara* or sword-play movie, though there's plenty of colorful action in the first third of its running time. Unlike most samurai films, which are typically set during the shogunate of the sixteenth to nineteenth centuries, this takes place in the earlier Heian period of the twelfth century, when the relationship between the imperial noble class and the samurai warrior class was still evolving. During a military rebellion against the imperial court, Morito (Kazuo Hasegawa), a fierce fighter, sides with the samurai loyal to the emperor and in the chaos is assigned a diversion mission, escorting a lady impersonating the empress in an apparent attempt to escape the rebel soldiers. The mission succeeds, but in the process Morito is smitten with the beauty, poise, and courage of Lady Kesa (Machiko Kyo), the woman who performs the imposture. When the battle is over, she disappears, and Morito doesn't see her again until after the rebellion is put down, when he encounters her by chance and his feelings are rekindled.

Peace restored, when the samurai who stayed loyal are being rewarded by Lord Kiyo-mori, Morito asks him for Lady Kesa's hand and only then learns that she's already married to a noble of the Court. Morito, reckless and obsessed, vows to win her for himself regardless, and matters quickly go from bad to worse. Director Teinosuke Kinugasa's pacing is masterful, ratcheting up the tension as the story marches toward its crushing end. This was Japan's first big-budget color film, and even by today's standards it's drop-dead gorgeous, simply exquisite, a painting come to life. Kinugasa deliberately contrasts the serenity of nature with the violence of human emotions, but without judgment or sentimentality, allowing the characters and their actions to speak to the viewer for themselves. And all in 86 minutes, without a second wasted. What a treasure.

THE GAUCHO

Rating: ★★★★☆ • *Origin:* USA, 1927 • *Director:* F. Richard Jones • *Source:* Kino Video DVD

The Gaucho was a very different swashbuckler for Douglas Fairbanks Sr. In his mid-40s by the time he made this silent film, he could no longer convincingly play the endearingly earnest youthful hero, and besides, such roles were increasingly passé. By the late 1920s, the vogue was for darker and more openly erotic characters as exemplified by Rudolph Valentino and John Barrymore, the latter of whom had already challenged Fairbanks on his own turf with *Don Juan* and *The Beloved Rogue*. Was it perhaps time for Fairbanks to take a turn as a danger-ous Latin lover?

This seems to have been the thinking behind *The Gaucho*, in which the hero is a mock-ing, womanizing, hard-drinking, chain-smoking, bolas-swinging outlaw, a bandit chief known only as—you guessed it—the "Gaucho." He and his gang come across the Andes and swarm into a mountain town, where the Gaucho finds an ardent young admirer in a fiery local woman, who cuts out a rival by doing a torrid tango with the Gaucho while bound tightly to him by his bolas. This "Mountain Girl" (the only name she's given) is played with hot salsa by Lupe Velez—better known later in her career as the "Mexican Spitfire"—here in her American film debut.

Meanwhile, a South American comic-opera tyrant named Ruiz has sent his troops to occupy the City of the Miracle, a town built around a holy shrine, to confiscate the wealth brought there by pilgrims and enslave the poor peasants who depend on the shrine's generos-ity. But the Gaucho comes over the mountains to take that wealth for himself. The bandit chief, disguised in a captured Ruiz trooper uniform, sneaks into the occupied city to scout it out. He reveals himself to test the troops, and an acrobatic pursuit ensues. After a half dozen swashbucklers, you'd think we'd have seen every aerial trick Douglas Fairbanks could perform, but no—he continues to astound, still doing all his own stunts.

By means of a clever stratagem, the Gaucho's bandits take the city, but when he goes to loot the shrine, he meets its beatific holy-virgin-nun-lady and for the first time feels the power of purity and sanctity. But the Mountain Girl is jealous, the shrine's loot is in play, Ruiz is on the march, and the pot is soon bubbling over with passion, envy, treachery, and betrayal. The morality play that follows doesn't go quite the way you might expect, and though the religious aspect gets a bit mawkish, there are some clever twists and turns before it ultimately resolves for the best. (Hey, rogue hero or no, it *is* still a Doug Fairbanks swashbuckler.)

Interestingly, here we are at almost the end of the silent era, and yet this story—written by Fairbanks, by the way—is told almost entirely with visuals, and sometimes many minutes pass between one cue card and the next. But with this master at the height of his cinematic game, you truly don't miss the words. Happy discovery: Lupe Velez fights and rides as well as she dances!

GENGHIS KHAN

Rating: ★★★☆☆ • *Origin:* UK/West Germany/Yugoslavia/USA, 1965 •
Director: Henry Levin • *Source:* Columbia Blu-ray

Mongols-à-go-go! The tribe of Temujin (Omar Sharif) is slaughtered and he's enslaved by Jamuga (Stephen Boyd) of the Merkits. While toiling with a yoke around his neck, Temujin falls for Jamuga's intended, Bortai (Françoise Dorleac). Then, with the help of wise advisor Geen (Michael Hordern) and mute warrior Sengal (Woody Strode), he escapes and, aided by the wily Shan (Telly Savalas), gathers around him a tribe of raiders, the nucleus of the Mongol hordes to come.

Notice any Asians in the cast named above? Why, no. The white karst mountains of Yugoslavia stand in for the peaks of central Asia here in the same way that white Europeans and Americans (with the exceptions of Sharif and Strode) stand in for Mongols. It gets worse when Temujin and his barbaric buddies get to China, where James Mason appears as diplomat Kam Ling while the Emperor of All China is played by Robert Morley, no less. Now, Morley is a great comic actor who is never less than entertaining, but he's English all the way to the points of his absurdly long fingernails, and casting him as the emperor of China is just insulting. And James Mason, to his eternal shame, is even more embarrassing, squinting with an overbite and playing Kam Ling as a cartoon Chinee out of *Terry and the Pirates*. Ugh.

Okay, enough about the whitewashing: How is this film as a spectacle of sword-waving horsemen sweeping across the endless steppes? Mostly pretty good. It was shot by the great Geoffrey Unsworth, so it's plenty scenic, and director Henry Levin had a long history of helming B pictures, which gives him a good feel for the action scenes; the two big cavalry battles here are surprisingly tight and punchy, and Temujin's raid on a camp of slavers is tense and suspenseful. Levin is less impressive with the character scenes, which are sexist even for 1965, and the movie slows to a crawl when it gets stuck in China for most of its second hour. Eventually Temujin, now dubbed Genghis Khan, shows the Chinese what gunpowder is really for and busts out of Peking, taking all his now well-armed troops with him. A narrator and some burning lines on a map then describe his series of mighty conquests, all leading up to his final confrontation with Jamuga.

There isn't much real history to this noisy melodrama, though it's better in that regard than John Wayne's *The Conqueror*. But does that matter when you've got Eli Wallach in a sparkly silver fez weaseling away as the Shah of Khwarezm? Shrug and roll with it.

THE GIANT OF MARATHON (OR *THE BATTLE OF MARATHON*)

Rating: ★★☆☆☆ • *Origin:* Italy/France, 1959 • *Director:* Jacques Tourneur •
Source: Amazon streaming video

You know what the Italian filmmakers who created the peplum genre really wanted? Respect! After the runaway success of *Hercules* and *Hercules Unchained*, producer Bruno Vailati followed up with this serious sword-and-sandal film about the first Persian invasion of Greece in 490 BCE. He hired the stylish Jacques Tourneur as director but had enough commercial sense to keep Steve Reeves as his star and add the Bardot-esque Mylène Demongeot as his love interest, as well as hundreds of extras to fill out the ranks of the Persian, Athenian, and Spartan armies.

Marathon is a sprawling historical epic, handsome to look at but deadly serious and self-important. Reeves's Hercules could crack a joke now and then, but his Olympic athlete Philippides never smiles and is often downright sullen. Sergio Fantoni is appropriately sinister as the Athenian traitor Theocritus, but I liked him better as the unhinged and maniacal Eteocles in *Unchained*. And Demongeot has little to do but bemoan her situation and get abducted.

The story is an earnest melodrama of dirty politics and soap-opera romance that, once King Darius arrives with his club-helmeted Persians, dissolves into a series of battles. To make sure all the armies show up to meet each other at Marathon, Philippides has to race across eastern Greece not once but three times. It's exhausting. The great battle itself is impressively staged and Tourneur shows that he's studied both Eisenstein and Olivier, though the part where Reeves rolls giant boulders down on the Persians is, I think, original. The last act ends with an amphibious invasion of the port of Piraeus that includes an underwater battle scene that won't be topped until *Thunderball*. Plus it's an opportunity to follow the peplum trope of having the good guys fight shirtless, as Reeves leads the Athenian Sacred Guard in disrobing before diving into the waves. A very busy movie, but in the end, not much fun.

GIANTS OF ROME

Rating: ★★☆☆☆ • *Origin:* Italy/France, 1964 • *Director:* Antonio Margheriti •
Source: Mill Creek DVD

This is a hybrid peplum adventure/Roman war movie inspired by *The Guns of Navarone* (1961), about a commando raid of legionaries into enemy territory in Gaul as a prelude to Julius Caesar's victory at the Battle of Alesia (52 BCE). It's an action film and nothing but, with only perfunctory nods to motives and characterization between fight scenes, and though the dialogue is weak, the combat director knew his business and the theatrical fights are exciting and dynamic. Good thing, too, because there are plenty of them.

To attack the Gauls, Caesar plans to bring his army through a mountain pass, but he's heard that it's defended by a great weapon devised by the druids, so he sends a team of four elite Roman warriors to infiltrate the pass and clear away the weapon. His handpicked and super buff team consists of swordsman leader Claudius (Richard Harrison), shirtless strongman Germanicus (Ralph Hudson), lightning-fast knife thrower Varus (Goffredo Unger), and rope-and-garotte man Castor (Ettore Manni)—and that's all there is to know about them, because weapon specialization stands in for personality here. The team looks great, eschewing armor because they have to travel fast, and besides, armor just hides your pectorals and biceps. They plunge into their mission behind enemy lines, but they are the Worst Infiltrators Ever, falling into one ambush after another, which is fine since this film's purpose is to show how good these Romans are at beating up Gauls. They pick up some extra allies along the way—a spunky Roman lad, a legionary broken by torture, a captive patrician lady as love interest for Claudius—and then, to make sure we know that this is a serious war movie, characters start to die.

The pacing is hit or miss, tight for a while and then suddenly slack as the characters march through the forest and then march through more forest. But then along comes another fight, which like most of the others is at least interestingly staged, including an amphibious attack on a couple of Gaulish rafts that features some pretty good underwater combat photography. There's some decent spectacle in the final act when they get to the secret weapon, but no real twists, and everything works out exactly as you expected it would. Ave Caesar!

THE GIANTS OF THESSALY

Rating: ★★☆☆☆ • *Origin:* Italy/France, 1960 • *Director:* Riccardo Freda •
Source: Amazon streaming video

You can't have too many retellings of the story of Jason and the Argonauts, or so the Italian filmmakers of the peplum era seemed to think, because here's another one. Thessaly has been cursed by Zeus with offscreen volcanoes that will destroy the island unless Jason, King of Iolcus (Roland Carey), quests to Colchis and returns with the Golden Fleece. The *Argo* sails, but Hercules, Castor, Pollux, and most of the usual crew are missing, though Orpheus is aboard for some reason, making doomy remarks about love and loss. The plot is a weird mix of elements from various ancient sources; for example, there's no Ulysses either, but Jason fights a giant ape-like cyclops and contends with a witch who is Circe in all but name.

However, let's not give the impression there's a lot going on here, because most of the time, there isn't. After every one of Jason's brief adventures, the story shifts for about twice as long back to politics in Iolcus, where Jason's wicked cousin Adrastus plots to seize his throne and his wife. He does this mainly by meeting with a tedious group I call his Council of Exposition, or his spunkier Committee of Conspiring. In fact, for an action-adventure film the pacing is strangely deliberate, even weirdly dreamlike during the fantasy episodes. Characters often give solemn speeches while staring into the middle distance, as if that will add significance. American bodybuilder Roland Carey, the ostensible star, has no charisma to speak of, or even personality. No one delivers lines with much conviction except for Orpheus (Massimo Girotti), who seems to have wandered in from a different picture.

And then, in the last 20 minutes, things suddenly get interesting. The *Argo* arrives at Colchis and Jason, as foretold by prophecy, goes ashore alone, mainly to climb stuff: first a towering wall of unstable cut stone and then a 100-foot statue that holds the Fleece in its open hand. The dreaminess, so goofy in the earlier fantasy scenes, is strangely compelling here. In no time, the *Argo* is back at Iolcus, there's a brief interval of strategy, and then a climactic melee ensues between the Argonauts and Adrastus, backed up by his bronze-helmed goons. Whoever choreographed the swordplay knew his business, so the movie ends on a satisfying note, but it sure took its time getting there. If you just fast-forward through the first hour, I promise not to tell.

G. I. SAMURAI (OR *TIME SLIP*)

Rating: ★★☆☆☆ • *Origin:* Japan, 1979 • *Director:* Kosei Saito • *Source:* Mill Creek DVD

A small Japanese Defense Forces unit armed with modern weapons accidentally time travels back to the Warring States period, where samurai warriors kick their asses. But it takes the samurai well over two hours to do it.

There's not much more to this film than that. The JDF unit, two dozen men with a tank, a helicopter, a patrol boat, a halftrack, a jeep, a truck, and a whole lot of ammunition, endure cheap special effects as they find themselves transported to about 1561 and right into a conflict between warring daimyo. They immediately have to defend themselves against attacking samurai, because this is an action movie and nothing but. However, the JDF commander, Yoshiaki Iba (Sonny Chiba), parleys with General Kagetora (Isao Natsuyagi), and the two immediately hit it off. After some shallow soul-searching between pointless action scenes, Iba decides to join Kagetora to try to conquer Japan, on the ostensible rationale that if his modern troops radically change history, history will somehow spit them out and send them back to their own era. It's a questionable decision, but pretty much every decision made in this movie is questionable, so hey.

The samurai warriors look great, and a company of mounted samurai with a troop of ashigaru foot soldiers, sashimono back banners flapping, leading a twentieth-century armored column across war-torn Japan makes a compelling and memorable image. But that's it as far as compelling and memorable go for this film. Though Iba is excited about the challenge of finding himself in the sixteenth century, most of his soldiers are pretty bummed about it. The script goes out of its way to attempt to make their plight relatable, but the fact is, their personal stories are boring. The Iba-Kagetora warrior bromance likewise goes nowhere, and the film just chugs along until it arrives at its reason for existence, the 40-minute set-piece battle pitting the JDF unit against the entire army of famed warlord Takeda Shingen at the Battle of Kawanakajima (think samurai Gettysburg). The soldiers' automatic weapons slaughter untold numbers of their opponents, but the samurai are fearless and inventive, and one by one they manage to take out the JDF vehicles and whittle down their number of soldiers. But somehow, Lieutenant Iba, adept with both modern and ancient weaponry, manages to fight his way to Shingen's headquarters, where he challenges the great general to personal combat. If Iba manages to kill Takeda Shingen and change history, will his troops be zapped back at last to their own time? Nah.

THE GOLDEN BLADE

Rating: ★★☆☆☆ • *Origin:* USA, 1953 • *Director:* Nathan Juran • *Source:* Universal DVD

Every year for a while, Universal popped out another of these quickie Arabian fantasies, amortizing the costumes and sets they'd built for *Arabian Nights* in 1942. It's a tribute to Piper Laurie that she managed to star in three of these things in succession and still go on to have a distinguished cinematic career. By the time of this production, her former costar Tony Curtis had left Bagdad for Camelot, so Universal roped in the rising star Rock Hudson to play the male lead, Harun. The story is rudimentary: Harun's father, the Sultan of Basra, is slain by mysterious assailants whom Harun tracks to Bagdad. There, in a used-clothing shop, he encounters both Khairuzan (Laurie), the incognito daughter of the caliph who likes to go slumming among the commoners, and a magical golden blade, the Sword of the Prophecy of the Destiny of Fate or something, that only exhibits its powers when wielded by Harun. This is never really explained, like at all, but that's par for the course in this sloppy farrago. For example, Harun's quest to avenge his father is conveniently forgotten for most of the picture, as he gets drawn by Khairuzan into improbable shenanigans at the caliph's court. Most of the running time is spent on a dumb palace conspiracy involving an evil vizier inevitably named Jafar (the always reliable George Macready, looking embarrassed), his dim-witted and brutal son, a scheming noblewoman, a Greek merchant, giggling half-clad harem girls, and an endless supply of disposable palace guards.

Sounds like a total loss, right? Not quite: the bad guys wear scorpion medallions (you heard me: scorpion medallions!), Piper Laurie has got the Adorable turned up to 11, and there's one amazing, essential scene where Harun, at a palace party, gets totally stoned smoking whatever's in that tall, pink hookah while watching a dancer undulate in front of him. In his hallucinatory state, the dancer transforms into Khairuzan, and Harun pursues her staggering through an endless hall hung with filmy, fluttering salmon-pink curtains. Far out! I had to watch it twice.

Meanwhile, in a plot engineered by Jafar, Harun's magic golden blade is stolen and replaced by an imitation so Jafar's doofus son can win a tournament that . . . nah, never mind, it's just too dumb to recount. At least Hudson's smarmy grin is wiped off his face for a while, as without his magic sword, he becomes a sad-sack loser who can't do anything right. Then the golden blade gets stuck in a marble pillar. (Tony Curtis may have run off to Camelot, but he left Excalibur behind in Bagdad.) Nobody can pull the blade out, not no how, except for, guess who? When Harun finally draws the magic blade, everything wraps up double quick in a spasm of bloodless mayhem, and Harun is reunited with Khairuzan, who was only pretending to hate him. She has a nice smile.

THE GOLDEN HAWK

Rating: ★★★★☆ • *Origin:* USA, 1952 • *Director:* Sidney Salkow •
Source: Cinema International DVD

Top-billed Rhonda Fleming gives Maureen O'Hara and Jean Peters serious competition here for the crown of Queen of the Swashbucklers, missing out only because she never picks up a sword. If you can swallow the ultra-American Sterling Hayden as a Frenchman, you'll have a fine time with this classic Hollywood pirate adventure. It's based on the best-selling novel of the same name by Frank Yerby, who wrote romantic historical potboilers that were ideal for adaptation to the screen. Setting: the Caribbean in the late seventeenth century, and Kit Gerardo, known as Captain Hawk (Hayden), is a French privateer who's in it mainly in hopes of meeting—and killing—Spanish captain Luis del Toro (John Sutton), whom he blames for his mother's death. He finally catches up to del Toro's galleon and is pounding its sterncastle from his more maneuverable ship when a female prisoner (Fleming) escapes the Spanish brig, swims to Gerardo's ship, and tells them to knock it off, as the galleon is loaded with innocent captives. Gerardo sheers off, takes the woman aboard, and is smitten. After several nights he makes a pass at her, but she shoots him in the shoulder and then dives overboard, swimming for a nearby island, leaving a note identifying herself as Captain Rouge, the notorious female pirate. Scuppered, bigad!

Aye, it's a love/hate relationship, and there are further complications when Gerardo captures Bianca del Valvida (Helena Carter in a strong performance), Captain del Toro's fiancée. Gerardo holds Bianca for ransom long enough for her to fall for the bluff privateer, which will lead to jealousy, deceit, and Bianca's unexpected hand in Gerardo's reconciliation with Rouge.

Director Sidney Salkow shot more than 50 Hollywood B movies, but this may be his best. You have to love a movie that opens on a piratical raiding montage with flame consuming a map of Jamaica! This is sheer melodrama but a good one, and if the characters are no deeper than they seem, it's only because more character development would just slow down the action. Gerardo's tactics are superb when he has only Spanish enemies to deal with, but when the ladies are involved, love clouds his mind and he goes all stupid; he decides to infiltrate the fortified Spanish port of Cartagena on his own and gets captured, and Bianca and Rouge have to pull his chestnuts out of the fire. There's a best-of-class climactic battle between a fine flotilla of miniature French ships and a miniature Spanish fort, backstory revelations that will surprise no one who's familiar with the genre, and a final, lingering kiss so hot that Captain Rouge's flintlock pistol drops, forgotten, from her languishing fingers. Raise anchor and stand by the braces!

THE GOLDEN HORDE

Rating: ★★☆☆☆ • *Origin:* USA, 1951 • *Director:* George Sherman •
Source: YouTube streaming video

The plot of this tale of English knights versus Mongols on the Silk Road comes from a story treatment by Harold Lamb, the adventure fiction expert on Central Asia, so it has good bones, but we have to blame George Drayson Adams for the appalling script. Lamb is known for his evenhanded treatment of Asians and Europeans, but that got lost somewhere along the way: the Asians here are all caricatures of one flavor or another, while the English are noble, forthright, and convinced that their innate superiority entitles them to be condescending and rude to all the Persians and Mongols. It doesn't help that there are zero Asians in the cast except for one (1) "exotic" dancer.

Anyway. It's the year 1220, and the Mongols and their allies the Kalmuks, "a tidal wave of death and destruction," are threatening the city of Samarkand. Queen Shalimar (Ann Blyth) has a scheme to pit the Mongol and Kalmuk leaders against each other for the right to marry her, but everyone's plans are upset by the arrival of a dozen English ex-Crusaders led by Sir Guy of Devon (David Farrar), who also takes a shine to Shalimar and decides on the spot that to keep the queen from giving herself away, Samarkand will fight to the death under his command. When Shalimar objects that she's got everything under control, Sir Guy calls her a "pigeon-brained halfwit"—twice!

Adventures ensue, half in a Samarkand palace set that's honeycombed with secret passages, and half out in California's Death Valley standing in for the high steppes. The director, George Sherman, had helmed nearly 50 Westerns before making this film, so you can bet there's plenty of galloping. Much is made of the superiority of European heavy armor and the English longbow over the gear of the lightly armed horse warriors, but when they do come to grips, the fights are just weak stage combat. The plot might be more complicated than it needs to be, but at least that keeps the interest level up. You can choose to be upset because Farrar's Sir Guy is an arrogant and bossy mansplainer, or you can prefer to admire Blyth's

Shalimar, who plays all sides against the middle without once simpering or acting helpless, though the story does require her to fall in love with Sir Guy, despite (or because) of the fact that he refers to her as "that wench."

As the only other character with any brains, you also have to admire the ever-treacherous George Macready as Mongol agent Raven the Shaman, a fine villain. When his boss, Genghis Khan (Marvin Miller), looking more like a Neanderthal than a Mongol, finally shows up at the gates of Samarkand with his horde behind him, he finds that his son is dead, his advance troops have been slaughtered, and his alliance with the Kalmuks is in tatters—most of that the handiwork of Queen Shalimar, though Sir Guy takes the credit, of course. Faced with such unexpected resistance, how does the mighty khan respond? Watch it and see.

GOLDEN SWALLOW (OR *THE GIRL WITH THE THUNDERBOLT KICK*)

Rating: ★★★☆☆ • *Origin:* Hong Kong, 1968 • *Director:* Chang Cheh •
Source: Dragon Dynasty DVD

After director Chang Cheh's success with *One-Armed Swordsman*, Hong Kong's Shaw Brothers selected him to direct this sequel to the seminal *Come Drink with Me*, once again starring Cheng Pei-pei as female *wuxia* hero Golden Swallow, though this film gives her a backstory that has no connection to the previous movie. In the opening combat, coyly viewed by a nameless observer through gaps in wooden shutters, Golden Swallow fights off vengeance-bound bandits, is poisoned, and is then saved by the intervention of swordsman Golden Whip (Lo Lieh), who forces the bandits to give him the antidote. Whip takes Swallow off to his secluded mountain cottage to recover. There they are visited by Whip's friend Golden Flying Fox, who tells them of the exploits of a white-clad swordsman called Silver Roc (Jimmy Wang of *One-Armed Swordsman*) who has been making a name for himself as a fighter, though he only kills bad folks who have it coming. Swallow tells Whip that it sounds like her childhood friend Little Roc (yep, sorry), whom she hasn't seen for years. Whip, who is falling for Swallow, can tell that Swallow still has feelings for Roc. Angst!

And that's the plot: the whole thing is a puerile high-school love triangle. To attract Swallow's attention and get her to come to him, the arrogant Silver Roc goes around attacking various bandit groups and leaving Golden Swallow's signature yellow darts behind to implicate her, so that when they go after Swallow for revenge, she'll have to turn to him for aid. Nice valentine, Silver Roc. But really, this is Silver Roc's film, perhaps because Chang Cheh has little interest in female characters. Roc is meant to be hot: in addition to being a human killing

Golden Swallow AUTHOR'S COLLECTION

machine, he's also a poet and calligrapher, a melancholy romantic hero whose thwarted love for Golden Swallow is what drives him to slaughter bandits and hang out in brothels. Right.

Okay, but how's the action? Quite good, actually. I lost count of how many sword fights there are, but Cheh keeps them interesting by interjecting handheld camera and in some cases shooting from directly above, which gives the swirling combats a flavor of old Busby Berkeley musicals. Cheng Pei-pei holds up her end well, but the male characters get most of the screen time, alas. Though the mass melees can be rather chaotic, the one-on-one combats are shot for clarity of action; the inevitable duel of romantic rivalry between Silver Roc and Golden Whip is particularly excellent. There's a lot of unconvincing fake gore that was much more shocking in 1968 than it is now, but ignore that and enjoy the leaping fights staged in colorful locations such as ancient tombs and the headquarters of the Golden Dragon bandit gang, fully equipped with handy and convenient torture implements. Lurid!

THE GOLDEN VOYAGE OF SINBAD

Rating: ★★★★☆ • *Origin:* UK, 1973 • *Director:* Gordon Hessler • *Source:* Viavision Blu-Ray

Golden Voyage is beloved by fantasy film fans for its fabulous creatures animated in stop-motion by Ray Harryhausen, but its hallmark monsters aside, this is one strange movie. The story is a sort of stately parade of wonders with a plot that makes sense only in the terms of dream logic. Sinbad (John Philip Law, bland but with a nice smile) happens upon one-third of a magical golden amulet and thereafter is led by visions and visitations on a quest for . . . what? Some goal that, despite a superfluity of prophecies and portents, is never really made clear. Wealth? Power? Experience points?

Maybe it's the latter, because Sinbad and company are basically a *Dungeons & Dragons* adventure party, his crew reminiscent of the clichéd squad members in every war movie, only with *Arabian Nights* names like Haroun and Omar. They're joined by Caroline Munro as Margiana because she's the hottest thing in harem pants and because she has an eye tattooed on her hand that Sinbad saw in a dream, so she must join their crew because Fate or something. The party is rounded out by a grand vizier who conceals his features behind a golden mask because they were destroyed by a fireball from the evil wizard Koura. This masked vizier joins the quest because *somebody* has to utter portentous warnings and explain What It All Means.

Which brings us to the aforementioned evil wizard Koura, and here's where the movie gets interesting. This sorcerer, Sinbad's archrival on the amulet quest, is played by Tom Baker—the Fourth Doctor Who!—though he's almost unrecognizable in a black turban and face kerchief. But he does more emoting with just his eyes than the rest of the cast put together. Koura is the wizard who magically animates all the creatures that bedevil Sinbad and company, but every time he casts a spell, he visibly ages, dwindling toward death, and soon it becomes clear that he wants the magical amulet's prize because it will restore his lost youth and stave off his suicide-by-sorcery. This makes Koura the only character in the picture with clear and comprehensible motives, and Baker plays him with such energy and verve that about halfway through the film, you find yourself starting to root for the villain.

Koura won me over in the scene where, with a mandrake root, alchemy, and a dollop of his own blood, he animates a tiny, winged homunculus, and suddenly we see that the putative villain is the real heart of this fantasy, a man of passion who breathes life into inanimate matter, creating wonder before our eyes. Yes, you've got it: Koura is really Ray Harryhausen himself, literally pouring his life into his creations. This is even more clear when Koura animates a statue of the six-armed goddess Kali, making it dance for him purely so he can revel in his artistry—or rather Harryhausen's artistry, for whether dancing or wielding six swords against Sinbad, the slyly smiling Kali is a masterpiece so wonderful it's easy to forgive those stretches where the film falls flat.

The script is by Brian Clemens, the English screenwriter behind most of the best moments of the British *Avengers* TV show, but this outing is weak work, recycled adventure-film tropes and orientalist clichés. The dialogue is studded with phony wise sayings like "You cannot pick up two melons with one hand," in which you can hear the snotty British intellectual sneering at the Wisdom of the East. It's embarrassing. Eventually the quest leads to the long-lost island of Lemuria, which is cluttered with ruins evoking every ancient Asian culture at once: India, Tibet, Cambodia, China, and so on. It's meant to imply that the questers have discovered the source of all the cultures of the Mysterious East, but it feels more like, "All those bally foreign temples look alike to me, eh, what what?" It doesn't help that the Lemurians, when they appear, are a tribe of green-skinned ooga-booga cannibals with skulls on sticks. Ouch.

But those animated monsters, though! So fabulous. Plus there's some wonderfully lush music by Miklós Rósza, contributing one of his last great film scores, and a couple of epic dungeon crawls that I guarantee helped inspire Gary Gygax. Despite its lapses and eccentricities, as fantasy films go, *Golden Voyage* is still almost indispensable.

GOLIATH AND THE SINS OF BABYLON

Rating: ★★★☆☆ • *Origin:* Italy, 1963 • *Director:* Michele Lupo • *Source:* Retromedia DVD

If you like any of the later peplum epics, you'll like this one, because it's as good as they get. It stars one of the best strongman heroes, Mark Forest, as Goliath/Maciste, and the visuals are an undeniable success on the level of sheer spectacle. Oh, sure, the story is utterly clichéd: the ancient city of Nefir is ruled by a puppet king controlled by the tyrannical Babylonians, whose tyranny is opposed by a desperate group of rebels who also happen to be shirtless muscleman gladiators. There's a comic dwarf sidekick who's even more embarrassing than most, and the tone varies wildly between wacky slapstick and grim vengeance, but the good stuff more than balances that out. Drawing inspiration from *Ben-Hur* (1959), there's a sea battle between a galley with a lion-headed ramming prow and a towering Babylonian trireme that's genuinely exciting, though the fighting savors more of professional wrestling than of gladiatorial combat. And in a full-scale hippodrome, there's a deadly chariot race that the rebels must win because if the victor beats the Princess of Nefir, who drives her own chariot, he gets to wed her and become Nefir's new king. (I'm sure that's a historically authentic practice. Well, pretty sure.) And there are any number of dark dungeons with plummeting portcullises, steel-spear death traps, and inflammable bridges over abysses.

The gaudy costumes are less *Ben-Hur* than *Flash Gordon*, gleaming with barbaric bling; the black-clad Babylonian royal guard wear Evil Armor™, but the good guys just need leather straps and half-tunics (at best), because gladiators. The direction is actually pretty sharp and dynamic, the scenes are well framed, and the action pauses only to build tension before the next outburst of rebel guard-thrashing. There's even an obvious but serviceable romantic sub-plot in which the rebel chariot-driver Xandros (Giuliano Gemma) falls for the handmaiden of Princess Regia (José Greci) without realizing she's really the princess in disguise. But then he's wounded by assassins, so Goliath has to take his place in the race. Angsty!

After the rebels put things right in Nefir, the struggle moves to Babylon, and the plot unravels under the weight of its many improbabilities. But Mark Forest is still charming even when he's angry, there's another pitched battle in the palace dungeons, and Nefir's cavalry comes galloping across the deadly Desert of Gore ("Impossible!" cry the bad guys) just in time to save the day and, um, sack the city and put the Babylonians to the sword. But hey, they had it comin'.

GOR

Rating: ★★☆☆☆ • *Origin:* USA/South Africa, 1987 • *Director:* Fritz Kiersch •
Source: MGM DVD

Edgar Rice Burroughs published the first sword-and-planet story in 1912 with *A Princess of Mars*, establishing a genre in which a sword-wielding hero typically finds himself on a distant planet where he must contend with barbarians, humanoid aliens, and bizarre ancient cultures. John Lange, writing as John Norman, wrote a popular sword-and-planet series about a world called Gor starting with *Tarnsman of Gor* in 1966. The books were notorious among SF and fantasy fans for their regressive attitudes toward slavery and the domination of submissive women, but they found an audience despite general intellectual disapproval. In 1987, late in the '80s barbarian boom, the series finally made its way to the movie screen; the resulting film, while it had plenty of slavery and the abuse of partially clad women, was milder in that regard than other films of the period, such as *Barbarian Queen* (1985). For all the opprobrium heaped on the Gor books over the years, the movie when it came was mainly just . . . boring.

Tarl Cabot (Urbano Barberini) is a nerdy university professor with a mystic ring inherited from his father said to be able to open a way to another world, a "counter-Earth." After being humiliated by a cooler dude who drives off with his girlfriend, Cabot is heading out alone on a camping trip when the ring starts to glow and he is transported, John Carter–style, to Gor. The hapless Cabot wanders a barren wasteland until he stumbles upon a slave raid in progress, gets mixed up with Talena (Rebecca Ferratti), a fugitive warrior, and then accidentally kills the nasty son of the nasty slave lord, Sarm (Oliver Reed, nooooo!), who vows vengeance. However, Sarm has already gotten what he wanted from the village in addition to slaves: the town's mystic "home stone," a glowing piece of melty pink plastic that resembles the stone in Cabot's ring.

Cabot joins the fugitive villagers on a quest to free the slaves and retrieve their home stone, which he's assured has the power to return him to Earth, but he's petulant and useless, which is supposed to be funny but is just tiresome. No problem! Cue a three-minute training montage, at the end of which Cabot is skillful enough with a sword and bow to be a match for any fighter on Gor.

An aside about the swords in this movie: a lot of low-budget fantasy films feature cheap-looking and unbelievable medieval weapons, but the swords in *Gor* are the cheapest and most unbelievable *ever*, looking like plywood laths wrapped with foil, which maybe they are. Ugh. A second aside, this one about Oliver Reed: before getting up in arms about the great artist lowering himself to participate in this trash, remember that he started out dedicating his art to acting in Hammer exploitation films. And only a real actor like Reed could wear that ridiculous protuberant slave-king's helmet and still keep a straight face as he orders helpless sacrifices to their deaths.

Anyway, there's really nothing going on here but an ill-conceived and poorly executed action flick with an overwrought soundtrack—no story, and no characters. Don't blink, or you'll miss Jack Palance at the end being set up as the villain for the sequel.

GOYOKIN

Rating: ★★★★★ • *Origin:* Japan, 1969 • *Director:* Hideo Gosha • *Source:* Toho DVD

This may well be the masterpiece of director Hideo Gosha (*Three Outlaw Samurai*), and though not easy to find in America and Europe, it's worth the effort. Set in 1831, late in the period of the Tokugawa shogunate, it's a story of moral bankruptcy and the inherent conflicts in the Way of the Samurai that led to the end of the dominance of that class. It starts out like a horror movie: on the coast of a small island in deep winter, young Oriha (Ruriko Asaoka) returns to her fishing village after an absence of several years. But all she finds are ruins and squawking carrion crows—everyone has vanished, and there are not even any bodies except for one overlooked human head. "Kamikakushi!" she cries. *Taken by the gods.*

The scene changes, to the capital of Edo, where we meet Samon (Kinnosuke Nakamura), a charming charlatan with a dangerous sword show, and his reluctant star Magobei (Tatsuya Nakadai), a surly and shabby ronin whose conversation consists mainly of grunts. After the show Magobei is ambushed by samurai of the Sabai clan, but he cuts them down and escapes. Next is the castle of the Sabai, where we meet the ruthless Chamberlain Tatewaki (Tetsuro Tamba), whose subordinate sent the hit team to kill Magobei. Gradually, through a series of flashbacks, we find out why.

Magobei once belonged to the Sabai and was married to Shino (Yoko Tsukasa), Tatewaki's sister. Three years before, the clan was about to default on its debts to the sho-gunate, but Tatewaki had come up with a scheme to recoup their fortunes: every winter a ship full of *goyokin*, "official gold," passed their rocky island on its way to Edo. With the help of the fisher folk of Oriha's village, Tatewaki engineered a shipwreck, stole the gold, and slaughtered all the villagers to hide the Sabai clan's crime. When Magobei learned what Tatewaki had done, rather than accept complicity, he turned his back on his clan and became a ronin. Flash forward to the present: the Sabai are once again out of money, Tatewaki plans to repeat his shipwreck theft and massacre with a different village, and Magobei is determined to stop him.

A compelling story, but what really sells it are Gosha's epic visuals. *Goyokin* was filmed in wide-screen Panavision, the first Japanese movie to use that format, and Gosha took full advantage of the expanded canvas to portray sweeping, windswept winter vistas, an icy coast with thundering waves, mounted samurai blowing clouds of breathy vapor into the frigid air, their horses stamping in the snow. It was the late 1960s, the broad vision of David Lean crossing with the action-movie aesthetic of Spaghetti Western maestros Leone and Corbucci. There's plenty of Kurosawa's *Yojimbo* in here as well. Makes sense, considering the film was originally conceived of as a vehicle for Toshiro Mifune's Yojimbo character, but Mifune couldn't get along with Gosha and didn't want to freeze his ass off filming in the snow.

So we got Tatsuya Nakadai instead, and in this case lost nothing by the exchange. All the principal actors in *Goyokin* turn in fine performances, but Nakadai is remarkable: Magobei, his dead face enlivened only by his expressive eyes, resembles the sociopath Nakadai played in Okamoto's *Sword of Doom* (1966), but here, instead of unhinged, he is haggard and haunted. Magobei, so stricken with guilt as to be almost inarticulate, says everything through eyes and

REJECTING BUSHIDO

After militant nationalism in Japan during the 1920s and 1930s led to the disaster of the 1940s, many Japanese blamed the country's march to war on an excessive reverence for Bushido, the samurai's martial code of honor. Media that glorified Japan's military history was prohibited during the American occupation, but in the 1950s, movies and TV shows featuring heroic samurai began returning to the mainstream. However, a significant segment of Japan's creative community regarded this as a woeful development, and nonconformists opposed to the innate conservatism of Japanese society began making alternative samurai films that, subtly at first and then openly, accused Bushido culture of oppression and cruelty. Two films from 1962 illustrate the difference: *Chushingura*, which extols the virtues of samurai honor, and *Harakiri*, which is a virtual mirror image of it, examining the same themes through a different lens and reaching diametrically opposite conclusions.

body language. The fighting, and there's quite a bit of it, is harsh and relentlessly brutal, not at all stylized. And Magobei, good as he is, is no superhero: one man against overwhelming odds, he is frequently beaten, only time and again to be covertly given a chance to escape by Tatewaki. Their final duel, in deep snow and air so bitingly cold they struggle to keep their hands warm enough to hold their swords, to the beat of drums pounded by frenzied, masked demon dancers, is a classic of the genre. You won't watch this one only once.

HANNIBAL

Rating: ★★☆☆☆ • *Origin:* Italy, 1959 • *Directors:* Edward G. Ulmer and Carlo Ludovico Bragaglia • *Source:* YouTube streaming video

Are there war elephants? Yes, there are. As the American movie poster screams, "Jump on! Hang on! Here comes the avenging Hannibal and his crazed elephant army!"

If only this Italian historical epic delivered that level of energy. It starts with a brief but tedious debate in the Roman Senate and then quickly cuts to Hannibal (Victor Mature) and his Carthaginian army crossing the Alps in winter to invade Italy from the north. This is what most people know about Hannibal, so the film gets right to it, spending a quarter of an hour on Carthaginian officers shouting, "March! Get those elephants moving!" in the mountains while Victor Mature watches with solemn approval from a soundstage in Belgrade. When some of the elephants stray onto the stage set and run mad from fear, we find out that Hannibal is not just the greatest general of the Punic Wars but a genuine action hero, as he grabs up a firebrand and waves off the pachyderms.

After his army makes it down into Italy and starts kicking legionary butt, we learn that in addition to being an action hero, Hannibal is a general with a heart, a man who hates war and only wants to free Carthage from Roman domination. Which is why when the Lady Sylvia (Rita Gam), the niece of a Roman senator, is captured by Hannibal's soldiers, she falls in love with the big lug. This unlikely and entirely fictional romance is intended to be the beating heart of the film, which is good because it needs one, the rest of the time being spent on rather dull skirmishes between Carthaginians and Romans and even duller debates in the Senate, where the actors display all the animation of roman statuary.

The movie sags badly in the middle, and it wasn't exactly gripping to start with. Hannibal's right eye gets infected and removed, after which he gets to wear a bitchin' black eye patch, and there's exactly one good gladius fight in the film, when Hannibal duels one of his own generals with a short sword after the man tries to kill Sylvia with an elephant stampede because she's made Hannibal go soft. He's not wrong.

At last, we finally get to the only other thing anyone knows about Hannibal: his great victory over the Roman legions at the Battle of Cannae (216 BCE), where he gives up being an action hero and goes back to general-ing. Director Edward Ulmer does a decent job of organizing the action to depict Hannibal's entrapment and envelopment of the Roman army, including the final decisive charge of the Carthaginian cavalry. No elephants appear in the battle, though—I mean, come on, if you put those beasts on a battlefield, somebody might get *hurt*.

HARAKIRI (OR *SEPPUKU*)

Rating: ★★★★★ • *Origin:* Japan, 1962 • *Director:* Masaki Kobayashi •
Source: Eureka! Blu-ray

This is a great film, but be warned: it's as bleak as cold, dry ashes, and while there's some fine swordplay in it, it's all in the last 20 minutes; the previous nearly two hours of talk and angry glaring serve as the grim setup to that socko ending.

The 1600 Battle of Sekigahara left Japan firmly under the control of the Tokugawa shogunate, and with the land at peace, the ruling samurai class was left without a purpose. In the 20 years that followed, a number of clans were dissolved, throwing many thousands of warriors out of work. By 1630 their plight was desperate, and in the capital of Edo some of them, faced with a life of ever-worsening poverty, chose instead to commit hara-kiri, ritual suicide. Hara-kiri was a feudal act that really needed to be carried out in a samurai lord's courtyard, which was a nuisance for the clans of Edo. Some masterless samurai took to requesting the use of a lord's forecourt for hara-kiri in hopes of being fobbed off instead with a few coins and sent away. When one desperate young warrior approaches the Iyi clan with this scam in mind, the proud and cruel Iyi samurai insist he go through with the act—and when they find that his sword blades have been pawned and replaced with bamboo lathes, they force him to disembowel himself with his own dull wooden dagger.

The rest of the story details the vengeance taken on the Iyi by Tsugumo, the youth's father-in-law (Tatsuya Nakadai, excellent as usual), another indigent samurai but one driven to strike back at the Iyi even if it costs him his life. He does this by strictly following the warrior's code of Bushido to trap the clan in a web of their own dishonor. This is not done as a celebration of Bushido but as an indictment of it.

Though its dark tone is unremitting, this is a beautiful film, masterfully composed. Unwavering in its conviction, it never strays into sentimentality. However, despite the top-notch fight scenes at the end, this is not a *chambara* adventure flick, so caveat emptor.

HAVE SWORD WILL TRAVEL

Rating: ★★★★★ • *Origin:* Hong Kong, 1969 • *Director:* Chang Cheh •
Source: Black Hill Blu-ray

King Hu's innovation in *Come Drink with Me* was to portray sword fighting not as a martial art but as choreographed dance inspired by Chinese opera. In his third film, Chang Cheh takes this two steps further, imbuing the entire production—costumes, sets, and lighting—with the theatricality of Chinese opera. The result is a colorful fairy tale told with subtle glances and stylized violence.

On a sunny day in a flowering meadow, kute kung fu kouple Piau Piau (Li Ching) and Brother Siang (Ti Lung) are teasing each other about their upcoming wedding when they are stumbled upon by bandits of the Flying Tiger gang. After driving the bandits off, the kouple trail them to their lair in a pagoda tower and decide they're up to no good. However, before they can return to Invincible Village to report to Siang's Uncle In, the kouple encounter a mysterious young stranger with impressive sword skills—though he won't tell them his name, which makes them suspicious.

Meanwhile, Lord In (Cheng Miu) has got trouble. Every year the government engages In and his martial artists to protect their annual silver shipment to the capital, but this year Lord In is so sick, he can't even hold up his signature cleaver sword. He's sent for Piau Piau's mother, a famous sword teacher, to lead the escort in his place, but she can't come, so Piau Piau and Brother Siang volunteer to do it. Then the mysterious stranger (David Chiang) appears at Lord In's door, broke and looking for food and lodging. His name is Lo (for lone and lonely), and when he and Piau Piau start making eyes at each other, Siang draws his sword and accuses Lo of working with the Flying Tigers. In a brief exchange, Lo demonstrates that his skills are superior to Siang's, but then Ghost Shadow, an actual Flying Tiger spy, is spotted at the window, there's a confused melee, and both Lo and Ghost Shadow disappear into the night.

As in Cheh's *Golden Swallow*, we're in high school romance territory here, but the story is much better told this time around. Misunderstandings occur and are sorted out, there are lingering looks and flashing blades, and Brother Siang grows ever more jealous. Piau Piau reveals Lord In's infirmity to Lo, and he decides he must join Piau Piau and Siang to help escort the silver, much to Siang's displeasure. But it's a good thing he does, because the silver shipment's path is past the Flying Tigers' pagoda tower and right into the bandits' elaborate ambush.

This pagoda tower is a brilliant setting for a running *wuxia* combat: eight floors of balconies, wooden platforms, and stairways, a perfect video game–level design decades before such a thing existed. It's the stage for the story's final bloody ballet of jealousy and sacrifice, every shot perfectly composed as Siang and Lo defeat the Flying Tiger minibosses one by one, growing ever more wounded in the process. After the big boss is finally thrown from the highest balcony, the bleeding rivals stagger down to be reunited with (the also wounded) Piau Piau, and the romance concludes in the way that it must. So fine.

HAWK THE SLAYER

Rating: ★★☆☆☆ • *Origin:* UK, 1980 • *Director:* Terry Marcel • *Source:* Network DVD

Hawk the Slayer Author's Collection

This was the first movie of the 1980s barbarian boom, released fully a year and a half before *Conan the Barbarian.* It's fondly remembered by fantasy fans of a certain age, but beyond nostalgia it doesn't have much to offer. The film establishes its allegiance to the sword-and-sorcery genre in its first 30 seconds, which show a lone armored warrior riding through dark woods toward a castle where an old wise man sits by a glowing, mystic pool. The warrior is the evil Voltan (Jack Palance) and the wise man his father, who refuses to give him the "secret of power," so Voltan deals him a mortal blow, laughs, and leaves. As the old man is dying, in comes his second son, Hawk (John Terry, in his first role), to whom his father bequeaths a magic weapon, the Mindsword, which can do . . . magic stuff. "Voltan, you will die!" Hawk vows, his sword's green gem glowing luridly.

Voltan is a bad man, and he has a bad son, Drogo (Shane Briant), and a gang of bad warriors. They slaughter a village, but one good crossbowman escapes, and though wounded, he goes to warn an abbey of good nuns that the bad men are approaching. Voltan invades the abbey and kidnaps the abbess, despite the crossbowman's attempts to defend her, demanding 2,000 gold pieces as the abbess's ransom. The crossbowman sets out to find the one man who can save the abbess and stop Voltan: his brother Hawk, who is in the north woods protecting innocents from evil bandits by acting like a Spaghetti Western badass (only with a magic sword). When he hears about Voltan's warrior band, Hawk decides he needs backup and calls together his old *D&D* party, adding to the crossbowman a dwarf, an elf, a giant, and a spooky sorceress who comes and goes as needed. There follows a confused series of back-and-forth fights between Hawk's party and Voltan's thugs, interrupted by flashbacks explaining why Hawk and Voltan hate each other (thwarted jealous love, as usual), leading to a final confrontation between the brothers.

The main thing this film has going for it is a charming earnestness, a belief that you can hang a python on a branch and throw a handful of dry ice into a pool and thereby turn an English woodlot into a fantasy forest. Producer Harry Robertson and director Terry Marcel, who wrote the script together, are in love with the tropes of the sword-and-sorcery genre and just thrilled to be able to put them on the screen. However, though their American stars have some capable support from British character actors like Roy Kinnear, Harry Andrews, and Patrick Magee, it's just not enough. John Terry aims for badassery but has all the charisma of a plank, while Jack Palance, at a low point in his career, is just awful, his delivery consisting of two levels of shouting: angry and angrier. The swordplay is perfunctory at best, and Hawk's party has just one trick: an elf with a repeating crossbow, machine archery that mows down the bulk of their enemies before the melee boys wade in. This is kind of cool when done once, but then they keep repeating it, which is not cool. The sorcery employs the same zero-budget special effects seen in thousands of post–*Star Wars* student movies, while the synthesizer soundtrack just recycles themes from Ennio Morricone. The costumes are adequate, but you'll see better at any Renaissance Faire. Lesson: Halloween decorations do not a haunted forest make.

HELEN OF TROY

Rating: ★★★☆☆ • *Origin:* USA/Italy/France, 1956 • *Director:* Robert Wise •
Source: Premier DVD

This is a triple-A sword-and-sandal epic, a big international production conceived in Hollywood and executed in Italy with a pan-European cast. It's meant to be first and foremost a love story between knockout leads Paris of Troy (Jacques Sernas) and Helen of Sparta (Rossana Podestà), but with stiff and unconvincing performances around a flat script, the romance is dead in the water, a surprise from director Robert Wise of *West Side Story*. (It doesn't help matters that both stars' voices are dubbed, albeit discreetly, for the English-language version.)

The action sequences of the Trojan War come off better, which makes sense given that the second unit directors are Yakima Canutt and Sergio Leone. The Greeks' initial assault on the walls of Troy, with phalanxes, war chariots, and ox-drawn siege towers, is a grand spectacle, and the Bronze Age swordplay is exciting and pretty persuasive. (Authentic? Who knows?) The Greek and Trojan warriors look tremendous in armor right off period ceramics, and wait until you see the towering horsehair crests on the helmets of the Greek kings, simultaneously majestic and ridiculous. Stanley Baker and Harry Andrews as the heroes Achilles and Hector are godlike, but somebody has to be, because the classical gods have been strangely excised from the story, which plays fast and loose with Homer's *Iliad*. I guess when you need to turn Paris from a selfish weasel into a romantic action hero and make the Greek kings nothing but pirates out for Troy's plunder, then Homer, shmomer, am I right? Just shoehorn "the face that launched a thousand ships" and "beware of Greeks bearing gifts" into the screenplay somewhere, and you're good to go.

But don't worry; though most of the dramatic scenes are wooden posturing, there's good stuff in here, including a surprisingly endearing performance by Janette Scott as King Priam's prophecy-haunted daughter, Cassandra. But the person who's having the most fun is Ulysses (*not* Odysseus—this production mixes Greek and Roman proper names with gay abandon). He's played with gusto by Torin Thatcher (the sorcerer Sokurah from *The 7th Voyage of Sinbad*) as a wily reprobate who is just waiting for his fellow Greeks to suffer a setback so he can gleefully persuade them to put his mad plan for the Trojan Horse into action. And it works! After a 10-year siege, the Trojans, giddy with victory and desperate for a good time, draw the great wooden horse in through their gates and then celebrate—and as this movie has a screen credit for "Bacchanal Choreography," there's no need to tell you what kind of a party they throw. Trust me, though, if you put on a frenzied Trojan bacchanal, you want your music to be composed and conducted by Max Steiner, fair recompense for any number of dull debates in Daddy Priam's throne room.

HENRY V (1944)

Rating: ★★★★★ (Essential) • *Origin:* UK, 1944 • *Director:* Laurence Olivier •
Source: Criterion DVD

George MacDonald Fraser, Richard Lester's screenwriter for *The Three* and *The Four Musketeers*, and therefore our patron saint, thought the Olivier version of Shakespeare's *Henry V* was the finest movie ever made. It's a wonderful film, justly celebrated, and there are plenty of sources available that explain why it's so admirable. For the purposes of this book, we'll

BOY TOYS OF TROY

Our major source for stories of the legendary Trojan War is Homer's *The Iliad* (eighth century BCE, more or less), which includes a huge cast of characters from both the besieging Greeks and the defenders of Troy, as well as the many Olympian gods who meddle in the mortals' affairs. For focus, a screenwriter telling a story based on this epic needs to pick a few major characters to follow and relegate the rest to supporting roles. In films made in the middle of the twentieth century, that usually meant leaving the gods out entirely, because including them would have meant your film was considered a fantasy (the horror!), and the Western moviegoing audience was deemed too Christian to regard classical polytheism as anything but benighted superstition.

Still, that left plenty of warrior heroes to choose from, particularly the big names like Achilles, Hector, and Odysseus (though he appears in the *Iliad* as more of a manipulative schemer than a hero). But some films chose different heroes for their protagonists, such as *Helen of Troy*, which focused on Paris and his romance with Helen. Unsurprisingly, they chose strikingly handsome actors to fill those roles, and the backup actors, male and female, were mostly gorgeous as well (Brigitte Bardot, for example, in an early minor role). Hey, if you're going to be traipsing around in a short chiton, I guess you'd better have good legs.

confine ourselves to just two aspects of this classic. First, the armor: ever since Mark Twain's *A Connecticut Yankee in King Arthur's Court* (1889) made a mockery of knights in shining armor, it became the received wisdom that a medieval warrior in full plate was awkward, encumbered, and a lumbering clod when off his horse. Most mid-century Hollywood historical epics paid deference to this idea, showing warriors in heavy armor clanking around ponderously. But the knights and nobles of *Henry V* wear their plate armor lightly, as if it was tailored for them—as of course it was—seeming completely comfortable and at home while wrapped head to toe in metal, their movements unencumbered, even elegant. More recent scholarship and reconstructions inform us that, in fact, that was the way of it: battle armor, though heavy, was made to move and fight in.

Second, there's the play's sprawling set piece in the next to last act, the re-creation of the Battle of Agincourt. In 1944 the Luftwaffe was causing problems in England and even Wales, so Olivier filmed the battle in Ireland, the rolling fields of County Wicklow standing in for the Pas de Calais. Agincourt, a decisive battle in the Hundred Years' War between France and England, pitted a much larger army of French knights and men-at-arms against King Henry's badly fatigued force of footmen and English and Welsh longbowmen. The French knights, the flower of European chivalry, charged the English across muddy plowed fields and were slaughtered by the archers. Henry's men-at-arms then closed in from both sides, and the battle became a general melee, but the English never lost the upper hand and the French were trounced.

Olivier's depiction of the battle's opening scenes was a landmark for its time, unmatched in its clarity and power. The initial charge of the French heavy cavalry draws on Eisenstein's charge of the Teutonic Knights in *Alexander Nevsky* but goes it one better: a tracking camera follows the French vanguard from the side as the knights advance, going from a walk to a trot to a full gallop that seems unstoppable—until they hit the muddy fields and a wall of English and Welsh arrows. The battle then becomes episodic, reverting to Shakespeare's structure of jumping to encounters between various combatants, English and French, whom we'd been introduced to earlier in the story. It all ends in a final clash between King Henry and the constable of the French army, with Henry, of course, victorious.

Watch for Robert Newton—Long John Silver himself—hamming it up as Ancient Pistol, an English hedge knight who's become the leader of Prince Hal's old band of rogues since the death of John Falstaff. He's hilarious.

HENRY V (1989)

Rating: ★★★★★ (Essential) • *Origin:* UK, 1989 • *Director:* Kenneth Branagh •
Source: MGM DVD

This is not only one of the finest Shakespeare films ever made, it's a damn fine swashbuckler, too. Starring, scripted, and directed by Kenneth Branagh in his first feature, it's kind of a miracle, an economical adaptation of the sprawling history play that focuses on King Henry's dramatic invasion of France without neglecting the reasons behind the conflict nor its consequences, all shot on a modest budget with a small but absolutely first-rate cast. And it moves at a breakneck pace without ever dragging for a minute, even when Henry goes incognito from campfire to campfire to take the temperature of his weary troops on the night before the Battle of Agincourt.

All right, some context: Henry V (Branagh), who suddenly assumed the throne of England upon the death of his father after a youth spent in frivolous pursuits among low companions, is determined to show all the doubters that he is nonetheless a worthy king. He receives the crown after generations of war with France and is persuaded that, due to the victories of his ancestors, he has a legitimate claim to rule France as well as England. In 1415 he mounts an expeditionary force to invade France and pursue his claim, but the campaign doesn't go as planned; after exhausting most of his troops, Henry retreats toward the Channel coast and runs right into a much larger French force waiting for him in the fields near Agincourt.

The tale is told not just through Henry's point of view but through the eyes of a number of colorful characters who surround him, from dukes and peers down to officers and common soldiers. To keep the story tight, Branagh chooses to focus on just a few of these many characters to carry the weight of the narrative and its themes: the Duke of Exeter (Brian Blessed), Henry's uncle and chief advisor; Fluellen (Ian Holm), an argumentative Welsh officer; and Bardolph (Richard Briers), one of the dissolute friends of Henry's youth, with the scenes bridged and the story held together by the narrator Chorus (Derek Jacobi). Each of these parts is perfectly cast, with Blessed making a powerfully physical impression striding about in full plate like an armored tank. But while the visuals are strong and memorable, it's in its treatment of language that this movie is most successful. Instead of the actors declaiming Shakespeare's speeches like Elizabethan orators, Branagh has them simply speak the Bard's lines in a natural, conversational manner, and as a result the meaning and emotion comes through even when the archaic vocabulary is unfamiliar. It's a brilliant approach, one that requires a director like Branagh who's thoroughly comfortable with the material to pull it off.

And as mentioned, it's a fine swashbuckler into the bargain, with action at the siege of Harfleur and then in the set-piece medieval battle at Agincourt. Unlike Olivier's 1944 version, which has scores of armored knights thundering across a broad battlefield, Branagh's budget is much more constrained; the great battle is represented by a few dozen combatants mainly seen in tight shots and close-ups, and arguably there are too many scenes of desperate knights splashing through the bloody mud in slo-mo. But Branagh's approach is to make a virtue of his modest budget, giving all characters their own individual intimate and horrific battle of Agincourt, to keep the conflict personal and meaningful.

In the final scenes, the tone changes as Henry, victorious, comes to the French court to dictate his terms and to claim as his prize the French king's daughter, Princess Katharine (Emma Thompson), whom Henry woos and wins in a delightful scene that ends the play on an up note. Just as Willy S. intended.

HERCULES (1958)

Rating: ★★★☆☆ • *Origin:* Italy, 1958 • *Director:* Pietro Francisci • *Source:* GAIAM DVD

In the 1950s Hollywood was churning out big-budget biblical epics, wide-screen extravaganzas that did quite well when exported to Europe. Italian producer Federico Teti wondered why these sword-and-sandal flicks should all be made in California when he could shoot them in actual Rome, so he hired director Pietro Francisci and American bodybuilder Steve Reeves to make *Hercules*.

And thus the Italian genre of "peplum" movies (named after the brief tunics worn by the ancients) was born. It would dominate Italian film production until the mid-1960s, when the industry switched overnight to making so-called Spaghetti Westerns. Peplum films mostly follow the formula of cheesy low-budget wrestle-fests in which shirtless muscle men in ancient Rome, Greece, or Babylonia battle the minions of bosomy tyrannical queens wearing gauzy gowns—villains who are backed up by dungeons full of torturers and arenas full of beasts. Though *Hercules* establishes the pattern for these films, it doesn't set out to be cheesy; it aspires to compete with the Hollywood epics, with a substantial budget, a good cast, and decent production values. Its cheesiness is just an incidental result of the decision to lose the inward-looking finding-faith aspect of the biblical flicks and replace it with sheer, gaudy spectacle.

Steve Reeves as *Hercules* (1958) Utente / Wikimedia Commons

THE BIRTH OF PEPLUM

The peplum movie, or Italian sword-and-sandal craze of 1959–1965, was a phenomenon that had its immediate origin in three films: *Ulysses*, which showed that there was a postwar Italian market for adventure films from the era of myth; *Hercules*, which proved you could make such a movie popular on both sides of the Atlantic; and *Hercules Unchained*, which demonstrated there was a formula for repeated success. These were well-crafted movies that aimed much higher than most of their successors and provided solid and, occasionally, even thoughtful entertainment. But after them, the genre rapidly dived deep into the cheese.

And it works: the film was a big hit on both sides of the pond, begetting the dozens of ever-cheesier imitations that followed.

It helps that Steve Reeves can genuinely act, sort of. (He's also handsome, charismatic, and big—really, really big. If any actor ever looked like he was born to play a demigod, it's Steve Reeves.) And he's surrounded by a cast of top-notch Italian actors overseen by a competent director. The story is a loose interpretation of the familiar tale of Jason and the Argonauts questing for the Golden Fleece, with a couple of the 12 labors of Hercules tacked on in act one to get things moving. In this version Hercules gets to be the protagonist and Jason, though heroic, is demoted to second fiddle. Herc also gets most of the romance when Princess Iole of Iolcus (Sylva Koscina, drop-dead gorgeous) falls for him, though her father is inconveniently the king who stole the throne from Jason's father.

Reeves's Hercules is a straight-up demigod with superhuman strength, but though there's a lot of talk about the gods, the divines don't show their faces at all, and things stay pretty down to earth: when Herc fights a lion, or the Cretan bull, he's pitted against an actual beast, and you can see Reeves working hard to defeat it. Occasionally there are minor magical shenanigans, which are always announced by a theremin sting that sounds like it came from *Forbidden Planet*. Hercules has come to the kingdom of Iolcus supposedly just to train their youths (Ulysses, Castor and Pollux et al.) in the martial arts but soon gets involved in dynastic politics and comes out in favor of Jason as the true heir. King Pelias decrees that Jason can prove he's the heir only by recovering the Golden Fleece, and soon all the heroes are off to sea in the *Argo*, represented by a lovely full-size sailing galley. Treachery, of course, sails with them.

After they lose all their cargo in a sudden storm, the *Argo* puts in to an island to reprovision, and everybody gets captured by the Amazons, a tribe of warrior women. Queen Antea tells Jason the Amazons permit no men to live on their island because they know all about male brutality and their unchecked desires, but Jason just tells her, "Not all men are alike!" You might not think that's persuasive, but he follows it with, "A woman is incomplete without a man," and apparently that works because soon all the Amazons have Argonaut boyfriends. But clever Ulysses learns that their sibyls have decreed that on a certain dawn, all the men must be murdered, so he puts poppy seeds in the Amazons' wine, and while the woman are sleeping it off the men escape with a ship full of Amazon loot. Good thing not all men are alike!

From there it's a short hop to Colchis, where they find the Golden Fleece, Jason defeats the one fantasy creature in the film—a really disappointing dino-dragon that looks like it's made of chicken wire and old carpeting—and then it's back to Iolcus to install Jason on the throne. However, the king's treacherous agent steals the fleece, Jason is declared an impostor, Hercules is dropped through a trapdoor into a dungeon, and Pelias orders his soldiers to attack the Argonauts. (This film, by the way, establishes the peplum visual shorthand where the good guys who are fighting for justice and freedom are always shirtless, while the goons of the evil tyrant wear armor and helmets.) Things look bad until, with Princess Iole's help, Hercules escapes and tears into the king's helmeted goons, swinging a 15-foot iron chain from each hand. The final fight, an impressive finale, includes some thrilling demigod feats of strength: it wowed 'em in 1958 and still looks pretty good more than 60 years later. Sneer at the peplum genre if you must, but this film, which started the craze, is worth a look even today.

HERCULES (1983)

Rating: ★★☆☆☆☆ • *Origin:* Italy/USA, 1983 • *Director:* Luigi Cozzi (Lewis Coates) • *Source:* MGM DVD

Another American bodybuilder-turned-actor comes to Italy—time to see if we can reboot the '60s Hercules craze! "But, listen, Menahem, baby, here's the concept, here's the twist: it's Hercules à la *Star Wars*! Genius, am I right?"

Nope. But it is a testament to the success of *Star Wars* (1977) and its sequels that by 1983, even a peplum revival had to be set against a background of stars and planets, with techno-monsters, zap effects, and spacy synthesizer stings at every turn. For example, you may be surprised to learn that the gods of classical myth lived not on Mount Olympus but among the craters of the moon. And when Hercules gets mad, he throws things so hard they fly off . . . into spaaaace! (Just look at those planets go by! Zap!)

The story is a grab bag of mythic names and plot elements tossed together at random. Hercules (Lou Ferrigno), prince of Thebes, is orphaned as a baby when his parents are killed by the wicked Ariadne (Sybil Danning), the daughter of King Minos (William Berger) of Thera, the miniature-model capital of Atlantis. But really, they're all just pawns being manipulated by the gods Zeus (Claudio Cassinelli) and Hera (Rossana Podestà). Herc is raised humbly on a farm by adoptive parents, until Minos discovers his location and sends the mecha-monsters of Daedalus (Eva Robin's) after him and his adoptive parents. These are robots that look like tin-plate Bionicle toys and are about as menacing, shooting zap-beams just as Imperial Stormtroopers do but falling over and disintegrating in starry sparks when Herc hits them hard enough.

With two sets of parents dead but no idea why, Herc sets out to find his fortune, performing the usual Mighty Feats of Strength and falling in love with Princess Cassiopeia (Ingrid Anderson), who is promptly kidnapped by Ariadne and taken off to Thera to be sacrificed to the Phoenix for . . . reasons. Hercules goes after them and does more fighting and more Mighty Feats until he meets the sorceress Circe (Mirella D'Angelo). Thanks to more divine meddling, Circe falls in love with Herc, which causes her to lose her powers but not before she gets them to Atlantis where she's immediately zapped by a Bionicle.

The actors in this are terrible, most particularly when they think they're good, arching an eyebrow while delivering a stale zinger. Herc does the usual clobber-six-guys-at-once stuff, but whenever Ferrigno picks up a sword, it's clear he has no idea what to do with it. He should stick to tree trunks. Ferrigno has two expressions, smug and petulant, though when he gets really upset the flesh on his bulging pectorals begins to twitch. The only cast member who can match him chest-to-chest is Sybil Danning, whose exposed and upthrust bosoms ride majestically before her like two tanned moons rising over a stormy sea. At the climax, when Ferrigno and Danning face each other inside the inevitable erupting volcano (Atlantis, remember?), it's a divine vision of dueling diaphragms that even Homer would have been hard pressed to pay poetic justice to.

HERCULES II (OR *THE ADVENTURES OF HERCULES II* OR *NEW ADVENTURES OF HERCULES*)

Rating: ★★☆☆☆ • *Origin:* Italy/USA, 1985 • *Director:* Luigi Cozzi (Lewis Coates) •
Source: MGM DVD

A sequel nobody asked for! This Lou Ferrigno vehicle reprises the absurd *Star Wars*–y approach of the 1983 film, with an even lower budget and cheaper effects. They even reused the music from the prior movie without changing a note.

To be fair, this sequel is less confusing and easier to follow because writer-director Luigi Cozzi removed all pretense of backstory and character development and simply made it a straight-up collection quest. Zeus (Claudio Cassinelli) rules the stars by virtue of his seven thunderbolts, and when they're stolen by a cabal of rebel gods and hidden inside seven mythic creatures, calamity ensues big-time—like, the moon-is-going-to-collide-with-the-earth-and-destroy-it level calamity. So Zeus calls Hercules down from the constellation he inhabits in the heavens, and Lou Ferrigno once again walks the earth shirtless.

The rebel gods aren't happy about this, so they bring King Minos (William Berger) back to life by draining the blood of a loyal worshipper onto his bones, and in no time he's up to his old shenanigans, acquiring a magical ice sword from Daedalus (Eva Robin's again) that can threaten the gods themselves! Uh-oh.

This time Hercules has *two* comely female sidekicks in short skirts, the priestesses Urania (Milly Carlucci) and Glaucia (Sonia Viviani), who act as expository foils and get rescued a lot. (Whatever happened to Cassiopeia, Herc's great love from the first movie? Don't ask—Herc's a son of Zeus, after all.) To collect the seven thunderbolts, Herc has to defeat a spider queen, a rotoscoped, glowing fire monster, a knight with a zap halberd, a guy in a ghillie suit who knows kung fu, a gorgon that's a bad knockoff of Harryhausen's Medusa from *Clash of the Titans* (1981), and more. He even must walk through a forest hung with articulated papier-mâché mannequins. So scary! Best of all, Herc gets turned into an animated gorilla so he can wrestle a glowing T. rex. Ferrigno is acting hard here, often deploying both of his facial expressions in the same scene, and once he gets to tell his sidekicks, "Quick! Inside the stone mouth!" So I guess it was money well earned. Hey, it was good gig, and he was lucky to get it. Fortunately, you have other options.

HERCULES AGAINST THE MOON MEN

Rating: ★★☆☆☆ • *Origin:* Italy/France, 1964 • *Director:* Giacomo Gentilomo •
Source: Mill Creek DVD

"Earth's Mightiest Titan Battles Moon Monsters!" screamed the posters, and movie posters never lie—well, not this time, anyway. Whoa, the mighty Hercules in a sci-fi fantasy—sounds great, right?

It's not great. It's not even good. In ancient times, evil moon dudes with alien powers plummet to Earth in a meteor and take up residence under the Mountain of Death, demanding for generations the sacrifice of children and youths from the nearby city of Samar. The Samarans get fed up with feeding their kids to a glowing rock face every full moon and send for Hercules/Maciste (Alan Steel) to help—but what the plucky rebels don't know is that their queen, Samara (Jany Clair), has gone full evil and is planning to sacrifice her sister, Princess Billis (Delia d'Alberti) to the moon dudes so they can drain her blood to restore their Queen Selene (also Delia d'Alberti) to life and . . . *conquer the world!* Cool idea, especially if you have a platoon of eight-foot-tall Stone Men at your command. However, if your queenly accomplice has a love potion in her necklace, you'd better not trust her when Hercules is around, because you just know she's going to try to make him her love slave instead of killing him as the Moon Men demand, and then there goes that whole world domination thing.

Okay, points awarded for breaking from the peplum formula by bringing in Moon Men with a blood transfusotron controlled by a giant, swelling brain, but the pacing in this movie is so wretched, it's a dreadful slog to stick it out and get to the good stuff. Most of it is the usual rigmarole of captures, escapes, and secret passages with death traps under the palace, with Herc performing Mighty Feats of Strength to escape the death traps and then mauling Queen Samara's royal guards six ways from Sunday. (Seriously, though, if you ever find yourself in an ancient city ruled by an evil queen, *do not* enlist with her royal guards, no matter how badass their armor is. At some point you're going to get your ass kicked by a demigod.)

Nobody cares anymore about royal guards and death traps once the moon starts approaching the earth and the dreaded stock footage of storms and volcanoes is unleashed, but then Herc rips open the Mountain of Death and gives the Moon Men what for, and boy howdy. Was it worth the wait? No, it wasn't.

HERCULES AND THE CAPTIVE WOMEN
(OR *HERCULES AND THE CONQUEST OF ATLANTIS*)

Rating: ★★★☆☆ • *Origin:* Italy/France, 1961 • *Director:* Vittorio Cottafavi •
Source: Mill Creek DVD

This is a strange one, even for an Italian Hercules movie. The first half hour is surprisingly dull, but then things start to get weird, and as the weirdness notches up, the film keeps getting cooler. Weird, but cool.

It stars Reg Park, the English bodybuilder (and mentor to Arnold Schwarzenegger) in the first of the four Hercules films he made at the height of the peplum sword-and-sandal craze. Park was a personable guy with just enough charisma and range to manage Hercules's three basic moods, a perfectly adequate hero, but at first it seems like his starring vehicle here just can't decide what it wants to be.

Story time! Androcles, the King of Thebes (Ettore Manni), and his best friend Herc are riding through ancient Greece when they are confronted by a vision from the gods, who use crappy special effects to foretell an apocalypse coming to Greece from the west. Androcles gravely vows to face this horrible doom, but then the movie slips sideways into a comedy, and not a very good one. Androcles is unable to persuade his doofus Greek fellow kings to join his expedition, and even Hercules turns Andy down because he wants to stay home with his wife and son. Cut to Herc waking up on Androcles's westbound ship after having been drugged and shanghaied by the king and his "humorous" dwarf sidekick. Ha-ha, some joke!

Herc just smiles, refuses to help and goes all passive-aggressive. He even sleeps through the crew's mutiny and wakes up only just in time to save the ship, exerting himself with a Mighty Feat of Strength. And about damn time, too.

They sail west into an uncanny fog, there's a supernatural storm, and the ship wrecks on the coast of what turns out to be Atlantis. Herc washes ashore alone and immediately has to save a trapped maiden from a shape-changing monster. As monsters go, it isn't very impressive, but at least it's a step in the right direction.

The maiden leads Herc to the Atlantean capital, and as soon as Bad Queen Antinea (Fay Spain) arrives in a chariot drawn by 12 snorting stallions, we know we're finally in for a good time. Atlantis is just solid weird: it's got a stone-faced and somnambulant bad queen who's the rescued maiden's mom, a company of invincible, identical guards in ominous black armor that looks like it was designed by Hugo Boss, chanting priests of Uranus (insert joke here), and shipwrecked King Androcles, who's been zombified by mystic mind-wipe mist. There are also child sacrifices, leprous slaves, a vizier with glowing eyes, an acid pit—and why, you ask? Because in a forbidden cave atop a mountain, there's a glowing green rock formed from the blood of a dead god that emits vibes of evil, that's why. Duh.

Labors! Herc leaps into action, and one must admit he looks good doing it. He stops the sacrifices, frees the slaves, rejects the Bad Queen's love, rescues Androcles and the dwarf and the maiden and his son (did I forget to mention his son?), and finally destroys the evil vibes rock by his favorite expedient of pulling the ceiling down. It never fails! Cue stock footage of Vesuvius erupting, and then—well, it's Atlantis. Do I have to spell it out for you?

HERCULES AND THE MASKED RIDER

Rating: ★★★☆☆ • *Origin:* Italy, 1963 • *Director:* Piero Pierotti • *Source:* Mill Creek DVD

This is a weird genre mash-up of a strongman peplum picture crossed with a masked outlaw adventure, a combination that shouldn't work but does. In Spain circa 1630, wicked Don Ramiro (Arturo Domenici) covets the neighboring domain of Don Francisco (Renato Navarrini), and intimidates the aging Francisco into letting him marry his daughter, Dona Blanca (José Greci). But Blanca loves her cousin Don Juan (Mimmo Palmara), who's just returned from the war in Flanders; he tries to spirit Blanca away to get her out of the marriage, gets caught, and is banished by Don Francisco. On his way to exile, he's captured by a gang of bandits, who challenge him to survive three minutes in a fight with "Hercules" (Alan Steel, called Goliath in the Italian original). Don Juan and Hercules forge a manly bond by beating the stuffing out of each other, so Juan joins the band and immediately starts figuring out how to use them to save Blanca. Since the bandits' Queen Estella (Pilar Cansino) falls for him at first sight, her subjects are all in. Idea! Juan dons a crimson domino mask, cape, and gloves and becomes . . . the Masked Rider!

Outlaw cavalier adventures ensue, drawing liberally from the traditions of both Zorro and Robin Hood. The Masked Rider is an invincible swordsman, and Hercules is just plain invincible, but Don Ramiro seems to have unlimited morion-helmed soldiers, and affairs are nip and tuck until Ramiro's lieutenant, Captain Blasco (Ettore Manni) falls for Queen Estella and comes over to the good guys, tipping the balance. In the process we're served up every Spanish, Romani, and flamenco stereotype imaginable plus regular Mighty Feats of Strength from Hercules. It's especially impressive when he rips out the gallows upon which Don Ramiro intended to hang the Masked Rider and uses it to sweep away his morioned goons. The acting here is adequate, the pacing is decent, and the fencing is passable. Will noble passion win out over avarice and cruelty in the end? Could be!

HERCULES AND THE PRINCESS OF TROY

Rating: ★★★☆☆ • *Origin:* Italy/USA, 1965 • *Director:* Albert Band •
Source: Mill Creek DVD

This is a pilot for a *Hercules* TV series that didn't get picked up—which is a shame, because it's pretty good. It's got Gordon Scott, the second-best peplum Herc after Steve Reeves, in the title role, tight direction from Albert Band, and decent production values. At 47 minutes, it's short for a feature, but was released to TV and then also to theaters as part of a double or triple bill, likely at your nearest drive-in.

Troy is being terrorized by a sea monster, a punishment from the gods for some unknown transgression: each month a maiden is chosen to be tied to an offshore rock to be taken by the creature. (Yes, it's the myth of Andromeda repurposed.) Some Trojan families try to escape by fleeing out to sea, only to be captured by pirates. Fortunately for them, Hercules happens by in his ship the *Olympia*, along with his comrades Ulysses (Mart Hulswit) and Diogenes (Paul Stevens). There's a sharp boarding action—this Hercules is armed with a Greek short sword, and he's not afraid to use it—Herc rescues the Trojans, and then learns of the menace that drove them away. He resolves to put an end to the monster's depredations, and just in time, too, as the Princess Diana (Diana Hyland) has been chosen as the next victim!

There's no time for shilly-shallying, so the story races ahead, with enough twists and turns plus opportunities for Mighty Feats of Strength to keep the viewer glued to the screen. There's treachery, of course—never trust the ruler of an ancient city!—plus nods to Greek myth: a pair of invulnerable white wonder horses, the Grotto of Minerva, and of course that sea monster, a really big lobsteriffic puppet that Herc has to fight mano-a-clawo after Diogenes's Greek fire drives it ashore. Good stuff. Watch for Italian action star Gordon Mitchell in a brief appearance as the pirate captain, fighting Herc in a Duel of Two Gordons.

HERCULES AND THE TYRANTS OF BABYLON

Rating: ★★☆☆☆ • *Origin:* Italy, 1964 • *Director:* Domenico Paolella •
Source: Mill Creek DVD

If you enjoy sword-and-sandal movies and are also a fan of the 1960s *Mission: Impossible* TV series, then this film is a treat, as it stars Peter Lupus (Willy Armitage in *M: I*) as Hercules. Lupus, appearing here under the name Rock Stevens, is just as modest and mighty as in *Mission: Impossible*, plus as Hercules he wields a comically gigantic club when clobbering squads of Babylonian soldiers, which is hilarious fun. Score!

There's also more depth to this film than the usual peplum epic, because there's political intrigue to the story beyond the usual plucky-rebels-versus-evil-monarch plot. Babylon has not one but three wicked rulers, all siblings: a warlike brother, a scheming brother, and a seductive sister. The wicked Babylonians and the King of Assyria are all looking for the queen of the Hellenes, who's hiding among her fellow Hellenic slaves in the dungeons under

Babylon, where they wait till Hercules can come and rescue her. Herc's been off doing hero stuff, but now he's returned, and all those plotting tyrants had better look out!

Political intrigue ensues as everybody tries to co-opt Hercules, and it might even matter if it wasn't for the Big Winch. Object lesson to evil tyrants: when you build your ancient city, of course you must construct dungeons under the palace that are accessible from secret passages, but for the love of dog don't equip your dungeon with an urban doomsday device that links your city's infrastructure to mighty chains attached to a winding wheel that can be turned by 100 slaves—or by a single straining and well-oiled demigod. Because nobody cares about you and your political intrigues once your city collapses on top of you. D'oh!

HERCULES IN THE HAUNTED WORLD

Rating: ★★☆☆☆ • *Origin:* Italy, 1961 • *Director:* Mario Bava •
Source: YouTube streaming video

Hercules goes to hell! In most ways this is no better than the average peplum strongman flick: production values are low, the acting is mostly terrible, the plot is a grab bag of elements from Greek myth flung together at random. And yet there are reasons to watch it. First, it was directed by Mario Bava, the master of stylish Italian 1960s horror movies, and Bava combines the peplum and horror genres with an easy confidence. Second, it has Christopher Lee, the master Dracula of Hammer Horror films, as the vampiresque main villain, though they did dub his voice for the English version. And third, oh Lordy, there's that monster Procrustes—but we'll get to him in a minute.

Hercules (Reg Park) is returning from his adventures to Acadia to marry his sweetheart Daianara (Leonora Ruffo) with his buddy, the hero Theseus (George Ardisson), who looks and acts just like a blond, skirt-chasing surfer dude, and his other buddy Telemachus (Franco Giacobini), the requisite goofball comic sidekick. But upon arrival Herc finds that Daianara's father, the king, has suddenly passed away. However, instead of Daianara assuming the throne, it's been taken by her uncle Lico (Christopher Lee), because the princess is too ill to rule. Herc's ladylove Dai doesn't even recognize him; she's wandering around in a dazed trance that might maybe have something to do with the fact that Lico keeps her at night in a stone coffin in his subterranean shrine to the Gods of Darkness. Just guessing here.

But Herc doesn't know about that, so he consults with a creepy oracle who tells him Daianara can be saved only by going on a quest to Hades itself! Herc must enter the realm of the god Pluto to obtain the Stone of Forgetfulness, but to get out again he'll first need to get the Golden Apple from the cursed Garden of the Hesperides. Double MacGuffins? Why not? Let's go!

Bava conjures up an eerie tone for Hercules's journey into Hades mostly with nothing more than the brilliant use of lighting and clever lap-dissolves to fade images in and out— it's cheap, but it works. The story stops making much sense around the time the heroes are shipwrecked on the shore of Hesperides, but Herc picks up the pace with his Mighty Feats of Strength, throwing great boulders as if they were mere painted chunks of foam, plus being nonstop forthright and courageous even when everyone else falters. There are lots of spooky hell caves, and just when you're starting to tire of them, Theseus and Telemachus get captured by the monster Procrustes, who by himself is worth the price of admission. He's a tall stone man in a heavy stalactite suit; he laughs real slow, "Ha. Ha. Ha," ties Telemachus to a too-short stone bed, and rumbles, "You. Should be. Shorter. I will. Make you. Fit the bed." What a card!

Hercules throws him through a wall.

Anyway, the MacGuffins get got and the heroes return to Acadia, but Christopher Lee isn't about to surrender to a musclebound lug like Reg Park; he abducts Daianara, carrying her in a white, gauzy dress to his underground lair, where the Gods of Darkness have commanded him to do unspeakable things. Herc pursues, fighting hordes of zombies; during a lurid lunar eclipse, he finally catches up to them at an altar surrounded by standing stones. But if there's one thing Hercules knows how to use, it's a really big stone. Sorry, Lico.

HERCULES UNCHAINED (OR *HERCULES AND THE QUEEN OF LYDIA*)

Rating: ★★★☆☆ • *Origin:* Italy/France, 1959 • *Director:* Pietro Francisci •
Source: Amazon streaming video

Hercules Unchained comic book adaptation
DELL COMICS / WIKIMEDIA COMMONS

Hercules was such a breakout international hit in 1958 that producer Bruno Vailati immediately reassembled its director, stars, crew, and even props (that full-size sailing galley!) to make a sequel. *Unchained*, almost as successful as its predecessor, reinforced the dramatic conventions of the peplum genre established by *Hercules* and made it a full-on craze, as every studio in Italy turned to making epics about ancient shirtless strongmen.

The movie's prologue immediately adds a new staple to the genre, the bosomy tyrant queen in a gauzy gown, in this case Omphale, Queen of Lydia (Sylvia Lopez), who has *plenty* of omph. Her hobby is taking a handsome male lover into her lurid palace until she tires of him and then sending out her soldiers to abduct a replacement. The old lover, we later learn, is then killed, embalmed, posed, and added to Omphale's weird trophy dungeon. Ooh, she's a bad one.

Opening titles, and then cut to our wholesome heroes, Hercules (the charismatic Steve Reeves once again), his new wife Iole (reprised by Sylva Koscina), and their young pal Ulysses (Gabriele Antonini), who's smart as a whip and cute as a puppy. The gang are on their way to Herc's home city of Thebes when they happen to ride past the gaping cave entrance to hell and encounter a couple of Herc's old friends: Oedipus, King of Thebes, and his son Polynices. But Oedipus is no longer king because, Lear-like, he's given up the throne to his two sons, who are supposed to take turns as ruler. However, Eteocles, the other son and current ruler, won't give up his seat, so Polynices, vexed, has invited in the brutal army of the Argives to overthrow him. Herc persuades Poly to hold off on the bloodshed until he gets a chance to talk to Eteocles, and Poly gives him a week. (Meanwhile, Oedipus gets dragged down into hell. Don't hang around near gaping hell maws, people.)

Herc's negotiations between the princes actually go pretty well until, like a complete boob, he drinks from the Well of Forgetfulness. (Look, when your screenplay is adapted from Greek myths, these things happen.) Herc, his mind a blank, gets carried off to Lydia by Omphale's soldiers, who were out looking for a new boy toy for their queen. Thus, act two is all Hercules, love slave to the bosomy tyrant queen, while Ulysses, in disguise, tries to restore Herc's memory. Meanwhile, there's lots of gratuitous, mostly naked "oriental" ballet dancing, *en pointe* even.

Then Ulysses summons the Argonauts by carrier pigeon, Herc recovers his memory, and the Mighty Feats of Strength begin, which is how you know act three is *on* and it's going to be Mighty Feats all the way down to the bloody end. Decadent Lydia is quickly dealt with, but back at Thebes the war between the princes is in full swing and Iole is being held hostage, which gets Herc hopping mad. He wrestles tigers, he topples siege towers, and entire companies of soldiers are crushed beneath massive statues. The big final battle between the princely factions is well staged, well paced, and entirely successful on the level of sheer spectacle. There's a satisfying chariot duel between the two Theban princes that ends in the movie's best sword fight, and then somehow it all resolves in a solution satisfactory to everyone. (Hint: everybody who was mean to Iole winds up dead.) It's a shame that this was Reeves's last outing as Hercules, because over the next five or six years, a whole lot of strongmen will try to fill his oversized sandals, but no one will quite match the original.

THE HEROIC ONES

Rating: ★★★☆☆ • *Origin:* Hong Kong, 1970 • *Director:* Chang Cheh •
Source: Well Go USA Blu-ray

China, toward the end of the Tang dynasty: the imperial capital of Changon is occupied by the rebel army of Wang Chao, and the weakened Tangs must turn to the fierce border warriors of Prince Li Jin for aid. Prince Li arrives with his 13 generals, all adopted sons, and a considerable army, but there is friction between the hard-riding, hard-drinking "wild savages" of Li's generals and the officers of the imperial Tangs. Worse, there's friction between some of the 13 generals as well.

Thirteen starring heroes! During the opening titles, each is introduced by name, in a medium shot on horseback so you can't even identify them by their features. How to keep them straight? Fortunately, they refer to each other by number, such as "Fifth General" or "Seventh Brother," and there are only four of them who matter: Thirteenth (David Chiang) and Eleventh (Ti Lung), who are the good brothers, and Fourth (Nam Seok-hun) and Twelfth (Wang Chung), who are the bad generals. Thirteenth is the most heroic Heroic One, a charismatic natural leader who performs impressive martial feats that earn him the most praise from Daddy Li, to the fury of Fourth and Twelfth. These latter are plenty tough as well, and as their minor betrayals gradually grow into lethal treachery, their combat skills and glib tongues keep getting them out of trouble until the trouble is just too deep.

And that's about all the plot there is, really. This film is kind of an experiment: What if you shot a two-hour movie with just 30 minutes of story and a full 90 minutes of relentless action? Though they're supposed to represent army corps and guard troops, in addition to the 13 generals there are only about 40 other combatants in this picture, all changing their outfits and weaponry and going at each other with swords, spears, poles, and chains in every combination director Chang Cheh can think of. Those 40 fighters die about 50 times each to the heroes and villains, as the generals and leaders of the various factions, who don't get to come back, are gradually whittled down to a few.

There are more ancient Chinese weapons here than you can shake a qiang at, but you know what's really impressive? The grappling hooks. You will never again see so many walls scaled by so many guys with so many, many grappling hooks. Plus getting down on the other side is no problem, because in slo-mo unison they all somersault to the ground with a whoosh.

Snark aside, this is a good-looking film with solid, even spectacular, action sequences, but the character development is so cursory it's hard to care about anybody. The 13 general-bros are all macho louts high on testosterone, while their enemies are either one-note brutes or weaselly aristocrats. But if you've got an appetite for martial-arts weapon battles that go on for 10, 15, or 20 minutes at a time, you'll get a full plate of that here—plus a hefty side of grappling hooks.

HERO OF ROME (OR ARM OF FIRE)

Rating: ★★★☆☆ • *Origin:* Italy/France, 1964 • *Director:* Giorgio Ferroni •
Source: Mill Creek DVD

Gordon Scott had Tarzaned a lot in the 1950s and then gone to Italy and Macisted for a while, but here he finally gets to put on a tunic. In this historical epic of early Rome, Scott plays Roman General Mucius, and in the first scene he fights off an Etruscan ambush on a food convoy almost single-handedly, wielding his gladius with skill. But he also does Mighty Feats of Strength, like throwing whole tree trunks at the attackers, so at first the film looks like it's shaping up to be just another strongman adventure.

But then things get interesting. The Romans have revolted against their Etruscan over-lords, thrown out their last king—Tarquin (Massimo Serato, always a dependable villain)—and declared themselves a republic. Tarquin has joined up with Etruscan King Porsenna (Roldano Lupi), and their army has placed Rome under siege. Outnumbered, supplies dwindling, Mucius decides Rome's only hope is for him to sneak into King Porsenna's camp and kill him. But Mucius slays the wrong man, a mere aide, and is captured. Threatened with torture unless he reveals Rome's military secrets, Mucius bravely thrusts his own hand into a flaming brazier and holds it there until Porsenna, impressed, begs him to take it out.

There follows an engaging tale of romance, political intrigue, betrayal, and vengeance, as Porsenna and Mucius try to negotiate a peace but are repeatedly foiled by the plots of Tarquin, who not only wants Mucius dead but also wants his fiancée, the lovely and spirited Cloelia (Gabriella Pallotta). The story twists and turns, but Mucius, his sword hand crippled, can't gain control over Tarquin until Porsenna's son, Prince Arunte (Gabriele Antonini), persuades him to learn to fight left-handed—and to clad his useless right hand in a heavy metal gauntlet that can serve as both shield and truncheon. Cool! When speaking his lines, Scott is pretty wooden, but he's a fine physical actor, and the training sequence is convincing. Mucius, his mojo restored, leads a commando raid to rescue Cloelia from Tarquin, followed by a pitched battle between the Romans and Etruscans and a climactic single combat between Mucius and Tarquin. And it's a tough fight, but the victor finally wins . . . handily.

THE HIDDEN FORTRESS

Rating: ★★★★★ • *Origin:* Japan, 1958 • *Director:* Akira Kurosawa •
Source: Amazon streaming video

The sound bite on *The Hidden Fortress* is that it's the Kurosawa film that inspired *Star Wars*, but if you go into it expecting to see some kind of samurai cognate to the Skywalker saga, you're going to be disappointed and, worse, you may overlook the very real pleasures this film has to offer. Yes, *Hidden Fortress* did inspire some aspects of George Lucas's approach to *Star Wars*, but just put that aside and let this movie win you over on its own terms.

This is the director working firmly within the tropes of the *chambara*, or historical swordplay film, but he can't resist subverting those tropes even as he displays his mastery of them. Kurosawa does this from the very beginning: a bombastic march plays over the opening credits, dissolving into a shot of a country road. But instead of a masterless samurai striding into a new adventure, staggering down the road come a couple of losers, two failed would-be warriors fleeing the aftermath of a battle. These clownish peasants, Matashichi (Kamatari Fujiwara) and Tahei (Minoru Chiaki), are greedy and

The Hidden Fortress AUTHOR'S COLLECTION

feckless cowards who bicker constantly. But this pair of clowns will provide the picture's point of view, and we'll view the actions of the ruling samurai-class characters, heroic and not so heroic, through the eyes of these ordinary folk.

The two losers, lamenting their fate, are on the run after the Akizuki clan was defeated and nearly destroyed by the Yamana. Though they'd intended to fight for the Yamana, the pair are soon swept up with the fugitive Akizuki and pressed into forced-labor gangs digging through the ruins of the Akizuki clan's castle, seeking its hoard of gold. The Yamana samurai treat the captive workers like animals, and they rise up (with no help from Matashichi and Tahei) in a brilliantly depicted night revolt in the ruins. (This is Kurosawa's first wide-screen film, and he uses the format's scope and depth of field to great effect.) The clowns take the opportunity to escape and soon revert to the status of fugitives starving in the countryside. They try to return to their home province of Hayakawa, but they are foiled because the Yamana guard the border. Desperate, they make their way into the mountains, where they build a campfire to cook some stolen rice. But inside the firewood, hidden in a thick branch, they unexpectedly discover a slim gold bar stamped with the Akizuki crest. Have they discovered a clue to the lost Akizuki hoard?

Indeed they have, and more than that, they discover the hoard's guardian, the Akizuki general Rokurota Makabe (Toshiro Mifune), as well as the clan's sole surviving leader, Princess Yuki (Misa Uehara), both of whom have taken refuge in a mountaintop "hidden fortress." Rokurota presses the clowns into service by exploiting their greed for the gold, but the searching Yamana are closing in, so the four, with the two samurai disguised as commoners, set out to try to get across the border to Hayakawa.

Now we are firmly in chambara adventure territory, and Kurosawa alternates scenes of exciting samurai action with poignant interludes among the peasantry, where the disguised princess, who's been raised in a castle, learns what life is like outside the samurai's rigid and duty-bound warrior class. These scenes are wonderful, moving and sharply drawn, but the pace doesn't flag, and in between them we're treated to the greatest samurai spear fight ever filmed, as Rokurota duels and defeats Hyoe Tadakoro (Susumu Fujita), a Yamana champion. Tension grows as the Yamana close in on the fugitives, and the movie rushes toward its climax, which I won't reveal, but it's both exciting and satisfying. The film ends as it started, with the two rueful peasants walking away from the deadly, honor-driven milieu of Japan's rulers, heading home to their village at last.

HIGHLANDER

Rating: ★★★★☆ • *Origin:* UK, 1986 • *Director:* Russell Mulcahy • *Source:* Weltkino DVD

Highlander AUTHOR'S COLLECTION

The story of this enormously entertaining action fantasy doesn't bear close inspection, but it only takes itself seriously enough to keep you hanging on through the thrill ride. Director Russell Mulcahy made his name on music videos for early MTV, and his stylistic use of quick cuts and orbiting Steadicams, while standard now, was a revelation in 1986.

The story is set in Scotland in the sixteenth century and in New York City in 1985, cutting back and forth between the two. Highlander Connor MacLeod (Christopher Lambert) goes to battle with his clan mates where he faces a mysterious bone-clad knight called the Kurgan (Clancy Brown) who impales MacLeod with his broadsword. He's rescued by his friends, and his lethal wound heals overnight. Accused of witchcraft and driven from his village, MacLeod, living alone but for his wife Heather (Beatie Edney), has no idea what this all means until he's tracked down by an ebullient Spaniard, Ramírez (Sean Connery). Ramírez explains to MacLeod that he's one of an elite group of immortals who live only to kill each other and absorb their extrahuman energy in an event called the "Quickening." The Spaniard trains MacLeod in swordplay to withstand the inevitable return of the Kurgan, until one day their nemesis shows up while MacLeod is away.

In 1985 in the current-day storyline, MacLeod, still alive after over four centuries, is attacked in a parking garage by Fasil (Peter Diamond), another immortal. After a furious sword fight, MacLeod beheads him, the only way an immortal can be slain, and absorbs his power. Then the cops arrive. MacLeod is arrested and released for lack of evidence, but he's attracted the attention of forensic scientist Brenda Wyatt (Roxanne Hart), who also happens to be an expert on ancient swords and who finds Fasil's exotic blade. Obsessed, Brenda tracks down MacLeod and they fall for each other, but the Kurgan tracks down MacLeod as well, because it's finally time for the Gathering, when the last two immortals must fight to the death. (You know the meme: There Can Be Only One.)

This is solid, silly fun, with scenery chewed by all concerned, because in addition to threats of decapitation, there's also the Angst of Doomed Romance. The exaggerated broadsword combats are not what you'd call historically authentic, but these immortals are not so much swordsmen as badass superheroes who happen to wield swords. This is just as well, because none of the actors is a credible fencer except for Peter Diamond who, along with Bob Anderson, is responsible for choreographing the sword fights—the same team who performed that service for *Star Wars*. And there are definite visual echoes of *Return of the Jedi*'s lightsaber battle in the final clash between MacLeod and the Kurgan, under a giant electric sign at night on a downtown rooftop and then in the dark and empty warehouse below. However, watch this if only to savor Connery's over-the-top performance as an Egypto-Spanish immortal with an inexhaustible lust for life and an impossibly anachronistic Japanese *katana*. You won't be sorry.

HITOKIRI (OR TENCHU)

Rating: ★★★★☆ • *Origin:* Japan, 1969 • *Director:* Hideo Gosha •
Source: Fuji Telecasting DVD

It's worth noting up front that one of the stars of this film is Yukio Mishima, the celebrated Japanese writer, provocateur, public intellectual, and nationalist who tried (and failed) to inspire a right-wing coup d'état in Japan in 1970. By all accounts a thorough narcissist, it's fascinating to see him here playing a character who's strong, stoic, honorable, and ruthless, traits that align so closely with how Mishima saw himself. He definitely has a magnetic screen presence, though he appears in this film for less than five minutes all told, despite being fourth-billed behind Shintaro Katsu, Tatsuya Nakadai, and Yujiro Ishihara.

The story is set in 1862, a time of conflict between samurai clans supporting the failing shogunate and those who want to restore power to the emperor. However, if you're hoping to learn about the fascinating politics of that era, this isn't the movie for you. This is a character study of one of the samurai who opposed the shogunate, an angry and ignorant man named Okada (Katsu), who at the start of the film is at the end of his resources. The local pawn shop won't even take his family suit of armor, and he's all at sea until he's taken up by Takechi (Nakadai, exuding cold megalomania), an officer of the Tosa clan who's forming a death squad to murder the political enemies of the emperor. Takechi praises Okada's sword work, which though untutored is wild and effective, but since Okada's never killed a man, Takechi sends him along to observe the assassination of a clan regent by three of his swordsmen. The murder

SHOGUNATE'S END

The Tokugawa shogunate of the samurai military caste ruled Japan for over 300 years, keeping the island nation in a sort of stasis enforced by rigid regulation and an entrenched hierarchy. But outside, the rest of the world was changing, as the Western powers of Europe and America developed economies based on global trade on terms backed up by military might. In 1853, when the United States came knocking on Japan's door insisting on trade concessions, the shogunate had only swords and matchlock muskets with which to oppose armored warships and had to comply with the American demands. Other Western nations followed suit, and Japan began to open its borders, resulting in economic and political instability that the shogunate was too weak and hidebound to manage successfully. This period before the imperial restoration of 1868, known as Bakumatsu, was a sort of slow-burning civil war in which a number of factions struggled for ascendancy, all sides resorting to death squads and assassinations. The time of the sword, which had ruled Japan for almost 1,000 years, was coming to an end.

is a slow horror in the pouring rain as Takechi's men bungle the job; Okada, watching from the shadows, sneers, "Damn, I could do better than that. I could kill."

And so he does: Okada quickly becomes the Tosas' most feared killer, ritually crying out, "*Tenchu!*" ("Heaven's punishment!") as he cuts men down with his extralong *katana*. Okada is well paid for his murders and comes to see himself as a big man in the Tosa clan, respected and responsible for Takechi's increasing influence. Only gradually, and with great reluctance, does he realize that Takechi, far from respecting him, regards him as nothing but a tool, to be discarded when Okada becomes an embarrassment by drawing too much attention to himself.

Katsu is excellent as Okada, a man of low rank whose only skill is fighting but whose character is otherwise opposite in every way to Katsu's signature role of Zatoichi. When Okada is chastised by Takechi for not following orders, he angrily quits the Tosas and goes looking for another patron. He's even befriended by his rival Shinbei (Mishima), the leading killer of the Satsuma clan, but no one will hire him. Eventually he goes crawling back to Takechi, who assigns Okada to kill a government official and frame Shinbei for the murder. When Shinbei is presented with the evidence of his guilt, his own, stolen sword discovered at the crime scene, he draws the blade and instantly commits seppuku. This breaks Okada; he goes on a drunken binge, gets in a fight with a whole squad of police, and ends up in jail—and Takechi, to his horror, leaves him there. When he's finally released, Okada is a changed man, but his relationship with Takechi must still be resolved.

This film is about 20 minutes too long, and while Hideo Gosha's direction is as good as you'd expect, his eye when shooting in color isn't as sharp as in black-and-white, and night scenes are often murky. But the performances of the leads are outstanding, and that alone makes this well worth watching.

One year after the release of *Hitokiri*—which means "killer"—Mishima's attempted right-wing coup was a failure, and, like Shinbei, he committed seppuku with his own sword.

IF I WERE KING

Rating: ★★★★☆ • *Origin:* USA, 1938 • *Director:* Frank Lloyd •
Source: Universal Vault Series DVD

Justin Huntly McCarthy's 1901 novel romanticizing the life of French poet and petty criminal François Villon (1432–1463) was so popular, it spawned a play, an operetta, and a 1920 silent film, and it was the uncredited source material for John Barrymore's *The Beloved Rogue* (1927). Paramount decided to revive it as a starring vehicle for Ronald Colman following his success with *The Prisoner of Zenda*. It was intended to be a top-of-the-line prestige picture, no expense spared, and the studio hired enfant terrible Preston Sturges to write the screenplay. This was an inspired choice, and his script for the film was one of Sturges's favorites. Much of Villon's poetry in the film was translated from French by Sturges himself.

It's midwinter in the mid-fifteenth century, and Paris is under siege by the Burgundians. Villon (Colman) is being pursued by the city watch for robbery and seeks refuge in the rectory of the priest who raised him. The priest drags the abashed but unrepentant poet into the church to pray for his sins, but his attention is diverted by a beautiful penitent, Katherine de Vaucelles (Frances Dee). He falls in love at first sight and writes a poem for her on the spot, which persuades her to give him an alibi when the city watch catches up to arrest him.

We follow Katherine back to the palace where, after a little more exposition, we're introduced to the legendary King Louis XI, and—*omigod*—it's Basil Rathbone, barely recognizable as he completely inhabits the role of that fearful, cunning, cackling, conniving, but ever-brilliant monarch. No wonder Rathbone was nominated for an Oscar for Best Supporting Actor for it.

There's no tale about Louis XI that isn't about plots, treachery, and betrayal, and that's where this one goes immediately. King Louis, investigating a conspiracy while incognito, gets embroiled in a situation that Villon accidentally gets him out of—by killing the constable (i.e., head general) of France. So Louis, for wily and devious reasons of state, appoints Villon the new constable.

Hilarity ensues. And it's time to talk about Ronald Colman's performance, as Villon and as the impostor constable of France. At the beginning of the film, Colman's Villon is high-strung, voluble, and twitchy, as if suffering from delirium tremens, but as soon as he falls in love with Katherine, he grows calmer and more responsible, and once Louis appoints him constable, he becomes suave and urbane—basically back to his Rudolf Rassendyll (*The Prisoner of Zenda*). It's not really a very convincing transformation, but Colman is so charming and clearly having so much fun, it's better to just go along and enjoy it. Sturges updated McCarthy's old stage play by leaving its hoary clichés intact but giving it plenty of witty, self-aware dialogue that lets Colman mock the source material while bringing the audience in on the joke. He doesn't quite break the fourth wall and wink at the viewer, but it's awfully close.

Highlights: one of the best castle dungeons in a genre full of them, Frances Dee's amazing two-and-a-half-foot-tall, pointed hennin hat, and her cool sedan chair suspended between two horses, something I'd never seen before. But really, Rathbone's performance is reason enough to watch this film, and if you're a fan, it's worth seeking it out just for that.

THE IRON MASK

Rating: ★★★★★ • *Origin:* USA, 1929 • *Director:* Allan Dwan • *Source:* Kino Video DVD

The Iron Mask (1929) WIKIMEDIA COMMONS

The Man in the Iron Mask is the conclusion of Alexandre Dumas's long tale of d'Artagnan and company that began a million words earlier with *The Three Musketeers*. Here all the characters are 30 years older than in that first story, which makes it a fine valedictory for Douglas Fairbanks Sr.'s last silent swashbuckler. Fairbanks reprises his role as d'Artagnan, as do many other members of the cast of the 1921 *Three Musketeers*, with the exception of Eugene Pallette, who'd grown too portly to play Aramis and was replaced by Gino Corrado. (We'll next see Pallette as Friar Tuck in the 1938 Errol Flynn *Robin Hood*.)

The story, involving young King Louis XIV and his imprisoned identical twin brother, is one of Dumas's greatest tales, exceeded only by *The Count of Monte Cristo* and *The Three Musketeers* itself. Fairbanks, who wrote the screenplay, wisely tacked on an extended prologue set back when the Inseparables were all still musketeers, to remind the audience of their characters and camaraderie. This adds some jolly roistering to what is otherwise a relatively somber story and incorporates elements from the latter half of the first novel that didn't appear in the 1921 adaptation.

The second half of *The Iron Mask* is more faithful to the spirit of Dumas's novel than it is to the details of its plot, but even to this Dumas fanboy, Fairbanks's deviations make sense from the cinematic standpoint. We still get gloomy secret passages, a dark conspiracy to replace King Louis XIV, and his ultimate salvation thanks to d'Artagnan's courage and unswerving loyalty. The pacing of the film never flags or falters, the acting is consistently solid, and it's gorgeous to look at. As noted in the opening credits, "This entire production was under the supervision of Maurice Leloir," the veteran French artist who was the most celebrated of the many illustrators of *The Three Musketeers*, and an expert on the period. The costumes and sets, therefore, are visually sumptuous and historically impeccable. A fine production in every way. Watch for Nigel de Brulier reprising his role as the domineering Cardinal Richelieu and totally nailing it.

IVANHOE (1952)

Rating: ★★★★☆ • *Origin:* USA, 1952 • *Director:* Richard Thorpe •
Source: Amazon streaming video

In 1814 the poet Walter Scott began publishing his popular *Waverly* novels of recent Scottish history and then switched, with *Ivanhoe* in 1819, to the medieval era and the history of England, in the process coinventing (along with Jane Porter) the modern genre of the historical adventure novel. *Ivanhoe* was a landmark in other ways as well: for its sympathetic treatment of Jews in Western societies, for establishing the character and tone of our modern version of Robin Hood, and for promoting the medieval background as a setting for adventure tales, still as popular today in the twenty-first century as Scott made them in the nineteenth. (That's right: no *Ivanhoe*, no *Game of Thrones*.)

This blockbuster 1952 MGM film was also something of a landmark: its success made movies of knights in shining armor a Hollywood staple for years to come, it brought Scott's treatment of the plight of the Jews to the big screen, and it launched Elizabeth Taylor to the heights of stardom. Its titular hero, however, is another Taylor—Robert—in the role of Sir Wilfred of Ivanhoe, a knight in the service of King Richard Lionheart who has newly returned from the Crusades. King Richard has been imprisoned by Leopold of Austria, so Ivanhoe has vowed to raise the money for his ransom and to fight for the Saxons against Prince John and Norman oppression while he's at it. As if that weren't enough, he also wants to marry the Lady Rowena (Joan Fontaine), but to do that, he'll have to regain the lost favor of his fierce Saxon father, Sir Cedric (Finlay Currie, with an amazing head of hair). To get anywhere on this impressive list of goals, Ivanhoe must first win the Big Tournament, but he can't enter without money for horse and gear—which is how he meets Rebecca (Elizabeth Taylor), the daughter of a moneylender. Do sparks fly? Yes, they do.

Of course, a hero is only as good as his villains, and Ivanhoe has some dangerous foes in Prince John (the wolfish, sneering Guy Rolfe) and the foremost of the Norman knights, the arrogant Sir Bois-Guilbert—played by George Sanders, so now you know you're in for a good time! The movie was filmed in and among the castles of Scotland, so the scenery is fabulous, and the castle interiors are properly cramped, stony, and asymmetrical. Some of the weapons are wrong for the period, but the knights' armor is right, all suits and coifs of chain mail rather than the plate armor of later times. The film is bookended by two knightly tournament scenes, both classic in their way, but they're outdone in the middle by the exciting siege and assault on a castle, as the Saxons, led by Robin Hood (Harold Warrender), finally rise against the Normans. If you've ever looked at a medieval castle and wondered how the devil attackers could get across a moat and up a sheer wall in the face of bolts and boulders, *Ivanhoe* shows you how.

The movie's not without flaws: except for a few weak jokes from Wamba, Ivanhoe's jester-turned-squire, it's a humorless affair, and here and there it drags a bit. Robert Taylor looks the part, but his acting is rather dry and stiff, and the same can be said of Joan Fontaine. Of the leads in the love triangle, only Elizabeth Taylor as Rebecca the Jewess really shines, almost literally; when she's onscreen you can't look away. And it's not just because she's stunning; she's also far and away the best actor in the picture. Only Sanders comes close: after villain Bois-Guilbert loses his black heart at first sight of Rebecca, he's conflicted at every turn and never sure of himself again. Kudos must also be paid to Felix Aylmer for his fine performance as the Jewish patriarch Isaac, and to Miklós Rósza for the rousing score, one of his best. A whole series of medieval movie epics will follow in the wake of *Ivanhoe*, but few will be as good.

IVANHOE (1970, MINISERIES)

Rating: ★★★☆☆ • *Origin:* UK, 1970 • *Director:* David Maloney •
Source: Simply Media DVDs

I've read Walter Scott's *Ivanhoe* (1819) because it's in my line of work, but if you haven't, trust me, it's a lot of hoary old hifalutin bombast, and you're better off watching a decent screen adaptation; the story is ripe for the cinematic treatment because it has the good strong bones of a melodrama that's serious about its excesses. This BBC TV adaptation devotes ten 25-minute episodes to the novel, which is enough time to include nearly all the plot, and because it's the BBC, it's pretty faithful to the book.

It doesn't start off very well: Cedric the Saxon is played by Peter Dynely as a one-note, obstreperous blowhard, and the main qualifications of Eric Flynn to play his son Ivanhoe seem to be blond good looks and a cleft chin. But then the villains weigh in, and they're mostly played by the fine, stage-trained British actors you expect in a BBC production: Roger Bizley as the Norman knight de Bracy and Noel Coleman as Fitzurse are particularly good. However, they're both outdone by Anthony Bate as Bois Guilbert, the lead villain, who is arrogant and cruel but tormented by his illicit love for a good woman. Juicy!

The story is a knightly love quadrangle between the noble Ivanhoe, who loves his father's ward the Lady Rowena (Clare Jenkins) and the healer Rebecca (Vivian Brooks, quite good), the daughter of Isaac the Jew, who is loved by the wicked Templar Bois Guilbert. The problem is that both women love Ivanhoe and despise Bois Guilbert, while Ivanhoe and Bois Guilbert are locked in a blood feud that started when they were both on crusade in Palestine. Got that? Moreover, Cedric wants Rowena to marry Athelstane, the last royal Saxon, while Prince John wants to steal the throne from Richard the Lionheart, who is on his way back from the Third Crusade, so the Norman villains capture all the Saxon and Jewish heroes and imprison them in Torquilstone Castle. It's up to the Black Knight and Robin Hood and Friar Tuck to get them out . . . of course.

Scott's genius as a storyteller is that this claptrap all makes sense in the moment, and if things slow down, somebody just rings a bell or blows a horn to signal another attack or ambush. Sadly, the knightly combat here is awful, complete crap, though the archery and quarterstaff action aren't bad. The costumes and sets are bottom of the barrel, but hey, it's the BBC. The script is by Alexander Baron, and to his credit, he deals with the woeful racism of the novel by putting all the prejudice front and center and letting it stink for itself. Refusing to soft-pedal the wretched attitudes of even the sympathetic characters is a brave decision that opens a window to the past—by which I mainly mean Scott's 1819 rather than Ivanhoe's 1194. If you're interested in the popularization of tales of chivalry in the Romantic era and in the 19th-century revival of the Robin Hood legend, you need to start with *Ivanhoe*—but do yourself a favor and watch this instead of reading the book.

IVANHOE (1982)

Rating: ★★★☆☆ • *Origin:* UK/USA, 1982 • *Director:* Douglas Camfield •
Source: Sony Pictures DVD

This is a TV movie adaptation of Walter Scott's 1819 novel that harks back to the 1950s Technicolor epics of knights in shining armor, and within the limitations of its budget it actually approaches that goal. It helps that it has a strong cast of mostly British actors, led by Anthony Andrews in an earnest performance as Sir Wilfred of Ivanhoe, with Michael Hordern as his father, the crusty old Sir Cedric, Olivia Hussey as Rebecca the Jewess, and Michael Gothard as the Saxon lord, Athelstane. Best of all are the trio of villainous knights who oppose Ivanhoe, depicted here as Norman frat-boy pals who are like an arrogant and selfish Three Musketeers: Stuart Wilson as Maurice de Bracy, Sam Neill cast against type as Brian de Bois-Guilbert, and John Rhys-Davies as Reginald Front-de-Boeuf outshining them both with his hearty brutality. Less impressive are James Mason as the Jewish moneylender Isaac of York, giving a performance both unenthusiastic and unconvincing, and Lysette Anthony as Lady Rowena, whose main asset is that when she's all dolled up, she looks exactly like a princess from an illuminated medieval Book of Hours.

The screenplay by John Gay, who specialized in literary adaptations, is quite faithful to the novel, but unlike the 1970 BBC version, which focused on the story's literary qualities, the emphasis here is on action. From a cinematic standpoint, the main problem with the novel is that Ivanhoe spends so much of it hors de combat, recovering from his wounds in the opening tournament. This version mitigates that by spending a lot of screen time on the Tournament of Ashby right up front, so we get plenty of Ivanhoe while he's still hale and heroic. The knightly combat with lance and broadsword is decent, and the centerpiece siege of Front-de-Boeuf's Torquilstone Castle is effectively staged, using Northumberland's magnificent Alnwick Castle as its setting. Unfortunately, the love quadrangle, which smolders in the 1952 version, is a damp squib here, and the colorful cinematography too often just serves to highlight how weak the costumes are—really, that phony fabric chain mail is about as bad as it can be. And giving Sir Bois-Guilbert a shield displaying a carrion crow perched atop a skull is overselling his villainy rather hard, especially when he's supposed to be a pious Knight Templar.

However, this production's old-school Richard the Lionheart, Robin Hood, and Friar Tuck (Julian Glover, David Robb, and Tony Haygarth) pluck pleasantly at the strings of nostalgia, and Andrews works at putting what character he can into his squeaky-clean knight, edging out the wooden Robert Taylor to take the crowned helm as "Best Screen Ivanhoe." You could do worse.

Fun fact: this film's first airing on Swedish TV was on New Year's Eve 1982, and its annual broadcast has been a New Year's tradition in Sweden ever since.

JABBERWOCKY

Rating: ★★☆☆☆ • *Origin:* UK, 1977 • *Director:* Terry Gilliam • *Source:* Columbia Tristar DVD

Though he had codirected *Monty Python and the Holy Grail* (1975), this is really Terry Gilliam's first film as full director (and cowriter). Visually, it's much more ambitious than *Holy Grail*, displaying many of the directorial hallmarks of the man who would go on to create such brilliant classics of imaginative film as *Time Bandits* (1981), *Brazil* (1985), and *12 Monkeys* (1995).

Unfortunately, *Jabberwocky* isn't a very good movie.

A comic medieval fantasy, *Jabberwocky* expands upon some of the themes of *Holy Grail*, such as the venality of knights and nobles, the ignorance and filth of the Middle Ages, and the ignoble brutality of knightly combat, while adding scathing critiques of organized religion and disaster capitalism. Unlike *Holy Grail*, it also attempts to have a coherent story, and here the film falls flat. The storytelling is weak: the only sympathetic character, would-be medieval entrepreneur and hapless boob Dennis Cooper (Michael Palin), is shallow and uninteresting, the pacing from scene to scene is terrible, the timing of the gags is frequently off, and the sound recording is often muddled and muffled. What the movie does have going for it is Gilliam's striking visuals and intriguingly cockeyed compositions and camera angles. Most scenes are shot with natural lighting, effectively immersing the viewer in Gilliam's medieval world.

If only the story matched up to the imagery. The kingdom of King Bruno the Questionable (Max Wall) is being menaced by the Jabberwock, a horrible monster that's eating peasants alive and destroying whole villages. Refugees are crowding into the squalid capital city, enabling the greedy merchants who run the place to profit by jacking up their prices. But the king feels he must do something about the monster, so he holds a comically lethal tournament to choose a champion to face the beast. Into this chaos wanders the feckless Dennis, who's come to the city in hopes of joining the ranks of its predatory businessmen. Instead, he bumbles around, falling in and out of various dangerous predicaments, until he accidentally becomes the squire of the knight champion sent out to face the Jabberwock. The monster itself, when it finally appears, is a towering and ragged human-operated puppet, so crappy that it's thoroughly delightful. John Tenniel, who drew the original portrait of the Jabberwock in Lewis Carroll's *Through the Looking-Glass,* would have been pleased.

Like *Holy Grail,* this isn't so much an adventure as an anti-adventure, intended to skewer the pretentious heroics of typical medieval epics, but the punch doesn't really land. It also stumbles as a comedy because the jokes just aren't that good. For the film historian, *Jabberwocky* is a fascinating look at a unique auteur learning his trade—but as a box o' yocks, it's a flop.

JACK THE GIANT KILLER

Rating: ★★★☆☆ • *Origin:* USA, 1962 • *Director:* Nathan Juran • *Source:* 101 Films Blu-ray

This movie has a curious history. After Columbia Pictures had a big hit with Ray Harryhausen's *7th Voyage of Sinbad,* indie producer Edward Small decided to try to cash in by imitating it, which is, after all, what Hollywood does best. He hired the director and stars of *7th Voyage* but couldn't replace Harryhausen because he was irreplaceable, so instead he brought on three apprentice stop-motion animators and told them to get as close to Harryhausen's effects as they could. So they did—and they got so close that Columbia threatened Small with legal action. Whether Columbia had a case or not, it definitely had more lawyers, so Small pulled his film from distribution, recut it, added some songs and rereleased it . . . as a musical!

Small was an old-school moviemaker who genuinely misunderstood why *7th Voyage* worked, deciding that because fantasy appealed only to kids, he needed to make a fairy tale—and since the Harryhausen film had a one-eyed giant, in imitation Jack the Giant Killer was the obvious tale to tell. The result is unabashedly a kid flick, but all in all not a bad one (if you avoid the musical version), with everyone in brightly colored theatrical costumes suitable for a fairy tale. Kerwin Mathews as hero Jack is possibly even duller than he was as Sinbad, but Torin Thatcher as yet another evil wizard is just as awesome as before. The creatures, which consist of two giants, a dragon, a kraken, and a gaggle of demon witches, are mostly fanboy homages to Harryhausen, but you can see worse in every fantasy peplum, so it would be churlish to complain. Director Nathan Juran had by this time a half dozen SF and fantasy films under his belt, so he was used to juggling the special effects while keeping the story moving along. It's good times—if you avoid the musical version.

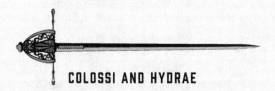

COLOSSI AND HYDRAE

The early 1960s was a time of giants on the movie screen. In Japan, inspired by *King Kong* (1933) and *The Beast from 20,000 Fathoms* (1954), the *kaiju*, led by Godzilla, were wreaking swaths of destruction across the modern world. Ray Harryhausen, though, who'd animated *The Beast*, was looking backward to the ancient world, where the giants of myth had their origins, and other filmmakers in America and Europe were following the same path. Hissing hydras raised their many heads in tales of Jason and Sinbad, while Sergio Leone re-created the Colossus of Rhodes, and though he didn't bring it to life, it was as much mechanism as statue. To see what it would be like if that colossus actually walked, we are indebted, once again, to Ray Harryhausen.

JASON AND THE ARGONAUTS

Rating: ★★★★★ (Essential) • *Origin:* USA/UK, 1963 • *Director:* Don Chaffey • *Source:* Viavision DVD

This is the finest fantasy film of the 1960s and Ray Harryhausen's favorite of all his features. We'll get to why it's so good later, but first, the basics. The story is adapted from Greek myth as told by Appolonios of Rhodes in the third century BCE, a tale of prophecy, fate, and the interactions between gods and mortals. The hero Jason (Todd Armstrong), son of the slain King of Thessaly, wants to reclaim his throne, but more than that he wants to inspire his people to recover from the tyranny of King Pelias (Douglas Wilmer), so he decides on a grand quest to bring back a divine treasure, the Golden Fleece. He stages the first Olympic Games to attract Greece's greatest athletes, the prize being a place with him in Greece's greatest ship, the *Argo*. His final crew includes not only the demigod Hercules (the wonderful Nigel Green) but also Pelias's son Acastus (Gary Raymond), who secretly plans to sabotage Jason's quest.

Jason and the Argonauts Columbia Pictures / Wikimedia Commons

Like *The Odyssey*, the journey of the *Argo* is a series of fantastic episodes, and like Odysseus, Jason is a hero of brains as well as brawn. The marquee attraction here, of course, is Harryhausen's fabulous creatures—the harpies, the animated bronze statue Talos, the hydra, and the skeletons—but they're joined by the more mundane pleasures of the *Argo*, a full-size Greek galley, the natural settings of the coasts and isles of southern Italy, and the towering interiors of the temples of Hera in Thessaly and of Hecate in Colchis, their ancient splendor enhanced by masterful and magical lighting. Plus the fight with the harpies is set in an actual ruined temple rather than a purpose-built set—for a fantasy, you can't get realer than that!

So what makes *Jason and the Argonauts* better than Harryhausen's other epics, good as they are? I think there are at least four reasons why it takes the prize. First, the script by Beverly Cross and Jan Read is just smarter and sharper than that of any other Harryhausen fantasy, addressing what the Greeks felt they owed to their gods and what the gods owed to mortals in return. Jason's character shows significant development, growing from an overconfident youth to a responsible leader. Second, this film is a career best for director Don Chaffey, who keeps tight control over the 80 percent of the film that doesn't belong to Harryhausen and even arts it up with interesting compositions and dynamic camera angles. Third, the acting here is mostly quite good, both among the humans mentioned above and among the gods, such as Honor Blackman as Hera and Niall MacGinnis as Zeus. In most Harryhausen epics, the performances of the human actors seem almost an afterthought, but that's not the case here. Fourth and forever, there's Harryhausen's stop-motion animated creatures, always excellent, but these are among his best, especially the seven skeleton swordsmen in the climactic battle. The actors playing the Greek warriors work hard at it, but somehow, compared to the life and expressiveness of the warriors of animated bone, it's the Greeks who seem like mere puppets. It's an unparalleled work of artistic imagination, and you can't see it too many times.

JULIUS CAESAR AGAINST THE PIRATES

Rating: ★★★☆☆ • *Origin:* Italy, 1962 • *Director:* Sergio Grieco • *Source:* Cheezy Flicks DVD

"Based on True Events!" In 75 BCE, the young Julius Caesar was captured by pirates in the Aegean Sea and held on the island of Pharmacusa. Released after paying his ransom, he returned with a fleet and wiped out the pirate stronghold. Yes, that's right: Julius Caesar, action hero!

Don't mistake this for a cheap, quickie Italian peplum; this is a medium-budget historical epic, and a pretty good one. Lucius Sulla seizes Rome, declares himself dictator, and starts eliminating his political enemies, including Caesar (Gustavo Rojo). Wounded, Caesar escapes to sea on a raft with a noble friend and a comic sidekick. Eventually he is picked up by a Bithynian ship, which has also captured Plauzia (Abbe Lane), the consort of the pirate king Hamar (Gordon Mitchell). Caesar protects Plauzia from assault by Bithynian louts, and she falls for him. Fearing Sulla's enmity, the Bithynians betray Caesar to Hamar, and Caesar, his friends, and Plauzia are all taken to the pirate haven of Pharmacusa. Famously, Hamar demands a ransom of 20 gold talents for Caesar and company, but Caesar scoffs and says they're worth 50. While his friend is sent off to raise the ransom from the freedom-loving opponents of Sulla in Rome, Caesar scouts out a secret underground back door into the pirates' cove—and when the Romans return, Caesar is ready to lead an attack on Hamar to free Plauzia and his friends.

There's a lot going on here, and most of it's good. The direction is solid, the lead actors are all pretty convincing, the romantic melodrama is standard but serviceable, plus there's

Aegean pirate revelry, big-ass Roman galleys with towering stern castles, a pirate gal catfight, and a lurid torture dungeon. What do you want, a chariot race?

KAGEMUSHA

Rating: ★★★★★ • *Origin:* Japan, 1980 • *Director:* Akira Kurosawa • *Source:* Criterion DVD

Kagemusha means "shadow warrior," an apt name for a film about seeming, about the pretense of reality and how it can come to seem real, though it is not. In 1573, late in the Warring States period, a petty thief (Tatsuya Nakadai), so unimportant he's never even named, is saved from execution by Lord Nobukado (Tsutomu Yamazaki) because of his uncanny resemblance to Nobukado's elder brother, the daimyo Takeda Shingen (also Tatsuya Nakadai). Nobukado thinks the thief might be useful as a double for his brother. Shingen, a great general in an age of great generals, dreams of marching on the capital of Kyoto and declaring himself military ruler of Japan, but he is blocked by the alliance of Oda Nobunaga (Daisuke Ryu) and Tokugawa Ieyasu (Masayuki Yui), two other daimyo with brilliant strategic minds.

At a siege of one of Ieyasu's castles, Shingen is shot by a sniper and badly wounded, though the extent of his injury is covered up. Shingen and Nobukado decide to deploy the humble double to cover for the wounded clan lord until he can recover—but then Shingen dies, a fact that is hidden from everyone, even the thief. According to Shingen's last wishes, his death is to be concealed for three years so the Takeda clan's enemies can't take advantage of the loss of their greatest general.

The thief starts to enjoy his new role, but when he tumbles from Shingen's horse and his imposture is nearly discovered, he decides he's had enough and plans to rob Shingen's castle and escape. In the treasure room he finds a great jar and, thinking it must contain something valuable, he stealthily cracks it open, only to be struck down in terror when he finds his own face staring back at him from Shingen's pickled corpse. Disgusted with the thief, the Takeda officers decide to give up on the deception and send him away. But when the thief realizes what the dead daimyo really meant to his people, he begs the officers for another chance. Over time, the double grows into his role, learns to love Shingen's young grandson, and

Kagemusha AUTHOR'S COLLECTION

THE KUROSAWA CHECKLIST

Akira Kurosawa (1910–1998) is probably the Japanese director best known to Western movie-goers: you likely know of him as a director of samurai action films frequently starring Toshiro Mifune, even if you're not particularly a fan of such films. But Kurosawa was far more than that; he was hands down one of the greatest filmmakers of the twentieth century, a man who to our great good fortune happened to set many of his finest movies in Japan's historical samurai era. His incredibly influential *Seven Samurai* (1954) set a standard for intelligent action movies that has rarely been equaled, while *Yojimbo* (1961) exemplified the trope of the lone hero against overwhelming odds with setups and scenes that are still being mined for new movies today. If you're new to Kurosawa, you have a wonderful series of discoveries ahead of you—and if you're an old fan, you know how endlessly rewatchable his best films are.

- *Rashomon* (1950)
- *Seven Samurai* (1954)
- *Throne of Blood* (1957)
- *The Hidden Fortress* (1958)

- *Yojimbo* (1961)
- *Sanjuro* (1962)
- *Kagemusha* (1980)
- *Ran* (1985)

almost forgets that he's nothing more than an imitation. But when he has to appear to lead the Takeda army during a frightening night battle, and he watches as Shingen's retainers give their own lives to protect the life of their dead lord's double, the reality of his false position is brought home to him.

Though there's a lot of warfare here, many battles beautifully staged, this is not a samurai action movie, so don't expect *Yojimbo* or *The Seven Samurai*. This is a superbly acted period drama stunningly depicted with Kurosawa's consummate visual poetry. Though it was the most successful Japanese movie of 1980, the director had a long, hard road to get it made, finally having to turn to fans George Lucas and Francis Ford Coppola to find extra American money to fund it. There were other problems: Kurosawa had written the dual lead role for star Shintaro Katsu, best known for his *Zatoichi* series, but Katsu and Kurosawa clashed on the first day of shooting and Katsu either quit or was fired, depending on whom you ask. Kurosawa finally settled on Tatsuya Nakadai to fill the part, and it was the right choice—his moving performance is one you won't soon forget.

KILL!

Rating: ★★★★☆ • *Origin:* Japan, 1968 • *Director:* Kihachi Okamoto • *Source:* Criterion DVD

There are a lot of comedic Japanese samurai movies; of course, you just wouldn't know it based on which films get English-language versions distributed in the United States and Europe. This picture, cowritten and directed by Kihachi Okamoto (*Samurai Assassin*), is a hilarious mash-up of clichés and tropes from samurai films of the '50s and '60s, including the finest *chambara* movies of Akira Kurosawa. And yet, it's also a solid story well told with a point to make, as often touching and exciting as it is funny. It also doesn't hurt that it has the great Tetsuya Nakadai in the lead role. Let's go!

It's 1833, and the wheels are coming off the shogunate. In a town twice as ruined as the one in *Yojimbo*, in a dust storm twice as dusty and fierce, not one but two strangers drift into the wreckage, both looking for any work that will get them a decent meal. The first one, Tabata (Etsushi Takahashi), is a farmer pretending to be a samurai, a good-hearted but rather dim man who's sold his farm for a sword but never really used it. The second, Genta (Nakadai), is a down-on-his-luck samurai who's pretending to be a yakuza because the crime families always look after their own, right? Only not in this town. In this town, even the old woman who ran the last noodle shop has hanged herself, because, as the last yakuza tells Genta, the samurai ruin everything.

And they're not done with their ruining, because not even this wreck of a town can avoid clan politics. Seven young samurai appear, determined to reform their clan by ambushing and slaying a corrupt chancellor, though Genta warns them not to be rash. Too late! After a terrific melee, the corrupt chancellor and his guards are slain. And then, as the seven young zealots congratulate themselves, the betraying begins—because the idealistic young swordsmen have been used as cat's-paws by Chamberlain Ayuzawa (Shigeru Koyama), who is eliminating all his rivals for complete clan control and now must make sure everyone who can betray him to the government in Edo is likewise removed. (Sound like *Sanjuro*? It was adapted from the same novel on which Kurosawa's film was based.)

Tabata and Genta get caught up in this deadly intrigue, Tabata because he's eager to prove himself a warrior and gain samurai status, and Genta because what's happening to this clan is all too similar to what happened to his own, the tragedy that made him want to give up the samurai life. Though they almost immediately end up on opposite sides, the would-be samurai Tabata and the ex-samurai Genta keep saving each other, as Genta adopts one ridiculous guise after another to try to rescue the young idealists and bring down Ayuzawa. Nakadai is slyly hilarious as Genta (is there any role he couldn't play?), and Koyama as Ayuzawa is icily villainous while maintaining absolute respectability. The jokes are funny, the swordplay is top-notch, the skewering of samurai culture is on point, and this is also one of the best-looking chambara films of the late '60s. If you get a chance to see it, don't miss it.

KILLER CLANS

Rating: ★★★★☆ • *Origin:* Hong Kong, 1976 • *Director:* Chor Yuen •
Source: Dragon Dynasty DVD

Killer Clans is a *wuxia* martial arts adventure crossed with a spy thriller, and it's quite good. Adapted from a novel by Ku Lung, the clans of the title are "secret societies," which in this case means organized crime families, and the tale is of a war to the death between two of them, the predominant Lung Men Society, led by Uncle Sun Yu (Feng Ku), and the rising Roc Society, led by Wong Pan Wong. Caught in between is an assassin-for-hire, Meng Sheng Wen (Chung Wang), a handsome loner with a code of honor who only kills those who've got it coming.

Meng is hired to assassinate Uncle Yu, but his mission is really just a diversion to distract Uncle from his real enemies, the traitors hidden in the Lung Men ranks. But Uncle has his own agents lurking in the Roc Society, and a war of bloody murder commences as the leading martial artists of both sides are betrayed one by one and slain. The plot has all the hallmarks

WUXIA IN THE TIME OF KUNG FU

Hong Kong directors King Hu and Chang Cheh had revived the *wuxia*, or chivalrous hero genre for the modern era in the late 1960s, dominating Asian box offices until Bruce Lee burst on the scene in 1971 with his weaponless kung fu films set in contemporary times. The biggest Hong Kong studios, Shaw Brothers, Golden Harvest, and Seasonal Film, all began churning out kung fu thrillers as fast as they could. Historical wuxia movies were eclipsed during the kung fu boom, but the studios kept making them, and following the trend of the times they increasingly included unarmed action sequences amid the sword, spear, and axe fights. And as the martial arts bar was raised, the action kept getting faster.

of a superspy movie, with sleeper agents, false identities, secret escape tunnels, murder-by-seduction, and death traps, along with the wuxia genre staples of acrobatic duels with exotic edged weaponry, kung fu leaps, drunken warriors, and old men with extravagant facial hair. There's even a tragic romance.

Amid all this betrayal and bloodshed, Meng, under an assumed name, infiltrates Uncle Yu's household but then gains a grudging respect and admiration for the man he was hired to assassinate. And Uncle Yu finds that "the only person I can trust now is the one who came to kill me." The film is well paced, the fights are exciting, the costumes and sets are visually striking, the double crosses come thick and fast but not too quick to follow, and there's even a surprise dungeon crawl. Most versions of this film clock in at 91 minutes, but look for the 102-minute Dragon Dynasty version—the extra 10 minutes make the plot much clearer.

KINDAR THE INVULNERABLE

Rating: ★★☆☆☆ • *Origin:* Italy/Egypt, 1965 • *Director:* Osvaldo Civirani •
Source: Mill Creek DVD

American bodybuilder Mark Forest made 10 Italian peplum movies in the early '60s, mostly playing Hercules and/or Maciste, but by 1965 the fad for shirtless ancient strongmen was waning, and it was time to try something different. Some Egyptians wanted to co-fund an action film, so how about an Arabian adventure fantasy? Kindar (Forest), a child of prophecy and son of the King of Utor, is struck by lightning while his mother is giving birth to him, and the divine fire renders him invulnerable to normal weapons. But the day after he's born, he is abducted and taken to the desert nomads, whose chieftain, Seymuth (the inevitable Mimmo Palmara), raises him as his own son, training him for the day when Kindar will lead the nomads against Utor and his real father. Kindar's training includes raiding Utor-bound caravans, and from one he captures Princess Nefer (Dea Flowers), who is betrothed to his younger brother Prince Siro of Utor (Howard Ross). Seymuth gives Nefer to Kindar as his slave, but he treats her with respect and love blooms. Then things get awkward.

There's the germ of a classic story here, but the pacing is poor, the acting is awful, the combat is mostly just guys waving scimitars at each other, and there are no surprises, because every turn of the plot is telegraphed in advance. The movie has some good points: the exteriors are all shot in the Egyptian desert, and the locations are striking; there's a traditional Arabian adventure climbing-the-princess's-balcony scene; and the nomad raiders have their own nomad raider riding song. But it should have been called *Kindar the Predictable*.

KING RICHARD AND THE CRUSADERS (OR *THE TALISMAN*)

Rating: ★☆☆☆☆ • *Origin:* USA, 1954 • *Director:* David Butler •
Source: Amazon streaming video

This movie has the reputation of being one of the worst Hollywood epics of all time, and I'm here to tell you its reputation is well deserved: this one's a real stinker, folks. Oh, on paper it sounds like a good idea: adapt *The Talisman* (1825), Walter Scott's classic novel of the Crusades, cast George Sanders as King Richard Lionheart and Rex Harrison as Saladin, throw in Laurence Harvey and Virginia Mayo as the romantic leads, get Max Steiner to do the music, and the rest is cake! However, as soon as we're past the opening titles, it all starts to go wrong: a faceless narrator (ugh!) explains the historical situation of the Third Crusade, but the narration script is just awful—and then people start to talk, and it gets worse. The screenplay's pompous blowhardery (yes, that's a word now) is just unbelievable—oh, Lordy, the stuff these poor actors have to say! The romance plot goes on the rocks in record time, not just because Harvey and Mayo can barely stand to look each other in the eye but also because they clearly can't believe how crappy their lines are.

Top-billed Rex Harrison made a career out of playing smugly superior characters so self-satisfied you want to punch them (a lot), and his role here, as the too-clever Saracen who's always the smartest guy in the room, constantly putting one over on the doofus Christians, is made for him . . . though to be fair the Christians, to the last man and woman, *are* complete doofuses. The boring villains' plots are ham-handed and obvious, but the putative good guys are so dense they barely know which end of the sword to hold and spend all their time angrily blaming each other instead of the clumsy bad guys. The villains try to help identify themselves as villains by wearing matching black uniforms, but nope!

As for poor George Sanders, he gets poisoned in the first few minutes and then spends half the movie on his back, grumpily making snarky remarks from the horizontal. His King Richard is nominally in charge of this Crusade, but there's hokey political conflict with his rivals Ludwig of Austria and Philip of France, both ridiculous national caricatures: Ludwig is always drunk, while Philip limp-wristedly waves a fan of lavender feathers, fer Chrissake. There are brief spasms of combat in which everyone flails around with heavy weaponry as if there were no such thing as skill or finesse. There's a contrived trial by combat and an absurd abduction of Mayo, and then everyone stops pretending they're telling a coherent story, and the film is reduced to Hollywood's lowest common denominator of frantic galloping through the California hills. It ends in the Worst Final Duel Ever, with Harvey and the boring chief villain atop a drawbridge three-quarters closed, hanging by their arms and kicking at each other ineffectually. Come on! Screenwriter John Twist inexplicably continued to get work after this fiasco, but it was the end of David Butler's career as a director of feature films. He had to flee to television, where he directed 58 episodes of *Leave It to Beaver*. So maybe there is a God after all—and an Allah.

KNIGHTS OF THE ROUND TABLE

Rating: ★★★☆☆ • *Origin:* USA, 1953 • *Director:* Richard Thorpe •
Source: Amazon streaming video

Thomas Malory's *Le Morte Darthur* (1485) was the first comprehensive collection of the legends of King Arthur and his Knights of the Round Table in English, and according to the opening credits of this film, Malory was the source material for the story—though considering the script, *The Boy's King Arthur* by Sidney Lanier (1880) is a more likely candidate. This is producer Pandro Berman's follow-up to the hugely successful *Ivanhoe*, with the same director, crew, male lead (Robert Taylor), and composer (Miklós Rózsa)—but this time the team barely puts it across. There are two problems that this movie doesn't successfully solve: it's harder to boil down a collection of tales into a coherent story than it is to adapt a novel, and Merlin, Guinevere, Arthur, and his knights are more archetypes than fleshed-out characters.

Let's just get the failings of this flick out of the way so we can focus on what's worth watching. First of all, the dialogue is atrocious, stilted Ye Olde Englishe, and the actors deliver it dead on arrival, as stiff as slabs of oak. The characters are all simple and shallow, allowed just about one note apiece (archetypes, remember?). The knights move awkwardly in their foolish Hollywood plate armor, and the knight-on-knight combats are reduced to painfully artless flailing that goes on way too long. And though the heart of the story is the Arthur-Guinevere-Lancelot love triangle, as it should be, Sir Percival's quest for the Holy Grail is clumsily and intrusively shoehorned into the narrative, possibly to give the film some moral cover in the staid '50s, because otherwise it's basically a tale of medieval adultery. Moreover, Percival stopping everything to have divine visions is disturbingly out-of-tone, as it's the only supernatural aspect retained from Malory: Merlin here is just a wise old advisor, not a wizard, and Morgan le Fay uses poison rather than magic.

But this movie is still worth your time for two reasons. First, it succeeds as a visual spectacle. Based solely on looks, the casting is perfect: Taylor is proud, upright, and stern as Lancelot, and Ava Gardner as Guinevere would make any knight forsake his vows. Mel Ferrer is earnest and leonine as King Arthur, Stanley Baker sneers convincingly as Modred, and Gabriel Woolf as Sir Percival looks like he stepped out of a pre-Raphaelite painting. There are two large, pitched battles that are surprisingly effective—clearly director Richard Thorpe had studied his Eisenstein. And Thorpe's composition and staging of scenes and individual shots is impeccable: sharp, painterly, and memorable.

Finally, as dumb as the script is—and it's real dumb—the basic plot of the rise and fall of Camelot as embodied in the love triangle of the three principals is such a strong story that it works anyway, despite the crappy dialogue. There's real emotion in this timeless tragedy, and Gardner and Taylor manage to wring it out by heroically underplaying their roles while everyone around them is hamming it up. Surprising, but there it is: go figure.

KNIVES OF THE AVENGER

Rating: ★★★☆☆ • *Origin:* Italy, 1966 • *Director:* Mario Bava • *Source:* Starz DVD

This taut little Viking melodrama was directed by Mario Bava in six days after he took over from a previous, faltering director. It's a small production on a modest budget, and besides some killer lighting work, Bava isn't able to include many of his trademark stylistic flourishes, but the scene composition is excellent and the action is tense.

The setup is Shakespearean: in a Norse village, Prince Arald (Giacomo Rossi Stuart) is marrying his bride Karin (Elissa Pichelli) when raiders headed by the brutal Hagen (Fausto Tozzi) burst in with his wedding presents: the heads of the wife and child of Rurik, neighboring chief and longtime enemy. However, Arald's village had just made an alliance with Rurik, so Hagen and company are angrily banished—but too late to prevent the vengeance of Rurik, who comes to the village that night with his carls on a mission of blood and fire. Rurik, in a face-concealing helm, wounds Arald and then goes in and rapes Karin (offscreen). When he comes out, one of his carls asks if Arald should be killed, but Rurik replies, "He's already been punished."

Twelve years later: Arald has been gone for three years, lost and presumed dead when his longship wrecked on the English coast, and Karin, still waiting for Arald, rules the village in his stead with their son Moki. Then Hagen and his raiders return from piratical exile, the leader intent on marrying Karin and ruling the village with an iron fist. Fortunately, a nameless stranger (Cameron Mitchell) rides into town on a white horse, equally determined to protect Karin and Moki and repay Hagen for the evil he's done. This stranger is as deadly with his big throwing knives as a sharpshooter, and like a video game hero, he seems to have unlimited ammo in his black leather jerkin—which he'll need, as Hagen has plenty of goons.

There are no surprises here, just solid visual storytelling supported by a lively Morriconesque score by Marcello Giombini. There are swords as well as those flying knives, and the final confrontation ends in a moody dungeon crawl that wraps up the story with admirable economy. Plus it was a winning double-header at the drive-in with *Gamera the Invincible*. Rawr!

KRULL

Rating: ★★☆☆☆ • *Origin:* UK/USA, 1983 • *Director:* Peter Yates • *Source:* Columbia Pictures DVD

Where to start with *Krull?* Let's try with the beginning, where the title sequence clearly informs us that this is a *Star Wars*–style space fantasy—but then we land on the planet Krull, and it seems it's actually a sort of *Dungeons & Dragons* film. No, wait, it's a Brothers Grimm fairy tale, but then it's back to *Star Wars*, and then we're in Greek myths and *Clash of the Titans* territory, then on to *Robin Hood*, to *Excalibur*, to *Thief of Bagdad*—even *The Beastmaster* rears its feline head.

Krull AUTHOR'S COLLECTION

If Columbia Pictures' idea was to make a film that rolled every '80s fantasy movie into one, laden with every kind of special effect available at the time, it reached that goal. But did the studio, as the wizard-mentor Ynyr asks, use its power wisely? You be the judge. The medieval fantasy planet Krull is invaded by a flying mountain space cathedral bearing armored alien warriors called Slayers that are for all intents and purposes Imperial Stormtroopers, only slower and kind of goofy. They are ruled by a giant reptilian titan called the Beast who likes to conquer worlds and abduct princesses, just 'cause. To resist the Beast, the two warring states on Krull decide to unite by wedding their heirs, Prince Colwyn (Ken Marshall) and Princess Lyssa (Lysette Anthony), who fall in love at first sight. And it's a good thing they don't need any more time than that, because before the ceremony can be completed, Lyssa is captured by the Slayers and whisked off to the Black Fortress. Colwyn, the lone survivor of the Slayer raid, is rescued by Ynyr (Freddie Jones), the aforementioned wizard-mentor, who informs him that his only chance of slaying the Beast and recovering Lyssa is to go on a quest to retrieve the Glaive, a legendary magical weapon. That turns into about four successive fantasy quests, action that takes up the bulk of the picture before the inevitable climactic battle.

The viewer is offered precious little context for any of this. There's almost no history or background of the Beast or of the planet it's invaded, and even in the vast sets where everyone runs around waving weapons, the walls are bare and virtually unornamented, as if built by a people without a culture. The place is a nullity. As he proceeds on his heroic quest, fighting Slayers and changelings, quicksand and traps, Colwyn acquires an entourage of assorted side-kicks, some grim, some humorous, but none of them has more than one-sentence motivations, and it's hard to feel upset as they sacrifice themselves one by one for their callow young leader. The near exception is a tall cyclops named Rell (Bernard Bresslaw), who blinks wryly at all the hijinks and whose plot function is repeatedly to save Colwyn's butt, a sort of cyclops ex machina.

Krull is basically a two-hour parade of wonders, one fantasy obstacle after another until Colwyn finally gets his trusty band to the Black Fortress, where Lyssa has spent the whole time wandering around in a wedding dress while listening to the Beast say stuff like, "Love is fleeting, but power is eternal!" Colwyn had acquired the Glaive, a sort of starfish switchblade frisbee, about 90 minutes earlier, and now he finally whips it out and in short order makes hash of the Beast in an orgy of special effects. Cue the victory fanfare.

Speaking of which, the soundtrack, by James Horner in full-on John Williams mode, is catchy and memorable, though loud and ever present. And though the leads, Marshall and Anthony, are shallow, the supporting actors are mostly pretty decent, including Francesca Annis as a mournful spider-queen and Liam Neeson, charming as usual, in a bit part as a bandit. Plus there's one really lovely sequence in which Colwyn's merrie men have to corral and tame a herd of magnificent and spirited Clydesdale horses. It stands out as the most real thing in the film, which otherwise is a mere collection of unrelated scenes, loud and colorful though they are. Mediocre.

LADYHAWKE

Rating: ★★★★☆ • *Origin:* USA, 1985 • *Director:* Richard Donner •
Source: 20th Century Fox DVD

This is a historical fantasy, less a sword-and-sorcery adventure than a romantic fable. In the late Middle Ages or early Renaissance, in the northern Italy hill town of Aquila, a teenage thief known as Mouse (Matthew Broderick) escapes from the dungeons of the tyrannical Bishop of Aquila (John Wood)—something that has never happened before, so the bishop sends Marquet (Ken Hutchison), his ruthless guard captain, to recapture Mouse lest the bishop's reputation suffer. Nearly caught by the guards, Mouse is rescued by a knight, Etienne Navarre (Rutger Hauer), who has a spirited hunting hawk, a great black charger named Goliath, and

Ladyhawke AUTHOR'S COLLECTION

an impressive begemmed bastard sword. Navarre also has a secret: after dark he's cursed to become a large black wolf, while during the day, his ladylove Isabeau (Michelle Pfeiffer) must assume the shape of the hawk. Thus they can never meet in human form.

They encounter an outrageously scruffy fallen friar named Imperius (Leo McKern) who reveals to Mouse the secret of the curse: in Aquila, the bishop had conceived an obsessive desire for Isabeau, but she loved Navarre, his captain of the guard, so the bishop had pledged a Satanic pact to curse the pair. Desperate for release, or at least revenge, Navarre wants to use Mouse's knowledge of the secret ways of Aquila to help him assassinate the bishop, though that will make the curse endure forever—but Imperius believes he's figured out how the curse can be broken.

Ladyhawke is a fine, self-contained fantasy fable, well written, superbly cast, and beautifully filmed amid the mountains and castles of northern Italy. The story is told from the viewpoint of the young thief, and Mouse, an inveterate liar who carries on an ironic one-sided dialogue with God, could have been overarch and irritating, but Broderick pulls it off in a performance that's equal parts canny and endearing. He carries the film, which is just as well, as the gorgeous Pfeiffer and Hauer spend most of their screen time in yearning looks (though Hauer swings a mean sword). Bonus: if you have an eccentric monk in your cast, Leo McKern should be at the top of your list to play the part.

The task of counterweight to all these adorable good guys goes to John Wood as the villainous Bishop of Aquila, and fortunately he's more than up to the task. At first, he seems a man with a nearly impassive stone face, until you realize that beneath the surface, he's consumed by passions conveyed by tiny flickers of expression, subtle quivers that convey his inner seething more effectively than if he foamed with rage and chewed the scenery. He's remarkable. Wood seems carved from sandstone, an integral part of his domain, the brooding hilltop castle of Torrechiara (near Parma).

The film has its flaws: the pacing is erratic, it sags a bit in the middle, and the Alan Parsons–style prog-rock soundtrack is a trifle incongruous, though it's not as distracting as some make it out to be. The leads' outfits are all fine, but the costumes and weapons of the bishop's guards look gaudy and cheap. However, the fight direction is by the great William Hobbs, and if you've always wanted to see two mounted knights clashing in the crowded nave of a cathedral during an eclipse, your wish has been granted.

LADY IN THE IRON MASK

Rating: ★☆☆☆☆ • *Origin:* USA, 1952 • *Director:* Ralph Murphy •
Source: Turner Classic Movies

This is a deservedly obscure Dumas pastiche, a reimagining of *The Man in the Iron Mask* in which, rather than twin princes, twin princesses Anne and Louise are born to King Louis XIII. To preserve the stability of the realm, Louise is locked away in a dungeon in an iron mask to hide her resemblance to Anne. When Princess Anne (Patricia Medina) reaches adulthood, her uncle, the Duc de Valdac, plans to marry her against her will to Prince Philip of Spain and rule from behind the throne. D'Artagnan (Louis Hayward), sensing the realm is in trouble, gathers his companions Athos, Porthos, and Aramis and rides to Paris to save the day.

There's nothing inherently wrong with this plot, but the execution of it is dreadful—this is a career low for the otherwise reliable Louis Hayward, and when I tell you that Athos (Steve Brodie) and Aramis (Judd Holdren) are outacted by the execrable Alan Hale Jr. as Porthos, that should give you a hint as to how bad this is. The only excuse for this movie to exist is the 15 minutes d'Artagnan and Porthos spend in the dungeon rescuing the princess. There the creepy iron mask does its usual visual voodoo, and worse, the musketeers find that the guardian of the dungeon is the massive Tor Johnson (*Plan 9 from Outer Space*)! Tor (as Renac) and Porthos give each other the stink eye from the moment they meet, and you know it's only a matter of time before they'll be wrestling over the gaping maw of a bubbling lime pit. Spoiler: one of them goes in.

The rest of the film is a lot of routine galloping through Southern California and perfunctory sword fights with foils instead of proper rapiers—though at least Hayward knows how to handle a blade—plus an absurd romance between d'Artagnan and Princess Anne that's like weak musketeers fan fiction. Fortunately, this film is hard to find, so you probably won't be tempted to waste 78 minutes on it.

But that leaves us time for Musketeers movie trivia! Hayward, of course, played both twin princes in the 1939 version of *The Man in the Iron Mask* and had a lot more fun there. And the role of Porthos was something of a Hale family heirloom: Alan Hale Sr. played the giant musketeer in that 1939 version of *Iron Mask*, while his even-less-talented lookalike son took the same role in *Lady in the Iron Mask*, *At Sword's Point* (1952), and *The Fifth Musketeer* (1979).

LADY SNOWBLOOD

Rating: ★★★☆☆ • *Origin:* Japan, 1973 • *Director:* Toshiya Fujita • *Source:* Criterion DVD

This bloody revenge drama was one of the primary inspirations for Quentin Tarantino's *Kill Bill*, and it's easy to see why, as it's equal parts artistic and cheesy. Yuki, or Lady Snowblood (Meiko Kaji), is born in Tokyo Prison in 1874 where her mother, Sayo, has been imprisoned for killing one of the men who raped her and killed her husband and son. Dying, Sayo bequeaths to her newborn daughter the mission of slaying the three other criminals who got away, confiding Yuki and her mission to another prisoner, Tajire (Akemi Negishi), who takes the girl to be trained in martial arts by a fierce ex-priest with a grudge against the world. Flash forward 20 years: Yuki confronts a Tokyo crime boss and his three sword-armed escorts on a dark street. She seems to carry nothing but an umbrella, but it has a sword blade concealed in its handle, and with that and some astonishing leaps, Yuki kills them all.

Only later do we learn why. The story is told in a series of flashbacks, stylish but not confusing, and after some establishing exposition, it becomes clear that Yuki slew the crime boss because he was an enemy to the ragged Matsuemon (Hitoshi Takagi), leader of an extensive network of beggars, a clan of the unseen who may be able to track down Yuki's three targets for her. Though the ex-priest had tried to make a heartless *asura* death-demon out of her, Yuki is far from emotionless and is desperate for leads to help her complete her life's mission. In fact, her life story seems to belong to almost everyone but herself: to her dead mother, whose last words were, "I will die, and my spirit will possess her"; to her foster mother Tajire; to the angry ex-priest; and to a muckraking young journalist Yuki meets who seems to know everything about her. Yuki has nothing for herself except her mission of blood and is increasingly driven to escape by completing it.

The story is adapted from the manga series by Kazuo Koike (writer of *Lone Wolf and Cub*) and Kazuo Kamimura, which depicts Japan at the end of the 19th century as a society that has descended into greed and rampant corruption, against which Lady Snowblood stands with her purity of purpose, grim though it may be. Despite the film's low budget and shallow characters, the sharp direction by Toshiya Fujita and the blushing charisma of star Meiko Kaji pull it through. At the climax, during a snowstorm, Yuki tracks her final target to a masked ball in a house of pleasure replete with deranged assassins, revolving secret doors, and one-way mirrors, and you can't really ask for more than that.

LADY SNOWBLOOD: LOVE SONG OF VENGEANCE

Rating: ★★★☆☆ • *Origin:* Japan, 1974 • *Director:* Toshiya Fujita • *Source:* Criterion DVD

This sequel is even wilder than the first movie. It's 1906, 10 years after the first film, and Yuki (Meiko Kaji) has continued working as Lady Snowblood, assassin for hire. Following the wartime defeat of Russia the previous year, Japan is in the grip of nationalistic and militaristic euphoria, but this is not shared by the poor and the wounded veterans who are jammed into Tokyo's slums. Yuki is constantly on the run from swordsmen out for revenge for her murders, and from the brutal Tokyo police, who are worse than the swordsmen. A hunted fugitive, she is saved from a bear trap by a mysterious dreamboat doctor but then is surrounded again by the police, this time on a beach. Sick of fighting, she throws away her sword and surrenders.

Then things take a bizarre turn. Yuki is tried, convicted, and condemned, held in the same Tokyo prison where she was born—but on the way to the gallows, assassins wearing bizarre baby masks slaughter her guards and take her to an ominous estate where she meets Kikui (Shin Kishida, terrifying), the head of the secret police. She is to be freed and allowed to continue her murderous career if she agrees to spy on the notorious anarchist Tokunaga (Juzo Itami) and get from him a confidential document.

Trapped, Yuki picks back up her umbrella sword and takes a job as a maidservant in Tokunaga's household, where she searches for the document and instead discovers . . . class consciousness. Tokunaga recognizes her as Lady Snowblood and teaches her about the horrors the capitalist government is inflicting on its poorest citizens. Yuki is radicalized.

But it's not all about politics—not yet, anyway. First there's a soap opera: Tokunaga's loyal wife Aya (Kozuko Yoshiyuki) was once married to Tokunaga's brother Shusuke (Yoshio Harada), but Tokunaga "stole her away" while Shusuke was in the trenches in Manchuria. Shusuke is also the heartthrob doctor who saved Yuki from the bear trap—but he won't save his brother when the secret police come for him.

Meanwhile, Tokunaga has given the document that could "bring down the government" to Yuki for safekeeping; she is wounded when trying to defend him against the police, and she escapes to bring the document, and her wounds, to Shusuke. And it does bring down the government, or at least its fist in the form of the secret police, who set fire to the slums and deliberately infect Shusuke with plague. (That's how bad they are.)

From this point on, there's nothing left for Yuki but vengeance, and the blade comes out of the umbrella for good. Star Kaji's high-wattage charisma notwithstanding, the final orgy of carnage is noteworthy more as a gore fest than as a display of sword-wielding martial arts. And be warned, a lot of the gruesome injuries inflicted by both sides verge on torture porn. But the direction by Toshiya Fujita is brisk and bracingly weird, with some scenes you won't soon forget.

LAST HURRAH FOR CHIVALRY

Rating: ★★★★☆ • *Origin:* Hong Kong, 1979 • *Director:* John Woo • *Source:* Eureka! Blu-ray

This *wuxia* film written and directed by John Woo is broad, almost cartoonish, and very entertaining. Before making his name with action crime films, Woo directed kung fu and wuxia movies for Hong Kong's Golden Harvest studio. He made *Last Hurrah* as a sort of tribute to his mentor, Chang Cheh, especially referencing Cheh's *Have Sword, Will Travel*, but adding the kind of double crosses and plot reversals that would become hallmarks of Woo's later works.

In ancient China, Kao Peng (Lau Kong), the son of a respected gang boss, is getting married at his father's fortified hilltop estate when the festivities are crashed by a rival boss, Pai Chung-tien (Hoi Sang Lee), killing the father and driving away the son, who escapes vowing revenge. Kao Peng is advised that only retired fighter Chang San the Divine Blade (Wai Pak) has the chops to defeat the bandit boss, so Kao Peng decides to test Chang San by hiring another famous swordsman, An Tien-ming, to take him on. But Chang San, though young, has hung up his sword, is working as a humble horse washer, and refuses to fight. An Tien's provocations are amusedly observed by the bibulous and sardonic Ching I (Damian Lau), another sword-for-hire who decides he likes Chang San—though not enough to help him.

Meanwhile, Kao Peng is trying to bully his father's old weapons master into giving him a legendary blade, the Moon Shadow Sword, but the grandmaster insists his paltry skills are unworthy of it. Frustrated, Kao Peng focuses on his first plan, deceitfully befriending Chang San for his own ends. Chang San is finally aggravated by An Tien into picking up the Divine Blade and meeting the swordsman for a spectacular duel, which Chang San wins, but meanwhile Kao Peng fakes an attack on his own house by Pai Chung, in which the old grandmaster is wounded. Chang San, outraged by the slaughter of Kao Peng's retainers, swears to get revenge on Pai Chung for his new friend.

After some humorous intrigues, Ching I, who has been spying on Pai Chung's headquarters, joins Chang San for the big raid on the bandit stronghold. Before the pair can get to Pai Chung, however, they first must defeat his 36 first-level goons and then a half dozen colorful martial arts experts, including such notables as Yellow Weasel, the Phantom Spear, and the Mad Blade of the Sleeping Buddha. This is hot stuff, but the relentless final combat with Pai Chung, which inexplicably takes place in an underground vault lit with 1,000 candles, is even better. However, the treacherous Kao Peng, who's finally gotten his hands on the Moon Shadow Sword, intends to be the last martial artist standing.

This is a richly colorful film with inventive and intensely theatrical swordplay, replete with snappy dialogue and deft comic touches. Everyone involved seems to be having a good time. So will you.

LAST OF THE BUCCANEERS

Rating: ★★★☆☆ • *Origin:* USA, 1950 • *Director:* Lew Landers •
Source: Turner Classic Movies

In the late 1940s, leading man Paul Henreid was blacklisted in Hollywood, accused of sympathy for the Communist Party and unable to get cast in his former serious dramatic roles. However, he'd made a successful pirate move, *Spanish Main*, in 1945, so independent producer Sam Katzman was willing to cast him in another. And thus the urbane Henreid, Victor Laszlo himself, was reinvented as a swashbuckler.

So how's the movie? Fair to middling. Henreid is pirate Jean Lafitte, and the story picks up right after the Battle of New Orleans, as this is a sort of sequel to Cecil B. DeMille's *The Buccaneer* (1938), and the story replicates many of the elements of the DeMille film, so it isn't particularly original. Henreid as Lafitte is a reasonable replacement for Fredric March, but instead of the mighty Akim Tamiroff as gunner Dominique You, here we get Western sidekick character actor Jack Oakie as "Dominick the Pirate from Kentucky"—he even sings that as a song about himself. Ugh!

After helping defeat the British, Lafitte receives official thanks, but his ships are confiscated, so he takes letters of marque against Spain from Venezuela, then fighting for its independence, and seizes a Spanish ship right off the New Orleans docks, sailing it away after making its crew walk the plank 100 yards from shore. Harsh! But Lafitte has a personal reason for harassing Spanish shipping: most of the merchant ships are owned by Spanish magnate George Mareval (Edgar Barrier), who refuses to let his niece Belle Summers (Karin Booth) marry Lafitte. The privateer relocates west to Galveston, establishing a settlement despite the opposition of the Karankawa Indians, and Mareval plots to trick the American garrison at New Orleans into marching against it.

There isn't much piracy in this film—frankly, just a couple of boarding-action montages before a final battle of cavalry sabers versus cutlasses—and there's even less history in it than piracy. Henreid does fine, of course, but the best thing in the picture is the performance of Mary Anderson as the sassy pirate lass Swallow, who swings a cutlass with confidence and loves Lafitte hopelessly, while despairing about the captain's pretensions as he pursues his society gal. And alas, in the end blond respectability prevails over brunette sass.

LAST OF THE VIKINGS

Rating: ★★★☆☆ • *Origin:* Italy/France, 1961 • *Director:* Giacomo Gentilomo •
Source: Mill Creek DVD

This is a solid Viking adventure film, a cut above most Italian action movies of its day. It stars Cameron Mitchell and George Ardisson as the male Viking leads in parts similar to their roles later in the year in the even better *Erik the Conqueror*. The film opens with a sea battle, after which Harald (Mitchell) and his brother Guntar (Ardisson) return to Norway after 10 years of sea roving, only to find that all the free Viking chieftains have been crushed under the heel of Bad King Sveno (Edmund Purdom, *Sword of Freedom*)—who, to add insult to injury, has adopted the effete ways of civilized Europe. Harald vows vengeance, because that's what Vikings do, and begins gathering the surviving warriors under his banner.

Meanwhile, Bad King Sveno, smug in his impregnable castle, is plotting to marry his niece Hilde (Isabelle Corey) to the King of Denmark in return for enough troops to exterminate the remaining Viking holdouts. Purdom as the sneering Sveno overacts atrociously, aiming for Olivier as Richard III but winding up closer to Snidely Whiplash. He's so terrible you can hardly wait for Harald to take him down.

The plot and characters here are pretty standard, serviceable but familiar. The only interesting twist comes when Harald infiltrates Sveno's castle by impersonating the Danish ambassador, which puts a strain on Mitchell's limited acting abilities, but he pulls it off. Harald and Princess Hilde fall in love at first sight, but then brother Guntar gets captured, Sveno crucifies him in the castle dungeon, and everything rapidly goes to hell. Cue the final orgy of death and vengeance!

Director Gentilomo does an adequate job of keeping things moving and is reputed to have been assisted by Mario Bava (who so memorably directed *Erik the Conqueror*) in an uncredited role. There's no convincing evidence of Bava's distinctive style until the movie reaches its final apocalyptic battle, but that has Bava's fingerprints all over it: inspired compositions, quick cuts, acute camera angles, and shocking violence building to a triumphant climax. And Bad King Sveno dies horribly. Vengeance accomplished!

THE LAST VALLEY

Rating: ★★★☆☆ • *Origin:* UK/USA, 1971 • *Director:* James Clavell •
Source: MGM Home Entertainment DVD

Nowadays we think of James Clavell as a novelist, but early in his career, as a screenwriter and director, he made more films than books. After *To Sir, With Love* (1967) was a huge hit, he had enough leverage to produce, write, and direct this movie, based on a 1959 novel by J. B. Pick. *The Last Valley* is set during the middle of the Thirty Years' War (1618–1648), one of the most horrific episodes in European history, a religious conflict between Catholics and Protestants that slaughtered nearly half the population of Germany. It was no fun at all, so in that regard at least, this movie is historically accurate.

Vogel (Omar Sharif), an intellectual refugee who survived the annihilation of Magdeburg, flees through the war-torn countryside, but everywhere he's confronted by more death: starvation, plague, and most of all murder by ravaging soldiers on both sides. He runs into the deep forest, crosses a mountain, and finds . . . paradise, a valley, peaceful and prosperous, that has somehow been untouched by the war. But on his heels comes a hard-boiled mercenary troop with a leader known only as the Captain (Michael Caine). He is determined to plunder the valley, but Vogel persuades the Captain to simply occupy it and spend the winter there, safe for a time from the war.

However, there are factions and personality conflicts among both the mercenaries and the villagers, and things get complicated. The village headman Gruber (Nigel Davenport) plots the murder of the mercenaries, the town's overzealous Catholic priest wants to root out heresy, the soldier Hansen (Michael Gothard) wants to rape and pillage as he pleases, the young villager Inge (Madeleine Hinde) falls for Vogel, and the Captain falls for Erica (Florinda Bolkan), who's a secret satanist. Most of these characters are nuanced and multisided, and their stories are interesting, but impending doom haunts every relationship. Eventually, after trying to force himself on Inge, Hansen escapes the valley, only to return leading a mercenary company larger than the Captain's. However, his return is expected, and the villagers and Captain's men join to ambush and slay the invaders.

But now things are spinning out of control. News comes that the Protestant army paid by Catholic France is on the advance, and the Captain decides to join them. When he leaves with most of his men, the détente in the village unravels, and Vogel's life is once more in peril.

This movie looks great; the scenery is majestic, the costumes and gear are authentic and even striking, it has a memorable soundtrack by John Barry, and you have to admire the performances of Caine, Sharif, Davenport, and Bolkan. But it's a two-hour-plus bummer with no redemption for anybody, and it's no wonder that it was a complete flop at the box office. Okay, we get it, there are no winners in wars of hatred, only losers. That includes Brian Blessed, who's in the beginning of the film for about four minutes as a mohawked thug named Korski whom the Captain kills with the pointy spike on his helmet. Brian, nooooo . . . !

After this film's resounding failure, James Clavell gave up on moviemaking and returned to books, because he thought he had an idea for a good one. It was *Shogun* (1975), which turned out to be the biggest historical fiction bestseller of the '70s.

LEGEND

Rating: ★★★☆☆ • *Origin:* USA, 1985 • *Director:* Ridley Scott • *Source:* Universal DVD

Director Ridley Scott (*The Duellists, Blade Runner*) is brilliant but not infallible, as this movie demonstrates. Scott wanted to shoot a fairy tale, a film with the fanciful air and gemlike colors of an animated Disney fable, and in that he was largely successful: the visuals, particularly in the first half of the film, are rich and sumptuous, every scene a painting. The problem is that beneath this glossy surface, there just isn't much going on.

Into an enchanted forest singing enchanting songs comes Princess Lili (Mia Sara), looking for her special friend, forest child Jack o' the Green (a young Tom Cruise), who tells her he has a surprise for her. Intrigued, Lili allows Jack to blindfold her and take her to meet a pair of magical unicorns—but though she's warned to stay away from them, Lili insists on approaching and touching the stallion. Unbeknown to Lili and Jack, the Lord of Darkness (Tim Curry), who also knows of the coming of the unicorns, has sent his goblins to kill them and harvest

Legend Author's Collection

their horns, for with the power of those "alicorns" he can plunge the world into eternal night. Lili's fatal distraction of the unicorn stallion enables the goblins to shoot it with a poisoned dart. Chaos ensues, the goblins take the stallion's alicorn, and the forest freezes in a sudden blizzard. Lili, following the goblins, is captured along with the unicorn mare and dragged off to the Lord of Darkness's Big Tree of Evil. Meanwhile, Jack falls in with fairies Honeythorn Gump, Tom Brown, Screwball, and Oona, who tell him (often speaking in rhyme) that he must absolutely be the hero fated to undertake the quest to recover the horns, rescue Lili, and save the world.

This film is mostly gorgeous, a delight to look at, though once the questers enter Darkness's evil underworld, the visuals get rather muddy and some clarity is lost. A bigger problem is that the characters are all mere archetypes and, frankly, they have nothing interesting to say. They look wonderful, the costumes are spectacular, but their lines are uniformly flat and dull. There's great potential here: Darkness falls for Lili and tries to woo her to become his queen, which is a fabulous setup. Here's Tim Curry in the infernal costume and makeup of a lifetime, playing tempter and having a conversation that should sparkle with witty repartee, and instead we get a flat exchange of desire and refusal. It ranks as one of the greatest failed opportunities in the history of fantasy cinema.

To sum up: beautiful but shallow and unsatisfying. Look for the director's cut, which has 20 extra minutes of shallow beauty, and best of all, the bewitching original soundtrack by Jerry Goldsmith, which was replaced by '80s synth pop for the American theatrical release. (Sorry, Tangerine Dream.)

LEGEND OF THE EIGHT SAMURAI

Rating: ★★★☆☆ • *Origin:* Japan, 1983 • *Director:* Kinji Fukasaku • *Source:* Mill Creek DVD

This is the kind of movie where you might ask yourself, "If the villains always had giant flying snakes they could send out to abduct the princess, why didn't they do so earlier?"—or you can just roll with it. In this case, I advise the latter approach. *Eight Samurai* was a major success in Japanese theaters, and you'll soon see why.

Eight Samurai is a sprawling *chambara* fantasy of warriors and wizardry based on Toshio Kamata's novel *Shin Satomi Hakkenden* (1982), itself an updated version of Kyokutei Bakin's classic *Nanso Satomi Hakkenden* (1842). It tells of a century-long feud between rival samurai clans, a struggle that, as the film starts, seems to have come to an end with the victory of the evil Hikita. The Satomi leaders' heads are all sacrificed to the Hikitas' patron Eternal Spirit—and yet, the victory is incomplete, as Princess Shizu (Hiroko Yakushimaru) of the Satomi has somehow escaped! Furious, the undead Hikita lord Motofuji (Yuki Meguro) and his equally undead magician mom Tamazusa (Mari Natsuki) send their armor-clad warriors, shiny as scarabs, out to capture her. On the run, Shizu encounters Shinbei (Hiroyuki Sanada), a vagabond would-be samurai who decides to capture her when he hears that there's a reward, but the princess is saved by a pair of warriors in white—Dozetsu (Sonny Chiba) and Daikaku (Minori Terada)—devoted defenders of the Satomi, who've been looking for her. They're two of eight ancient, loyal dog spirits now reborn as humans, each with a mystic crystal—but to defeat the Hikita, they'll have to find the other six, some of whom are in unexpected situations.

Next comes two hours of pursuits, escapes, sword fights, abductions, and magical transformations, with the occasional expository interruption of legendary backstory. So much stuff happens it would be exhausting to detail it, but director Kinji Fukasaku is a master of action pacing who keeps everything moving, though not so fast that you can't keep up. There're plenty of swords and sorcery in this old-school fantasy, with magic spells, undead reanimations, flying snakes, and centipede demons portrayed mainly with practical effects. There's also a fair amount of Hong Kong–style wire work, as the eight heroes and their enemies swoop around through haunted caves and the elaborate set of the Hikitas' sinister mountaintop castle.

As the eight dog warriors are gradually collected, there are inevitable echoes of Kurosawa's *Seven Samurai*, especially when super bossy Dozetsu initially rejects Shinbei from their number, but he follows them across the countryside anyway. Alas, there are so many characters here that none of them gets a chance for development (except Shizu and Shinbei, who become lovers). But that doesn't stop some of the players, particularly the villains, from outrageous overacting, bwa-ha-ha-ha-ha-ha! Moreover, some of the sudden plot reversals that keep the pot boiling are considerably less than credible. However, it all comes to a satisfying conclusion as Shizu's eight disparate magic samurai, now a team, storm the evil castle to attack the Eternal Spirit with the divine Bow of Light. Even the doomed romance works out somehow.

LIFE OF A SWORDSMAN (OR *LIFE OF AN EXPERT SWORDSMAN* OR *SAMURAI SAGA*)

Rating: ★★★☆☆ • *Origin:* Japan, 1959 • *Director:* Hiroshi Inagaki • *Source:* Samurai DVD

On a stage before an audience of commoners and nobles, a celebrated singer begins a performance. A voice rings out from the crowd, commanding the singer to leave the stage. Hasn't she been forbidden to perform? The singer, shaken, looks to the nobles for support and upon receiving their nods, continues her performance. The owner of the voice strides onto the stage, a swordsman whose face is distorted by a grotesque nose. He chases the singer away, and when the nobles draw their weapons to chastise him, the swordsman defeats them handily while simultaneously composing a poem about it.

Sound familiar? It's the opening of Edmond Rostand's *Cyrano de Bergerac*, rendered here as a samurai melodrama by top director Hiroshi Inagaki, with Toshiro Mifune in the Cyrano role! The play fits the Edo period like a gauntlet, with scarcely anything needing to be changed other than proper names and background politics. It's 1599 in Edo (i.e., Tokyo), and the samurai Komaki (Mifune), swordsman and poet, belongs to the faction supporting Lord Hideyoshi, but the Tokugawa samurai are increasingly aggressive, targeting Komaki and his friends for death in street skirmishes. The young and handsome Jurota (Akira Takarada), another Hideyoshi supporter newly arrived from the provinces, catches the eye of Lady Ochii (Yoko Tsukasa). Beautiful, sensitive, and poetic, Lady Ochii's sure Jurota must be the same, and asks Komaki, who's known her since they were young, to introduce her to the newcomer. Komaki, though secretly in love with Ochii himself, does so, but Jurota is so inarticulate that Ochii dismisses him. Jurota is smitten, however, and begs the famously eloquent Komaki to write his love letters and speeches for him.

You probably know where it goes from there, as this is a closer adaptation of *Cyrano* than most. Mifune's prosthetic nose, while broad and ugly, wouldn't warrant a second look on a European street, but in Edo it's a deformity, and Komaki is extremely sensitive about it. Mifune delivers a theatrical but nuanced performance that's appropriate for a samurai Cyrano, but sadly no one else in the cast is in his league. This is a lesser Inagaki film, but that still puts it head and shoulders above most of its competition of the time. The soundtrack by the always excellent Akira Ifukube is particularly good.

This adaptation has considerably more action in it than Rostand's play—the *katanas* come out early and often, and the swordplay is quite good. Instead of a siege between French and Spanish cavaliers, here the conflict between factions ends in the decisive Battle of Sekigahara (1600)—with Komaki and his friends on the losing side. The finale takes place 12 years later, in the same month in which Sasaki Kojiro was defeated in a famous duel by Musashi Miyamoto . . . as portrayed in *Samurai III* (1956) by Inagaki and Mifune!

LONE WOLF AND CUB 1: SWORD OF VENGEANCE

Rating: ★★★★☆ • *Origin:* Japan, 1972 • *Director:* Kenji Misumi • *Source:* Criterion Blu-ray

The manga series *Lone Wolf and Cub*, written by Kazuo Koike and drawn by Goseki Kojima, began publication in Japan in 1970 and was an instant success. Shintaro Katsu of *Zatoichi* fame decided to produce a series of films based on the stories, scripted by Koike himself, directed by Kenji Misumi, one of Katsu's favorites, and starring Tomisaburo Wakayama, Katsu's elder brother and a martial artist himself. Under the influence of Hong Kong *wuxia* films and reflecting the source material, the movies were more violent and bloody than the *Zatoichi* series and had more sexual content. Yet these were not mere exploitation films.

Under the Tokugawa shogunate, the shogun's spy agency was run by the Yagyu clan, while the position of shogun's official executioner was an office held by the Ogami family. The film starts with Itto Ogami (Wakayama) performing his cruel duty with rigorous precision, taking the life of a two-year-old lord whose clan the shogun had decided to dissolve. Itto then goes home to his wife and his own infant son, Daigoro, whom he loves and intends to raise in the rigid code of the samurai. However, the greedy and ambitious Yagyu want to add the prestigious position of executioner to their own portfolio, so they assassinate Itto's wife and frame Itto with a phony treason charge. He is ordered to commit seppuku.

But Itto is unwilling to die before having his revenge on the Yagyu and attempting to clear his name, which requires defying authority and becoming a fugitive. He tests his tiny son by offering him two options: a gaudy ball and a shiny sword. If Daigoro chooses the ball, Itto will send him to the afterlife to join his mother—but he crawls to the sword, and Itto takes it as a sign that Daigoro should join him in the life of an assassin. When the shogun's officers, the Yagyu included, come to witness Itto's self-suicide, he proclaims himself no longer bound by samurai law, cuts himself free with his sword in one hand and his son in the other, and disappears.

Two years later, Itto has become a masterless ronin, an assassin known only as Lone Wolf. Grim and ragged, he pushes a baby cart carrying three-year-old Daigoro while wearing a banner proclaiming himself as a sword for hire. The chamberlain of the Oyamada clan whose lord is threatened by traitors within offers him a job: assassinate the leaders of the traitors and the ronin ruffians they've hired to attack the lord, gathering now at a remote hot springs resort. After hearing the chamberlain's reasons for the job, Itto accepts.

The Lone Wolf is a grimly efficient assassin, but his Cub takes a child's delight in the world and what it has to offer, and we often see things through his innocent eyes rather than his father's: roadside flowers, children playing, the beauties of nature. Itto enters the resort as a simple traveler with a child, but the ronin who've taken it over are brutal thugs, raping and killing, so Itto shields Daigoro from seeing their worst excesses. And though the thugs take Itto's executioner's sword from him upon arrival, Daigoro's cart turns out to contain a number of lethal, hidden weapons. The thugs, and the disloyal samurai who've hired them, don't stand a chance.

LONE WOLF AND CUB

Lone Wolf and Cub, the celebrated samurai manga series by writer Kazuo Koike and artist Goseki Kojima, began in 1970 and, wildly popular, eventually ran to many thousands of pages and was adapted to both film and television. However, it was virtually unknown in America and Europe until 1980, when the compilation *Shogun Assassin* was released, drawing on the first two motion pictures. But *Shogun Assassin* emphasized the series' brutal violence and was regarded by most in the West as trash cinema, a reputation that was unchanged until 1987 when the *Lone Wolf and Cub* manga series was finally republished in the United States and the UK by First Comics. With covers and endorsements by then–fan favorite Frank Miller, the comics were widely acclaimed, and the movies finally found release in the United States and Europe in their original forms. Despite their level of gore and carnage, which was considered extreme at the time, these are serious films, adapted from the manga by Kazuo Koike himself. Their success is all the more remarkable because star Tomisaburo Wakayama, middle-aged and heavy, looks so little like a samurai matinee idol. But Wakayama had been a dedicated martial artist before he became an actor, and his surprising athleticism adds depth and credibility to the role.

LONE WOLF AND CUB 2: BABY CART AT THE RIVER STYX

Rating: ★★★★☆ • *Origin:* Japan, 1972 • *Director:* Kenji Misumi • *Source:* Criterion Blu-ray

This is even better than the first one: without the burden of recounting an origin story layered in flashbacks, writer Koike and director Misumi are freed up to tell a straightforward tale of one of Lone Wolf and Cub's assassination missions. Well, it's as straightforward as such a tale can be when it includes Kurokuwa clan ninja, Yagyu female samurai assassins, a burning ship as a nautical death trap, son Daigoro dangling over a bottomless well, naginata pole-vaulting, knives concealed in daikon radishes, ambushers hiding under the sand in seaside dunes, and the Three Monks of Death.

Once again, Itto Ogami (Tomisaburo Wakayama) is approached by a clan chamberlain to perform an assassination, this time by the Awa clan, who are trying to protect their indigo dye secrets from the shogunate, who want to steal them and reap the profits for themselves. The Awa dye master, who hopes to defect, is in hiding, and Itto, after hearing all the "secrets and reasons" for the job, agrees to kill him. But the Yagyu clan are still after the former shogunate executioner, and they detail their Akashi female killers, led by Lady Sayaka (Kayo Matsuo), to "use any means" to end Itto's life. Sayaka is disdainful of employing dishonorable means to kill Itto, but the orders of Yagyu Lord Retsudo are explicit. So Sayaka sends wave after wave of her disguised assassins after Itto, and he kills them all—even little Daigoro gets in on it, loosing a spring-loaded blade from his baby cart. Finally, only Sayaka is left, and she escapes.

The Kurokuwa ninja are equally unsuccessful, and the last of their number insists that Sayaka join in a plot to distract Itto by abducting Daigoro. This they do while Itto is recovering from his ninja-inflicted wounds, but their threats to his son don't deter him: Itto informs his opponents that he and Daigoro are on the Demon Road to Hell, and though they will fight to avoid death, they accept their destiny. Sayaka wavers. Will she stand by and let Daigoro die?

There's still that mission to accomplish: the shogunate is sending three brothers, martial arts killers known as the Monks of Death, to collect the Awa defector and bring him to Edo. With their great wicker hats, they are a striking trio, and anyone looking for the visual inspiration for the Three Storms in *Big Trouble in Little China* (1986) need look no further. Each Monk of Death uses a different cruel weapon, and they slaughter about 30 Awa samurai in two mass ambushes before they must face a more formidable opponent: Itto Ogami, standing alone waiting for them in the blowing sand atop a tall dune.

(This film, by the way, was the primary source for the notorious *Shogun Assassin*, the reedited, sensationalist *Lone Wolf and Cub* movie concocted by American director Robert Houston in 1980, covered separately.)

LONE WOLF AND CUB 3: BABY CART TO HADES
(OR *LIGHTNING SWORDS OF DEATH*)

Rating: ★★★★☆ • *Origin:* Japan, 1972 • *Director:* Kenji Misumi • *Source:* Criterion Blu-ray

Another fine entry in the series, with something for everyone, from the serenity of nature and its creatures, as seen through the eyes of young Daigoro Ogami, to the brutality of sudden death, as seen through the eyes of a rolling just-severed head.

On his wanderings with his son, Itto Ogami (Tomisaburo Wakayama) encounters disgraced samurai Master Kanbei (*chambara* heartthrob Go Kato), who is traveling with a band of lowly mercenaries. The mercenaries molest two innocent women, Itto and Kanbei come into the quarrel on opposite sides, and Kanbei formally demands a duel with Itto. Upon drawing their swords, the former executioner recognizes Kanbei's qualities and declares the duel a draw so that Kanbei will survive and have the opportunity to live on as a "true samurai."

After cutting down a few more vengeance-crazed ninja, who jump out of the woodwork every time things slow down, Itto finds his next big assassination mission. He defends a country woman who'd been bought for a brothel and then killed her abusive pimp, which puts Itto in conflict with Torizo (Yuko Hamada), the hard-boiled brothel mistress, who insists the young woman must suffer the traditional yakuza punishments. Itto demands to act as her proxy and suffer the tortures himself, which he does so stoically that he earns the admiration of Torizo. More importantly, she recognizes him as the assassin Lone Wolf, whom her father has been searching for.

Torizo's father is a former officer of a fallen clan that was sold out to the shogunate by Genba (Isao Yamagata), who now rules the clan's lands as the shogun's governor. This villain also raped Torizo's twin sister and drove her to suicide. Itto agrees to assassinate Genba and is able to get close to him because Genba wants to hire the Lone Wolf himself to take out a rival. But Genba, with the insight of the paranoid, realizes that Itto has already been hired to kill *him*, and he escapes.

Genba has a couple of colorful bodyguards whom he sends after Itto, a quick-draw swordsman and a gunman with twin American revolvers, but Itto dispatches them both, so Genba goes for quantity over quality, calling in favors to gather dozens of defenders, including the mercenary band that includes Master Kanbei among their membership. But Itto prepares for the encounter by outfitting Daigoro's baby cart with some lethal new tricks, and Genba and his men are scythed down like wheat at harvest time. The last man standing is Master Kanbei, who once again demands a formal duel—and when Itto hears his reasons for courting death, he agrees.

LONE WOLF AND CUB 4: BABY CART IN PERIL (OR *SLASHING BLADES OF CARNAGE*)

Rating: ★★★★☆ • *Origin:* Japan, 1972 • *Director:* Buichi Saito • *Source:* Criterion Blu-ray

With this entry the series changes, as star Tomisaburo Wakayama takes over the producer role from his brother Shintaro Katsu, bringing in a new director, Buichi Saito, and ratcheting up the sensationalism with more nudity and gore. There's also an increased *wuxia* influence, with Itto Ogami and his ninja opponents making 10-foot aerial leaps.

And notably, where the first three films were about the Lone Wolf, this film belongs as much to the Cub, as Daigoro Ogami becomes more of a partner in the action and less of a mere observer. The story also reverts to the more complex structure of the first film, employing lots of flashbacks, though they're always strongly cued and easy to follow.

Itto (Wakayama) is hired by the Owari clan to kill a renegade female assassin named Yuki (Michie Azuma) who fights topless, her torso covered in startling tattoos, the better to distract her male opponents. The Lone Wolf sets out on his mission, but during a town festival, young Daigoro chases after some street clowns, gets lost, and wanders off into the country, where he meets a grim swordsman at a temple. The swordsman is struck by Daigoro's "death life eyes," and follows him on his wanderings, astounded by his survival skills, until Daigoro finds his father. Itto recognizes the swordsman as Gunbei Yagyu (Yoichi Hayashi), who once competed on behalf of the Yagyu clan against Itto for the position of shogunate executioner, losing out because during the bout he carelessly pointed his sword at the shogun. The Yagyu clan faked his subsequent ritual suicide and then sent the disgraced Gunbei into internal exile. He demands a rematch with Itto, but the Lone Wolf refuses, saying, "It's no use killing a dead man."

Itto knows that before Yuki became an Owari "sword mistress," she was a street performer of the Gomune guild, so he visits their secluded refuge to speak to Jindayu, the boss of the Gomune. Jindayu reveals that Yuki is his daughter but tells Itto to seek her at a remote hot springs resort. Yuki, meditating at the springs, reveals via flashback her reasons for becoming a tattooed assassin: she had been raped by Kozuka, an Owari swordsman-illusionist with a flaming sword and a mesmerizing gaze. As Itto arrives, she kills another half dozen Owari samurai sent to slay her, taking their topknots to send back to their clan to goad them. Itto disapproves: shamed in that way, a samurai's entire family is banished from the clan, but her taunts work, as the Owari are finally provoked into sending Kozuka to kill her. This time, Yuki kills the illusionist, and then Itto reluctantly kills Yuki, giving her the best death he can.

But the vengeful Yagyu clan are now hot on Itto's trail, and their villainous leader Retsudo (Tatsuo Endo, who played several vile yakuza bosses in the *Zatoichi* series) misleads the Owari daimyo, telling him Itto had joined with Yuki to kill the Owari samurai. Incensed, the daimyo calls out his troops, and there's an exciting climax in which Itto must face the Owari clan as well as the killers of the Yagyu and their allies, the Torugawa ninja. There's no need to spill all the details, but some of the stunts in this extended final melee are spectacular, and the body count is very high indeed.

LONE WOLF AND CUB 5: BABY CART IN THE LAND OF DEMONS
(OR *FIVE FISTFULS OF GOLD*)

Rating: ★★★★★ • *Origin:* Japan, 1973 • *Director:* Kenji Misumi • *Source:* Criterion Blu-ray

If this is the best of the *Lone Wolf and Cub* films, it's probably because it has the most interesting and thought-provoking story, adapted once again by writer Kazuo Koike from his manga series. Itto Ogami (Tomisaburo Wakayama) is hired by different elements of the Kuroda clan—not once, but twice! A series of five Kuroda samurai test themselves to destruction against Itto, each giving him one-fifth of the payment for an assassination and one-fifth of the "secrets and reasons" behind it: the Kuroda lord has substituted his mistress's young daughter for his legitimate son and in atonement given a letter confessing his actions to a holy Buddhist priest—but the priest, Abbot Jikei (Hideji Otaki) is actually a secret ninja boss for the Yagyu clan and plans to turn over the letter to the shogunate, which will mean the end of the Kuroda. Itto agrees to kill Jikei and recover the letter, and he is then hired by another Kuroda agent, a woman called Ghost-Fire (Michiyo Okusu), to kill the Kuroda lord, his mistress, and daughter, so the legitimate prince can inherit the lordship.

Pretty cool, but it gets even better. During a town festival, Itto leaves his son Daigoro in his baby cart and goes to Abbot Jikei's temple to kill him but is stunned to find that he can't do it. Jikei tells him why: the abbot has "merged with nothingness," and Itto won't be able to slay him until he perfects the assassin's art and passes through the "gateless barrier." Disconcerted for the first time in his career and unsure how to proceed, Itto returns to the baby cart only to find that Daigoro is gone, having followed some excited children to the festival. In the town, we watch the larcenous activities of a charming female pickpocket called Quick-Change O-yo (Tomomi Sato), who is being pursued by a master detective from Edo. With the detective hot on her heels, O-yo gives a stolen wallet to Daigoro to hold and has him promise to tell no one where he got it. The detective spots Daigoro with the wallet, arrests him, and takes him to a public platform where he threatens to flog the toddler unless O-yo turns herself in. O-yo surrenders, but when the detective asks Daigoro to identify her as the one who gave him the wallet, he refuses and steadfastly goes on refusing, even when the detective flogs him hard. Meanwhile, Itto, watching silently from the crowd, finds in his own three-year-old son the determination he needs to pass the gateless barrier and become the perfect assassin.

The rest of the film is pretty much nonstop action. In an amazing scene that shouldn't be spoiled, Itto assassinates Jikei and recovers the scroll. (When the abbot realizes he's about to be murdered, he says quietly, "Is it not good, he who perfects his path?") The Yagyu ninja and the Kuroda Mask-Men are no match for Itto, and the Lone Wolf completes his second assassination task as well before his final meeting with Ghost-Fire. For this movie, the great Kenji Misumi returns to the director's chair for his next to last film before his untimely death at the age of 54. He, too, had perfected his art.

LONE WOLF AND CUB 6: WHITE HEAVEN IN HELL

Rating: ★★★★☆ • *Origin:* Japan, 1974 • *Director:* Yoshiyuki Kuroda •
Source: Criterion Blu-ray

By late 1973 it looked like the *Lone Wolf and Cub* movie series was over. Making five movies in quick succession, they had run through adaptations of the full manga series published since

1970 and were out of stories to tell. Lead director Kenji Misumi felt that, visually, the series had said all it had to say and declined to sign on for another entry. But star and now producer Tomisaburo Wakayama wasn't ready to give up. Reputedly disappointed at not getting the lead role in the *Lone Wolf and Cub* TV series, but with enough funding for a sixth film, Wakayama decided to go big and make the wild, over-the-top movie he'd been dreaming of. He hired Tsutomu Nakamura to write an all-new script to meet his needs, and Yoshiyuki Kuroda, known for his yokai fantasy-horror films, to direct. And the series went out with a bang.

The previous films had mostly stuck to the structure of the Lone Wolf and Cub taking an assassination job and then somehow completing it despite interference from Itto Ogami's nemesis, the Yagyu clan. This film dropped that formula, devoting itself to a final showdown between Itto and the Yagyus, led by the relentless Lord Retsudo (Minoru Ohki). Retsudo is called on the carpet by the shogun because the Yagyus' repeated failure to capture or kill Itto Ogami is a public embarrassment for the government. Though in previous encounters Itto had slain Retsudo's three sons, he begs for more time from the shogunate because Retsudo still has one child, his daughter Kaori (Junko Hitomi), who also has been trained as a formidable martial artist. Kaori, who fights with throwing knives that she juggles hypnotically to confuse her opponents, sets out to get at Itto through his son, Daigoro. But the boy proves as fearless as his father. Kaori fails, and she falls.

Now things get good and strange. Wait, says Retsudo, I still have an *illegitimate* son, Hyoei (Isao Kimura), who's been adopted by the Tsuchigumo, a pariah clan of demon-worshipping weirdos who skulk in the remote mountains. Hyoei receives his father with scorn but agrees to kill Itto Ogami, not to do Dad a favor, but to show him up for a failure. Hyoei's chief weapon is to be three Tsuchigumo warriors who were buried alive and have been resurrected with creepy powers. These undead samurai can burrow through the ground like moles, and they like to slaughter innocents wholesale to strike terror into the hearts of their enemies. Itto and Daigoro are visibly shaken by the depredations of the three Tsuchigumo, and the former executioner realizes he must find a new strategy to deal with them.

So Itto puts skis on Daigoro's baby cart and retreats into the snowy north, where the Tsuchigumo will be out of their comfort zone. And indeed, burrowing through snow is more difficult than moling it through the warm loam of central Japan, and the half-frozen Tsuchigumo are slowed just enough that Itto, with the help of Daigoro in his deadly baby sled, is able to take them down.

However, Lord Retsudo, desperate, has followed Itto into the north with all his remaining warriors and ninja, now mounted on skis and sleds, and there's a final mass confrontation on the snowy mountain slopes. This climactic fight in the deep snow took six weeks to film, but Wakayama persisted and got the epic conclusion to the series he wanted. There's nothing else like it.

LONE WOLF AND CUB (TV), SEASON 1
(OR *FUGITIVE SAMURAI* OR *THE IRON SAMURAI*)

Rating: ★★★☆☆ • *Origin:* Japan, 1973 • *Directors:* Various • *Source:* Tokyo Shock DVDs

It would be easy to complain that the *Lone Wolf and Cub* TV show isn't as good as the movie series: the stories are less expansive and somewhat repetitive, production values are much lower, the direction is merely adequate, and star Kinnosuke Yorozuya lacks Tomisaburo

LONE WOLF AND CUB [PART 2]

Let's look at the influence of the *Lone Wolf and Cub* films on the *Star Wars* series *The Mandalorian*. I'm far from the first person to point out the connections between the two, but as they show the continuing relevance of *Lone Wolf and Cub* even 50 years later, I think it's worthwhile to consider them.

To state the obvious, *The Mandalorian* draws most of its inspiration from the Western genre, especially the Italian variety known as Spaghetti Westerns, and of course from the *Star Wars* saga itself. But the *Lone Wolf* influence is strong: the visual archetype of the solo martial artist fighting off waves of enemies with a young son by his side or in his arms is powerful and was adopted in whole. And there are thematic similarities as well: when Itto Ogami, the shogunate executioner who lives by a rigorous warrior code, is betrayed by a rival clan, his wife slain and his son threatened, he breaks the rules, refusing to commit seppuku and taking his son with him into an outlaw career as an assassin for hire. The Mandalorian has a tribal warrior code and belongs to a guild of bounty hunters with strict rules—but when the child who has adopted his heart is threatened with death, he abandons his guild and its rules and goes on the run, his new son by his side.

As in the *Lone Wolf* films, the bond between father and son is virtually wordless, but we are often shown the world, not through the slits of the Mandalorian's helmet, but through the wide and innocent eyes of his adopted child. And like Itto Ogami's son Daigoro, little Grogu is not as helpless as he seems.

Wakayama's gravitas and burly athleticism. But the show is still pretty good, and it wins on sheer quantity: 26 episodes (27 were broadcast, but episode 2 has never been available on home release), each 45 minutes in length, just long enough for Itto Ogami to accept an assassination job and carry it out with room for a twist or two and some time spent with three-year old Daigoro, Itto's son. The Cub is played with remarkable expression for a toddler by Katzutaka Nishikawa, his large, limpid eyes and drooping lip making up in puppy gravitas for whatever Yorozuya lacks. He's surprisingly good.

Most of the episodes fall into a common formula: a clan leader contacts the Lone Wolf and Cub to complain of a plot by the shogunate to ruin them and take over their lands and wealth, a plot that can only be forestalled by the death of a traitor. Once he takes the job, Itto Ogami typically has to deal with treachery from within the clan as well as some sort of government hit team, often drawn from the ranks of Itto's archenemies, the Yagyu clan. The stories are usually adapted from the manga series written by Kazuo Koike, who coproduced the TV show, often drawing from the same serials adapted for the movies: for example, the manga story adapted for the first film was also used, in shorter form, for episode 3 of the TV show, "Fangs of the Wolf."

There are other differences from the movie adaptations: the TV show has far less gore and nudity than the films, though considerably more than you'd see in commercial shows from the United States and Europe during the early '70s. Itto Ogami's philosophy is less nihilistic than in the manga and movies, and he has a softer side rarely seen in the films—heck, sometimes he even smiles! And no matter how many people get murdered in an episode, a way is usually found to end it on some kind of up note.

There are a few episodes that break the formula, and perhaps unsurprisingly they're among the best. Look for episode 7, "Cloud Tiger, Wind Dragon," in which the Lone Wolf turns down the job of killing a stubborn samurai retainer of a daimyo he'd beheaded when he was the shogun's executioner, ultimately befriending him and helping fight off his enemies. And the season ends in an epic three-part story pitting Itto against Lord Retsudo, the head of the Yagyu clan, in which the Wolf and his Cub are separated and face a desperate struggle to be reunited. These outstanding entries make up for a lot of the cookie-cutter episodes that went before.

LONG JOHN SILVER (OR LONG JOHN SILVER'S RETURN TO TREASURE ISLAND)

Rating: ★★★☆☆ • *Origin:* USA/Australia, 1954 • *Director:* Byron Haskin • *Source:* American Home Treasures DVD

Sure, it's cheap and it's cheesy, but this film's just chock-full of piratical goodness, and pirate-movie fans owe it to themselves to dig up a copy.

How did this thing even happen? It starts back in 1950, when Disney makes a new version of *Treasure Island*, which Walt thinks is pretty clever because it's a beloved property that's in the public domain, so he doesn't have to pay for it. Jump forward three years and Byron Haskin, who'd directed *Treasure Island* for Disney, realizes that because the source is *still* public domain, Disney can't stop him from shooting a sequel to it. (This is a lesson Disney will never forget.) Haskin contacts Robert Newton, who made such an impression as Silver in the Disney version; Newton, who didn't handle Hollywood success very well, has fled back to England to escape his debts, so he's happy to come aboard. Haskin proposes shooting on the cheap in Australia, where he'd made *His Majesty O'Keefe* the year before, Newton agrees, and Bob's your uncle!

The winning formula for this production is to recycle elements from *Treasure Island*, but add more pirates and lots more Long John Silver—Newton, in high form, is in almost every scene. The first third of the movie is set in and around Porto Bello, which is inexplicably under British rule. (The Brits sacked it four times but never governed it.) Silver hangs out there in a low dive with a crew of sea dogs, and it's immediately established that, though glib and plausible, he's just as big a scoundrel as ever. (Huzzah!) All he needs is an opportunity, and it comes when another pirate crew, led by a Captain Mendoza, kidnaps the governor's daughter. (It's a genre rule that if the governor has a daughter, pirates must kidnap her.)

Silver knows Mendoza, and he persuades the governor to let him handle the ransom transfer. He then performs a double double cross, retrieving both daughter and ransom money while plundering the governor's warehouse and blaming it on Mendoza. Not so incidentally, he also liberates young Jim Hawkins (*Treasure Island*'s protagonist, played adequately here by Kit Taylor), who should have been enjoying his newfound wealth back in England but for some unexplained reason was serving as Mendoza's enslaved cabin boy.

MacGuffin time! Jim, who's still "smart as paint" (requotes from *Island* are common), has a medallion that holds the key to the location of a second hoard hidden on Treasure Island. The movie veers briefly into farce as Silver tries to trick Jim into giving him the medallion while avoiding being maneuvered into wedlock by the proprietress of his low dive, but soon Jim, Silver, Mendoza, and two scurvy pirate crews are off across the Caribbean to dig up

NOT-SO-WHOLESOME BUCCANEERS

The role of Long John Silver in Disney's 1950 *Treasure Island* finally launched the talented English actor Robert Newton into international stardom. As Silver, Newton popularized the broad West Country accent that's become the default talk-like-a-pirate voice of buccaneering rogues ever since. (You can blame—or acclaim— Newton for the ubiquitous piratical "Ahr!") But fame ruined the actor, enabling endless rounds of drink, gambling, and the kind of wild behavior that made him a role model for Oliver Reed and Keith Moon. And Newton was never able to escape the shadow of the one-legged pirate with the parrot on his shoulder—but typecast though he was, you can still see that he enjoyed the role even while repeating it. Newton died from alcohol-related heart failure in 1956, and his ashes were buried at sea in the English Channel off Cornwall: "Ahr-men."

Cap'n Flint's second treasure. The last half of the film shamelessly plunders and recombines elements of *Treasure Island*, unburdened this time by any tiresome good guys except for Jim. It's a real scoundrel-fest, sudden reversals are the order of the day, and "those who die are the lucky ones." I won't reveal how it ends except to say the finale hinges on two words: *doubloon grenades!*

One caveat: it seems there's no good restored version of this film available digitally; all the prints floating around are pan-and-scan, and most of them are in terrible shape. Ye be warned!

THE LONG SHIPS

Rating: ★★★★☆ • *Origin:* UK/Yugoslavia, 1964 • *Director:* Jack Cardiff • *Source:* Columbia DVD

Also known as *The Vikings, Jr.*, in which Kirk Douglas and Tony Curtis are traded for Richard Widmark and Russ Tamblyn—it's by no means an even trade, but we do get Oscar Homolka in exchange for Ernest Borgnine, and that almost makes up for it.

This film is 126 minutes of glorious nonsense, not even slightly credible but delivered with such reckless, deadpan glee that it just doesn't matter. Though theoretically based on a respected historical novel by Frans G. Bengtsson, the story is pure pulp: legend tells how Byzantine monks collected an unholy quantity of gold and cast it in the form of a great bell, the "Mother of Voices," solid gold and three times the height of a man. Moorish prince Aly Mansuh (Sidney Poitier) is obsessed with finding this bell, and when Rolfe (Richard Widmark), a shipwrecked Norseman, is heard telling a tale about the bell in the marketplace of Mansuh's Barbary Coast town, the prince has him arrested and threatened with torture unless he tells what he knows. But Rolfe escapes by leaping out a window into the sea and then apparently swims from the Mediterranean to Norway, because the next time we see him, he's climbing out of the water in the fjord of King Harald Bluetooth's seacoast town. I am not making this up.

Harald has just taken delivery of the finest longship ever made by his ship-building thane Krok (Oscar Homolka, in a deliriously bonkers performance), who is also the father of Rolfe and his brother Orm (Russ Tamblyn, athletic but terrible). Rolfe has ruined Krok's fortunes by losing his ship and crew in a storm, but he begs his father for another ship, because of course the legend of the golden bell is true: Rolfe heard it tolling while his ship was breaking up. With Krok's connivance, Rolfe and Orm rustle up a crew and steal Harald's new *drakkar*, while they're at it abducting Harald's daughter Gerda (Beba Lončar) as a hostage for Rolfe and love interest for Orm. Hostage or no, Harald sets out in pursuit with a whole Viking flotilla.

Dress-up at the Dutch premiere of *The Long Ships* Jack de Nijs for Anefo, CCO 1.0 / Wikimedia Commons

On the verge of being caught, Rolfe's longship desperately sails into a howling maelstrom for some vintage just-too-cheesy-to-be-convincing special effects and then wrecks on the Barbary shore. It's at this point that Jack Cardiff's direction, which has been perfunctory, suddenly becomes sharp and on point—literally so, as the shipwrecked Viking crew is attacked by a troop of Moorish cavalry. In a thrilling fight, the Norsemen defend their position with a reasonable facsimile of authentic Viking tactics and kick the cavalry's collective ass. It's the best scene in the picture, though the Norsemen's victory is short-lived as the cavalry comes back in overwhelming numbers and the Vikings are taken prisoner.

It was Aly Mansuh's cavalry, of course; he's still determined to find the Mother of Voices, and the next 30 minutes are a dance of negotiations at scimitar point between various factions among the Moors and Vikings, all vying for the upper hand. This is where we find one of the film's most striking and lurid visuals: the Steel Mare, a giant scimitar-blade fun slide that splits a man in two when he takes the Mare for a ride. Oog! Rolfe is threatened with just such a ride, but at the last minute a deal is cut whereby all parties can go together to find and bring back the great golden bell. And do they find it? What, are you serious? Of course, they do, but it's just the beginning of the climactic shenanigans.

Beware: at one point the Viking crew gets loose in Aly Mansuh's palace, stumbles on the prince's harem, and the Nordic barbarians go lust mad and assault the concubines with evil intent. It's attempted rape played for laughs, but it isn't the least bit funny. Just wince, shake your head, and be glad it's no longer 1964. Yeesh.

THE MAGIC CARPET

Rating: ★☆☆☆☆ • *Origin:* USA, 1951 • *Director:* Lew Landers •
Source: Amazon streaming video

This is quite terrible. In a cheesier-than-usual Arabian palace set, the Good Caliph is just naming his newborn son his sole heir when he's assassinated by the Evil New Caliph. The nurse escapes with the child and sends him flying away on a magic carpet. (This is the only fantasy element in the film and is completely unexplained, because Mysterious East or something.) The baby is taken to a doctor, who hides the carpet and decides to raise the child as his own, not telling him that he's the Rightful Caliph. The child grows up to be legendarily awful leading man John Agar, who has all the screen presence and charisma of an Idaho potato. There's a guards-oppressing-the-people montage, and Agar, now called Dr. Ramoth, sees some of this oppression and says a few lines to show he disapproves, though that's the only way you can tell, because his face doesn't change. To fight the Evil Caliph's oppression, Dr. Ramoth becomes the Scarlet, or maybe Crimson, Falcon and leads a band of freedom fighters in a freedom-fighting montage. He keeps raiding the wrong caravans that don't have the weapons he needs to arm the people to overthrow the Evil Caliph, so Agar decides he should infiltrate the palace to get inside information. His cunning plan is to kill a bunch of palace guards as a diversion, so his comic sidekick can get inside, take the place of the Evil Caliph's wine taster, and dose him with a permanent-hiccups potion. Nobody pays any attention to the guards Dr. Ramoth killed as a diversion, because it's just routine, I guess, so he breezes in, cures the Evil Caliph of permanent hiccups, and becomes the new palace physician.

Yeah. Now that he's inside the palace, Agar meets the Evil Caliph's Evil Sister, who is played by, I am not kidding even a little bit, Lucille Ball. With her red hair and green eyes, she's about as Arabian as a leprechaun, but I suppose what matters is that she wears harem pants and a midriff-exposing top like the (I guess the word is) *bevy* of giggling starlets prancing around the palace and its blue plastic in-ground pool. Cast as a seductive villainess, Ball's talents are completely wasted, as she never does anything the least bit funny or, for that matter, seductive or villainous. More stuff happens: Agar finally learns he's the Rightful Caliph and then flies around on his carpet, the effects for which are so awful they're almost endearing. There's a bunch of "swordplay," with people waving around thin curved sticks that are supposed to represent scimitars, but confusingly there are always some guys waving actual sticks, I guess because the props department didn't make enough scimitars. Also, everybody knows that when you run someone through, you pass the sword *behind* the person's body, but Raymond Burr didn't get the memo and impales people on the wrong side. Oh, right, Raymond Burr is in this, too, as the Evil Caliph's Evil Grand Vizier, wearing black facial hair that must be darned stiff, because his lips barely move when he speaks. Only his eyes look alive, the eyes of trapped animal shifting this way and that, desperately seeking an escape.

THE MAGIC SWORD (OR *ST. GEORGE AND THE DRAGON*)

Rating: ★★☆☆☆ • *Origin:* USA, 1962 • *Director:* Bert I. Gordon • *Source:* MGM DVD

This is a children's fantasy with story, direction, and special effects by Bert I. Gordon, who was mainly known for his cheesy low-budget '50s monster movies such as *King Dinosaur* and *The Amazing Colossal Man*. It's just two points north of terrible, those two points being its cheerful enthusiasm for fairy tale knights and monsters, and its casting of the aging Basil Rathbone as the evil wizard Lodac. The hero, Sir George, is played, in his first starring role, by a young and baby-faced Gary Lockwood—yes, Lt. Cdr. Gary Mitchell from *Star Trek* and astronaut Frank Poole from *2001: A Space Odyssey* but at this point still very much a shallow surfer dude from Van Nuys, California.

The story is kinda-sorta based on the legend of St. George and the Dragon. The Princess Helene, whose royal father appears to be the King of Cartoons from *Pee-Wee's Playhouse*, is magically abducted by Lodac as payback for his sister having been put to death as a witch by a previous king. In seven days, Helene will be fed to Lodac's ever-hungry dragon unless someone dares the Dark Journey and its Seven Curses to save her. George, the feckless foster son of feckless sorceress Sybil, has fallen in love with Helene by viewing her in Sybil's magic pool while she bathes in the palace's nonmagic pool, which isn't creepy at all. George swipes Sibyl's magic sword, magic armor, and magic horse, reanimates six magic knights, and sets out to save Helene. But he has a rival in the treacherous Sir Branton, who also seeks to rescue the princess and is determined to eliminate George on the way.

The next 70 minutes are a parade of Gordon's cheeseriffic monsters, mostly actors in terrible costumes magnified or glowified by cheap special effects. There's an orthodontically challenged ogre, a vampire hag, spooooky ghosts, evil dwarves, and cone-headed goons, all as prelude for a feeble two-headed puppet dragon. Rathbone just about saves the flick by gleefully threatening doom and curses at every turn, though even he can't overcome the plodding pace of Bert Gordon's direction. But you know what? If you were eight years old, you'd love it.

THE MAN IN THE IRON MASK (1939)

Rating: ★★★★☆ • *Origin:* USA, 1939 • *Director:* James Whale •
Source: Hen's Tooth Video DVD

This is the first sound version of *Iron Mask* and stars Louis Hayward in the dual role of King Louis XIV and Prince Philippe. Hayward was a leading man who appeared in a variety of parts, heroic and romantic, from the late 1930s to the early 1950s, but if he's remembered today, it's as the star of eight or nine small- to medium-budget swashbucklers made mainly for independent producer Edward Small (of which this is the first). The genial Hayward didn't have the compelling screen presence of Errol Flynn or Tyrone Power, but he was likeable and determined and had enough handsome charm to carry off the romances.

The Man in the Iron Mask is the final tale in Alexandre Dumas's long Musketeers Cycle, which tells the stories of d'Artagnan and his three friends Athos, Aramis, and Porthos from youth to old age. However, no movie version of *Iron Mask* has ever told the tale the way Dumas wrote it. Oh, you always get a plot to switch King Louis XIV with his twin Philippe, who was spirited away at birth and raised somewhere secretly, and somebody always winds up wearing a welded-on full-helm iron mask, and of the musketeers, you can count on at least d'Artagnan putting in an appearance. Other than that, all bets are off. This adaptation is no closer to Dumas than any other version, so let's just toss the source material out a tower window like an old tin plate and look at this movie on its own merits. These are considerable: first, it was directed by James Whale, best known for his classic horror movies *Frankenstein* and *Bride of Frankenstein*, and he does a fine job making the dungeon scenes with the iron mask quite chilling. He also turns out to have a touch for costume drama, and this movie moves right along, never flagging until just before the end.

Other pleasures include the sharp byplay between the king's rival advisors, Walter Kingsford as Colbert and Joseph Schildkraut as Fouquet; any number of secret passages in the Louvre and the Bastille; the genuinely touching scene in which the elderly Queen Anne finally meets her long-lost son; and a guard captain who lives the dream by getting to shout *both* "Seize them!" *and* "Take them away!"

In this version, Prince Philippe is given as an infant into the care of d'Artagnan, who takes him to distant Gascony to raise him with his three musketeer friends as tutors. D'Artagnan is

LOUIS HAYWARD, EVERYMAN WITH A SWORD

Independent Hollywood producer Edward Small had his biggest hit in 1934 with a version of *The Count of Monte Cristo* and was determined to follow it up with more swashbucklers. But he needed a leading man, and after several years' delay, Small finally found him in Louis Hayward, an actor trained on the British stage who'd come to America in the early 1930s, where he mainly played romantic leads in light comedies and the occasional prestige drama. Hayward was charming, well-spoken, good-looking in period costume, and he had a deft hand with a sword, so Small signed him to a three-film contract. Small's new star ending up making a half dozen swashbucklers for him and several more for other producers. Some of these are forgettable, but most of them are pretty good or better and are nowadays unfairly overlooked.

played by Warren William, who was popular earlier in the '30s but whose star is by this time fading. He's a curious choice for the role: he's not very athletic, which had been a hallmark of the part since Fairbanks (and still is), and though his long, droll face looks good with a pencil 'stache and goatee, he's not a convincing swashbuckler. Worse, he doesn't always remember to act engaged and engaging or even interested.

Hayward, on the other hand, is clearly enjoying himself, switching back and forth between the cruel and tyrannical King Louis and the bold and boisterous Philippe. As a bonus, when he's playing the impostor, he gets to romance Queen Maria Theresa (Joan Bennett), who is sadly ignored by the real Louis XIV—possibly the only touch of historical accuracy in the picture.

So there's plenty of good stuff. On the downside, the awful Alan Hale Sr. is inflicted upon us, though if he's suited to play any famous character, I suppose it would be Porthos, as he does here. Also, though the costumes are good for a B picture, everybody fences with these flimsy little foils that are no substitute for an honest rapier. Finally, this movie just has one climax too many, an unnecessary carriage chase through the too-familiar woods of Southern California before the musketeers finally save the day. But that's nitpicking: this may be no *Adventures of Robin Hood*, but it's 100 minutes well spent.

THE MAN IN THE IRON MASK (1977)

Rating: ★★★☆☆ • *Origin:* UK, 1976 • *Director:* Mike Newell • *Source:* Network DVD

Dumas's novel *The Three Musketeers*, especially its first half, is a self-contained story that's almost made for screen adaptation. But *The Man in the Iron Mask*? Not so much: at the very end of Dumas's long Musketeers Cycle, *Iron Mask* is the final 90 chapters of a 280-chapter mega-novel, with 600,000 words of setup before it unfolds the conspiracy to replace King Louis XIV with his twin brother, Philippe. A screenwriter couldn't possibly summarize that lead-in and shouldn't even try; there's no choice but to pick a few characters and themes from Dumas's oversupply and try to make a tidy tale of it. William Bast, who wrote the script for this version, did a reasonable job at that task, but this TV movie, despite its excellent cast, doesn't entirely succeed at putting Bast's story across.

The cast, as mentioned, is excellent: Richard Chamberlain doubling as King Louis and Prince Philippe, Louis Jourdan in a ridiculous page-boy haircut as d'Artagnan, Ralph Richardson as his ally Colbert, Patrick McGoohan as their opponent Fouquet, and Jenny Agutter surprisingly good as Louise de La Vallière, whom Louis, Philippe, and Fouquet all love. The costumes and production values are above average for a TV movie, and astoundingly, they shot it at the actual historical sites of King Louis's palace of Fontainebleau and Fouquet's estate of Vaux-le-Vicomte, settings that add a great deal of credibility to the story. The film even reuses some of the extravagant ballet costumes from Richard Lester's *Three Musketeers*.

In Bast's version of Dumas's story, Louis XIV is a terrible king, lazy and lecherous, so Colbert and d'Artagnan scheme to replace him with his modest twin brother Philippe, who has been raised in the country with no knowledge of his royal heritage. But Fouquet learns of their plot and has Philippe taken from Paris and imprisoned on the Île Sainte-Marguerite (also using the actual location), clamping his face in an iron mask so no one will see his resemblance to the king. Fortunately, d'Artagnan gets him out, persuades Fouquet that Philippe was killed in the escape, and Philippe is then trained for the big switcheroo, falling in love with Louise de La Vallière along the way.

There are some good times to be had here. Chamberlain is clearly enjoying himself when playing King Louis, and the royal ballet scene, in which he flounces about as Apollo in gold glitter makeup, is almost worth the price of admission. Ralph Richardson and Patrick McGoohan twitch their eyebrows and curl their lips at each other in majestic disdain, and the great Vivien Merchant has a couple of excellent scenes as Louis's acerbic Spanish wife, Queen Maria Teresa. The problem is the direction and pacing: Mike Newell, much acclaimed later in his career for movies such as *Four Weddings and a Funeral* and *Donnie Brasco*, is directing his first feature film here. It's apparent he doesn't yet have a grasp of building and maintaining suspense, so much of the movie just limps along from one scene to the next until it all ends rather abruptly. But watch it anyway for the cast and for those fabulous sets.

THE MARK OF ZORRO (1920)

Rating: ★★★★★ (Essential) • *Origin:* USA, 1920 • *Director:* Fred Niblo •
Source: Kino Video DVD

Douglas Fairbanks Sr., on his way to Europe on his honeymoon after marrying screen darling Mary Pickford, had brought a stack of *All-Story Weekly* pulp fiction magazines with him to read during the crossing on the steamer *Lapland*. He was struck by the hero of Johnston McCulley's *The Curse of Capistrano*—Zorro, of course—and decided that he'd found the subject of his next movie. The next year Fairbanks played the starring role in the story he'd retitled *The Mark of Zorro*; it was a gigantic hit, and Fairbanks was to enjoy the next 10 years as a movie swashbuckler, appearing in lavish productions as Zorro, d'Artagnan, and Robin Hood.

The Mark of Zorro is a genuinely great film, the movie that elevated Doug Fairbanks from star to superstar. His athleticism and charisma are legendary, of course, but damn it, the man could act: his foppish Don Diego is as hilarious and nuanced as his heroic Zorro is rousing and romantic. The villains are also uniformly excellent: Robert McKim's Captain Ramon is every bit as mocking and arrogant as Basil Rathbone would be later, and Noah Beery's swaggering rodomontades as Sergeant Gonzales even steal the scenes he shares with Fairbanks.

All the elements of the Zorro legend are here, fully formed: the black mask and cape; the hidden cave under the hacienda; the mute servant, Bernardo; even the black stallion, trained to follow its master's orders. Plus the action scenes are great—Fairbanks famously did all his own stunts—the cinematography and direction are sharp and free from the theatrical staginess that plagued a lot of the silents, and the period details are spot on.

Not to mention that this film is indisputably the direct inspiration for the Batman. If you're a Batman fan but haven't seen *The Mark of Zorro*, you're just not fully aware of that character's origin. Seriously.

THE MARK OF ZORRO (1940)

Rating: ★★★★★ (Essential) • *Origin:* USA, 1940 • *Director:* Rouben Mamoulian •
Source: Fox Studio Classics DVD

Tyrone Power's family had been on the stage for generations, and he considered himself a serious actor. He finally broke into the movies in the mid-1930s and became a popular leading man for 20th Century Fox in parts both serious and not so serious. Meanwhile Warner Bros. was making a pile from Errol Flynn's swashbucklers, and though Fox didn't have Flynn, it did have Power, so Darryl F. Zanuck decided Power was going to be Fox's sword-swinging hero. To launch him in that new role, they chose to remake *The Mark of Zorro*, the film that had launched Douglas Fairbanks Sr.'s swashbuckling career. It wasn't the kind of part Power really wanted to play, but he dutifully agreed, and the result was a classic that typecast him, rightly or wrongly, for the rest of his career.

This new *Mark of Zorro* was no slavish remake: the screenwriters rewrote the story from top to bottom, retaining its familiar and iconic elements but adding new ones, such as naming the ruler of colonial Los Angeles the "Alcalde," a title that became standard thereafter. But first they tacked on a prologue, showing Don Diego as a cadet in the cavalry hussars in Madrid, romancing the ladies and dueling the other young hot-bloods. Then his father summons him back to California, where he expects there'll be no one at all to fight—so he abandons his sword by thrusting it into the ceiling (a nice callback to Fairbanks, who did the same thing at the *end* of his *Mark of Zorro*).

However, California is not the peaceful backwater Diego remembers. His father, the Alcalde, is Alcalde no more, forced out and replaced by the brutal Don Luis Quintero, who runs Los Angeles as a private fief for the enrichment of himself and his enforcer, Capitan Esteban. But it's not all bad, for the new Alcalde has a sweet, clever, and beautiful niece named Lolita.

Meanwhile, the peons are taxed into destitution, those who can't pay are whipped, and even the sanctuary of the church is violated—so Zorro must ride! And it

The Mark of Zorro (1940) Distributed by 20th Century Fox / Wikimedia Commons

turns out Power is tailor-made for the part: he's dashing, romantic, and swordsman enough for the role of Zorro, and he has the sly comic touch needed to play the effete fop Don Diego. In this sort of film, the hero is key, of course, but all the best swashbucklers feature a top-notch supporting cast, and this is no exception. To help launch their rival to Errol Flynn, Zanuck cannily hired two of the standouts from *The Adventures of Robin Hood*, namely, Basil Rathbone for the role of the arrogant Capitan Esteban, and Eugene Pallette to play Fray Felipe, who is essentially Friar Tuck transported from Old England to New Spain. Linda Darnell also does fine as the dewy love interest Lolita, but the prize goes to Gale Sondergaard arching her astounding eyebrows as Inez Quintero, the Alcalde's lascivious wife, who's set her sights on Don Diego. She's just delicious.

The two best scenes in this film are polar opposites: the first is where Power and Darnell bandy words while Zorro, disguised as a monk, flatters Lolita as she gradually catches on to what's happening; and the second is nearly the last, when Power and Rathbone cross swords for the final duel. It's exciting, and even better, it's convincing: "Tyrone," said Basil Rathbone, "could have fenced Errol Flynn into a cocked hat."

THE MASTER OF BALLANTRAE

Rating: ★★★★☆ • *Origin:* USA, 1953 • *Director:* William Keighley •
Source: Warner Bros. DVD

This movie shouldn't be any good. It's adapted from Robert Louis Stevenson's darkest and most complex historical novel, not exactly apt fare for the Hollywood treatment. It's the last Warner Brothers film for star Errol Flynn, by 1953 widely considered a washed-up has-been. And it's the final movie directed by the ailing William Keighley, who was famously replaced on *The Adventures of Robin Hood* by Michael Curtiz because Keighley didn't have a good grasp of filming action scenes. So this should be a mediocre and obvious potboiler, a mere 100-minute rehash of tired clichés.

But it isn't. Oh, it doesn't start out very well: it's set during the battles and aftermath of the final Scottish rebellion of 1745 (the same background as Stevenson's *Kidnapped*), and the historical events are mostly conveyed in montages voiced over by a faceless narrator, everyone's least favorite expository device. But someone had the bright idea of shooting the film on location in Scotland, and the Highland glens and castles frame the story convincingly. This also had the happy side effect of getting Flynn away from his Hollywood haunts, and he looks engaged and invigorated here, deepened and matured but still lit by the old charisma. Flynn's role is tailor-made to both his talents and his tabloid reputation: Jamie Durie, in amazing plaid trousers, is the reckless, hell-raising and womanizing elder son of a Scottish laird who sides with Bonnie Prince Charlie in the Rising, while his stodgy brother Henry (Anthony Steel) holds down the debt-ridden home castle in support of England's King George—thus the family fortunes are covered no matter the outcome of the rebellion, d'ye see. The disastrous Battle of Culloden goes down (in narrated montage), the Scots' hopes are dashed, and Jamie, now a fugitive, must flee overseas—but not before he's betrayed and nearly captured by the English redcoats. He assumes his brother Henry, who desires his fiancée Lady Alison (Beatrice Campbell, fine in her few scenes), is responsible for this treachery, and he vows vengeance as he sails away.

But his vengeance is deferred, because the skipper of the hired sloop is a villain who robs Jamie of his money and presses him and his sidekick, the Irish Colonel Burke, into forced

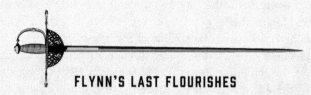

FLYNN'S LAST FLOURISHES

Errol Flynn's late-career swashbucklers are widely considered mediocre efforts, desperate attempts by an aging and fading star to recapture his youthful popularity, but that sells the films short. It's true that by the late 1940s, Flynn could no longer match the vigor and charm of his performances in *Captain Blood* (1935), *The Adventures of Robin Hood* (1938), and *The Sea Hawk* (1940) . . . but really, who could? Compared to any other standard, Flynn's later sword-slingers are average at worst and mostly better than that. Flynn wasn't keen to make most of these pictures; he was well aware that he wasn't the athletic rascal he'd been almost 20 years before, but he was still a solid leading man and now and then the old charm shone through. *The Master of Ballantrae, Against All Flags, The Warriors* . . . enjoy these films for what they have to offer, and you won't be sorry.

labor before the mast. They sail to the West Indies where—hooray!—the sloop gets attacked by a pirate bark! During the boarding action, Jamie attacks the skipper who'd shanghaied him, which so impresses the pirate captain that he takes Jamie and Burke into his crew as officers. The glorious episode of Caribbean pirate adventure that follows is only a few chapters in the novel, but it's the throbbing heart of the middle of this film. Captain Arnaud, a mincing French dandy played by Jacques Berthier, is a delight, especially in contrast with his brutal ox of a first mate, appropriately named Bull (Francis de Wolff). This is also a good place to mention the fine work of Roger Livesey, who plays Colonel Burke with a sly grin. Flynn's old pal Alan Hale Sr. had died a couple of years before or he would inevitably have had this role as Jamie's sidekick—and the movie would have been the poorer for it. Livesey's Burke is a perfect foil for Flynn's roguish Jamie, able to change in two seconds from smiling camaraderie to scowling menace.

And scowling menace is just what's needed when they arrive in Tortuga (lovely scenes filmed in Sicily), where Jamie talks Captain Arnaud into a bold plan to steal another buccaneer captain's prize, a captured Spanish galleon. Piratical antics ensue, with a fight through town, across the harbor, and aboard ship, ending with a top-notch duel between Jamie and Arnaud (and Burke and Bull) for the ship's command and possession of the Spanish treasure. (Kudos here to Patrick Crean, the uncredited fight director, who was a master.) The Scots win the day, and Jamie sets out to return to Scotland with enough loot to get the Durie castle out of hock and enough swords to enact his vengeance. I won't spoil the last act, which takes some unexpected turns, but it wraps up in a satisfying ending that's reasonably true to the novel. It's a fine swan song to Flynn's 35-film career at Warner Bros. and a solid wrap-up for the underappreciated veteran Keighley, as the screen fades on Flynn literally riding off into a Scottish sunset. Bon voyage, laddie!

MASTER SWORDSMAN HIRATE MIKI (OR *HIRATE MIKI*)

Rating: ★★★☆☆ • *Origin:* Japan, 1951 • *Director:* Kyotaro Namiki • *Source:* Shintoho DVD

This austerely beautiful film tells the tale of the legendary Hirate Miki, a samurai whose pride in his sword skills leads him to ruin. In the 1840s, at the end of the Tokugawa era, at the Chiba sword school in Edo, young student Hirate Miki (So Yamamura) exceeds all his classmates, but the age of the shogunate is over, nobody needs swordsmen anymore, and finding a place in a prosperous clan depends more on family connections than on ability in the martial arts. Hirate's social skills lag far behind his skill with a *katana*, and he's too proud to curry favor with the wealthy students; though he becomes the school's leading student instructor, Japanese society no longer values swordsmanship. Frustrated, he takes to drink, which interferes with his instruction and worse, brings on the early onset of tuberculosis. But his romantic melancholy attracts the attention of Masuji, a talented independent geisha who also refuses to trade her art for preferment, and together they leave Edo to find success on their own terms somewhere else.

But with Japan's old social contract fraying, the only place for swordsmen is in the organized crime gangs of the yakuza, and Hirate finds himself reduced to working as a bodyguard and sword trainer for the Sasagawa crime family. His prowess keeps the rival Iioka gang at bay, and a healthy routine in the country air puts his TB into remission, but eventually bitterness sends Hirate back to the bottle, and his malady returns. The master of the Chiba school calls on him to return to Edo, and Hirate decides that he and Masuji should accept, but the Iioka gang, learning that Hirate's sickness has made him an invalid, decides it's time to make their move.

After World War II, under the American occupation, Japanese filmmakers were forbidden to make "violent" movies; this film was produced just as those limitations were loosening up, and so the swordplay, though well represented, is semicensored: combat is shot from a distance or the camera cuts away or tall bamboo boles are sliced down to stand in for the slashing of men. It hardly matters; the final fight in a cemetery between the staggering Hirate and the Iioka yakuza is an early landmark of the genre. At 62 minutes, it's short and sweet: the tight screenplay, by Shinobu Hashimoto (*Rashomon*, *Seven Samurai*, *Harakiri*, et al.) makes its point about the value, and futility, of the warrior code of Bushido without a word wasted, in perfect harmony with the clean visuals of director Kyotaro Namiki. (For another take on the character of Hirate Miki and the Sasagawa-Iioka gang war, see *The Tale of Zatoichi*.)

MONTE CRISTO (1922)

Rating: ★★☆☆☆ • *Origin:* USA, 1922 • *Director:* Emmett J. Flynn • *Source:* Flicker Alley DVD

Here's another silent adaptation of Dumas's *The Count of Monte Cristo*, a remake of the 1913 version, shot from the same basic script (to which Fox bought the rights) but greatly expanded to create a film a half hour longer than its predecessor. Lead John Gilbert is a rising star at this point, though he hasn't yet gained the popularity he will with *The Big Parade* (1925) and *Flesh and the Devil* (1926). Once again, Edmond Dantès succumbs to a conspiracy of envy and is imprisoned in the horrific Château d'If, only to escape and achieve his revenge, outconspiring the conspirators as the chameleonic Count of Monte Cristo. The villains, each a different flavor of sleazy, are thoroughly despicable, and the innocent Mercédès, Dantès's lost love, is wide-eyed and appealing. Gilbert looks and moves well in the role of Monte Cristo and inhabits the count's various guises convincingly.

This version avoids the stage-play feel of its predecessor by employing frequent close-ups and switching camera distance and angle often. And it does a better job of explaining how Dantès comes by not just his great wealth but also the knowledge and culture that enable him to pass as the elegant and noble count. With its extra running time, there's room to include more of the characters and twists of Dumas's novel, adding robberies, lurid murders, duels, and impersonations. In fact, it's somewhat *over*ambitious, trying to jam in more of the novel than is comfortable in less than two hours. In the end it feels too contrived, and not even a final spate of swordplay and highway robbery can quite save it. It's just too hokey.

MONTE CRISTO (1929)

Rating: ★☆☆☆☆ • *Origin:* France, 1929 • *Director:* Henri Fescourt •
Source: Grapevine Video DVD

Except for the Mister Magoo version from 1965, at 40 minutes this must be the shortest *Count of Monte Cristo* ever filmed. The main thing it has going for it is that many of the scenes from the novel were shot at their actual locations, so if you're a fan of the book, that's a reason to watch it. Otherwise, not so much. There's time for no more than a précis of the events of the novel, but at least we get to see Edmond Dantès, in the shroud of the Abbé Faria, tossed into the sea from the parapet of the actual Château d'If. This is for *Monte Cristo* completists only.

MONTY PYTHON AND THE HOLY GRAIL

Rating: ★★★★★ (Essential) • *Origin:* UK, 1975 • *Directors:* Terry Gilliam and Terry Jones •
Source: Netflix streaming video

There'd be no point in trying to say something new about the comedy in this rightfully revered Arthurian farce, even if its gags hadn't been quoted to death by two generations of nerds. No, we're here to talk about *Holy Grail* as a historical adventure film, a company in which it is as comfortable and welcome as the rude jester in a king's court.

The Pythons were intent on skewering tales of knights in shining armor, a goal they achieved in part because they understood those tales so well, not just from Hollywood epics but from Arthurian literature studied at Oxford and Cambridge. They knew exactly what tropes they wanted to subvert and turned them inside out with relish and gusto.

The cliché of the knightly duel, two heavily armored warriors hammering each other with greatswords, is disposed of early in the film with the challenge of the Black Knight at the ford, where the trope is literally dismembered. So much for knightly duels. Next comes the rescue of the imprisoned maiden, in which Sir Lancelot (John Cleese) charges into a castle and indiscriminately slaughters the guests of a wedding feast. So much for the lone hero facing impossible odds. Then comes the chaste Sir Galahad (Michael Palin), tempted by seductive maidens . . .

The film is remarkably well paced and composed, considering directors Terry Gilliam and Terry Jones hadn't previously made anything longer than a TV comedy sketch. They clearly had a solid grasp of the classics: scene 24, in which King Arthur (Graham Chapman) and Sir Bedevere (Jones) meet a creepy soothsayer in a haunted forest is clearly based on the similar scene in Kurosawa's *Throne of Blood*, while the preparation-for-battle montage at the end, with its grim-faced veterans lining up in the mist, callused hands gripping their weapons, evokes the prelude to the Battle of Agincourt in Olivier's *Henry V*. All so it can be taken down for a laugh, of course.

The medieval adventure tropes the film doesn't upend for comic effect it instead doubles down on, also for comic effect. The common folk of the Middle Ages are depicted as wallowing in abject squalor, prey to ignorance, superstition, and fear of the word "Ni!"—except when they're members of anarcho-syndicalist communes or connoisseurs of suburban shrubbery, the Humor of Incongruity being a Python specialty.

This movie *is* nearly a half-century old, so one supposes it's remotely possible that you haven't seen it. If so, it's a (doubtless inadvertent) lapse that should be corrected immediately. Get thee to thy streaming service, varlet.

THE MOONRAKER (OR *BLOOD ON THE SWORD*)

Rating: ★★★★☆ • *Origin:* UK, 1958 • *Director:* David MacDonald •
Source: StudioCanal DVD

This is a British swashbuckler set during the English Civil War, one of the few that's sympathetic to both sides. In 1651, after the Royalists have lost their last battle to Cromwell's New Model Army, an unknown cavalier known only as the Moonraker helps fugitive Royalists escape arrest by the Roundheads. The Moonraker, secretly Anthony, Earl of Dawlish (George Baker), has his greatest challenge in trying to help the fugitive Charles II (Gary Raymond) evade the ever-tightening net of Cromwell's troops, led by the implacable Colonel Beaumont (Marius Goring, of *The Adventures of the Scarlet Pimpernel*). The Moonraker plans to help Charles escape from a smuggler's inn on a headland on England's south coast, but the tides of fate bring all his friends and enemies to the inn at the same time—and some of them are not what they seem.

Sounds like a stage play, doesn't it? That's because it *was* a stage play before it was a screenplay, but fortunately the writers opened the story out with a full act of alarums and excursions in the pursuit of Charles Stuart before anyone arrives at the inn, which is where all the speechifying between the major characters takes place. At the inn, the surprises, reversals, and revelations of the original drama get a chance to play out, with a romantic interlude and a duel or two tossed in, and then finally Colonel Beaumont shows up with a troop of horse, and it's time for everyone to make their escape—or try to prevent it. Those clever screenwriters added a fine extended climax that bursts the inn's bounds and culminates in a rapier duel between the hero and his nemesis on the sea-girt rocks below. There are some striking English locations, the costumes are good, and so is the fencing, and the acting is better than average for a medium-budget historical adventure. It's all quite satisfying, and if the story might be a touch too tidy, well, that's a stage play for you.

PIRATES—ITALIAN STYLE!

We tend to think of pirate tales as mainly an English-language thing, since the earliest modern histories of pirates were in English, as were the genre-defining stories of Robert Louis Stevenson (*Treasure Island, Kidnapped*), Rafael Sabatini (*The Sea Hawk, Captain Blood*), and Howard Pyle. But pirate stories were extremely popular in Continental Europe as well, especially in Italy, where Emilio Salgari (1862–1911) wrote as many as 200 adventure novels, his most famous being *The Black Corsair* (1898), which has been filmed at least five times.

During the period of 1960 through 1965, the Italian film industry was famously focused on making peplum, or sword-and-sandal films, but it also dabbled in other historical adventure genres—and in the case of pirate movies, more than dabbled. At lot of them are quickies that might not be worth your time, but Italy loves a good keelhaulin' cutthroat, and some of the Italian pirate films of the early '60s were standouts.

MORGAN, THE PIRATE

Rating: ★★★★☆ • *Origin:* Italy/France, 1960 • *Directors:* André DeToth and Primo Zeglio •
Source: Turner Classic Movies

This is a fine Franco-Italian production, one of the best Continental pirate movies, starring Steve Reeves as Henry Morgan and Valérie Lagrange as Doña Inez, his daughter-of-the-Spanish-governor love interest. Its taut direction is primarily credited to the Hungarian American director André DeToth, who (you can't make this up) later in life lost one eye and wore a black eye patch. But seriously, *Morgan*'s production values are good, it has top-notch cinematography by Tonino Delli Colli, excellent costumes and locations, and a rolling nautical score by Franco Mannino.

But it does throw history to the winds. The story begins in the Spanish colonial port of Panama, where captive Englishman Henry Morgan is kicking up a fuss in the slave market. In a scene reminiscent of *Captain Blood* (1935), the governor's daughter, Doña Inez, buys Morgan for her household and assigns him to handle her horses—but when he steals a kiss in the stables, he's arrested and condemned to work as a slave hand on a Spanish galleon. Predictably, Morgan leads an uprising, takes over the galleon, and is acclaimed its new captain. He sails with his uprisen crew to the pirate port of Tortuga and a tense relationship with its brutal commodore, François l'Olonnais (Armand Mestral), who has, incidentally, captured Doña Inez. Morgan demands supplies, clothing, and Inez from l'Olonnais, and fights a fine rapier duel with him to win them—but then he finds he's been given only women's clothing, ha ha ha. So Morgan clothes his crew in dresses to deceive a Spanish treasure ship, his men conduct a boarding action in drag, and he returns to Tortuga wealthy and in triumph.

And we're not even halfway through the picture! Still ahead are Morgan's frustrated romance with Inez, an alliance with England, a failed attack on Panama, a bold James Bond–ish trespass on a Spanish victory ball, Morgan burning his own pirates' ships so they can't retreat from an overland raid, and his final revenge on the Spanish as he leads his pirate army to take Panama from the landward side. The resulting sack of Panama is one of the best piratical 20 minutes on film.

About the only thing that keeps this film from being an utter classic is the flat performances of the leads, who just don't seem to be into it. Reeves is handsome and charismatic as always, but unlike the magnificent Laird Cregar in *The Black Swan* (1942), Reeves's Henry Morgan has no sense of humor—and even worse, no chemistry with costar Valérie Lagrange, who is beautiful but bland. But lawdy mama, the locations, shot off the Neapoli-

Steve Reeves as *Morgan, The Pirate* Indeciso42 / Wikimedia Commons

tan coast on the Italian island of Procida, are simply fabulous, with Tortuga a rollicking town of shanties and limestone caves filled with Caribbean loot and, after dark, the best buccaneer beachfront revels ever. Blow me down! I'm ready to sign the Articles. Aficionados of pirate films have got to see this one.

NINJA WARS (OR *DEATH OF A NINJA*)

Rating: ★★★★☆ • *Origin:* Japan, 1982 • *Director:* Kosei Saito • *Source:* Mill Creek DVD

This is a lavish and exuberant fantasy set in Japan's Warring States period, in which the evil scheme of a sorcerer and his five mystic ninja is opposed by a single ninja hero who chooses to fight for love.

But it sure ain't simple. Lady Ukyo (Noriko Watanabe), the fiancée of Lord Myoshi (Noboru Matsuhashi), is desired by the ambitious Lord Danjo (Akira Nakao)—all the more so once he hears a prophecy from the sorcerer Kashin (Miko Narita) that whoever possesses Lady Ukyo will rule the nation. All Danjo has to do is accept Kashin's advice and the services of his five nasty magical ninja warriors, and they promise they'll get him Lady Ukyo. Danjo's loyal samurai advisor Shinzaemon (Sonny Chiba) objects to this and is dismissed.

Cut to a flowery meadow where two young ninja in love, Jotaro (Hiroyuki Sanada) and Kagaribi (Noriko Watanabe again), as cute as two bugs, are planning their marriage. Tragedy intrudes when the Five Nasties appear to kidnap Kagaribi, despite Jotaro's best efforts, because she's the separated-at-birth twin of Lady Ukyo, and the sorcerer needs to add her tears to the sinister magical Spider Pot to brew the love potion that will make Ukyo fall in love with Danjo. However—stick with me, here—to foil their plans, Kagaribi uses her mystic ninja powers to *cut off her own head*, but the Nasties just decapitate a handmaiden, reattach the heads to the wrong bodies, and abuse the body with Kagaribi's head until it cries the tears they need, before the body with the handmaiden's head (but Kagaribi's soul) steals the Spider Pot and takes it to Jotaro, explaining everything before dying.

Then things get weird.

Jotaro vows to protect Kagaribi's twin Lady Ukyo, the Five Nasties pursue him, each with his own bizarre power; Kashin bewitches an entire army of monks and sends them after Ukyo and Jotaro. There's a spectacular temple fire which the pair survive by hiding in the hollow interior of a headless Buddha statue, Ukyo and Jotaro fall for each other, masked mounted samurai appear out of nowhere and temporarily rout the Nasties, Lord Miyoshi is driven mad by seeing both Ukyo and her double, and Ukyo is literally crucified on a flaming altar of love. Don't worry, though, it's fine.

This is a quick-paced, colorful, and stylish film featuring impressive practical effects, with flying wirework inspired by Hong Kong *wuxia* movies. The fights are well staged and wild, and if they sometimes end abruptly as other characters suddenly interfere, the brief confusion is immediately explained. The romantic leads are attractive and sympathetic, the sorcerer is wryly creepy, his five nasty ninja are each awful in their own way, and the samurai Shinzaemon is honorable and forthright. Plus there's a flying boomerang sickle—better duck!

THE NORSEMAN

Rating: ★☆☆☆☆ • *Origin:* US, 1978 • *Director:* Charles B. Pierce • *Source:* MGM DVD

Around the year 1000, Vikings sailing west reached the coast of North America at Newfoundland, dubbing the coast "Vinland." Writer-producer-director Charles B. Pierce made an action movie about two follow-up Norse expeditions to Vinland, but filmed it on the west coast of Florida. This squares well with star Lee Majors's Kentucky accent, which renders Norseman as "Norzman." It also fits with hiring a bunch of Tampa Bay Buccaneers as extras and dressing them up as cartoon Vikings out of *Hagar the Horrible*. Seriously, their costumes, with plastic, Roman-inspired muscle-breastplates, could not be worse. Things could only be worse if Charles B. Pierce decided to dress the Native Americans the Norz encounter as outright savages in ragged loincloths and war paint.

Does Pierce go there?

Yes, Pierce goes there.

In 1006 CE the Vikings, a "lusty horde of blond giants," according to Pierce, conquer Europe and then head west, lusty for more conquering. King Eurich (Mel Ferrer) went lustily conquering west and never came back, so his sons Thorvald (Lee Majors) and Eric (Pierce's 12-year-old son Chuck) find another longship and set out after him. This ship, which Pierce borrowed from somewhere in North Carolina to make the film, is actually pretty cool, so props for that prop. However, no points awarded for the Vikings' plastic horned helmets or modern metal crossbows.

Thorvald and Eric bring with them their shipmaster Ragnar, played by Cornel Wilde, who looks pained and embarrassed, possibly hoping no one will recognize him behind his bristling Norz beard. They also bring a hunchbacked Norz wizard named Death Dreamer played by Jack Elam, which is okay because nothing can embarrass Jack Elam.

The Vikings land by wading ashore onto a Florida beach, where they are immediately attacked by the local Native Americans, who are all howling savages who say "Yah!" a lot. They don't speak any English, which in this film is a definite advantage, because that means they don't have to utter Pierce's wooden dialogue. Example: Thorvald wants to chase the Indians into the Florida woods and make them tell him where his father can be found, but Death Dreamer solemnly warns Thorvald, "To go into the forest after them is worse than crossing the high Alps to kill the white bear with empty hands." Right. There's a lot of that stuff, except when the dialogue is replaced by flat and intrusive narration by the adult Eric, which would be unwelcome except that it has the virtue of suppressing the dialogue.

With the help of a young, underclad Native American woman named Winetta (Susie Coelho), the Vikings eventually find King Eurich and his crew, who have been blinded and enslaved by the Indians, because savages. There's a tedious chase through the forest in which Pierce displays his one directorial trick of cutting back and forth from pursuers to pursued, and a dumb fight on the beach in which ferocity is conveyed by slo-mo. This must at least have felt familiar to *Six Million Dollar Man* Lee Majors. Perhaps he requested it.

Anyway, don't watch this unless you think it would be funny to see former Olympic fencer Wilde hacking away at Native Americans with a fake broadsword as if he were chopping wood. To save you the trouble: It isn't funny. It's just sad.

ONE-ARMED SWORDSMAN

Rating: ★★★★☆ • *Origin:* Hong Kong, 1967 • *Director:* Chang Cheh • *Source:* 88 Films Blu-ray

King Hu reinvented the modern *wuxia* film in 1966 with *Come Drink with Me* and then left the Shaw Brothers Hong Kong film factory for Taiwan. But the Shaw Brothers had another top-notch action director in Chang Cheh, who began his own series of historical martial arts movies with *One-Armed Swordsman*, which broke new ground with its dynamic and colorful swordplay and was an even bigger hit in Asia than *Come Drink with Me*.

It's sometime in China's past. Master Qi's Golden Sword School is a leading training ground of martial artists, but Qi Ru (Tien Feng) has made enemies of bandits Long-Armed Devil (Yeung Chi-hing) and his son Smiling Tiger Cheng (Tang Ti). The bandits launch a surprise attack on Qi's school, and his servant Fang throws himself in front of the attackers, dying over his broken sword to save the master, so Qi honors his sacrifice by taking his son, Fang Kang (Jimmy Wang), to be one of his disciples. Years pass, and Fang distinguishes himself as Qi's best student, but the other students are jealous, including Qi's spoiled daughter Pei (Angela Pan), who's peeved that Fang won't court her. The jealous students ambush Fang one winter night, and when Fang dismissively defeats Pei without using weapons, she suddenly picks up a sword and severs his right arm!

Fang staggers away and falls unconscious from a bridge into the canal boat of Xiao (Lisa Chiao Chiao), a young peasant woman who takes him home and nurses him back to health, falling in love with him as she does so. Alas, Fang is in despair because martial arts were his life, but now he's crippled—he can't properly wield Qi's heavy golden sword left-handed. Fortunately, Xiao has an ancient book of kung fu that had belonged to her father that includes methods for wielding a shorter blade in the left hand—perfect for use with his father's broken sword!

Xiao hates martial arts, though, blaming the pursuit for her father's death, and extracts a promise from Fang that he'll give it up. But then Long-Armed Devil and Smiling Tiger reappear with a new weapon, the sword-lock, that enables them to beat Master Qi's Golden Sword style, and they begin ambushing and killing Qi's students. Fang's new left-handed short-sword style enables him to defeat the sword-lock; can he keep his promise to Xiao when his adoptive family is threatened? You know he can't.

CHANG CHEH

Though visionary director King Hu established the elements of the modern *wuxia,* or Chinese historical swordplay film, it was fellow Hong Kong director Chang Cheh who really took the ball and ran with it. He followed hard on Hu's *Come Drink with Me* and *Dragon Inn* with his own wuxia action movies and quickly became one of Asia's top-grossing directors, with a style that drew on Hu but also Japan's Akira Kurosawa, America's Sam Peckinpah, and Italy's Sergio Leone. After about a dozen swordplay films, he turned to unarmed martial arts, helping to define the burgeoning kung fu film genre. All told, he made over 90 films for Hong Kong's Shaw Brothers studio and was a major influence on later directors such as John Woo, Robert Rodriguez, and Zhang Yimou.

The swordplay in the final act is sensational and relentless, often shot with a handheld camera, unusual for the time. Director Cheh takes King Hu's method of quick cuts and improves upon it, driving the action while keeping events crystal clear. Long-Armed Devil has more tricks up his sleeve than the sword-lock, and Fang performs amazing martial feats but always with effort, as if barely pulling them off. The villains are menacing and despicable, the lead actors are appealing, and their victories feel both well-earned and satisfying. Scores of Hong Kong action films will come after, all doing their best to follow the example of Chang Cheh's *One-Armed Swordsman.*

PIRATES

Rating: ★☆☆☆☆ • *Origin:* France/Tunisia/Poland, 1986 • *Director:* Roman Polanski •
Source: BLU RAY R Blu-ray

There are only three legit reasons for watching this woeful travesty: (1) You want to see every film in which the swordplay is choreographed by the great William Hobbs; (2) you are actually its director, Roman Polanski; or (3) you have been very, very naughty and feel you should be punished.

This film is a strong candidate for Worst Pirate Movie Ever Made. Its star, Walter Matthau as Cap'n Red, is shockingly miscast; his RP (received pirate) accent is dreadful, and he gargles half his words in the back of his throat so that he's often unintelligible. The romantic leads, Cris Campion as Frog (because he's French, ha-ha) and Charlotte Lewis as María-Dolores, are bland, uninteresting, and uninterested in each other. The antagonists, an assortment of nonentities as villainous Spanish dons, are paper-thin caricatures. The only actors who do anything whatsoever with their characters are Roy Kinnear as Dutch, a corrupt merchant, and Olu Jacobs as Boomako, an ex-slave piratical sidekick.

What serves as the story, fragmented folderol about a golden Aztec throne everyone wants, is excruciatingly slow, stupefyingly dull, and it has an ending that's even worse than everything that's gone before. It must be intended to be funny, but like the rest of the labored and tasteless attempts at humor in this film, it falls utterly flat.

Galleon from Roman Polanski's *Pirates* Zıl—Own work, CC BY-SA 3.0 / Wikimedia Commons

This movie cost 40 million 1985 dollars to make and took in only $6 million in global receipts, making it one of the biggest theatrical flops in cinema history. You can certainly see where a lot of those millions went: the costumes are stellar, the sets are detailed and elaborate, and they built a gigantic Spanish galleon in Tunisia that must be just about the biggest sailing-ship prop every created. (If you're ever in Genoa, Italy, it's down at the docks and you can tour it for nine euro.) The cinematography is flawless.

And there's an 11-minute joke about eating a boiled rat. It's an apt metaphor for watching this thing.

THE PIRATES OF BLOOD RIVER

Rating: ★★★☆☆ • *Origin:* UK, 1962 • *Director:* John Gilling • *Source:* Columbia Pictures DVD

Adultery and piranhas in the first five minutes—must be a Hammer film! In the seventeenth century, Huguenots (French Protestants) fleeing persecution founded a secret haven on a tropical island. A hundred years later, their Puritanical town elders have become complete jerks, so when their refuge is discovered by a crew of ruthless pirates, it's impossible to sympathize with them. Plunder and pillage, me lads!

Jonathon Standing (Kerwin Mathews), the son of the mayor, is caught dallying with another elder's wife, and after the fleeing wife is eaten by piranhas, Jonathon is sentenced to the island's penal colony by his own father. This brutal prison in a sand quarry contains about as many prisoners as there are residents in the town, so you know the town is not governed by nice guys. Jonathon makes a daring escape but is then captured by a newly arrived pirate crew, who think the Huguenots' island is just the hideout they're looking for. But Captain La Roche (Christopher Lee) promises Jonathon the town will be spared if he leads them to the treasure the Huguenots must have brought from France.

HAMMER ~~HORROR~~ HISTORICALS!

Hammer Films was a London studio founded in 1934, but it didn't really make much of a mark until the mid-1950s, when it hit its stride with a revival of the Gothic horror genre. With dependable leads in Peter Cushing, Christopher Lee, and (later) Oliver Reed, they just about owned the horror category from 1955 through 1965 but were successful enough to branch out into other genres as well, including historical swashbucklers, all with that distinctive Hammer look and feel. Batten down the hatches, it's Christopher Lee in an eye patch, ye swabs!

Like most Hammer films, this was made on the cheap and on the quick but with an unrestrained and lurid glee that makes it entertaining despite the low production values. Its chief pleasures are watching buccaneers La Roche and Brocaire (Oliver Reed) sneer and glower piratically at the captive Huguenots while their drunken maties roister and fight with one another. Lee, all in black leather including eye patch, strides around like he was born with a rapier on his hip. The Huguenots, Mathews included, are earnest but boring, and it's hard to cheer for them even as their piratical enemies dissolve into acrimonious anarchy. Come for the piranhas and stay for the blindfolded sword duel.

THE PIRATES OF CAPRI (OR *THE MASKED PIRATE*)

Rating: ★★★☆☆ • *Origin:* UK/Italy, 1949 • *Director:* Edward G. Ulmer • *Source:* FilmRise DVD

It's 1798 and French-style revolutions are breaking out all across Europe, which puts us squarely in Scarlet Pimpernel territory—only this time, the noble outlaw with the secret identity is on the side of the revolutionaries rather than the aristos. Maria Carolina, Queen of Naples (Binnie Barnes, in an uncharacteristically timid role), is terrified there will be a people's revolution in southern Italy and her head, like that of her relative, Marie Antoinette, will end in a basket. Her fears are stoked by her evil chief of police, Baron Holstein (Massimo Serato, suave, handsome, sinister, and cruel), to whom she gives sweeping powers. Meanwhile Count Amalfi, amusing fop and wit-about-court, tries to calm the queen's fears, but every time he does, the daring raids of the masked pirate Captain Scirocco set her off again.

Louis Hayward plays both Count Amalfi, fopping it up by day, complete with quizzing glass and a series of ridiculous wigs, and the revolutionary outlaw Captain Scirocco, rabble-rousing by night with black mask and sword. At this point Hayward had been playing gallant swordsmen fighting oppression for over a decade, and one can see he's a bit weary of it, though he still manages to work up some of the old charm for his scenes with the count's fiancée, Lady Mercedes (Mariella Lotti, surprisingly good), whom he romances as both Amalfi and Scirocco, thus becoming his own rival.

This was shot on location in Naples and the nearby island of Capri, plus the first scene is set at sea aboard a sweet period 60-gun three-masted man-o'-war, which Scirocco loots of a weapon shipment to arm his rebels. The film makes the most of these authentic locales, and the director, fan favorite Edward Ulmer, a low-budget Orson Welles, does wonders with light and shadow on a shoestring. The police raid a gathering of revolutionaries, so to draw them away, Scirocco leads the guards off in a breathtaking chase across the tiled rooftops of Naples, scrambling across famous façades like someone right out of *Assassin's Creed*. The story makes a hash of the actual history of the Neapolitan revolution of 1798–1799, but we forgive it because of the brilliantly shot final duel, acrobatic and brutal, between Scirocco and Holstein in a Naples theater, as brawling rebels and guardsmen pour into the building through the shattered doorways. Hot stuff.

PIRATES OF TORTUGA

Rating: ★★☆☆☆ • *Origin:* USA, 1961 • *Director:* Robert D. Webb • *Source:* 20th Century Fox DVD

Ex-pirate Henry Morgan, though appointed governor of Jamaica by the British Crown, has returned to piracy and relocated to the island of Tortuga. (Morgan totally never did that, but whatever.) In London, the admiralty call in privateer captain Bart Paxton (Ken Scott) and charge him with taking Morgan down, though it must be done so as not to violate the new treaty with Spain. But before leaving London, Captain Bart saves spunky street thief Meg (Letícia Román) from hanging for petty theft, so she stows away aboard his ship.

Ready for action? Not yet, sorry. The movie's next hour is spent on the adventures of Meg, a petite blonde with a broad, mischievous smile, as she tries to seduce Captain Bart, then his officers, and then the new Governor of Jamaica. It's supposed to be funny and charming, and Román does her best, but frankly nobody here is sharp enough to make it work.

Then we're into the pirate action as Captain Bart schemes to defeat Morgan, with ship captures and impostures, but that's not convincing either. The script kind of wants Bart and his lads to be dangerous buccaneers but at the same time to be clean-cut and square-jawed American heroes, and it never makes up its mind. (Oh, another thing: everybody in this film who's pretending to be English isn't English at all but instead all too obviously American or Italian.) Alas, Robert Stephens's sadly epicene portrayal of Henry Morgan just make things worse—it's impossible to take him seriously. Hasn't he seen the guy on the rum bottles? Moreover, Captain Bart's scheme to capture Tortuga from Morgan is easily the Worst Plan Ever, so it's no surprise when it goes wrong and he ends up in irons. The only thing less believable is the way Meg turns up and saves him with nothing but a smile. Shoals ahead, mates—steer clear!

THE PRINCE AND THE PAUPER (1937)

Rating: ★★★☆☆ • *Origin:* USA, 1937 • *Director:* William Keighley • *Source:* Warner Bros. DVD

Thirties child actors: threat or menace? Warner Bros. had the cloying Mauch twins, Bobby and Billy, under contract, and bought the rights to Mark Twain's 1881 novel, *The Prince and the Pauper*, as a vehicle for them. And after his success in *The Charge of the Light Brigade* (1936), Warners threw in their new action hero, Errol Flynn, for good measure. Flynn plays Miles Hendon, a down-at-his-heels gentleman who takes in the prince (Bobby, or maybe Billy) after he's been switched with the pauper (Billy, or maybe Bobby). The film actually follows the novel's plot pretty closely, which means Flynn doesn't come onstage for nearly an hour, a considerable wait. Fortunately, not all of that hour is wasted on the twins, as much of the time is spent with Claude Rains, well cast as the suave villain of the piece, the Earl of Hertford.

The presence of Flynn and Rains notwithstanding, this movie is mainly a kids' fable, broadly played, but adults can still enjoy the fine Tudor-period costumes, Flynn's indelible charm and charisma, and the occasional razor-sharp line retained from Twain's novel. The ending is quite absurd—but it's a fable, isn't it? Plus we get one of Erich Wolfgang Korngold's best film scores, the main theme of which was so good he reused it as the final movement of his violin concerto. Watch for Fritz Leiber Sr. as a saintly friar, and enjoy Flynn finally getting to swashbuckle in the last 20 minutes. Guilty pleasure: the execrable Alan Hale Sr., not yet promoted to the role of Flynn's permanent sidekick, plays a minor villain who comes to a well-deserved bad end.

(For another adaptation of *The Prince and the Pauper*, see *Crossed Swords*.)

PRINCE OF FOXES

Rating: ★★★★★ • *Origin:* USA, 1949 • *Director:* Henry King •
Source: Fox Cinema Classics DVD

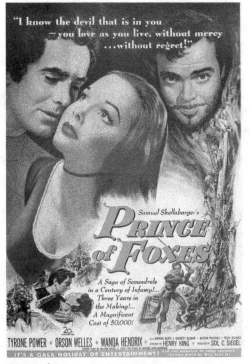

Prince of Foxes 20TH CENTURY FOX / WIKIMEDIA COMMONS

This, like *Captain from Castile*, is based on a novel by the popular American historical fiction author Samuel Shellabarger, and once again it's directed by Henry King. It's set in 1500 amid the warring states of northern Italy, where Cesare Borgia (Orson Welles!) has a cunning plan: gain the control, or at least the neutrality, of the principality of Ferrara by marrying his sister Lucrezia to nominal enemy Prince Alfonso D'Este. Borgia needs a sly and capable agent to undertake this diplomatic mission, and from a number of rivals he selects Capt. Andrea Orsini (Tyrone Power) for the task. It's clearly a test for Orsini, and if he succeeds, greater honor—and challenges—await. Along the way, Orsini thwarts an attempted murder, and then co-opts the assassin (Everett Sloane) into his own service . . . because according to the Borgias' maxim, "The end justifies the means."

This film succeeds brilliantly everywhere *Castile* failed, giving us a protagonist who is morally compromised but in command of his own destiny, who navigates the dangerous intrigues of Renaissance Italy and changes as a result of his choices. It's one of Power's most complex roles, a solid performance, plus Welles and Sloane are both great in their supporting parts; of the leads, only Wanda Hendrix as love interest Madonna Camilla Verano is a bit out of her depth. Add in the fact that the movie is entirely shot in Italy at the historically apt locations—Venice, Rome, Ferrara, among others—and you have one of the finest depictions of Renaissance romance and intrigue ever put on film. Its sole flaw is that, due to a shortfall in its international funding, it was shot in black-and-white instead of the full color it deserved.

So how is it as a swashbuckler? The movie's all politics for the first hour, but then the swords come out of their scabbards and they never go back. The siege and storming of the mountaintop fortress of Città del Monte is particularly stunning, as it's staged not at some phony walls on a Hollywood backlot but on the actual medieval battlements on Monte Titano in San Marino. Shortly after Orsini's climactic longsword duel on the tower stairs with Borgia's henchman Don Esteban, it all wraps up with a thoroughly satisfactory conclusion. Two stilettos up!

PRINCE OF THIEVES

Rating: ★★☆☆☆ • *Origin:* USA, 1948 • *Director:* Howard Bretherton •
Source: Columbia Pictures DVD

This is loosely based on Alexandre Dumas's *Le Prince des Voleurs* (1872), itself loosely based on Pierce Egan's *Robin Hood* (1840), a story from which can be found in my *Big Book of Swashbuckling Adventure*. It was adapted for the screen by Charles H. Schneer, better known later as Ray Harryhausen's frequent producer and partner; this is Schneer's only screenwriting credit. In Sherwood Forest, which has never looked more like Southern California, Robin Hood (Jon Hall) saves a traveling noble couple from assassination by an unknown archer. Robin takes them to his camp, where the nobleman reveals that he's one of the retainers of King Richard, who's still in France; the woman is his sister, and her name is Lady Marian. Her brother has come to claim the hand of the daughter of the Lord of Nottingham, but the lord has reneged on his promise and intends to marry his daughter to Prince John's nephew—and suddenly, that nephew's soldiers stage a surprise attack. And this is all in just the first 10 minutes! Fortunately, Robin has another hour in which to get things sorted out.

Jon Hall is one of those square-jawed but modestly talented leading men who made three or four movies a year in the 1940s for the smaller studios, playing stalwart heroes in formulaic adventure films. He's adequate enough, though about as English as baseball. The rest of the cast—lords, ladies, and Merrie Men—are mostly pretty tepid, except for Alan Mowbray as Friar Tuck and Robin Raymond as the saucy lady's maid, Maudie; they're quite engaging, and do a lot of the heavy lifting with the gags and trickery that move the plot forward. Nottingham Castle uses the same set we saw in *The Bandit of Sherwood Forest*, so we're not surprised that Robin knows how to get into it. Getting out isn't as easy, since they closed that leaky postern gate, but fortunately they added a secret escape passage through the dungeon. (Strangely, Robin forgets about this later, when the bandits need to get back into the castle again.)

This is another one of those cowboy Robin Hood pictures, where everyone rides horses—except for Friar Tuck, who rides a cute little donkey to good comic effect. The swordplay is ludicrous, the knife-fighting is worse, with everybody doing that stupid-looking overhand stab, but the archery is pretty good, probably because all the guards and bandits have played Indians in low-budget Westerns. On the other hand, the pole-arm work with those sad halberds—by my halidome, what an embarrassment! All in all, meh: this is one for Robin Hood completists only.

THE PRINCESS AND THE PIRATE

Rating: ★★★☆☆ • *Origin:* USA, 1944 • *Director:* David Butler • *Source:* Warner Bros. DVD

You wouldn't know it from his later career, but there was a time when Bob Hope was genuinely funny. His movies in the 1940s followed a formula: Hope, a genial but cowardly schmoe stuck in a Hollywood genre film—Western, gangster, monster movie—fouls up and gets in trouble with the bad guys. Trying to avoid whatever doom is at hand, he falls in with an Aspirational Blonde who's also threatened by the creeps, and having to save her gives him the spine and spunk necessary to outwit the villains. This time 'round, the villains are a crew of cartoonish Caribbean pirates led by a captain known as Hook because—do I have to tell you? Hope plays a comically bad itinerant actor called Sylvester the Great, which gives him an excuse to adopt various guises over the course of the story (including, of course, a fop with a quizzing glass). The Aspirational Blonde is Margaret (Virginia Mayo, fittingly pale, bland, and cloying), who's been abducted by the pirates and held for ransom because she's actually the Princess of . . . somewhere, we're never really told. Facts, meh: the story's just a framework for a torrent of gags. The jokes start to get good when Walter Brennan shows up in the pirate crew, playing a crazy coot named Featherhead with unholy glee. He helps Sylvester and Margaret escape and sends them off on a cockamamie mission to dig up Hook's buried treasure.

The escapees sail their dinghy to the pirate port of Casarouge, where after various mock-frightening encounters with the town's scurvy citizens, they run afoul of the colonial governor, the oleaginous La Roche, who's played by the fine Austrian actor Walter Slezak making his Hollywood debut in a comic role tinged with menace—his specialty. In fact, he made such a strong impression in this film that he spent the rest of the '40s playing wily villains in historical adventures. Pirate Hook reappears and bellows a lot, Featherhead pops out of a wardrobe and tattoos a treasure map on Sylvester's chest, Margaret sings a song, and there's a good deal of chasing around inside the governor's mansion. It's pretty funny, actually, until a dumb deus-ex-machina ending invalidates all of Sylvester's reluctant heroism. Walk the plank for that one, writers.

THE PRINCESS BRIDE

Rating: ★★★★★ (Essential) • *Origin:* USA, 1987 • *Director:* Rob Reiner • *Source:* MGM DVD

There are very few near-perfect films, particularly in action genres like swashbuckler movies, which are often fun but a shade less than smart. *The Princess Bride* exceeds all such expectations—for our kind of film, it's as good as it gets, and that's very, very good, indeed.

William Goldman's classic 1973 novel had been optioned early and often for movie adaptations, and there were several attempts to bring it to the screen that fell through before director Rob Reiner was able to pull a production together with the backing of Norman Lear—the lesson here being that if something's worth doing, it's better to do it right than to do it fast. Reiner, who had loved the book ever since his father, Carl Reiner, had given him a copy as a gift, worked closely with Goldman to adapt his novel to a screenplay. The casting was handled with similar care: Cary Elwes was approached to play Westley, and as he'd grown up with the novel and dreamed of playing its hero, he jumped at the chance. The rest of the ensemble fell into place quickly, thought it wasn't until almost the last minute that novice Robin Wright was found for the part of Buttercup. With her addition, the cast was perfect.

The Princess Bride Author's Collection

That set the pattern. Costumes, sets, and locations, mostly in Derbyshire, England, are also perfect. The film's pacing, never rushed but never slow, with just the right amount of time spent on each scene, is likewise perfect. The signature rapier duel between Inigo Montoya (Mandy Patinkin) and Westley as the Dread Pirate Roberts, directed by Bob Anderson and Peter Diamond (*Star Wars, Highlander*), is a perfect distillation of every cinematic duel of the twentieth century, Anderson and Diamond's magnum opus. Goldman's sharp and endlessly quotable script, witty and light yet touching and even moving, is perfect. Even the monster puppets, the shrieking eels and the Rodents of Unusual Size, could not be improved upon.

But the most important perfect thing about *The Princess Bride* is its tone—so hard to define, so very difficult to maintain. The tone of this film, passionate, heroic, lighthearted in the face of deadly danger, perfectly encapsulates not just the swashbuckling genre, but its ethos. The brilliant framing sequence in which Peter Falk reads the story to his grandson couches the tale as a fable, but its characters and events reflect the challenges of the real world, and they offer a solution: sticking to a personal code of behavior that enables someone to be a hero when facing evil and injustice. When you're a true swashbuckler—like Westley, like Inigo, like Fezzik, and like Buttercup—you do what you know is right regardless of opposition, you stick with your friends, and you face danger with a laugh and a quip.

But you know all that already: that's why you're here. It was kind of you to read this, since it tells you things you already know. It's the movie that matters: go watch it again.

PRINCE VALIANT

Rating: ★★★☆☆ • *Origin:* USA, 1954 • *Director:* Henry Hathaway • *Source:* 20th Century Fox DVD

When I was a kid, Sunday morning meant the eagerly awaited color comics section of the *Akron Beacon Journal*, and the comic I always turned to first was *Prince Valiant*. Hal Foster's adventure tale, set "In the Days of King Arthur," was gorgeously designed, told an endless story of nearly adult caliber, had engaging characters, and was epic in scope yet ambitious in its attempt to get the details of medieval life credible and accurate. (Its historical setting was highly fictitious, of course, but the Arthur tales are legend, not history.) *Prince Valiant* was arguably the greatest American adventure strip of the twentieth century.

The movie adaptation is . . . not as great. However, it's also not nearly as terrible as its reputation, which rests mainly on how doofy Robert Wagner looks in a black pageboy wig, and how badly miscast the talented Sterling Hayden is as Val's mentor, Sir Gawain. The rest of the cast is quite good, led by James Mason as the treacherous Sir Brack and Janet Leigh as the feisty Aleta, backed up by Debra Paget as Princess Ilene and the ursine Victor McLaglen as Boltar the Viking. The direction by Henry Hathaway is solid, especially in the action sequences, and Franz Waxman delivers his usual top-notch score.

So why is this movie so roundly sneered at? Its problems are twofold. First, it seems somebody at the studio thought that because it was adapted from a comic strip, its tone needed to be juvenile, like a *Boy's Own* adventure book, with everything clichéd and obvious. Second, though there's nothing more English than King Arthur and the Knights of the Round Table, there was nobody more gosh-darned American than Sterling Hayden and Robert Wagner (unless it was Tony Curtis, who almost got Wagner's part). Every time they open their mouths, you hear New Jersey.

The first two-thirds of the movie are basically a standard Hollywood squire-learning-to-be-a-knight picture but with dialogue that's even worse than usual. The only twist on the formula is that Val is a Viking prince from "Scandia" (clever, eh?), so there's extra snobbery because he's a northern barbarian. The flick briefly turns into a silly romantic farce when both Val and Gawain fall for Aleta, and for 20 cringe-worthy minutes, the movie looks doomed—until James Mason saves the day by being a right evil, scheming bastard.

Literally. Though illegitimate, Sir Brack has royal blood, and he's been plotting to usurp Arthur's throne. Brack's cut a deal with the wicked Viking Sligon—the same brute who deposed Val's father, which is why Dad had sent Val to Camelot. The deal is to lend Brack a Viking army in exchange for Prince Valiant, the last heir to Sligon's stolen throne. The scheming Sir Brack tricks Val into leaving Camelot, whereupon he's captured and taken to Scandia.

And suddenly it's like we're in a whole different movie, an exciting action-adventure that's not doofy at all. Val, his parents, and Aleta (who'd gone after him) get clapped by Sligon into a grim dungeon, condemned to be tortured and then crucified. Boltar is outside in the town, rallying the loyal Vikings to attack Sligon's castle and save their true rulers, but the effort is doomed without someone on the inside to change the odds. Val, locked in a dungeon cell with no way out, suddenly transforms from a naive patsy into the bold and clever trickster of the comic strip—it's like a switch got flipped. In a thrilling extended action sequence, Val escapes from his cell, signals the loyal Vikings to attack, drenches half of Sligon's defenders in their own flaming whale oil, duels Sligon to the death for possession of the Singing Sword, his birthright, and frees his parents and Aleta before the burning fortress can collapse on top of them. It's brilliant. After that, returning to Camelot to challenge Sir Brack to trial by combat seems almost an afterthought.

As a final aside, let's take a moment to address the controversial yet hilarious subject of horned helmets. They'd been part of the popular image of Vikings since Wagner's operas, and there had been quite a few modestly horned helms in the 1928 silent epic *The Viking*, though historians had little or no evidence for them. Since Prince Valiant was a Nordic prince, there were plenty of Vikings in Foster's comic strip, though the only character to sport a prominently horned helm was Boltar, whose role was, after all, to be a larger-than-life jovial giant. But the costume designers on this feature film seemingly looked at Boltar's headgear and decided that was the way to go, and boy howdy, did they go there: so many horned heads! When the Vikings come ashore in *Prince Valiant*, it looks like a stampede of longhorn cattle. It's kind of adorable, really.

THE PRINCE WHO WAS A THIEF

Rating: ★★★☆☆ • *Origin:* USA, 1951 • *Director:* Rudolph Maté •
Source: ATI Entertainment DVD

This is the first of many sword-swinging starring roles for Tony Curtis, whom you really can't avoid if you're watching historical adventures made in the 1950s. Everybody mocks Curtis, and it's somewhat deserved, since he didn't have the smarts of a Burt Lancaster or even a Louis Hayward, but he wasn't terrible so much as mediocre. Somebody was persuaded that Curtis was movie star material, but it took Hollywood about 10 years to figure out that he was best employed as a reliable second banana. Fortunately, he's offset in this film by engaging performances from Everett Sloane and Piper Laurie, who even this early in her career knew exactly what she was doing.

As he had done in *Prince of Foxes*, Sloane excels at playing a thief and assassin, though here he does so with a comic touch he didn't get to show in the earlier film. Hired to kill the infant Dey of Tangier so the child's wicked uncle can assume the throne, when the time comes, he can't do it, so he fakes the murder and takes the child to raise as his own. As in all tales of a rightful monarch raised in obscurity, we know how it's going to end, so the pleasures or disappointments come in getting from here to there, and this time the trip is mostly worthwhile. The boy grows up to become Julna (Curtis), the city's greatest thief, who is fixated on its greatest prize, the treasury vault where the false dey stores the gold his tax collectors wrest from the people. The business of thieving gets a proper workout in this movie, and Julna's exploits evoke the young Conan the Barbarian or a *Dungeons & Dragons* rogue. The whole thing is shot on soundstages, with no exteriors at all, just the ever-dark city streets and the moody lamp-lit interiors that surround and tower over them.

In proper *Thief of Bagdad* fashion, while escaping some guards, Julna goes where he shouldn't and casts his eyes on forbidden fruit: his beautiful cousin the Princess Yasmin (Peggie Castle). The thief is smitten with the snotty princess, but as soon as he cute-meets another thief, Tina (Piper Laurie), during a bungled jewel robbery, we know she's really the one for him. The barely legal Laurie, slippery as an eel and cute as a bug, is a wide-eyed naïf who speaks of herself in the third person like an *Elder Scrolls* Khajiit and is just as adorably avaricious. Lissome and energetic, she effortlessly matches Curtis's considerable athleticism, usually while squealing with glee. She's a delight.

Though based on a story by Theodore Dreiser (of all people), the plot is standard-issue claptrap, with mistaken identities, intrigue in the dey's court, and an egg-sized pearl the possession of which is the key to marrying the snotty princess. There are several unnecessary scenes of "oriental" dancing by scantily clad women, but to be fair there's also a lot of gratuitous swimming by the bare-chested Curtis. The thefts and pursuits are interspersed with gags, but about half of them fall flat, often because they rely on lines such as "Begone, you sons of she-camels!" Sad stuff, but the scene where the thieves use geese as projectiles is charming. After enough hijinks, Julna is revealed as the rightful dey—he has a tattoo *and* a scar, to make doubly sure—the snotty princess is packed off, and Tina is forced to take a bath so she can be properly married. Ending with a marriage: in classical terms, that's what makes it a comedy, right?

THE PRISONER OF ZENDA (1922)

Rating: ★★★☆☆ • *Origin:* USA, 1922 • *Director:* Rex Ingram • *Source:* Warner Bros. DVD

Ramon Novarro as Rupert of Hentzau in *The Prisoner of Zenda* (1922) WIKIMEDIA COMMONS

This film, the third silent movie adaptation of Anthony Hope's best-selling 1894 novel (the first two are lost, alas), features craggy-faced Lewis Stone in the dual parts of Rudolf Rassendyll and King Rudolf, parts he had also played in the theatrical version this film was based on. Even better than Stone is Ramon Novarro, in his breakout role as the villain Rupert of Hentzau. Every version of *Zenda* is stolen by the engaging rogue Rupert, and this is no exception—and Novarro's raffish charm in the part made him a star. The movie starts slow, and its talky set pieces betray the production's origins as a stage play, but the emphasis on interiors and close-ups gives plenty of scope for mugging by an array of fine silent-screen character actors. A great deal of effort was put into Ruritanian pomp and display that hasn't aged well, and the story doesn't really pick up until over an hour into it— but once the action starts, there's actually more swordplay than in the better-known 1937 and 1952 versions. The last 40 minutes definitely redeem the previous 70, and the fencing in the climax is better than anything seen previously in the silent era. Visual bonus: monocles and jodhpurs!

THE PRISONER OF ZENDA (1937)

Rating: ★★★★★ • *Origin:* USA, 1937 • *Director:* John Cromwell • *Source:* Warner Bros. DVD

David Selznick bought the rights to *The Prisoner of Zenda* as a starring vehicle for Ronald Colman, who was at the height of his fame just after *Lost Horizon* (1937). Colman plays the dual role of Rudolf Rassendyll and King Rudolf, and Selznick surrounds him with a first-rate cast, including the glowing Madeleine Carroll as Princess Flavia, and C. Aubrey Smith and his whiskers as the king's loyal Colonel Zapt. But best of all are the villains: Raymond Massey, looming and ominous as the would-be usurper Black Michael, and Douglas Fairbanks Jr., as the raffish rogue Rupert of Hentzau, stealing every scene he appears in (as Rupert does in every version of *Zenda*).

The story sticks pretty closely to that of Anthony Hope's 1894 novel—and if you're not familiar with it, why are you wasting time reading this? (Side note: the best of Hope's Zenda short stories is included in my anthology, *The Big Book of Swashbuckling Adventure.*) On the eve of his coronation, King Rudolf of Ruritania is kidnapped, but his loyal aides convince his lookalike English cousin to stand in for him. While impersonating his royal cousin, Rassendyll falls in love with the king's betrothed, Princess Flavia—and she with him. Heartbreak ahead! Meanwhile, good guys Colonel Zapt and Fritz von Tarlenheim (a very young David Niven) engage in a desperate dance with the villains, as nice and nasty try to outmaneuver each other before their various threats and ultimatums erupt in violence.

Besides the brilliant performances, there's so much to love in this movie: drugged wine, secret passages, throwing knives, and brooding Castle Zenda, so medievally murderous it's practically a character unto itself. The outrageous helmets and embroidery-crusted uniforms of the Ruritanian nobility and guards cannot be improved upon. And everybody wears monocles! So fine.

In the end it all comes down to swordplay, of course, in a climactic duel filmed by James Wong Howe, who projected the duel-

The Prisoner of Zenda (1938) WIKIMEDIA COMMONS

ists' shadows thrice life-size on the inner walls of Castle Zenda. (Yes, this is where that trope originated.) The Oscar-nominated soundtrack by Alfred Newman was so good it was reused in the 1952 remake. Fun fact: when the first theatrical production of *Zenda* was the hit of the London stage in 1896, the dual role of Rudolf and Rassendyll was played by . . . C. Aubrey Smith (pre-whiskers!).

THE PRISONER OF ZENDA (1952)

Rating: ★★★★☆ • *Origin:* USA, 1952 • *Director:* Richard Thorpe •
Source: Warner Bros. DVD

If you want to recapture the essence of a classic movie in a new version, I guess a shot-for-shot remake is one approach. The 1952 *Zenda* used the same shooting script as the 1937 version with just a few changes, and even a cursory comparison shows that scenes, setups, and shooting angles are virtually the same in both. They even repurposed Alfred Newman's excellent score from the earlier film. But though the newer version is just as well made as its predecessor, it lacks some of the spark or spirit of the Ronald Colman film. Why is that? The qualities of the '37 version certainly weren't the result of spontaneity or serendipity—it was shot, cut, reshot, and recut until the studio finally had what it wanted. And *Zenda* already had a long history in stage and film, with three previous silent versions. Perhaps it was that the '37 version aspired to be better than what had gone before, while the '52 version only aimed to be as good—and that just wasn't aiming high enough.

The story is still great, and there's no denying that Ruritania and its comic-opera uniforms look better in Technicolor, even if we miss James Wong Howe's dueling shadows. But a *Zenda* stands or falls on its hero, the twin cousin Rudolfs, and their nemesis, Rupert of Hentzau. The '37 version had the mature Ronald Colman as Rudolf playing off the brash young Douglas Fairbanks Jr. as Hentzau. The '52 remake flips this, pitting the energetic young Stewart Granger as Rudolf against the seasoned and sophisticated James Mason as Hentzau—and yes, it works. Granger is confident and likeable and lithe enough for some acrobatic swashbuckling. Furthermore, like Basil Rathbone and Cornel Wilde, he's a serious fencer: Mason had to be doubled by an expert in the final, heart-stopping saber duel in Zenda Castle, but it's Granger all the way. Put a sword in Granger's hand, and Colman is eclipsed.

Ah, but when it comes to the love story, the sly and nuanced Colman easily outdoes the new guy. Nonetheless, Deborah Kerr as the new Princess Flavia holds her own compared to Madeleine Carroll and maybe even edges her out. As for the rest of the supporting cast—Louis Calhern, Robert Douglas, and others—they all carry their weight, but can they compare with Raymond Massey, David Niven, and C. Aubrey Smith? Sorry—there the '37 entry gets the nod. That said, the Granger version is still top-notch entertainment, and who doesn't want to pop a monocle over one eye and spend another two hours in Ruritania? Bonus: watch for craggy old Lewis Stone playing the Cardinal of Strelsau—Stone, the man who starred as the twin Rudolfs in the silent 1922 version!

THE PRISONER OF ZENDA (1979)

Rating: ★★☆☆☆ • *Origin:* US, 1979 • *Director:* Richard Quine • *Source:* Fabulous DVD

Peter Sellers was one of the greatest comic actors in the history of film. It's a shame to see him, at nearly the end of his career, involved in this tedious and ill-considered mistake.

This movie attempts to take Anthony Hope's Victorian-era romantic adventure and make it a comedy by inverting some of its key assumptions. But then they forgot to make it funny. In the original story, the double of imperiled King Rudolf of Ruritania is a dashing English gentleman; here, as a twist, the double is a stolid and rather dull London cabdriver named Sydney Frewin. Sellers plays both Rudolf and Frewin, but where the king is a hilariously irresponsible aristocratic twit, the cabby is a matter-of-fact salt-of-the-earth workman who greets danger with a shrug and drains the zest out of every situation. After the king is kidnapped and the cabby takes his place, Frewin must face not only the assassins sent by the king's half brother Prince Michael (Jeremy Kemp) but also the jealous husband of a countess (Elke Sommer) who keeps trying to get into his bed. Yes, they added a bedroom farce. Sound like a good time? It isn't.

Another inversion is to take Michael's scoundrel accomplice, Rupert of Hentzau (Stuart Wilson), and change him from one of the most engaging rogues in swashbuckler fiction into an arrogant private-school bully with an irritating laugh. (His laugh is so irritating that Frewin even points it out, just in case you'd missed it.) Thanks for that.

In general, the jokes are weak, every gag is telegraphed a mile off, and worse, this movie just plods. Okay, there is exactly one funny scene, when two groups of conspirators get confused signaling to each other in the dark woods with owl hoots and chicken clucks. Lionel Jeffries is fine as the mutton-chopped old royal retainer Colonel Sapt, and Kemp is pretty good as Prince Michael. And they spent a jillion dollars on the costumes and sets, which include Schönbrunn Palace in Austria, but elaborate costumes and sets don't make a comedy any funnier. Toward the end, the movie gives up on the jokes and tries to slide back into romantic adventure, but Peter Sellers, for all his many talents, is no swashbuckling action hero, and it just doesn't work out. What a misbegotten mess.

THE PRIVATE LIVES OF ELIZABETH AND ESSEX

Rating: ★★★☆☆ • *Origin:* USA, 1938 • *Director:* Michael Curtiz • *Source:* Warner Bros. DVD

This film tells the story of the doomed romance between Queen Elizabeth I (Bette Davis) and the Earl of Essex (Errol Flynn), their love thwarted by the machinations of rival courtiers and by the lovers' own unbending pride. Based on a hit 1930 play by Maxwell Anderson, it's darker and talkier than most Flynn vehicles, and Bette Davis famously didn't want him for the male lead role, afraid he didn't have the dramatic chops for it. She preferred Laurence Olivier—but as it happened the part suited Flynn and he did just fine, as Davis herself admitted years later.

Elizabeth and the much younger Essex adore each other but can't get along because each is ambitious to rule. As a result, Essex is always getting sent away from Court, and when separated he and Elizabeth gnash their teeth and pine and yearn. Meanwhile in the halls of the palace, quarreling and conspiring, are the royal courtiers, vicious rivals to Essex

Errol Flynn in *The Private Lives of Elizabeth and Essex*
Jrodsquad—Own work, CC BY-SA 4.0 / Wikimedia Commons

played by a fine bunch of English actors, including Henry Stephenson, Donald Crisp, and Henry Daniell—though all are overshadowed by the delightfully supercilious Vincent Price as Sir Walter Raleigh. Wow, he's good, even when wearing ridiculous silver armor and pink trunk hose for the purpose of being mocked for it by Essex. Also at Court is Olivia de Havilland as a lady-in-waiting who's pining for Essex, but her brains and poise are mostly wasted here, as the role gives her little scope for them. At least she gets to be called a "brazen wench" and "shameless baggage" by Davis.

This is a top-of-the-line production, in brilliant Technicolor, with fabulous costumes by Orry-Kelly and a swooning score by Erich Wolfgang Korngold. It looks great. The bickering between Elizabeth and Essex does get tiresome, though to their credit Davis and Flynn manage to carry it off. By the time the smirking courtiers manipulate Essex into undertaking a hopeless invasion of Ireland, we're ready for some swordplay as a break from the wordplay. Of course, it all goes wrong, as invading Ireland is always a sucker move. And there among the bogs, Essex is defeated by—oh, ignominy of ignominies—the wretched Alan Hale Sr. as Lord Tyrone. Beaten, Essex returns to England and yet more angst. There's still a good deal of playwright Anderson's talk before the final, tragic end—and fine talk it is too. You might like it.

RAIDERS OF THE SEVEN SEAS

Rating: ★★★☆☆ • *Origin:* USA, 1953 • *Director:* Sidney Salkow • *Source:* MGM DVD

Pirate captain Barbarossa (John Payne), in service to the sultan of Morocco, gets too frisky in the harem and escapes just ahead of the headsman. He captures a Spanish slave ship by freeing the enslaved convicts and sails it to the Caribbean, where he accepts French letters of marque so he can harry the Spaniards further. (They were mean to him in his backstory.) Putting the freed slaves into phony breakaway irons, Barbarossa brings them into Tortuga to "sell" and then frees them again and takes Tortuga away from the Spanish—in the process capturing the haughty Countess Alida (Donna Reed), the port's acting governor. (No, really.) Barbarossa falls for the countess, which gives her the opportunity to escape to her rotten Spanish fiancé— but she'll be sorry she did. Crosses and double crosses ensue.

It's pretty entertaining for an indie-produced Hollywood B picture, a bit sloppy here and there but overall quite solid. Donna Reed takes the acting prize, summoning her inner spitfire to try to measure up to her model Maureen O'Hara. John Payne is rather stiff, not looking as comfortable here as he did in Western and detective flicks except when he goes into disguise as a one-eyed sea dog out to collect a ransom—really, he would have made a decent character actor. Speaking of which, good ol' Lon Chaney himself appears as a peg-legged mate named (what else?) Pegleg. The fencing is decent, the color cinematography is good, the mocking and merciless Spaniards get what's coming to them, and if the ship models are a trifle cheesy and the cannons the pirates haul ashore to assault Havana with seem to be painted balsa wood, well, we can shrug it off just this once, eh, matey?

RAN

Rating: ★★★★★ • *Origin:* Japan/France, 1985 • *Director:* Akira Kurosawa •
Source: StudioCanal Blu-ray

Writer-director Akira Kurosawa's final historical epic, *Ran* is at the same time one of the greatest war and antiwar movies ever made. Though set in Japan's Warring States period, this is not a samurai *chambara* adventure like *Seven Samurai*, but a grand Shakespearean tragedy—in fact, its story is adapted from *King Lear*, though Kurosawa's initial inspiration was a tale from Japanese history.

The aging Lord Hidetora (Tatsuya Nakadai) has spent his life in warfare, conquering his neighbors step by bloody step until finally he rules the entire fertile Azusa plain and the mountains that surround it. But Hidetora is tired of war and decides to abdicate his power to his three adult sons, dividing his holdings between them while retaining his privileges and title as Great Lord. His eldest son Taro (Akira Terao), who will receive the greatest inheritance, is in favor of this, as is the next son, Jiro (Jinpachi Nezu), but the third son, Saburo (Daisuke Ryo), bluntly denounces it as the irrational act of a madman—for isn't Hidetora's world based on nothing but the gaining and holding of power? Hidetora is outraged, banishes Saburo, and then goes to live in glorified retirement at Taro's castle. But Taro is married to Lady Kaede (Mieko Harada), the vengeful daughter of the lord Hidetora slew to complete his conquest of Azusa. Kaede agitates Taro into driving Hidetora away—and when he tries to relocate to Jiro's domain, he finds himself unwelcome there as well. Hidetora and his last few retainers are granted Saburo's old castle, but it's a trap—he's betrayed by one of his own vassals, who is working for Kaede, and his men are slaughtered, his castle sacked and burned. In the fighting, Taro is treacherously killed by one of Jiro's men, leaving the second son on top, but Hidetora, stricken, escapes the fire and staggers off unseeing into the volcanic wasteland that surrounds the castle.

There's a lot more to follow, and by the end everyone receives their comeuppance (Shakespearean tragedy, you know), but before that are some of the most magnificent samurai battle scenes ever filmed. The horrific siege and massacre at Hidetora's castle are shown almost entirely without sound except for the heartrending music of Toru Takemitsu's dark, searing soundtrack, and it is unforgettable. That grim episode is offset later by the bright victory of Saburo's troops over Jiro's much larger force, who are out to take the raving Hidetora's head. Here Kurosawa delivers a master class in how massed troops in formation moving against each other in combat can be depicted with absolute visual clarity. Much of this is due to Kurosawa's striking use of color to identify the four different forces involved, despite the inevitable tumult of battle.

The great Tatsuya Nakadai as Lord Hidetora, his face makeup like a rigid Noh mask of age, plays his demanding role almost entirely physically, through posture and gesture. The most intense performance comes from Harada as Lady Kaede who, icy one moment and fiery the next, dominates every scene in which she appears. The famously androgynous entertainer Peter appears in the important role of Hidetora's fool Kyoami, who laments the madness of human pride and treachery. But the real star is always Kurosawa's unerring eye for composition, movement, light, and color—you could take any shot from this film and frame it on the wall. It's a masterpiece.

RASHOMON

Rating: ★★★★★ • *Origin:* Japan, 1950 • *Director:* Akira Kurosawa • *Source:* Criterion DVD

Although this is director Akira Kurosawa's first famous samurai film, it arguably doesn't belong in the Cinema of Swords as it's not really a *chambara*—a swordplay movie—but rather a historical crime tale. You probably have a general idea of what it's about even if you've never seen it, as its title has come to stand for the principle of the unreliable narrator, the same story told differently from several different viewpoints. In this case it's the history of a crime, a rape and a murder in a lonely grove on a remote wooded mountain. The tale is told from four different points of view, and viewers are left to tease out the truth for themselves.

The film stars Kurosawa's favorite leading man, Toshiro Mifune, as a fierce and antic bandit, a character that prefigures his unforgettable Kikuchiyo in *The Seven Samurai*, and several other actors familiar from that masterpiece show up as well. It's a striking movie, gorgeously shot in a sun-dappled forest and a relentless downpour, displaying the firm grasp Kurosawa had of the moviemaking art even this early in his long career. There's even a touch of the ghost

Rasho-Mon RKO Radio Pictures / Wikimedia Commons

story to it, as the murdered man tells his own version of events. And of course, there is that one pivotal sword duel between the samurai (Masayuki Mori) and Mifune's bandit—which is one more than you'll find in swashbuckler *The Scarlet Pimpernel* (1935), so I guess this film qualifies after all.

RED LION

Rating: ★★★★☆ • *Origin:* Japan, 1969 • *Director:* Kihachi Okamoto • *Source:* Warrior DVD

Kihachi Okamoto, who directed the excellent *chambara* parody *Kill!*, returns with what seems to be, at first blush, an outright samurai comedy. It's coproduced by and stars Toshiro Mifune, who we've seen can be slyly funny in movies such as *Sanjuro*, but here he plays a straight-up comic character, a warrior named Gonzo who is as strong as he is dimwitted, speaks with an awkward stutter, and is emotional about everything. He's brilliant.

It's 1868, and the Tokugawa shogunate is finally falling to the forces of the Imperial Restoration, starting in the capital of Edo, where crowds of commoners dance in delirious celebration, chanting, "It's alright! It's alright! Why not?" Gonzo is a soldier in the Sekiho Brigade, which supports the emperor's restoration, a unit known as the Red Lions for the shaggy scarlet helmet covers worn by their officers. The imperial troops are gradually spreading their revolution to rural Japan, and when Gonzo sees that they're planning to march through his home village, he boldly requests permission to ride ahead and bring them the good news—and can he please borrow his captain's red headpiece?

Gonzo, armed with leaflets proclaiming that land taxes will be halved and debts forgiven, rides for his village, where he finds that the old, corrupt ways of the shogunate are still in force: the local deputy is extorting double taxes out of the peasants, the yakuza moneylender charges predatory rates, and families who can't pay are coerced into selling their women into bondage at the brothel. With his news of a New World Order, Gonzo hits his hometown like a hurricane, encouraging the local young idealists to fight for the imperial cause, redistributing the stolen rice from the tax collector's warehouse, and liberating the debt-ridden prostitutes from the brothel—one of whom is Tomi (Shima Iwashita), Gonzo's childhood sweetheart. The villagers are thrilled. But though the old bosses are intimidated by this stuttering force of nature, there are others who aren't impressed. This includes ronin-for-hire Hanzo (Etsushi Takahashi), who accepts money from the bosses to kill Gonzo, and a secret cadre of shogunate agents known as Mobile Unit One, who are waiting to assassinate the leaders of the advancing imperial forces.

And suddenly the story's tone grows darker, as the agents and the bosses start to turn the villagers against Gonzo, playing on their fears and suspicions and hoodwinking the simple warrior. However, Gonzo fights back, proving himself, and even sends some of the young idealists out to welcome the oncoming Sekiho Brigade and guide them into town. But the young villagers ride into the imperial camp to find no Red Lions, only white lions—the Sekiho Brigade is no more, disbanded, its officers beheaded after being accused of overreaching and pandering to the peasants. Tax cuts and debt forgiveness are all repudiated, and it's clear the new masters will be no better than the old ones, if not worse. The young villagers are shot down, all but one who rides, mortally wounded, back to town to warn Gonzo what's coming.

A squad of imperial riflemen follow the rider back to the village, and though Gonzo, joined by Hanzo, cuts them down, he has no chance against an entire advancing army. Utterly betrayed, things can't end well for Gonzo—but his legacy will live on, as he's taught the villagers how powerful they can be if they all act together. "It's alright! It's alright! Why not?"

RED SONJA

Rating: ★☆☆☆☆ • *Origin:* Netherlands/USA, 1985 • *Director:* Richard Fleischer •
Source: StudioCanal DVD

Set in Conan-creator Robert E. Howard's Hyborian Age, with Arnold Schwarzenegger top-billed, this is essentially the third Conan movie, and it shows how a series can go from self-important to self-parody in just three pictures. A number of talented people worked on this movie, but nonetheless it stinks like a dead fish from head to tail.

The backstory of title character Red Sonja (Brigitte Nielsen) is such a sword-and-sorcery cliché that the film doesn't even bother to expend a full scene on it; it's just summarized in a quick flashback: An evil tyrant burns her family farmstead, kills her parents, and leaves Sonja for dead. She's awakened by a goddess who looks like a cloudy version of Glinda the Good Witch and who magically endows Sonja with strength and fighting skill, which is condescending as fudge: can't a woman learn to fight well without divine intervention? Vengeance is duly vowed, plus Sonja swears, "No man may have me unless he has beaten me in a fair fight"— which elevates her sexual availability above her fighting skills, so don't feel threatened by the strong woman, lads, this film has its priorities in order. Plus there's eye candy: Sonja may not wear a chain mail bikini like in the comics, but her outfit is still plenty skimpy without any of that unbecoming armor stuff.

There's a plot, of sorts: evil Queen Gedren (Sandahl Bergman, who'd turned down the role of Sonja), the tyrant who'd killed Sonja's parents, sends her troops to a temple shaped like a traffic cone to slaughter its priestesses and obtain a glowing green beach ball called the Talisman, which has the power to destroy the world. Coincidentally, Sonja's sister is one of the priestesses and the only one to escape, though she lives just long enough to tell her tale to a beefy warrior named Kalidor (Schwarzenegger), who sets out to find Sonja and bring her up to speed. Sonja has just completed her weapons training in the arena of the Statue of the Pooping Buddha, and she thanks Kalidor for his warning but then, in a few wooden and emotionless lines, refuses his aid in going after Gedren.

As soon as she opens her mouth, it's clear that Brigitte Nielsen is awful, possibly the worst actor to appear in any of the three Conan-et-al. films, and that's saying something. As for the rest of the cast, look: at this point in his career Schwarzenegger is still learning his trade as an actor, yet he has more screen presence than everyone else in this picture put together. Veteran director Richard Fleischer, faced with this script and this cast, seems to have simply shrugged and given up. He made only one more movie after this one, a promotional tie-in for Glad-Lock trash bags, the final act of a broken man.

Fortunately for Sonja, Kalidor won't take no for an answer and keeps showing up to help her out every time she gets in a fix. Sonja collects two other sidekicks, a child ruler whom Gedren has dethroned, but who's meant to be endearing, and his pudgy bodyguard, who keeps talking about going on a diet. Are there worse sidekicks in any 1980s barbarian movie? I don't think so. Meanwhile, Gedren hasn't figured out that a plan to conquer the world with a weapon that will destroy the world is the worst plan, so Sonja and her sidekicks decide to infiltrate her Evil Palace to steal the Talisman just as the world-destroying earthquakes start shakin'. Cue the climax! Alas, in addition to being unable to act, Brigitte Nielsen can't fence a lick; in their final confrontation it's clear that Sandahl Bergman is holding herself back from mopping the floor with her. In fact, the only person who comes out well from involvement in this travesty is composer Ennio Morricone, who delivered a jaunty and adventurous score. Go look for his soundtrack album and give the movie a hard pass.

RED SUN

Rating: ★★★★☆ • *Origin:* France/Italy/Spain, 1971 • *Director:* Terence Young •
Source: Evergreen Entertainment DVD

Given all the cross-fertilization between the *chambara* and Spaghetti Western genres, in hindsight it seems inevitable that someone would make a Spaghetti Western with samurai in it. This one stars Charles Bronson and Toshiro Mifune as the protagonists, with Alain Delon as the villain and Ursula Andress as the female lead.

The American West in 1860: a steam locomotive chuffs across the wild country pulling passenger cars, a mail car with a shipment of government gold, a cavalry troop to protect it, and a diplomatic car transporting the first Japanese ambassador to the United States. Among the passengers are members of a bandit gang led by Link (Bronson) and Gauche (Delon) who stop the train; a diversionary attack gets the cavalry out of their car, and then the bandits drive off with the train and leave them behind. They steal $400,000 in gold, rob the passengers and then the ambassador, taking his money and a gold-hilted Japanese sword meant as a gift for the US president. One of the two samurai guards is shot and killed by Gauche, and the other, Kuroda (Mifune), vows revenge.

Meanwhile, Gauche casually betrays Link, blowing him out of the train with dynamite, and rides off with the loot. But Link jumped when he saw the TNT coming and survived, only to be captured by Kuroda when he revives. The ambassador tasks Kuroda and Link with recovering the sword and gives them seven days to do it, or Kuroda will have to commit ritual suicide. "That's something I'd like to see," says Link, but Kuroda promises him he won't be alive to see it.

And now comes the real fun, as the captive outlaw leads the samurai warrior, very much out of his element, in pursuit of Gauche, the gold, and the sword. The two are initially contemptuous of each other, and Link isn't shy about showing it. Though unarmed, the gunfighter is confident he'll be able to escape Kuroda, but he finds that he can't outrun him, outfox him, or even outfight him when he challenges the samurai to put down his swords and battle it out on equal terms. (Jiu jitsu, y'all.) By the time they catch up with some of Gauche's gang and appropriate their guns and horses, Link has learned respect for the samurai and doesn't shoot Kuroda out of hand—though he does insist that the samurai promise not to kill Gauche until Link has had enough time to force him to say where he's hidden the bulk of the gold.

They lose Gauche's trail, so Link decides to go to the small town of San Lucas because he's sure Gauche will show up there to visit his lover, a prostitute named Cristina (Andress). But Gauche doesn't come personally, instead sending some of his toughest men to pick up Cristina, and in the ensuing fight in a brothel, Link's own skills earn Kuroda's grudging respect. They take Cristina hostage and set off to lure Gauche out of his mountain lair, a plan complicated by crossing paths with a war band of Comanche renegades.

This is a fine action film, confidently overseen by the British director Terence Young, who'd helmed three of the first four Bond movies starring Sean Connery. Despite being a pair of stone-faced grunters, Bronson and Mifune have real chemistry together and show some wry wit as their disdain changes to mutual regard. Delon is a stylish villain in his dapper gambler's suit and black gloves, someone you can't root for but have to admire. Despite being second-billed behind Bronson, Andress isn't given much to do, and her role is mostly ornamental. Bronson was at the height of his fame in Europe and Japan, and this film played for a record-setting 35 weeks at a first-run theater in Tokyo. Give it a squint.

THE RETURN OF MONTE CRISTO

Rating: ★★☆☆☆ • *Origin:* USA, 1946 • *Director:* Henry Levin •
Source: Firecake Entertainment DVD

Louis Hayward spent the war in the US Marines, and was at Tarawa; afterward he returned to making swashbucklers but with an edge he hadn't had before. Interestingly, though produced by the same company and with the same star, *The Return of Monte Cristo* is *not* a sequel to 1940's *Son of Monte Cristo*. The latter, set in 1865, was about the late count's son (obviously), while *Return*, which begins in 1868, features another heir entirely, the count's grandnephew. Thus Edward Small, who produced the hit 1934 *Count of Monte Cristo*, made two alternative and mutually exclusive sequels to it in the '40s. Do their inconsistencies matter? Not at all!

The intro to *Return* features a bogus letter from Alexandre Dumas explaining why he decided to tell this story—which he totally didn't, but the tale's a pretty good Dumas pastiche, crafted in emulation of the original *Monte Cristo* novel (1844). When the count's grandnephew and heir, also named Edmond Dantès, goes to court to claim his vast inheritance, he's cheated out of it by three corrupt officials and sentenced, under a false name, to life imprisonment on Devil's Island. This tropical French penal colony is even worse than the Château d'If (which will make an appearance in act two), and there's no Abbé Faria to help him, so the younger Edmond Dantès is on his own. Spoiler: he manages to escape and return to France to commence a campaign of revenge. To deceive and entrap his prey, Dantès assumes various guises, such as a bank auditor, an Imperial nobleman, and a hunchbacked private investigator. To give Hayward his due, these impersonations are darned entertaining, but they can't quite carry the film, which is otherwise fairly pedestrian.

The Return of Monte Cristo is a darker film than *Son*, or even *Count*, almost a historical film noir in feel. In fact, it's probably the least swashbuckling *Monte Cristo* of all the novel's many adaptations and sequels. That said, its emphasis on vengeance is thematically more fitting than the Zenda-esque *Son of Monte Cristo*, though the latter film was a lot more fun—and it had a top-notch villain in George Sanders, something this movie lacks. In short, though Louis Hayward does his best with the material, this isn't his most successful film. Better ones will follow.

THE RETURN OF THE MUSKETEERS

Rating: ★★★☆☆ • *Origin:* UK/France/Spain, 1989 • *Director:* Richard Lester •
Source: Universal DVD

This is the belated sequel to *The Three* and *Four Musketeers* of 1973–1974, those highlights of director Richard Lester's career, an attempt to recapture the magic of those films with the same writer and largely the same cast as the originals. There have been scores of screen versions of *The Three Musketeers*, but Dumas's sequel, *Twenty Years After*, is rarely filmed, as its broad scope and wide-ranging plot aren't easily shoehorned into the feature film format. Reviews often refer to *Return* as a "loose" adaptation of the novel, but actually George MacDonald Fraser's script is remarkably faithful to Dumas's story. And that faithfulness is where it goes wrong, because trying to jam the whole book, plus new scenes featuring Cyrano de Bergerac (added, apparently, just because he could), into less than two hours was a big mistake. Fraser is one of my literary heroes, but he's blundered badly here; where his adaptation of *The Three Musketeers* unrolls across two movies and four hours at just the right pace for the material, *Return* is rushed and confused and even has added (and awkward) voice-over narration by d'Artagnan here and there to try to explain what the hell is going on. That kind of desperate ploy in a movie is nearly always an admission of storytelling failure, and it doesn't succeed here.

The original films were a near-perfect balance of drama and comedy, of action and character scenes, tense where they needed to feel dangerous and loose when conveying the happy camaraderie of the heroes. Here the balance is off, leaning too heavily on slapstick, which often feels forced and just isn't very funny. Reprising their roles as d'Artagnan, Aramis, and Porthos, Michael York, Richard Chamberlain, and Frank Finlay all seem vaguely embarrassed at being involved in what amounts to tiresome self-parody. Even the usually unflappable Christopher Lee, returning as Rochefort, seems to be wondering what he's doing in this thing. Only Oliver Reed plays his part with conviction, and as a result his Athos is the anchor to the whole picture. Reed is spot on, never lets up, and has more stature and gravitas than the rest of the cast put together.

The plot isn't easily summarized; suffice to say it involves the musketeers in exploits in civil wars in both France and England, while they try to avoid falling prey to the vengeful assassination attempts of Justine de Winter (Kim Cattrall), the now-grown daughter of Milady, archvillain of the original films. Athos's adopted son Raoul (C. Thomas Howell) is thrown into the mix to provide a young love/hate interest for Justine, but he's barely fleshed out, and his character is just as much a stuffed shirt as he is in Dumas's later novels. The less said about Howell's acting the better, and while Cattrall is energetic, she doesn't have one-tenth the screen presence of Faye Dunaway as Milady. Even the swordplay is off: though the fights are arranged by the great Bill Hobbs, who did the original films, Lester seems to have lost the touch for desperate mayhem that served him so well in *Robin and Marian* and the first *Musketeers* movies. Once in a while there are flashes of his former greatness, as in the woodland encounter between Justine and Raoul, reminiscent of Ridley Scott's work in *The Duellists*. And there's one great character scene near the end where Athos and Aramis finally get the better of the wily Cardinal Mazarin (Philippe Noiret) and extort from him the musketeers' long-overdue rewards. But mostly this movie will just make you want to go back and revisit those career-defining masterpieces whose magic it tries—and fails—to recapture.

THE RETURN OF THE SCARLET PIMPERNEL

Rating: ★★★☆☆ • *Origin:* UK, 1937 • *Director:* Hanns Schwartz • *Source:* PRS DVD

Though the celebrated 1934 version of *The Scarlet Pimpernel* is justly famous, few are aware that the film had a sequel less than three years later. There's a reason for that: though produced by the same studio, almost no one who made the first movie was involved with the second, and the journeyman cast and crew of *The Return of the Scarlet Pimpernel* were unable to recapture the magic of the original.

The story is based loosely on *The Triumph of the Scarlet Pimpernel* (1922), one of Baroness Orczy's dozen sequels to the first novel. Sir Percy has promised Lady Blakeney not to return to France and spends his time in England playing cricket, but in Paris under the tyranny of Robespierre, heads continue to fall to Mam'zelle Guillotine. Though the Scarlet Pimpernel has been exposed and confined to England, Robespierre is convinced that he's still remotely managing a network of traitors in Revolutionary France and orders Citizen Chauvelin to find a way to induce Sir Percy to come to Paris, where he can be taken and executed. Raymond Massey was busy in 1937, appearing in other costume dramas as Black Michael, King Philip

II, and Cardinal Richelieu, so Chauvelin is played this time around by the baby-faced Francis Lister, who was quite good as Prince Gaston in *Cardinal Richelieu*. But though Lister's Chauvelin is smart enough for the role, he entirely lacks Massey's menacing edge.

Before she was Lady Blakeney, Marguerite St. Just was an actress from the theatrical demimonde of Paris, so Chauvelin hatches a plot involving another actress, Theresa Cobarrus (Margaretta Scott), and sends her to England to lure Marguerite into an abduction—and so, in Brighton under false pretexts, Theresa tests her wits against those of the Blakeneys. Sir Percy is played by Barry K. Barnes, Marguerite by Sophie Stewart, and unfortunately, Leslie Howard and Merle Oberon they ain't. The script doesn't give them much to work with either—especially poor Lady Blakeney, who seems to have lost about 40 IQ points since the first film. Sir Percy comes off rather better, but Barry Barnes simply doesn't have Leslie Howard's ability to convey several simultaneous levels of nuance, and the script isn't as sharp.

To save his wife, Sir Percy is drawn back into the fray of Revolutionary Paris, and the requisite impersonations, pursuits, intrigues, and daring escapes duly follow. It's not bad—but as Sir Percy remarked in the first film, "Really, there's nothing quite so bad as something that's not bad." Watch for the young James Mason making his mark in a minor role as a revolutionary parliamentarian—radiating intensity, he stands out as the only real actor of stature in the picture. Ironically, this just diminishes the earnest but inadequate performances of the lead actors, forever eclipsed by Howard, Oberon, Massey—and Mason.

RETURN TO TREASURE ISLAND (OR *JOHN SILVER'S RETURN TO TREASURE ISLAND*)

Rating: ★★★★☆ • *Origin:* UK, 1986 • *Directors:* Piers Haggard et al. • *Source:* Network DVDs

Robert Louis Stevenson never wrote a sequel to his most influential novel, *Treasure Island* (1883), but over time plenty of others have pitched in to fill that need, including Ivor Dean, who played Long John Silver in the popular 1966 German miniseries *Die Schatzinsel* (no English-language version, alas). Dean died before he could make his *Return to Treasure Island*, but his carefully worked-out story was adapted by John Goldsmith into a screenplay for the Welsh HTV network, cofinanced by Disney for broadcast on their cable channel. And we're glad they did.

The result is a miniseries of ten 50-minute episodes that has many fine qualities, the chief of which is the casting of Brian Blessed as Silver. The best-remembered depiction of Silver is, of course, that of Robert Newton in the early 1950s, but Blessed's performance comes in a close second. The larger-than-life role of Silver calls for a characterization that plays to Blessed's strengths as a charismatic personality but also requires him to rein in that charisma and be sly, for this version of Long John is a thoroughgoing rogue. The second protagonist is the now fully grown Jim Hawkins (Christopher Guard), and he's in a tough spot holding his own opposite Blessed. It isn't easy to play a character who's earnest, well-meaning, and forthright yet not a fool, but Guard manages it. And he has the good fortune to be opposed by two delightfully ruthless and despicable villains, English scoundrel Joshua Hallows (Donald Pickering) and Spanish slave driver Superintendente Garcia (John Bennett). The rest of the cast does all right without particularly standing out, except for Kenneth Colley as Jim's sidekick, the aging and addled Ben Gunn, whose repertoire of eccentricities rapidly becomes tiresome.

The story is set 10 years after *Treasure Island,* when Jim Hawkins has just come home to the Admiral Benbow Inn from Oxford (where I believe he took a First in cutlass fencing), just as John Silver reappears with some scurvy maties intent on taking possession of Captain Flint's old treasure map. The pirates are captured and tried, and then Squire Trelawney (Bruce Purchase) persuades Jim to sail to Jamaica to sort out disturbing reports from the squire's plantation there—and when he sails, Silver, sentenced to transportation to the East Indies, sails with him. And you can bet he doesn't stay in chains for long.

This miniseries is one long, continuous story, and though every episode has plenty of intrigue and action in it, most of it sharply directed, the tale is arguably too long and gets a trifle repetitive in the middle episodes—Hawkins is framed for murder in Jamaica and has to flee, passes through a pirate haven, and arrives in Mexico, where he is once again framed for murder and has to flee. Ah, but that interim stop in the pirate haven, the Crow's Nest, is one of the most authentic and convincing depictions of life under the black flag in a century of piracy on the screen, a precursor in tone to the *Black Sails* series of almost 30 years later. It's surprising that the Disney company was involved with anything this dark.

Shot in Wales, Jamaica, and Spain (standing in for Mexico), the rest of the sets and settings are just as authentic and convincing, making a clear statement that you can create an exciting tale about Caribbean pirates without abandoning history and veering into fantasy. Special kudos for use of the gorgeous Danish three-master *Kaskelot* which takes the role, under different paint jobs, of several of the series' ships. This is a top-notch production for a TV show, by the pow'rs, and it's a shame it isn't better known outside the UK.

ROBIN AND MARIAN

Rating: ★★★★★ (Essential) • *Origin:* UK/US, 1976 • *Director:* Richard Lester •
Source: Columbia Pictures DVD

Robin and Marian is the first major feature about the Outlaw of Sherwood to step out of the long shadow of Errol Flynn's *Adventures of Robin Hood*, made almost 40 years earlier, and it does so by revisiting the lives of its major characters when they are well into middle age. Robin Hood (Sean Connery) and Little John (Nicol Williamson) have been following King Richard Lionheart (Richard Harris) on his foreign conquests for 20 years, growing increasingly fed up

Robin and Marian Author's Collection

AVE RICHARD LESTER

A Jewish American from Philadelphia, Dick Lester had to go to the UK to make his mark in the movies, though he worked first in television, short subjects, and commercials. His early work was in comedy, and he was part of the gang of English comics, among them, Spike Milligan and Peter Sellers, who created *The Goon Show*, a direct predecessor to *Monty Python*. John Lennon was a huge fan of the Goons and of Lester's hilarious short, *The Running Jumping & Standing Still Film*, and Lester got his big break when he was tapped to direct the Beatles' first feature, *A Hard Day's Night*. This kicked off what you might call the Swinging London portion of Lester's career, during which he made some of the funniest movies of the '60s, including *Help!* (1965) and *A Funny Thing Happened on the Way to the Forum* (1966).

Lester made some antiwar films that were dogs at the box office, and his career bogged down until his surprise second act as a director of action films, beginning, of course, with *The Three* and *Four Musketeers* (1973, 1974). The resounding success of the musketeers films was followed by more action movies, some better than others but all watchable: *Royal Flash* (1975), *Robin and Marian* (1976), *Butch and Sundance: The Early Days* (1979), *Superman II* (1980), and *Superman III* (1983). After a hiatus, he came back to swashbucklers with *The Return of the Musketeers* in 1989. It was not a success. Worse, Lester's close friend, Roy Kinnear, who was playing d'Artagnan's lackey Planchet, died during the shoot from complications due to a fall from a horse. Kinnear's family sued Lester and the production company, accusing them of negligence and slipshod safety procedures. Lester, heartbroken, never made another full feature film, and he lives in retirement.

And I must thank him here for his work, because without it, this book wouldn't exist.

with the futility of his wars. When the king dies of sepsis from a freak arrow wound, Robin and John return to England and Sherwood Forest, where they find their outlaw exploits have become the stuff of legend. Will Scarlet (Denholm Elliott) and Friar Tuck (Ronnie Barker) are now scruffy, aging deer poachers, and Robin's old love Marian (Audrey Hepburn) is the abbess of the local convent.

Only the Sheriff of Nottingham (Robert Shaw) still seems formidable, and Robin arrives at Kirkly Abbey in search of Marian just as the Sheriff is on his way to arrest her on the orders of King John (Ian Holm), who is closing the monasteries. Robin decides he's going to save Marian from the Sheriff whether she wants saving or not; swords are drawn and bows are strung, and soon everyone has fallen back into their old roles.

But their youth has gone, and Robin's rescue of the kidnapped nuns from Nottingham, with wall-climbing and acrobatic swashbuckling just like in the old days, leaves everyone wheezing and tottering. However, Robin, Marian, and company do make their escape back to the greenwood, and the Sheriff makes his plans to go after them—but not in the way that Robin expects.

The excellence of this film starts with its script by the acclaimed James Goldman (brother of William of *The Princess Bride*), an alternately wry and moving tale of lost youth and the endurance of love. Director Richard Lester trades in most of his signature slapstick comedy for elegiac, autumnal visions of the woods and hills, with a stirring but tender score by John

Barry and warm cinematography by David Watkin. But what really makes the movie work is the tart chemistry between Connery's Robin and Hepburn's Marian, who glows with warmth and intelligence. The two are perfectly set off by Shaw's acerbic Sheriff of Nottingham, who may be the sharpest sword in the armory, but he still can't resist Robin's challenge to settle all their differences in single combat. That duel, choreographed by the great William Hobbs, wordlessly encapsulates everything the film has to say about the glory and stupidity of men of war. Only Marian has the wisdom to see that the days of futile fighting must come to an end, and she takes firm steps to ensure that love will not be defeated by age and death. The romance of Robin and Marian, like this film, is undimmed by time.

ROBIN HOOD

Rating: ★★☆☆☆ • *Origin:* USA, 1922 • *Director:* Allan Dwan • *Source:* Kino Video DVD

Douglas Fairbanks Sr. as *Robin Hood* WIKIMEDIA COMMONS

After Douglas Fairbanks's worldwide success with *The Mark of Zorro* and *The Three Musketeers*, no expense was spared for his next silent swashbuckler, 1922's *Robin Hood*. The film is a spectacular saga of medieval chivalry, a lavish production on an epic scale, but is all about lords, ladies, and kings with strangely little Robin Hood in it. It's a weird boys' club of a movie that's mostly about the manly bromance between Fairbanks's Earl of Huntingdon and King Richard Lionheart, played with wearying brio by beefy Wallace Beery. Huntingdon is the knightliest knight when it comes to trouncing the others at tournament, but he's strangely leery of the ladies, and when Richard tells him to take his prize from Lady Marian, he says (no kidding), "Exempt me, Sire. I am afeared of women." Spoiler: he gets over it, as least as regards Marian.

There follows about an hour of royal intrigue involving King Richard, evil Prince John, and Huntingdon, as the king leaves England to lead an army to the Crusades. There's a fair amount of regrettable nonsense about militant Christianity marching off "with high purpose" to wrest the Holy Land from the infidels. However, once Richard leaves Prince John to rule as regent until he returns, John immediately becomes an oppressive tyrant who turns England into Mordor. Peasants are robbed of all they possess, women are abused, and capering torturers burn and lacerate for John's dour amusement.

The movie's more than half over before Huntingdon returns to England to set things aright by donning Robin Hood's cap and tights. As a knight Huntingdon was stolid and earnest, but as Robin he's suddenly as merry and active as Zorro and d'Artagnan. Fairbanks leaping like an acrobat was a revelation in *The Mark of Zorro*, but in Sherwood Forest, a hundred Merrie Men imitating him and bounding about like kangaroos is ludicrous.

In fact, *Robin Hood* is the least effective of the Fairbanks swashbucklers, because it's so overblown in every way. All the sets are colossal, every tableau is teeming with extras, the language is hifalutin and purple, and everybody overreacts to everything. Every actor overplays his role (except Sam De Grasse as Prince John, whose relative restraint actually makes him seem more sinister). Except for Little John—played by the talentless Alan Hale, who will assume the role twice more over the next 30 years—the familiar Merrie Men barely make an appearance, and none of the famous tales is even referenced, so it barely resonates as a Robin Hood movie. And gah, the hairstyles are terrible.

The film was a big hit in its day but just doesn't hold up particularly well 100 years later. Can't recommend it.

ROBIN HOOD AND THE PIRATES

Rating: ★☆☆☆☆ • *Origin:* Italy, 1960 • *Director:* Giorgio Simonelli •
Source: Amazon streaming video

The first major Robin Hood feature film was the Douglas Fairbanks vehicle of 1922, and over the next 40 years, there were at least a dozen more. *Robin Hood and the Pirates* is a leading contender for the worst of the lot. In the late 1950s, Lex Barker, a handsome but bland American leading man (Tarzan, Westerns) found his star setting in Hollywood, so he went to Europe where he made a half dozen or so low-budget swashbucklers. Some of these films eventually got dubbed into English for the American drive-in market, but many never made it back over the pond—Barker spoke Spanish, French, and Italian, so the films didn't need to be shot in English. But they're nearly all terrible, so this is no great loss unless you're a swashbuckler completist (like me).

Robin Hood is on his way to the Crusades in the twelfth century when he gets captured by pirates from the eighteenth century and is held for ransom. There's a storm and the pirates' ship wrecks (offscreen, because shipwrecks are expensive to film), and Robin washes up on the shore of the County of Sherwood. There are no forests to be seen, and the terrain looks more like Sicily, but hey—he's home at last! However, his father's domain, Sherwood Castle, has been taken over by a seeming sixteenth-century Florentine whose name, unaccountably, is Brooks, so Robin has to team up with the castaway pirates to overthrow the usurper.

That's it: that's the whole story. Oh, there's an evil, hunchbacked jester named Goliath, and the good dark-haired lady and the bad fair-haired lady have a catfight in a mud wallow, but those are just grace notes. The one thing that differentiates this film from an overlong episode of a weak 1960 TV show is that four of the pirates are Black African women, escaped slaves, and they're feistier and have more fun than the rest of the lackluster crew put together. Also, there's an implied romantic relationship between the leading Black woman and the white Captain One-Eye (clever name, eh?), which is certainly something you wouldn't see in an American picture from 1960. But otherwise, bleah.

ROBIN OF SHERWOOD, SEASON 1

Rating: ★★★★☆ • *Origin:* UK, 1984 • *Director:* Ian Sharp • *Source:* Acorn DVDs

Robin of Sherwood AUTHOR'S COLLECTION

The British reinvention of the Robin Hood legend onscreen that began with *Robin and Marian* (1976) continues here and goes much, much further. This Robin is no dispossessed noble, he's a commoner, the son of a Saxon rebel orphaned when the former Sheriff's men-at-arms murdered his father in a hilltop stone circle and took from him an ancient, silver arrow—a magical arrow, because this version of the story is a full-on fantasy. Autocrats and satanists all want the silver arrow, but it belongs to the worshippers of Herne the Hunter, a deity of pre-Christian Britain whose hero, the Hooded One, rises again and again as a leader who fights injustice. And in the late twelfth century, the newly chosen Son of Herne is young Robin of Loxley, Robin i' the Hood (Michael Praed), an outlaw in Sherwood Forest.

The show's first season is structured like a hybrid regular and miniseries, with a three-hour opening episode, "Robin and the Sorcerer," that mixes standard elements of the legend with new twists to make the story fresh again, ending in an unstable balance between the outlaws and their enemies that sets up the weekly stories to follow. As usual, Robin first meets Little John (Clive Mantle) in a quarterstaff bout on a river-spanning log—but this John is possessed by the sorcerer, placed in a murderous trance that Robin must dispel after incapacitating him. And as usual the Sheriff of Nottingham (Nickolas Grace) tries to trap Robin with an archery contest, but the prize isn't a golden arrow, it's Herne's silver shaft, which Robin must take back from the aristocrats. Escaping from Nottingham Castle, Robin encounters Lady Marion (Judi Trott), they fall in love pretty much at first sight, and rather than be treated like chattel by the Sheriff, she joins Robin in the greenwood, along with John, Friar Tuck (Phil Rose), and Will Scarlet (Ray Winstone), an angry and vengeful ex-soldier whose wife was raped and murdered by a nobleman's men-at-arms. These classic members of the band are joined by Nasir (Mark Ryan), a mostly silent Saracen assassin whom Robin frees from his master, the sorcerer.

This core band of outlaws are pitted in grim struggle against the corrupt Sheriff and his soldiers, commanded by the murderous Guy of Gisburne (Robert Addie, Mordred in *Excalibur*). Though there's some cheerful camaraderie among these new, young Merrie Men, these aren't lighthearted tales of bloodless derring-do, the outlaws and their accomplices are in regular danger of death, and the Sheriff's men go down before volleys of arrows a half dozen at a time. Praed's Robin, with his rock-star good looks, is a charismatic leader, and his judgment is sound until the final episode of the season, "The King's Fool," in which King Richard Lionheart (John Rhys-Davies, i.e., Gimli) returns to England. Riding incognito, the king encounters Robin and company in Sherwood and demands they swear fealty to him in return for a general pardon. Even Robin is starstruck by the king, so they agree (all but the untrusting Will Scarlet). But this Richard doesn't live up to the Lionheart legend, as Robin and his band discover. (Richard's royal failings had been explored before in *Robin and Marian*, but it's one more part of the standard Robin Hood story that showrunner Richard Carpenter seems to have been eager to overturn.)

ROBIN OF SHERWOOD, SEASON 2

Rating: ★★★★☆ • *Origin:* UK, 1985 • *Directors:* Robert Young, James Allen, Alex Kirby • *Source:* Acorn DVDs

Robin Hood's merry band of outlaws, with their mix of skills and personalities, is the original hero team from which all others descend. (Arthur's Knights of the Round Table never really act as a coordinated group.) Robin's company of comrades is the template for Dumas's musketeers, for Doc Savage's aides, for the Justice League, Ocean's Eleven, the A-Team, the Fellowship of the Ring, the Avengers, and many more. *Robin of Sherwood*, particularly the second season, is successful largely due to the expression of the bonds and tensions between the seven core outlaws of Robin's band, all distinct and comfortable in their roles and forming a whole greater than the parts. Michael Praed may be the charismatic lead, but it's the full band that gives Robin's adventures depth and context. And it's the chemistry and cohesion of the team that carry it through the big change at the end of this season.

The settings count for a lot as well. Has any screen Robin Hood story ever been in woods so vibrantly green as those of England's west country, where this series was shot? The forest, fields, villages, castles, and towns of Nottinghamshire feel genuinely medieval, a far cry from Hollywood backlots (though the fog machines are a bit overexercised at times). Two other elements deserve particular mention: the gritty fight arrangements by Terry Walsh, which keep the fighting relatively credible, and the theme and incidental music by Irish band Clannad, which does so much to set and maintain the tone.

This is another short season, only six or seven episodes, depending on how you count the double episode "The Swords of Wayland"—but these are the strongest stories of the series, each episode feeling consequential and building on the one before. If you weren't happy with the series' rough treatment of King Richard in season 1, you'll be pleased that Prince John returns in the first episode of season 2, and he's still the paranoid sociopath we all love to hate. Episode 2 could have been filler from the first season, but with episode 3 the series begins its rising arc toward its rather mystical ending: "The Enchantment" starts out in an Arthurian vein but quickly veers into Hammer horror territory, where matters stay through the two-part "Swords of Wayland" story with its demonic rituals and coven of deranged Satan-worshipping nuns. Robin is in dire straits, and Herne himself has to step in to help out.

Partway through season 2, it was clear that showrunner Richard Carpenter had a hit on his hands—and then star Michael Praed gave notice that he was taking his newfound fame elsewhere and wouldn't be available for season 3. So, for the final episode, Carpenter simply wrote Praed, and his character, out of the series entirely. (Don't mess with writers, I'm warning you.) The result turned the rather simple story of Praed's swan song into one of the most memorable of TV moments of the '80s.

(What happened to Michael Praed? He went to Broadway to star as d'Artagnan in a big-budget revival of Rudolf Friml's musical version of *The Three Musketeers*. It flopped.)

ROBIN OF SHERWOOD, SEASON 3

Rating: ★★★☆☆ • *Origin:* UK, 1986 • *Directors:* Robert Young et al. • *Source:* Acorn DVDs

A new Robin Hood: changing not just lead actor but lead character from one season to the next is a bold move, enabled by the setup that Robin i' the Hood is adopted as Herne's Son by that pagan deity, not born into the role. It could have worked, but the new Robin here is Jason Connery (son of Sean, who played an older Robin Hood in *Robin and Marian*), a pleasant but indifferent actor who lacks the commanding screen presence the role requires. He has little chemistry with the strong personalities of the outlaw band developed in the first two seasons and none at all, sadly, with Lady Marion: Connery and Judi Trott mime affection for each other but neither seems to believe it, and their romance sputters throughout the 13 episodes.

Thirteen episodes: as many as the first two seasons combined, but showrunner Richard Carpenter has a success on his hands and runs with it. Carpenter had written the entirety of the first two seasons, but now other writers are brought in, there's a revolving slate of directors, and the show chugs along but loses its consistency, especially in the middle episodes. The season is bookended by a pair of two-part stories written by Carpenter, full-on heroic fantasies featuring fierce bands of barbaric border Welsh right out of Conan's Hyborian Age. They're led by Owen of Clun (Oliver Cotton), a brute who runs pit-fighting games in his dungeon and whose right-hand accomplice is a satanic alchemist, Gulnar (Richard O'Brien, Riff Raff in *Rocky Horror Picture Show*), who potion-whammies Marion so she falls for Owen. In his origin story as the new Robin Hood, Robert of Huntingdon (Connery) puts the old gang back together, cleans out Clun, and rescues Marion.

A number of episodes follow that are neither here nor there, except insofar as they feature the villainous schemes of the Sheriff of Nottingham (Nickolas Grace) and Guy of Gisburne (Robert Addie), still locked in a codependency of mutual loathing. You gotta love 'em. Gulnar returns in the two-part season wrap-up with a new gang of barbaric Welsh, the Sons of Fenris, a curious creed for Celts to follow but hey: wolf cult! The sneering Gulnar has a strong gloating game, with a playbook full of lines like "Fool! Did you think you could oppose *me?*" There's a bestial Robin-golem, an oversized half-ton wolf skull, and a weak-ass plan by Robin that results in part 1 ending with the outlaws and all their villager allies captives of Gulnar, quite the best cliffhanger in the whole series.

The Sons of Fenris get sorted out in part 2, but the season ends with a number of important plot threads incomplete, so it lacks a real conclusion. The show was doing well in both the UK and North America, and everyone expected there would be a fourth season, but the business office bungled the funding and production collapsed at the last minute—an unhappy end for the best screen take on Robin Hood for many years to come.

ROB ROY, THE HIGHLAND ROGUE

Rating: ★★★☆☆ • *Origin:* USA/UK, 1954 • *Director:* Harold French •
Source: Amazon streaming video

Rob Roy MacGregor (1671–1734) was a Scottish outlaw who took part in two Jacobite rebellions against the English, was in and out of trouble his entire life, and seems to have been a pretty tough customer. Romanticized accounts of his exploits began appearing in the popular press as early as 1723, in his own lifetime. He became a hero of Scottish legend, and even the title character of a novel (1817) by Sir Walter Scott. This Disney live-action film follows that tradition, presenting a lively though highly fictionalized account of the outlaw's career. It was mostly shot in the gloomy grandeur of the Highlands, and that suits the tone of the picture, which is darker than that of most Disney adventure films. In fact, *Rob Roy* was a disappointment at the box office, due I think to this somber tone and to the portrayal of the hero by star Richard Todd, who puts aside his toothpaste-commercial smile and delivers a hard-bitten Rob Roy who's a bit too grim and vengeful to be truly sympathetic.

The story is the time-honored tale of the doughty but disorganized Scots, brave warriors with swords and shields beaten again and again by the perfidious English with their serried ranks of muskets and bayonets—not to mention their horse dragoons and artillery, the big cheaters. The victorious English oppress the Scots, the clansmen exact reprisals, and the cycle of violence continues. The Scots here are mostly broad caricatures, hard-fighting and hard-drinking, the camera dwelling on their colorful celebrations of wedding and burying, the pipes skirling at every opportunity. To be fair, the wicked English are cartoon parodies as well, their bewigged officers taking snuff and curling their lips as they sneer in contempt at the barbaric Scots. The halting English speech of their imported German king, George I, also comes in for its share of mockery, so no nationality goes unscathed.

In truth, the only sympathetic and three-dimensional people in this film are Glynis Johns, lovely and heartbreakingly earnest as Rob Roy's ladylove Helen MacPherson, and the massive James Robertson Justice as the Duke of Argyll, a Scottish noble seeking an honorable way to end the eternal bloodshed. Whenever Justice shows up, his commanding presence dominates the screen, and we know he's going to win in the end by dint of sheer moral authority—but not before the requisite number of ambushes and escalades, pursuits and escapes, and pitched battles with howling swordsmen and roaring cannon. Scotland Forever, right?

ROGUES OF SHERWOOD FOREST

Rating: ★★☆☆☆ • *Origin:* USA, 1950 • *Director:* Gordon Douglas •
Source: Columbia / Sony DVD

Like *The Bandit of Sherwood Forest* (1946), this is another story of the son of Robin Hood, of King John, and of the Magna Carta. Young Robin (John Derek) has inherited the title of Earl of Huntingdon and has just returned from the Crusades with Little John (Alan Hale Sr., reprising the role he played opposite Fairbanks in '22 and Flynn in '38). He encounters treachery at a tournament where, under the eyes of the exceedingly blond royal ward, Lady Marianne (Diana Lynn), Robin is to joust against a Flemish knight with the absurd name of Sir Baldric. (Right?) Baldric's lance is secretly pointy where Robin's is bated, but Robin wins anyway, which vexes evil King John (George Macready). Curses!

Angry John repairs to the same castle set we see in all these postwar Robin Hood flicks, bringing his henchmen along so he has somebody to snarl exposition at: thanks to the foolishly liberal policies of the late King Richard, it seems the barons have acquired a measure of autonomy that John wants to crush. But he needs money to hire mercenaries, so he resorts to the usual means to pay for a bloated military budget, that of raising the commoners' taxes to oppressive levels. Soon Robin and Little John have given up their Crusader armor for green tights and are riding around resisting tax collectors. They get captured in a brawl in Nottingham square, and we're off on the usual routine of defiance, imprisonment, escape, and rallying the yeomen.

This is another of those California Robin Hood films in which everyone has horses and there's a great deal of gratuitous galloping, troops of charging horsemen splitting left and right just before they ride over the camera. The movie breaks no new ground, and in fact goes out of its way wherever possible to evoke and emulate *The Adventures of Robin Hood*, which had been rereleased to great success in 1948. But apparently no one thought to hire Fred Cavens to coach the fencers, because the swordplay here is embarrassingly weak. The too-handsome John Derek looks pretty in his jerkin and tights, but he can't act worth a farthing. Alan Hale Sr., making his last appearance in a feature film, is visibly tired and barely getting through it. Only the ever-reliable George Macready shows any fire, so much so that toward the end you almost start to root for him. But he can't fight history, not in a film that's based on one actual-factual event, and he's finally forced to affix the royal seal to the Magna Carta that delimits the monarch's powers. Curses!

ROMEO AND JULIET

Rating: ★★★★★ • *Origin:* USA, 1936 • *Director:* George Cukor • *Source:* Warner Bros. DVD

Romeo and Juliet MGM / WIKIMEDIA COMMONS

What's *Romeo and Juliet* doing in the Cinema of Swords? Isn't that a love story? It is, but this version is a love story punctuated by four superb rapier duels, three of them involving Basil Rathbone, and one of those is against Leslie Howard—that's right, Sherlock Holmes crosses swords with the Scarlet Pimpernel!

In 1935 Warner Bros. had just released Shakespeare's *A Midsummer Night's Dream* with an all-star cast, and MGM didn't want to be out-Barded, so they opted to make *Romeo and Juliet*, which producer Irving Thalberg conceived of as a starring vehicle for his wife, Norma Shearer. Then-popular Leslie Howard was cast as Romeo, John Barrymore as the droll Mercutio, and Basil Rathbone as the fiery Tybalt; they were all too old for the roles of hot-headed teenagers, especially Barrymore at age 54, but Thalberg wanted actors who could handle both the Shakespearean language and a sword, which narrowed the field.

This is a prestige production for which MGM pulled out all the stops, and sumptuous doesn't even begin to describe it. The astounding costumes alone, theatrical but inspired by authentic Renaissance designs, are reason enough to watch this, and even if Shakespeare isn't to your taste, the acting is so good you might just like it anyway. At the Oscars, the film was nominated for Best Picture, Best Actress (Shearer), and Best Supporting Actor (Rathbone), but it was a dog at the box office, and Hollywood wouldn't touch Shakespeare again until the late 1940s. But, hey, it still has those tasty, tasty duels.

ROYAL FLASH

Rating: ★★★☆☆ • *Origin:* UK, 1975 • *Director:* Richard Lester •
Source: 20th Century Fox DVD

The best swashbuckler farces work because, behind the jokes, they show a love for the genre they're lampooning, and that's certainly the case here. Director Richard Lester and screenwriter George MacDonald Fraser followed up their collaboration on *The Three* and *Four Musketeers* with this adaptation of Fraser's second Flashman novel, and it has many of the virtues of the previous films. If it's less effective, it's mostly because it leans too heavily into the comedy: a lot of the jokes are heavy-handed, and the slapstick scenes run on too long.

Another difference from the Musketeers films is that there are no heroes here, only an antihero, the cowardly rogue Captain Harry Flashman (Malcolm McDowell) and the series of villains who threaten him. Leading these is the great Oliver Reed as the ruthless German statesman Otto von Bismarck, whose best scene is near the beginning, when the smarmy Flashman humiliates him by maneuvering Bismarck into a fistfight with a retired English heavyweight boxer, who makes short work of the overconfident Prussian diplomat. Bismarck coldly assures Flashman that he'll have his revenge.

His opportunity comes four years later, when he embroils Flashy in a deadly political plot on the Continent. The story is a close adaptation of Fraser's novel, which reworks Anthony Hope's *The Prisoner of Zenda* and sets it on the northern German border during the 1848 Schleswig-Holstein affair. Flashman is summoned to Bavaria by an old lover, the notorious Lola Montez (Florinda Balkan)—another historical character—but is framed for a crime by Bismarck's aide, the rakish and rascally Rudi von Sternberg (Alan Bates), and tricked into fleeing to the fictional Duchy of Strackenz. Bismarck wants to add Strackenz into his German confederation via an elaborate plot that involves Flashman impersonating the Danish prince who is to marry Strackenz's icy Duchess Irma (Britt Ekland). It all goes outrageously wrong, of course, and Flashy ends up getting pursued around a grim old German castle by Sternberg and Bismarck's other minions, comic-opera villains all, including Lionel Jeffries as Kraftstein, who has an awesome three-fingered iron hand.

Malcolm McDowell is particularly well cast as Captain Harry Flashman, displaying the appropriate mix of smug arrogance and brash cockiness when he's on top and servile groveling when he's threatened. Alan Bates is good as Sternberg, this story's analogue to Hope's Rupert of Hentzau, but not good enough to steal his scenes the way Rupert does in *Zenda*. There are a number of excellent half-serious duels with cavalry sabers, all choreographed by the brilliant fight director William Hobbs, who'd performed the same service for Lester's Musketeers films. And with veteran cinematographer Geoffrey Unsworth behind the lens, it looks great. But at the time, *Royal Flash* had only a limited release to theaters and didn't review well, which has left it with a reputation for mediocrity that's not entirely justified. It doesn't help that it fell between Lester's greatest film swashbucklers, the Musketeers movies and *Robin and Marian* (1976), but taken on its own terms, it's well worth watching.

SAMSON AND THE 7 MIRACLES OF THE WORLD

Rating: ★★☆☆☆ • *Origin:* Italy, 1961 • *Director:* Riccardo Freda • *Source:* Mill Creek DVD

Despite its American title, this isn't a biblical epic but rather a peplum flex-fest retitled from *Maciste at the Court of the Great Khan*. It's what in Italian cinema was called a "recovery" film, a low-budget quickie made with the assets from an expensive epic to recoup part of the cost of the big-budget film, in this case 1962's *Marco Polo*. Thus its costumes and sets are first-rate, but nothing else about this production lives up to that standard. Though it's set in China in the thirteenth century, almost every actor with a speaking part is a European or American in awkward makeup, and the orientalism is in fifth gear. Moreover, Samson/Maciste (Gordon Scott) looks exactly like Tarzan, which isn't surprising as Scott spent the latter half of the '50s playing that role in movies and TV. To avoid being typecast as a jungle lord, Scott moved to Italy to make sword-and-sandal adventures, but they still made him wrestle a tiger in this one.

The plot is the familiar rescue-the-imperial-heirs-from-the-invaders thing, with plenty of abductions, escapes, and pursuits punctuated by fights with the Mongol invaders. The action is all pretty perfunctory, and none of the performances really stands out, especially that of leading man Scott, who's particularly bland. Scott's Samson is modest and agreeable but not very engaged except when performing a Mighty Feat of Strength, and then he sweats a bit. In the last half hour, the film gives up its pretensions to historicity and goes full-on fantasy, and that almost saves it before it's sunk by a weak and abrupt ending. Nice sets, though.

Samson and the 7 Miracles of the World Reynold Brown / Wikimedia Commons

SAMURAI I: MUSASHI MIYAMOTO

Rating: ★★★★☆ • *Origin:* Japan, 1954 • *Director:* Hiroshi Inagaki • *Source:* Criterion DVD

Toshiro Mifune, still relatively early in his career, stars as Musashi Miyamoto, the Japanese culture hero who virtually defines Bushido, the warrior code of the samurai. This is the first movie in a trilogy adapting Eiji Yoshikawa's long (*really* long) novel fictionalizing Musashi's early life, originally serialized from 1935 to 1939. Director Hiroshi Inagaki was such a big fan of the work that this is the second trilogy he made from it: unfortunately, the first three films, made in 1940 to 1942, are now lost.

Though we Westerners most often associate Mifune with the classic films of the great director Akira Kurosawa, he actually made more movies with Inagaki, working with him from the mid-1940s to the end of the '60s. This prestige film for the Toho studio was their first big-budget production together, and it was a hit even overseas, where it won the Best Foreign Film Oscar in 1955. It's certainly gorgeous: Inagaki was a master of color, though unlike Kurosawa his compositions tend to be more pretty than striking. He was as adept with character scenes as with action, and his establishing shots of the Japanese countryside are beautiful.

The film opens with Musashi in his late teens, a country samurai still known as Takezo. He and his friend Matahachi (Rentaro Mikuni) naively leave their small town to find fame and glory as warriors, joining the local army on the eve of the Battle of Sekigahara (1600). Unfortunately, the side they join is the losing one, and they must flee to avoid the massacre of their army's survivors. They fall in with petty criminals, a woman and her daughter who've been fencing stolen goods for a band of brigands, and for the first time Takezo shows his talent for fighting by driving the brigands away and killing their leader—all with a wooden sword! We then enter soap opera territory for a while as the female crooks vie with hometown girl Otsu (Kaoru Yachigusa) for the affections of Takezo and Matahachi. This sets up Takezo's long, hopeless love affair with Otsu, which will be the romantic pulse of the rest of the trilogy.

On his way to see Otsu, Takezo is detained at a checkpoint, rashly cuts his way through the soldiers, and from that point on, he's a hunted outlaw. He goes from bad to worse, a feral fugitive in the woods lashing out at the hapless peasant troops sent to capture him, until a Buddhist priest named Takuan (Kuroemon Onoe) uses Otsu as bait and takes him into his personal custody. Sensing a powerful spirit beneath the savagery, Takuan sets out to tame the wild Takezo, hanging him bound for a tree for days to teach him humility and eventually locking him in a castle attic with nothing but a library of books.

Mifune is great as Takezo, angry at the world yet unsure of himself and vulnerable, perfectly offset by Onoe as the jovial but steely priest. And Yachigusa is appealing and determined as Otsu, initially afraid of Takezo yet inescapably drawn to the wild man's vulnerable heart. The priest's firm persistence wins out, redirecting Takezo's strength and spirit until he's transformed and renamed into the self-controlled Musashi, who then sets out to find wisdom as a wandering swordsman. (Like you do.)

The historical Musashi, who fought his first duel at 13, avoided all romantic attachments, never served a samurai lord, and eventually wrote the classic *Book of Five Rings* (c. 1643), was a far more unorthodox man than the rather conventionally noble samurai represented in Inagaki's trilogy. But *Samurai I* nonetheless does a fine job of setting up Musashi's spiritual journey (with swordplay interludes) to follow.

SAMURAI II: DUEL AT ICHIJOJI TEMPLE

Rating: ★★★★★ • *Origin:* Japan, 1955 • *Director:* Hiroshi Inagaki • *Source:* Criterion DVD

Samurai II: Duel at Ichijoji Temple EVERETT COLLECTION / ALAMY STOCK PHOTO

For a movie less than two hours long, there's an awful lot going on here. As the second film in a trilogy, this one has to do the heavy lifting of supporting the central arc of the hero's character development, as well as marching the story forward and setting up the climactic final movie, and it does all this with clarity, economy, and finesse. And that's important, because this is the part of the story where the legendary Musashi Miyamoto, played once again by Toshiro Mifune, must evolve from an angry and arrogant bully into a humble and honorable samurai warrior.

As far as Musashi is concerned, the story is a succession of combat encounters separated by meetings with surprising mentors—a caustic old monk, an accomplished geisha, a reverent sword-polisher—who teach him to find himself by looking within. For the rest of the ever-burgeoning cast, it's a frantic dance of deceit, adoration, conspiracy, rape, greed, ambition, calculation, and murder, in a carefully orchestrated flow of short, sharp scenes that keep the story moving so deftly you can almost ignore its frequent mind-boggling coincidences. All the characters introduced in the first movie return to be joined by an equal number of new faces, most of whom make it to the end of this film with their plots still unresolved. The most important new character is Kojiro Sasaki (Koji Suruta), a wry and cynical young swordsman who seems to dog Musashi's every footstep, showing up whenever there's trouble, sometimes fomenting it, sometimes defusing it, but always with an eye toward an inevitable showdown with Musashi.

Speaking of showdowns, there's a lot of fighting in this entry, much more than in the previous picture, and director Inagaki shows himself to be a master of the form. But of all the combats in the film, significantly only the first and last are shown from beginning to end, because they bookend Musashi's character arc; all other fights are only partially depicted, mere links in the chain of the story's progress.

The movie opens on the first duel, in which Musashi has been challenged by Baiken, a master of the *kusari gama* (chain and sickle). Musashi, facing an unfamiliar weapon, is unsure of himself, gets caught by the chain, and wins only through audacity and desperation. An aging monk who witnesses the duel tells him disapprovingly that though victorious, he is no samurai, as he didn't win by art or skill, only sheer force. "You are decidedly too strong," he says.

Only as events unfold does Musashi begin to glimpse what the monk means. He gets into a protracted squabble with the many swordsmen of the Yoshioka fencing school, whom he repeatedly defeats while demanding a match with the young samurai who has inherited the school's mastery—a duel which is always denied him, because the Yoshioka students secretly fear their master is no match for Musashi. They keep trying to kill him in failed or mistaken ambushes, and the wrong people die. Meanwhile all the secondary characters pursue their agendas of love and avarice in and around this feud, and hostilities sharpen and harden.

Finally, a duel between Musashi and Seijuro Yoshioka (Akihito Hirata) is set for dawn at Ichijoji Temple—but once again the master is diverted, and some 80 of his students set an ambush for Musashi. Forewarned by Akemi, one of the three women pining for his affections, Musashi defies the ambushers and then battles the lot of them in a magnificent fighting retreat, carefully choosing his terrain so they can come at him only a few at a time. After dropping two dozen adversaries, Musashi eventually breaks away into the forest, nearly exhausted, only to be confronted by Seijuro at last. Musashi can barely contain his rage: after taking the measure of his opponent, he defeats Seijuro in a single pass, but then refrains from killing him as all his recent life lessons combine to restrain his hand. Which leaves all the elements set up to perfection for resolution in the final film.

SAMURAI III: DUEL AT GANRYU ISLAND

Rating: ★★★★★ • *Origin:* Japan, 1956 • *Director:* Hiroshi Inagaki • *Source:* Criterion Blu-Ray

This is the final film in Inagaki's epic trilogy adapting Eiji Yoshikawa's biographical novel of the early life of Musashi Miyamoto, the exemplar of Bushido. It leads up to the inevitable duel between Musashi (Toshiro Mifune) and his archrival Kojiro Sasaki (Koji Tsuruta), introduced in the previous movie. But more than that, the purpose of this film is to draw a contrast between the vainglorious Kojiro and the increasingly humble and thoughtful Musashi. It does this from the very beginning, the first scene showing Kojiro at a waterfall, a location of great natural beauty; but this beauty is ignored by the samurai, who sees a passing swallow as nothing more than a challenge to his sword skill, bringing it down with a single lightning stroke. Meanwhile, Musashi, when challenged by a boastful spear-wielding monk, declines to draw his own sword, and instead neutralizes his opponent by grabbing the end of his spear and using his own strength against him.

This sort of thing continues: Kojiro defeats his adversaries in flashy duels, burnishing his reputation, while Musashi avoids a brawl with a gang of thugs in a famous scene where he awes them with his skill by using chopsticks to grab flies on the wing. Though Kojiro has never lost a duel, neither has Musashi; realizing that only Musashi is a match for him, Kojiro challenges him, but Musashi temporizes, putting him off for a year "to train further."

Musashi's idea of further training is to return to the simple life of the soil. He becomes a farmer at a village where the peasants, repeatedly raided by bandits, are giving up in despair. But the complications of his old life pursue him into the countryside: Otsu (Kaoru Yachigusa), who's loved him since he was a youth, shows up at the village, as does the bandits' moll Akemi, who also pines for Musashi. Jealous of Otsu, she calls the bandits down on the village, and Musashi must fight to defend the peasants.

At last, the reckoning with Kojiro can be put off no longer. Inagaki's depictions of the fights in this film are impeccable, but the final duel at dawn on the beach at Ganryu Island is a thing of beauty, a ballet of light, water, and weaponry, a few simple elements the director combines into a scene both elegant and unforgettable, exemplifying all that's gone before. So good, it bears rewatching.

SAMURAI ASSASSIN

Rating: ★★★★☆ • *Origin:* Japan, 1965 • *Director:* Kihachi Okamoto • *Source:* Warrior DVD

This is a film that aims high but doesn't quite hit all its targets. Set in 1860, during the unrest of the Bakumatsu period, its subject is the Sakurodamon Incident, in which an elder lord of the shogunate is ambushed by dissidents—or so it seems at first. For there's a lot more involved here, maybe too much for one movie.

The film starts with the events of February 17, 1860, presented in documentary style, complete with narrator, in high-contrast black-and-white. Samurai of the Mito clan, who've decided that Lord Naosuke must be assassinated for making a humiliating treaty with the Western powers, are gathering in the snow outside Edo Castle's Sakurodamon gate. As they wait, tense, blood pounding, other lords' processions one by one enter the castle, but not Naosuke's. As the time for the castle ceremony passes, the Mito must face the fact that Naosuke isn't coming; furtively, they withdraw, regathering at a nearby tavern to discuss what went wrong.

The Mito leaders, who've been betrayed before, conclude that Naosuke didn't show because he'd been tipped off about the ambush. One of their number must be a traitor! Their suspicions quickly settle on two outsiders among them: Kurihara (Keiju Kobayashi), a scholar from another clan who joined their cause for ideological reasons, and Niiro (Toshiro Mifune), an angry and drunken ronin who joined because he is desperate for action and for the rewards of its success. More suspicious yet, these two polar opposites are good friends.

As the Mito investigate the background of the suspected traitors, the nature of the story changes into the discovery of Niiro's secret history and how he descended from promising young fencing expert to bitter loner. Piece by piece, we learn of his background as the unrecognized son of a high lord secretly born to a samurai concubine, of his frustrated romance foiled because he doesn't know his father's name, and of his violent reactions to a succession of disappointments, until finally he joins the Mito dissidents and finds a friend in the scholarly swordsman Kurihara.

And it is that friend, Kurihara, whom the Mito leaders conclude must be the traitor who'd warned Naosuke: Kurihara, whose sword skills are so great that among the Mito, only Niiro is his match. Niiro is ordered to either execute Kurihara or be expelled from the patriotic cause. Meanwhile, the secret of Niiro's parentage, long suppressed, is finally on the verge of being revealed. And then another great procession to the castle, to include Lord Naosuke and his retainers, is announced, and the assassination is on again!

Coproduced by and starring Mifune, *Samurai Assassin* is directed by Kihachi Okamoto, who had made an impression with *Warring Clans*, his debut, two years earlier. Okamoto's mastery of black-and-white filmmaking is on full display here, and the resulting look is beautiful one moment and utterly grim and stark the next. For the final assassination attempt, the movie reverts to its documentary approach, and it's a rather jarring transition, frankly. However, the climactic mass melee in a driving snowstorm outside the gates of Edo Castle is brilliant, one of the most harrowing samurai sword battles ever filmed. It's too bad that it's followed by an ending of unbelievably heavy-handed, in-your-face irony. Otherwise, *Samurai Assassin* would be a must-see.

SAMURAI BANNERS

Rating: ★★★☆☆ • *Origin:* Japan, 1969 • *Director:* Hiroshi Inagaki •
Source: Samurai Cinema DVD

Produced by and starring Toshiro Mifune, *Samurai Banners* was directed by Hiroshi Inagaki, with whom Mifune made more films than for any other director. It's Inagaki's penultimate feature, and in accord with his penchant for filming the stories of Japan's national epics: he'd tackled the story of Musashi Miyamoto in the *Samurai* trilogy (1954–1956), the Forty-Seven Ronin in *Chushingura* (1962), and here the rise of Takeda Shingen, renowned daimyo of the Warring States period, as told through the story of his leading general and strategist, Kansuke Yamamoto (1501–1561, by Western reckoning).

Kansuke (Mifune) came from obscure origins but was already an experienced warrior who had lost his master and thus went looking for a new position as a retainer for the promising young warlord Takeda (Kinnosuke Nakamura). In the first scene Kansuke shows both his talent for strategy and his ruthlessness by persuading another

Toshiro Mifune in *Samurai Banners* FurinKazan69—
Own work, CC BY-SA 4.0 / Wikimedia Commons

ronin to ambush one of Takeda's traveling officers. Kansuke then intervenes, killing the other ronin, and the officer takes him into Takeda's service. Kansuke proves his worth to his new lord when he advises Takeda to assassinate a rival daimyo of the Suwa clan, a bold move that Takeda was already considering but which didn't occur to his more conventional advisors. Kansuke then advises Takeda to take Suwa's daughter, Princess Yu (Yoshiko Sakuma), as his concubine, to bind the Suwa to him and in hopes that Yu will bear Takeda a son and heir— which she does, but not before falling into a love/hate relationship with *both* Kansuke and Takeda. It's extra poignant.

As you've probably picked up, this isn't a *chambara* swordplay adventure but a doomed romance wrapped in a historical military epic, and soon the armies are on the march, in all the panoply of sixteenth-century Japanese warfare. The battle scenes are bloody gorgeous, and if Inagaki has trouble making it clear what's going on when all these thousands of fabulously armed and armored soldiers wheel, charge, and clash, well, not everybody is an Eisenstein or Kurosawa. What we chiefly care about is Mifune as Kansuke, a stoic veteran with a caterpillar-like scar over one eye and a pronounced limp that has him leaning on a cane. However, in the saddle the years melt away and he's young again, wearing amazing armor with great curving horns sprouting from his helm as he directs the mayhem of battle with stentorian commands and flashing *katana*.

Eventually Takeda's victories bring him up against another talented warlord, Uesugi Kenshin, and Kansuke directs Takeda's strategy in a 10-year duel with Takeda's great rival. It all culminates in the Fourth Battle of Kawanakajima, in which Kansuke makes his first—and last—strategic mistake.

So, watch it or not? The samurai politics aren't very compelling if you're not already well versed in this stuff, but the doomed romance almost works, and the battles make for fine spectacles. Mifune's performance tips the balance: he's in fine form here, caterpillar scar and all, and his Kansuke Yamamoto is a standout, even in a career of remarkable roles. Verdict: watch it.

SAMURAI REBELLION

Rating: ★★★★★ • *Origin:* Japan, 1967 • *Director:* Masaki Kobayashi • *Source:* Criterion DVD

Sometimes, all you can do is refuse.

This is director Kobayashi's follow-up to his *Harakiri* (1962), and it bears some similarities to that film: it's a story about resistance to the cruelty of the rigid samurai social system, it spends most of its length carefully and artistically setting up an explosion of violence at its climax, and it features the always excellent Tatsuya Nakadai in a key role. But *Samurai Rebellion* is more densely layered than *Harakiri*, with a larger cast to depict its complex conflicts of duty and morality. And most importantly its pivotal character is not a samurai warrior but a samurai wife.

In 1725, Isaburo (Toshiro Mifune) is a midlevel functionary in the Matsudaira clan whose only real skill is swordplay, which during the peaceful Tokugawa shogunate, nobody has much need for. His clan's daimyo, or warlord, decides to dump his young mistress Lady Ichi (Yoko Tsukasa) in favor of another, but because Ichi has borne the lord a son, she must be honorably placed somewhere in the clan. The daimyo chooses to marry her to Isaburo's son Yogoro (Go Kato), but Isaburo's family is reluctant to accept, as Ichi is said to have lost her temper and actually slapped the daimyo. However, eventually they agree, and surprisingly the marriage between Ichi and Yogoro is a happy one, blessed by a daughter, Tomi. Then the daimyo's eldest son unexpectedly dies, his child by Ichi is declared the new heir, and she is summoned back to the castle to care for him. But first she must divorce Yogoro and leave behind their infant daughter.

Isaburo and his family feel trapped by law and duty into giving Ichi up, but she turns out to be stronger than they and refuses to surrender. Isaburo and Yogoro join Ichi in defying the daimyo's authority, the clan starts tightening the screws, and events begin to bend toward the inevitable break. Differing opinions within the clan are represented by Isaburo's friend Tatewaki (Nakadai), who deplores the daimyo's arbitrary cruelty but sees no option but obedience, and by Takahashi, the cruel clan steward (Shigeru Koyama) who relishes the opportunity to break Isaburo's family to the daimyo's will. Koyama is great in this villainous role, so coldly repellent that from the first moment he appears, you can scarcely wait until meets his well-deserved end.

Unlike the lush visuals of Kobayashi's art-horror film *Kwaidan* (1964), here he returns to the austerely striking compositions of *Harakiri*, providing simple, clear backdrops for his characters' complex emotions. The climactic combats, two melees and a duel, are passionate and affecting, even poignant. As in *Yojimbo* and *Sanjuro*, Mifune and Nakadai face off at the end, but the harsh strictures of Bushido mean that this time there can be no winners.

SAMURAI SPY (OR SPY HUNTER)

Rating: ★★★★☆ • *Origin:* Japan, 1965 • *Director:* Masahiro Shinoda • *Source:* Criterion DVD

The year 1965 was a big one for spies and secret agents, so why not make a samurai spy movie? This has all the hallmarks of the spy genre: mirror-image espionage agencies locked in a cynical dance of deceit, double agents selling out to both sides, mysterious women who fall into the hero's arms, a secret mastermind pulling the strings behind the murders and betrayals, and a spy hero who's had enough of the soul-crushing game and just wants out. *Samurai Spy* is a darling of the serious critics because it's artsy and dark and poses a critique of society's culture of hypocrisy, but what the serious critics don't mention is that it's also some goofy fun, I'm here to tell you.

In 1600 the Battle of Sekigahara ended the era of warring states with a victory for the Tokugawa clan, but the defeated Toyotomi continued a shadow war to try to recover their power and influence. Under a façade of peace, the covert espionage clans of the Tokugawa and the Toyotomi conduct a war of spies, while neutral clans such as the Sanada and Suwa try to increase their leverage by dealing with both sides. The samurai Sasuke (Koji Takahashi) is a top spy for the Sanada who's growing sick of the eternal conflict, cruelty, betrayal, and death, but when Tokugawa spy chief Tatewaki (Eiji Okada) disappears in an apparent defection, Sasuke gets caught up in the pursuit because everyone thinks *he* knows where Tatewaki has gone.

Events go over the top immediately, and about all you can do is enjoy the ride. There are throwing stars and hooked chains, assassins in animal masks, a hallucinogenic episode, a clan of crypto-Christians, and an unexplained recurring beggar boy who walks through scenes dragging a dead raven. Best of all is the depiction of the other Tokugawa spy chief, Sakon (Tetsuro Tamba), a sort of ninja-in-white who appears and disappears and fights in a theatrical two-sword style. Sakon's spy clan is the Yagyu, who were the original ninja, so there are lots of early ninja tropes and even proto–kung fu high leaps in slo-mo. It's a hoot.

All of the above is not to diminish the artistry of director Masahiro Shinoda, who has an eye for composition that compares with Kurosawa's and who stages combats with a bracing mix of long shots and close-ups in gorgeous natural environments that almost upstage the swordplay. The story is complicated, a five-sided treachery-fest, and though you may lose track of who's who, it's still a rich visual feast. However, if you pay attention, it hangs together and you can follow it, reversal after reversal, all the way to the end, when it finally makes sense. (Except for the beggar boy with the raven: what's up with that?)

SAMURAI VENDETTA (OR HAKUOKI)

Rating: ★★☆☆☆ • *Origin:* Japan, 1959 • *Director:* Kazuo Mori • *Source:* AnimEigo DVD

Some regard Kazuo Mori's tale of a tragic love triangle as a masterpiece of samurai cinema, but I'm not among them. I find Mori's direction pretentious and haphazard, compelling in one scene and awkward in the next. The visual style switches from natural to overwrought impressionism without warning, which is jarring rather than emphatic. And there's an over-reliance on narrative voice-overs to move the plot forward or tell us what the characters are feeling when a well-acted dialogue scene would do the job better. That said, with dialogue like "Ours is a twisted world of warring titans," maybe we're better off with the voice-overs.

The film nonetheless has several points of interest. First of all, it's a prequel of sorts to the Japanese national epic of Chushingura, or the 47 Ronin, telling the backstory of one of those famous martyrs to the samurai warrior code. Raizô Ichikawa does a fine job as the first male lead in the role of Tangé Tenzen, a dishonored fencing instructor forced to separate from his wife. Even more interesting is the second male lead, one of the 47, named Yasubei, who's played by a young Shintaro Katsu, years before his international stardom as Zatoichi the Blind Swordsman. Katsu has the best fencing moves in the picture, plus he gets to weep in the rain and be the only survivor of a scene of horrific slaughter—good training for the future Zatoichi.

SANJURO

Rating: ★★★★★ • *Origin:* Japan, 1962 • *Director:* Akira Kurosawa • *Source:* Criterion DVD

Nine idealistic young samurai are meeting in a lonely barn. They've banded together to oppose corruption in their clan, and they're listening to their leader report on his meeting with his uncle, the chamberlain. The chamberlain had genially fobbed off his nephew's complaints, so the nephew had taken them to the clan superintendent. The superintendent told the nephew that he took his corruption complaints seriously, and the nephew had revealed to him that the chamberlain had not. But hooray, because the superintendent is definitely on the side of the young samurai!

There's a grunt from the next room, and a scruffy warrior emerges from the darkness, where he'd overheard their conversation. It's Sanjuro (Toshiro Mifune), the wandering ronin, or masterless samurai, from director Kurosawa's previous film, *Yojimbo*. Humorously gruff, he tells the youngsters that they're fools, that it sounds to him like the chamberlain is a great man, and that under no condition should they trust the superintendent. "But we're meeting him here tonight!" says the nephew.

The ronin's bleary demeanor instantly changes. Suddenly alert, he peers out between the shutters and informs the youngsters that the barn is surrounded by the superintendent's men. The young samurai draw their swords, ready to fight and die—but the ronin has a better idea.

The grim and gritty *Yojimbo* had been a big hit for Kurosawa, but though *Sanjuro* has the same protagonist played by the same star, facing off against the same actor (Tatsuya Nakadai) who'd played the lead villain in *Yojimbo*, the sequel has a very different tone from its predecessor. This is largely because it didn't start out as a sequel at all but as a standalone story, a humorous historical crime tale about a clever hero with more brains than brawn. But *Yojimbo* was such a success that Kurosawa's studio, Toho, encouraged him to make his next film a follow-up, and they didn't have to twist his arm very hard to get him to do it. The film's detective hero morphed into Sanjuro, the story was reconfigured to play to the scruffy ronin's strengths, and action scenes were added that made it less of a humorous *jidaigeki* (historical drama) and more of a *chambara* (story of swordplay). But it retained a lot of its original ironic tone and may be Kurosawa's funniest film.

The heads of the nine young samurai are filled with the honor code of Bushido and romantic notions of heroism, and to keep them from getting killed, Sanjuro is repeatedly forced to intervene in their foolhardy plans, in scenes that are both thrilling and hilarious. Sanjuro reluctantly assumes leadership of the effort to save the chamberlain, whom the youngsters have compromised, and take down the superintendent. But the superintendent commands scores of armed warriors, the most dangerous of whom is Muroto (Nakadai), a veteran rogue almost as experienced as Sanjuro. Nonetheless, after many twists and turns, the ronin, relying

Sanjuro AUTHOR'S COLLECTION

more on misdirection than on martial prowess, manages to turn the situation in favor of the youngsters. But there will be a final, and shocking, confrontation with Muroto that you'll never forget. Don't miss this one.

SASAKI KOJIRO, PARTS 1 & 2

Rating: ★★★☆☆ • *Origin:* Japan, 1957 • *Director:* Kiyoshi Saeki • *Source:* Samurai DVD

Considering how many stories and screenplays there are about the fencer Sasaki Kojiro, the great opponent of the legendary Musashi Miyamoto, you'd think there must be plenty of biographical material about him, but on the contrary: historians aren't even sure he really existed. However, thanks to his appearance in Eiji Yoshikawa's epic meganovel *Musashi* (1939) and its many subsequent film adaptations, Kojiro is as well known in Japan for appearing in Musashi's story as Doc Holliday is in the West for appearing in Wyatt Earp's saga.

This three-hour tale, released in two parts in quick succession to Japanese theaters in 1957, is based not on Yoshikawa's more famous work but on Genzo Murakami's 1949 novel about the life of Kojiro, which features only occasional appearances by Musashi. It's a tragedy from the start, if only because Japanese audiences know how it will end, as well as you know that a movie about the *Titanic* has to conclude with the ship going down. In this version of the story, Kojiro is a sensitive and artistic young samurai with an elegant sword style, a ronin of no family who aspires to fame as a fencer so he can marry Tone (Shinobu Chihara), his ladylove of higher rank. But Kojiro's attempts to make a name for himself by dueling the masters of well-known fencing schools are initially a frustrating failure, as nobody famous wants to cross swords with a nobody. This is partly due to Kojiro's appearance, as he presents himself as a romantic youth who wears eccentric clothing and won't shave his forelock, which in a samurai context seems effeminate; indeed, he's even mistaken once for a male prostitute.

But Kojiro persists in his ambitions without compromising his appearance, and along the way he makes both enemies and friends. The time is the early 1600s, at the beginning of the Tokugawa shogunate, and Japan is still riven by political intrigue; Kojiro tries to avoid becoming a pawn of the rival factions but can't entirely escape clan politics. Fortunately, he is guided by his loyal friend Shimabei, a ninja spy (with a nagging ninja spy wife!) who masquerades as a street puppeteer, and by Okuni, the nation's most famous dancer, who moves freely through the dangerous world of the conflicting clan lords. Kojiro's heart is lifted by song, and his soul is inspired by dance, and it's by watching Oman, a dancer who falls in love with him, that

Kojiro develops the "turning swallow" sword style with which he finally makes a name for himself. After that he has only one more ambition: to defeat his rival, Musashi Miyamoto.

This is a big-budget wide-screen epic from Toei Studios with high-end production values and strong performances from all concerned. Former kabuki actor Chiyonosuke Azuma cuts an appealing figure as Kojiro, and Chiezo Kataoko is a formidable screen presence as Musashi. Having played the role a half dozen times before in previous films, he steals every scene in which he appears. Watch this for a different take on the same characters portrayed in Inagaki's *Samurai* trilogy with Toshiro Mifune.

SCARAMOUCHE (1923)

Rating: ★★★★☆ • *Origin:* USA, 1923 • *Director:* Rex Ingram • *Source:* Warner Bros. DVD

You know a film adaptation is good when it makes you want to go back and reread the book. *Scaramouche* is a real gem and a close adaptation of Rafael Sabatini's novel, which had been a recent (1921) bestseller. This silent production has the same director and cast as the previous year's *Prisoner of Zenda*, but with a swap at the top: Ramon Novarro cast this time as romantic lead André-Louis Moreau, and Lewis Stone taking the part of the supporting villain, the Marquis d'Azyr. It's a good move, as the fiery young Novarro is perfect for the role of Moreau/Scaramouche—in fact, much better suited than the rather stolid Stewart Granger in the better-known 1952 version.

It's France under Louis XVI, and we're back in Mordor again, with the populace ground down by the oppressive nobility. Many of the bloated aristocrats are hilarious caricatures—the Minister of Justice could pass for Baron Harkonnen. The movie starts out a little slow, establishing its characters and Moreau's reasons for revenge on the aristos but really gets moving once he's on the run and joins a troupe of traveling actors. As a stage performer, Novarro gets to unleash his undeniable charm, and once he dons the striped outfit of Scaramouche, we're off to the races. The film spends an hour covering the same ground as the '52 version—the first, more personal half of the novel—and then goes beyond into the politics, glories, and horrors of the French Revolution, which are depicted convincingly. The costumes and makeup are superb, and in a series of dueling scenes, we see the first really good fencing of the silent era, swordplay both persuasive and exciting. Instead of the usual contrived happy ending, the film is true to its source and retains the rather dark finish of Sabatini's novel. *Aux armes, mes camarades!* Visual bonus: snuff boxes and quizzing glasses!

SCARAMOUCHE (1952)

Rating: ★★★★☆ • *Origin:* USA, 1952 • *Director:* George Sidney • *Source:* Warner Bros. DVD

Born in Italy, the novelist Rafael Sabatini lived in England beginning in 1892; when World War I broke out, faced with Italian conscription, he finally naturalized and then served throughout the war as a translator for British Intelligence. Though he never said why, working for the spy service darkened Sabatini's worldview, and when he returned to writing after the war, his first novel was the bitter and scathing *Scaramouche* (1921), a best-selling story of romance, revolution, and above all, revenge. This MGM adaptation leaves out most of the politics, but the romance and revenge are front and center.

"He was born with a gift of laughter, and a sense that the world was mad": this famous first line of the novel, the epitaph on Sabatini's tomb, also starts the film, though it will be a while before we see the protagonist to whom it applies. First we're introduced to the Duc de Maynes (Mel Ferrer), a sneering aristo whose hobby is picking fights with other men and then slaying them "honorably" in sword duels. The duke is gently scolded for this lethal pursuit by the Queen of France, who thinks he needs to settle down and selects one of her demoiselles, Aline (Janet Leigh, radiant), to be his future bride. Her Majesty also complains about the rude political pamphlets written by a revolutionary under the pseudonym Marcus Brutus, and the duke vows to discover and deal with him in his usual fashion.

Background established, we finally meet André Moreau (Stewart Granger), a scapegrace young wit, romancer, and philosopher of life, as he pays a midnight visit to a traveling commedia dell'arte troupe to make love to its leading lady, Lenore (Eleanor Parker). Moreau is also besties with Philippe de Vilmorin, who is secretly the writer Marcus Brutus, who's being pursued by the duke's goons. Moreau promises to help him but is unable to prevent de Maynes from maneuvering Philippe into a duel and killing him before his eyes. Moreau swears to avenge Philippe but barely escapes himself and is forced to hide in Lenore's comedy troupe, adopting the insolent role and impudent mask of Scaramouche. The laughing scoundrel finds a purpose at last.

Though Granger, coming to MGM, stipulated in his contract that he must get the lead in *Scaramouche*, he isn't ideal for the role: his mockery is joyless, and he lacks the comic touch for his bits with the commedia. In short, he isn't funny enough to be Sabatini's scornful clown—and the less said about his unconvincing love scenes with Leigh and Parker, the better. However, Granger brings two powerful assets to the part: a feel for grim vengeance and the skilled swordplay that's central to the movie's final third. There are several fine learning-to-fence montages in the film as Moreau trains with two master swordsmen, scenes that reflect the serious training Granger himself undertook in preparation for the picture. He does his own stunts, and both Granger and Ferrer (a dancer, and it shows) do all their own fencing, most notably in the justly famous seven-and-a-half-minute duel in a Paris theater that serves as the climax of the story. That duel alone is worth the price of admission and is a thoroughly satisfying payoff to the 90 minutes of setup that give it weight. It's probably the best scene with a hero clad in skintight striped leggings in all of cinema!

THE SCARECROW OF ROMNEY MARSH (OR DR. SYN, ALIAS THE SCARECROW OR DR. SYN: THE SCARECROW OF ROMNEY MARSH)

Rating: ★★★★☆ • *Origin:* USA, 1963 • *Director:* James Neilson • *Source:* Golem Video DVD

English novelist Russell Thorndike created outlaw hero the Scarecrow and wrote seven books about him from 1915 through 1944; there were three screen versions of the story, but the best known is this Disney adaptation, starring Patrick McGoohan in between his runs as the spy Drake in TV's *Secret Agent*. Disney was on the lookout for a swashbuckling follow-up to *Zorro* and found it in this tale of another disguised hero with a secret identity who fights against oppression—at least that's the positive spin it put on the Scarecrow, though he's a smuggler boss who rules through terror and deceit while wearing a scary mask and howling a horrifying laugh. But he's on the side of the rebellious Americans against the villainous King George III and his redcoats, so all is fine and family-friendly.

As the Scarecrow, the Vicar of Dymchurch (McGoohan) runs a secret smuggling operation that evades the revenue imposts and enables the local farmers to pay off their oppressive debt burdens. But the crown demands its import fees and sends the ruthless General Pugh (Geoffrey Keen) and a brigade of redcoats to burn farms and press-gang the locals into the navy, promising to continue until somebody turns in the Scarecrow and his masked accomplices, Hellspite and Curlew. It's a tale of conflicting loyalties and quick reverses; at first Pugh has an ally in the local justice of the peace, Squire Banks (Michael Hordern, excellent as always), but Pugh's brutality alienates Banks and his aide, Lieutenant Brackenbury (who wants to marry Banks's daughter), and they switch to side with the smugglers. Pugh's plans to turn the Scarecrow's own men against him come to naught, and though some are captured, the Scarecrow and his men, in the guise of a press-gang, manage to free his allies from Dover Castle and send them off to America with the smugglers.

This was produced as both a three-part miniseries for Disney's *World of Color* TV show and as a feature film for overseas release. It opens with a catchy tune reminiscent of the *Zorro* theme but punctuated by McGoohan's eerie laugh, which is so alarming it was edited out on rerelease. McGoohan, ominous and intimidating even as the mild-mannered vicar, is born for the role, and the direction by James Neilson, who'd worked on *Zorro*, is taut and suspenseful, especially during the dramatic escape from the dungeon of Dover Castle. The show was shot on location in Romney Marsh on England's south coast, and the authentic sites add considerably to the authentic ambience. If it wasn't popular enough to warrant a sequel, it may be because the grim tone of the Scarecrow and his gang was just too dark for Disney's early '60s audience. (It could also be because the first Scarecrow episode debuted on TV opposite the first appearance of the Beatles on *The Ed Sullivan Show*. Curse the fates!)

THE SCARLET PIMPERNEL (1934)

Rating: ★★★★★ (Essential) • *Origin:* UK • *Director:* Harold Young • *Source:* PRS DVD

After Alexander Korda's success with *The Private Life of Henry VIII*, he was ready to produce another costume drama on an even larger scale and with more action in it. He decided to adapt Baroness Orczy's 1905 novel, *The Scarlet Pimpernel*. Though it had already been filmed several times in the silent era, it was the perfect choice: the Pimpernel, the original noble outlaw with a secret identity, was the direct precursor to Zorro, and he was also a most English hero for a thoroughly British production. (Interestingly, both Orczy and Korda were Hungarian.)

You know the story, at least in outline: an outlaw mastermind leads a band of English gentry on perilous missions to save condemned French aristocrats from the guillotine during the period of the French Revolution known as the Terror. Though in this adaptation the duels are all fought with words and wits and not a single sword is drawn, it's nonetheless an iconic swashbuckler, with a hero who holds to his own code of honor in the face of tyranny and death and in defiance of all the ordinary rules. The story bristles with suspense, betrayals, reversals, and deadly menace: the threat of violence is ever-present but never quite erupts, though death hovers over every deceit. It's masterly. And if that weren't enough, it's also a ravishing romance!

The witty script is endlessly quotable, and the cast is perfection. The great Raymond Massey plays Citizen Chauvelin, the Pimpernel's nemesis, with cold, reptilian malice and penetrating intelligence. Merle Oberon is pitch perfect as Lady Blakeney, the former French actress whose heart is torn between conflicting loves and loyalties, but who in the end is as

SINK ME! SCARLET PIMPERNELS!

The Baroness Orczy (1865–1947)—but really, we must give her full name: Emma Magdolna Rozália Mária Jozefa Borbála Orczy de Orczi (no wonder they called her "Emmuska" for short) was a Hungarian noble by birth whose family left Hungary after her father's farm was burned by rioting peasantry. That may have had something to do with her later decision to write about the persecution of aristocrats during the French Revolution.

One day in 1903, the image of Sir Percy Blakeney appeared, fully formed, in Emma Orczy's mind's eye, and she knew she was seeing the protagonist of her next novel. She wrote *The Scarlet Pimpernel* in five weeks and sent it out with high hopes, but a dozen publishers turned it down. With her husband's collaboration, she crafted a version of the story for the stage and found a company willing to produce it. After a slow start, the play took off and became a huge success, after which selling the novel was suddenly easy.

Sequel followed sequel for the next 30-plus years; and over more than a dozen novels and collections, the dashing Scarlet Pimpernel probably saved more aristocrats from Mam'zelle Guillotine than were actually executed in the historically brief period of the Terror. But the baroness wasn't a historian, she was a storyteller, and few storytellers have created a character as indelible as Sir Percy Blakeney, the Scarlet Pimpernel—or one more perfect for translation to the silver screen.

brave as the outlaw hero himself. And though Leslie Howard is superb as the steely-eyed and indomitable Scarlet Pimpernel, he's simply immortal in the role of that simpering, blithering, farcical fop with a cunning gleam in his eye, the Right Honorable Sir Percy Blakeney (Bart.). Sink me! It's a triumph.

THE SCARLET PIMPERNEL (1982)

Rating: ★★★★★ • *Origin:* UK • *Director:* Clive Donner • *Source:* Acorn DVD

This is an outstanding remake of the 1934 *Scarlet Pimpernel*—and we call it a remake because although it's an original adaptation by screenwriter William Bast that's half-again as long as the earlier version, Bast was careful to include all the most memorable scenes of Alexander Korda's film, and because star Anthony Andrews's portrayal of the Pimpernel and his alter ego, Sir Percy Blakeney, is firmly based on Leslie Howard's characterization. As well it should be.

Once again, the Scarlet Pimpernel mixes the high adventure of saving French aristocrats from the revolutionary guillotine during the height of the Terror in Paris with romantic melodrama, as his beloved but unaware French wife, Marguerite St. Just (Jane Seymour), is blackmailed into betraying the Pimpernel to Citizen Chauvelin of the Committee of Public Safety (Ian McKellen). This version goes much more deeply into the characters' romantic backstory, showing Percy's courtship of Marguerite, who had formerly been engaged to Chauvelin, thereby establishing Blakeney and Chauvelin as romantic as well as political rivals. Tautly directed by Clive Donner, this TV movie maintains its pace despite its length, breaking the

The Scarlet Pimpernel (1982) Author's Collection

suspense only for heavy-breathing scenes of tragic love and angst d'amour. Andrews and Seymour are excellent, but McKellen steals the show; adding barely suppressed sexual jealousy to the role of Chauvelin enables McKellen to outshine even the great Raymond Massey in the role.

Bast adapted the story from Baroness Orczy's *The Scarlet Pimpernel* (1905) and *Eldorado* (1913), drawing from the latter the plot of the rescue of Prince Louis, the Dauphin of France, which is where a lot of the film's additional running time comes from. This extra material is the weakest part of the movie, as it doesn't really add more to the story except to distract viewers from what they really want, the hot romantic tension between the three leads. But Bast does add a fine climactic saber duel between Chauvelin and Sir Percy, an element that was missing from the 1934 version.

Production values are top-notch, especially for a TV movie, and the costumes are superb (they'd better be, in Percy's case). It was shot on location at lux historical sites in the UK, including Blenheim Palace, and looks succulent. Prepare to swoon.

THE SEA HAWK (1924)

Rating: ★★★☆☆ • *Origin:* USA, 1924 • *Director:* Frank Lloyd • *Source:* Warner Bros. DVD

The Sea Hawk (1924) First National Pictures / Wikimedia Commons

The silent era turns to tales of pirates! *The Sea Hawk* features Wallace Beery as a piratical rogue a full 10 years before his star turn as Long John Silver in *Treasure Island*. Here he also plays a lovable villain named Captain Jasper, opposite star Milton Sills as Sir Oliver Tressilian, who I'm convinced was cast mainly for his burning gaze and the fearsome way he slowly clenches his fist when contemplating revenge on his betrayers.

The story is based on Rafael Sabatini's 1915 novel, which had been revived in the wake of the worldwide success of his *Scaramouche* and *Captain Blood*. This film hews much more closely to the novel than the later version with Errol Flynn. It tells the story with an old-fashioned melodramatic staginess that was already going out of style, especially in the movie's first act, an Elizabethan soap opera (with dueling) that sets up why Tressilian, one of the queen's former "sea hawks," gets himself shanghaied onto a pirate ship. That's when the rapscallion Beery enters the picture, and the real fun begins.

Suddenly, sea battles! And not filmed with models or miniatures, either, they built real ships for this, a barque and two galleys, and the clashes between them are pretty spectacular. Betrayed in England and made a galley slave by Spain, Tressilian renounces Christianity and joins the pirates of Algiers to take his revenge on the world. He becomes a corsair captain, and in due time he captures the rogue Beery, who originally captured him. The two join forces, and rascally antics ensue—also alarums, excursions, abductions, impersonations, leering lechers, spying eunuchs, and vengeance-turned-to-ashes-in-one's-very-mouth. That slow and stagy start? Entirely forgotten.

THE SEA HAWK (1940)

Rating: ★★★★★ (Essential) • *Origin:* USA, 1940 • *Director:* Michael Curtiz • *Source:* Warner Bros. DVD

Shortly after the success of *Captain Blood* (1935), Warner Bros. optioned *Blood* author Rafael Sabatini's *The Sea Hawk* as a follow-up vehicle for Errol Flynn; but production was postponed, partly because the plot of *Hawk* was too similar to that of *Blood*. Several years passed, war between Britain and Germany began to appear inevitable, and the British production of *Fire over England* (1937) provided a model for an American approach to the same historical events. The *Sea Hawk* project was revived, retaining the title but with a new story by Howard Koch and Seton Miller (who a year later would

Errol Flynn in *The Sea Hawk* (1940) WIKIMEDIA COMMONS

write *Casablanca*), setting the tale during the run-up to the Spanish Armada and sending Flynn back to Elizabethan England for the second time in two years. Besides providing the model for the story, *Fire over England* also gave *The Sea Hawk* its queen in the form of Flora Robson, reprising her memorable role as Elizabeth I.

The film starts with the English queen's opponent, Spain's King Philip II, sending his suave ambassador Don Alvarez (Claude Rains!) to England to string Elizabeth along while Spain builds her Armada for an invasion. Only England stands between a ruthless tyrant and his conquest of the world. (Sound familiar? The movie was released just before the beginning of the London Blitz.) However, when approaching England the ambassador's galley, rowed by English slaves, is attacked by an English privateer captained by Geoffrey Thorpe (Flynn). Superior English gunnery, followed by a fierce boarding action ("It's cutlasses now, men!"), carries the day; the slaves are freed, and Don Alvarez and his niece (the tepid Brenda Marshall) are captured. Thorpe wryly promises to deliver them to the queen—along with the treasure looted from their sinking galley. It's just about the best first 20 minutes of any swashbuckler.

Meanwhile, England's royal court teems with the schemes and intrigues of the queen's ambitious advisors. Here comes the excellent Henry Daniell again, treacherously plotting once more—why wasn't he run out of London after *Elizabeth and Essex*? But the queen is his match; when Daniell and Rains complain about the privateers, Elizabeth publicly reproaches the Sea

Hawks, especially Thorpe—and then congratulates him in private. She even allows Thorpe to persuade her to give him tacit permission to attack the annual Spanish treasure convoy in Panama.

But there is treachery, and Thorpe is betrayed, though the ambassador's niece, who's fallen in love with him, tries too late to warn him. In Panama Thorpe and his crew are captured, and the Inquisition sentences them to life as galley slaves. And then things get serious.

With the great Michael Curtiz directing, Orry-Kelly on costumes, and a soundtrack, possibly his most magnificent, by Erich Wolfgang Korngold, Warners had their A-team on this picture, and it shows. Flora Robson is tremendous as Elizabeth, the escape of the galley slaves is taut and suspenseful, and Flynn gets to do some of his finest swashbuckling in the exciting finale. Watch for Fritz Leiber Sr. in a brief role as the vulturine Inquisition judge, fine supporting work from Gilbert Roland as Captain Lopez, the only honorable Spaniard, and a mischievous pet monkey that will feel familiar to fans of the *Pirates of the Caribbean* series.

SECRET OF NARUTO (OR A FANTASTIC TALE OF NARUTO)

Rating: ★★★★☆ • *Origin:* Japan, 1957 • *Director:* Teinosuke Kinugasa •
Source: YouTube streaming video

This intricate samurai spy thriller is based on a story by the celebrated historical novelist Eiji Yoshikawa, and it's got pretty much everything you want in a *chambara* tale. It starts with a series of five quick vignettes, each only a minute or so long, introducing the major characters: Ryutaro (Raizô Ichikawa), an arrogant young swordsman; Otsuna (Chikage Awashima), a nimble female ninja; Norizuki (Kazuo Hasegawa), a monk wearing a basket hat who is more than he seems; Yone (Fujkio Yamamoto), out to avenge her father's death by killing Norizuki; and Chamberlain Waki (Osamu Takizawa), a scheming and ruthless Awa clan official. After that pause to set the stage, it's right into the action.

In the western province of Awa, across the Naruto Strait, clan leaders secretly plot to unite with other disaffected clans to topple the shogunate. Imprisoned in a mountain cave, a dying old man writes a letter in his own blood exposing the plans of the Awa—but the shogunate already suspects something, and Chamberlain Waki receives word that an inspector is being dispatched from the capital to investigate. Waki decides to cover up by ordering the death of the mountain prisoner and by framing another clan leader for the Awa's schemes, a man whose death will divert government suspicion from the other plotters. But agents of the shogun have already arrived in the province and are ferreting out the Awa's secrets, among them the ninja Otsuna, who is the daughter of the dying prisoner on the mountain (and secretly in love with Norizuki, the pretended monk).

This is a handsome film, set mainly in the mountains of Tokushima, and ably directed by Teinosuke Kinugasa (*Gate of Hell*), who keeps the story moving while missing no opportunity for visual splendor. The ensemble cast is strong, and if no one stands out enough as to draw attention away from the others, there are also no weak performances that break immersion. The characters they play are well drawn and nuanced, avoiding cliché and caricature, and there are some surprising reversals to trip up your expectations. There's plenty of swordplay, including some extended melees around the "monk" Norizuki, who turns out to be a total badass when he puts down his basket hat and flute. Plus there are ninja shenanigans, frustrated love affairs, diplomatic double-dealing, and a surprise ending around that blood-letter MacGuffin everyone chases throughout the third act. Recommended: see if you can find it.

THE SECRET OF THE BLACK FALCON

Rating: ★★☆☆☆ • *Origin:* Italy, 1961 • *Director:* Domenico Paolella •
Source: Amazon streaming video

This Italian pirate adventure is a throwback to the Saturday matinee movies of the early 1950s, so it's appropriate that its lead is Lex Barker, another former Hollywood Tarzan gone to Europe to prolong his cinematic career. The story is a series of pirate movie clichés strung like the pearls on a captive Spanish señorita's necklace. It's the Caribbean in the Age of Piracy: the costumes, accurate but cheap-looking, say it's 1625, the presence of Calico Jack Rackham says it's closer to 1700, but the setting in the made-up Spanish colony of "Melida" means it's really in the realm of pure fiction. A document that's very, very (very) important to both the Spanish and the English was on a ship that's been captured by pirates, so the noble Captain Herrera of Spain (Barker) pretends to get cashiered to go undercover, join the buccaneers, and recover it. His aide and guide, the roguish Sergeant Rodriguez, is drolly played by the bald and mustachioed Livio Lorenzon; you'll recognize him, as he was in nearly every Italian peplum and historical adventure of the early '60s as a hero or villain, and here he gets to play both, with a comic turn into the bargain. Lorenzon has a good old time with this piratical folderol and is the main reason to watch it. Barker, though? He's just earning a paycheck on his good looks and can't be bothered to work hard beyond that. But at least he can fence (more or less).

The only other person enjoying himself here is Walter Barnes (Rolf the Viking in *Captain Sindbad*), appearing in the role of Calico Jack and chewing the scenery at every opportunity. Jack, of course, is the pirate who's captured the Very Important Document, and Herrera and Rodriguez must persuade him to let them join his crew so they can find it. Dumb jokes ensue as the pair go in and out of favor with Rackham while searching for the document, but then Calico Jack captures a Spanish ship simply chock-full of highborn Spanish ladies, including Herrera's ladylove Leonora (Nadia Marlowa), and things get serious (more or less).

But what about the eponymous Black Falcon? He's another pirate captain who's also after the document, and he shows up a time or two in his cool all-black outfit, including cloak and hood, but then gets forgotten about for an hour until he finally reappears to bedevil Herrera, Jack, and even Leonora. Who can he be under that mysterious black cowl? Well, he isn't Herrera or Calico Jack, so he must be . . .

THE SECRET SWORD (OR HIKEN)

Rating: ★★★★★ • *Origin:* Japan, 1963 • *Director:* Hiroshi Inagaki • *Source:* Samurai DVD

The secret thrust is a common trope in swashbuckling literature, an attack that, under certain conditions, is unbeatable and cannot be parried and is usually passed down as the final lesson between master and student, father and son. The idea of the secret sword thrust occurs in all fencing traditions, including, of course, Japan's.

Director Hiroshi Inagaki is best known to Americans and Europeans for lush historical epics such as the *Samurai* trilogy and *Chushingura* (1962). After completing the latter, Inagaki cleansed his palate with this intimate and intense *chambara* character study, shot in moody black-and-white, like a film noir. Like Okamoto's *Sword of Doom* (1966), it follows the descent of a dedicated swordsman into cruelty and obsession as he loses his humanity to his devotion to the sword.

Based on a novel by Kosuke Gomi, the story is set in 1633, early in the Tokugawa shogunate, when peace has idled thousands of samurai warriors and at the same time made it illegal to fight matches with real blades. Young Tenzen (Koshiro Matsumoto), though a samurai of the lowest rank, is his clan's most talented swordsman and is determined to become a famous practitioner of the martial arts, though he's allowed to practice only with wooden or bamboo weapons. An orphan, Tenzen was raised in the house of Chojuro (Hiroyuki Nagato), who considers him a brother, and his talent has already won for Tenzen an engagement with a higher-ranking daughter of the clan. But someone among the young samurai has been murdering untouchables, lowly street workers, with a sword, and when the clan inspector decides Tenzen should take the blame and accept a nominal punishment to cover it up on the clan's behalf, Tenzen angrily refuses, because the untouchables were clumsily slaughtered rather than cleanly slain.

About this time famous duelist Musashi Miyamoto (Ryunosuke Tsukukigata), now a retired sage, comes to the clan to visit an old friend and is confronted by the clan's young firebrands, who demand that Musashi support their sword-wielding ambitions. Musashi chides them for the murders of the untouchables, saying the Way of the Sword is not about killing, it's the way of all arts, and then whips up a heavy floor mat and bisects it vertically with a single blow of his sword. Tenzen, unimpressed, calls it a stunt and does the same trick—horizontally, which seems even more impressive.

But Tenzen has now shamed his clan: his engagement is broken off, and he's confined to his quarters in house arrest for 100 days. He escapes to visit and upbraid his former fiancée, and when he's caught by clan enforcers, he cuts them down and flees. His stepbrother, Chojuro, is charged with bringing him back to commit suicide, or Chojuro must commit seppuku in his place.

The character of Chojuro, fearful but determined, now comes to the fore as he searches for Tenzen, who has found refuge in the mountains. Obsessed, Tenzen practices alone in the woods every day until he invents a secret sword thrust that defeats opponents by severing their thumb behind the sword guard. Chojuro finds him, but instead of killing or capturing Tenzen, he joins him, and his stepbrother teaches him his secret thrust. But the clan has not relied solely on Chojuro to bring Tenzen in, and when a squad of samurai track him down, Tenzen kills or cripples them all and then flees again. Chojuro visits Musashi to ask for advice on how Tenzen can be redeemed and his talent saved for the clan, but Musashi tells him he cannot, as the secret thrust is an abomination: "The sword is not used merely for winning—it is a mirror that reflects the soul." And so, the stage is set for a tense confrontation between the stepbrothers amid the bizarre lava forms on the slopes of an active volcano.

This superb film is hard to find in a version with English subtitles, but you won't regret the trouble it takes to track it down.

SEVEN SAMURAI

Rating: ★★★★★ (Essential) • *Origin:* Japan, 1954 • *Director:* Akira Kurosawa •
Source: Criterion Blu-Ray

When your profession is killing people, messily, with hand weapons, how do you reconcile that with trying to do right in the world?

My father, an engineer from the Bronx who aspired to culture, first took me when I was 12 or 13 to a then-rare showing of *Seven Samurai*. It mostly went by in a blur, but some of

Director Kurosawa sets up a shot in *Seven Samurai* Eiga no Tomo / Wikimedia Commons

the more vivid scenes stuck with me, indelible, embedded, and when I saw it again as an adult many years later, I was amazed by how clearly I remembered parts of it.

Nowadays I rewatch it about once a year, and every time—*every time*—new details leap out at me, touches that were deliberately placed by Kurosawa, each designed to reveal some aspect of the humanity of the farmers, the bandits who prey on them, and the seven samurai who come to defend them. And I shake my head and wonder, *How have I always missed that?*

If you're reading this, it must be because you're interested in the kinds of movies I write about—but maybe you've never seen this film, despite its reputation. Maybe you've been put off by the fact that it's subtitled or in black-and-white or because it's over three hours long, and who wants to sit through all that? Believe me: *you* do. With this film, director Akira Kurosawa set out to create a historical epic that would be unfailingly entertaining and at the same time truthful: about its time and place, about the people who lived through it, and about how people of all times try to find the heart and courage to face up to danger and fear. And he succeeded.

Technically, this film is a marvel of performance, of composition and photography, and most of all, of genius-level editing: long as it is, every scene moves the story relentlessly forward, and there's not an ounce of fat on it.

And the characters, so sharply drawn, so unforgettable: Takashi Shimura as Kambei, the imperturbable but warm and wise veteran who leads the samurai in their hopeless and thankless task; Toshiro Mifune as Kikuchiyo, the wild-man of no background who earns his place among the haughty warrior caste; even the farmers, such as Bokuzen Hidari as Yohei the terrified, who has the world's saddest face but finds capabilities within himself he never suspected. And that's just a few of many remarkable performances, because a film about how a society at odds with itself manages to survive that conflict needs a big cast to carry such a theme off—and that cast must come across as real people living real lives, not play-actors going through the motions. A large part of Kurosawa's genius as a storyteller is that he loves every one of these characters, as much for their flaws as for their strengths, and you can see that love on the screen.

Much of the rest of Kurosawa's genius is his feel for movement. As mentioned above, every scene moves, and none more so than the amazing combat sequences, which despite being muddy, bloody, rain-drenched, and fast as hell, are marvels of cinematic clarity that are also completely convincing. Exhausting. Draining. Exalting. And horrible.

Who wins? You know the story, even if you've seen it only in remakes such as *The Magnificent Seven* or *Battle beyond the Stars* or even *A Bug's Life*. The warriors fight and die, because that's what warriors do, while the farmers, who survive to carry society on, are the winners. The farmers—and us.

Next year I get to watch it again.

SEVEN SEAS TO CALAIS

Rating: ★★★☆☆ • *Origin:* Italy, 1962 • *Director:* Rudolph Maté • *Source:* Llamentol DVD

This movie really wants to be *The Sea Hawk* (1940), and it gets closer to the mark than you might expect for an Italian swashbuckler made during the height of the peplum craze. It's a fictional biography of the life and adventures of Francis Drake, compressed and simplified to fit into 100 minutes, the story hinging on the relationship between Drake the privateer and Elizabeth I the queen. Drake is played by Rod Taylor, who does everything he can to evoke Errol Flynn, and by and large the effort pays off. Elizabeth is portrayed by the Shakespearean stage actress Irene Worth, and while she's no Flora Robson, she comes close. British actors fill most of the other speaking roles, so at least they get the accents right.

The film opens on a running sword fight through the back alleys of the port of Plymouth and goes on from there all the way to the defeat of the Spanish Armada, the action ably overseen by veteran director Rudolph Maté, who never lets the pace flag. This is a busy movie, as the ambitious story attempts to include the highlights of Drake's long and eventful career, including forestalling a mutiny off Argentina, the epic journey around the tip of South America into the then-Spanish Eastern Pacific, Drake's taking of Spanish treasure ships, his claiming of the coast of California as New Albion, and his return to England with treasure equal to twice the nation's annual budget. Without that treasure Elizabeth would have had to give in to Spain's threats and sign a treaty amounting to a surrender of sovereignty, a plot point supported by involving Drake in bonus fictional events such as foiling a Spanish scheme to assassinate the queen, preventing the escape of Mary, Queen of Scots, and looting a Chilean gold mine that's decked out like something from a lurid 1930s pulp adventure. History is compressed, so all this happens in two years instead of ten, but who's counting? Bear away and prepare to fire broadside!

One caveat: a bit over halfway through, there's a "comical" sequence involving the Miwok tribe that's incredibly insulting to Native Americans; it's hard to see how it could have been considered funny even in 1962. Just . . . skip past it. It's super cringey.

THE 7TH VOYAGE OF SINBAD

Rating: ★★★★★ (Essential) • *Origin:* USA, 1958 • *Director:* Nathan Juran •
Source: Viavision Blu-ray

Before *7th Voyage*, Ray Harryhausen was just the creature guy for black-and-white monster movies; after this big-budget full-color fantasy adventure, he was the premier special-effects wizard of his time, not simply because he presented the most convincing and magical fantasy creatures in world cinema but also because it proved he was a top-notch storyteller to boot.

THE *7TH VOYAGE* AND ITS CHILDREN

Nowadays you can't walk down a store's DVD aisle without tripping over a stack of fantasy films, but not that long ago they were as rare as roc's teeth, and finding a good one was like stumbling on a magic lamp. In that regard, Ray Harryhausen's *7th Voyage of Sinbad* was a watershed, a top-notch fantasy that seemed to leap out of nowhere into magical life (though it had predecessors in the 1924 and 1940 *Thief of Bagdad* films). Hollywood didn't quite know what to make of it, so *7th Voyage* was followed by just a handful of copycats that were pitched at children. But it inspired an entire generation of young filmmakers, special effects artists, and game designers, whose work would bear fruit in the fantasy boom that would begin in the early 1970s.

This film delights the child, adult, and professional storyteller in me equally, and I love it without reservation.

Even if you've never seen *7th Voyage*, you know the film's iconic cyclops, the roaring one-eyed giant with the hoofs and digitigrade legs, its face more expressive than even the movie's human actors. And you've very likely heard Bernard Herrmann's pounding and melodic score, probably his best-known non-Hitchcock soundtrack, evoking the surge of ocean waves at one moment and the growling of behemoths in the next. The story is also a familiar one, but I won't recapitulate it, because there must be some readers who haven't seen this film yet, absolute classic though it is. Suffice to say it's based on the Sinbad stories from the *Arabian Nights* and has two main settings: the fabulous city of Bagdad, from the *Tales*, and the

The 7th Voyage of Sinbad Columbia Pictures / Wikimedia Commons

mythical island of Colossa, home of fantastic creatures like the aforementioned cyclops. Without going into detail on the plot, I do want to draw attention to its tight, classical structure: an action-packed 10-minute prologue that establishes the characters and situation followed by three quick, 20-minute acts (Bagdad; Colossa; the wizard's lair) jammed with colorful incidents—and then bang, it's over, and the audience goes home thrilled and happy. All kudos to writer Kenneth Kolb and director Nathan Juran for pulling that off.

I mentioned a wizard, didn't I? There's always a sorcerous antagonist in a Sinbad movie, a tradition established with this film, and though Sinbad may be the titular hero, the wizard always gets the juiciest part. This time it's the duplicitous Sokurah, played with gusto by Torin Thatcher. He drives every twist and turn of the story before meeting his inevitable fate, completely eclipsing Kerwin Mathews, this outing's Sinbad. Mathews is the usual clean-cut 1950s hero; he isn't asked to be anything more than handsome, active, and forthright, and for that he's just fine. However, Kathryn Grant as Princess Parisa has more fun and is thoroughly adorable, especially in the scenes she shares with Richard Eyer as Barani, the young genie of a magic lamp.

But all the human actors, even the wizard, are outshone by the creatures, especially Sokurah's fire-breathing dragon, easily the most persuasive dragon seen on film up to that date (and for many years thereafter). And Sinbad gets to wave his scimitar at a half dozen other wonderful, mythical opponents animated by Harryhausen, the most impressive scene being a sword duel with a fencing skeleton, a fight so memorable that Harryhausen restaged it in *Jason and the Argonauts*—but with *seven* skeletons!

And don't forget that cyclops! Look, there's not a moment wasted in this Arabian Nights fable, and you'll enjoy every minute of it no matter how many times you've seen it before. Cue it up!

SHINSENGUMI: ASSASSINS OF HONOR (OR *BAND OF ASSASSINS*)

Rating: ★★★☆☆ • *Origin:* Japan, 1970 • *Director:* Tadashi Sawashima •
Source: Toho Video DVD

Just the year before, Toshiro Mifune had coproduced and starred in *Samurai Banners*, a historical epic about the beginning of the Tokugawa era; here he does the same in a film about the era's end. In the 1860s Japan went through a civil war in which the samurai of the shogunate, who wanted to continue running the country as they had for three centuries, were opposed by samurai who wanted change and supported a restoration of the power of the emperor. This film is about Isami Kondo (Mifune), who rises to command the Shinsengumi, a paramilitary force of formerly masterless samurai who band together to help defend the shogunate. Kondo, a poor country samurai who ran a sword-training school, initially comes to the capital Kyoto when he hears there are threats to the shogunate, the institution that to him represents all that is meaningful about the samurai tradition. He joins an early band opposed to the imperial "loyalists" run by the obstreperous Kamo Serizawa (Rentaro Mikuni) and quickly distinguishes himself, so when the group is reconstituted as the Shinsengumi, Kondo becomes one of the commanders.

As an unofficial arm of the shogunate, it soon develops that the role of the Shinsengumi is to use spies and informers to identify adherents of the imperial faction and then murder them. At this the band is all too successful, and soon co-commander Serizawa becomes an embarrassment, killing and looting indiscriminately and spending the spoils on sake and women. Kondo tries to get Serizawa to reform but eventually joins with the other commanders to assassinate him. After that, Kondo is the undisputed leader of the band.

This film takes no sides in the politics of the opposing factions; it just observes the character of Kondo as he gradually grows sick of all the killing and realizes that it changes nothing. Kondo is a stoic, reserved and restrained, and Mifune is brilliant at conveying his thoughts and feelings through the tiniest changes of expression. Kondo's world is harsh and brutal, but he's convinced that if he maintains self-discipline and adheres to the warrior code, then surely by example he will lead his men to do what is right. But he's only human, he makes mistakes, and even when he finally sees that the code of the samurai is no longer the solution to Japan's problems, he stays true to it. Unfortunately, modern warfare has arrived, and bringing a *katana* to a gunfight doesn't work out well for the Shinsengumi.

The swordplay in this film is realistic and brutal, as harsh and unforgiving as civil war usually is, especially when Kondo leads a raid on a clan planning an arson attack, saving Kyoto from burning down. But the shogunate is weak and failing, and though Kondo finally sees that his end is inevitable, he faces it forthrightly. Alas, inevitability doesn't necessarily make for a compelling story, and in this case, it deflates the last act of the film. Mifune is great, and the depiction of Japan at the end of the Tokugawa era is excellent, but this movie won't be for everybody.

SHOGUN

Rating: ★★★☆☆ • *Origin:* USA, 1980 • *Director:* Jerry London • *Source:* Paramount DVDs

Dude. Nine hours.

If you were alive in 1980 and over the age of 10, you probably watched this blockbuster TV miniseries along with everybody else in America and Europe. For American TV of its time, it was daring for its treatment of adult themes, and it served to introduce most viewers to the samurai period of Japanese history, which up till then had been rarely depicted in Western mass media. After the broadcast, James Clavell's novel, on which it was based, sold over two million copies in paperback. (I bought one.)

It hasn't aged well. Viewed 40 years later, this is a slow, talky soap opera set against historical events that are never clearly explained, a backdrop of samurai politics that's murky at best. Only a few of the many characters are portrayed in enough depth to make them interesting, giving the viewer little investment in whether they come or go. And though there are ninja assassins and a lot of talk about what it means to be a samurai, there's not much samurai action in all those nine hours, and what action there is doesn't compare well with Japanese jidaigeki films made around the same time.

Clavell's novel is a fictionalized account of a true story, that of William Adams, an English navigator shipwrecked on the shores of Japan in 1600, when the country was completely unknown to Europeans save for a few traders and missionaries from Portugal and Spain. This English pilot, here called John Blackthorne (and played by Richard Chamberlain), has to negotiate the strange and deadly culture of the samurai with no prior knowledge of the society or its language. His seafaring skill makes him a pawn in conflicts between warring daimyo until he is taken up by the wily Lord Toranaga (Toshiro Mifune). Toranaga is served by the Lady Mariko (Yoko Shimada), who has learned European languages from Portuguese Jesuit missionaries, and she becomes Blackthorne's guide to Japanese ways—and eventually his lover, despite Mariko being married to one of Toranaga's leading retainers.

THE YEAR OF *SHOGUN*

Before 1980 few people in America and Europe knew much about Japan's samurai era—if anything, they associated its warrior ethos with the hostile mindset that had led the country into its big mistake in World War II. The unarmed combat skills of judo and karate were popularized during the 1960s, but little was known about the martial arts of the samurai that had preceded them until *Shogun*, James Clavell's blockbuster novel and subsequent TV mini-series, hit the American and European mainstream. Suddenly samurai were top-of-mind for mass market consumers, from low-culture exploitation videos (as they were regarded then) like *Shogun Assassin* to high-culture art-house darlings like *Kagemusha*, the triumphant return of director Akira Kurosawa to the genre of his breakthrough film *Seven Samurai*. After 1980, "samurai" was nearly as recognizable a historical concept as "cowboy."

Much angst ensues. Chamberlain as Blackthorne is regularly gobsmacked by the harshness of samurai culture, staring in consternation with furrowed brow as events beyond his control unfold in front of him. After a career in 1960s TV shows, in the '70s Chamberlain had graduated to B-level leading roles in the movies, mainly historical adventures in which he acquitted himself well. *Shogun* made him a top star, but it's far from his best work. The Japanese leads come off better: Mifune oozes gravitas and sly humor as Toranaga, while Shimada as Mariko delivers a complex and moving performance that steals every scene from Chamberlain. A few of the supporting actors are memorable as well, particularly John Rhys-Davies (you know him as Gimli) playing Spanish navigator Rodrigues, and Frankie Sakai as one of Toranaga's vassals, Lord Yabu.

But the pacing plods for most of the miniseries, and after running on for so many hours, it wraps up with an abrupt and unsatisfying ending. Production values are okay but still below the quality of feature films. The show does make one bold move by refraining from translating the spoken Japanese except when respoken by one of the European-speaking interpreters, which effectively conveys Blackthorne's incomprehension when suddenly immersed in a foreign culture. However, sometimes no interpreter is around to explain events conveyed in Japanese, necessitating a voice-over to explain things, an awkward imposition that's partly forgiven because they got Orson Welles to serve as narrator. Mostly, though? Meh.

SHOGUN ASSASSIN

Rating: ★★★☆☆ • *Origin:* Japan/USA 1980 • *Directors:* Kenji Misumi/Robert Houston •
Source: Criterion Blu-ray

In the 1970s, the *Lone Wolf and Cub* movies (1972–1974) were almost entirely unknown outside of Asia, deemed too violent for the American and European markets. In 1980 producer David Weisman paid Toho studios $50,000 for the American rights to the films, and his partner, avant-garde filmmaker Robert Houston, recut the first two *Lone Wolf* movies into *Shogun Assassin*, dubbing the dialogue to an entirely new script by Houston and Weisman. The result used part of the origin story from the first movie in the *Lone Wolf* series, *Sword of*

Vengeance, and nearly all of the second, *Baby Cart at the River Styx*. Beyond just editing the two original films together, the new movie's story was significantly altered, simplifying the plot to cut out nearly all the period politics and reducing it to a duel between the assassin Lone Wolf (Tomisaburo Wakayama) and Lord Retsudo of the Yagyu clan (Yunosuke Ito), here renamed the Shogun. Why that latter simplification? The year 1980 was that of the hugely successful *Shogun* TV miniseries, which introduced mass American audiences to samurai history, so "shogun" was a magic word to conjure with.

Moreover, Houston and Weisman gave their version a narrative voice-over by Lone Wolf's three-year-old son, Daigoro, in which the toddler explains his father's life and career of sudden death, calmly keeping a count, for example, of the hundreds of the "Shogun's ninja" that the Lone Wolf has slain. It's a daring move, edgy and hilarious, and it *works*, elevating *Shogun Assassin* from a mere violent exploitation flick into a cult classic. Moreover, Houston's reediting is sharp; the dubbing, often deliberately humorous, is clever and well done; and the film has a cheesy but tense soundtrack by Mark Lindsay, the former lead singer of Paul Revere & the Raiders.

The film was released to the American grindhouse circuit in 1980, where it was an instant niche success. It became a notorious gotta-see-it violent video in America and Europe during the VHS years of the early '80s, molding the tastes and ambitions of later directors such as Quentin Tarantino and Robert Rodriguez. Even today, *Shogun Assassin* holds up as sheer entertainment—and if it gets the viewer to take a look at the outstanding original films it was adapted from, that alone justifies its existence.

SIEGE OF THE SAXONS

Rating: ★★★☆☆ • *Origin:* UK, 1963 • *Director:* Nathan Juran •
Source: Ambito Domestico DVD

This is another Arthurian adventure from the year of Camelot, but there's nothing particularly Arthurian about the title *Siege of the Saxons*, which probably contributes to why it was overlooked and is now nearly forgotten.

In the 1950s and '60s, movies were often packaged and sold to distributors as double features, with a lead marquee title and a lesser opening film. This picture was the opening feature to *Jason and the Argonauts*, both made by the same producer, Charles H. Schneer, and directed by Nathan Juran of *The 7th Voyage of Sinbad*. *Saxons* was shot in 15 days by Juran with a small cast and recycled costumes, sets, and footage from *The Black Knight* and *Sword of Lancelot*. It's a curious sort of Arthurian film: King Arthur (Mark Dignam) has no round table, his wicked son Mordred has been replaced by a loyal daughter named Katherine (Janette Scott), and his only knight champion is Edmund of Cornwall (Ronald Howard), who turns out to be a rotter. Edmund is plotting with the invading Saxons to kill Arthur, forcibly marry Katherine, and seize the throne, and he'd have gotten away with it, too, if it wasn't for a meddling outlaw from the greenwood named Robert (Ronald Lewis). Yep, there's at least as much Robin Hood in this movie as King Arthur, despite the eventual appearance of an aging and unmagical Merlin (John Laurie).

The story isn't much, the leads are likeable but unmemorable, and the combat is mostly weak sauce until the final battle between the Saxons and the English knights, where director Juran shows what he can do despite his tiny budget. This is for Arthurian fans only, and even they could be forgiven for giving it a pass.

THE SIGN OF ZORRO

Rating: ★★★★☆ • *Origin:* USA, 1958 • *Directors:* Lewis R. Foster/Norman Foster •
Source: Disney+

Disney's *Zorro* TV series has continued stories like an old-time serial, structured in what we'd now call story arcs of 13 episodes each. This feature is a compilation of the "Monastario" story arc from the start of the first season. Though it's episodic and it's easy to see the seams where the chapters were stitched together, compressing thirteen 25-minute episodes into one 90-minute story definitely sharpens and improves the storytelling.

Not that it needs much improving. The *Zorro* series is the pinnacle of the Disney studio's live action productions, well acted, sharply written, and tightly directed; if you've never seen it, this is a fine introduction, with all its virtues presented in capsule form. The basic story doesn't stray from the one told in *The Mark of Zorro* in its 1920 and 1940 incarnations: in 1820, Diego de la Vega (Guy Williams), the son of one of the leading landholders of Southern California, returns from his studies in Spain to find that the pueblo of Los Angeles is under the tyrannical rule of a corrupt *comandante*. The crimes of Capitán Monastario (Britt Lomond) are so outrageous that the rancheros, led by Don Alejandro de la Vega (George Lewis), are ready to rise in open revolt. Diego realizes this will lead to their defeat and his father's death, so he adopts the guise of the outlaw Zorro to oppose Monastario in their place.

Williams is a fine Zorro in the athletic swashbuckler tradition of Doug Fairbanks Sr. and Tyrone Power, climbing adobe walls, leaping from tile roofs, and rearing against the horizon on Tornado, his famous black stallion. The swordplay, with period-appropriate small swords and cavalry sabers, is solid, which is no surprise as the fencing master is Fred Cavens, who also coached Fairbanks and Power. The wicked Monastario is a worthy opponent, clever and courageous, and after a series of clashes, he deduces who Zorro must be behind his black mask and nearly exposes him to the visiting viceroy of Mexico; however . . . but no, see it for yourself.

SINBAD AND THE EYE OF THE TIGER

Rating: ★★★★☆ • *Origin:* UK, 1977 • *Director:* Sam Wanamaker •
Source: Viavision Blu-Ray

After the success of *Golden Voyage of Sinbad*, Columbia Pictures and Ray Harryhausen decided to up their game by shooting the third Sinbad movie at eye-popping locations in Spain, Malta, and Jordan, including the actual ruins of Petra. Then I guess they figured no further improvements were needed, because they hired mediocre director Sam Wanamaker, a journeyman unable to mitigate the pacing problems of the story, which was already burdened by a dull and generic script from Beverly Cross. The cast is bland as well, featuring the charisma-free Patrick Wayne (son of John) as Sinbad and the vacant Taryn Power (daughter of Tyrone) as Dione, the wizard's telepathic daughter. Jane Seymour as Princess Farah gets to do some decent acting in a couple of early scenes, but then the movie forgets she has any character and demotes her to the role of not-many-clothes horse. The best actors, as usual, are cast as the magicians: Margaret Whiting as the transforming sorceress Zenobia and Patrick Troughton (the Second Doctor Who) as Melanthius, gray and looking just like Gandalf minus the hat. The film's saving grace, as always, is the stop-motion artistry of Harryhausen and his marvelous creatures.

The plot follows the tried-and-true quest structure, with Sinbad and company on a peril-ous journey to find a cure for Farah's brother, Prince Kassim, whom Zenobia has transformed into a baboon. This animated primate, with its humanlike gestures and expressions, is entirely convincing and ranks with Harryhausen's best work. Zenobia also gets a first-rate animated minion in Minaton, a bronze minotaur golem with a clockwork heart and an endless reservoir of superhuman strength. With the baboon in almost every scene with Sinbad, and Minaton ever-present with Zenobia, *Eye of the Tiger* probably features more onscreen creature time than any other Harryhausen epic.

The journey is the usual parade of wonders interrupted by fantasy melees. It's a tribute to Harryhausen's skill—and an indictment of Wanamaker's failings—that the animated combats are far better choreographed than the live-action fights. In the middle of the film, as Sinbad's ship sails toward Arctic Hyperborea, pursued by Zenobia in a bronze boat powered by the untiring Minaton, the pacing sags in a miasma of fog and stock footage of icebergs, alleviated only by a dumb battle with a giant walrus, possibly the least-cool Harryhausen creation ever. The pace picks up again when they reach Hyperborea, where Sinbad and friends encounter an oversized protohuman they call Trog. Instead of the expected combat pitting Trog and his great bone club against the scimitars of Sinbad's crew, Kassim the baboon befriends the primi-tive creature, and it trustingly joins their party. The friendly nonverbal interactions between Trog and the baboon that follow are delightful, and the animated creatures establish an emo-tional connection stronger than any between the movie's "real" actors.

As usual, the climactic scene is set in an ancient temple, an Arctic pyramid with a magic, ever-swirling whirlpool bath inside. This confrontation between good and evil is overlong and entirely predictable; and some big-time monster-wrestling notwithstanding, one just wishes they'd hurry up and get it over with. The wrestling comes courtesy of an ice-locked saber-toothed tiger, which in accordance with the Law of Frozen Prehistoric Beasts, gets thawed out to menace the heroes. Once the final fight is over, the film blessedly cuts straight to the end credits, which play over the coronation of the rehumanized Prince Kassim, while the rest of the good guys smile in bland approval. That's fine: we don't really need any character closure with them anyway, since none of them has half the heart and soul of Harryhausen's noble beasts.

SINBAD OF THE SEVEN SEAS

Rating: ★☆☆☆☆ • *Origin:* Italy/USA, 1989 • *Directors:* Luigi Cozzi and Enzo G. Castellari • *Source:* MGM DVD

Harryhausen this ain't. After making *Hercules* (1983) and its wretched sequel with "star" Lou Ferrigno, writer/director Luigi Cozzi shot this Sinbad movie with the ol' Hulk, but it was such a dreadful mess that not even Cannon Films could release it. After the footage sat fester-ing in its film cans for a couple of years, producers Golan and Globus hired director Enzo Castellari to try to salvage it. Inspired perhaps by the recent success of *The Princess Bride* (1987), Castellari added a framing sequence of a modern mom reading a bedside story to her daughter, providing a narrator to patch up the holes in the clumsy storytelling of Cozzi's film, but there are so many problems to solve with this mechanic that the narrator quickly becomes intrusive and tedious. But really, what else could they do?

The opening credits claim the story is adapted from Edgar Allan Poe's "The Thousand-and-Second Tale of Scheherazade," but that's bogus, it really just cops ideas from the classic

Thief of Bagdad films (1924 and 1940), adding a few cheesy peplum tropes topped off with gratuitous racism and sexism. There's an evil vizier/wizard named, as usual, Jaffar (John Steiner), who wants to supplant the Caliph of Basra and marry his daughter, Princess Alina (Alessandra Martines). But the princess longs only for Prince Ali (Roland Wybenga), who sails with Sinbad (Ferrigno) as one of his crew of ethnic caricatures that includes a Viking, a Greek alchemist, an Asian who's either Chinese or Japanese (they can't decide), and a "humorous" dwarf—one of those unfortunate cheesy peplum tropes. The plot is incoherent nonsense about collecting four or five (they can't decide) magic gems that Jaffar has hidden in dangerous locations, protected by superdumb monsters like a guy in a rubber rock suit and a slime golem that shoots lasers. Ferrigno flexes and does Mighty Feats of Strength, and his enemies pop like balloons.

Sinbad of the Seven Seas ranks up there with the oeuvre of Ed Wood Jr., as one of the most technically incompetent movies ever made. It tries to be outrageously campy but doesn't know how. Every aspect of it is simply woeful. In fact, this film regularly shows up on lists of movies-so-bad-they're-good, and on that basis, you might enjoy it. I (your illustrious author) have been known to be amused by the occasional utter cinematic failure, and even my mouth gaped when Sinbad, dropped into a dungeon infested by cobras, sweet-talks the snakes into allowing him to tie them into a rope of serpents so he can climb out and save his Five Caricatures from being cast into a piranha pool. Word of honor. Plus there's an evil twin encounter, which is never wrong. Even so, the real test here may not be whether you can find some fun in this botched and bungled flop but whether you can stick it out for the full 93 minutes. Warned or challenged, it's up to you!

SINBAD THE SAILOR

Rating: ★★★☆☆ • *Origin:* USA, 1947 • *Director:* Richard Wallace •
Source: Warner Bros. DVD

After making *The Corsican Brothers* in 1941, Douglas Fairbanks Jr. joined the US Navy for five active and much-decorated years. Following his wartime service, the return to mere moviemaking must have seemed anticlimactic. He took his time in picking the vehicle that would relaunch his acting career and finally settled on *Sinbad the Sailor*. Strangely, though there had been a couple of animated two-reelers in the '30s, this film is the first full Sinbad feature. It's amazing that it took until 1947 for that to happen, especially considering how many Sinbads there have been since, but the success of *A Thousand and One Nights* (1945) had established the Arabian fantasy subgenre as a dependable moneymaker, and by this point they were coming thick and fast.

Fairbanks decided to make the movie a conscious homage to his late father, performing a lot of his own stunts and adopting some of Doug Sr.'s exaggerated silent-movie gestures and mannerisms. Unfortunately, the result feels forced and affected, and the performance seems out of place, as if Fairbanks is making a moving in 1927 while the rest of the cast is in 1947.

But what a cast it is! The story follows the Arabian Nights convention of telling a tale within a tale, with a framing sequence in which Sinbad purports to tell his buddies in Basra the story of his hitherto-unknown eighth voyage. Unknown or not, it's a familiar story, a treasure hunt built of standard elements but supremely useful as a setting for the lead actors to show their chops. And so, let us praise Maureen O'Hara, Queen of the Swashbucklers, who plays the clever and conniving Shireen, a Kurdish beauty with brains to spare. She's proud and ambitious but must somehow choose between wealth, power, and love (for Sinbad, of course!).

Further, O Best Beloved, let us praise the worthy Walter Slezak, he of the waggling eyebrows, who as the barber-surgeon Melik (among other guises), serves as the evil genie of this morality play, a corrupter and tempter so cunning and sly you can't help but admire him, even when you know he's up to no good. As usual with Slezak, the best part of his portrayal is the way he shares how much fun he's having with us, the audience. O'Hara's intelligence lights up her performance, but Slezak's razor wit gives his role a darker edge. His Melik knows he's a villain and will probably come to a bad end, but he accepts that as his nature and revels in it.

Which brings us to the movie's other villain, the ominous Emir of Daibul, as played by Anthony Quinn in his best role to date. Usually cast before as a sidekick or second banana, in *Sinbad* he comes into his own as a charismatic ruler of men and women, a confident commander both smart and ruthless. Like Sinbad, Shireen, and Melik, Quinn's Emir is after Alexander the Great's treasure on the lost island of Deryabar, and he means to have it at any cost. So do the others, of course, and between them there are plenty of temporary alliances and inevitable betrayals along the way, as well as romantic intrigue, stolen maps, virulent poison, Greek fire, and much waving around of those long, curved *katar* knives they all seem so fond of. Ultimately this is a fable, so expect the ending to turn on a moral before going back to Sinbad's framing sequence where we started—and may Allah's blessings be upon you!

SIREN OF BAGDAD

Rating: ★☆☆☆☆ • *Origin:* USA, 1953 • *Director:* Richard Quine •
Source: Turner Classic Movies

Paul Henreid and Hans Conried star in a sort of Arabian fantasy Road Picture, and you know what, I love those guys, but Henreid and Conried are no Hope and Crosby, especially with a script as weak as this one. Henreid is Kazah the Great, a magician with a traveling show featuring doofus assistant Ben Ali (Conried) and a bevy of dancing chorines in harem pants. The gag is that stage magician Henreid can do real magic but only when it's funny. And you know what, in this film, that's not very often. Bagdad is ruled by an old usurper sultan who's controlled by an evil grand vizier, and the real sultan's daughter Zandi (Patricia Medina) is the true heir to the throne, but Kazah . . . aah, you know what, forget it. Allakazam! It never happened.

SIR FRANCIS DRAKE

Rating: ★★☆☆☆ (first half) / ★★★☆☆ (second half) • *Origin:* UK, 1961 •
Directors: Clive Donner, Terry Bishop et al. • *Source:* Network DVDs

This British TV series is a segue between two entertainment eras, harking back, on the one hand, to the popular swashbuckling shows of the late 1950s and, on the other, to the new spy shows just coming to the fore at the start of the '60s. Sir Francis Drake is Queen Elizabeth's action hero at sea with cannon and sword, when not engaging in intrigues at the royal court and secret missions in foreign capitals that could have been written for *Danger Man* a.k.a. *Secret Agent*—whose hero is also named Drake!

The series, twenty-six 25-minute episodes, takes a while to find its feet, and the first half of the season is pretty weak, with ridiculous stories in which Drake takes castles and rescues captured royals by sneaking in the back way, clobbering a few guards, and declaring victory.

Drake is played by Terence Morgan, an actor who'd made his name in British cinema playing handsome scoundrels. The historical Drake was certainly a handsome scoundrel, but his namesake here is too squeaky clean, the only honest man at Elizabeth's court, and at first Morgan isn't really into it, sometimes on the verge of phoning it in. Though they built a 100-ton replica of Drake's *Golden Hind* for the naval scenes, the sailing and gunnery is all folderol, quite unbelievable. Fortunately, the fencing, directed by Peter Diamond (*Star Wars*, *Highlander*), is excellent—fast and furious—and Morgan looks like he enjoys plying a rapier.

There are a few worthwhile episodes directed by Clive Donner early in the season, but the series really picks up in the second half: the stories turn taut and tense, and the scripts start giving the actors lines worth speaking. For example, in episode 15, "The Irish Pirate," the queen sends Drake to the ragged shores of County Mayo to capture Hugh O'Neill, the Earl of Tyrone, who's planning to set himself up as the King of Ireland, but Drake gets entangled with the historical pirate Grace O'Malley (Elspeth March), represented here as a thoroughly unscrupulous and cunning old harridan. Episode 18, "The Bridge," written by Brian Clemens (*The Avengers*, *Captain Kronos*), is a good example of a swashbuckler/spy crossover, as Drake must rescue the Portuguese Prince Gazio (Patrick Troughton) from a Spanish prison; Drake gets himself arrested and thrown behind bars but while wearing a hidden utility belt filled with lockpicks, skeleton keys, and small lock-exploding gunpowder charges. John Keir Cross wrote two strong episodes with historical literary slants: 19, "Johnnie Factotum," in which Drake meets both Shakespeare and his Dark Lady; and 24, "Gentleman of Spain," another spy intrigue in which Drake must save captured Welsh slaves from Tripoli on the Barbary Coast and teams up with Don Miguel de Cervantes (Nigel Davenport), Drake's exploits helping to inspire the creation of *Don Quixote*. Throughout the series the stories often turn on the (respectful, alas) relationship between Drake and Queen Elizabeth, played by Jean Kent with the right mix of sentiment and majestic petulance, never better than in episode 20, "Mission to Paris": Elizabeth falls for a French prince, the Duke of Alençon, and Drake is sent to the French court to find out if the duke was just toying with her. This episode also includes Pamela Brown in a chilling performance as the murderous Catherine de Medici. Brrr!

SON OF ALI BABA

Rating: ★★☆☆☆ • *Origin:* USA, 1952 • *Director:* Kurt Neumann •
Source: Universal Vault DVD

After *The Prince Who Was a Thief* (1951), Universal decided to make another Arabian Nights–style adventure starring Tony Curtis and Piper Laurie, but this time around they got a dud. Thanks to his ex-thief father Ali's vast wealth, Kashma Baba (Curtis) is enrolled with the sons of the nobility as a cadet in Bagdad's Military Academy—which, except for the dark-haired Curtis, is entirely filled with WASP-looking frat boys straight from the country club. (As usual in these films, only merchants, thieves, and the caliph's goons look like actual Persians or Arabs.) Trying to fit in, Kashma throws himself a rowdy birthday party in his opulent Bagdad house, but the caliph's boorish son gets thrown into Kashma's indoor pool. Uh-oh! Vengeance is sworn, and the next morning Kashma is embroiled in a plot to ruin him and his father by foisting upon him an escaped slave girl, Kiki (Laurie), only she's really a princess who's been promised to the shah unless she can find Ali Baba's treasure for the caliph to save her mother—but it's impossible to care because this thing is a mess, okay?

I always hate to blame the writers, as they've got it hard enough, but in this case, I feel obliged to point the finger of shame at Gerald Drayson Adams, who concocted this goofy story and wrote all the terrible, terrible dialogue. There's a definite high style to the classic Arabian Nights stories, and adapting that poetic diction to a movie script can be done, and done well, but based on this clunker, Adams had no idea how to go about it. These poor actors are only human, and no one can say a line like "I sense an evil hand has wrought this chain of circumstances!" without looking at least a little embarrassed. Poor Tony Curtis has it the worst, having to utter junk like "Perished I would have, had not the princess dragged me from the flames," all with a pronounced Noo Yawk accent. Yeesh. (Fun fact: "This is the palace of my fadda, and yonda is the Valley of the Sun" is actually from this film rather than the later *Black Shield of Falworth*.)

The only real point of interest in this otherwise dull and derivative exercise is the character of Tala (Susan Cabot), a bow-wielding huntress and friend of Kashma's youth. At first it seems her only purpose is to make Princess Piper jealous of her connection to Kashma, but then she saves the day several times in succession with her deadly talents at archery. Tala is genuinely intriguing and capable, and how she wandered into this fiasco is anybody's guess. Her role should probably have been combined with that of the princess so Laurie would have something to do other than look ornamental, because as it stands, her considerable talents are wasted. Skip this one and watch *The Prince Who Was a Thief* a second time instead.

THE SON OF MONTE CRISTO

Rating: ★★★☆☆ • *Origin:* USA, 1940 • *Director:* Rowland V. Lee •
Source: American Home Treasures DVD

Independent producer Edward Small's biggest hit was *The Count of Monte Cristo* (1934), with star Robert Donat. Small planned to follow up with a sequel, but Donat bailed and went back to England, so the producer set the project aside until he found a charming new star in Louis Hayward. Sadly, this middling sequel doesn't live up to its memorable predecessor, never really rising above pretty good. Much of the problem lies with screenwriter George Bruce's story, a predictable cape-and-sword potboiler that's more Anthony Hope (i.e., *Zenda*) than Alexandre Dumas, with a protofascist villain anachronistically thrown in for good measure.

Fortunately, the protofascist, Gen. Gurko Lanen, is played by the lethally arrogant George Sanders, the only man in Hollywood who could outsneer Basil Rathbone. The tale is set in 1865 in the fictional central European country of Lichtenburg, whose young ruler (Joan Bennett) is Grand Duchess Zona, a name that cannot be improved upon. Lanen and his jackbooted thugs threaten to usurp Zona's power, so she attempts to escape to Paris to call for French intervention. But her attempt is foiled: it's stopped in a border incident that draws in the dashing Count of Monte Cristo (Hayward)—or his son, anyway, who now bears the title. Zona is taken back to Lichtenburg, and Monte Cristo, smitten, follows her.

The ensuing intrigues in Lichtenburg, though predictable, are entertaining enough, but the only thing Monte Cristo–ish about them is that the count adopts several guises and impersonations in his campaign to rescue Zona and her grand duchy from Gurko Lanen. The film checks most of the swashbuckler boxes, with secret passages, a masked outlaw, a grim castle dungeon, a fop with a quizzing glass, a secret treaty, a slimy sewer, a treacherous servant, forged documents, and an interrupted wedding, plus there's plenty of lively swordplay—nothing new in any of it, but at least it's enthusiastic. Hayward is likeable and energetic, Bennett is appealing and determined, and Sanders steals his every scene with sheer supercilious effrontery. Director Rowland V. Lee, who helmed the original *Monte Cristo*, keeps this sequel moving along, and it's a good time, mostly. Watch for Clayton Moore—yes, the Lone Ranger—as an earnest young guard captain loyal to Zona, who allies with Monte Cristo.

SON OF SINBAD

Rating: ★★☆☆☆ • *Origin:* USA, 1955 • *Director:* Ted Tetzlaff • *Source:* Turner Classic Movies

Bagdad buddy picture, with Dale Robertson as the skirt-chasing Sinbad, son of Sinbad, and Vincent Price as his wisecracking poet pal Omar Khayyam. This is one of the last films produced by Howard Hughes, so it's also a jiggling boob-fest that was condemned by the Catholic Legion of Decency, featuring about five-score would-be Jane Russells, the stripper Lili St. Cyr, and four "exotic" dance routines right off the burlesque stage. Nobody in this film is from the Middle East, or even east of New Jersey: cowboy star Robertson's Oklahoma accent is as broad as the Panhandle, and Price even imitates it mockingly in their first scene together. But Robertson's not the only one, as Murad, the envoy of the Mongols, sounds like he just rode in from Dodge City, and the guards running around in turbans and waving scimitars were just the week before wearing cowboy hats and waving six-guns in Westerns.

But is there any swashbuckling? A bit. Sinbad's hobby is intruding into the harem of the Caliph of Bagdad, a practice that eventually gets him and his pal Omar captured and condemned. Fortunately, next to them in the line of captives is an old friend of Sinbad's father, a sage who knows the secret of Greek Fire and has passed it along to his daughter Kristina (Mari Blanchard). This suddenly becomes important when the aforementioned Murad arrives as herald of the host of Tamerlane, demanding "submission or the sword!" Sinbad proposes that the caliph free Kristina and her father, with him and Omar in the bargain, so they can use the sage's Greek Fire to fend off the Mongols. However, the caliph's jester Jiddah (Jay Novello) is a spy for Tamerlane, so Kristina gets abducted and things get complicated. Sinbad and Omar set out to save both Kristina and the secret of Greek Fire, scimitars are duly waved, and Mongols are incinerated offscreen. Plus, there's dancing.

If you're one of those viewers who can't get enough of Vincent Price, I sympathize with that, and this movie is very much for you, because Price fires off poetical quips and does wide-eyed double takes in nearly every scene. But if you're not a Price fan, steer clear and find yourself another caravan. "The moving finger writes, and having writ, moves on."

SORCERESS

Rating: ★☆☆☆☆ • *Origin:* USA/Mexico, 1982 • *Director:* Jack Hill •
Source: Square Classics DVD

"This movie is so bad that it's good!" You hear that a lot, usually when someone is defending a thoroughly mediocre film that the person happens to enjoy. But can it really be said to be true? Well, here it is, folks, the exception that proves the rule, a movie so terrible that you can only gape at it and savor its unremitting terribleness.

This is a sword-and-sorcery flick shot at the same time as *Conan the Barbarian* but so far beneath *Conan* as to be barely visible from it. In an unnamed ancient land, a woman is pursued by the soldiers of the evil wizard-king Traigon (Roberto Ballesteros), who fathered her infant twin children. To become all-powerful, Traigon has offered to sacrifice his firstborn child to the evil goddess Kalghara, but the mother of the twins refuses to tell him which babe was born first. This vexes Kalghara, so he wounds her mortally, only to die himself thanks to the tardy appearance of the good wizard Krona (Martin LaSalle), who always shows up a little too late. As Traigon dies, he vows he'll be reborn when the stars are right and will sacrifice that firstborn yet. The dying mother of the twins makes Krona swear they'll be raised as warriors and avenge their mother. But, surprise twist time—the twins are girls!

Twenty years pass, and the now-mature twins, Mira and Mara (Leigh and Lynette Harris), are introduced to us in a nude swimming scene, because . . . of course. Meanwhile, Traigon has been reborn and sends out his beak-helmeted goons to search for "the two who are one," which they do by burning, raping, and murdering, because that's how you know they're bad. The goons kill the peasant family who had raised the twins in ignorance of . . . well, everything, including the difference between boys and girls, which will lead to some boffo yocks later on, you betcha. The twins had been granted combat powers by Krona, and they use them to slay the goons, just before the aging Krona, with a random Viking named Baldar (Bruno Rey) and his friend, a leering, baa-ing satyr, show up too late to help. Krona gives the twins the powers he already gave them plus some exposition, tells them to remember the name "Vetal," and dies. The twins and Baldar instantly decide to go after Traigon. They sneak into Traigon's generic fantasy town, where they also pick up the film's leading man, a surfer-dude barbarian prince named Erlick (Bob Nelson), who throws in his lot with the twins after taking a good look at them topless.

Then a lot of stuff happens in more-or-less random order. Traigon has an evil girlfriend named Delissia who is served by an evil ape-person in the worst ape-person costume ever, Baldar has a super iron sword whose powers are mentioned once and then forgotten, Mara and Erlick are given a glowing green aphrodisiac drink so that when they bang, Mira will feel it by sympathetic magic and writhe around, Baldar and Mira go on a dungeon crawl with zombies, and the satyr, with his pan-pipes, leads a platoon of sheep and goats to the rescue. Plus more partial nudity.

A lot of low-budget fantasy films buff up their casts by hiring a few decent character actors, but not this one: in *Sorceress*, players act like they've never acted in anything before, and based on this they never will again. The costumes are a random mixture of ancient, medieval, and barbaric, rented off the rack for about a dollar apiece, and the special effects—oh, lord, the special effects. The final celestial battle between Kalghara and the god Zetal, who looks like a sort of winged lion squeezy bath toy, will be seared into your cortex until the sweet release of death.

THE SPANISH MAIN

Rating: ★★★★☆ • *Origin:* USA, 1945 • *Director:* Frank Borzage • *Source:* Warner Bros. DVD

This is a fine Technicolor pirate epic, grand and satisfying, the story carried by the energy of its three marquee stars and a surprise standout fourth. Paul Henreid, best known as Victor Laszlo in *Casablanca*, is the heroic lead, a Dutch ship captain who is captured and enslaved when a storm drives his peaceful ship aground in Spanish colonial waters. He escapes and becomes a feared pirate captain known as the Barracuda, preying exclusively on Spanish shipping. You might not think the stiff and rather serious Henreid could buckle a swash like Errol Flynn or

Tyrone Power, but you'd be wrong: his Captain Barracuda displays an edge of mocking arrogance that enables him to command buccaneers and defy Spaniards, he looks good in pirate garb, and he knows what to do when you put a sword in his hand.

The Barracuda captures a Spanish ship bearing our second star, the radiant Maureen O'Hara as the Condesa Francisca, on her way to marry the Viceroy of New Granada—the very man who is the particular target of the Barracuda's campaign of revenge. When the Barracuda meets Francisca, sparks fly, and he decides to marry her just to spite the viceroy—or is there another motive? The condesa initially refuses, but then she finds a reason of her own to agree, sort of. The two maneuver around each other toward marriage like a pair of tall ships tacking in to a boarding action. Here, as with her role in *The Black Swan*, O'Hara's character has to find a means to give herself away without giving herself up. She does it, though, and O'Hara has the chops to make you believe it.

The viceroy, Don Juan, isn't happy about any of this—but when Don Juan is unhappy, we're delighted, because he's played by Walter Slezak, and boy, do we love him when he's angry! Slezak is basically reprising his governor's role from *The Princess and the Pirate*, but the viceroy here is much smarter, more menacing, and equipped with a wicked sense of humor. He's quick-witted, mean, and oozes contempt for his inferiors, that is, everyone. It takes everything the Barracuda and Francisca have to defeat him, and even so it's a near-run thing.

However, before our two romantic leads run afoul of the wicked viceroy's final trap, they put in to Tortuga for some roistering, revelry, and a spot of getting-betrayed-by-your-allies-because-what-do-you-expect-from-pirates? One of these allies is Binnie Barnes playing the historical female pirate Anne Bonny, and *The Spanish Main* is worth watching for her performance alone. This is, I believe, the first appearance of Anne Bonny onscreen, and in Barnes's portrayal she's tough and jealous but fiercely independent and takes no guff from anyone. In this she resembled Barnes herself, who had a long career in the movies from the 1920s to the '70s but always refused to play submissive roles: give me anything, she said, "as long as I don't have to be a sweet woman." Amen to that.

SPARTACUS

Rating: ★★★★★ • *Origin:* USA, 1960 • *Director:* Stanley Kubrick •
Source: Universal Blu-ray

Spartacus is a meme, of course—but more than that, it's a remarkable motion picture, arguably the best of the grand historical epics of Hollywood's studio era. Its subject is the evils of human slavery (and if you're an apologist for slavery you can stop reading now, because you're not welcome here). Like all great stories about injustice, it makes the matter relatable by personalizing it, making it the story of a few representative characters.

The setting is in Italy in 72 BCE, the late Roman Republic, and the three representative characters are Spartacus (Kirk Douglas), a condemned slave being trained as a gladiator, Varinia (Jean Simmons), a slave and body servant at the gladiator school, and Marcus Licinius Crassus (Laurence Olivier), a wealthy Roman senator and would-be dictator. We're introduced to these characters in the first hour of the movie, which is entirely set at the gladiator school of slave merchant Lentulus Batiatus (Peter Ustinov in the role of a lifetime, but more about him later). At the school the slaves, already treated as mere possessions, are dehumanized even further by being turned into hopeless machines desperate enough to fight each other to the death for the amusement of the masters. This is depicted in an extended martial skills training montage to end all martial skills training montages; there we first see director Stanley Kubrick's visual mastery in a bravura sequence that displays his particular kind of genius. The camera starts every scene perfectly placed, and as the scene moves, no matter where the action goes, in close, out wide, slowly or quickly, the camera follows—and no matter where it goes, the camera is. Still. Perfectly. Placed.

It's as well that the story is in the hands of a visual maestro, because for that first hour, Douglas and Simmons barely speak. Douglas might not have the most expressive face in Hollywood, but Kubrick gets him to tell the entire tale of Spartacus's restrained anguish, fierce spirit, and growing love for Varinia entirely with his eyes. And he's matched by Simmons, whose eyes are so eloquent she scarcely needs speech. It is, as I said, quite remarkable.

Olivier's Crassus comes into the picture when he shows up at the gladiator school with his son-in-law and a couple of patrician ladies to demand a private show: a duel to the death. Before the match, Spartacus is asked by his friend Crixus if he would really kill Crixus if he had to, and Spartacus says, "Yes." The fight, which pits Spartacus with a Roman gladius against Draba (Woody Strode), a tall Ethiopian armed with trident and net, is exciting, dramatic, and as authentic as historical research could make it. Spartacus loses to Draba and expects to die, but instead the Black man refuses to kill his fellow slave and sacrifices his own life in a hopeless attack on their masters.

Draba's sacrifice infuses Spartacus with the principle he lacked and the purpose he needed. When Varinia is sold to Crassus, Spartacus leads a violent revolt that overruns the gladiator school in a few thrilling minutes, and Spartacus is transformed from a sullen slave to the inspiring leader of an ever-broadening slave rebellion. He forges the former slaves into an army with gladiator training and one simple truth: all men and women die, but if they all fight together, win or lose, they'll die free.

And many die, though for quite a while the rest survive and win. Spartacus's army grows ever larger as they march toward a port where a hired pirate fleet is waiting to take them away from Italy. This part of the film isn't perfect; Kubrick does a fine job of putting human faces on the swelling throng of ex-slaves as they march in their thousands toward the sea, but really a little marching-of-thousands goes a long way, and there's way more than a little. The Romans try to stop Spartacus's army, but their legions are repeatedly defeated in battles of which we see only the aftermath. After a while this feels like a cheat, but Kubrick knew what he was doing, building the suspense toward one final battle in which all the might of Rome is arrayed against Spartacus's vast but ragtag horde. It's a huge but convincing spectacle, and as confidently filmed as if the 32-year-old director had been making movies about ancient classical warfare for decades.

You know the meme, so you know how it ends—but there's much more to *Spartacus* than that. The story of the slave rebellion is echoed by a parallel plot in the Roman senate about the decline of the Republic and the rise of authoritarianism, a plot that pits Crassus against Gracchus (Charles Laughton), the voice of the plebeians, who is ugly and corrupt but brilliant, with an undeniable, oily charisma. Laughton is tremendous, and yet he's outdone by Ustinov as Batiatus, the obsequious but engaging scoundrel who moves back and forth between the worlds of the slaves and the patricians. Ustinov won a Best Supporting Actor Oscar for the role, and he deserved it.

If you haven't seen *Spartacus*, or haven't seen it lately, you'll want to watch the 2015 digital restoration of this classic, which includes deleted scenes and composer Alex North's magnificent full score. Trust me.

SPARTACUS AND THE TEN GLADIATORS

Rating: ★★★☆☆ • *Origin:* Italy/France/Spain, 1964 • *Director:* Nick Nostro •
Source: Mill Creek DVD

Writer-director Nick Nostro thought it would be a good idea to use the heartbreaking saga of Spartacus's slave revolt as the background for a lighthearted adventure romp, a buddy picture with 10 shirtless pals beating the tar out of slavers and Roman guardsmen. And, son of a wolf, he was right!

The gladiator Rocca (Dan Vadis) and his nine interchangeable gladiator pals put on a good show in the arena at Capua but then watch as a dozen mutinous Thracian gladiators are ordered to fight each other to the death. Halfway through that combat, one of the Thracians refuses to continue, and the rest throw down their weapons as well. Despite Rocca's protests, the impresario of the games wants the mutineers immediately put to death, but instead a brute named Chimbro (Milton Reid, you'll recognize him) buys the Thracians for his master, Senator Varro (Gianni Rizzo). Thwarted, the impresario takes out his anger on Rocca and company, telling them they'll never work in Italy again.

Ten unemployed gladiators in the Italian countryside, looking for love and a chicken dinner! Being good-hearted lugs, they rescue a snooty patrician woman from a gang of bandits; she turns out to be Senator Varro's daughter, and she takes the gladiators home for supper. During the meal, Chimbro comes in to report that he's been unable to find the camp of the bandit Spartacus, so Varro recruits Rocca and company to take on the task, and since they don't like bandits, they accept.

This movie is basically one exaggerated fight scene after another, with just enough connective tissue in between as a pretext for the next fight. Director Nostro is refreshingly unembarrassed about this: Chimbro tells Senator Varro that these gladiator dopes will never find Spartacus's camp, and then cut! Rocca and company are looking down at Spartacus's camp. The gladiators infiltrate the camp in an attempt to capture Spartacus (Alfredo Varelli), but he turns out to be the Thracian who refused to fight in Capua, and his ex-gladiator buddies quickly surround Rocca and company. Spartacus challenges Rocca to single combat and they fight . . . for a really long time, so long that everybody from both sides sits down to watch and enjoy it, as Rocca and Spartacus bond in manly fashion by waling on each other until they're staggering like drunkards. The fighters embrace, Rocca admits he was wrong about Spartacus, he falls in love with one of the ex-slave women at first sight, he and his buddies join the slave revolt, and everyone cheers.

The plot is even less credible from this point onward, but everyone's having such a good time, it would just be mean to complain. There are more captures, betrayals, escapes, gladiator commando raids, and clobbering of slavers on the regular, building up to a big set-piece battle between a Roman legion and Spartacus's slave army. Things look dark for a while, young love is in peril, but the laughing gladiators win through, and it's entertaining despite being dumb. This is actually the third *Ten Gladiators* movie, but the first two don't seem to be available in English versions, so you'll have to be satisfied with this one.

STAR WARS (OR *STAR WARS—EPISODE IV: A NEW HOPE*)

Rating: ★★★★☆ • *Origin:* USA, 1977 • *Director:* George Lucas •
Source: 20th Century Fox DVD

Star Wars made swords cool again.

You already know what you think about *Star Wars*, so this entry isn't going to be a full review of the film, just the part that matters to this book, which is the swordplay. Writer-director George Lucas was a fan of Akira Kurosawa's samurai films such as *The Hidden Fortress* (1958), and when he was creating his space fantasy, he knew he wanted it to include science-fiction *katanas* so he could get the striking look of classical Japanese fencing but with energy weapons.

From the standpoint of realistic melee weapons, lightsabers are ridiculous, but from a cin-ematic point of view, they're genius, probably the single element of *Star Wars* with the great-est visual appeal. And not just visual: their sound, that hungry energy hum as they're swung about, added convincing credibility to their lethal effect. It all makes the lightsaber seductively appealing as a power fantasy, because it looks like even a wielder with little skill could do horrific damage with one, since the weapon does nearly all the work. Obi-Wan Kenobi uses his to take off a thug's arm in the Mos Eisley cantina, which is a feat an ordinary katana could do as well, but not with a mere flick of the wrist.

Considering the outsize impression made by lightsabers, it's surprising how little they actually appear in the first film. Luke practices with his aboard the *Millennium Falcon* against a hovering "remote" that fires mild zap blasts, and then the weapon doesn't really appear again until the climactic duel between Obi-Wan and Darth Vader. This fight was directed by stunt coordinator Peter Diamond, who had experience with stage fighting and devised a two-handed style reminiscent of Japanese kendo, with the fighters feeling each other out, seeking advantage, until suddenly attacking with moves mostly of the arms and wrists. This made sense given the apparent properties of the weapons but also took into account the capacities of actors Alec Guinness and David Prowse, who were neither fencers nor very athletic.

And so it was that, by the end of May 1977, youngsters around the world were putting down their toy guns, picking up broom handles and cardboard tubes, and once again miming heroic swordplay, albeit with *vverrroum-herrroummm* noises rather than the clash of steel.

STAR WARS: THE EMPIRE STRIKES BACK (OR *STAR WARS—EPISODE V: THE EMPIRE STRIKES BACK*)

Rating: ★★★★★ • *Origin:* USA, 1980 • *Director:* Irvin Kershner • *Source:* 20th Century Fox DVD

After *Star Wars* was a global blockbuster, there was a long laundry list of what was desired in its sequel, but on one subject everyone was agreed: give us more lightsabers!

The sequel delivered—and this time, George Lucas got an actual saber fencer to act as sword master. Bob Anderson was a former Olympic fencer who had worked in the back-ground in filmmaking for many years, finally making a mark when he choreographed the smallsword duel in *Barry Lyndon* (1975) for Stanley Kubrick. Though his fight direction work on *Empire Strikes Back* was uncredited at the time and largely unrecognized for years afterward,

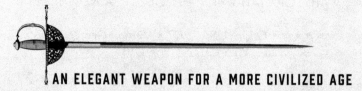

AN ELEGANT WEAPON FOR A MORE CIVILIZED AGE

In adventure movies throughout the twentieth century, swords had been losing ground to guns as the hero's weapon of choice. Though films of knights, pirates, and cavaliers had a strong start in the silent era, they were gradually sidelined over the decades as Western, gangster, and war movies came to the fore. By 1971, Dirty Harry and his ultramacho Smith & Wesson .44 magnum seemed to have put the nail in the coffin.

Then came *Star Wars*. And suddenly, out of the left field of Japanese samurai movies via the imagination of George Lucas, swords resumed their prominence. In the decade that followed they even dominated for a while, falling back again during the '90s to second place before Peter Jackson brought them back, seemingly for good, with the *Lord of the Rings* trilogy. So from those of us who are sword fanciers, a hearty *thank you* to George Lucas, Peter Jackson—and Akira Kurosawa.

it was Anderson who came up with the more fluid and dynamic lightsaber dueling style seen in that film and its sequel, *Return of the Jedi*. He even doubled for David Prowse in the role of Darth Vader for the more athletic fight sequences and is responsible for the brilliant sword choreography that added so much impact to the *Star Wars* sequels.

As if to make up for how little he used the weapon in the first movie, this time around Luke Skywalker (Mark Hamill) wields the sword in every lightsaber scene, showing its use as a standard Jedi tool in the episodes set on the planet Hoth (where it once again lops off an arm, this time from a wampa snow beast). On the planet Dagobah, during a Force-related vision quest, Luke then crosses lightsaber blades with a mind-illusion of Darth Vader, a foreshadowing of their climactic battle at the end. It's in that final long, multistage duel between Luke and Vader that the Force first becomes a major element in the swordplay, adding a telekinetic wild card to the saber fencing.

Bob Anderson would go on to become a major figure in cinematic sword fight direction, choreographing the duels in *Highlander* (1986), *The Princess Bride* (1987), *The Mask of Zorro* (1998), and the *Lord of the Rings* trilogy (2001–2003)—but arguably it was his work on *The Empire Strikes Back* that made the greatest and most lasting impression.

STAR WARS: RETURN OF THE JEDI
(OR STAR WARS—EPISODE VI: RETURN OF THE JEDI)

Rating: ★★★☆☆ • *Origin:* USA, 1983 • *Director:* Richard Marquand •
Source: 20th Century Fox DVD

For *Return*, Luke Skywalker (Mark Hamill) picks up his lightsaber yet again, but Luke has changed between the second movie and the third, and his mastery of the lightsaber shows this more than any other aspect of the film.

However, first we must have the sword-and-planet adventure of Luke and company rescuing Han Solo (Harrison Ford) from Jabba the Hutt on Tatooine, with Skywalker bounding

Star Wars: Return of the Jedi AUTHOR'S COLLECTION

around atop Jabba's Barsoomian flyers going full Mifune on the crime lord's many goons. Luke intermixes use of the Force with rapid swordplay, and if the sequence goes on a bit too long, we forgive it for its enthusiastic sense of fun and triumph over the forces of cartoonish evil.

After that the film gets darker, as the stakes in the fight between Empire and Rebellion reach an existential level. As the personifications of the two sides, Darth Vader (David Prowse) and his son Luke inevitably face off in an extended, climactic lightsaber duel. As in *The Empire Strikes Back*, the swordplay is choreographed by Bob Anderson, who sometimes dons the Vader suit for the more physical moves. Taking advantage of the fact that the energy blades are also light sources, the duel is atmospherically set on a series of darkened stages lit mainly by the clash of the lightsabers. Director Richard Marquand's use of quick cuts increases the feeling of danger from previous duels in the series. This sharpens the fight's dramatic function, which is to point out how Luke has internalized the lessons of the first two films in order to show what it really means to be a Jedi Knight. Vader toyed with Luke in *Empire Strikes Back*; this time the son holds his own against the father, and more. It's a classic lesson in how cinematic swordplay can be used, not just to embellish a film, but to effectively tell its story through motion and emotion.

THE STORY OF ROBIN HOOD AND HIS MERRIE MEN

Rating: ★★★☆☆ • *Origin:* USA/UK, 1952 • *Director:* Ken Annakin •
Source: Disney DVD

After the success of *Treasure Island*, Walt decided to continue the Disney studio's live-action adventures with Robin Hood, another popular (and public domain) property. Since 1938 every Robin Hood movie had stood in the shadow of the towering Errol Flynn film, but the Disney version set out to be a reboot, a resetting of the legend for the safe and conformist 1950s. In this telling Robin (Richard Todd) is infantilized: when we meet him, he's a lad playing juvenile archery games with Maid Marian (Joan Rice) while his father Fitzooth, the chief forester for the Earl of Huntington, meets with the other grown-up, bearded, manly men to prepare for what manly men do, which is go to war. The earl—Marian's father—is eager to follow his own father-figure, King Richard, off to fight in the Crusades. Big Daddy Richard leaves behind Prince John (Hubert Gregg), in this version hardly older than a lad himself, enjoining him to mind the kingdom in his absence, and the Earl of Huntington does the same for his domains with his forester, Fitzooth.

The kids had been warned to play nice while the daddies are gone, but John would rather be a bully, so there. Since Richard took the manly, bearded Sheriff of Nottingham with him on Crusade, John appoints his crony Guy of Gisbourne (Peter Finch) to be the new sheriff (a convenient combining of two legendary characters) and orders him to build a force of the finest archers in the land. The sheriff hires a few ruthless goons who begin plundering the peasants to collect John's new extortionate taxes but he needs more, so he organizes an archery tournament to awe the serfs and attract more bowmen. Now, in the Robin Hood legend, Robin is usually the finest archer in all England, but here it's his own father who splits Robin's arrow and wins the tournament. However, still loyal to King Richard, Fitzooth refuses to join John's tax collectors. The wicked sheriff has Fitzooth murdered, Robin kills the assassin, and then, proscribed, has to go off into the woods and play outlaw with the other bullied boys.

The wild and dangerous edge that Flynn brought to Robin Hood is lacking here: Todd is a Boy Scout with a junior executive haircut and a smile from a toothpaste commercial, and Basil Rathbone would eat him for lunch and carry off Maid Marian for dessert. But aside from that, on its own terms this movie is a solid retelling of the Robin Hood story, successfully establishing the tone and template that would rule further remakes for a decade or so, especially the hit *Adventures of Robin Hood* TV show that would run from 1955 through 1959. Shooting the film in the forests of old England rather than the California woods gives the film an authentic feel, and director Ken Annakin is equally adept with character development and action scenes. The Merrie Men are all charming and well cast, especially James Robertson Justice as Little John, and the clever use of the minstrel Alan-a-Dale (Elton Hayes) to provide segues in song from one scene to another works well. The climactic fight between Robin and the sheriff is genuinely suspenseful, and if the violence isn't as gritty as in *Treasure Island*, it's less bland and bloodless than it will be later in the '50s. Marian even gets to join with the Merrie Men for a while and play in their secret clubhouse—so long as she dresses up like one of the lads and agrees not to do any icky girl stuff.

SWASHBUCKLER (OR *THE SCARLET BUCCANEER*)

Rating: ★☆☆☆☆ • *Origin:* US, 1976 • *Director:* James Goldstone • *Source:* LL DVD

We all like a good pirate adventure. This is not a good pirate adventure. This is a pirate adventure made by people who seem to think everything you need to know about pirate adventures can be learned from a 10-minute Disney theme park ride.

The star, the great Robert Shaw, is wasted here, miscast as a reckless, thoughtless, jolly frat boy of a captain, a role he plays with an appropriate lack of conviction, cackling joylessly at bawdy limericks. The talented Peter Boyle is utterly miscast as Lord Durant, a cartoonish villain who says things like "There is no lord but Darkness." (Like, whoa.) Geneviève Bujold is miscast as the spunky ingenue who is meant to fall in love with Shaw's Ned Lynch, but the two have zero or even negative chemistry together, and Bujold just looks angry all the time, probably at her agent for getting her into this role with its demeaning catfight and gratuitous nude swim. A young Beau Bridges is miscast as a dopey and unfunny British officer named Major Folly, say no more. In fact, everyone in the film is miscast, because none of them should be in this film.

The plot, about opposition to the ludicrously cruel and evil Lord Durant, who rules Jamaica in 1718 as a despot, is nonsense and doesn't bear summarizing. The script is wretched, and the pacing of the direction is terrible. The tone of the movie veers widely from campy comedy to horrific torture, sometimes in the same scene. The score for the action sequences is literally circus music. The fencing is a bad joke. The costumes resemble nothing worn by anyone in 1718 or, for that matter, anyone anywhere at any time in history. There's a food fight in the town market. Bananas are thrown. James Earl Jones, as Shaw's piratical first mate, tries desperately to maintain a shred of dignity. Poor devil; look away from his suffering and remember other, better nights at the movies.

THE SWORD AND THE DRAGON (OR *ILYA MUROMETS* OR *THE EPIC HERO AND THE BEAST*)

Rating: ★★★☆☆ • *Origin:* Russia, 1956 / UK, 1960 / USA, 1963 •
Director: Aleksandr Ptushko • *Source:* YouTube streaming video

The *bogatyrs* were legendary culture heroes of the Kievan Rus, precursors of the later Russian Empire that was centered on Muscovy. One of the mightiest of the bogatyrs was Ilya Muromets, who was said to fight the Mongol invaders with superhuman strength and a magic sword; the old epic poem about Muromets was revived in the 19th century, and in the 20th century the bogatyr was adopted as a protopatriot of the fatherland by Soviet Russia. That made his larger-than-life adventures a perfect subject for Russia's leading filmmaker of the fantastic, Aleksandr Ptushko, who made the colorful fable *Ilya Muromets* in 1956. With the growing popularity of Harryhausen-style fantasies, in 1960 the film was issued in an English-language version in the UK as *The Epic Hero and the Beast* and was then redubbed and reissued by American producer Roger Corman in 1963 as *The Sword and the Dragon*. The Corman version is what's usually seen today, though there's a cleaner Russian version restored by Mosfilm that has decent English subtitles.

This film is an epic fantasy with big medieval battles, colossal sets, extravagant costuming, sorcery, demons, and a three-headed fire-breathing dragon. It's also so simple it's almost a child's fairy tale, which is how it was marketed by Corman, and like much Soviet art, it's as subtle as a sledgehammer. The Mongols, called Tugars in the film, are dreadful barbarians, all bad habits and bad hygiene, and Muromets (Boris Andreyev) is a gigantic hero of goodness whose only flaw is that he's a wee bit short-tempered. But at the start, Ilya is a mere farmer stricken with paralysis who can't even raise his arms to fight when the Tugars raid his village and carry off his beloved Vilya (Ninel Myshkova). Meanwhile, a giant bogatyr, called Invincor in the Corman version, wearies of fighting and passes on, metamorphosing into a mountain of rock, but not before giving his magic sword to some pilgrims and charging them with finding a hero who will wield it for the cause of good. The pilgrims find Muromets, cure him with a magic potion, give him Invincor's sword, and it's look out, Tugars! He raises up a magical horse called Chestnut Gray, declaiming, "Serve me well, noble steed!" (All his lines are like that.) Advised by talking ravens, Muromets captures a hideous wind demon, impresses Prince Vander of Kiev, and when an arrogant half-ton Tugar envoy, borne on the backs of slaves, appears at the gates to make demands of the noble prince, Muromets kills him outright.

The depiction of the Tugars here is both fabulous and disturbing. Brutal caricatures of Central Asians, they're all cruel slaves of their even crueler Khan (Shukur Burkhanov), who does stuff like command hundreds of his minions to pile into a human pyramid so he can climb to the top to get a better view. The Tugars' fantastic outfits and vile practices are outsize, outrageous, and appallingly racist on an epic scale. Hundreds of them come sweeping across the steppe for the final battle with Muromets and his proto-Ukrainians, for a climax that features the aforementioned dragon, a mix of stop-motion animation and a giant puppet whose heads are mounted with actual military flamethrowers. Quite a spectacle, all in all. Just don't hope for subtlety.

THE SWORD AND THE ROSE

Rating: ★★★☆☆ • *Origin:* UK/USA, 1953 • *Director:* Ken Annakin •
Source: Walt Disney Home Video

This is based on the popular 1898 novel *When Knighthood Was in Flower* by Charles Major, a Victorian historical romance that had been filmed twice before in the silent era, a story that has just enough swashbuckling in it for inclusion here. Despite its title, the novel isn't set in medieval times but during the early reign of King Henry VIII, telling the story of his sister, Princess Mary Tudor, and her (largely unhistorical) love for Charles Brandon, a mere captain of the guard. Brandon is played by Disney's chosen leading man of the time, Richard Todd, in perhaps his best performance, though he's better known for *Dam Busters* (1955). Princess Mary is played by Glynis Johns, who has the impossible task of making her willful and selfish character seem adorable, but she's so good she almost pulls it off. The leads are supported by a cast of fine British actors that includes James Robertson Justice as King Henry, Michael Gough as the Duke of Buckingham, and Rosalie Crutchley as Queen Katherine, all benefiting from a strong script with a lot of cutting gibes and haughty rejoinders.

To the plot! King Henry wants to marry his sister to King Louis XII of France, but Mary wants no part of that dynastic nonsense and instead sets her heart on the dashing but far-from-royal Brandon; Buckingham, however, wants Mary for himself and is lethally jealous. Cue the court intrigue and illicit love. Brandon ends up in the Tower of London, while the princess is married off to the aged Louis of France but not before she extracts a promise from Henry that she can choose her own second husband when the time comes. Buckingham engineers a phony jailbreak from the Tower so Brandon can be killed while escaping, but he survives. In due course Louis of France dies, but his son by a previous marriage, the new King Francis, wants Mary for himself and means to have her. Buckingham and Brandon go separately to France to retrieve Mary and meet in the inevitable duel in the Channel surf to settle who will bring her home.

It's a good-looking film, shot at evocative English locations, but mention must be made of the magnificent background paintings by Peter Ellenshaw that give it so much of its authentic-seeming period character. There's not much action in it, but the escape from the Tower of London is suspenseful, and the final rapier duel between Todd and Gough is quite well done. This was the third of four Disney historical adventures shot in Britain in the early 1950s; it was a handsome picture, slick and well made, yet for some reason it was a disappointment at the box office. Disney would make one more British historical, *Rob Roy*, and then lay off the swashbucklers until the *Zorro* TV series some years later.

THE SWORD AND THE SORCERER

Rating: ★★★☆☆ • *Origin:* USA, 1982 • *Director:* Albert Pyun • *Source:* Laser Paradise DVD

After *Conan the Barbarian*, this movie is the second essential pillar of the 1980s barbarian boom, because it proved there was a ready market for heroic fantasy films even if they were low budget, indifferently acted, and rather cheesy. Released nearly coincident with *Conan*, *The Sword and the Sorcerer* is true to its name, a largely successful attempt to incorporate every trope and stereotype of the sword-and-sorcery genre into a single feature, shamelessly plundering the works of Conan's creator Robert E. Howard and his many pulpy imitators.

THE BARBARIAN BOOM (PART 2)

Filmmakers jump on a hot new genre with alacrity if it looks like it can be reduced to an easily replicated formula. That was certainly the case with 1980s sword-and-sorcery films, which were happily adopted as a replacement for the dying genre of Westerns. Producers of formulaic genre and exploitation movies, such as the notorious Roger Corman, practically started an assembly line to produce quickie barbarian pictures. Following the heroic fantasy formula probably reached its qualitative peak with 1984's *Conan the Destroyer*, which has a story by Marvel comics writers who had already worked out every variation of standard sword and sorcery plots and characters, so they knew what worked best. Following that film, the best fantasy movies of the later '80s would be those that broke formula to a greater or lesser extent.

It's not that this is a bad movie, it's just that it doesn't bother to aim for good, settling in every aspect for good enough. Director Albert Pyun, a journeyman specializing in B movies, doesn't have an original bone in his body, and every scene is swiped from somewhere else, a relentless succession of clichés presented with the absolute confidence that that's exactly what you came to see. The hero, a prince-turned-mercenary named Talon (Lee Horsley), is a swaggering Spaghetti Western badass with a sword instead of a gun—and what a sword: an oversized triple-bladed aluminum contraption that looks more like a kitchen implement than a weapon. Bonus: it's spring-loaded and can shoot its extra blades as missiles—but that's fine, given that the combat here is on the level of Saturday morning live-action TV shows. Talon's enemies are the evil King Titus Cromwell (Richard Lynch), who killed Talon's parents (of course), Cromwell's evil war chancellor Machelli (George Maharis), who lives for treachery and sneering, and the slime-covered demon wizard Xusia (Richard Moll), who lives for vengeance and comes back from the dead on the regular to get it.

The Sword and the Sorcerer AUTHOR'S COLLECTION

Talon's allies are likewise right off the sword-and-sorcery rack: Mikah the Rightful Prince of Ehdan (Simon MacCorkindale), who never wears a shirt despite being a prince, Alana the Rightful Prince's Hot Sister (Kathleen Beller), who promises her virtue to Talon if the hero will save her brother from Cromwell, and Brave but Feckless Stripling Rodrigo (Anthony De Longis), who wants to join Talon's hard-bitten mercenary band. Some of these folks, such as Maharis and MacCorkindale, are actually decent actors, but given lines like "Let's finish this" and "No! It lives!", they just mug their way through it without working too hard.

Nonetheless, this movie is nearly essential if you want to understand the cinematic origins of the genre, because it set the standard for the decade of budget fantasy films to follow. It was a big, fat surprise hit, the most successful independent film of 1982, earning over 10 times what it cost to make, and producers of quickie genre films like Roger Corman and his ilk took notice. Everything in it may be utterly predictable, but the film's insouciant disregard for being anything but an enthusiastic cheese-fest gives it an undeniable charm. Assuming you like cheese.

THE SWORD OF DOOM

Rating: ★★★★★ • *Origin:* Japan, 1966 • *Director:* Kihachi Okamoto •
Source: Criterion DVD

This extraordinary film tells the story of a samurai who trusts only his sword; he has no principles but its use, and his sword's only purpose is killing. If this sounds like the most antiheroic, nihilistic 1960s thing ever, you're not wrong, but *Doom* isn't just another film about the hollowness of the Bushido warrior code that led the previous generation to disaster in World War II. This story is older, based on a popular Japanese serial novel by the pacifist Kaizan Nakazato that began publication in 1913 and had been filmed at least four times before. But Okamoto's version, distilling the events of that very long novel into under two hours, is a punch in the gut you won't soon forget.

Ryunosuke, the protagonist—we can't call him the hero—is played by the great Tatsuya Nakadai, and he gives the swordsman the empty eyes and vacant expression of a soulless sociopath. We first see him appear behind an old man at a mountain shrine praying to die well—so Ryunosuke kills him, leaving the body to be found by his granddaughter Omatsu (Yoko Naito). Ryunosuke returns home to prepare for a demonstration duel with Bunnojo (Ichiro Nakaya), a match Bunnojo must win to earn a position and provide for his family. Ryunosuke's aging father urges his son to let Bunnojo win, as does Bunnojo's wife, Ohama (Michiyo Aratama), who comes in private to plead with him. Ryunosuke promises Ohama he'll lose but then rapes her (offscreen—it's the one mercy this film affords us) and sends her home to Bunnojo. He divorces her and goes to the match with rage in his heart, enabling Ryunosuke to lure Bunnojo into a deadly attack that gives him a pretext to kill him. Ryunosuke escapes prosecution but is now a pariah, and what's left of his humanity begins to crumble away.

There isn't much fun to be had in this film—indeed, it denies the very possibility of the existence of fun—but there is beauty. Director Kihachi Okamoto's every shot is meticulously composed, the pacing is masterful, and the performances are restrained and all the more striking for that. The one-on-one duels are suspenseful, as Ryunosuke seems almost to slowly collapse before his opponents, drawing them in to an attack that will be their last. The mass combats are both savage and balletic, the moves elegant but the resulting injuries cruel. Okamoto's eye is precise and spares us nothing.

Having lost everything, Bunnojo's widow Ohama follows Ryunosuke and becomes his common-law wife as he seeks a living as a sword-for-hire. The story is set in the 1860s, during the dying days of the shogunate, and Ryunosuke joins the Shincho group, a death squad of samurai who murder the shogun's political enemies. But the killer is also being stalked by Bunnojo's younger brother Hyoma (Yuzo Kayama), who studies swordplay at the school of Master Shimada (Toshiro Mifune—yes!). Ryunosuke learns from Omatsu, whose grandfather he'd murdered in the first scene, that Hyoma is after him, but he has no fear, because he's never lost a fight and he considers himself invincible. He believes that he and his sword are supreme, until the night the Shincho group attacks Shimada, mistaking him for someone else, and Ryunosuke watches in frozen amazement as Shimada cuts down every single Shincho but him. Faced with visible proof that he is neither supreme nor invincible, that his every achievement is hollow, Ryunosuke begins to unravel. Haunted by visions of those he's slain, including his own wife Ohama, he descends into a final mad frenzy of blood lust. What, you expected a happy ending?

SWORD OF FREEDOM, SEASON 1

Rating: ★★☆☆☆ (first half) / ★★★☆☆ (second half) • *Origin:* UK, 1958 •
Directors: Terry Bishop et al. • *Source:* Network DVDs

This is another swashbuckler series from Hannah Weinstein's Sapphire Films, which also produced *The Adventures of Robin Hood* and *The Buccaneers*. It's set in Renaissance Florence during the late 15th century, after the Florentine Republic was essentially usurped by Lorenzo de' Medici, known as the Magnificent. The hero is an artist and fervent republican, Marco del Monte (Edward Purdom), with a studio on the Ponte Vecchio, who must balance his covert activities on the behalf of restoring the Republic with his need to please wealthy patrons such as . . . Lorenzo de' Medici.

The series has a rocky start, taking a while to find its footing and establish a consistent tone. At first it leans toward comic swashbuckler, a sort of sitcom-with-swords in the mode of British comedy in the Those Funny Foreigners genre; this isn't very good, but it suits the talents of star Purdom who, if he'd been a sandwich, would have been a ham rather than a hero. But eventually the tone settles on intrigue with a touch of humor, and that more ironic than broad, after which the series becomes dependably watchable. Its supporting characters are particularly strong, one or more of them often carrying an episode despite Purdom's histrionics. The best is Adrienne Corri, a talented comic actor with a broad range, in the role of Angelica, Marco's regular model and a reformed pickpocket. Also excellent are Martin Benson as villain Lorenzo de' Medici, and Kenneth Hyde as Niccolò Machiavelli, who plays for both sides; whenever one or both of them are onscreen, a good time is guaranteed. Monica Stevenson frequently appears as Lorenzo's sister, the adorably duplicitous Francesca de' Medici, and the ever-reliable Patrick Troughton shows up in a number of character roles. Swords are drawn in every episode, usually cheap-looking protorapiers, but there are also plenty of Italian stilettos and the occasional authentic matchlock musket.

Most of the better episodes occur in the second half of the season, after the writers and cast have figured out what they're doing. These include two highlighting Angelica, "The Ambassador," her best comic episode, and "Angelica's Past," which delves into Florence's thieves' guild and where she gets to show her dramatic chops. Machiavelli shines in "The Besieged Duchess," a sort of Renaissance ghost story, and Francesca gets to strut her stuff in

"Strange Intruder," where she plots to replace her brother Lorenzo with a French nobleman. And don't miss "Forgery in Red Chalk," in which Medici tries to get hold of Leonardo da Vinci's advanced weapon plans, and "Marriage of Convenience," which turns on Renaissance science scams such as perpetual motion and turning lead into gold. All the later episodes are worth watching.

SWORD OF FREEDOM, SEASON 2

Rating: ★★★☆☆ • *Origin:* UK, 1960 • *Directors:* Peter Maxwell et al. •
Source: Network DVDs

All 39 episodes of *Sword of Freedom* were shot in 1958, but only 27 appeared in the first season, the last 12 appearing in a final demiseason in 1960–1961. These second season episodes are all worthwhile, particularly "Chart of Gold," in which Florence's former admiral, long thought dead, returns to his estranged family with a map to the treasure of Eldorado, and "The Assassin," in which an amoral sellsword hired by Lorenzo de' Medici to kill Marco del Monte gets tangled in a web of conflicting obligations and finds he isn't so amoral after all. Also excellent are "Adriana," a gothic terror tale in which a predatory widow from Rome is assigned as Francesca de' Medici's new governess, and "Vendetta," in which Marco kills a Corsican assassin in a fair duel, only to be targeted for vengeance by the Corsican's younger brother. Oh, and there's "The Reluctant Duke," in which a noble threatened with assassination abdicates his responsibilities and runs away to join a troupe of commedia dell' arte buffoons. Big noses for everyone!

SWORD OF LANCELOT (OR *LANCELOT AND GUINEVERE*)

Rating: ★★★★☆ • *Origin:* UK, 1963 • *Director:* Cornel Wilde • *Source:* Alpha Video DVD

This is a worthy attempt to film the tragedy of the doomed love triangle of Arthur, Guinevere, and Lancelot, and if it falls short of greatness, it isn't because writer, director, and star Cornel Wilde didn't give it his all; it's just that he wasn't David Lean or Sergei Eisenstein.

Cornel Wilde was an Olympic fencer who became an action movie star during the studio era, but he didn't like being typecast and he wanted to control his own career, so in the mid-1950s he formed his own production company with his wife Jean Wallace and began making independent films, appearing in dramatic roles as often as fighting heroes. Camelot was a popular subject when Kennedy was in the White House, and there was a brief boom of Arthurian pictures, of which this was one of the best. The story has all the classic elements of Thomas Malory's *Le Morte Darthur*, with King Arthur (Brian Aherne) deciding to marry Princess Guinevere (Wilde's wife Jean Wallace), his finest knight Sir Lancelot (Wilde) becoming Guinevere's champion and secret lover, and Arthur's son Modred (Michael Meacham) plotting to bring Camelot down by revealing the treasonous love between Arthur's wife and his closest friend. The movie has a bit of a split personality, oscillating between the drama of its tragic love story and Lancelot's deeds of knightly valor, which include fighting in a tournament, a skirmish, an ambush, and two pitched battles. The love story is daring for its day, with a scene of lingering and sensuous adultery; Wilde's Lancelot, who is French, after all, speaks

THE YEAR OF CAMELOT

It's 1963: Lerner and Loewe's Broadway musical *Camelot* finally closed after almost 900 performances, Disney's *The Sword and the Stone* was preparing for release at the end of the year, and President John F. Kennedy's administration was being compared to King Arthur's. This didn't go unnoticed in Arthur's Great Britain, and the British movie industry obliged with two Camelot movies, *Siege of the Saxons* and *Sword of Lancelot*. And though one of these was quite ambitious, both have now largely been forgotten.

with a pronounced French accent, unusual in movie depictions of the character but sensible if you want to portray him as an illicit lover. The combat is also pretty daring for 1963, with an attempt to depict medieval combat as realistically as was possible at the time, such as when Lancelot wins his first tournament by splitting his opponent's skull with a greatsword. The battles are likewise valiant attempts to portray medieval warfare clearly and convincingly, with Lancelot leading his knights and men-at-arms first against a warband of invading Saxons and finally against Modred and his rebel army. In both battles the English longbow tactics of a later era figure prominently, and director Wilde does a good job of giving the audience a clear idea of what's going on as the various units wheel and charge. It all ends in tragic death and pious renunciation, but that's true to the source material, which is more than you can say for most Arthurian movies. Kudos for that.

SWORD OF SHERWOOD FOREST

Rating: ★★★★☆ • *Origin:* UK, 1960 • *Director:* Terence Fisher •
Source: Columbia Pictures DVD

For a low-budget movie made by a small studio just establishing its style—the UK's Hammer Films—this is quite good. The marquee draw is Richard Greene as Robin Hood, coming off his four-season star turn in the same role on the popular *Adventures of . . .* TV show; at the time, starring in a feature film, even a modest one, carried far more prestige than even a hit television series, so in some ways this movie is the capstone of Greene's career. However, this is a standalone Robin Hood movie whose story is unconnected with the show, and none of the other TV cast members appear in it—which is a bit of a shame, because their replacements in the corresponding parts aren't always better. There's one conspicuous exception: Hammer stalwart Peter Cushing plays the Sheriff of Nottingham, and his cold, blue stare brings a menace to the role never seen in the TV show. Indeed, the tone of this production is two shades darker than that of the series, grimmer and with higher stakes.

At story's start Robin is already the benevolent chief of an outlaw band in Sherwood, and unusually, he's given no backstory—he's just a good outlaw pursued by a bad sheriff and has yet to meet Marian Fitzwalter or get involved in the affairs of the realm. The story, scripted by Alan Hackney with spare and serviceable dialogue, starts off a bit slowly as we meet Robin, the Sheriff, and Marian (Sarah Branch, pleasant but unmemorable), but it picks right up once it introduces a political intrigue involving the unscrupulous Earl of Newark (Richard Pasco) and the honest and upright Hubert Walter, the King's Chancellor (Jack Gwillim). Fancy archery is a key plot point here, a delight for us traditional fans of the Outlaw of Sherwood, and Robin's skill with a bow comes to the attention of Newark, who tries to hire him for a mission. Robin plays along until it becomes clear he's being employed to carry out an assassination, and then suddenly the Sheriff comes along and recognizes him, Robin flees, and for the rest of the film, events move quickly.

The production is ably directed by Terence Fisher, taking a break from making a name for himself establishing the Hammer horror brand. I'll say this for Fisher, he has a sharp eye for composition, and even his simple shots are often beautifully set up. The movie was filmed in the bucolic Irish countryside, which gives it the authentic Merrie Olde England look that California lacks. The costumes, gear, and weaponry are reasonably authentic, the swordplay is credible, and the fights themselves are exciting. Plus we get the ever-excellent Oliver Reed stealing several scenes in an uncredited bit part as a nasty and arrogant young noble, just a year before his breakout role in *Curse of the Werewolf*. It was only 1960, but this may be the best Robin Hood movie of its decade. Recommended.

THE SWORD OF THE BARBARIANS (OR BARBARIAN MASTER)

Rating: ★★☆☆☆ • *Origin:* Italy, 1982 • *Director:* Michele Massimo Tarantini •
Source: YouTube streaming video

This is a standard Italian peplum, a formulaic sword-and-sandal film from the 1960s given a sword-and-sorcery paint-over to update it to the '80s. It's cheap, lurid, enthusiastic, and shameless, utterly unoriginal but nonetheless sporadically fun.

An opening narration informs us that some people are good, but there are others who are just plain bad. With that matter settled, we proceed to the story of one of the good ones, the barbarian hero Sangraal (Pietro Torrisi), who is leading his oppressed people, including his wife Lenna, across a wasteland in search of a place where they can live in peace. They find a likely looking valley, but there's a fight going on there: hunchbacked priests of Rani, the topless goddess of fire (Sabrina Siani), are attempting to capture some peaceful valley folk to sacrifice to their insatiable deity. In a gory fight, Sangraal and company slaughter the priests and rescue Ati (Yvonne Fraschetti), the daughter of the local chieftain: Ati and Sangraal lock eyes, sparks fly, and you just know Lenna isn't long for this world.

Sangraal's good people join Ati's good people, but the goddess Rani demands vengeance on Sangraal from her bad people, who are led by the ruthless warlord Nantuk (Mario Novelli). The bad people threaten the village of the good people; Sangraal rides out to defend them, falls into a trap like a complete dope, and is captured. Nantuk crucifies Sangraal on the hill above the village and makes him watch while Lenna and assorted extras are massacred. Fortunately, a random Asian stealth archer named Li Wo Twan (Hal Yamanouchi) happens along and helps Ati decrucify Sangraal and escape. Twan is an embarrassing caricature with a "funny" Asian accent, but he's also the only one of the good people with a lick of sense, so you kind of like having him around for as long as he lasts.

Time for mystic quests! To get his revenge, Sangraal must find Rudak, the Wizard of the Black Mountain, who says pompous stuff like "Ask for justice rather than vengeance." Right. Rudak sends Sangraal on *another* quest, to the Forest of Aranda, to seek the Ark in the Cavern of the Templars. Along the way Sangraal must fight blind troglodytes in a mystic cave, anthropoid tree-men who capture him in another simple trap (he never learns), and a topless witch in another mystic cave who looks like his dead wife Lenna. Whew! Finally, he reaches the Ark of the Templars, where his reward is . . . an oversized crossbow. This is confusing, because the name of the movie is *Sword of the Barbarians* and not *Oversized Crossbow of the Barbarians*, but whatever. Sangraal is now ready for his final confrontation with Nantuk, which is surprisingly well choreographed, the only decent fight in a film full of combat.

Director Tarantini tries to make up for his rock-bottom budget by swiping gimmicks from Italian horror films, shooting from weird perspectives and using wide-angle lenses, and that does help keep the visuals from being completely flat. Just don't expect Mario Bava. In fact, keep all your expectations at moderate or below, and you might get through this all the way to the end.

SWORD OF THE BEAST (OR SAMURAI GOLD SEEKERS)

Rating: ★★★★☆ • *Origin:* Japan, 1965 • *Director:* Hideo Gosha • *Source:* Criterion DVD

Cowriter and director Hideo Gosha's follow-up to *Three Outlaw Samurai* takes an even less forgiving view of society than its predecessor: individuals may be good, bad, or both, but hierarchical authority cares only for power and does only ill.

It's 1857, the shogunate is in tatters, and samurai Gennosuke (Mikijiro Hira) is on the run, pursued by members of his own clan because he slew a counselor who rejected reform. We learn in flashback that the naive Gennosuke had been suckered into killing the counselor by a lower officer who then betrayed him, so now he's turned his back on society. While hiding in a shabby gambling hall, he learns of a government preserve, a mountain where outlaws are illegally prospecting for gold, and decides to seek escape, and perhaps his fortune, up the valley of gold. Meanwhile, a band of crooked thugs are also planning to loot the mountain, but they're blocked by another samurai, Jurota (Go Kato), and his wife, Taka (Shima Iwashita), who are there ahead of them. Jurota has been secretly gathering gold on the orders of his own unnamed clan and will stop at nothing to succeed in his mission, even when Taka is abducted by the thugs. Gennosuke comes up the valley, and though he wants Jurota's gold, he saves Taka from the thugs and comes to an uneasy détente with the clan swordsman. But then Gennosuke's pursuers arrive, followed by Jurota's clan assassins, who've been ordered to get Jurota's gold and then kill everyone on the mountain.

This grim tale is shot in beautiful mountain wilderness deliberately to contrast the humans' bestial behavior with the serenity of nature. Combat is authentically brutal, a stain on the natural world. Gennosuke refuses to face his pursuers directly, forswearing samurai honor and vowing to become an animal who lives like a wolf, but when confronted with threats from genuine animals like the gang of thugs, he can't sink to their level. When he learns that Jurota and Taka have been targeted for death by their own clan, though they've done nothing but risk their own lives to follow orders, Gennosuke chooses to fight on their behalf, even as his own clan's pursuers catch up to him. In the end, Gosha says, individuals can depend only on their own integrity, because to maintain power their clan will always betray them.

SWORD OF THE CONQUEROR

Rating: ★★★☆☆ • *Origin:* Italy, 1961 • *Director:* Carlo Campogalliani •
Source: Cheezy Flicks DVD

What we have here is a pretty good early medieval soap opera with bad action interludes. Veteran moviemaker Carlo Campogalliani, who wrote and directed, had an undeniable talent for melodrama, but his scenes of swordplay are so embarrassing, you just want them to be over so you can get back to the talking heads.

The story is set in sixth-century Italy, where a civilized king is advised by his treacherous minister to conquer the Lombards, a neighboring tribe of barbarians. But these barbarians are lucky enough to have Jack Palance as their chieftain, Alboïn, and his horde of long-haired and mustachioed Sonny Bonos easily defeat the king's army. Okay, deep breath: the king's daughter, Rosmunda (Eleonora Rossi Drago) loves the king's general, Amalchi (Guy Madison), by whom she's secretly had a baby boy, but the king decides to make peace with the Lombards by marrying Rosmunda to Alboïn. Then the warlord's brother, who is sent as an envoy to the king, is killed by Amalchi in a wholly anachronistic joust, and Alboïn vows vengeance on the king, whom he beheads in front of Rosmunda after an embarrassing battle in which the Sonny Bonos are victorious. Bloody conquest ensues.

To give Campogalliani credit, casting Jack Palance as a barbarian warlord was an inspired choice: Palance's features look like they were carved from oak with a chainsaw, and his eyes glitter with grim intelligence. And fortunately, Drago as Rosmunda is easily his match, for among all these strutting macho tough guys, only she shows any real insight or strength of character. Smoldering one moment, haughty the next, she steals every scene she's in, easily outacting her American costars.

Best not to reveal the ending, but the last act takes a turn for the gruesomely Gothic that wraps up the soap opera with satisfying finality. Now, where can *I* get a flagon made from my archenemy's skull?

Jack Palance in *Sword of the Conqueror* WIKIMEDIA COMMONS

SWORD OF THE VALIANT: THE LEGEND OF SIR GAWAIN AND THE GREEN KNIGHT

Rating: ★★☆☆☆ • *Origin:* UK, 1984 • *Director:* Stephen Weeks •
Source: Koch Media DVD

Sword of the Valiant AUTHOR'S COLLECTION

This isn't a good movie—flawed in script, acting, and direction, but it is a sincere attempt to capture the feel of medieval Arthurian romances in a film. Shot in striking period locations such as Cardiff Castle and the Château de Pierrefonds, it's loosely based on the fourteenth-century epic poem *Sir Gawain and the Green Knight*—heck, they even hired noted novelist Rosemary Sutcliff, who wrote a whole shelf of Arthurian literature, to help with the dialogue.

All for naught: mistakes were made. Director Stephen Weeks wanted Mark Hamill for the role of Sir Gawain, but producers Golan and Globus insisted on Miles O'Keeffe, a dimpled muscleman in a blond page-boy haircut with no discernible talent. The part of the magical Green Knight goes to Sean Connery, who clearly knows he's in a junk flick but puts what gusto he can into it anyway. Certainly, the glitter frosting his beard and outrageous wig do him no favors. The fine John Rhys-Davies and Peter Cushing are utterly wasted in bit parts, while the rest of the cast is filled out by nonentities except for Trevor Howard, who plays the grumpiest King Arthur ever.

The story starts as the epic poem does: King Arthur, at his midwinter feast, decries the sloth and gluttony of his knights and is asking if any still have the spark of heroism in them, when his court is invaded by a glowing knight in green who challenges all present to a bizarre game: try to behead him with a single blow, and if he survives, he gets to do the same to his would-be executioner. No one accepts this challenge until Gawain, a squire, steps forth, and Arthur knights him on the spot so he'll be a fit representative of his court. Sir Gawain takes up the Green Knight's axe and duly lops off his head, but the knight just laughs, reaches down and replaces his head on his body. Then he gives Sir Gawain a riddle and one year to solve it before he must face his own beheading.

So Gawain goes a-questing in a series of episodes that evoke the Arthurian tales but are undercut by cheap special effects, a cheesy all-synthesizer soundtrack, and weak, anachronistic jokes. Gawain is fooled by Morgan le Fay (Emma Sutton), falls in love with Lady Linet of Lyonesse (Cyrielle Clair), fights a Black Knight and a Red, loses his love and goes mad in the forest for a while, and collects both enemies and allies, who all fight for or against him in a pointless skirmish near the end. Despite having directed several episodes of *The Adventures of Robin Hood* in the late 1950s, action director Anthony Squires seems unaware that medieval combat consisted of anything other than graceless hacking, so the fight scenes are rather silly. To quote Peter Cushing as the Seneschal: "Take me away."

SWORD OF VENUS

Rating: ★★☆☆☆ • *Origin:* USA, 1953 • *Director:* Harold Daniels •
Source: Amazon streaming video

As a novel, *The Count of Monte Cristo* was complete unto itself, and Alexandre Dumas never felt moved to write a sequel to it. Plenty of others did, however, and this is one more pastiche about an heir to the novel's Edmond Dantès, in this case a son named Robert. It's set in 1832 and starts in Paris, where Robert lives the carefree life of a wealthy playboy. The story is by Jack Pollexfen and Aubrey Wisberg, a team who produced a number of low-budget pictures in the 1950s in several genres, including *The Man from Planet X* (1951) and *Son of Sinbad* (1955). This film neatly turns the revenge theme of the original novel on its head, being largely told from the viewpoints of three conspirators, their families ruined by Edmond Dantès, who set out to destroy his heir.

The result is a story in which Robert (Robert Clarke), the ostensible protagonist, largely plays the role of dupe and victim for the first three-quarters of the film, which would usually be irksome, but the quality of the writing makes up for it—it's pretty sharp, and the plotting is tight. But after a long sequence involving a lady in distress, a lonely inn, a vengeful husband, a falsely loaded pistol, and a feigned murder, Robert Dantès ends up behind bars. And once you throw a Dantès into prison, then, by dog, you know you've got a story. The final act is propelled by dramatic reversals as identities are switched, secrets are revealed, and swords come out of their sheaths at last. It's a familiar tale well told, and nobody seems embarrassed by the fact that they aren't saying anything new.

THE SWORDSMAN

Rating: ★★★☆☆ • *Origin:* USA, 1948 • *Director:* Joseph H. Lewis •
Source: Columbia Pictures DVD

It's late seventeenth-century Scotland, and the clans are a-feudin'. This film has two matinee-idol lookers as stars in Larry Parks and Ellen Drew, and if you guess that means we're in for a cross-clan *Romeo and Juliet*–type romance, well now, but you're good guessers, lads and lassies, aren't you so? The Glowan and MacArden clans have been stealing each other's livestock and cutting each other's throats for a century, but when Alexander MacArden (Parks), under an assumed name, cute-meets Barbara Glowan (Drew), bonny eyes start a-twinklin', and young Alex vows it's time to make peace between the families. Under his false name, he attends the Glowans' highland games, winning the javelin throw (tossing an eight-foot boar-sticker—some javelin!) and Barbara's heart. But he's recognized as a trespassing MacArden, and soon the killings, both fair duels and foul murders, begin.

I've never quite understood Parks's appeal, and at first glance Drew doesn't do much besides smile and look adoringly at Parks, but I admit that they both eventually show enough depth to win me over. I have no such reservations about George Macready as Barbara's villainous cousin Robert Glowan, who's as dedicated to war as Alexander is to peace. He's nasty and smart, manipulating his younger brothers into dishonor and death, and he's never slow to go for his basket-hilt broadsword. But Alexander, though reluctant, is a dab hand with a broadsword himself, and as you might expect from a film entitled *The Swordsman*, blades flash with some frequency. The swordplay is good, too, and the leading Glowans and MacArdens, Parks included, are all credible fencers.

This is a handsome production that makes good use of Technicolor. Northern California stands in for the Scottish Highlands, and it's scenic enough for the part, especially with the addition of a few herds of sheep and some judiciously placed matte paintings. The cast's Scottish accents are hit or miss, but at least there are only a few golf and whiskey jokes. Given this tale's series of abductions, ambuscades, betrayals, and warnings of betrayals, there's an awful lot of riding along the shores of the "lochs," all conducted at a gallop—I swear, there must be a full 15 minutes of sheer galloping in this flick. And b'god, these haughty Scots are stiff-necked and proud, which accounts for all the deadly misunderstandings in act two. However, by act three everyone's decided whether they're for war or peace, which leaves Parks and Macready to sort things out in a fine rough-and-tumble climactic duel. Will peace and love prevail in the end? Och, aye.

SWORDSMAN OF SIENA

Rating: ★★★★☆ • *Origin:* Italy/France, 1962 • *Director:* Étienne Périer •
Source: Warner Bros. DVD

If this swashbuckler seems a trifle old-fashioned for 1962, that could be because it was stuck in development hell for a decade. But eventually it got filmed, and though star Stewart Granger might be a bit old for the lead role, he manages to pull it off regardless.

The story is set in the Tuscan city of Siena in the late 1550s during the Italian Renaissance, shortly after Siena's long-standing republic has been overturned by the conquering Spanish, who have installed their own governor. Granger plays English mercenary Thomas Stanswood (modeled on the historical John Hawkwood), who hires out his sword arm to the rulers of Italian city-states. The opening scene establishes him as a charming but amoral rogue being pursued by his previous employer for having dallied with his duchess. After some acrobatic swashbuckling and quick-change artistry, he eludes his pursuers and arrives in Siena, home of his next employer, the hated Spanish governor. The city is seething with intrigue as the old republican nobles, who call themselves "The Ten," plot against their new Spanish overlords.

The former leader of the nobles, Lord Arconti, got himself killed by the governor's hatchet man in the city's no-holds-barred annual horse race, leaving behind two daughters: the young and idealistic Serenella (Christine Kaufmann), and the elder Orietta (Sylva Koscina), who seems resigned to having to marry the Spanish governor. Stanswood is hired as bodyguard to Orietta; he's quickly caught up in a web of plots and politics, and finds that Orietta *needs* a bodyguard, because she's playing a double game.

The swordplay in this movie is simply superb, its centerpiece an extended duel in a grain mill between Stanswood and a member of the Ten that shows Granger has lost none of the skills he'd developed for *Scaramouche* (1952). In the first half of the movie, Stanswood (or perhaps it's just Granger) is so smug that he's almost insufferable, but once he starts to fall for Orietta, he becomes more likeable. The film is pleasant to look at, shot in and around Bracciano Castle near Rome, and the colorful Renaissance costuming is particularly gorgeous. Most striking is the deadly climactic horse race, which is based on the Palio, a contest that dates back to medieval times and to this day is held twice a year in Siena; the film takes full advantage of its visual spectacle. A tidy package, all in all; add this to your watchlist.

TALES OF ROBIN HOOD

Rating: ★☆☆☆☆ • *Origin:* USA, 1951 • *Director:* James Tinling •
Source: YouTube streaming video

After *The Adventures of Robin Hood* (1938), a generation of children in America and Europe mimed Errol Flynn and Basil Rathbone fighting it out with wooden swords, dueling in schoolyards and empty lots while calling each other knaves and varlets. This production by Hal Roach Jr., an unsold TV pilot released to theaters, is just one step up from those schoolyard dramas. With a running time of less than an hour, it still manages to tick off all the usual Robin Hood check boxes: the theft of the Locksley heritage, the quarterstaff fight with Little John on the log, and the trap of the archery contest with the golden arrow as a prize, all calculated to evoke warm memories of the 1938 version.

Unfortunately, the cast Roach assembled, mostly cardboard C-list nobodies, isn't up to its simple task. Robert Clarke as Robin Hood bears a superficial resemblance to Errol Flynn, but the likeness stops there: he has the charisma and acting chops of a mannequin with a painted smile. Mary Hatcher is a passive and pudding-faced Maid Marian, Wade Crosby as Little John makes the mistake of imitating the awful Alan Hale Sr., and Tiny Stowe may be the least imposing Sheriff of Nottingham ever to blot the silver screen. As is so often the case, only the villains are worth watching, and Paul Cavanagh, as Sir Gui de Claremont, and Keith Richards (not that one), as Sir Alan de Beaulieu, are the only members of the cast who can say "methinks" and "milady" without embarrassment.

Look you, methinks there are a lot of other Robin Hood movies ahead of this one in the queue, and if you never get as far as *Tales of Robin Hood,* that's a good hour saved.

TARAS BULBA

Rating: ★★★★☆ • *Origin:* USA, 1962 • *Director:* J. Lee Thompson •
Source: KL Studio Classics DVD

If you're in the market for an epic Cossack cavalry spectacle, this is your one-stop shop. Like the Vikings, the Cossacks were big jerks, but they had an undeniable flair. And nobody ever embodied that flair better than Yul Brynner as Taras Bulba. He's unforgettable.

The story, based on a short novel by Nikolai Gogol, is set in the sixteenth century on the Ukrainian steppes (but was shot on the vast expanses of the Argentine pampas). It opens with a cavalry battle, but this isn't just gratuitous action; rather, it establishes the situation. The Ottoman Empire, attacking from the south, has run into the Polish Empire, expanding from the west, and the Poles are getting the worst of it until their new allies, the Cossacks, charge onto the scene. The Cossacks rout the Turks, but then the Polish artillery, held in reserve to this point, treacherously blows the Cossacks to smithereens—but not before Cossack leader Taras Bulba severs the Polish governor's right hand.

The Cossacks are defeated and must bow to Polish sovereignty, but Taras swears the situation is only temporary. He has two sons, the eldest of which is Andrei (Tony Curtis), and when they're old enough, Taras sends them to the Polish academy in Dubno to learn the ways of their enemies. But what Andrei mainly learns is to fall in love with Natalia (Christine Kaufmann), a Polish princess. Kaufmann might be a fine actress but you can't tell it from this film, because all she's given to do is look dewy-eyed at Andrei. (Apparently that was good enough for Curtis: he married her.) When Andrei's forbidden relationship with Natalia is discovered, he and his brother are driven out of Dubno, arriving back at home just in time to learn that the Cossack war banners are being raised in a call for vengeance on the Poles. And you can bet Andrei's love affair will cause tragic complications.

Besides Brynner's commanding screen presence and the cavalry battles, of which there are plenty, the fun here is in vicariously hanging out with the rough and rowdy Cossacks at their barbaric revels, which include plenty of Stupid Cossack Tricks like blanket-tossing, bull-ox-riding, crossing a balance beam over a bear pit while chugging vodka, and leaping a narrow gorge on horseback to prove who's the *real* coward. We also get the ever-villainous George Macready as the vile Polish governor and what many consider composer Franz Waxman's greatest movie score, a rollicking gallop that evokes the mounted Cossacks sweeping across the steppes. There are issues with director Thompson's confusing management of close-ups in the battles, but the striking long shots of the Polish and Cossack troop movements make up for it. And when plague strikes Dubno after the Cossacks put it under siege, the driver of the corpse wagon actually gets to ring a bell and call, "Bring out your dead!" Talk about living the dream.

THE TARTARS

Rating: ★★☆☆☆ • *Origin:* Italy/Yugoslavia, 1961 • *Director:* Richard Thorpe • *Source:* Warner Bros. DVD

Barbarian smackdown: Victor Mature versus Orson Welles—it's the Crush-a in Russia!

This just isn't any good. On the Russian steppes, sometime in the Middle Ages, a mini-horde of Tartars invites a tribe of Vikings to join them in attacking their pals the Slavs, but the Vikings refuse, and Tartars . . . they just don't handle disappointment well. Arrows and axes fly, and Viking chieftain Oleg (Victor Mature) kills the brother of Khan Burundai (Orson Welles), taking his daughter hostage as a bonus. In retaliation Burundai takes Oleg's wife hostage, rapes her offscreen, and then everything goes rapidly and brutally to hell. The minihorde attacks the Viking stockade, Oleg and Burundai meet in ridiculous single combat, and it's so bad it's not even funny.

The stereotypes are strong here: right in the opening narration we're informed that the Vikings, who are forthright and friendly, are Good, and the Tartars, who have droopy mustaches and sinister shifty eyes, are Bad. The orientalism is over the top, featuring giant gongs, acupuncture torture, and scandalous "exotic" dancing. This film is pretty much a career low for everyone involved, especially director Richard Thorpe, who less than a decade before had helmed near-classics *Scaramouche* (1952) and *Ivanhoe*. Every single person involved with this picture was phoning it in, including the entire nation of Yugoslavia where the exteriors were filmed. In the end almost everyone dies—but from a fiasco like this, death is sweet release.

THE THIEF OF BAGDAD (1924)

Rating: ★★★★★ (Essential) • *Origin:* USA, 1924 • *Director:* Raoul Walsh • *Source:* Cohen Film Collection DVD/Blu-Ray

Douglas Fairbanks gets his swashbuckling mojo back after *Robin Hood* in this fabulous, dream-like, silent fantasy that features the star at his most expressive and balletic, swaggering, leaping,

The Thief of Bagdad (1924) Anton Grot / Wikimedia Commons

and pantomiming through a fable from the Arabian Nights. The costumes are eye-popping and opulent, with towering hats—I mean, they look like actual towers—and curly-toed shoes to die for. The fanciful sets (by William Cameron Menzies) are fairy-tale tall and studded with grips so Fairbanks can clamber all over them. In its own way, the film is as excessive as *Robin Hood,* but this time every excess is in service to the story, which moves quickly and stays focused, even with a running time of almost two and a half hours. A lot of the credit for this should probably go to the director, the great Raoul Walsh, in an early effort from a long career that would later include such classics as *High Sierra* and swashbucklers like *Captain Horatio Hornblower.*

Even after almost a century, the Thief's visual gags in this film are outstanding, a combination of Fairbanks's inspired gymnastics and some imaginative camera tricks. Fairbanks's dancelike movements and broad gestures are compelling and eloquent, but he's just as effective with his facial features in intimate close-ups. The star still had many fine films ahead of him, but *The Thief of Bagdad* has to be regarded as his masterpiece. The story, about wooing and winning a princess, is negligible, a flimsy pretext for infiltrations, escalades, abductions, and rescues involving such enchanted adjuncts as a fakir's vertical trick rope, a flying carpet, and a wondrous winged horse. Also sleeping potions, mystic talismans, and a Valley of Fire. Plus secret panels, walking tree-men, giant bats, crystal balls, a cloak of invisibility, an underwater city of sirens, a spider the size of a grizzly bear, and the Old Man of the Midnight Sea. The film just keeps unrolling this rapid cavalcade of wonders, but somehow it stays fresh all the way to the end. Immortal line: "Fling him to the ape!"

Warning: this film has long been in the public domain, and there are a lot of crappy digital transfers out there. A lot of care went into restoring the Cohen Film version, and that's the one to watch.

THE THIEF OF BAGDAD (1940)

Rating: ★★★★☆ • *Origin:* UK, 1940 • *Directors:* Ludwig Berger, Michael Powell, Tim Whelan • *Source:* Criterion DVD

Everybody loves this movie. It's got heart, magic, music, adventure, romance, and ambitious special effects that alternate between stupendous and hilarious. Hang it, even *I* love this movie. And yet, to be perfectly frank, it's a bit of a mess.

Given its production history, it's a wonder it was ever made at all. Hungarian English producer Alexander Korda was determined to create a grand epic, a career-defining masterpiece, and inserted himself into every aspect of the film's production, sometimes causing chaos.

The Thief of Bagdad (1940) United Artists / Wikimedia Commons

Shooting started in early 1939 with German director Ludwig Berger, but he wasn't delivering a story on the scope that Korda wanted; and then that war thing happened, so Berger was replaced by three other directors, all English or American. Throughout production the film's story was in flux, constantly changing, with new elements added and other parts cut. When war actually broke out in September 1939, further production in the UK was suspended, and the whole thing was picked up and moved to Hollywood, with side shooting in the Grand Canyon.

Whew! Somehow Korda took all these disparate assets and assembled a mostly coherent whole, but one can see the seams where he stitched it together in the film's continuity lapses and sudden changes of tone. And yet, all that hardly matters, because this *Arabian Nights* fable is so vivid and fanciful that dream logic seems to hold it together.

Certainly, the romance that's ostensibly the plot's driving wheel is flat and rather dull, as John Justin (King Ahmad) and June Duprez (Princess—that's all the name she gets) don't provide much heat, chemistry, or interest. Perhaps they knew they were hopelessly outclassed by the real stars: the young thief, the evil vizier, and the mighty djinni. In truth, this is their movie. The thief, Abu, is played with engaging panache by the 15-year-old Sabu (that's all the name he gets), a lad of genuine charm from India. The great German actor Conrad Veidt is Jaffar—wizard, tyrant, lecher, and the archetypal wicked vizier—and he has a fine old time with the role. But no one has as much fun as the African American actor Rex Ingram as the Djinni, whose energy and gusto would make him seem 90 feet tall even if he wasn't already being depicted as 90 feet tall.

The story is loosely based on Doug Fairbanks's 1924 silent epic, with a half dozen other familiar *Arabian Nights* elements tossed into the stew to keep things bubbling. There's a flying carpet, magical curses and transformations, grotesque monsters, and voyages to unknown lands: picking up from its silent predecessor, this is the film that set the style and tone for all Arabian fantasy films to follow, up to and *especially* including Disney's *Aladdin*.

But be warned: the European colonialist gaze is strong here. There are people of all different skin shades in Bagdad, but lightness of color is the infallible guide to status. This is somewhat offset by the prominent casting of brown Sabu and Black Rex Ingram—but damn.

As for the film's look, "sumptuous" doesn't even begin to describe it. Visual wizard William Cameron Menzies, whose credits stretched back to the 1924 *Thief of Bagdad*, was Korda's associate producer and uncredited fourth director, and his eye for form and color deserves much of the credit for the film's visual appeal. The excellent score is an early effort by Miklós Rósza, best known for his soundtrack for *Ben-Hur* (1959). There are some hokey songs—during part of the production cycle Korda thought he wanted the film to be a musical—but the orchestral pieces are dynamic and memorable.

Guilty pleasure: the picture's screenwriter, Miles Malleson, gets to play the delightful part of the dotty old Sultan of Basra, who collects magical toys. I have to say, seeing the script guy having such fun warms my writer's heart. And even C. Aubrey Smith would be envious of his amazing whiskers.

THIEF OF DAMASCUS

Rating: ★★☆☆☆ • *Origin:* USA, 1952 • *Director:* Will Jason •
Source: Turner Classic Movies

This is another of Paul Henreid's blacklist-era swashbucklers for independent producer Sam Katzman, and whoa, it's mostly a stinker. Good General Andar (Henreid) is besieging Damascus for Bad King Khalid (John Sutton), as depicted by jarringly inappropriate footage of European soldiers storming European battlements yoinked from films such as *Joan of Arc* (1948). Good General Andar fools the Damascene defenders, and the city falls to his troops, but Bad King Khalid repudiates Andar's generous surrender terms and orders him arrested. Andar is pursued by Khalid's goons through the four streets of Columbia's Arabian backlot set, running through it in six directions filmed each time from a different angle. Henreid, or anyway his stunt double, does some acrobatic swashbuckling and fights his way free, thanks to an amazing sword of Damascus steel he picked up along the way.

Damascus steel? Check! Familiar *Arabian Nights* characters? On it! Andar makes new allies of Sheherazade, Sinbad, Aladdin, and Ali Baba, but only the latter gets to be cool because he has a secret cave lair with a magic door (which makes this technically a fantasy, but meh). And Andar *needs* allies, because he must rescue his love-at-first-sight Zafir (Helen Gilbert), the Princess of Damascus, from Khalid before he either marries her or cuts off her head (he's flighty like that). There are a lot of weak jokes that depend on Hollywood character actors talking like gangsters instead of Arabians, gratuitous "oriental" dancing by half-clad starlets, and guards running about waving ridiculous scimitars. The only reason to watch this is to admire Paul Henreid, because about half the time he seems to actually be having fun, and when he is, his Continental charm makes up for any number of American goons in turbans speaking lines like "Did your eyes behold what mine just did?"

THOR THE CONQUEROR (OR THE MIGHTY THOR)

Rating: ★☆☆☆☆ • *Origin:* Italy, 1983 • *Director:* Tonino Ricci •
Source: YouTube streaming video

You can argue about which movie of the 1980s barbarian boom was the best, but when it comes to which is the worst, there's no debate: it's the Italian film *Thor the Conqueror*.

If you'd just seen *Conan the Barbarian* and had 500 bucks, a camera, and some smoke bombs for atmosphere, this is the movie you'd make. It's so utterly bad that its badness would be entertaining in itself if the film wasn't also appallingly misogynistic. It starts as a barbarian warrior named, er, Kunt (Angelo Ragusa) marches resolutely across the wilds followed by his heavily pregnant wife and an obnoxious shape-changing wizard called Etna (Luigi Mezzanotte). Arriving at some standing stones dedicated to the god Teisha, the wife gives birth to the infant Thor just as they are attacked by another warrior, Gnut (Raf Baldassarre), and his tribe of white-faced barbarian mimes, who want Kunt's magic sword. Kunt and his wife are slain, but the magic sword turns into a snake and escapes, as does Etna with the newborn baby. The obnoxious wizard raises Thor (Bruno Minitti) to shirtless adulthood and then sends him off to, you guessed it, avenge his parents' murder.

Everything about this is terrible, predictable, and terribly predictable. Thor talk like caveman, except when he speaks in full sentences before he suddenly talk like caveman again. Because Etna says so, Thor must fight three "Warrior Virgins" wearing ridiculous straw helmets, killing two of them but sparing the third so he can rape her, saying, "You will bear the fruit called children!" Naturally, Ina (Malisa Longo) adores her rapist and becomes his loyal helpmeet. Thor comes to a stupid village and gets into a stupid fight and conquers it, eating their stupid roast squirrels and then planting some magic seeds he found earlier that are immediately forgotten. Then Gnut and the barbarian mimes find him, capture both Ina and Thor, and blind Thor by coating his eyes with cheap black eyeliner. They release him back into the wild, but Etna magically sends Thor a nonvenomous python and (surprise!) Thor milks its nonvenomous fangs onto some moss, uses the moss to rub away the cheap eyeliner, and his vision is restored! He blesses the god Teisha and then finds his dad's magic sword, and you know where it goes from there.

The sets here consist of some huts made of branches, a few carved stones, and a bunch of skulls on sticks. There are unexplained cheap SFX ghosts, for some reason. The costumes are burlap sacks and fur, because barbarians, and even the weapons have fur on them because I guess that makes them barbaric. Everyone, Thor included, says "Rahh!" a lot while waving their weapons. Drink responsibly, friends—except when watching this movie.

A THOUSAND AND ONE NIGHTS

Rating: ★★★☆☆ • *Origin:* USA, 1945 • *Director:* Alfred E. Green •
Source: Amazon streaming video

Now we get wacky. This is a tongue-in-cheek Arabian Nights fantasy that falls somewhere between send-up of and homage to *The Thief of Bagdad*, especially the 1940 version. Aladdin of Cathay(?), played by Cornel Wilde, is a vagabond street singer whom we first see crooning an ode to the desirability of a row of women for sale at a slave auction. This is tasteless by current standards, but it does serve to inform us that in this film, the role of women is strictly ornamental—with a notable exception which we'll get to shortly. This singing Aladdin has a comic sidekick, a pickpocket named Abdullah, played by Phil Silvers—yep, it's Sergeant Bilko, black-framed glasses and all. Everyone calls him crazy because he says he was born 1,200 years too soon, makes jokes about television and gin rummy, and tells the palace guards their turbans are "groovy."

Some story happens: in a scene lifted right out of *The Thief of Bagdad*, mounted guards clear everyone from the street at the approach of a princess's elaborate sedan chair because "no man may gaze upon her and live." That, of course, makes Aladdin determined to see her— and one daring trespass and two songs later, the vagabond and the princess (Adele Jergens, strictly ornamental) have fallen in love. He serenades her in a palace garden that, like many of the sets, is a virtual duplicate of the one from the equivalent scene in *Thief of Bagdad*. In fact, the whole look of the film, the architecture, the props, the bright costumes against the pastel backgrounds, is practically a love letter to William Cameron Menzies.

Soon enough the guards are shouting, "Seize him!," and Aladdin and Abdullah are on the run. In a mystic cave they meet a mystic mage with a mystic crystal who sends them after a mystic treasure guarded by a mystic giant—Rex Ingram himself, 50 feet tall and looking exactly as he did playing the Djinni in *Thief of Bagdad*, once again pursuing his puny prey and doing *that laugh*. The treasure turns out to be a magic lamp (oh, right: Aladdin) that contains the best thing about this movie, a sassy red-headed genie played by Evelyn Keyes and named (ahem) "Babs." Keyes, who is lively, clever, and ornamental in the bargain, effortlessly steals the rest of the picture, and no wicked vizier, sultan's evil twin, or mystic mage can stand against her. All the bad jokes are worth it just to savor her performance. Bonus: in the action-packed finale, Cornel Wilde, who'd been an Olympic fencer in the '30s, gets a chance to show us what he can do with a sword, and it's quite impressive. Groovy, even.

THE 300 SPARTANS

Rating: ★★★☆☆ • *Origin:* USA, 1962 • *Director:* Rudolph Maté •
Source: 20th Century Fox DVD

Any account of the Battle of Thermopylae is a bit like the story of the *Titanic*—you know how it ends, but you want to see how it gets there. This movie was filmed in Greece near the site of the battle, and it feels much more genuine than if it had been shot in, say, Santa Barbara. In 480 BCE the quarreling city-states of Greece are threatened by the huge invading army of the Empire of Persia, and a small contingent of Greek warriors led by King Leonidas of Sparta must hold off the Persians in a narrow pass, defending it long enough for the city-states to pull together an army of their own. The movie, the swan song of the veteran director Rudolph Maté, moves quickly and capably through the setup to the battle, presenting just enough of the politics on both sides to give the conflict meaning while adding a forbidden romance between a couple of young Spartan lovers to personalize the stakes. Then it devotes over half its running time to depicting the battle itself in five distinct phases, which is, after all, what we came for.

On the eve of battle, the Spartans stage a nighttime amphibious raid on the Persian camp, which infuriates King Xerxes and drives him to make hasty decisions in his attacks. The Persian cavalry fails to break the Spartan line; then the war chariots fail; even an assault by Xerxes's bodyguard, the legendary Immortals, fails in the face of Leonidas's superior tactics. Finally, after three days of fighting, the Greek traitor Ephialtes leads a force of Persians around the pass on a mountain goat path, and the situation changes.

The battle is well staged, mainly in long and medium shots so the viewer can clearly follow the troop movements, with just enough chaotic close-ups to convey the grim butchery of the combat. The costumes are convincingly authentic, the music by Manos Hadjidakis is effective, and the speeches are kept short. The only real problem is that, except for David Farrar as Xerxes and Ralph Richardson as Themistocles of Athens, the acting is all as stiff and wooden as the Spartans' spears, including that of cowboy star Richard Egan as Leonidas. We won't go into detail about how it ends, because there are probably a few people who don't even know what happened to the *Titanic*.

THE THREE MUSKETEERS (1916)

Rating: ★★★☆☆ • *Origin:* USA, 1916 • *Director:* Charles Swickard •
Source: Alpha Home Entertainment DVD

This early silent version of Alexandre Dumas's greatest swashbuckler is enjoyable and, at only 50 minutes long, quite fast paced, though it adapts only the first half of the novel, the affair of the queen's diamonds. D'Artagnan (Orrin Johnson) is active, Richelieu (Walt Whitman, not that one) is imposing, and Queen Anne (Dorothy Dalton) is majestically pouty. As will be typical of American film versions to follow, it makes d'Artagnan's love interest Constance (Rhea Mitchell) into something other than Bonacieux's wife—in this case, his daughter—and has Rochefort (Arthur Maude) play both his role and that of the Comte de Wardes, a doubling that occurs in almost every film version. A good early effort.

THE THREE MUSKETEERS (1921)

Rating: ★★★★☆ • *Origin:* USA, 1921 • *Director:* Fred Niblo • *Source:* Kino Video DVD

Douglas Fairbanks Sr.'s *Three Musketeers* is far and away the best of the seven versions filmed in the silent era—but more about that in a moment. First, I want to gush about this production's costumes, which are fabulous, both historically accurate and theatrically gorgeous. This film was another Fairbanks production, and after the worldwide success of *The Mark of Zorro*, no expense was spared in an attempt to duplicate that triumph. And boy, did they succeed. The costumes and sets show that serious attention was paid to getting the details right, including settings and

The Three Musketeers (1921)   PKM / WIKIMEDIA COMMONS

tableaux inspired by nineteenth-century paintings of the period, as well as the engravings of Maurice Leloir, Dumas's most celebrated illustrator.

Fairbanks was nearly 40 in 1921, far too old for the part of the youth d'Artagnan, but instead of trying to look young, he *plays* young, in his expressions and body language, and does so brilliantly. Fairbanks made his Zorro an acrobat, and he does the same for d'Artagnan, leaping and fencing with a buoyant athleticism that has been attached to the role of the young musketeer ever since. But beyond that, Fairbanks's d'Artagnan exhibits the sharp wits and quick thinking on display in Dumas's novel, crucial aspects of the character that are often overlooked in lesser adaptations.

As usual, the film covers only the first half of the novel, the affair of the diamond studs, but with 121 minutes to do it, this version has plenty of room for character interplay, romance, and joyous musketeer shenanigans. There is roistering, roguery, and even outright piracy on the English Channel. This time around, Constance (Marguerite De La Motte) is Bonacieux's niece rather than wife, and she gets a generous amount of screen time in a movie that's otherwise a boys' club. But the real supporting-actor prize goes to Nigel Brulier as Cardinal Richelieu, whom he plays as a cold and calculating automaton with a genuinely ominous screen presence. In the end Richelieu reacts to his defeat with dignity and even generosity but is rebuffed by d'Artagnan and the musketeers, who prefer their camaraderie and half-drunken revelry to the sober demands of the state. You go, frat boys!

THE THREE MUSKETEERS (1935)

Rating: ★★★☆☆ • *Origin:* USA, 1935 • *Director:* Rowland V. Lee •
Source: Vertice Cine DVD

This is the first English-language "talkie" version of Alexandre Dumas's classic story, which means it's also the first version with an integrated musical score, and the soundtrack, by the great Max Steiner, is arguably the best Musketeers music ever written. Steiner had been laboring in the Hollywood trenches for years before he finally broke through with his score for *King Kong* in 1933, and still riding on that high, his music for *The Three Musketeers* is confident, muscular, and catchy—the main march even has lyrics so the musketeers can sing it as they stride, triumphant, through Paris after defeating the Cardinal's Guards! If you're into this sort of thing, the soundtrack is well worth seeking out, in the original or a rerecorded version.

Beyond that, there's not much about this adaptation that's really memorable. Studio RKO usually turned out second-rate B movies, and though this was an expensive production for them, it's not exactly up to Warner Bros. standards. Most of the cast were journeyman actors who are now forgotten, the only real standout being the fine Hungarian actor Paul Lukas in the role of Athos. D'Artagnan is played by Walter Abel, a silent screen star who'd made the transition to talkies but still lets his unsubtle facial expressions do most of the acting work—which is just as well, as he has scarcely any lines for the first 20 minutes: he just gapes in naive wonder at the marvels of Paris. He also just mimes romance with the bland Heather Angel as Constance, but nonetheless you're still kind of embarrassed for him by how badly he gets conned late in the film by Margot Grahame as the archvillain Milady de Winter. He gets tied up and carried off in Milady's carriage, and Athos, Porthos, and Aramis have to rescue the poor sap.

The plot of *The Three Musketeers*, of course, is incredibly sturdy and will stand any amount of manhandling. It's pretty much played straight here, as usual covering only the first half of the novel, the affair of the queen's diamonds, streamlined to keep the running time under 95 minutes. There are two carriage chases through the eucalyptus woods of Southern California and some mediocre fencing, but it all ends in a surprisingly well-staged duel between d'Artagnan and Rochefort (Ian Keith, meh). Kudos for that to director Rowland V. Lee, who had gotten this job based on his helming the previous year of the hit version of *The Count of Monte Cristo* for United Artists. He'll go on to direct Monte Cristo sequels and Charles Laughton in *Captain Kidd* (1945).

Special treat for Musketeer nerds: Nigel de Brulier plays Cardinal Richelieu, a role he'd enacted twice before, in the Douglas Fairbanks silent versions of *The Three Musketeers* (1921) and *The Iron Mask* (1929). In looks, at least, he was the Cardinal incarnate.

THE THREE MUSKETEERS (1939)

Rating: ★★☆☆☆ • *Origin:* USA, 1939 • *Director:* Allan Dwan •
Source: Fox Cinema Classics DVD

This is the first filmed *musical* version of *The Three Musketeers* (there are others!): it's a musical comedy swashbuckler, believe it or not. So the first question is, Is it any good as a musical? Well, Don Ameche, who plays d'Artagnan, can certainly sing and deserves credit for that. But the songs aren't particularly worth singing, and they don't really add much fizz to the story. As a musical, then, it's pretty much a bust.

How is it as a comedy? In that regard it's mainly a vehicle for the Ritz Brothers, a comic trio briefly popular in the 1930s; some compare them to the Marx Brothers, but that isn't really apt, because each Marx had his own distinctive character, while the three Ritzes, like the crackers, are indistinguishable and interchangeable. Also, they aren't funny, which is kind of a liability in a comedy. So no joy there.

Finally, then, how is it as a version of *The Three Musketeers*? Surprisingly, it's one of the more faithful adaptations of Dumas's novel, which is amazing since, if they were already jamming songs and the goofball Ritz Brothers into the story, why did they bother? At a guess, it's because the original story is so sturdy and resilient, it can support the insertion of Ritzes and songs-es and still carry on just fine. Ameche is too old for the part of the young Gascon, but he's energetic and far from the worst d'Artagnan ever cast—and the beguiling Binnie Barnes is one of the best-ever Milady de Winters. She kills. Bonus: watch for the fun early appearance by John Carradine as Naveau (i.e., Bonacieux), Constance's treacherous guardian.

THE THREE MUSKETEERS (1948)

Rating: ★★★★★ • *Origin:* USA, 1948 • *Director:* George Sidney •
Source: Warner Bros. DVD

There were a lot of movie and TV adaptations of *The Three Musketeers* in the twentieth century, but three of them tower above all the others: the Fairbanks film from 1921, Richard Lester's 1973 version, and, falling almost exactly in between them, MGM's star-studded entry from 1948.

This is an interesting adaptation: it starts out as a typical Hollywood vehicle for star Gene Kelly, bright, colorful, charming, and lighthearted, a musical without songs, as d'Artagnan (Kelly) finds camaraderie with the musketeers and romance with Constance (June Allyson).

But the top-billed actor is actually Lana Turner, at the height of her fame, who, based on her roles as femme fatales in films noir, is cast as the wicked Milady de Winter. Now Milady appears mostly in the second half of Dumas's novel, so to give Turner enough screen time, the movie races through the affair of the diamond studs in its first hour, enabling it to spend its second hour on the schemes of Milady. These schemes take the story into darker places than most screen versions of *T3M*, and toward the end the tone becomes quite grim. The emphasis on Milady also explains the elevation of Athos (Van Heflin), her bitter estranged husband, nearly to the level of coprotagonist with d'Artagnan. Heflin, an actor of stature and gravitas, ranks up there with Oliver Reed for Best Athos Ever, but Turner doesn't seem entirely engaged with the part of Milady—though when she does get into it, it works.

One thing the aforementioned best versions of *T3M* all have in common is a recognition that the novel is not only full of adventure, intrigue, and romance but is also funny as hell. The humor in the MGM version is mainly delivered by Kelly, who puts in a broad and unrestrained performance, adopting some of the exaggerated silent-film mannerisms of Douglas Fairbanks Sr. as well as all of his athleticism. Kelly even goes Fairbanks one better, because he's not just an acrobat, he's a dancer, and his swordplay owes as much to the school of ballet as it does to the academy of arms. Of course, at age 35, Kelly is too old for the part of d'Artagnan, but that's true of every screen incarnation until Michael York took the role in '73, and Kelly makes up for it with energy and dexterity. All the fencing in the film is with slender foils rather than period rapiers, but the swordplay, Kelly's especially, is more theatrical than realistic: it's choreographed to the split second and very entertaining indeed.

And we must note that in addition to Turner and Heflin, Kelly is backed up by a top cast. On the male side, we get Frank Morgan (the Wizard from *Oz*) waffling adorably as the ineffectual King Louis XIII, and sly, malicious Vincent Price gives us the best Cardinal Richelieu since Raymond Massey's turn a decade earlier. On the female side, Angela Lansbury is perfect as Queen Anne, while June Allyson gives Constance more depth than the character usually gets. (As is usual in a Hollywood *T3M*, Constance is single here, goddaughter to the landlord Bonacieux, rather than his wife.)

Playwright Robert Ardrey's script is very good, tight and fast moving without ever feeling rushed, and includes the inspired idea of giving Constance the role of jailer-in-chief when Milady is imprisoned in England, a vast improvement over the weak coincidence that throws them together in the novel. We get some scenes from the book that are rarely filmed, and for once all four of the musketeers' lackeys make an appearance, though only Planchet (Keenan Wynn) gets any lines. Even minor villain the Count de Wardes shows up, mainly so d'Artagnan can impersonate him later. The ending, as alluded to earlier, is dark, but Richelieu's revenge on d'Artagnan is forestalled by the famous carte blanche: "It is by my order, and for the good of the State, that the bearer has done what has been done." *Exactement.*

THE THREE MUSKETEERS (1950) (OR *THE SWORD OF D'ARTAGNAN*)

Rating: ★☆☆☆☆ • *Origin:* USA, 1950 • *Director:* Budd Boetticher •
Source: Amazon streaming video

Over the opening title card, the Magnavox Theater announcer intones, "The Three Musketeers: the first full-length film made in Hollywood especially for television!" Magnavox Theater was a brief series of seven one-hour dramas broadcast in the fall of 1950, all of which were live TV except this episode, which was produced by Hal Roach Studios. These kinds of early

TV "prestige" productions were a lot like Classics Illustrated comic book adaptations—earnest and well-meaning, but stiff, flat, and awkwardly abridged. The abridgment here consists of throwing out nearly everything in the novel except the duel between the musketeers and the Cardinal's Guards, Buckingham's secret visit to the queen, and the gauntlet d'Artagnan and the musketeers must ride to Calais to recover the diamond studs, with narration by Athos to fill in the gaps. Production values are better than usual for 1950 television—that is, just two notches above terrible. For once, Porthos is well cast, played here by Mel Archer, a giant of a man with a booming voice, but the rest of the actors are forgettable. For Dumas completists only.

THE 3 MUSKETEERS (1953)

Rating: ★★★☆☆ • *Origin:* France, 1953 • *Director:* André Hunebelle • *Source:* Pathé DVD

This action-comedy was the first major French production of *The Three Musketeers* since Diamant-Berger's epic two-part adaptation of 20 years before, and though it borrows a few bits from that predecessor, it owes far more to the first half of the 1948 MGM version with Gene Kelly. Unlike the 1932 French version, which presented the whole novel, this entry takes the usual approach of adapting only its first half, the affair of the queen's diamonds. It does so with a decidedly light touch, though it employs the regrettable device of an intrusive narrator, not just at the beginning but all through the film, helpfully explaining the jokes so you won't miss them. Moreover, the cast just isn't that impressive, the only standout being sad-sack comedian Bourvil as d'Artagnan's lackey Planchet; he gets plenty of screen time, but that's okay because he's much funnier than the narrator. The other high point is that the film is shot on location at the French royal châteaux of Fontainebleau and Vincennes, so the settings are both opulent and authentic. The swordplay is enthusiastic and theatrical without looking dangerous, which is in keeping with the movie's tone, the story moves along capably enough, and there are plenty of jokes—even, *mon Dieu,* a pie fight with the Cardinal's Guard! It must have been what the French cinema audience was looking for, because it was a sizeable success, so much so that director Hunebelle made several more light swashbucklers before the end of the 1950s.

THE THREE MUSKETEERS (1966, MINISERIES)

Rating: ★★★★☆ • *Origin:* UK, 1966 • *Director:* Peter Hammond • *Source:* Koch Vision DVDs

Brian Blessed as Porthos! . . . You need more than that? Well, if you *insist.*

The BBC was in the business of literary adaptations, and after the success of writer-director Peter Hammond's teleplay of *The Count of Monte Cristo,* the BBC turned to him for a follow-up with a version of Alexandre Dumas's other best-known novel, *The Three Musketeers.* As with *Monte Cristo,* it has all the strengths and weaknesses of a BBC miniseries: a literate script, fine performances by stage-trained actors, and lots of grainy close-ups to divert the viewer's attention from the low-budget sets and bare-bones production values. Unlike most Hollywood versions, the story is played straight, without a touch of camp or a wink at the audience, except for the twinkle in Brian Blessed's eye. Dumas's long novel is boiled down to ten 25-minute episodes, or just over four hours—the length of two features, the approach of those adaptations, like Diamant-Berger's in 1932 or Richard Lester's in 1973, that really intend to do justice to the source material. And since the novel was originally published in serial form, breaking it into 10 chapters does it no harm; in fact, it may be the most authentic approach.

What a wealth of fine actors this version presents: Jeremy Young is a memorable and commanding Athos, Gary Watson is a dry and droll Aramis, and a young Jeremy Brett—yes, the great Sherlock Holmes of the 1980s Granada TV series—makes a fine and passionate d'Artagnan, though it takes him a couple of episodes to really grow into the role. Screen versions of *The Three Musketeers* are often fortunate in the actors chosen to play Cardinal Richelieu, and this adaptation is no exception, with Richard Pasco of the Old Vic and the Royal Shakespeare Company nailing the role. It's harder to find a good Queen Anne onscreen, but this version has one in Carole Potter, who gives the character an inner strength missing in most portrayals.

There was no swashbuckling in Hammond's adaptation of *Monte Cristo*, but there's plenty in his *Musketeers*, and though the swordplay is indifferent in the early episodes, it improves as the series goes on. Several scenes from the novel show up here that I believe are seen in no other screen versions, including d'Artagnan's duel with Lord de Winter behind the Palais Luxembourg, and Porthos's courtship of the wealthy attorney's wife Madame de Coquenard, most welcome because it gives us more of the vainglorious Blessed preening and curling his mustachios. Plus this extended adaptation includes plenty of time for scenes of camaraderie between d'Artagnan and the musketeers, most of which come straight from Dumas. In short, despite its threadbare budget, this is one of the best *Three Musketeers* available, highly recommended to aficionados of swashbuckling cavaliers.

And Brian Blessed is the best screen Porthos *ever*. (Duel me!)

THE THREE MUSKETEERS (1973) (OR *THE QUEEN'S DIAMONDS*)

Rating: ★★★★★ (Essential) • *Origin:* UK/US, 1973 • *Director:* Richard Lester •
Source: StudioCanal Blu-ray

In the last 110 years or so, there have been dozens of screen adaptations of Alexandre Dumas's greatest novel. This one is the best.

Director Richard Lester had shown a deft hand for comedy with *A Funny Thing Happened on the Way to the Forum* and the first two Beatles movies and had first thought about adapting *T3M* when it was briefly considered as a vehicle for the Fab Four. Lester reread the novel and realized it offered much more to the screen than its comedic elements; in fact, it reminded him of *Flashman*, a humorous historical adventure novel that he'd also considered filming, and he hired its author, George MacDonald Fraser, to write a *T3M* screenplay. It was an inspired choice: Fraser understood *T3M*'s balance of adventure, suspense, comedy, and camaraderie and wrote a script that captures all those elements, a screenplay so sharp and dynamic and with such juicy roles that top-notch actors clamored for the parts.

And what a cast it was, when finally assembled: Michael York as d'Artagnan, with the youth and activity the part demands and the acting chops of the stage trained; the glowering Oliver Reed as Athos, the finest actor ever to fill that role; Charlton Heston, utterly convincing as the many-sided Cardinal Richelieu; Christopher Lee as his arrogant and ruthless hatchet man Rochefort; Raquel Welch, showing an unexpected talent for slapstick as d'Artagnan's love Constance; and a dozen more, including Faye Dunaway, Richard Chamberlain, Geraldine Chaplin, Spike Milligan, Simon Ward, and Roy Kinnear, all perfectly cast for their parts, large or small.

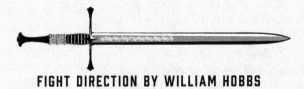

FIGHT DIRECTION BY WILLIAM HOBBS

William Hobbs (1939–2018) was the greatest director of European-style stage fencing of his generation. An English actor trained to the stage at the Old Vic, Hobbs was fight director at Laurence Olivier's National Theatre Company in the 1960s before making his first big splash in films with Richard Lester's *The Three Musketeers* in 1973. As a fencing choreographer, he was known for his more realistic, rough-and-tumble approach to cinematic fighting, depicting combat as a desperate and fearful endeavor, often having the actors expend effort to exhaustion. This was a revelation that overturned the Hollywood standard of elegant and balletic fencing as exemplified by the sword work of actors like Basil Rathbone, Stewart Granger, and Cornel Wilde. In a William Hobbs fencing match, an actor was as likely to strike a blow with a handy broomstick as with a rapier.

Hobbs's most influential work was certainly the swordplay he choreographed for Ridley Scott's *The Duellists*, after which he was the go-to guy for decades for any British or American production that featured fencing, his credits including *Excalibur* (1981), *Ladyhawke* (1985), and *Rob Roy* (1995), all the way through to *Game of Thrones* (2011). In between he continued to work as a director for stage fencing, mainly for productions of Shakespeare plays—he directed the sword work in *Hamlet* over two dozen times, including the 1990 film with Mel Gibson. "I do think, what the hell am I going to do this time to make it different?" Hobbs said in 2008. "A fight has to grow out of the situation of the play. There's the text, and you've got to follow it truthfully and honestly."

The Three Musketeers (1973) AUTHOR'S COLLECTION

The costumes and sets, even 50 years later, are simply astonishing. One of the reasons this film is endlessly rewatchable is that there is just *so much* going on, nearly every scene jammed with historical details, every character fully alive, every activity in street, tavern, or royal court fascinating. Pomanders, dog chess, torturers cooking potatoes in their braziers, tavern games, street dentists, cupping, hawking . . . it goes on and on.

The action, and there's plenty of it, is both comical and thrilling, usually both at the same time. Every fight, for love or for glory, is a perfectly choreographed roughhouse brawl arranged by dueling master William Hobbs, with all of the gratuitous acrobatics we expect from d'Artagnan and company. The night duel in the forest between d'Artagnan and Roche-fort, both using dark lanterns, could have been filmed by Terry Gilliam.

The novel, of course, is big and packed with plot, and Lester originally intended to make a three-and-a-half-hour epic complete with intermission like *El Cid*. But when it became clear that approach was no longer commercially viable, it was split into two films, *The Three Musketeers* (*The Queen's Diamonds*) and *The Four Musketeers* (*The Revenge of Milady*), released the following year. (Famously, the actors, who'd been paid for only one film, sued the production company, and a clause forbidding the splitting practice became standard in the industry thereafter.)

And crucially, Lester's *T3M* revitalized the entire genre of the swashbuckler movie, sharpening the action and modernizing the dialogue while winking at the clichés and turning new twists on the old tropes. It was an approach George Lucas would use to good effect several years later in a film called *Star Wars*.

THREE OUTLAW SAMURAI

Rating: ★★★★★ • *Origin:* Japan, 1964 • *Director:* Hideo Gosha • *Source:* Criterion DVD

This is acclaimed director Hideo Gosha's first feature after he cut his teeth directing shows such as the earlier *Three Outlaw Samurai* TV series, every episode of which is now lost, alas. This film serves as the origin story of how the three mismatched ronin came to be comrades of the road, and it is superb.

In a district with a corrupt magistrate (aren't they all?) where the harvests have failed for several years running, some peasants, desperate for relief, have kidnapped the magistrate's daughter to force him to present their petition to the clan lord. A roving samurai, Sakon Shiba (Tetsuro Tamba), stumbles on the mill where the three peasants are holding the daughter hostage, criticizes their amateurish efforts with an ironic smirk, but then, moved by their desperation, joins their cause. Shiba drives off the magistrate's goons when they attack, so the officer orders his best hired samurai, Kikyo (Mikijiro Hira), along with a vagabond ronin released from jail, Sakura (Isamu Nagato), to handle the situation. Once the earthy Sakura realizes what's going on, he switches sides to join the peasants, at which the effete Kikyo withdraws in disgust. The magistrate then sends Kikyo to collect the daughter of one of the rebellious peasants to serve as a hostage to trade for his own daughter and also hires 12 more scruffy ronin as hatchet men. Outnumbered, Shiba offers to turn himself in and release the magistrate's daughter if the peasants are set free, and the magistrate accepts, pledging his samurai honor— but he's a big fat liar, and Shiba is betrayed. This is too much for Kikyo: he goes over to the opposition, and then it's three mismatched fighters against an entire clan.

After the disaster of blind devotion to Bushido that was World War II, many samurai films were made about distinguishing honor from unquestioning loyalty, but Gosha takes it two steps further, decrying loyalty as a trap and honor as a figment. His three outlaws learn that, in a world of corruption and cowardice, they can be true to nothing but themselves and each other. Gosha's direction is striking and dynamic, often in dark scenes carefully lit to highlight cruelty and danger, with more than a touch of film noir to them. The swordplay is exciting, just as choreographed as in a Kurosawa film, but wilder and more naturalistic and thus almost more convincing. Characterizations are strong, vivid, and conveyed in broad strokes, with sudden close-ups nailing home reaction shots to express violent emotion. The performances are strong, and the peasants and villains all get nuanced scenes, not just the samurai heroes. The twists and turns of the story play out with a sort of deadly inevitability, leading to a final confrontation with the clan's famous leading swordsman, ultimately exposing the futility of the three outlaws' effort to change the world they live in. It's kind of a masterpiece.

THRONE OF BLOOD

Rating: ★★★★★ • *Origin:* Japan, 1957 • *Director:* Akira Kurosawa • *Source:* Criterion DVD

This is a stark, brutal, black-and-white adaptation of *Macbeth* that relocates the story from medieval Scotland to samurai Japan, replacing Shakespeare's sonorous language with the stylized imagery of classical Noh theater—so, yeah, it's not a movie for everybody. It's a fast ride to hell on the horses of greed, ambition, and betrayal, with few (if any) sympathetic characters, shorn of even the lukewarm reassurance found in Shakespeare's moralistic finale. Bummer.

But if you can get past, or even better, embrace all that, you'll find that director Kurosawa's third major samurai film is rich with vivid scenes you'll never forget. To name a few: the encounter in the haunted forest between Generals Washizu (Toshiro Mifune) and Miki (Akira Kubo) with the pale and malevolent witch who foretells their fates; the brooding intensity of the murder scene in which Washizu's wife, Lady Asaji (Isuzu Yamada), hands him the spear with which he is to assassinate their guest, his reigning lord, and her tense wait for him to return, shaken, his hands clotted with blood; the siege of the great black castle on the barren slopes of Mount Fuji where Washizu, now the reigning lord himself, pays the price for his betrayals in a hissing storm of hurtling arrows.

Most of all, you'll remember the coldly poisonous voice of the relentless Lady Asaji, and Lord Washizu's panicked glances from behind his fierce martial visage, the look of a trapped animal who sees no way to go except deeper into the trap. Yes, it's very different from an uplifting action movie like *Seven Samurai*, in which heroic warriors fight desperately against the odds, but on its own terms, *Throne of Blood* is a very great film indeed.

TIME BANDITS

Rating: ★★★★☆ • *Origin:* UK, 1981 • *Director:* Terry Gilliam • *Source:* Arrow DVD

This superbly imaginative fantasy was director and· cowriter Terry Gilliam's breakout success, the hit that ensured his continued career as a cinematic visionary. It's an episodic series of adventures across history and myth told from the viewpoint of Kevin (Craig Warnock), an 11-year-old boy struggling to make sense of society and its rules. Kevin falls in with a gang of would-be "international robbers," a half dozen raffish dwarves who worked at repairing flaws in the fabric of creation for the Supreme Being until they stole his map of the time holes that riddled reality. Alternately pursuing and pursued, Kevin follows the gang to the Napoleonic wars, medieval England, ancient Greece, and the Time of Legends, where the band is lured to the Fortress of Ultimate Darkness by the Evil One (David Warner), who wants the Creator's map for his own nefarious purposes.

Nowadays casting a group of dwarf actors as a joke about their shortness would be at best tasteless, but it illustrates Gilliam's theme that against the rule of arbitrary authority, adults have no more stature than children. In further justification, Randall (David Rappaport) and his gang are all fine character actors with more personality and definition than, say, the Merrie Men of Robin Hood (John Cleese), who are one-joke medieval brutes right out of *Holy Grail* or *Jabberwocky*. Likewise, Napoleon (the ever-excellent Ian Holm) is no more to be admired or respected than Kevin's gadget-greedy and materialistic parents or Cleese's smarmy Robin Hood. However, not all heroes are frauds: King Agamemnon (Sean Connery) is brave, kind, and just, the kind of wise and caring father denied to Kevin back in suburban reality. If there's any hope for humanity, it's in the like of Connery's character.

So *Time Bandits* is an exuberant visual romp, funny, fast-moving, and with at least a few ideas behind its roller-coaster ride—but is it a swashbuckler? Hey, it has Robin Hood, medieval knights, and a Bronze Age duel with a minotaur, so I think we're on solid ground for including it here. To top it off, who else would you cast as the Supreme Being if not Ralph Richardson? If you've somehow escaped seeing it before now, add this to your short list (er, no pun intended).

A TOUCH OF ZEN

Rating: ★★★★☆ • *Origin:* Taiwan, 1971 • *Director:* King Hu • *Source:* Mubi streaming video

This movie is writer-director King Hu's statement that a *wuxia* film can have artistic significance without straying outside the bounds of the genre, a claim he pretty much makes good on. Originally released in two parts, this is a three-hour epic that takes its time developing its characters and telling its story. Fortunately, it's time well spent.

During the Ming dynasty, in a remote village near a ruined fort, unambitious artist and calligrapher Gu Shengzai (Shih Chun) lives contentedly with his nagging mother amid a stack of ancient scrolls. But when two groups of strangers appear in town, furtively keeping an eye on each other, he is intrigued and investigates, becoming even more interested when he finds one of the strangers, Miss Yang (Hsu Feng), is an attractive young woman. But these strangers are dangerous folk, martial artists from opposing factions, and noncombatant Gu might be getting in over his head.

Almost everything is seen from the viewpoint of the scholarly artist, and a wuxia fan could be forgiven for wondering when the fighters are going to step forward as protagonists, sending the inoffensive calligrapher back to his brushes. However, though Yang Huizhen emerges as the most important of the martial arts characters, she never usurps Gu's central role. Yang and her allies, renegade generals Shi (Bai Ying) and Lu (Xue Han), are on the run from the murderous Eastern Group, and Gu, smitten with the fiercely independent Yang, gets drawn into the fugitives' affairs. The inoffensive artist, filled with purpose for the first time in his life, emerges as the band's battle planner because he's spent so many years studying the scrolls of the masters of strategy. And they're going to need strategy, for the Eastern Group is sending General Men Da (Wang Rui) after them with a company of 200 soldiers.

Gu plants a story that the fugitives are hiding in the ruined fort, spreads a rumor among the troops that the fort is haunted, and then devises tricks and traps that will panic the soldiers in the night and concentrate them where they can be slaughtered by multishot standing cross-bows. It all works just as Gu had planned, and the morning after the battle, he triumphantly surveys his clever tricks and fright devices, laughing delightedly at how effective they'd been, until he suddenly comes upon the crossbows' killing field of dead soldiers and faces the true consequences of lethal violence. And where is Miss Yang? She's disappeared! Grim-faced Buddhist monks arrive to clean up after the carnage, and though Gu begs them to tell him if they know where Miss Yang has gone, none will say. He will have to leave his village and search for her himself.

Though it's almost an hour into the film before anyone draws a sword, there are plenty of classic wuxia combats in this movie, with all the exotic weapons, aerial leaps, and arrow catching you could ask for, especially in the clashes between the steely Wang Huizhen and relentless Ouyang Nian (Tien Peng), the Eastern Group's most dangerous agent. Buddhist themes gradually become more prominent as Abbot Hui (Roy Chiao) intervenes to give the fugitives protection at his Chan monastery, and once Gu goes on his search for Yang, the story gets increasingly allegorical. (With a straight face, Abbot Hui utters lines like "His evil is not yet expunged," so you know he's a serious dude.) In the last hour the story also leaves the small town's sets and opens out into the gorgeous natural scenery of Taiwan, where the director composes his shots like paintings on ancient triptychs. King Hu even finds a way to give the story a happy ending, though it's just as unconventional as his lead characters. Epic!

TREASURE ISLAND (1934)

Rating: ★★★★★ • *Origin:* USA • *Director:* Victor Fleming • *Source:* Warner Bros. DVD

Robert Louis Stevenson's classic 1883 novel established the entire genre of pirate swashbuck-lers, so naturally it had been filmed in the silent era—five times, in fact. However, none of those older films has survived, so the earliest adaptation we have is this one—but this one's all we need. It's a wonderful film that has a lot going for it, but what makes it endlessly rewatch-able is the larger-than-life performance of Wallace Beery as Long John Silver.

Conversely, it has one major liability that, despite Beery's best efforts, makes the modern viewer cringe and wince: the inclusion of child actor Jackie Cooper as young Jim Hawkins. To be fair, Cooper delivered exactly what was asked of him, which was to be painfully over-earnest and sentimental, like every other 1930s child star. It's just that by current standards and sensibilities, the performances of this period's child actors—Jackie Cooper, Shirley Temple, and their ilk—are so damned grating that you just want to fast-forward right past them.

All right, we got that little rant out of the way. On to the movie: *Treasure Island* is a pretty close adaptation of Stevenson's novel, which means it starts slowly, with the first act that establishes the backstory centered on the fugitive pirate Billy Bones at the Admiral Benbow Inn. Fortunately, this production has the great Lionel Barrymore (brother of John) in the role of Billy Bones, and he leaves no scenery unchewed in a bravura performance that ends in his death from equal parts terror and rum. But in death he unwittingly bequeaths to Jim Hawkins the map to the plunder buried on Treasure Island, and avast! We're off to the Caribbean.

But how to get there, eh? Eh? Enter Squire Trelawney as played by Nigel Bruce (later to be Dr. Watson to Basil Rathbone's Sherlock Holmes—harrumph, harrumph!). He takes Jim off to Bristol Port, perfectly depicted with a forest of masts above a row of docked ships.

Jackie Cooper and Wallace Beery in *Treasure Island*
(1934) Metro-Goldwyn-Mayer (MGM) / Wikimedia Commons

On the wharf there, we meet Long John Silver, and from that point the rest of the film belongs to Wallace Beery. Silver is the original engaging scoundrel, and Beery plays him broad, smiling, squinting, rolling his eyes and looking around furtively, making sure the audience is in from the beginning on the joke of his duplicity. Young Jim and Squire Trelawney are completely hornswoggled, allowing Silver to pack the crew of the *Hispaniola* with pirates. But Captain Smollett (craggy Lewis Stone) isn't fooled by Silver's smarmy ways and spots him as a cunning rogue.

But by that time, they've arrived at Treasure Island, and it's mutiny, mates, so serve out the cutlasses! The plot adheres closely to the twists and rapid reversals of the novel, and the action scenes are staged well, their imagery striking and memorable. The tense scene in which Jim Hawkins is pursued around the drifting *Hispaniola* by a wounded pirate, Israel Hands, is particularly fine. One can almost forgive the swab for letting Jackie Cooper survive!

Incidentally, they used a genuine three-master for the *Hispaniola*, a beautiful ship, filming key scenes at sea, so the sailing's all true to life and the episodes shot high in the rigging are dizzying. And cackling, mad old Ben Gunn is the real treasure of the island. What a classic! Immortal line: "Them that die'll be the lucky ones!"

TREASURE ISLAND (1950)

Rating: ★★★★★ (Essential) • *Origin:* USA/UK, 1950 • *Director:* Byron Haskin •
Source: Disney DVD

Walt Disney liked to adapt well-known classic tales, so when he decided to make his first live-action feature, it's not surprising that he chose Robert Louis Stevenson's *Treasure Island*, with its child protagonist and adventures in exotic locales. What is surprising is how hard-edged and gritty it is, considering Disney's later (well-earned) reputation for peddling bland conformist mediocrity. This 1950 film is as tense and dynamic as its pre–Hays Code, 1934 predecessor and just as closely adapted from the novel, though exact choices of scenes and dialogue vary between the two. Moreover, the Disney version is in vibrant full color.

The supporting cast isn't as strong: the Disney film's Billy Bones, Squire Trelawney, Dr. Livesey, and Captain Smollett can't match up to their 1934 incarnations, but Bobby Driscoll as 1950's young Jim Hawkins does just fine and is far less grating than the saccharine Jackie Cooper. And as good as Wallace Beery was in 1934 as Long John Silver—and he was very good indeed—Robert Newton in the Disney version simply blows him away. Newton is

DISNEY'S FIRST SWASHBUCKLER

After the box-office success of RKO's *The Spanish Main* (1945) and *Sinbad the Sailor* (1947), in 1948 Warner Bros. rereleased *The Adventures of Robin Hood* to theaters, where it did almost as well as its first time 'round in 1938. The rest of Hollywood took notice, and soon every studio had two or three historical adventures in the development pipeline. The postwar swashbuckler boom was on!

Walt Disney wasn't about to be left behind. With a pile of money parked in European banks, he decided to open a British studio to make his first live-action films, using *The Adventures of Robin Hood* as the template: historical adventures with broad appeal based on familiar stories from public domain sources (because why pay royalties?). And he hit a home run the first time at bat with *Treasure Island*.

Stevenson's consummate con man incarnate, all deference and false humility, constantly letting the mask slip just enough to show the audience the calculating schemer behind the smile—a trick he learned from Beery, to be sure, but Newton perfected it. Plus, the broad West Country accent he adopts as Silver has become the default talk-like-a-pirate voice of buccaneering rogues ever since. You can blame Newton for "Ahr," which he slips in everywhere; at the end of a funeral prayer for a man he's murdered, he even solemnly intones, "Ahr-men." And with a wink to the viewer, you know the mutiny will soon be on.

The film was shot almost entirely on location in Cornwall and the tropics, and it looks great, including the background matte paintings of Bristol Port and of a distant *Hispaniola* run aground on Treasure Island's shore. Speaking of the *Hispaniola*, the ship plays such an important role in the plot that in any adaptation of Stevenson's tale, it's practically a member of the cast, and for this version they got a fine square-rigged three-master that's completely persuasive.

The most important decision in the novel, and the most intense scene in the film, is when Jim Hawkins decides to leave the safety of the island stockade and go alone to cut the *Hispaniola* adrift, which leads to the nightmarish pursuit of the lad across the darkened deck and up into the rigging by the deranged and murderous pirate Israel Hands (Geoffrey Keen). It's the emotional climax of the movie, and after Jim wins though single-handed, there's no doubt but that in the end, the ragtag pirates will succumb to young Hawkins and the forces of right and decency, no matter how John Silver plies his deceitful silver tongue. Don't miss this one, mates, it's a winn-ahr.

TREASURE ISLAND (1972)

Rating: ★★★☆☆ • *Origin:* UK/France/West Germany/Italy/Spain • *Director:* John Hough •
Source: Prism Leisure DVD

They dubbed Orson Welles. They got Orson Welles to play Long John Silver, one of the foremost scoundrels in English literature, and then they dubbed his voice. SMDH.

That bizarre decision aside, the main problem with this version is its painfully low budget and weak production values. This film was shot in Spain in a mere seven days, and it looks it. Fortunately, the cast is decent: Welles as Silver and Walter Slezak as Squire Trelawney are past their glory days but still good, Italian action star Rik Battaglia is a properly gritty Captain Smollett, and they have a solid Jim Hawkins in child actor Kim Burfield. The pacing's a bit slow until the *Hispaniola* reaches the island where Flint's treasure is buried, but after that it picks up nicely and jogs right along to the end. The classic story holds up well to the indignity of cheap costumes and poor lighting, and despite everything, one still gets swept up in Jim Hawkins's desperate ventures and hairbreadth escapes. But compared to the superb 1934 and 1950 adaptations, this version is sadly lacking.

TRIUMPH OF THE SON OF HERCULES

Rating: ★☆☆☆☆ • *Origin:* Italy, 1961 • *Director:* Tanio Boccia • *Source:* Mill Creek DVD

The strongman Maciste, a.k.a. Hercules (Kirk Morris), ever wandering and ever shirtless, shows up this time in ancient Egypt, where Bad Queen Tenefi (Ljuba Bodina) makes daily sacrifices of young women to the Fire God, whose mechanical idol is tended by the monstrous Yuri Men. Maciste doesn't like this: he throws a lot of large, heavy objects, is briefly enchanted by a magic scepter to become Tenefi's love slave, and then throws more large, heavy objects until he ends Tenefi's reign of terror. Nothing about this is any good: the story is predictable, and the acting is terrible; this movie isn't even funny-bad, it's just boring-bad. The only point of interest is that the American version begins and ends with an incongruous Son of Hercules theme song that sounds like it was written by Frankie Laine for a Western. So wrong!

THE TROJAN HORSE (OR THE TROJAN WAR)

Rating: ★★★☆☆ • *Origin:* Italy/France/Yugoslavia, 1961 • *Director:* Giorgio Ferroni •
Source: YouTube streaming video

Say, this isn't bad. Oh, it has the starchy script and stale acting you see in most Italian historical epics, but a few standouts carry the rest of the cast. And as an action movie about ancient warfare, it's a winner.

We're back in that familiar 10th year of the Trojan War that Homer tells us about in *The Iliad*, a sprawling saga with a bewildering cast of heroes and gods. If you're going to make a movie from it, you have to pick somebody from the crowd to be your protagonist, and this is an Italian film, so they've picked Aeneas, because he's an honorable warrior who survives the war and goes on, at least in legend, to become one of the founders of Rome.

As the movie begins, the foremost Greek warrior, Achilles (Arturo Domenici), has just slain his great Trojan rival Hector and is dragging the body around the battlefield behind his chariot. This is watched from the walls of Troy with grim sorrow by Aeneas (Steve Reeves), who thinks the war has ground on long enough and that it's time to make peace, an opinion that pits him against his commander, the weaselly Paris (Warner Bentivegna) and his bitchy stolen wife, Helen (Edy Vessel). King Priam (Carlo Tamberlani) decides to go alone to the Greek war camp to beg for the return of his son Hector's body, and Aeneas defies Paris's orders to go with him. This gives Aeneas an opportunity to flex pecs against Greek muscleman Ajax (Mimmo Palmara) and cross verbal swords with Ulysses (John Drew Barrymore). However, for defying Paris, Aeneas is sent away from Troy to raise troops among the Dardanians, while jealous Helen insists that his pregnant wife, Princess Creusa (Juliette Mayniel), must be sent to the Greek camp as a Trojan hostage. When Aeneas gets back with his army of Dardanians, he's mighty pissed and defies Paris again to storm the Greek camp. Things get messy, much blood is spilled, and when the Greeks pretend to retreat, they leave behind this great, big wooden horse . . .

Reeves is no more expressive here than usual, but he's handsome, and the camera loves him, leaving the actors playing Ulysses (always a great part), Paris, and Cassandra to do the heavy lifting. Both Troy and the Achaeans field impressive armies whose maneuvers are beautifully filmed, with the troops all geared out in fine arms and armor and trained to look convincing using them. Reeves as usual looks his best when engaged in personal combat, and there's a fair amount of it, especially after Ulysses and company come out of that big horse and open the gates of Troy to the Greek infantry. Catastrophic endings with cities afire are standard fare in sword-and-sandal epics, but here the fall of Troy is thoughtfully, even movingly, staged, a sincere and mostly successful attempt to convey its human tragedy. Kudos to Mario Amonini and Giovanni Fusco for their stirring music, which runs the gamut from brassy fanfares to the ending's sorrowful dirge. A decent film, good enough for them to make a sequel the following year, *The Avenger*, continuing the adventures of Reeves as Aeneas.

THE TWO GLADIATORS (OR *FIGHT OR DIE*)

Rating: ★★★☆☆ • *Origin:* Italy, 1964 • *Director:* Mario Caiano • *Source:* Mill Creek DVD

Here's another Roman dynastic struggle involving Commodus, that gladiatin' son of Marcus Aurelius who becomes a Bad Emperor upon his father's death, oppressing the citizens while gratifying himself by fighting in the arena and forcing young patrician women to bow to his will. Fortunately for Rome, Commodus (Mimmo Palmara) has a secret twin brother separated at birth, Centurion Lucius Crassus (Richard Harrison), who has a Confirming Birthmark and is summoned to the imperial capital by the senator who knows his hidden history. Look, even Shakespeare used the twin-brothers-separated-at-birth trope, so is it a storytelling tradition or a genre cliché? It all depends on how it's executed—and this cheesy action film comes down firmly in favor of genre cliché.

Spies are everywhere, so Commodus soon knows that his good bro Lucius is coming to Rome, and the Praetorian Guard are sent to slay him—but don't worry, Lucius has two loyal legionary buddies who've got wrestling moves, so it's a fight. In fact, it's a lot of fights, all of them mediocre, plus the usual captures, rescues, ambushes, and escapes down secret passages, leading to an attempt to stage an uprising against Commodus, which fails because it was a really stupid plan. Really, it was never going to work, because the title of this film is *The Two Gladiators*, so it has to end with Commodus facing Lucius in gladiator gear in a sad low-budget arena watched by fully dozens of spectators. Gosh, who will win? (Note to directors of gladiatorial combats: don't put your combatants in identical masked outfits so the viewer doesn't know which one to cheer for, KTHXBAI.)

ULYSSES

Rating: ★★★★★☆ • *Origin:* Italy, 1954 • *Director:* Mario Camerini • *Source:* Lionsgate DVD

Kirk Douglas and Sylvana Mangano on the set of
Ulysses ANSA / Wikimedia Commons

Kirk Douglas made his reputation in Hollywood in the late 1940s as a leading man in a series of intense roles in prestige dramas. By 1954 he was ready for a change of pace: action hero! He signed on with Disney for *20,000 Leagues under the Sea* and with Dino De Laurentiis in Italy for the epic *Ulysses*, based, of course, on Homer's *The Odyssey*. This is a big-budget production, with lavish sets, exteriors shot on Mediterranean islands, and a lovely full-scale Greek galley. Plus, of course, a cyclops.

The movie starts and ends with a framing sequence set in Ithaca, where Queen Penelope (Silvana Mangano) waits for Ulysses (Douglas) to return from the Trojan War, meanwhile fending off the unwanted advances of a crowd of Greek nobles who are convinced her missing husband is dead. The most pressing of these suitors, Antinous (Anthony Quinn), is close to browbeating her into marrying him. Meanwhile, Ulysses washes up on the coast of nearby Phaeacia, bereft of memory after a shipwreck. (Neptune, god of the sea, has it in for Ulysses because of a little temple defilement incident during the sack of Troy.) The story unfolds in scenes of flashback as Ulysses's memory gradually returns: the Trojan Horse, Polyphemus the Cyclops, the Sirens, and the hero's enchantment by the witch Circe (also played by Silvana Mangano in a clever twist). Ulysses regains his memory just in time, returns to Ithaca and . . . well, you know how the story goes.

Douglas makes a fine Ulysses: he could maybe be a little more intellectual, but he nails the hero's reckless bravado, and as he proved many times thereafter, he's great in an action part. Quinn is charismatic and intimidating, as usual, while Mangano underplays both her roles, which is the right decision because it gives Penelope's final breakdown more weight. Director Mario Camerini, who cowrote the script (with six other guys), does a fine job with the mystical atmosphere, especially when he lets wunderkind Mario Bava codirect the cyclops fight. The movie was a substantial enough success that it inspired the making of the Steve Reeves *Hercules* film that kicked off the entire peplum craze, and when you see the buff and shirtless Douglas in his Greek wrestling scene, you won't wonder why. Special notice to Circe's pearl-studded octopus-tentacled cloche hat, which is to *die* for.

UNDER THE RED ROBE

Rating: ★★☆☆☆ • *Origin:* USA/UK, 1937 • *Director:* Victor Seastrom (a.k.a. Sjöström) •
Source: Alpha Home Entertainment DVD

This film is based on Stanley J. Weyman's 1894 novel of the same name, the most popular book by that now-forgotten English historical adventure author, a man whose work was greatly admired by his contemporaries Robert Louis Stevenson and Arthur Conan Doyle (and also by this author—I included one of his short stories in my anthology *The Big Book of Swashbuckling Adventure*).

The Red Robe refers to the ecclesiastical raiment of Cardinal Richelieu, portrayed here by the dour and domineering Raymond Massey, a perfect choice for the role. But his is actually a minor part: the hero is a veteran swashbuckler named Gil de Berault, played by the German actor Conrad Veidt, whom we know best as Major Strasser from *Casablanca*. Seeing past Strasser to accept Veidt as a French cavalier takes some effort, but after a while you get used to the idea. (You'll still laugh at his black page-boy haircut, however.) Berault is a notorious duelist nicknamed the "Black Death" who performs occasional missions for the cardinal. Returning from one such mission, Richelieu informs him of the new edicts that forbid dueling, and warns Berault that if he breaks them, he'll hang. Richelieu then orders a few arrests and plays his flute for a while to relax.

Meanwhile Berault takes his pay to a gambling hell where he's accused of cheating, challenges his accuser to a duel, runs him through, and is promptly arrested by the Cardinal's Guard. He's condemned, but on the way to the scaffold, he's reprieved by Richelieu, who suspends his sentence on condition that he accomplish an impossible task: infiltrate the castle of a rebellious southern duke and bring him back to Paris as a captive. The cardinal gives Berault an assistant—and watchdog—named Marius (Romney Brent), an engaging rogue with nimble fingers who's adept at sleight of hand. Cut almost immediately to the South of France—no time is wasted in this film—and to the grim and gothic Castle Foix. Berault, reluctantly rescued from drowning in the adjacent river, is reluctantly taken into the castle, where everyone is suspicious and unfriendly. How to gain their trust?

By the traditional method, of course: romance the lady of the castle! Enter Mademoiselle de Foix, played by French actress Annabella (yes, she has just one name, like Cher). Berault the spy inevitably falls for her, though she's the sister of the man he plans to betray. This sort of character development usually gives a plot focus, but instead the middle of this movie grows confused, with everyone wearing false names, while agents with mysterious MacGuffins mysteriously come and go, and motives get murky and unclear. It doesn't help that there's zero chemistry between Veidt and Annabella, which drains all credibility from their romance.

Oh, there are secret passages, scaling a castle tower, pursuits and escapes, and noble renunciations in the name of honor, but they can't quite save the thing once it's gone smash. The ending, when the cardinal comes back onstage, is an improvement but can't make up for the muddled middle. Too bad: Massey is awfully good as Richelieu.

THE VALIANT ONES

Rating: ★★★☆☆ • *Origin:* Taiwan/Hong Kong, 1975 • *Director:* King Hu • *Source:* Al!ve DVD

This is entertaining, but it's the least effective of King Hu's early *wuxia* films. During the Ming dynasty, the Chinese coast is plagued by pirates led by renegade Japanese samurai, in particular three ronin who are so persistent that General Yu Dayou (Roy Chiao) is tasked with bringing their depredations to an end.

Instead of a large force of troops, General Yu assembles a small team of martial artists to outwit and capture the pirate leaders, all of them military men who seem to know each other except for the modest and mysterious swordsman Wu Jiyuan (Ying Bai), "The Whirlwind," and his wife, expert archer Wu Reshi (Feng Hsu), who never speaks.

Except for a bit of double-dealing among the Chinese bureaucrats, there isn't much plot here, just a series of encounters, traps that succeed or fail, between the martial artists of General Yu and the "white tiger" pirates led by the ronin, whose strength is mainly in numbers. The story is told from the viewpoint of General Yu and his fighters, who are stripped to their essence, without much character beyond their individual fighting styles, communicating by gesture and by one fighter's melancholy flute tunes. In one amusing skirmish, Yu's orders are conveyed by the sudden and repeated rearrangement of stones on a go board, as the white-clad pirates move in to surround the dark-clothed defenders.

However, all the attempts to trap the pirates are inconclusive, so the whirlwind Wu couple decide to go incognito into the ranks of the pirates to discover their secret lair. This leads to the best scenes in the picture, when Jiyuan and Reshi, having penetrated to the ronins' headquarters, are tested by attacks from various martial arts experts in an inventive series of short, sharp combats. After defeating their opponents, the Wus are warily accepted among the pirates, but they escape at night to bring the location of the secret headquarters back to General Yu. This provokes the pirate leadership into pursuit, and at last they are drawn out of their lair and into a trap they can't evade.

There are some striking outdoor settings in this film, though less striking than those of King Hu's *Dragon Inn*, *A Touch of Zen*, and *The Fate of Lee Khan*. Most troubling is that the careful editing of the previous films, which often featured long and carefully composed establishing shots, has been abandoned in favor of a staccato style of abrupt cuts that rarely gives the eye a rest. The combat is similarly simplified from choreographed dance routines into rapid brushstrokes of sudden action. Writer-director Hu seems to be groping for the distilled essence of wuxia combat, but the result misses the careful balance of his earlier efforts.

VALMONT

Rating: ★★★☆☆ • *Origin:* USA/France, 1989 • *Director:* Miloš Forman •
Source: Metrodome DVD

The second cinematic adaptation of Choderlos de Laclos's novel *Dangerous Liaisons* (1782) in less than a year, *Valmont* suffers by comparison with its predecessor. Though visually lush, and with a historical depiction of eighteenth-century France that can scarcely be improved upon, its cast is weaker, and the story, scripted by Jean-Claude Carrière and director Miloš Forman, turns Laclos's deadly game of duels d'amour into little more than a mean-spirited bedroom farce. The Marquise de Merteuil (Annette Bening) and the Vicomte de Valmont (Colin Firth) are frenemies playing catch-and-release love games among the Paris aristos until Valmont has the misfortune to actually fall in love with his latest romantic target, the virtuous Madame de Tourvel (Meg Tilly). Meanwhile, Merteuil plots to get revenge on a former lover by having Valmont seduce his 15-year-old fiancée Cécile (Fairuza Balk). All their plans go wrong.

None of the leads gives better than a shallow performance, though that may be because the characters as written have little depth. Bening is stunning, of course, when she doesn't simper, but as a cold and calculating villain, she just doesn't sell it, while Firth and the wan Tilly aren't given any scenes that make their unlikely love affair believable. And Forman lards the story with slapstick comedy gags that don't sit well with its serious themes. Despite this, Fairuza Balk as Cécile and Siân Phillips (Livia in *I, Claudius*) as her mother Madame de Volanges deliver memorable portrayals, and there are two brief but excellent smallsword duels. And be sure to savor old warhorse Fabia Drake, Bertie Wooster's Aunt Agatha, in her final role as the roguish matron Madame de Rosemonde. Still, this is almost two and a half hours you can probably spend better elsewhere. (See also *Dangerous Liaisons*.)

VENDETTA OF A SAMURAI

Rating: ★★★★★☆ • *Origin:* Japan, 1952 • *Director:* Kazuo Mori • *Source:* Toho DVD

With a screenplay by Akira Kurosawa, Toshiro Mifune in the lead, and about half the cast of *Seven Samurai* in support roles, this very nearly qualifies as a Kurosawa samurai film, but there's more *High Noon* in this than *Seven Samurai*. Ably directed by Kazuo Mori, who oversaw a number of *Zatoichi* movies and TV episodes, as well as the similarly titled *Samurai Vendetta* (1959), this is a remarkable film, a revisionist *chambara* made while the genre was still establishing its tropes.

Kurosawa sets out to tell the story of the celebrated samurai showdown at Kagiya Corner in 1634, when the sword trainer Mataemon Araki helped his brother-in-law Kazuma achieve his revenge on the murderer Matagoro, despite the protection of a rival clan. At the start, we see the combat as it's been depicted in popular fiction, an exaggerated kabuki dance of orchestrated swordplay as Mataemon bloodlessly defeats a platoon of bodyguards. But before the fight is over, a narrator interrupts to tell us that what we've been seeing is just a figment, while the real story, and the real people behind it, are far more interesting.

The rest of the film is the historic backstory of the real participants in the showdown, leading to a shattering climax in a horrific street brawl (with *katanas*). After killing young Kazuma's brother, Matagoro (Minoru Chiaki) takes refuge with a clan in Edo into which he's married. The honor code demands vengeance, and because Mataemon (Mifune) is Kazuma's brother-in-law, he must help him, even though this pits him against his best friend Jinza (Takashi Shimura), who is related by marriage to Matagoro. The bulk of the movie takes place in the hour before the duel, as Mataemon and his three allies wait for Matagoro, Jinza, and company to arrive at Kagiya Corner and get ambushed. Facing possible death, the waiting samurai, none of whom has ever drawn a sword in real combat, contemplate their past lives in flashbacks that are elegiac and moving, between which Mataemon utters gnomic remarks like "Waiting is hard" and "Don't think about surviving." Gosh, thanks!

When the opponents do arrive and begin their final approach to the pair of teahouses where Mataemon and his comrades await them, the suspense is so thick you could cut it with a *wakizashi*. Fear is present like a fifth member of the attack team. The fight itself, when it breaks out, is utterly awful and utterly convincing. And all those personal flashbacks, with their songs and stories and hopes and dreams, seem suddenly significant.

THE VENGEANCE OF URSUS

Rating: ★★★☆☆ • *Origin:* Italy, 1961 • *Director:* Luigi Capuano • *Source:* Mill Creek DVD

This is smarter than your average shirtless strongman peplum. Though set in an uncertain classical time in two kingdoms lost to history, everything else about this tale is well grounded and relatively believable. Disappointed in love, Ursus the mighty warrior ("Samson" Burke) has retired after mighty warring to plow his modest farm and raise his young brother Dario (Roberto Chevalier). Their bucolic existence is disturbed by the arrival of Ursus's lost love,

Roberto Chevalier and "Samson" Burke in *The Vengeance of Ursus*
Utente / Wikimedia Commons

Princess Sira (Wandisa Guida), who is on her way to wed the neighboring monarch, King Zagro (Livio Lorenzon, always a pleasure). Suddenly, bandits! Ursus drives them off, but Sira's guards are decimated, so despite his heartbreak, Ursus offers to escort her to Zagro's capital.

Intrigue! Zagro is a scheming rat who plans to marry Sira, assassinate her father, and then rule both kingdoms, ha ha ha ha! Complications to this scheme include his jealous mistress Sabra (Nadine Sanders), the mighty Ursus, and the hero's young brother Dario, who unexpectedly turns out to be a clever and capable lad.

Ursus is a strongman on a more human scale that Hercules or Maciste: he can burst his bonds when he's captured by his perfidious enemies, but it doesn't look easy. And when he has to outmuscle eight other guys to avoid being pitched into a bonfire, he nearly doesn't make it. Burke isn't any better an actor than most of the American bodybuilders hired to star in these miniepics, but at least his Ursus is given sensible motivations and decent lines to say, and that makes all the difference. The rest of the cast does even better, especially the villainous Zagro, who's thoroughly convincing. Moreover, the action scenes are pretty credible, with soldiers wielding swords and shields as if they know what they're doing. Added bonus: an attack cheetah and an elephant! It may be hard to find a good surviving copy of this film, but it's worth the effort.

THE VIKING

Rating: ★★★☆☆ • *Origin:* USA, 1928 • *Director:* Roy William Neill •
Source: YouTube streaming video

As Leif Ericsson sails west from Greenland in search of the New World, on the deck of his longship are three men in love with his ward, the shield maiden Helga: his sailing master Egil the Black, Alwin the noble slave from England, and Leif himself. But the crew is more concerned about the likelihood of sailing off the edge of the world.

This was produced at the end of the silent era, made by the Technicolor corporation to show off its new full-color process, and it was mated with a nearly synced-up music track with accompanying sound effects, so it looks and sounds as good as a movie can that lacks only human speech. It's based on a 1902 novel by Ottilie Liljencrantz, though Wagner's Ring operas seem a bigger influence, given the extravagantly horned helms of the Vikings and the fact that Helga's musical theme is adapted from "The Ride of the Valkyries." This film incorporates every popular Norse Raider trope from the nineteenth century: bare-chested and fur-clad Vikings descending on the English coast to pillage, slaughter, and take slaves; drunken revelry in the mead hall; and manly duels of honor to settle even the slightest disagreements. It's all set against a largely ahistorical fight to the death between barbaric pagan Thor worshippers and those noble Nordics who have accepted the Cross.

They all keep slaves, however, and that's a historical fact the film faces directly. Alwin (LeRoy Mason), a Northumbrian noble, is captured in a raid and taken back to Norway, where Helga (Pauline Starke) sees him looking at her insolently and buys him to teach him a lesson. Or does she have a hidden agenda? Black Egil (Harry Lewis Woods) certainly thinks so, and he abuses the new slave until the generous and Christianized Leif Ericsson (Donald Crisp) steps in and makes him fight fair. Alwin's noble behavior, and good right arm, impress Ericsson, who decides to take him along on his voyage of discovery.

There are more fights in Greenland when Leif's brutal father, Eric the Red, learns that his son has become one of the hated Christians—it's all stage combat, unconvincing but mighty enthusiastic. Leif and his crew make a fighting retreat to their longship, and then they're off to the West,

The Viking Metro-Goldwyn-Mayer (MGM) / Wikimedia Commons

with Helga aboard as a stowaway so the boys will have someone to fight over. It must be said, Pauline Starke looks great in her operatic Viking armor, and as an actor she commands more nuance than her three suitors combined. Starke's Helga is far and away the best reason to seek out this old chestnut.

THE VIKING QUEEN

Rating: ★★☆☆☆ • *Origin:* UK, 1967 • *Director:* Don Chaffey • *Source:* StudioCanal DVD

This Hammer Films historical adventure set in Roman Britain should really be called *The Celtic Queen*, but apparently Vikings sell movie tickets while Celts do not, though the story is based loosely on that of Britannic warrior queen Boudica. Marketing, am I right? The aging king of the Iceni Britons, weary of war with Rome, decrees on his deathbed that the rulership of his kingdom be shared peacefully between the queen's daughter Salina (Finnish model Carita) and the Emperor Nero, represented in Britain by Governor General Justinian (Don Murray). However, Queen Salina's druid advisors want war to drive out the hated Romans, and Justinian's military advisors want war to send more enslaved Britons to Rome, but Salina and Justinian fall for each other after a super sexy chariot race through the woods and decide to make love, not war. With everyone else conspiring for conflict, this doesn't work out well for them.

A case could be made that Salina and her two sisters, who become warrior women driving battle chariots, represent female empowerment, but that case is badly undercut by a treatment that verges on exploitation, with gratuitous partial nudity, rapine, and whipping.

The film's lukewarm leads, Carita and Murray, turn in barely adequate performances, while Donald Houston as Arch-Druid Maelgan is just obnoxiously terrible, shouting every line and sputtering through his fake facial hair. Geez, dude, go hug a tree and chill.

Still, though Hammer films may be lurid, they're always well made, so there are compensations. Patrick Troughton, in his last role before *Doctor Who*, is a standout as Salina's wise advisor Tristram, and Adrienne Corri (*Sword of Freedom*) is fine as Salina's fiery sister Beatrice. The exteriors were shot in Ireland's lovely County Wicklow, and there's nothing like watching a column of legionaries winding their way through heather-covered hills to evoke the feel of the far-flung fringes of the Roman Empire. On the action side, the combat scenes of Britannic war chariots hurtling into shield walls of Roman cohorts, directed by Don Chaffey (*Jason and the Argonauts*), get the job done, and if the body count by the end includes just about everybody in the cast, well . . . what did you expect from a late '60s Hammer film?

THE VIKINGS

Rating: ★★★★★ • *Origin:* USA, 1958 • *Director:* Richard Fleischer • *Source:* KL Studio Classics Blu-ray

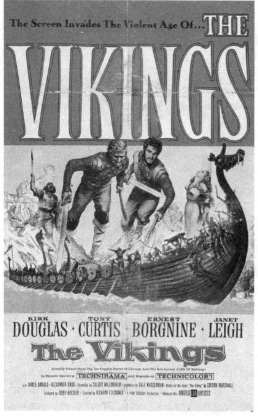

The Vikings REYNOLD BROWN / WIKIMEDIA COMMONS

You can complain about parts of this film if you want to—and with lines like "Love and hate are just horns on the same goat," you've got a point—but on the whole, *The Vikings* is a superb swashbuckling extravaganza, a production bursting with verve and enthusiasm, serious entertainment that never takes itself too seriously. It's a hell of a good time, and nobody had more fun making it than its producer and star, Kirk Douglas, who buoys it up with sheer gusto whenever it threatens to get too pompous.

The gusto starts right in the opening credits where, instead of setting the historical scene with scrolling text that reads like something from the King James Bible, we get a colorful animated storyboard depicting the depredations of the Vikings on the English coast. It's based stylistically on the Bayeux Tapestry and narrated (without credit) by Orson Welles, more of a classy cartoon than an illuminated manuscript. And then the film dives right into the action, cutting from cartoon Vikings to the real thing, murdering and pillaging in English Northumbria. They're led by the cheerfully ruthless King Ragnar (Ernest Borgnine), who callously rapes the local queen (the camera cuts away) and leaves her with child.

The movie then slows down for some exposition and the passage of 20 years, after which we're reintroduced to Ragnar and meet his son Prince Einar (Douglas, actually two months older than papa Borgnine), as well their English slave Eric (Tony Curtis), who unbeknown to all is the son Ragnar begot on the Northumbrian queen—and thus Einar's half-brother.

The movie's final lead is the English Princess Morgana (Janet Leigh, Curtis's wife at the time), who gets abducted a lot. She's the love interest for both Einar and Eric, and she looks great but unfortunately isn't given a lot to do other than to fail at teaching Einar the concept of romantic consent.

The three male leads really throw themselves into this fateful love triangle, acting their guts out—yes, Curtis could act—but they're almost overshadowed by the magnificence of the background their conflict is staged against. The production is splendid, shot in eye-poppingly gorgeous Norwegian fjords and on the coast of Brittany, and the costumes and sets are first-rate. They built a couple of fully functional Viking longships for the movie as well as several smaller vessels, and they weren't shy about putting them through their paces and showing you exactly how they worked. They also constructed an authentic Norse village with a capacious mead hall (we see a lot of the mead hall), the look of which, bold and rustic, defined the Viking era for a generation (and beyond: you'll see echoes of this film even in the video game *Skyrim*.) Add a bombastically memorable score by composer Mario Nascimbene, and you've got an audiovisual feast it would be hard to forget.

And now let us praise director Richard Fleischer, whom Douglas had met when shooting *20,000 Leagues* for Disney, and for whom *Vikings* was a career-making film. And rightly so: every shot is carefully composed, and every scene builds to maximum impact. This is as true for the action sequences—of which there are plenty—as for the scenes of sheer spectacle. For example, when Einar's ship returns in triumph to the home fjord, the crew, led by Douglas himself, "run the oars" by hopping above the waves along the row of outstretched timbers from stern to bow. It's both exciting and hilarious. (This was an actual historical feat that no one had attempted for nearly 1,000 years, and only the stuntmen were supposed to do it, but nobody could keep the grinning and athletic Douglas from joining in.)

We'll skip the details of the plot, which is the standard Viking saga mélange of attacks, abductions, arson, and amputation, and jump right to the final battle, where rivals Einar and Eric must team up to lead an assault on the castle of the treacherous English king who's captured Morgana. The whole prelude to this battle is silent except for the pounding of drums as the Vikings disembark from their longships, arm, and prepare for the attack. Fleischer borrows liberally from Eisenstein's *Alexander Nevsky*, and it pays off, the suspense building and building until the Norsemen are released to descend like a storm on the seemingly invulnerable fortress. Some top-notch gymnastic swashbuckling gets the Vikings through the castle's gates, and then the battle dissolves into convincingly bloody chaos. And yet, thrilling as this is, the whole sequence is really just a setup for the final confrontation between Einar and Eric that resolves their long-simmering romantic rivalry. It's tremendous.

A final note on tone: unlike most Hollywood epics of the big-studio era that featured conflicts between Christians and pagans, this movie is a sea change in that for once the vigorous, larger-than-life Odin worshippers win the day, ultimately triumphing over their effete Christianized adversaries. These Vikings are a warrior folk who live in a world ruled by doom and fate, and that gives them the strength to embrace whatever fate sends them. It doesn't make them admirable, but it does show why they were so often victorious.

VIKING WOMEN AND THE SEA SERPENT

Rating: ★☆☆☆☆ • *Origin:* USA, 1957 • *Director:* Roger Corman • *Source:* Lionsgate DVD

Viking Women and the Sea Serpent American International Pictures / Wikimedia Commons

Warning: here are 65 minutes you'll never have again. In the late 1950s, movies about giant monsters were all the rage, many of them produced by the shlock-meisters at American International Pictures, and filming a bevy of half-clad starlets had never gone out of style, so the young producer-director Roger Corman combined the two in this shoddy would-be epic. Its pompously overlong full title is *The Saga of the Viking Women and Their Voyage to the Waters of the Great Sea Serpent*, which is the only thing the least bit clever about this dud.

Let's get right to what passes for its story: in Norway, which you probably never realized looks exactly like Southern California, at a village whose men went off a-Viking and never returned, the women left behind are voting on whether to go search for them, using the traditional Nordic method of hurling their spears into the "Yes" tree or the "No" tree. The deciding "Yes" vote is cast by the priestess Inger, the only nonblonde, who is suspected of wanting to go on the mission so she can get her hooks into one of the missing men, a Viking who belongs to the blond woman with the ponytail. (None of the blond women has been granted a distinctive personality or any dialogue, so alas, the only way to tell them apart is by hairstyle.)

The women go to sea in a cheesy-looking fake longship, a prop so crappy that pieces are visibly falling from it as it's launched. (Apparently while filming, the whole crew of Viking women damn near drowned when the guy piloting the towboat fell asleep and they were all carried far offshore.) Once they're at sea, the only subject the women want to talk about is men, so you know this is a fantasy. Fortunately, the only man left in their town, a shirtless blond surfer dude, has stowed away and gone with them, so there's a responsible male on board who can make important decisions and deliver key exposition like "It's the monster of the vortex!" Said monster is the worst sea serpent ever back-projected in Hollywood, but it's monstrous enough to swamp the crappy longship, which for good measure is set afire by a gratuitous lightning bolt. The crew abandon ship, and we're treated to the sight of a flaming six-inch model of an entirely different vessel swirling down into a tiny whirlpool.

The crew wash ashore somewhere on the coast of Malibu, where they're promptly captured by a tribe of mounted barbarians and marched off to an unconvincing matte painting of a generic castle. There the barbarian chief tells them with a leer that they are now slaves who must do whatever the barbarians wish—but first, let's go on a boar hunt! And immediately the Viking women are given horses and spears, and off they all go. (Don't ask about the sad fake-tusked porker that plays the boar.) The rest of the film makes just as much sense. There's a rowdy feast with '50s "exotic" dancing, gratuitous woman-whipping, escape, betrayal by Inger (never trust the dark-haired one!), recapture, reunification with the lost and enslaved Viking men, more escape, more recapture, and a flaming sacrifice of the Vikings to the barbarian gods that gets snuffed out in a literal deus ex machina when Inger redeems herself by calling on the god Thor to save them. That leaves only the final battle with the titular sea serpent, who has apparently been able to terrorize the coast of Malibu for generations because nobody ever thought to stick a sword in its head. Well, I never.

WAR GODDESS (OR THE AMAZONS [1973])

Rating: ★☆☆☆☆ • *Origin:* Italy/France/Spain, 1973 • *Director:* Terence Young •
Source: Retromedia DVD

This is one of the later films in the career of director Terence Young (*Thunderball, Red Sun*), and lo, how the mighty have fallen. Robert Graves is named as one of the sources for the story, but *I, Claudius* this ain't. In the time of Greek myths, the Amazons are a warrior tribe consisting entirely of women, and the story starts with them slaughtering a band of barbaric Scythians so their warriors can complete their initiation rite of becoming an adult Amazon by killing a man. Immediate cut to their quadrennial games, in which their queen is chosen by athletic contest: javelin throw, obstacle course, horse racing, and archery, among others. There are two bitter rivals for the title, Antiope (Alena Johnston) and Oreitheia (Sabine Sun), and finally they are the last two in the running. The matter of rulership must be settled by . . . a topless, oiled wrestling match, and now we see what this movie's really about.

This film was made in the wake of the first flowering of Women's Lib, and it's both a put-down of that movement and an exploitation flick verging on soft-core porn. Antiope is named queen and immediately decrees that the Amazons have lost their way—why, some of them have actually been fraternizing with men. No more of that! For purposes of reproduction, the Amazon warriors will reluctantly submit to relations with men once a year, but that's it. And this year, the honor goes to the Greeks of Athens. The Athenian king, the hero Theseus (Angelo Infanti), comes along to the Love Camp of the Amazons and the Greeks and personally beds Antiope. Theseus is insufferably smug and condescending, but nonetheless Antiope is won over by his manly lovemaking. However, upon leaving the camp, Antiope takes his advice about returning home through the mountains, only to be ambushed by the Scythians. Theseus belatedly learns he gave Antiope a bum steer and rides to her rescue, but the queen believes he did it on purpose, and plot complications ensue. Oreitheia decides that Antiope's judgment is so badly affected by her dealings with Theseus that she must be replaced, a conflict that can only be solved by, yes, another extended catfight between the two, this time entirely in the nude.

This movie isn't 100 percent terrible, but it's close. Young is a competent enough director that the action sequences don't completely suck, and to give her credit, Sabine Sun as Oreitheia goes fierce and hard into her role as the bad girl. But the exploitation is tiresome, and the misogyny is dreadful. Do not go to Amazon Love Camp.

WAR GODS OF BABYLON

Rating: ★★☆☆☆ • *Origin:* Italy, 1962 • *Director:* Silvio Amadio • *Source:* Retromedia DVD

This quasi-historical epic is done in by its ponderous self-importance. Babylon has been conquered by Assyria and plots to throw off Assyrian rule. The wise Zoroaster, the mighty Hammurabi, Sardanapalus—basically everyone from the period whose name you might recognize—all get thrown into a stew of melodrama that comes down to a fight over the love of a cute young peasant woman named Mirra (Jackie Lane). The Assyrian king, Sardanapalus (Howard Duff) and the prophet Zoroaster (Arnoldo Foà) have some stage presence, but when actors have to say dumb lines like "Power digs deep trenches, even between brothers" and "When you weep, your beauty is magnified!," they're fighting a lost cause. Most of the film is just guys in ancient armor spouting lines like those at each other, and the eventual battles between Assyria and Babylon can't save it, especially since those clashes are perfunctory and uninteresting. When the dull fighting has gone on long enough, Sardanapalus blasphemes against the gods, there's a divine flood with cheesy special effects, the walls come tumbling down, and love dies on a pyre of hubris. I hate when that happens.

THE WAR LORD

Rating: ★★★★☆ • *Origin:* USA, 1965 • *Director:* Franklin Schaffner • *Source:* Eureka Blu-ray

This largely overlooked film may be the best depiction of medieval warfare from the 1960s. It stars Charlton Heston, who was instrumental in getting it made, and is based on a play by Leslie Stevens, so it has a script that's far more literate than you get in the usual knights-versus-Vikings movie. It has an excellent score by Jerome Moross (*The Big Country*), plus the action sequences were arranged by Yakima Canutt's son Joe, and they're tremendously good.

It's the eleventh century: war-weary Norman knight Chrysagon de la Crux (Heston) is sent by his lord, the Duke of Ghent, to take command of a remote coastal domain protected by a single round three-story tower. As he and his company of veteran warriors arrive in Chrysagon's marshy new holding, they pass stone menhirs and holy trees that clearly show that the locals, though nominally Christian, still hold with pagan religious customs. Suddenly a wounded peasant staggers out in front of the mounted knight and gasps that the village is being raided by Frisians (Lowland Vikings), and the Normans must ride instantly into battle. After a short, sharp skirmish, the Frisians are driven off, but the son of their chieftain is taken captive by Chrysagon's dwarf falconer Volc (Sammy Ross, excellent) and forced to become his page and servant.

Next comes the love story: the actors give it their all, but despite that, it still isn't entirely convincing. Chrysagon falls for dewy young peasant woman Bronwyn (model Rosemary Forsyth), but she's betrothed to hotheaded Marc (James Farentino), the son of the local headman. Though he wants her for himself, Chrysagon, in his capacity as the new local lord, gives Bronwyn and Marc permission to marry and is ready to suck it up as just one more disappointment in a life full of them, until his troublemaking brother Draco (Guy Stockwell) points out that by local custom, the lord has the right to bed a new bride on the night of her marriage. (Yep, here it is, the *droit de seigneur* which, no matter how often it's debunked, keeps rearing its head in historical fiction as an attractive male sex fantasy.) Chrysagon claims his right of a single night with Bronwyn, but when dawn comes, he—and she!—refuse to part. This is despite the disapproval of the knight's loyal bodyguard Bors (second-billed Richard Boone), who glowers and grunts like a surly bear. Meanwhile the outraged groom, Marc, runs off to inform the Frisian Chieftain that his son is held in the tower, the Vikings return in force, and the real trouble begins.

The second half of the film is mainly a top-notch small-scale siege action, as the Frisians deploy various stratagems to get into the Normans' stone tower, including a covered battering ram, flaming brush piles at the wooden door, and finally a great rolling wooden tower as tall as the fort it's attacking. It's all tautly and ingeniously directed by Franklin Schaffner, who though previously known for dramatic character studies, turns out to have genuine feel for exciting medieval warfare. This film was an attempt to get away from the Technicolor Camelot era of Hollywood films of knights in shining armor and portray the Middle Ages as they really were, and it mostly succeeds: the arms and armor on both sides are authentic to the period, and the combat is lethal and bloody. Heston wanted to shoot the film on location in the English marsh country, but Universal refused and insisted it be filmed in their expansive backlot, and though matte paintings and mist are used to give the impression the action is taking place in medieval Europe rather than Southern California, the results are pretty convincing. We won't tip the ending here, but it's just as grim and earthy as the story that precedes it. Look for Cecil B. DeMille's old leading man Henry Wilcoxon shaking his axe as the Frisian Chieftain. Director Schaffner and star Heston would team up again two years later to make a film that has over-shadowed this one, good as it is: *Planet of the Apes*.

WARRING CLANS

Rating: ★★★★☆ • *Origin:* Japan, 1963 • *Director:* Kihachi Okamoto • *Source:* Samurai DVD

It's the early 1570s, during the historic clash between the Oda and the Takeda—the warring clans of the title. On a lonely mountainside, a samurai, Ochi (Yuzo Kayama), is escaping from the Takeda when he's confronted by Suzumeno, the Takeda's boss ninja. The ninja is a cunning fighter, but Ochi slashes him across the face and throws him over a cliff. He's then congratulated for his feat by two other samurai who rise out of the underbrush: rugged Harima (Ichirô Nakatani), who salutes him ironically, and ragged Kinoshita (Makoto Sato), whose praises are rather more sarcastic and who suggests that, since he's left the Takeda, Ochi should find a new patron: himself. Ha-ha, just joking! But look, here comes a caravan of the Bashaku, an armed mercenary shipping company—maybe, Ochi, you could join them to escape your pursuers?

The three samurai, Ochi, Harima, and Kinoshita, united in mutual distrust and humor-ous skepticism, are the center around which this story of samurai intrigue and romance turns. Writer-director Kihachi Okamoto (*Samurai Assassin*, *Sword of Doom*), a master of the elements of *chambara* adventure, combines them here with a light touch, and sly irony is the order of the day. Taking Kinoshita's advice, Ochi and Harima pretend to be doofuses fighting over a stolen rice ball, and they cajole the caravan's leader, Lady Saghiri (Yuriko Hoshi), into letting them join the Bashaku. She takes them back to their forest compound, but that evening Kinoshita shows up in his true guise as an envoy of the Oda. He wants the Bashaku to smuggle 300 muskets stolen from the Takeda across the mountains, and he's willing to pay well for the job. The Bashaku run an honest caravan, but persuaded by the wily Kinoshita's gold, they agree.

As Ochi soon finds out, Kinoshita is hedging his bets, as he also hires a gang of pirates led by "Princess" Takihime (Kumi Mizuno) to carry another load of 300 muskets to Oda.

What is going on? Between the manipulations of the glib Kinoshita and the threats of the sinister Suzumeno (who survived his cliff dive, of course), can either the Oda or the Takeda be trusted? Ochi tells Harima that in these times, the only thing a samurai can really trust is his heart—and yet, what if Ochi loses his heart to the feisty Saghiri?

Serious questions, but Okamoto keeps the tone light and the action moving. Ochi is a fine young romantic hero, Harima is an engaging mentor-cum-sidekick, Kinoshita is a silver-tongued rascal, Saghiri is fiercely adorable, and the Bashaku are a bunch of lovable goofballs. There are traitors and sudden reversals, samurai archery tricks, a bandit with esoteric hypno-powers, jars of drugged sake—and best of all, by popular demand, a shipboard brawl of pirates versus ninja! Good times. And do you suppose those muskets are going to find a use in the slam-bang finale? Well, you know what Chekhov says about that gun you saw in the first act. Three hundred muskets? You do the math.

THE WARRIOR AND THE SORCERESS

Rating: ★★★☆☆ • *Origin:* Argentina/USA, 1984 • *Director:* John C. Broderick •
Source: Shout! Factory DVD

This is yet another remake of the classic *Yojimbo* (1961), with as usual no credit to Kurosawa or his screenwriter. This time the story is set on an alien desert planet that, like Tatooine, has two suns, which post–*Star Wars* became the standard signifier of an interplanetary setting. The warrior Kain (David Carradine) comes alone out of the desert to the hardscrabble town of Yamata, which has a single water well fought over by two gang lords, the militaristic Zeg (Luke Askew) and the bloated and decadent Bal Caz (Guillermo Marín). Yamata's other main resource is its starving population, whom the gang lords prey upon and occasionally sell to the nonhuman slaver Burgo (Armando Capo).

Kain, a former holy warrior for a dead god now reduced to the condition of mercenary, looks the situation over, decides he doesn't like either gang lord, and proceeds to play them off against each other, selling his services to one side and then the other. Complications arise when he discovers Zeg is holding Naja (María Socas), a sorceress of his former holy order, as a prisoner because she refuses to forge for him a legendary sacred sword. Kain helps Naja escape, which alerts Zeg to the game Kain is playing, and the warrior is drugged, captured, and beaten. However, when Kain manages to escape nonetheless, he finds that Naja has made the sacred sword but only for *him* to wield against the gang lords.

Despite the low budget and crappy production values, this film looks pretty good, atmospherically shot with a strong *Mad Max* vibe to it. Just before filming started, Carradine injured his right hand, so he wears a spiked black glove on it to conceal the cast, performing all his sword work with his left hand in a style taught by the noted fight director Anthony De Longis, who also plays the role of Kief, Zeg's guard captain. Though Carradine often looks tired, he still manages to muster enough charisma to carry off the role of the laconic Kain, sneering, evading guards, and scaling walls like an *Assassin's Creed* hero.

Short though the film is at 81 minutes, once its ending becomes obvious and inevitable, it still seems rather too long—one wishes the director would just get on with it. Extra points for the charming puppet monsters, which include Bal Caz's drooling lizard-headed advisor and a toothy tentacle beast defending Zeg's dungeon. Fair warning, however: if you're offended by female nudity, keep well away from this flick. There are so many breasts on display here, one woman even has four of them.

THE WARRIORS (OR THE DARK AVENGER)

Rating: ★★★☆☆ • *Origin:* USA/UK, 1955 • *Director:* Henry Levin •
Source: Warner Archive DVD

Allied Artists (formerly Monogram) was a minor studio known for inexpensive action-adventure films like the *Bomba, The Jungle Boy* series. In the mid-1950s Allied wanted to get a piece of the historical epic boom led by MGM, Warners, and Columbia with a big film of its own, so it rented the English studio MGM had used for Robert Taylor's medieval trilogy and bought a script about Edward, the Black Prince, and his adventures during the Hundred Years War. And for a bankable star Allied hired Errol Flynn for what would be his final swashbuckler.

This film's reputation is as the last hurrah of a has-been, but really, it's better than that. Oh, Flynn does look tired in the broadsword fights and is frequently doubled, but he still has much of the old charm. The story, though conventional, is economically told and kept moving by director Henry Levin (*The Return of Monte Cristo*). It's full of fine British actors like Michael Hordern, Peter Finch, and Rupert Davies, the combats are convincing and period appropriate, and the whole thing clocks in at only 85 minutes, so no time is wasted.

It's 1359, and after the English under Prince Edward (Flynn) have defeated the French and captured their king at Poitiers, King Edward III returns to England, leaving the prince behind to rule Aquitaine. But the French, led by the ruthless Comte de Ville (Finch), subvert the peace, and soon Aquitaine is at war again. To draw out Prince Edward, de Ville abducts Lady Joan Holland (Joanne Dru), Edward's childhood sweetheart. The prince falls into de Ville's ambush and there's a spirited cavalry skirmish, but Edward escapes the French trap. Separated from his men except for the loyal Sir John (Davies), Edward decides to rescue Joan himself by infiltrating de Ville's castle disguised as a nameless black knight. The story presents this credibly enough to make such a reckless plan believable, and derring-do ensues.

The fine castle built for *Ivanhoe* makes another appearance, or rather two, the interiors standing in for de Ville's medieval château, with the exteriors used as Edward's castle in the climactic siege. After a couple of attempts, Edward manages to rescue Joan and escape to his stronghold, but de Ville has been reinforced by the villainous Bertrand du Guesclin, who wants Edward's head, so the French have fun storming the castle. Mantlets and bombards are deployed, the English longbow wreaks its usual havoc on the French chivalry, and the laws of drama are obeyed as the principal antagonists meet in personal combat on the castle walls to resolve their differences the old-fashioned way. It's pretty good.

THE WIFE OF MONTE CRISTO

Rating: ★★☆☆☆ • *Origin:* USA, 1946 • *Director:* Edward G. Ulmer •
Source: YouTube streaming video

Haydee (Lenore Aubert) is practicing, sword in hand, on the fencing piste when her husband, the Count of Monte Cristo (Martin Kosleck), comes in, and the master-at-arms tells him, "Madame the Countess will soon be as expert as the best swordsman in France." Cool! Plus the movie poster promises, "She challenges men with her beauty . . . conquers them with her sword!" They have to pay off on that, right?

Wrong. Despite a promising beginning, and director Edward G. Ulmer's stylish visual touches, *The Wife of Monte Cristo* is a conventional costume thriller that starts strong but then goes to pieces in its second half. Its story, "suggested" by Dumas's novel, changes Edmond Dantès's origin to make the wealthy count into the Avenger, a masked vigilante along the lines of Zorro or the Scarlet Pimpernel, assisted by his wife Haydee, who's been whitewashed from Indian to European. In 1832, in a Paris caught in an outbreak of the plague, villain Danglars (Charles Dingle) and corrupt prefect of police de Villefort (John Loder) are making a fortune selling phony plague-cure medicine to the citizens. Their racket is opposed by Monte Cristo as the Avenger, but when he's slightly wounded during a raid on a medicine shipment, to protect his secret identity, the count must leave town until his wound heals. In his absence, his wife Haydee dons the mask (and skintight black leathers) of the Avenger, and for a while she does great, discovering who is behind the shipments and foiling the villains' plans to capture her husband. But then the plot requires her to get all stupid and drop her handkerchief where the police prefect will find it, she's caught and imprisoned, and Monte Cristo has to return to Paris to save her. Bleah. The husband even gets to have the final sword duel with the prefect, which isn't very convincing, but at least it looks good. By that time the screenwriters, Ulmer and Dorcas Cochran, have gotten their heroes into a hole so deep they can't figure out how to get them out, and the ending is an unsatisfying mess.

It's a shame, because the leads deserve better. Kosleck has striking features, narrow with high cheekbones, and a slender frame that makes Aubert's imposture of him credible. A refugee from Hitler's Germany, he spent most of his time in Hollywood getting his revenge by playing despicable Nazis; this is one of his few sympathetic lead roles. Lenore Aubert, from Vienna, Austria, had also fled the swastika to America, where her European accent brought her plenty of roles during the war, though her career stagnated afterward (unless you consider *Abbott and Costello Meet Frankenstein* a high point). Ulmer would go on to direct *The Pirates of Capri* and *Babes in Bagdad*.

WILLIAM TELL (OR *THE ADVENTURES OF WILLIAM TELL*)

Rating: ★★★★☆ • *Origin:* UK, 1958 • *Directors:* Ralph Smart et al. • *Source:* Network DVDs

William Tell, or "the other Robin Hood," the national hero of Switzerland, is known to Americans (if he's known at all) for the feat of splitting an apple atop his son's head with a bolt from his crossbow. For the Swiss, Tell is a freedom fighter of the early fourteenth century, when the cantons of what would become Switzerland were occupied by Austrians of the Hapsburg dynasty; Tell inspired a revolt when he refused to bow to the Austrians, was cruelly forced to shoot an apple from his son's head, and then assassinated Albrecht Gessler, the Austrian tyrant who made him do it.

For Hannah Weinstein's Sapphire Films, which had produced the successful *Adventures of Robin Hood* TV series and were looking to expand with additional small-screen swashbucklers, a series based on William Tell was a natural. Tell was portrayed as a leader of an underground resistance movement against the occupying Austrians, with themes that harked back to the then-recent World War II, with stories about espionage, betrayal, and guerrilla warfare. Though sometimes described as an adventure series for kids, *William Tell* had a harder edge than other Sapphire series such as *Robin Hood* and *Lancelot*, dealing with adult themes such as forced labor, extortion, and blackmail, and Austrian soldiers frequently met death at the hands of Tell and his partisan allies. This is a show about a country at war.

William Tell, played with activity and intelligence by the English actor Conrad Phillips, is a dead shot with a crossbow and equally effective as a brawler, wielding everything from a broadsword to a bench. However, his most important asset is a mind teeming with schemes for outwitting the Austrians. He's joined in his fight by his wife Hedda (Jennifer Jayne), no slouch with a crossbow or broadsword herself, and sometimes by his young son Walter (Richard Rogers), making resistance against the Austrians a family affair. They're most often pitted against local Austrian ruler Landburgher Gessler (Willoughby Goddard), a greedy and obese despot who's not without wits or courage, though Tell repeatedly outmaneuvers him. Gessler is frequently supported by the hapless Hauptman Hofmanstahl (Peter Hammond), while Tell often relies on the strength of the laconic former robber known only as The Bear (Nigel Green, Little John in *Sword of Sherwood Forest*). The 25-minute episodes mostly use stage sets, often with assets reused from *Robin Hood* and *Sword of Freedom*, but many exteriors were shot in striking locations in the mountains of Wales, which stands in for Switzerland more effectively than you might suppose.

The stories are surprisingly sharp and well written, and every one of the 39 episodes is worth watching. If you have time for only a few, recommended episodes include "The Trap," with Nigel Green as the Bear and guest-starring Robert Shaw in full-on sneering villain mode; "The Manhunt," with Christopher Lee as a mad Austrian prince who hunts humans; "The Castle of Fear," a Hammer-style Gothic melodrama; "The Master Spy," with Adrienne Corri (*Sword of Freedom*) as an Austrian femme fatale; and "The Spider," with Donald Pleasence as a creepy Austrian general who abuses women and children. Don't worry—William Tell settles *his* hash.

WILLOW

Rating: ★★☆☆☆ • *Origin:* USA, 1988 • *Director:* Ron Howard •
Source: 20th Century Fox DVD

J. R. R. Tolkien first found mass popularity in the late 1960s, and by the early '70s *The Lord of the Rings* was everywhere. Legions of readers devoured the trilogy and its prequel *The Hobbit* and then looked for more of the same—but there was no more, so certain fantasy novelists undertook to give those readers what they wanted by engaging in the sincerest form of flattery. Tolkienesque fantasy epics rolled out by twos, threes, and then dozens, thick paperbacks with colorful covers atop stories about humble but plucky heroes determined to save their imaginary worlds from dire, dark tyrants. Typically, these novels employed emulation more than originality, adding little to what they knew would be popular. With the same plot and character elements recycled over and over, these books came to be known as *generic fantasies*.

Derivative in every way, with scarcely an original idea to be found in its entire 126 minutes, *Willow* is a textbook generic fantasy. Its story, written by George Lucas and scripted by Bob Dolman, seems calculated to deliver everything an ardent Tolkien fan could desire. Like Hobbits? *Willow* has short folk called Nelwyns who live in peaceful farming villages. Like Gandalf? *Willow* has not one, but two charming and elderly good wizards, one male, one female. Like Galadriel? *Willow* has a prophetic and magical forest queen named Cherlindrea who even glows in the dark. Like Strider? *Willow* has a scruffy warrior hero who looks ill but means well. Like Frodo and Bilbo? *Willow* has a spunky but persistent half-sized hero named, well, *Willow*.

A Lucasfilm picture, this is a luxe production, no expense spared, with fantastic and evocative sets, warriors in exquisite fantasy armor, exteriors shot in exotic locations, and excellent-for-the-time special effects by Industrial Light and Magic. Lucas got Ron Howard to direct, the always reliable James Horner to compose the soundtrack, and Bill Hobbs, the best fight director of his generation, to choreograph the swordplay.

And yet, despite all that and the best of intentions, this movie is a stone drag. Other than Val Kilmer, who plays the Strider-ish character Madmartigan with surprising enthusiasm, the leads are dull, unappealing, and unmemorable, including Warwick Davis as Willow, who is supposed to be funny and appealing but mostly just comes across as irritable and petulant. The story is so predictable—in fact, its predictability is the point—that it's hard to stay interested as it unrolls in tepid inevitability, and there's little urgency to the plot, because the pacing just plods. Gratuitous action scenes like Indiana Jones–style headlong vehicle fights and downhill snow-sled escapes add nothing, even when Chuck Jones antics are added to Indiana Jones, because you know exactly how they'll end. And that dead-on-arrival romance between Madmartigan and Sorsha (Joanne Whalley), the evil tyrant's vapid daughter? Don't even start with me.

And then there's the brownies, two prancing four-inch loons with Monty Python French accents who are threatened, over and over, with being crushed flat by the battles going on over their heads, and yet somehow, no matter how much and how hard you want it, they are never crushed flat. The brownies. Ancient gods, preserve us.

THE WIND AND THE LION

Rating: ★★★☆☆ • *Origin:* USA, 1975 • *Director:* John Milius • *Source:* Columbia Tristar DVD

This is a curious piece of pure entertainment, a colonialist fable that revels in national caricatures of Americans, Moroccans, and Germans without believing its own depictions for a moment. It was written and directed by John Milius, who based his story loosely on the so-called Perdicaris affair, an international incident in 1904 in which a Moroccan tribal leader, Mulai Ahmed er Raisuli, kidnapped an American citizen from outside the city of Tangier and held him for ransom from the Moroccan government, a ransom the United States insisted Morocco must pay. Seven American warships were sent to Tangier harbor, a show of force that was backed up by England, France, and Spain, and eventually Ion Perdicaris was released—but not before President Theodore Roosevelt had politicized the incident, running for reelection behind the tough-guy phrase, "Perdicaris alive or Raisuli dead."

Milius adapts these facts to suit his story: the 64-year-old Mr. Perdicaris becomes an appealing young mother, Eden Pedecaris (Candice Bergen), who is kidnapped with her two children from within Tangier itself by Berber bandits led by the Raisuli (Sean Connery), a fierce but honorable freedom fighter. Teddy Roosevelt (Brian Keith) is portrayed as a bluff but wily rascal out to get whatever he can out of the incident for himself and the United States, two interests he regards as identical. And American marines under the bluff but wily Captain Jerome (Steve Kanaly) intervene directly in the sultan's affairs and attempt the rescue of the Pedecaris family, at one point getting into a firefight with a much larger force of predatory German troops. (Historically, the US Marines stayed on their ships, and German soldiers weren't present at all.)

However, these saber-rattling politics are secondary to the film's real concern, which is depicting the Raisuli as a reckless but courageous and charismatic war leader who is hilariously baffled by the pluck and sass of Eden Pedecaris. The woman just won't stay in her place—though eventually she comes to admire the Raisuli, who admits that he doesn't actually plan to harm her or her family and that the whole abduction is a great bluff. Eden's young son William (Simon Harrison) goes beyond admiration of the Raisuli to open hero worship, especially once the Berber chieftain single-handedly rescues the family with sword and horse from the ugly brigands who'd captured them after an ill-advised escape attempt. Indeed, we see the last scenes of the film largely through the boy's eyes, emphasizing how much the story is really a *Boy's Own* adventure tale with little grounding in reality.

Verdict: even with every character an exaggerated cartoon figure, the film still succeeds due to Connery's charm, a steady pace punctuated by timely action sequences, and the beauty of its Spanish scenery, which stands in effectively for Morocco. Just don't take it seriously, and when the film winks broadly at its own conceits, wink back.

WIZARDS AND WARRIORS

Rating: ★★★☆☆ • *Origin:* USA, 1983 • *Directors:* Bill Bixby et al. •
Source: Warner Archive DVD

This short-lived American TV series shows how influential the game *Dungeons & Dragons* had become on popular culture in less than 10 years. A fantasy comedy with an ensemble cast, it portrays a conflict between neighboring kingdoms with cartoonishly good and evil rulers. The Warriors are the nice Prince Erik Greystone (Jeff Conaway) versus the nasty Prince Dirk Blackpool (Duncan Regehr, the '90s TV *Zorro*), and the Wizards are the good but old and always late Traquil (Ian Wolfe) and Blackpool's evil henchman Vector (well-known voice actor Clive Revill), occasionally allied with the glamorous witch Bethel (Randi Brooks), who is barely clad in a few scraps of silver polyester.

All the trappings of heroic fantasy are duly included and broadly parodied: magic weapons and mystical gems, monsters grim and goofy, undead menaces, invisible dragons, even green slime. The deliberately tacky costumes are a hoot and won the show an Emmy. There are frequent dungeon crawls, and in episode 7, "Dungeon of Death," Prince Greystone even recruits a *D&D* party of variously skilled adventurers to brave the threats and traps under Castle Blackpool. There's a lot of action, all exaggerated and ridiculous, but the reason to watch this show is the witty and knowing dialogue, particularly the repartee between Greystone and his sidekick Marko (Walter Olkewicz), the darkly humorous exchanges between Blackpool and Revel, and the comic banter of Greystone with his fiancée, the vain and rather dim Princess Ariel (Julia Duffy), who is frequently hilarious.

The tenor of the humor might be most usefully compared to that of the British show *Blackadder*, which debuted just a few months after this series. Where *Wizards and Warriors* goes wrong is that its episodes are an hour long compared to *Blackadder*'s half-hour, and the result is comparatively slow paced and often padded, the comedy losing its momentum.

But when the characters get good lines, it's a laff riot. The best episode is probably the fourth, "Night of Terror," in which Greystone and Ariel are trapped in a haunted castle and confronted by skeletons, animated suits of armor, and illusory visions of their friends and enemies, all camping it up with evil laughter. Meanwhile, Blackpool and Vector, drinking in their own castle to celebrate their victory over the forces of good, get increasingly blotto while playing an absurd board game using '80s glow sticks as pieces, the stake being Vector's magic monocle, which he desperately wants back from Blackpool. The evil prince in his turn wants Vector's black and begemmed skullcap, and when he wins the game and drunkenly demands the hat, Vector just grimaces and says, "I don't wear a hat."

WIZARDS OF THE LOST KINGDOM

Rating: ★☆☆☆☆ • *Origin:* USA, 1985 • *Director:* Héctor Olivera • *Source:* M Square DVD

Gah. This Frankenstein of a fantasy film was shot on the cheap in Argentina and then padded out with extensive excerpts from two other Roger Corman productions, *Sorceress* (1982) and *Deathstalker* (1983). Even the soundtrack is largely recycled from James Horner's music for *Battle beyond the Stars* (1980). You might be able to overlook these invasive implant scenes but for the fact that their grim massacres and human sacrifices are completely at odds with the mild tone of the rest of the picture, which attempts to be a lighthearted parody like *Wizards and Warriors.*

The attempt fails. The main protagonist is a young wizard named Simon (Vidal Peterson, aged 15), who commands jaw-dropping magical powers one moment and then forgets all about them for 20 minutes at a time. An evil wizard named Shurka (Thom Christopher) has killed the realm's king and usurped the throne, and to defeat him Simon must get into the royal castle to retrieve a magic ring that he stupidly dropped just before being teleported out by his dying wizardly father. Simon finds help from a warrior hero named Kor the Conqueror (top-billed Bo Svenson), who isn't the usual long-haired barbarian muscleman—in fact, he's more like a has-been minor sports star turned amiable celebrity pitchman for infomercials, only with a sword. Simon also has a white polar-bear Wookiee sidekick named Halsak or Balsak or something, who moans like Chewbacca and does *absolutely nothing.* Their opponents include lizard goblins, a werewolf chimp dwarf, flimsy Halloween ghosts, a witch who turns into a giant bug, and a lady-cyclops-in-a-wedding-dress whom Kor left at the altar, which is supposed to be funny. (It isn't.) All their costumes are terrible.

Frankly, this thing is nearly unwatchable, below the bottom of the barrel, not even bad in an amusing way. Doing your laundry is a more satisfying experience; go do that.

YANKEE BUCCANEER

Rating: ★★☆☆☆ • *Origin:* USA, 1952 • *Director:* Frederick de Cordova •
Source: Universal DVD

This movie's story is based on some real American naval incidents that took place in 1823 and '24, albeit distorted almost beyond recognition. Yes, young Lt. David Farragut—later to be Admiral Farragut of Civil War fame—did sail with Commander David Porter in search of the Caribbean lairs of some pesky pirates, but they did not disguise an American ship-of-the-line and its crew as pirates to do it. And yes, Porter did illegally put ashore a crew on Spanish-held Puerto Rico to raid a port with the absurd name of Foxardo, but he didn't do it to rescue Farragut and a Portuguese countess from a lurid Spanish torture chamber. Everything else here is naught but a tissue of lies and deceit.

What we have in that tissue is a turgid naval bromance between Commander Porter (Jeff Chandler) and Lieutenant Farragut (Scott Brady), in which Farragut keeps getting into trouble and Porter keeps getting him out, huffing and pretending indignation, but really we know from the start that they're meant for each other. Chandler channels the bluff Gregory Peck as Hornblower and is adequate enough, considering what he has to work with, which isn't much; however, Brady, though good-looking, is talent-free and quickly becomes tiresome. Not even the officers' tepid romantic rivalry for the charms of the vapid Countess Margarita (Suzan Ball) can bring Brady to life. In truth, not much happens worth getting excited about, as the disguised ship sails around long enough without finding any pirates that it has to put ashore for some plot, I mean, *provisions*. They do this twice! Occasionally characters faux dramatically reveal their all-too-obvious secret backstories, or give each other MacGuffins for some reason or other, but it's hard to care.

Finally, the Americans, sailing around in their ridiculous pirate outfits, accidentally figure out that all the real pirates are gathered in a secret location preparing to ambush a treasure fleet (or something). But they don't do anything about it, really, except let Farragut get captured again, and we only ever see one actual pirate, a buffoon with the cartoonish name of Captain Scarjack. What is this, a *Scooby-Doo* episode? The fine character actor Joseph Calleia belatedly appears as a wicked Spanish aristocrat who's behind all the shenanigans, and he gets off a few good lines, but it's too little and too late to save this turkey. Abandon ship!

YELLOWBEARD

Rating: ★★☆☆☆ • *Origin:* UK, 1983 • *Director:* Mel Damski •
Source: Comedy Classics Blu-ray

This pirate comedy is a colossal disappointment. Comedy-by-committee can be quite successful—just look at Monty Python's entire oeuvre—but it can also go badly wrong, which seems to be what happened here. The ensemble cast reads like a who's who of '70s and '80s comedy films: Graham Chapman, Peter Boyle, Madeline Kahn, Peter Cook, John Cleese, Michael Hordern, Eric Idle, plus Spike Milligan and Marty Feldman in their final roles—even Cheech and Chong, but the less said about them, the better. The romantic lead is played by the bland Martin Hewitt, after the part was originally written for Adam Ant and then Sting. "Sting should have had my part," Hewitt later said. "For crying out loud, I would have hired Sting over me any day."

But Sting was deemed "too British" for the American market, and US distributor Orion Pictures contributed to the script's too-many-rewrites problem by insisting that the screenplay deemphasize the plot and inflate the parts of all those bankable supporting actors. Bad call, Orion. Director Mel Damski never made a feature film before and isn't able here to summon order out of the chaos. Moreover, the ostensible lead role, Graham Chapman's Yellowbeard, is a character with just one joke, which is that he's irredeemably bloodthirsty and awful. Funny once, but not for 96 minutes. To top it off, there are a bunch of rape and torture gags that haven't aged at all well.

The things *Yellowbeard* got right just emphasize what a huge missed opportunity it is. Even with rotten material, the actors are still frequently hilarious, and most of them are clearly enjoying themselves. The story, sort of an inverted *Treasure Island*, is a shambles, but it shows a real love for all the pirate tropes it's taking down. The costumes and sets are fine, including a real three-masted ship for the sailing sequences, the vessel built for the 1962 *Mutiny on the Bounty*. And the exaggerated swordplay is funny even when the jokes aren't. There's even a comic walk-on by David Bowie. If only this thing had a coherent script, sharp direction, and Sting in a lead role, how great it could have been.

YOJIMBO

Rating: ★★★★★ (Essential) • *Origin:* Japan, 1961 • *Director:* Akira Kurosawa •
Source: Criterion DVD

Kurosawa's *Yojimbo* TOHO / WIKIMEDIA COMMONS

Do you like badassery? Because *Yojimbo* is where the goody-two-shoes '50s end and the badass '60s begin.

Director Akira Kurosawa cowrote his story inspired by American Westerns and the hard-boiled crime novels of Dashiell Hammett—and boy, is it hard-boiled. A nameless, shabby ronin, or masterless samurai (Toshiro Mifune), wanders into a nameless, shabby town where the first creature he meets on the street is a dog running past with a human hand in its mouth. Clearly, this is a town with possibilities for a warrior-for-hire! The ronin soon learns that the town is consumed by a gang war, one gang run by Seibei (Seizaburo Kawazu), its long-time crime boss, and the other by Ushitora (Kyu Sazanka), Seibei's former right-hand man. The two sides have been hiring thugs and bandits in expectation of a showdown, but they're in a stalemate until the arrival of the ronin, who smells a profit and proceeds to upset the balance.

The ronin, who when asked his name picks "Sanjuro" out of the air, is so good with his sword that he could easily end the conflict by leading one side to victory, but it soon becomes clear that he has a greater challenge in mind: ridding the town of corruption entirely by exterminating both factions. He's dogged in pursuit of this goal, switching sides several times, waiting it out when a magistrate shows up in town, which enforces a truce for a few days, and then stirring up trouble between the factions when they contemplate a genuine truce.

The balance of power shifts again when Ushitora's younger brother Unosuke (Tatsuya Nakadai) returns to town armed with a six-gun. He's not only better armed, he's also smarter than the other goons; he figures out what Sanjuro is up to, and soon the ronin is captured and in a world of hurt. Desperate measures are called for.

This film is almost a stage play, set entirely on the town's main street, with a gang lair at either end and Sanjuro's headquarters in the middle, a rundown tavern run by the sourest old man on the planet. Despite this setup the film never gets stagy, thanks to Kurosawa's innovative compositions and fluid camerawork. It's also darkly funny, which keeps it from becoming unrelentingly grim. The film takes its time a bit in the middle, getting everything set up for the final confrontation, but wow, what an ending!

Hugely influential, *Yojimbo* was remade by Sergio Leone with Clint Eastwood as *A Fistful of Dollars*, the first big success of the so-called Spaghetti Westerns. From *Yojimbo* you can draw a straight line through *The Good, the Bad and the Ugly* to *The Wild Bunch*, *Escape from New York*, and *Conan the Barbarian*. If you like any of those, *Yojimbo* is for you, even if you think you don't want to watch a black-and-white movie with subtitles. Look, if you need a final nudge, there's this: one of the criminal thugs is a seven-foot giant with an enormous wooden mallet. How cool is that?

TALES OF ZATOICHI

During the American occupation of Japan after World War II, one of its many social restrictions was a prohibition on the making of violent movies, which meant no historical samurai adventures. When the occupation was lifted in 1952, the *chambara*, or swordplay action films, gradually returned, and by the late 1950s they made up a significant portion of the movies and TV shows made for Japanese domestic consumption. Based on a story by the novelist Kan Shimozawa, *The Tale of Zatoichi* was just one more minor chambara feature, but Shintaro Katsu's portrayal of the blind swordsman was surprisingly popular, and the Zatoichi films went on to become the longest running chambara series of all, running to 26 feature films and four seasons as a TV series. And yet its hero is no noble samurai, or even a masterless ronin, but a mere low-ranking member of the criminal yakuza. Nonetheless, he's a character you'll never forget.

ZATOICHI 1: THE TALE OF ZATOICHI

Rating: ★★★★★ • *Origin:* Japan, 1962 • *Director:* Kenji Misumi • *Source:* Criterion DVD

In Japan in the late 1950s and early 1960s, midlevel studios like Daei Motion Pictures churned out samurai action films and TV shows much like Hollywood did Westerns in the same period. These were largely disposable and forgettable, and most have been duly forgotten. You can be sure that nobody who worked on *The Tale of Zatoichi* thought they were making anything but one more quickie *chambara* feature, and yet somehow they created a story that transcended its genre limitations and spawned the longest-running samurai series in Japanese film.

What made this film stand out from its contemporaries? First, it was lucky in its writer: Minoru Inuzuka was a veteran screenwriter from the silent era on who had a firm grasp of tight plotting and strong characters. Second, it was lucky in its Director: Kenji Misumi was a visual master who'd been trained by the great Teinosuke Kinugasa (*Gate of Hell*), so good that he was often offered prestige dramas by the studio, but he just preferred to make action films. Third and most important, it was lucky in its lead actor: Shintaro Katsu had played character and lead roles in a number of films for Daiei, but his portrayal of the tough but vulnerable blind swordsman Zatoichi struck a chord with audiences in Japan and eventually around the world.

You heard me right: blind swordsman. Zatoichi is a sightless masseur (massage being one of the few careers open to the blind in samurai-era Japan) who travels in the lowest levels of Japanese society among the yakuza, or organized crime gangs. A wanderer tapping his way with a cane, he arrives in the town of Iioka and goes directly to the town's yakuza gambling den, where the local tough guys are wagering at dice. Zatoichi humbly asks if he can join the game and the thugs agree, eager to fleece the blind man of his money. And in fact, the masseur immediately loses half his coins to the cheating crooks but then uses sleight of hand to win the next throw and get all his money back, doubled. The thugs are incensed, but strangely, the blind man isn't intimidated by their threats. This mystery is solved by the return of local boss, who welcomes Zatoichi as an old acquaintance and warns his men that the blind man is actually an accomplished swordsman. But how can that be?

We learn as the story plays out: a gang war is imminent between the yakuza of Iioka and those of the neighboring town of Sasagawa, and the Iioka boss wants Zatoichi on his side to balance out the down-on-his-luck samurai Hirate (Shigeru Amachi) who's been hired by Sasagawa. However, Zatoichi strikes up an unlikely friendship with Hirate while they're both fishing in a local lake. The other pivotal character is Otane (Masayo Banri), a spirited young woman whose brother and ex-boyfriend are in the yakuza but who wants to escape the gang life. It's through the eyes of these people, the gang bosses, the hired samurai, and the hopeful Otane, that we gradually see and understand Zatoichi's many-sided character. When with the yakuza, he alternates between oily humility and curt bluster, demanding respect but according it only when he must. To the failed samurai, whom he senses is a gentle man of honor with a deadly disease, Zatoichi offers unconditional friendship. And to the wistful Otane, he reveals his loneliness and his guilt for the harm he's caused during his years in the underworld.

And always, when he isn't sniffing the plum blossoms or guzzling sake, Zatoichi is listening from the shadows. He puts together bits and pieces of overheard conversations until he understands all the intrigues, romantic, political, and criminal, of Iioka and Sasagawa, always with the aim of avoiding trouble, but inevitably coming to the aid of the innocent and helpless. And then his blindman's cane separates to reveal the straight sword blade hidden inside, and Zatoichi's preternaturally sharp senses enable him to dodge blows and slay attackers with blindingly quick short slashes.

Zatoichi explains that as a blind man among the yakuza, he'd suffered so much scorn that he took up the sword because that was the only thing that would compel their respect—but use of it has only made him more of an outcast and stained him with blood he can never wash clean. It all ends in the bloody gang war that both Zatoichi and Hirate had hoped to avoid, but destiny decrees otherwise. Afterward Otane awaits Zatoichi on the highway out of Iioka to pledge her love to him, but the blind yakuza knows he's unworthy of her and leaves by a side road, traveling ever onward to the next town.

ZATOICHI 2: THE TALE OF ZATOICHI CONTINUES

Rating: ★★★★☆ • *Origin:* Japan, 1962 • *Director:* Kazuo Mori • *Source:* Criterion DVD

It's clear that the first film wasn't intended as the beginning of a series, since at the end Zatoichi gives up the use of his cane sword and has it buried with his friend, the samurai Hirate. But the response to *The Tale of Zatoichi* was so positive that Daiei Motion Pictures rushed out this sequel to take advantage of it before the audience could forget and move on. What audiences loved most was the character of Zatoichi himself, so the second film makes him central to every aspect of the plot and reveals much more of his history. Written and directed by Kazuo Mori, it's fast and tight and packs a lot of plot into its 72 minutes; many fans consider it even better than the first one.

A year after the death of Hirate, Zatoichi (Shintaro Katsu) returns to the region where he's buried to commemorate him but gets enmeshed in new intrigues, old grudges, and complications from his past. The new trouble comes when Zatoichi is engaged in his capacity as a masseur to tend to a samurai lord; he notices that the lord's wits are badly addled, a fact the clan considers a closely guarded secret, so they decide to have Zatoichi killed. When he escapes their samurai, the clan hires Kanbei, the local yakuza boss, to track Zatoichi down and kill him, and Kanbei enlists the aid of his neighbor Sukegoro, the surviving boss from the first film, who has a score to settle.

Moreover, in addition to the two yakuza gangs, Zatoichi is being shadowed on his way to the cemetery by a wanted criminal named Yoshiro, played by Shintaro Katsu's brother Tomisaburo Wakayama, which is an apt casting, as later events will show. We know from the first film that Zatoichi is rueful about his violent life, but now we see that he's thoughtful and reflective as well. From Zatoichi's musings, we learn that what set him on his life of wandering was the loss of the love of his life, a woman named Ochiyo, who was stolen from him by a man they both despised. Returning to the town of Iioka, Zatoichi once more encounters Otane (Mazayo Banri), who is now engaged to an honest carpenter but who risks her life to warn Zatoichi of the approach of Kanbei's yakuza.

In the climax of the film, Zatoichi is pitted against an entire gang of goons in the kind of set-piece battle that will become a hallmark of the series, and for the first time his unique fighting style, in which he holds his sword in a reverse grip and moves to get inside his opponents' sword range, is displayed to its fullest. He also has a showdown with the criminal Yoshiro, and this time there's a clear setup for a subsequent film, as Yoshiro reveals a secret dear to Zatoichi's heart.

ZATOICHI 3: NEW TALE OF ZATOICHI

Rating: ★★★★★ • *Origin:* Japan, 1963 • *Director:* Tokuzo Tanaka • *Source:* Criterion DVD

Zatoichi, whipsawed between love and fate! The Zatoichi stories are set circa 1840, when over two centuries of stable rule by the Tokugawa shogunate is finally unraveling. Some samurai, no longer supported by the old social structure, take to crime, competing or collaborating with the yakuza, like the ex-samurai Tengu gang in this tale.

Zatoichi (Shintaro Katsu), wandering the highways, meets an itinerant musician from his hometown of Kasama and decides to return to his old environs. He makes it as far as neighboring Shimodate, where he's accosted by Yasuhiko (Fujio Suga), brother of that Boss

New Tale of Zatoichi Author's Collection

Kanbei whom Zatoichi had slain in the previous installment. Yasuhiko's revenge is forestalled by an interruption from a samurai named Banno (Seizaburo Kawazu), the sword master who originally taught Zatoichi how to fight. Banno is a master of *iaijutsu*, the attack on the draw, and Zatoichi learned his own mastery of the technique from him. The sword master takes Zatoichi home, where he meets Banno's younger sister Yayoi (Mikiko Tsubouchi), who has been waiting for Ichi, as she calls him, to return for four years. But Banno, down on his luck, plans to marry Yayoi to a wealthy samurai lord and has no patience for her romantic dreams about Ichi. There are other complications: Yasuhiko shows up in town, still bent on revenge, while Banno has been having secret dealings with the Tengu gang. Ichi just wants to avoid trouble and find happiness, but nearly everyone else has other ideas. He does find an ally where he expected only an enemy, but then is betrayed by someone he thought he could trust.

After the success of *Zatoichi Continues*, Daiei Motion Pictures finally realized it had a hit series on its hands and pumped up the budget for *New Tale*, shooting it in vibrant full color. Director Tokuzo Tanaka, who'd been an assistant director to Kurosawa, tells this tangled tale with complete clarity and an eye for composition and movement. The final fight between Zatoichi and the Tengu gang is superb, easily the best swordplay in the series so far, and it's followed by a climactic iaijutsu duel that compares well to the one at the end of *Sanjuro*. If you'd prefer to skip the two earlier black-and-white entries, you could easily start the Zatoichi series here.

ZATOICHI 4: ZATOICHI THE FUGITIVE

Rating: ★★★★★ • *Origin:* Japan, 1963 • *Director:* Tokozu Tanaka • *Source:* Criterion DVD

Zatoichi (Shintaro Katsu) arrives in a new town just as its annual festival is getting underway, and he throws himself into the celebration with gusto. This installment starts a pattern in which each film introduces a new skill or talent to Zatoichi's repertoire that was previously unseen, and this time it's sumo wrestling: at the festival Zatoichi enters a take-on-all-comers challenge and defeats five opponents, using when necessary a secret masseur grip like a Vulcan nerve pinch.

The festival town is run by Sakichi (Junichiro Narita), a young yakuza boss who's just inherited the territory and is surrounded by other, predatory bosses who covet his tract, especially Boss Yagiri (Toru Abe), who for unspecified offenses has put a price on Zatoichi's head, and also hired a fallen samurai named Tanakura (Jutaro Hojo) to be his hatchet man. Zatoichi has stumbled into a slow, multisided gang war with his own life on the line, but its real hub is the hearts and desires of two women: Onobu (Miwa Takada), the young daughter of a former yakuza boss who loves Sakichi, and Otane (Masayo Banri), the love from Zatoichi's past who is now the common-law wife of the samurai Tanakura. Tangled!

At this point Daiei Pictures was turning out Zatoichi features at a rate of one every three or four months, but their quality was still on an upward trajectory, and in many ways this is the best installment yet. Director Tokozu Tanaka opens the staging to a new, wider frame, setting much of the film outdoors and keeping the camera moving for a more expansive feel. And Katsu now fully inhabits the larger-than-life role of Zatoichi, humble one moment and proud of his skills the next, outraged by injustice but ashamed of his own sins. Though the blind swordsman skillfully picks his way through the criminal intrigues of the brutal yakuza bosses, he can still be deceived by the impulses of his own sentimental heart. It leads him to defend Sakichi against Boss Yagiri and the rogue samurai Tanakura in a beautifully shot melee in a moonlit forest, but then comes the final confrontation, a four-way battle on a windswept beach between Zatoichi, Tanakura, all the mob bosses, and about 50 yakuza thugs. The conclusion, after the battle, is masterful: Zatoichi consoles the forlorn, brings the estranged lovers together, and then cheerfully kabuki-dances off down the road to the sound of the festival flutes—but his face, when turned away from the others, is a mask of bitter sorrow.

ZATOICHI 5: ZATOICHI ON THE ROAD

Rating: ★★★★☆ • *Origin:* Japan, 1963 • *Director:* Kimiyoshi Yasuda • *Source:* Criterion DVD

Another solid entry, *On the Road* is grimmer in tone than earlier installments in the series and shows a darker side to Zatoichi than previously seen. Directed by Kimiyoshi Yasuda in the first of his six contributions to the cycle, it's a historical crime drama with swordplay interludes, though with a heavy helping of the romantic heartbreak that was becoming a hallmark of the series.

Zatoichi (Shintaro Katsu) is being escorted by an anxious yakuza to meet his boss in Doyama when he's spotted by a lieutenant from the rival boss in Shimozuma, who hires three masterless samurai to kill him. Zatoichi survives their ambush, killing the samurai, but is confronted by Ohisa (Reiko Fujiwara), whose husband he's just slain and who bitterly declares the blind swordsman her enemy. Zatoichi then encounters a dying man who begs him to "save Omitsu"—and if there's one thing Ichi can never resist, it's a dying request. The Omitsu (Shiho Fujimora) who needs saving is hiding nearby, a naive young lady being pursued by samurai for the crime of stabbing their lord in the face when he attempted to rape her. Zatoichi accepts the quest to escort her to her family in Edo, but he's dogged by Ohisa, who's bent on revenge . . . or is she?

Bound on keeping Zatoichi out of their imminent gang war, and on abducting Omitsu for a fortune in ransom, the yakuza this time are nearly all irredeemable scoundrels, and as Ichi gradually falls for the innocent Omitsu, their threats to her safety put him into a cold fury. After Zatoichi, the most interesting character here is Ohisa, who is complicit in Omitsu's abduction by the yakuza but then tries to protect her from their abuse. (It seems a perfect setup for a recurring character, but the series never sees her again.) The climax is the gang war between Doyama and Shimozuma, a running street battle that's more brutal than balletic, set in a windswept and deserted town like Kurosawa's *Yojimbo*—though the final three-way showdown between Zatoichi and the yakuza bosses is more reminiscent of Sergio Leone.

ZATOICHI 6: ZATOICHI AND THE CHEST OF GOLD

Rating: ★★★★☆ • *Origin:* Japan, 1964 • *Director:* Kazuo Ikehiro • *Source:* Criterion DVD

The James Bond–ish opening credits of this film announce a new visual presence for the series in young director Kazuo Ikehiro, clearly out to make his mark as a cinematic stylist. And he succeeds: the look of *Chest of Gold* is often daring and almost artsy without sacrificing clarity or the usual rocketing velocity of events, packing a lot of action and story into its 83 minutes.

Zatoichi (Shintaro Katsu) visits a small town's cemetery to offer rueful prayers at the grave of a yakuza warrior he'd unnecessarily slain two years earlier, but his guide turns out to be the slain yakuza's sister, who vows revenge. Ichi then joins in with the local peasants, who are celebrating "getting the tax man off our necks" by finally gathering enough gold to pay three years of tax debt. A chest filled with the tax gold is sent on the road to the local magistrate with an escort of locals, but the peasants are attacked by three scruffy ronin. Five fugitive yakuza and Zatoichi get involved in the scuffle, and in the chaos the chest goes rolling down a hill before somebody makes off with it—but who?

There are a lot of moving parts in this plot: the desperate peasants, the yakuza's sister, a corrupt magistrate, the brutal yakuza boss who is the magistrate's hatchet man, a noble but now-fugitive boss who's tried to help the peasants, main man Zatoichi, accused of stealing the gold and out to clear his name—plus the three scruffy ronin, whose leader, Joshiro (Tomisaburo Wakayama, Katsu's brother, back again in a different role), is a cruel but dangerous samurai who also happens to be a master of the bullwhip. Director Ikehiro does a good job of keeping all these characters distinct, but the story's too tight to give each of them a satisfactory resolution, and a couple of them get forgotten by the end. One extended sequence makes it all worthwhile: on a mountainside at night, dozens of the magistrate's goons, each one carrying a golden, glowing lantern, wind their way uphill in the darkness to try to catch the fugitive boss, only to encounter Zatoichi on his way down with a small child he must protect, fighting his way through the lantern cops with a crying toddler hanging on his back. Lone Wolf and Cub, anyone?

ZATOICHI 7: ZATOICHI'S FLASHING SWORD

Rating: ★★★★☆ • *Origin:* Japan, 1964 • *Director:* Kazuo Ikehiro • *Source:* Criterion DVD

Though it's less showy than his previous effort, director Kazuo Ikehiro provides another superior installment. Zatoichi (Shintaro Katsu) once again gets involved in a territory struggle between neighboring yakuza bosses, but this gang war is one of the most interesting in the series. Brutal Boss Yasugoro (Tatsuo Endo) wants the river-crossing business controlled by honorable Boss Bunkichi, whose daughter Okuni (Naoko Kubo) tends to Zatoichi after the blind swordsman was wounded by a musket shot by Bunkichi's prodigal son, the crass Seiroku (Takashi Edajima). Add five cutthroat ronin-for-hire, an adorable, aged fireworks maker, and Yasugoro's sister as mistress of an offstage corrupt magistrate, and you have one of the most colorful and memorable casts of the series.

The background plot is the battle of wits between the bosses, as Yasugoro tries to tempt Bunkichi into making a misstep that will give him a pretext to take over the river crossing. The foreground is Ichi falling for Okuni and her family, befriending the old fireworks maker, and gradually getting drawn into the escalating violence between the gangs. When he's jumped by six of Yasugoro's goons at the river, we learn that Zatoichi can fight just as well underwater as he does on land, blood billowing bright red behind the path of his blade. Eventually Bunkichi, a victim of his own code of honor, is tricked into sending Zatoichi away, heartbroken, on the verge of the fireworks celebration, and then Yasugoro makes his murderous move. When Zatoichi learns what's happened, he sends a message to his aged friend to launch his long-awaited fireworks, and in the darkness, he becomes a phantom of vengeance pursuing Yasugoro, cutting down his goons while lit by colored flashes from the explosions in the sky.

ZATOICHI 8: FIGHT, ZATOICHI, FIGHT

Rating: ★★★★☆ • *Origin:* Japan, 1964 • *Director:* Kenji Misumi • *Source:* Criterion DVD

Director Kenji Misumi returns with his more naturalistic style. The result is less frenetic than the previous few installments, almost relaxed, for despite its title, Zatoichi fights less this time than usual. (Oh, don't worry: a dozen or so ugly customers who've got it comin' will still go down before his sword.)

The sequence in *Chest of Gold* where Zatoichi had to fight while protecting a small child made such an impression that this time, he has to protect an adorable baby for damn near the entire length of the feature. Zatoichi (Shintaro Katsu) is being pursued by five assassins of the Monju clan of bounty hunters, who attack a palanquin they think is carrying the blind swordsman but instead kill an innocent woman traveling with an infant. The dead woman's papers show she was taking the child to his father in a distant village, so Zatoichi offers to carry the baby to his destination. But the Monju are still on his trail, and they enlist several yakuza gangs along the way to try to kill Ichi while he's encumbered with the child.

Of course, Zatoichi gets attached to the cute baby boy, becoming its tender guardian as well as its fierce protector. After he repeatedly encounters Oko (Hizuro Takachiho), an itinerant pickpocket and con artist, he eventually hires her to help him care for the child on the journey. Oko is a fascinating character with many layers, portrayed with real heart by Takachiho in one of the best performances yet in the series. But even she is outdone by Katsu, whose devotion to the child he knows he must give up is moving and endearing. Some will find this overly sentimental, but the steel under Zatoichi's soft exterior shows when he finally reaches the boy's father, Unosuke (Nobuo Kaneko), and the man, now a yakuza boss, cruelly repudiates his dead wife and living son. The last of the Monju bounty hunters then persuades Unosuke to help him kill Zatoichi with a cunning plan: trap him in a ring of warriors wielding flaming torches that will confuse the blind man's senses. Does it work? It at least provides a spectacular final fight scene in which Zatoichi is literally on fire. But what about that poor baby? Never fear, Buddha knows best.

ZATOICHI 9: ADVENTURES OF ZATOICHI

Rating: ★★★☆☆ • *Origin:* Japan, 1964 • *Director:* Kimiyoshi Yasuda • *Source:* Criterion DVD

With this installment, the series stumbles for the first time, slipping from the level of the earlier films. Oh, it's still enjoyable, but it's relatively slow, the sentimentality is forced and obvious, the story is overcomplex, and two damsels in distress is one too many.

Zatoichi (Shintaro Katsu) arrives at the town of Kasama just before the New Year's celebration, intending to welcome the first sunrise of the new year atop Mount Miyagi. The inns are crowded, and Ichi is thrust into acquaintanceship with two young women, one searching for her missing father, a village headman, and one trying to help her brother, a fugitive yakuza who wants revenge on Boss Jinbei (Kichijiro Ueda), who sold him out to the local corrupt magistrate. There are also two adorable young boys, traveling acrobats, who attach themselves to Ichi, a drunken old sot who might be Ichi's long-lost father, and the magistrate's samurai bodyguard, Gounosuke (Mikijiro Hira, of *Three Outlaw Samurai* and *Sword of the Beast*), who is determined to match his skill against the blind swordsman's.

Zatoichi's reputation among the yakuza as a dangerous man now precedes him, as the announcement of his name makes all the gangster goons recoil and rethink their choices. Ichi does his usual sword stunts, slicing dice in half before they can hit the mat and bisecting the go board in the middle of Jinbei and the magistrate's game, but there are no new tricks in his repertoire this time. Eventually Ichi learns that the stories of the two distressed women overlap in the worst possible way, and then one of them is kidnapped and taken to the magistrate's guard station to be silenced. Ichi goes all in to save her, and this leads to Gounosuke's showdown with Zatoichi, the best scene in the movie, as the deep New Year's bell tolls midnight and the two face off in a dark courtyard, snow falling softly around them as they draw their swords.

ZATOICHI 10: ZATOICHI'S REVENGE

Rating: ★★★★★ • *Origin:* Japan, 1965 • *Director:* Akira Inoue • *Source:* Criterion DVD

This is one of the finest installments in the series, stylishly overseen by TV director Akira Inoue on his first full feature, who somehow manages to strike the perfect balance between the suspense, pathos, action, and humor that define a Zatoichi movie.

Zatoichi (Shintaro Katsu) returns to Abazu, the town where he first learned the art of massage almost 10 years before, only to find that his teacher, Master Hikonoichi, has been murdered and his daughter Osayo (Mikiko Tsoubuchi) has been sold into a brothel to settle the teacher's trumped-up debts. The town is in the grip of an unholy alliance between Isoda (Fujio Harumoto), a corrupt magistrate, and Tatsugoro (Sonosuke Sawamura), a ruthless yakuza boss, who have been using tax scams to drive citizens into bankruptcy and then sell their daughters into prostitution. Zatoichi wants revenge for the murder of his teacher and freedom for Osayo, but he acts slowly and deliberately to make sure that in the process he tears down the entire rotten operation.

The crooks are protected by Kadokura (Takeshi Kato), the usual surly samurai bodyguard, but what really distinguishes this episode is the character of the allies Zatoichi makes along the way: Osayo, of course, but also the dice-dealer-with-a-conscience, Denroku the Sly Weasel (Norihei Miki), and his fearless 11-year-old daughter, Tetsuru (Sachiko Kobayashi), each of whom has a tight little character arc with a satisfying resolution. The direction is solid and brisk, bright and colorful in the peaceful scenes, bright and strident for the bursts of action. Katsu's performance is also among his best, as by this point, he completely embraces the role of Zatoichi in all its contradictions. The music by Akira Ifukube, who had scored several previous installments, incorporates a Spanish guitar sound that appropriately evokes Italian Spaghetti Westerns, just then nearing peak popularity.

High point: there's a scene toward the end where Denroku, through threats to his daughter, has been blackmailed by the yakuza into stealing Zatoichi's cane sword and is on his way to Boss Tetsugoro to turn it in. But guilt drives him to stop at every tavern on the way, and by the time he arrives at the last open noodle shop, he's staggering drunk. He lurches into the shop, orders yet more sake, blurts out his sad story, and then realizes that the shopkeeper who's serving him is none other than Zatoichi, who's hidden there while the magistrate's cops are combing the streets. It's 100 *ryo* worth of pure gold.

ZATOICHI 11: ZATOICHI AND THE DOOMED MAN

Rating: ★★★☆☆ • *Origin:* Japan, 1965 • *Director:* Kazuo Mori • *Source:* Criterion DVD

"Every time someone asks me a favor like this, I get in trouble." We know, Ichi. We know.

This is the weakest entry in the series so far. It isn't bad, but the story doesn't play to the lead character's strengths, and Zatoichi almost seems like he's stepping through the events of the plot because he's Zatoichi, and what other choice does he have?

Zatoichi (Shintaro Katsu), whipped and imprisoned overnight for illegal gambling, encounters a man named Shimazo in jail who's been condemned to death for crimes he swears he didn't commit. He begs Ichi to visit his home village and clear his name before he can be executed. Ichi is skeptical, and once he's released, he's indecisive about whether to help Shimazo, and that's the first problem: an indecisive Zatoichi seems out of character. It gets worse, as he runs into a series of con artists—a kid who tricks him into a clip joint, a woman who tricks him into getting her out of jail, a grifter who actually assumes his identity for a while—and as a result of their tricks, Zatoichi finds himself on the way to Shimazo's village after all. Zatoichi the wise, sly trickster railroaded by a bunch of amateurs just feels off. In the best installments, Ichi makes emotional connections with good people caught in tragic circumstances who need his help. Here he scarcely meets anyone worth caring about, so there's no meaning to his involvement, no pathos to his efforts on others' behalf, and little stake other than his life if he fails.

It does get better in the second half, as we get into the familiar territory of treacherous yakuza bosses betraying their own followers to expand their territories. Zatoichi is on firm footing when dealing with these scum, and after he solves the problem of the doomed Shimazo, he merely has to deal with the 50 goons Boss Jubei (Kenjiro Ishiyama) sends to kill him in a deserted fishing village at dawn. With the weak main plot out of the way, veteran director Kazuo Mori goes to town with this final mass melee, in which Zatoichi is nearly taken down by a combination of harpoons, a pit trap, nets, ropes, and muskets. But he wins through, in time to repay the woman who'd conned him into getting her out of jail with a final con of his own. It doesn't feel good.

ZATOICHI 12: ZATOICHI AND THE CHESS EXPERT
(OR *SHOWDOWN FOR ZATOICHI* OR *ZATOICHI'S TRIP TO HELL*)

Rating: ★★★★★ • *Origin:* Japan, 1965 • *Director:* Kenji Misumi • *Source:* Criterion DVD

This is a superb return to form after the stumble of *Doomed Man*, with a script by Daisuke Ito that's one of the strongest stories yet, and direction by Kenji Misumi that shows he's not only a master of action and emotion but of suspense as well.

Pursued by yakuza from one of the crooked bosses he's defeated, Zatoichi (Shintaro Katsu) takes passage on a boat across Edo Bay, trying to outrun his reputation. But there are goons from yet another yakuza family on the boat, and Ichi can't resist bilking them in a dice game, ensuring that he'll have new enemies among the Banyu gang when he reaches the other side. He also seemingly makes a new friend of a mysterious chess-loving samurai traveling under the assumed name of Jumonji (Miko Narita). Ichi is good enough at shogi, or Japanese chess, to give Jumonji a good game but not good enough to beat him more than once.

When Ichi is ambushed by some Banyu goons, Jumonji is able to witness his combat skill as Ichi drives off the Banyu without killing any of them. Ichi tells Jumonji that he prefers to avoid unnecessary killing, but the samurai's reply is that when he fights, he kills, because winning is what matters. In fact, he'll kill anyone who might defeat him at anything—but not Ichi, because, he says, "I don't kill opponents I like."

However, though no one was killed in the goon scuffle, a young girl got cut by one of the fleeing thugs and the next day she comes down with a fever: tetanus. Her name is Miki, and she's the niece of a traveling shamisen player called Otane (Kaneko Iwasaki), a name of ill omen to Zatoichi, as that was the name of his dead first love. He feels responsible for the girl's illness and offers to travel to get the expensive medicine she needs. And he does so, but in a marsh at night on the way back he's jumped by the Banyu, and there's a brilliantly choreographed fight in which Zatoichi tries to defend himself in the swamp without losing the box of medicine.

Miki's fever breaks, but to make sure she fully recovers, Zatoichi proposes that they take her to the hot springs at Hakone, and Jumonji, intrigued by Ichi, tags along as well. Otane is more than intrigued with Ichi—she's smitten—but there are further complications ahead: another dangerous samurai and his cross-dressing sister, pursuers from two gangs of yakuza, and revelations about Otane's true background. As the characters' intertwining pasts are gradually revealed, the story becomes a double murder mystery. Zatoichi, turning detective, deduces the solution—but it isn't going to make anybody happy. Except the viewer, who will go home completely satisfied.

ZATOICHI 13: ZATOICHI'S VENGEANCE

Rating: ★★★★★ • *Origin:* Japan, 1966 • *Director:* Tokuzo Tanaka • *Source:* Criterion DVD

Another top-of-the-line entry, with an exemplary script by Hajime Takaiwa and lovely direction by Tokuzo Tanaka, who returns to the series after a three-year absence. Korube (Shigeru Amachi), a down-on-his-luck samurai, kills a fugitive from the yakuza for a few gold ryo; Zatoichi (Shintaro Katsu) stumbles upon the murder scene, cuts down the goons who are looting the dying man, and then speaks to him. The man's name is Tamekichi; he gives Ichi a purse of money for someone named Taichi and then dies.

A dying request is a thing Zatoichi can never turn down. He takes the purse, and in the next town, he happens upon Taichi, a young boy being raised by Tamekichi's aging mother. The formerly peaceful town is being terrorized by Boss Gonzo (Kei Sato), whose gang is running a protection racket extorting payments from every business; only a few are still holding out. As usual, everywhere he turns, Zatoichi finds people who need help, but the only help he has to give is killing. The voice of his conscience, incarnated by a blind, *biwa*-playing priest, tells him he must restrain himself because his example is corrupting others, especially young Taichi. What to do?

Ichi goes legit, trying to earn money as a masseur; he's hired by a prostitute, Ocho (Mayumi Ogawa, in an affecting performance), who is haunted by a secret sorrow and is drinking herself into oblivion. Her sorrow is that she fell for the samurai Kurobe, who turned out to be unworthy of her love, and after he abandoned her, she turned to prostitution. Though Kurobe returns, pledging to make amends, Ocho rejects him—but he learns that he can buy out her debt to the brothel for 50 ryo. That's a lot of money, and the only way he can earn it is from Boss Gonzo, who will pay him that sum to kill Zatoichi, thus removing the obstacle to his protection racket.

Moral dilemmas on every side! Unfortunately for Ichi, he really does have only the solution of the sword, so when Gonzo's gang comes for Taichi's grandmother, the blade is once more drawn. A running battle with the yakuza leads to a final fight on a bridge, a melee shot entirely in silhouette against the predawn light. It's gorgeous. Though the goons try to deafen Zatoichi with thunder drums from the village festival, he finds the strength to defeat them anyway. But the battle isn't over: Kurobe arrives to challenge him so he can win the money to free Ocho, and they meet at dawn on a beach of shining pebbles.

The ending, as usual, is bittersweet, but it's entirely justified by the preceding events. And Zatoichi wanders on to yet another town without even taking his leave.

ZATOICHI 14: ZATOICHI'S PILGRIMAGE

Rating: ★★★★★ • *Origin:* Japan, 1966 • *Director:* Kazuo Ikehiro • *Source:* Criterion DVD

Zatoichi (Shintaro Katsu) feels remorse for killing all those yakuza goons in the first 13 films, but inside he doesn't feel like a killer, so in atonement he sets out on a pilgrimage to 88 temples, vowing to kill no more. Making his way across the idyllic Japanese countryside, he is dogged by an armed man on a horse, who eventually confronts him with drawn sword on a long bridge. He identifies himself as Eigoro, attacks suddenly, and Ichi kills him. So much for his vow.

In an affecting sequence, the horse paws at its dead master but then begins to follow Zatoichi as the blind swordsman continues his journey. Ichi is concerned, but it gets worse when they reach a fork in the road and the horse insists that he take the horse's route. Now Ichi is following the horse; eventually it leads him to its home stable, and a young woman comes out. Ichi asks if she's a relative of Eigoro; she senses that Ichi's killed him, suddenly grabs a sword, and slashes him in the arm. He could have dodged, but he felt moved not to move.

This protracted opening is as effective as it is unusual, but then the story moves to familiar territory. Eigoro had owed money to a gang boss, Tohachi (Isao Yamagata), but Tohachi saw Eigoro as an obstacle to his taking over the local village, so to cancel the debt he'd sent him to kill Zatoichi, assuming the notorious swordsman would instead kill him. With Eigoro out of the way, Tohachi thinks he can expand his territory safely, but he hasn't counted on Zatoichi's growing friendship with Eigoro's sister, Okichi (Michiyo Okusu). When Tohachi arrives to announce that he's now in charge and Okichi must marry him, she introduces him to her new guardian Zatoichi, and the whole playing field is changed.

Though in the end it deals with familiar themes, this film is a change of pace for Zatoichi, or at least a change of pacing; the story is given time to unfold gradually, and there are a lot of wide, lingering shots of lush summer farmland that are a refreshing contrast to the series' usual nighttime alleys and smoky gambling dens. The gangsters all ride horses, galloping across the countryside, and instead of a cowardly bully, Boss Tohachi is a confident conqueror who's also a dead shot with a horse bow. Tohachi is the most dangerous yakuza chief Zatoichi has faced yet, and Yamagata's performance is memorable, recalling that of Eli Wallach as Calvera in *The Magnificent Seven*.

It all leads to a showdown in the streets of Okichi's village, where the smiling headman has decided that the villagers' best chance lies in doing nothing and letting Zatoichi face Tohachi and his goons alone. And at first, no one comes to his aid, Tohachi's tactics are effective, and Zatoichi has to fight with increasing desperation just to stay alive. The direction is just grand, and the ending, when it comes, is in tune with everything that led up to it. Chef's kiss!

ZATOICHI 15: ZATOICHI'S CANE SWORD

Rating: ★★★★★ • *Origin:* Japan, 1967 • *Director:* Kimiyoshi Yasuda • *Source:* Criterion DVD

A son of gangsters who wants to leave the yakuza life behind; a brutal yakuza boss out to expand his territory; a corrupt official in league with the crooks; a vulnerable young woman who stands in their way. We've seen these elements many times before in previous Zatoichi installments, but *Cane Sword* makes them new again by giving these stock characters, both heroes and villains, enough space to establish themselves so their relationships feel real.

Most importantly, the story does the same for its protagonist, the blind swordsman Zatoichi (Shintaro Katsu). The wandering Ichi falls in with a troupe of traveling entertainers heading for the small town of Tonda for its New Year's celebration, but the fair has been taken over this year by the thugs of Iwagoro (Tatsuo Endo), a yakuza boss who shakes down Ichi's new friends. To teach the gang a lesson, Ichi figures out how Iwagoro's gamblers are cheating their customers, deftly turns the tables on them, and walks off with a pile of money. A little smug about his victory, Ichi befriends an old blacksmith named Senzo (Eijoro Tono) at a noodle house, but then has to defend himself against Iwagoro's thugs. When Senzo sees Ichi's sword, he insists the blind man come with him back to his house, and Ichi, needing a place to hide from the goons, is happy to comply.

Senzo, who was once a swordmaker, asks to see Ichi's sword. Inspecting it, Senzo declares that it's a legendary blade made many years before by his mentor, though now it's near the end of its life—there's a minute crack in the metal, and the next time Zatoichi uses it to kill someone, it will break! Ichi takes this as a sign that he should abandon his life of violence, and he gives his cane sword to Senzo, vowing to support himself henceforward as a masseur. Senzo says he knows just the place to ply his trade: the Shimotsuke Inn! Of course, it happens to be the refuge of the children of the yakuza boss whom Iwagoro murdered in order to take over the town, one of whom, the comely Shizu (Shiho Fujimura), is desired by the corrupt Inspector Kuwayama (Fujio Suga), but what of that?

With his sword gone, replaced by a mere wooden cane, Ichi loses his former swaggering confidence and does his best to stay out of trouble, but eventually the plight of Shizu and the threats to the honest owners of the inn move him to fight on their behalf. Ichi returns to Senzo to reclaim his sword, despite its fatal flaw, but by then events are moving fast: the old swordmaker has been murdered, Shizu has been abducted, and a band of murderous ronin hired by Kuwayama is closing in on our hero. And because this is a samurai movie, it starts to snow.

Up to this point, director Kimiyoshi Yasuda has let the story unfold at a deliberate pace, giving all these characters and situations time to set up and develop before the dénouement, but from here on it's all action to the surprising end. *Zatoichi's Cane Sword* is a master class in how to recombine a genre's familiar elements without succumbing to repetition or cliché. Great stuff.

ZATOICHI 16: ZATOICHI THE OUTLAW

Rating: ★★★☆☆ • *Origin:* Japan, 1967 • *Director:* Satsuo Yamamoto • *Source:* Criterion DVD

This installment in the series reaches for political significance, which isn't a bad thing as such, but the story and direction strain to make it work, missing the mark and hitting a sour note closer to nihilism than idealism. There are few sympathetic characters, and our hero fails to save all but one of them.

In the small town of Kiyotaki, Zatoichi (Shintaro Katsu) encounters two men whom he comes to admire. One is Ohara (Mizuho Suzuki), a ronin, or masterless samurai, who has become a pacifist and a sort of collectivist guru who is teaching the peasants how to farm together more effectively. The other is Asagoro (Rentaro Mikuni), a yakuza boss who seems more honorable than predatory. Asagoro's rival, who wants his territory, is Boss Tomizo (Tatsuo Endo again!), the usual ambitious and brutal thug in league with corrupt law enforcement. Oshino (Yuko Hamada), the sister of one of Tomizo's goons, is in love with another of his enforcers, Nisaburo (Toshiyuki Hosokawa)—Oshino wants Nisaburo to give up the yakuza life, but he refuses.

When Boss Tomizo sees Zatoichi siding with Asagoro, he sends his goons out on an ambush, but Zatoichi kills Oshino's brother and cuts off Nisaburo's right arm. (Like I said, this episode's tone is dark.) This attack provokes Asagoro into open war, which is exactly what Tomizo wants. Ichi, to keep Asagoro from falling into the trap, kills Tomizo and his lieutenants and then leaves town.

A year passes, and when next we see Ichi, he's working in another town as a humble masseur. This is a rather jarring discontinuity, and it's only after several less-than-compelling incidents unrelated to the previous act that Ichi finds a reason to return to Kiyotaki. There, everything has gone to hell: one of his two idols has betrayed his principles, evil is ascendant, and the world seems dark and hateful. As if to emphasize this, the lives of Oshino and Nisaburo have collapsed into ruin, degradation, and death that seem entirely gratuitous. Finally, Ichi is wounded, and victory is snatched from defeat only by the last-minute intervention of Ohara's collectivist peasants. It isn't satisfying.

That said, *Outlaw* does have its high points. Katsu, Suzuki, and Mikuni give fine performances, the settings are colorful and convincing, the swordplay is strong, and we're introduced to the tune that will become Zatoichi's theme song, a ballad in which Katsu laments Ichi's mistakes and informs the sun that they're both lonely. Nothing wrong with that.

ZATOICHI 17: ZATOICHI CHALLENGED

Rating: ★★★★☆ • *Origin:* Japan, 1967 • *Director:* Kenji Misumi • *Source:* Criterion DVD

After the overambitious *Zatoichi the Outlaw*, the series returns to form (and formula) with this installment, directed by the ever-reliable Kenji Misumi. Traveling again, Zatoichi (Shintaro Katsu) shares a room with a mother at death's door who has a six-year-old son, and Ichi, always a sucker for a dying request, agrees to take the boy, Ryota, to his father, the artist Shokichi (Takao Ito). Along the way, Ichi and Ryota fall in with a troupe of traveling entertainers who are menaced by a gang of yakuza thugs. Ichi intends to intervene but he's held back by Ryota, and a lone samurai, Akatsuka (Jushiro Konoe), does the job instead, sending the yakuza packing. Ichi and Akatsuka cross paths several more times in their travels, and they develop a grudging admiration for each other.

But Akatsuka is no mere wandering ronin: he's an undercover agent for the shogun investigating criminals who are producing and selling ceramics enameled with pornographic designs—a capital crime under the shogunate. To pay off his gambling debts, Shokichi has been forced to provide the crooks with the drawings the designs are based upon. Akatsuka tracks down the porn gang and executes them, one by one—and eventually he's going to get to Ryota's father, unless the blind swordsman gets in his way first.

Viewers' enjoyment of this episode is probably contingent on their level of tolerance for child actors. Unlike the two earlier films in which he had to escort a young child, Ryota is too large for Zatoichi to carry him into battle, so don't expect another *Lone Wolf and Cub* precursor. There's the usual romance between an innocent couple menaced by the crooks, but with an interesting twist this time, and the relationship between Ichi and Akatsuka is well drawn, especially since you know they inevitably must clash. Jushiro Konoe was a popular star of samurai *chambara* films, most notably as the lead in the *Yagyu Chronicles* series, and his charisma and stage presence here make him nearly a match for Katsu. He was also a notable screen swordsman, and the final duel between Akatsuka and Zatoichi (in a snowstorm, natch) is the finest in the series.

FYI: *Zatoichi Challenged* was updated to modern times and remade in 1989 as *Blind Fury* with Rutger Hauer. It isn't good, but it is amusing—for a fun evening, you could watch them back-to-back.

ZATOICHI 18: ZATOICHI AND THE FUGITIVES

Rating: ★★★★☆ • *Origin:* Japan, 1968 • *Director:* Kimiyoshi Yasuda •
Source: Criterion Blu-ray

The later films in the Zatoichi series show a lot of Spaghetti Western influence—and given what Leone owes to Kurosawa this is only fair—but this entry also owes more than a little to Japanese crime movies and American film noir. Usually, our blind swordsman hero is pitted against yakuza thugs, goons who are dangerous only because they come in packs, perhaps backed up by a broken ronin to give our hero some competition. However, this time he's up against a gang of hardened murderers, the fugitives of the title, who are so ruthless, brutal, and tough they even frighten the local yakuza boss into harboring them until the officers pursuing them move on. They're going to provide a serious challenge.

Zatoichi (Shintaro Katsu) encounters three members of this murder gang before he even reaches town: a pair of louts who harass him while he's trying to eat and the female face of the group, Oaki (Yumiko Nogawa), who watches as Ichi cut the louts down. Shortly thereafter Ichi encounters a man who's been wounded by yakuza thugs of Boss Matsugoro (Hosei Komatsu) and helps rush him to the town's doctor, Junan (Takashi Shimura—you'll recognize him as Kambei, the leader of the *Seven Samurai*). Junan has a lovely daughter, Oshizu (Kayao Mikimoto), and Ichi, admitted to the doctor's practice as a masseur and acupuncturist, is soon dreaming that he's found a home where he can give up his violent yakuza ways.

Of course, fate has different ideas, for unbeknown to Ichi, Ogano (Kyosuke Machida), the smartest member of the murder gang, is Oshizu's brother and Dr. Junan's estranged son. Ichi is drawn into helping the peasants oppressed by Boss Matsugoro, who runs a forced-labor sweatshop, and Matsugoro, intimidated by Zatoichi's skill and reputation, engages the murder gang to take him out: Ichi puts up a fight, but is badly wounded, shot and stabbed, and leaps into a river to escape. Peasants whom he's helped bring Ichi to the doctor, who patches him up and then sends him to a hidden shack to recover, but Matsugoro hears about it and abducts Junan and Oshizu, threatening them with torture and rape if they won't lead his men to Zatoichi. Unnecessary, of course: wounded though he is, Ichi takes the fight to Matsugoro to rescue the doctor and his daughter. This time he's been pushed too far, and the blind swordsman is ready for slaughter, reveling in murder as if he were himself a member of the gang of killers, and telling Matsugoro, "I came back from Hell to get you. The Lord of Hell is waiting for you." But so is the murder gang, once the yakuza goons are taken care of.

Directed by Kimiyoshi Yasuda, who also helmed the excellent *Cane Sword*, this is a tight and hard-hitting episode in which our hero, usually well defended by plot armor, finds himself horribly vulnerable, both physically and emotionally. Recommended.

ZATOICHI 19: SAMARITAN ZATOICHI

Rating: ★★★★★ • *Origin:* Japan, 1968 • *Director:* Kenji Misumi • *Source:* Criterion DVD

Samaritan Zatoichi AUTHOR'S COLLECTION

This is superb. Like all the best entries in the series, *Samaritan* is touching, ironic, suspenseful, exciting, and occasionally disturbing, but also, thanks to the capers of star Shintaro Katsu and his comical friend Takuya Fujioka, this film is also very funny, an aspect of the Zatoichi movies that hadn't been front and center for a while. The jokes are broad, but ace director Kenji Misumi keeps things taut and never overplays a gag.

Samaritan also packs a lot of story into its 84 minutes, but you're never in doubt as to what's going on. Zatoichi (Katsu), traveling as always, enters a new town and accepts the hospitality of its yakuza boss, Kumakichi, and in return is asked to accompany some of the boss's goons on a mission to collect a debt. The debtor, drunk and obstreperous, decides to fight the goons, and Ichi kills him just as his sister Osode (Yoshiko Mita) arrives with the money to pay off the debt. The goons take the money and try to take the sister into the bargain, but Ichi, guilt-ridden, drives them off, making an enemy of Boss Kumakichi.

Osode sets off to return to her hometown of Suwa, and Ichi appoints himself her unwanted protector and follows along. Also following is Kashiwazaki (Makoto Sato), a roguish ronin out for whatever he can get, including the gorgeous Osode, who is also desired by the local magistrate and by the brothel boss of Suwa. Kumakichi's thugs are in pursuit as well, hoping to abduct Osode for the magistrate, while ahead wait the yakuza of Suwa, who owe Kumakichi a favor. This amounts to a lot of moving parts, and when they collide, conflicts erupt; there's a good deal of swordplay in this picture, but the fights are all beautifully shot in a stunning variety of settings. There's also a wild chase scene involving Kashiwazaki the ronin, Osode carried in a speedy palanquin, five yakuza goons, and a desperate Zatoichi on a commandeered horse blindly galloping out of control. Whoa!

The acting is as good as the action. Katsu is at the top of his game, and Mita, one of Japanese cinema's leading female actors, is poignant as Osode, dealing with her guilt, self-loathing, and gradual, grudging admiration for Ichi. Sato also gives a fine, subtle performance as the sardonic ronin Kashiwazaki, and his encounters with Ichi are among the best in the series. Their final duel is fought against a background of thundering drums welcoming in the new year—and deafening Zatoichi, who can't hear the samurai coming.

In the end, as always, Ichi moves on, telling Osode he only wants her happiness, though she cries, "How can I ever be happy after you've gone away?" As Ichi shuffles off into the first sunrise of a new year, in a way Katsu himself is disappearing over the horizon, as he will take the next year off from the Zatoichi franchise to act in *Hitokiri* and other films. *Samaritan* is the last of a remarkable eight-year run of films, every one of which is worth watching. There will still be a lot more Zatoichi to follow, but the features are mostly special one-offs of one sort or another, interesting but inconsistent. However, with this film Shintaro Katsu ended his first Zatoichi run on a very high note indeed.

ZATOICHI 20: ZATOICHI MEETS YOJIMBO

Rating: ★★★☆☆ • *Origin:* Japan, 1970 • *Director:* Kihachi Okamoto •
Source: Criterion Blu-ray

Take the two leading *chambara* stars of their day portraying their signature characters, Shintaro Katsu as Zatoichi and Toshiro Mifune as the nameless "yojimbo," add in top-notch director Kihachi Okamoto (*The Sword of Doom*, *Kill!*), and the result should be a sure thing. Alas, instead we get one of the weakest films in the Zatoichi series.

Zatoichi, wandering and caught in a downpour, has to defend himself against a bandit gang who are preying on refugees. "Blood on my hands again," he laments. "I'm going home." Ichi returns to his home village, which he remembers as a pleasant heaven, but in the years since he left it, the place has become a dusty hell. Brutal gangsters have moved in and taken over, and even Ichi's childhood sweetheart Umeno (Ayako Wakao) now works as a prostitute. Though hardened and bitter, she seems to have feelings for the drunken samurai bodyguard (Mifune) who hangs out in her tavern. The yojimbo has been hired by the town's yakuza boss, Masagoro (Masakane Yonekura), to strong-arm his own father, businessman Eboshiya (Osamu Takizawa), into revealing where he's hidden a cache of stolen gold. Ichi runs afoul of Masagoro, takes up with Eboshiya, and soon he and the yojimbo find themselves on opposite sides.

That may sound clear on paper, but it isn't on film, as the introduction of all these people is slow, and their motivations are murky. There are almost no sympathetic characters here: for once both Katsu and Mifune are short on charm, and "everyone is corrupt" as a theme doesn't provide enough contrast and drive to get a plot moving. Even the harmless old ex-headman Hyoroku (Kanjuro Arashi) feels guilty for having invited the yakuza into town during a drought to defend it against starving refugees, and is expiating his sin by carving a statue of the Buddha for every refugee who was murdered. Jolly stuff.

This movie is also too long, but in the final third it finally pulls itself together and becomes pretty good. Two more characters come to town: Eboshiya's other son, Sanaemon (Toshiyuki Hosokawa), also corrupt, followed by a fearsome hitman from Edo named Kuzuryu (Shin Kishida). The yojimbo, whom Kuzuryu calls "Sasa," had worked with the hitman in the past, and it turns out they are both in the village on secret orders. Sasa the yojimbo and Zatoichi come to a sort of entente of mutual respect, calling each other "monster" and "beast," but Kuzuryu upsets the fragile balance and soon the swords are out. Everybody is after the hidden gold, and once our canny Ichi deduces where it is, there's nothing left but slaughter. Umeno, the only person both Ichi and the yojimbo hold dear, gets caught in the crossfire, and a face-off between the two is inevitable. But when top-grossing franchise characters have a showdown, is anyone really in danger?

Mifune would play his yojimbo character for the fourth and final time later in the year in *Ambush at Blood Pass*, which also costars Katsu. It's a much better movie.

ZATOICHI 21: ZATOICHI GOES TO THE FIRE FESTIVAL

Rating: ★★★★★ • *Origin:* Japan, 1970 • *Director:* Kenji Misumi • *Source:* Criterion Blu-ray

This is just marvelous—all the more so in that it follows the disappointing *Zatoichi Meets Yojimbo*. This entry in the series was produced and cowritten by star Shintaro Katsu, but perhaps most importantly it was directed by Kenji Misumi, who had directed the first Zatoichi movie and many subsequent episodes. This is Misumi's last Zatoichi film and it's a career high point, luminous and vivid, at times approaching the surreal. The sword duels in this film are among the most beautiful and imaginative of the series.

An alternative title for this movie could be *Zatoichi Meets the Sword of Doom*, because one of Ichi's antagonists is the great Tatsuya Nakadai playing essentially the same death-obsessed samurai killer as in Okamoto's classic *Sword of Doom* (1966). This is Nakadai's only appearance in Katsu's Zatoichi series and he makes quite an impression, glowering at Ichi from the shadows or walking past while intoning gems like, "You shall be killed by my hands only." As in Okamoto's film, Nakadai's nameless character is a total nutjob who hallucinates dire visions from his past and then has to kill somebody to exorcise them. He's terrifying.

And he's not even the Big Bad here. This time Ichi is up against a yakuza crime lord who rules the illegal activities of eight provinces, a "shogun of the underworld" who is coldly manipulative and cruel—and as blind as Zatoichi. Big boss Yamikubo (Masayuki Mori) is an opponent almost on the scale of a James Bond archvillain, but Ichi's abilities have grown to match, his skills at stealthy murder here verging on the supernatural. After Ichi offends the big boss by implying before a meeting of lesser bosses that Yamikubo's methods lack honor, the big boss sends a series of hit teams to take out the blind swordsman, all to no avail. One of these assassination attempts takes place in a bathhouse in which Ichi and his attempted killers are all naked but for their swords—it's an extraordinary sequence, simultaneously gruesome and hilarious.

After that Yamikubo gives up on strongarm tactics and goes for the honey trap, stating with an aggrieved smirk that "Blind men crave affection." But his tool, the beautiful Okiyo (Reiko Ohara), falls for Ichi's good-hearted simplicity, and that gambit fails too. So Yamikubo decides to attack Ichi in his pride, inviting him to a meeting of yakuza bosses that he can't fail to attend, even though it's obviously a trap. This is where the titular fire festival comes in, as the big boss tries to murder Ichi by trapping him on a narrow platform in the middle of a broad pool, its waters covered with flammable oil that is then ignited. How's the blind swordsman going to get out of this one?

With this movie, though, our hero passes beyond the human to the superhuman, and after that there's no going back. It's good training for director Misumi's next *chambara* films, the *Lone Wolf and Cub* movies, where he will direct four of that series' six films. The producer of those movies? Shintaro Katsu.

ZATOICHI 22: ZATOICHI MEETS THE ONE-ARMED SWORDSMAN (OR ZATOICHI AND THE ONE-ARMED SWORDSMAN OR THE BLIND SWORDSMAN MEETS HIS EQUAL)

Rating: ★★★★☆ • *Origin:* Japan, 1971 • *Directors:* Kimiyoshi Yasuda and
Hsu Tseng Hung • *Source:* Criterion Blu-ray

Mash-up, *chambara* + *wuxia*! The two most popular series characters in historical Asian swordplay in 1970 face off, mainly because neither can understand what the other is saying. It's one misunderstanding after another from beginning to end, which is actually the point of the whole thing.

A movie pitting Jimmy Wang Yu's Wang Kang, the one-armed swordsman, against Shintaro Katsu's Zatoichi could have been an exploitation quickie, but instead this is a serious entry in the Zatoichi series. It's ably directed by Kimiyoshi Yasuda, who'd directed four previous films in the series including the excellent *Cane Sword*, with Wang Kang's combat sequences arranged by Hong Kong director Hsu Tseng Hung.

Wang Kang comes to Japan seeking the fellowship of other martial artists at the Fukuryuji Temple, but he doesn't speak Japanese, so he's delighted to make the acquaintance of two traveling Chinese entertainers who speak both languages, as does their young son, Xiaorong. On the road, the four Chinese bow obsequiously before a procession of samurai of the Nanbu clan, but Xiaorong, chasing his kite, runs in front of them and the samurai draw their *katanas* to kill the child for this offense against propriety. Wang Kang wades in to protect him, and there's a wild melee that ends with the samurai slaughtering all witnesses to cover up their overreaction. Xiaorong and his wounded father escape while Wang Kang holds off the furious samurai.

Meanwhile, Zatoichi, being pursued by goons from yet another vengeful yakuza boss, stumbles across Xiaorong and his dying father, who asks Ichi to take care of the boy. Ichi, of course, cannot refuse a dying request and takes the child into a town, where he hears about a mad Chinese fighter who attacked the Nanbu clan and killed a bunch of innocents. Ichi and Wang Kang, both fugitives, encounter each other warily when they both try to use the same shack as a hideout, but Xiaorong translates for them, and soon Ichi gets the real story.

But there are more misunderstandings ahead. Tobei (Toru Abe), another yakuza boss, is in the pay of the Nanbu, and his thugs are looking for both fugitives. Ichi and Wang Kang find an ally in Oyone (Michie Terada), who seems to care for Xiaorong and maybe Wang Kang, but when her family is attacked by the yakuza, and Wang and the boy barely escape, the one-armed swordsman thinks Ichi sold him out. And indeed, Wang Kang runs into plenty of betrayal, including that of Kakuzen (Koji Nanbara), the martial arts monk who'd invited him to Japan, but Ichi stays true to protecting Wang and the boy.

The combat scenes of the one-armed swordsman facing the Nanbu are fascinating, because the samurai don't know what to make of him: Wang Kang leaps over their heads, runs across their shoulders, and mixes swordplay with kung fu in a manner that baffles his opponents. Only Zatoichi, who can't see these wuxia antics, is a match for Wang Kang. Who wins their final face-off? Hint: this is Jimmy Wang's last one-armed swordsman movie in the original series, and there are more Zatoichi films to come.

(The film reviewed here is the version made for the Japanese market. There is said to have been a variant version made for the Chinese market that has more wuxia combat and a different ending, but that version hasn't been seen since the film's original theatrical release. Dang it.)

ZATOICHI 23: ZATOICHI AT LARGE (OR *THE BLIND SWORDSMAN ON A MISSION*)

Rating: ★★★☆☆ • *Origin:* Japan, 1972 • *Director:* Kazuo Mori • *Source:* Criterion Blu-ray

Though this was made during the era of Zatoichi feature specials, there's nothing particularly special about it, other than it marks the transition of the series from medium-size Daiei Studios to Toho, the biggest motion picture company in Japan, home of Akira Kurosawa and

Godzilla. Perhaps Toho wanted a movie that contained all the elements that had made the Zatoichi series a success, which is why this feels like a greatest hits compilation. Dying request: check. Ichi burdened with caring for a small child: check. Comical traveling entertainers: check. Cruel yakuza boss extending his territory and terrorizing innocents: check. Women forced by debt slavery into prostitution: check. Vulnerable young woman menaced by yakuza: check. Dangerous dicing at the boss's gambling den: check. Samurai swordsman hired by boss to kill Ichi: check. Kidnapped young woman saved by Ichi at the last moment: check. Humiliation of the yakuza boss: check. Mass melee with dozens of yakuza goons: double check. Final showdown with samurai swordsman: triple check. Ichi shuffling off down the road, leaving adoring young woman behind—can I stop now?

That's not to say there aren't pleasures to be had here. Shintaro Katsu as Zatoichi is charming as usual, and there are fine performances from Rentaro Mikuni as Boss Tetsugoro, Hisaya Morishige as Tobei, the honest old constable, and Etsushi Takahashi as the samurai swordsman. There's a spectacular scene with a flaming death trap, and a touching redemption of the constable's ne'er-do-well son. Zatoichi even fights for a time while wearing a festival demon mask, which is extra cool. But the story feels perfunctory, and you won't see anything you haven't seen in the series several times before.

ZATOICHI 24: ZATOICHI IN DESPERATION

Rating: ★★☆☆☆ • *Origin:* Japan, 1972 • *Director:* Shintaro Katsu • *Source:* Criterion Blu-ray

By mid-1972, Zatoichi producer and star Shintaro Katsu's biggest competition was . . . himself. The *Lone Wolf and Cub* series he was producing, starring his brother Tomisaburo Wakayama, was taking off just as the Zatoichi series was winding down. The Lone Wolf movies were more sensational than the Zatoichi films, with more sex and violence, and perhaps Katsu was grasping for Lone Wolf's popularity when he decided to make a new Zatoichi film that went similarly over the top—and moreover, to direct it himself.

If so, it was a mistake, as *Zatoichi in Desperation* is easily the weakest film in the entire series. Abandoning the melancholy yet hopeful tone of the previous films, and throwing out comedy entirely, *Desperation* is unrelentingly grim, a series of events that start bad and just get worse until they end in pain and slaughter. To add injury to this insult, Katsu's direction is self-consciously arty and to no good result, muddy and confusing, with far too many awkward close-ups and shots often blocked by obstacles like curtains or occluded by passing figures. It's a mess.

There's a plot, of sorts. Ichi, wandering as usual, is crossing a dangerously rickety bridge when he meets an aging female shamisen player, who says that she's on her way to her home village to see her daughter. Ichi tries to give her a few coins to help her on her way and bumps into her, accidentally making her lose her balance and fall to her death. In atonement, Ichi takes up her instrument and sets out to find the musician's daughter.

In a raucous town run by Mangoro (Asao Koike), a nasty yakuza boss, Ichi finds the shamisen player's daughter, Nishikigi (Kiwako Taichi). She's a prostitute in a brothel, and for the sake of her dead mother, Ichi decides to raise the 50 ryo needed to buy out her contract. Unusually for the series, this prostitute has no heart of gold and doesn't want her freedom— but nonetheless Ichi is determined to liberate her, ignoring young Kaede (Kyoko Yoshizawa), the girl who really needs his help. It's all awful: the yakuza decide they want the 100 ryo reward for Ichi's head offered by another mob boss, Kaede's younger brother gets murdered for standing up to Mangoro's goons, Kaede kills herself in despair, Nishikigi helps betray Ichi to Mangoro, and everything goes to hell. There's exactly one satisfying duel, Ichi against Mangoro's hired samurai in the middle of a thunderstorm, but all the rest of the fights are darkened blurs. In the end, except for a few unnamed fisher folk who won't be exploited by the slain Mangoro, no one is saved or redeemed, and Zatoichi, bleeding and nearly mutilated, staggers away from town as uncaring waves pound the shore. No fun.

ZATOICHI 25: ZATOICHI'S CONSPIRACY

Rating: ★★★★☆ • *Origin:* Japan, 1973 • *Director:* Kimiyoshi Yasuda • *Source:* Criterion Blu-ray

With this movie, the final batch of films in the Zatoichi series ends on an up note. Tired of wandering, Zatoichi (Shintaro Katsu) decides to return to the small village where he grew up (apparently forgetting that he already returned to a different village where he grew up in *Zatoichi Meets Yojimbo*). As he arrives, the welcome mat is being rolled out for a returning prodigal, and at first Ichi mistakes this as intended for him, whereas actually it's for his childhood friend Shinbei (Eiji Okada), now a wealthy and successful rice merchant. Modest and friendly, in an act of apparent altruism, Shinbei goes to the magistrate and pays off all the peasants' back taxes—but in private he's also chummy with the local yakuza boss, Iwagoro (Tatsuo Endo again), and asks the boss to procure a young virgin for him, so he must be a bad 'un. Sure enough, Shinbei is conspiring with Iwagoro and the corrupt magistrate to take over the peasants' rock quarry and put the locals to forced labor there while helping the magistrate to sell his store of stolen tax rice.

But Ichi, in a warm haze of nostalgia, is oblivious to most of this. He pays a visit to the shack of the late Oshige, who'd nursed him as a child, meeting a young woman, Omiyo (Yukiyo Toake), who'd been her last infant client, and the two bond as together they visit the nurse's grave. Omiyo's father, the potter Sakubei (the great Takashi Shimura), remembers Ichi from when he was a young rascal; they both agree that Shinbei has become a skunk, but Ichi still isn't disturbed, just harassed by a gang of teenage delinquents who provide the comedy this time around.

Events go very sour very fast when Shinbei turns his lecherous eye on Omiyo and orders Iwagoro to procure her for him. Omiyo is abducted, Ichi goes to rescue her, he gives Shinbei 12 hours to get out of town, and finally, after probably the longest delay in any film in the series, the blind masseur draws his sword. But it was worth the wait, for the story has had time to develop its background, set up the antagonists, and give Ichi a believable emotional connection with the victims. The payoff is a long and inventive action sequence in which Ichi gradually whittles down his substantial opposition.

Instead of trying to direct this one himself, Katsu turned back to one of his reliable standbys, the excellent Kimiyoshi Yasuda, with stellar results, backed up musically by one of the celebrated Akira Ifukube's most poignant scores. With blood and slaughter once more in his wake, Zatoichi leaves town as usual without saying goodbye to those he's saved. But he'll be back, for though he's leaving the big cinema screen, he's headed for the smaller screen of television, where Katsu will blink and shuffle his way through four seasons of the *Zatoichi* TV show.

ZATOICHI 26: ZATOICHI (OR *ZATOICHI: THE BLIND SWORDSMAN* OR *ZATOICHI: DARKNESS IS HIS ALLY*)

Rating: ★★★☆☆ • *Origin:* Japan, 1989 • *Director:* Shintaro Katsu • *Source:* Arrow Films DVD

After starring in 25 films and four TV seasons of the original *Zatoichi* series, Shintaro Katsu's career went mostly on hiatus until he came out of near-retirement to make this final entry. Produced, directed, and cowritten by Katsu, this film is a nostalgic goodbye to his best-known character, breaking no new ground and largely repeating the tone, themes, and running gags of that outstanding *chambara* series. Older and perhaps a bit gentler, and now a yakuza legend, Ichi continues to roam from one small town to another, making friends among the downtrodden and enemies among their oppressors, still lonely, and still fast as lightning with the blade hidden in his blindman's cane.

After a brief stay in prison for defying a law officer, Ichi wanders to a seaside town that happens to be hosting a gathering of yakuza mob bosses, who are, as usual, quarreling about precedence and territory. While performing his usual sleight-of-hand tricks to scam the local gambling house, Ichi catches the attention of one of the bosses, Ohan (Kanako Higuchi), the young woman who heads the Bosatsu mob family, and they have a brief fling in a steamy bath. However, now he's been identified, and Ichi's loyalty or death becomes a matter of contention between the two leading yakuza firebrands, Akabei (Yuya Uchid) and Goemon (Ryutaro Gan). There are also a corrupt shogunate official, a nameless, down-on-his-luck ronin serving the bosses as a bodyguard, and an innocent young woman Ichi is fond of who is threatened with forced prostitution, all stock characters familiar from the original series.

Frankly, it's pretty formulaic, the cinematography is sadly murky, the yakuza politics are overcomplicated, and there's nothing new in the swordplay. And yet, Katsu still has it: his charm and talent are undiminished, and that's almost enough by itself to carry the picture. Add in memorable performances by Higuchi as the calculating lady mob leader and Gan as the rising young boss, a scary psychopath who will stop at nothing, and you have a worthwhile if elegiac capstone to Zatoichi's unparalleled long run. Essential, though? Not really.

ZATOICHI, SEASON 1 (OR *TALES OF ZATOICHI*)

Rating: ★★★☆☆ • *Origin:* Japan, 1974 • *Directors:* Kenji Misumi et al. • *Source:* Tokyo Shock DVDs

It's no surprise that the formula that worked in the *Zatoichi* movie series translates well to the shorter form of a TV show: 45 minutes is just enough time to introduce some sympathetic characters, menace them with heartless villains, and then have Zatoichi (Shintaro Katsu) sort things out with the blade of his cane sword. Episode 4, "The Kannon Statue That Was Tied," is a good example of this; it's actually two overlapping stories, one about an ex-convict mother trying to find her three-year-old child, and the other about two yakuza gangs fighting over a profitable territory while being played off against each other by a corrupt constable. And it looks great: it's one of the final works by master director Kenji Misumi.

However, by the middle of the season, the formula is getting a bit tired. Star and producer Katsu tries juicing it up by directing abridged remakes of some of the movies, including *Fight, Zatoichi, Fight* and *Zatoichi and the Chest of Gold,* but Katsu still hasn't found his feet as a director at this point and the results are muddled, over-artsy, and awkward.

So Katsu brings in a couple of other top-tier feature directors, Kazuo Mori and Kimiyoshi Yasuda, and changes gears. The stories in the last half of the season focus less on the blind swordsman and more on the current episode's other characters, samurai soap-opera plots in which Ichi features more as a sort of guardian angel than a key participant. With more room for non-Ichi character development, some of these are quite effective, particularly episode 22, "Song of the Father and Son," in which a ronin gone bad redeems himself in the eyes of his young boy. Also outstanding is episode 23, "Suicide Song of Lovers," which costars Ruriko Asaoka as a blind shamisen player in a doomed romance with a samurai and in which Katsu's directorial skills finally mature. Set unusually in the snowy north, this haunting story completely breaks the *Zatoichi* formula, and is arguably the best episode of the entire season.

ZORRO (1975)

Rating: ★★★☆☆ • *Origin:* Italy/France, 1975 • *Director:* Duccio Tessari •
Source: 101 Films Blu-ray

Alain Delon enjoyed starring in *The Black Tulip* (1964) so much that he decided he wanted to make another swashbuckler, and hey, Zorro was available. Because it's an Italian film shot in Spain, this is sometimes referred to as a Zorro Spaghetti Western, but it really isn't, as it draws its inspiration far more from Disney's *Zorro* TV series than from Sergio Leone.

Zorro gets an all-new origin that approximates the original but varies from it. In more-or-less 1820 in South America's northern cordillera, Don Diego (Delon), on his way to Spain, meets an old friend traveling to the fictional province of Nuevo Aragón to take the reins as its new reformist governor. But he's murdered by assassins, and though Don Diego kills them, his friend charges him to take his place in Nuevo Aragón—but he must give up killing. Diego reluctantly agrees.

Assuming the role of a feckless fop, Diego arrives in Nuevo Aragón as its new governor to find it grinding under the heel of the corrupt Colonel Huerta (Stanley Baker), who has the power of the military and the judiciary on his side. To fight on the behalf of the oppressed citizenry, Diego assumes the secret identity of Zorro, and the usual swashbuckling follows. A lot of this swashbuckling is played for laughs, and the slapstick gets pretty broad, especially after Huerta assigns the buffoonish Sergeant Garcia (Moustache—yes, that's the actor's name) to protect Governor Diego and track down Zorro. There are also various comic street urchins, comic annoying aristocrats, and a comic Great Dane dog. It's pretty comic.

On the good side, the story has a competent heroine and sassy romantic interest for Zorro in Hortensia Pulido (Ottavia Piccolo), a steadfast opponent of Colonel Huerta, and the jailbreak scene in which Zorro rescues her from durance vile is pretty good. The long, acrobatic final duel between Zorro and Huerta is said to have been inspired by the final duel in *Scaramouche* (1952), a good idea since Alain Delon is a credible fencer, but unfortunately Stanley Baker is not, so the combat cuts awkwardly between close-ups of Baker and long shots of his fencing double.

In summary: a minor effort, pleasant enough but essential only for Zorro completists. Also, fair warning, it has an *extremely obnoxious* pop tune theme by Oliver Onions that is played far too often during action scenes. Turn it down!

ZORRO, SEASON 1

Rating: ★★★★☆ • *Origin:* USA, 1957 • *Directors:* Norman Foster, Charles Barton et al. •
Source: Disney DVDs

A year after the hit British production of *The Adventures of Robin Hood* conquers television, Disney replies with *Zorro*, out-swashbuckling even the outlaw of Sherwood Forest. Latin heartthrob Guy Williams (born Armando Catalano) is perfectly cast as Zorro/Diego de la Vega, supported by two gifted comic actors, Henry Calvin playing Sergeant Garcia and mime artist Gene Sheldon playing the voiceless Bernardo, Diego's servant. The show is a successful mix of high adventure and low comedy, funny and suspenseful.

The series' structure resembles the movie serials of the 1930s and '40s, with the season's 39 episodes presented in three arcs of 13 episodes each. The first, the "Monastario" arc, shows Don Diego, newly returned from Spain, donning the cape and mask of Zorro to oppose the corrupt and arrogant Comandante Monastario. These episodes were edited into a feature film, *The Sign of Zorro*, and were covered under that title.

The second, or "Magistrado" arc, introduces a new villain, Magistrado Carlos Galindo (Vinton Hayworth), who has the new, honest comandante assassinated and then proceeds to misrule the pueblo of Los Angeles to some dark agenda of his own, causing strife and inciting unrest. Sergeant Garcia is elevated to the rank of acting comandante but must take his orders from the Magistrado, though he usually hates following them. To Garcia's relief, the Magistrado's plots are repeatedly thwarted by Zorro, whom Garcia begins to regard as more ally than enemy. Zorro discovers that the Magistrado is himself taking orders from someone else, a mastermind known as the Eagle, who sends messages by feathers that have been clipped in patterns to carry orders in code. Finally, another new and honest comandante arrives, so when Zorro exposes the Magistrado's schemes, he is brought to justice.

The third, or "Eagle" arc, reveals the plans of the really, really angry villain responsible for all the trouble, the ambitious aristocrat José de Varga (Charles Korvin), who hides behind the name of the Eagle. With Spain distracted by revolt in Mexico, Varga's plan is to foment rebellion in California, not to free its people from Spanish colonial domination but to declare it as a kingdom with Varga as its king. Worse than that, he then plans to sell his Kingdom of California to a foreign power, the bidders being agents from America and Russia. A single outlaw can't defeat such a broad conspiracy (no, not even Zorro!), so Don Diego must surreptitiously work with his father Don Alejandro's alliance of landowners to foil Varga's plans.

These are good stories, well told, and though some episodes are padded with the gratuitous comic antics of Sergeant Garcia, he's so lovable that he gets away with it. There's an occasional inconsistency of tone that comes from having a rotating stable of writers and directors, but these incongruities are easily overlooked. However, one could wish for stronger and more prominent female characters, but we get at least one in Suzanne Lloyd as Raquel Toledano, the ambitious wife of an honest comandante who falls for the false promises of the Eagle. She has a wicked smile.

ZORRO, SEASON 2

Rating: ★★★☆☆ • *Origin:* USA, 1958 • *Directors:* William Witney et al. •
Source: Disney DVDs

By the time of its second season, *Zorro* is a big hit, and Disney doesn't tamper much with the elements that make the series successful. However, the 13-episode story arcs of the first season gradually go by the boards; the "Monterey" arc, the first 13 episodes of season 2, is really three mini-arcs of four or five episodes each, and after it concludes, the rest of the season is a mix of short arcs and single, standalone episodes. Fortunately, each arc, no matter how short, is handled by a single director, which maintains internal consistency of tone and approach.

For the first arc, ably directed by William Witney, the story is relocated up the coast to the pueblo of Monterey, not that you can tell the difference, since they use the same sets as for Los Angeles. The plots reprise themes from season 1—a conspiracy of robbers employing secret information, false abuses of authority—but this time there's no real mystery about who's behind it. The main villain in the first episode is played by the formidable Lee Van Cleef, but he's replaced by a phony Native American named Pablo, who is frankly awful. At least Anna Maria Verdugo (Jolene Brand), Diego's on again, off again romantic interest, is spicy and courageous.

At the end of the "Monterey" arc, Diego's father, Don Alejandro (George J. Lewis), learns that his son is the wanted fugitive Zorro . . . and turns out to be all right with that. This removes one of the sources of tension from the situation, which eases the series' transition from a Western swashbuckler to a sort of outlaw situation comedy with bandit interludes. If anything, this only made the show even more popular, so Disney apparently knew what it was doing, though most of us will miss the edge of the earlier episodes. The latter part of season 2 features more gags, more songs, and considerably less lethal combat than before: villains are more likely to be put in the stocks and humiliated than shot or run through. And the cast begins to feature higher-wattage and more recognizable guest stars, which doesn't hurt, as that challenges Guy Williams (Zorro) to put more oomph into his performance to measure up. Episodes 16 to 19, known as the "Gay Caballero" arc, feature Cesar Romero as Don Alejandro's cousin, a charming rascal come to town to try to bamboozle Margarita (Hollywood leading lady Patricia Medina) into letting him marry her for her land and money. Even better are episodes 27 to 30, the "Man from Spain," with the wicked Everett Sloane in temporary command of Los Angeles. Both these arcs were directed a man with the resounding name of Hollingsworth Morse, who had a firm grasp of TV light adventure—he went on to direct 62 episodes of *Lassie*, which should tell you pretty much all you need to know.

One of the keys to this series' success, often overlooked, is the music by William Lava. In the '30s, the Disney animation studio had perfected the art of syncing the musical soundtrack with the onscreen action, and its mastery of this technique was carried over into the live-action *Zorro*, with near-continuous mood-setting melodies punctuated by stings and small fanfares that bring every scene alive. No one else at the time could match it.

ZORRO AND THE THREE MUSKETEERS

Rating: ★★☆☆☆ • *Origin:* Italy, 1963 • *Director:* Luigi Capuano •
Source: Amazon streaming video

There are many fine swashbuckling comedies. This isn't one of them.

MASH-UP OR SHUT UP

Everyone likes crossovers and mash-ups, right? If you're a fan of two heroes in the same genre, then of course you'd like to see a story in which they meet and confront a challenge together. That's the commercial calculation for crossovers in every medium, whether it's comics, games, TV shows, or movies. It's assumed a crossover or mash-up is a sure thing that will draw in the fans of both franchises. It's a no-brainer.

That's in principle, maybe, but not in practice. In practice, the story or personality elements that create the appeal of one character don't always fit comfortably with the elements of another. Zorro and the Three Musketeers, for example: all cheerful swashbucklers, but the musketeers are a disparate bunch that rely on teamwork, while Zorro is fundamentally a loner, so mashing them together in a coherent and credible plot is a task that shouldn't be underestimated, calling for a top-notch screenwriter. Or what if you put together two characters like Yojimbo and Zatoichi, each of whom usually functions as the fulcrum of the plot? What do you do with two fulcrums? Solving these problems can be a high bar to get over, and sometimes a low-budget genre picture just isn't up to it.

Though one has to admit, *Zatoichi Meets the One-Armed Swordsman* actually pulls it off.

Through the narrative magic of simply ignoring everything ever established about his origin and background, Zorro is whisked back two centuries to the 1600s. France and Spain are at war, with the Four Musketeers on the side of the French and Zorro intriguing for Spain, but even though they're on opposite sides, they manage to become the best of frenemies because that Zorro guy (Gordon Scott) is just so darned smart. Along the way we get the musketeers in gratuitous, slapstick bar fights, their four lackeys clowning around with Zorro's lackey, and Gordon Scott in his secret identity at the Court of Spain, fopping away and waving a limp handkerchief.

It's a shame the jokes aren't funny, because the story itself is actually rather clever. It manages to get Zorro into France to rescue a Spanish lady, Doña Isabella (José Greci), a prisoner the Four Musketeers have been ordered by Cardinal Richelieu to guard. Zorro dupes the Cardinal, the Cardinal's Guard, and all four musketeers and gets Isabella across the border into Spain, while she, of course, falls in love with her rescuer. However, d'Artagnan and company then are ordered to go to Madrid to kidnap her back, or they'll get sent to the Bastille. Fortunately, there's one big villain all the heroes can fight, a treacherous Spanish count who wants Isabella for himself, and Zorro and the musketeers must join forces to bring him down.

Gordon Scott (an ex-Tarzan) actually makes a decent Zorro, and he fences well in the bargain, but the musketeers are pretty weak, entirely interchangeable except for Porthos, played by peplum stalwart Livio Lorenzon, who always exudes character even when he isn't given one to portray. Otherwise, the musketeers just laugh and drink and laugh and fight and laugh, and it gets pretty tiresome. To be fair, there isn't much else for them to do, because the budget for this film was about 12 dollars, a constraint most evident in the execution scene, where a cast of tens mills around a scaffold in a square in "Madrid" that's about the size of a suburban backyard. I've had more people over for a barbecue. This movie is hard to find, but that's okay: some things are better left unfound.

ZORRO'S FIGHTING LEGION

Rating: ★★☆☆☆ • *Origin:* USA, 1939 • *Directors:* William Witney and John English •
Source: Hal Roach Studios DVD

Zorro's Fighting Legion REPUBLIC PICTURES / WIKIMEDIA
COMMONS

Before there were weekly TV shows, there were movie serials released as weekly episodes, typically in 12 installments, shown as part of the "short subjects" that preceded a feature film. Zorro film adaptations are usually set in a distinctive historical time and place, more colonial New Spain than Old West. Not so the Republic Zorro serials of the 1930s and '40s, most of which are basically standard Westerns that happen to feature an outlaw swashbuckler, with Zorro relying on a six-gun rather than a sword. The exception is *Zorro's Fighting Legion*, which is set in Mexico in 1824 and features the Zorro we know and love, the fop Diego Vega who dons black mask and sword to fight oppression and injustice. Unfortunately, it has all the flaws for which the Republic serials are notorious: the plot is thin, obvious, and repetitive; the characters are cardboard; production values are bottom of the barrel; and whoa, the acting. . . .

Zorro is played by Reed Hadley, an actor at the high school drama level—which puts him above the rest of the cast, whose only skills seem to be riding, fighting, running, fencing, and falling over when powder kegs explode. That's mostly okay, since frenetic action takes up 90 percent of this serial's screen time, and the actors just speak to each other briefly to set up the next deadly peril. The only exception is the villain who plays Don-Del-Oro, the Big Bad who thunders his orders in a stentorian announcer's voice from inside a golden god's awesome but towering and ungainly metal mask. The rest of the cast are just glorified stuntmen. But hey: good stunts!

The story is scarcely worth summarizing. The new Mexican republic needs gold from a certain mine to establish its administration, but disloyal politicians in the service of a criminal mastermind want the gold for themselves. The top crook masquerades as Don-Del-Oro, an ancient god of the Yaqui tribe of Native Americans, come back to lead them against the white men. Zorro arrives to save the day, and since the local government is corrupt, he forms a "fighting legion" of citizens loyal to the republic to oppose them. The best thing about this fighting legion? They have a theme song! Whenever Zorro summons them, they leap on their horses and gallop to join him, singing, "We ride . . . men of Zorro are we!" I think it's the first-ever Zorro song.

The portrayal of the Native Americans here is sad and unfortunate. In other films Zorro is a friend and defender of the oppressed natives, who are depicted with dignity and sympathy. Not here: the Yaqui are superstitious savages easily fooled and led astray by the villains. Only the good white men can straighten them out. Despite this, there's some stupid fun to be found in this three-and-a-half-hour gallop-fest, especially if you're under the age of 13 or under the influence of powerful cold medications. Gunpowder must have been easy to come by in old Mexico, because damn near everything gets blown up; if a wagon strays near a cliff, you can be sure it's going over it; there's a subterranean flood, beehive grenades, a peg-legged jailer, and a sort of Zorro-signal of brush arranged on hillsides in giant *Z*s that are set afire to summon the hero or his legion. Plus the music by William Lava, who composed a frantic Mexican-tinged gallop, is surprisingly good—so good that in the 1950s, he was hired by Disney to do the incidental music for its *Zorro* series!

ZORRO, THE GAY BLADE

Rating: ★★★☆☆ • *Origin:* USA, 1981 • *Director:* Peter Medak •
Source: Fox Home Entertainment DVD

After his comic turn in the vampire farce *Love at First Bite* (1979), dreamboat star George Hamilton went looking for another classic character to lampoon and decided on Zorro. The joke is, Zorro has a twin brother who is flamboyantly gay and stands in for him when he's sidelined by an injury. Ha ha, right?

This film is dedicated to Rouben Mamoulian, who directed the classic 1940 *Mark of Zorro*, a scene of which is shown at the beginning of this movie to establish that it's a direct sequel. It's 1840, and Don Diego de la Vega (Hamilton), the son of the original hero, is in Madrid seducing married women when he receives a letter from his father summoning him back to California. By the time he reaches Los Angeles, his father has passed away, leaving behind his Zorro outfit and weaponry for Diego—or for his twin brother Ramón, as one of them must be fated to don the cape and mask as needed. And the need is immediate, for Los Angeles groans under the tyranny of Capitan Esteban (Ron Leibman), Diego's childhood friend, who has matured into a heartless despot. In youth they were rivals for the heart of Florinda (Brenda Vaccaro), who is now married to Esteban but who throws herself at Diego. However, Diego is smitten with the meddling Bostonian reformer Charlotte Taylor-Wilson (Lauren Hutton) and vows he will clean up Los Angeles as Zorro if only to win her love.

And so, after a long absence, Zorro reappears at the captain's masked ball, where he crosses swords with Esteban, engages in a lot of classic athletic swashbuckling, and then falls out a window and injures his ankle. No more swashbuckling, just when LA needs Zorro the most! Conveniently, Diego's twin brother Ramón (also Hamilton) shows up to save the day, though instead of Spain, he's spent his life in Britain's Royal Navy under the name Bunny Wigglesworth—in which role Hamilton delivers a spot-on impersonation of Percy Blakeney, the alter ego of the Scarlet Pimpernel, complete with "Sink me!" and peering through a quizzing glass. Diego persuades Ramón to take his place as the hero while his ankle heals, and he does, clad in a series of increasingly outrageous Zorro outfits in bright rainbow colors.

If this sounds funny, it mostly is, in the then-prevailing Mel Brooks mode of comedy, primarily due to the sheer enthusiasm with which Hamilton embraces the material—he was nominated for a Golden Globe for his performance. His costars aren't up to his standard: Leibman as Esteban just shouts a lot and is tiresome, Brenda Vaccaro really wants to be Madeline Kahn but flops at it, and Hutton is vapid and shallow. Director Medak is good with the character scenes but doesn't know how to shoot action, and the swordplay is undistinguished. However, it was filmed in Mexico and looks authentic to place and period, and no movie that lists a "Whip Tutor" in its credits can be all bad. Right?

ZORRO, THE SPECIALS

Rating: ★★★☆☆ • *Origin:* USA, 1960 • *Directors:* William Witney et al. •
Source: Disney DVDs

After two successful seasons, Disney's *Zorro* series was suspended due to a rights dispute with the ABC network. In hopes that it would be resolved, Disney kept star Guy Williams on salary, and made four one-hour specials during the 1960 season that were broadcast on the *Walt Disney Presents* anthology show. These were the last of the Disney *Zorros*, as by the time the suit was resolved, the production company felt it had been off regular broadcast too long to renew. Too bad.

The specials were made with the same cast and crew as the regular show, and had all the strengths (and occasional weaknesses) of the previous series. The first two specials, the strongest, were a continued story that was shown back-to-back on successive weeks; Disney may have had in mind combining them into a feature for the overseas market, as it had with *The Sign of Zorro*, but that never eventuated. Ably directed by William Witney, they guest-star veteran Latino actor Gilbert Roland as El Cuchillo ("The Knife"), a bandit leader come up to California from Mexico who is nearly a match for Zorro, and whose code of honor, though somewhat flexible, gradually earns the masked vigilante's grudging respect. Roland makes a fine, sneering swashbuckler (though he has an unfortunate tendency to say, "Ay, chihuahua"), and moreover, he can fence: the spirited bouts between El Cuchillo and El Zorro are among the best in the entire series. Señorita bonus: Rita Moreno as Chulita, the tavern server who falls for El Cuchillo, one year before her breakout role in *West Side Story*.

The third episode is a limp Spanish colonial rom-com starring Annette Funicello which we'll shuffle past quickly with eyes averted to arrive at the fourth and last, "Auld Acquaintance," in which Don Diego meets Ramon Castillo, a rival swordsman he'd known in Spain who recognizes Zorro's fencing style as Diego's. Castillo and his sidekick Marcos are gentleman thieves out to rob the army's payroll, and they're played by none other than Ricardo Montalban and Ross Martin—yes, the Wrathful Khan himself and Artemus Gordon of *The Wild West*. Charming rogue Castillo tries repeatedly to prove that Don Diego is Zorro but is outsmarted by the team of Diego and Bernardo (Gene Sheldon). Señorita bonus: the return of Suzanne Lloyd, who made such an impression as Raquel Toledano in season 1, though in a different, less murderous role here. Summary: the specials are more elusive than the two regular seasons but worth it if you can find the Gilbert Roland episodes.

ZU: WARRIORS FROM THE MAGIC MOUNTAIN

Rating: ★★★★☆ • *Origin:* Hong Kong, 1983 • *Director:* Tsui Hark •
Source: Universe Laser & Video DVD

This is a wild fantasy *wuxia* adventure from the genre-smashing director Tsui Hark, who made it with American special effects wizardry previously unknown to Hong Kong cinema, in the process establishing the Hong Kong SFX industry. The tale is nominally set in China in the fifth century, but its real setting is the realm of legends and what in the West would be called fairy tales.

The plot is almost impossible to summarize. Ti-Ming (Yuen Biao), a scout in the endless wars between feuding East Zu and West Zu and a sort of kung fu everyman, falls afoul of his bad-tempered commander and is forced to flee both armies. He stumbles into a haunted temple where he's menaced by bat-demons until he's saved by the mysterious swordsman Ting Yin (Adam Cheng), who introduces him to a mystical mountain realm where heroes of good oppose the disciples of evil. While fighting the Blood Crows, they meet the good monk Hsiao Yu (Damian Lau) and his timid student, Yi Chen (Hoi Mang). Though the two heroes, the monk and the swordsman, are touchy and arrogant, their followers, the scout and the student, bond and become loyal friends. The pair encounters the elderly Long Brows, an avuncular martial artist who fights evil with his lambent Sky Mirror and his prehensile and adhesive eyebrows(!). While their masters are off arguing and trading insults, the followers help Long Brows imprison the erupting Blood Demon, who threatens nothing less than world destruction. Long Brows solemnly informs the friends that they must get to Heaven's Blade Peak and the Cave Beyond to collect the Twin Swords, for only they can defeat the Blood Demon, who will escape its bonds when the power of the Sky Mirror wanes.

And that's just the setup—the full quest lies ahead, a mélange of magic, martial arts, and monsters in which the action comes so fast and furious that, to be frank, it's often hard to tell what just happened. It sure looks cool, though, and the tone is mostly light and comedic, with plenty of slapstick gags to offset the imminent doom, an approach that John Carpenter cites as a primary influence on his film *Big Trouble in Little China* (1986).

Out of the flurry of near-constant action, the movie's themes gradually emerge. The heroes of good, such as the swordsman, the monk, and the countess of the Ice Fortress, are so full of themselves and caught up in proud bickering that they fall vulnerable to the disciples of evil, leaving the fate of the world in the hands of their humble apprentices. Together, the scout, the monk's student, and a spunky young Ice Priestess must take up the cause their elders have fumbled and somehow find the courage and determination to defeat evil with just a few hints from wise sources like Long Brows. That, plus a whole lot of vivid and hallucinogenic special effects. It's a lot of fun, a nonstop avalanche of creative invention from Tsui Hark, all deployed with a fearless confidence reminiscent of Terry Gilliam. You'll enjoy it.

INDEX BY TITLE

INDEXES BY SUBJECT

ARABIAN ADVENTURES

BARBARIANS AND HORDES

CAVALIERS AND MUSKETEERS

GLADIATORS AND CLASSICAL HEROES

HEROIC FANTASY

KNIGHTS AND FEUDAL WARRIORS

OUTLAWS AND ROGUES

PIRATES AND SEA DOGS

SAMURAI AND NINJA: FEUDAL JAPAN

VIKINGS, SAXONS, AND DANES

WUXIA: CHINESE FIGHTING HEROES

ACKNOWLEDGMENTS

Thanks as always to my family for their support and to my supremely capable agent, Philip Turner.

Thanks to Chris Chappell, Laurel Myers, and Ashleigh Cooke, the editorial team at Applause Books.

Thanks as well to Melissa Evarts, typesetter and interior text layout; Helen Subbio, copyeditor; Neil Cotterill and Devin Watson, the cover designers; and Christy Phillippe, proofreader. This wasn't an easy manuscript to wrestle into book form!

The cover image is from *The Golden Voyage of Sinbad* (1973). Go watch it.

Finally, thanks to the loyal Maryland members of the Wednesday night Cinema of Swords group—we watched a lot of great and terrible movies together!

Learn more about Lawrence Ellsworth and his work at his website, swashbuckling adventure.net, and at musketeerscycle.substack.com. See you there!

Lawrence Ellsworth
January 2023

ABOUT LAWRENCE ELLSWORTH

Lawrence Ellsworth is the historical fiction nom de plume of Lawrence Schick. Author of *The Rose Knight's Crucifixion* and editor of *The Big Book of Swashbuckling Adventure*, Ellsworth's current ongoing project is compiling and translating new, contemporary editions of all the books in Alexandre Dumas's Musketeers Cycle, a series that, when complete, will fill nine volumes.

Lawrence Schick is a writer and game designer primarily associated with narrative or role-playing games, a career he has pursued for over 40 years, starting in the late '70s working for *Dungeons & Dragons* cocreator Gary Gygax, moving into video games in the '80s, and then turning his attention to online, role-playing games in the '90s. He was lead writer and "loremaster" for *The Elder Scrolls Online* for over nine years and has now returned to the worlds of *D&D* as a narrative design lead for Larian Studios' massive *Baldur's Gate 3*.

ALEXANDRE DUMAS'S MUSKETEERS CYCLE

1. The Three Musketeers
2. The Red Sphinx
3. Twenty Years After
4. Blood Royal
5. Between Two Kings
6. Court of Daggers
7. Devil's Dance
8. Shadow of the Bastille
9. The Man in the Iron Mask

Volumes 1 through 7 are available now, the first five from Pegasus Books. Volume 8 is currently being published in serial form on the Substack platform at musketeerscycle.substack.com. Volume 9, *The Man in the Iron Mask*, is forthcoming.

CPSIA information can be obtained
at www.ICGtesting.com
Printed in the USA
BVHW060009280223
659268BV00004B/9